From Cooperation to Complicity

From Cooperation to Complicity is a study of the Degussa corporation, a firm that played a pivotal role in the processing of plundered precious metals in Nazi-occupied Europe and controlled the production and distribution of Zyklon B, the infamous pesticide used to gas the inmates of Auschwitz and Majdanek concentration camps, during the Third Reich. The author traces the extent of the corporation's involvement in these and other Nazi war crimes, including the Aryanization of Jewish-owned property and the exploitation of forced labor, and delineates the motivations for such conduct.

Peter Hayes is Professor of History and German and Theodore Z. Weiss Professor of Holocaust Studies at Northwestern University. He is the author of *Industry and Ideology: IG Farben in the Nazi Era* (new edition, Cambridge, 2001), which won the Conference Group on Central European History's biannual book award in 1988. He is also editor of *Lessons and Legacies: The Meaning of the Holocaust in a Changing World* (1991) and four other collections. He has written more than fifty articles published in German French, and Italian, as well as English. In 1997–98, he was the Shapiro Senior Scholar in Residence at the U.S. Holocaust Memorial Museum.

Advance praise for *From Cooperation to Complicity*...

"Bringing to bear a knowledge of business rare among historians, Peter Hayes has, on the basis of previously inaccessible company records, meticulously documented the moral corruption under Nazism of a venerable German firm whose executives allowed it to be drawn into ever-deeper implication in the crimes of Hitler's regime."
– Henry Ashby Turner, Jr., Stille Professor of History Emeritus, Yale University

"This outstanding study reaffirms Peter Hayes' claim to be the world's leading authority on business and the Third Reich. It proves that the most profound condemnation is always delivered by careful scholarship, not histrionic polemic."
– Neil Gregor, Department of History, University of Southampton, author of *Daimler-Benz in the Third Reich*

"*From Cooperation to Complicity* is an in-depth study of the Degussa Corporation, a firm whose wide-ranging commercial and technological interests and activities brought it into frequent and often intimate contact with the Nazi regime and its policies. Impeccably researched and elegantly written, the book is a fitting companion to Peter Hayes's classic study of IG Farben in the Nazi period, *Industry and Ideology*."
– Raymond G. Stokes, Professor of International Industrial History, University of Glasgow

"With devastating clarity combined with controlled moral outrage, Peter Hayes dissects Degussa's involvement in the most heinous crimes of the Third Reich, including the use of forced labor, the Aryanization of Jewish property, the refining of expropriated or murdered Jews' precious metals, and through its subsidiary Degesch the supply of Zyklon B gas utilized at Auschwitz. Hayes demonstrates that 'as so often in the history of the Holocaust, cooperating with its perpetrators was not the royal road to riches,' but this hardly stopped politically shrewd and 'materially and morally optimizing' executives from exploiting business opportunities offered by the government. Motivated by personal career ambition, ideological support, nationalist solidarity, or most banally seeking to preserve the firm's leading market position, Degussa executives ended up acting in 'morally indefensible' ways. This book is absolutely essential for anyone seeking to understand the roots and depths of corporate complicity during the Third Reich, but it should be read by anyone interested in business ethics and corporate responsibility."
– Jeffrey Fear, Harvard Business School

From Cooperation to Complicity

Degussa in the Third Reich

PETER HAYES

Northwestern University

CAMBRIDGE
UNIVERSITY PRESS

PUBLISHED BY THE PRESS SYNDICATE OF THE UNIVERSITY OF CAMBRIDGE
The Pitt Building, Trumpington Street, Cambridge, United Kingdom

CAMBRIDGE UNIVERSITY PRESS
The Edinburgh Building, Cambridge CB2 2RU, UK
40 West 20th Street, New York, NY 10011-4211, USA
477 Williamstown Road, Port Melbourne, VIC 3207, Australia
Ruiz de Alarcón 13, 28014 Madrid, Spain
Dock House, The Waterfront, Cape Town 8001, South Africa

http://www.cambridge.org

First published 2004

Printed in the United States of America

Typeface Sabon 10/12 pt.   *System* LATEX 2$_\varepsilon$ [TB]

A catalog record for this book is available from the British Library.

Library of Congress Cataloging in Publication Data
Hayes, Peter.
From cooperation to complicity: Degussa in the The Third Reich / Peter Hayes.
p. cm.
Includes bibliographical references (p.) and index.
ISBN 0-521-78227-9
1. Degussa (Firm) – History.   2. Gold industry – Germany – History.
3. Germany – History – 1933–1945.   I. Title.
HD9536.G44D42   2004
940.53'1813 – dc22   2004049742

ISBN 0 521 78227 9 hardback

To VSM, for having the heart, and MFB, for taking the liberty

I have made a ceaseless effort not to ridicule, not to bewail, not to scorn human actions, but to understand them.

Baruch Spinoza

Man will become better, when you show him what he is like.

Anton Chekhov

You say that [it is better to work from within the Party] because you reckon that you can still have a say in things. With a "Führerprinzip" orders come from above and then it is only: Obey! He who enters this tumbling avalanche only increases the plunging mass.

Pastor Kurt Rehling to Kurt Gerstein, 1932–33

Everything, even the future, must in the end fall into the hands of the historians.

Shmuel Niger

Contents

Illustrations

Abbreviations

archival references:

BAK	Bundesarchiv, Koblenz
BAL	Bundesarchiv, Lichterfelde (Berlin)
BU	Biographische Unterlagen
BUA	Bayer AG Unternehmensarchiv, Leverkusen
DUA	Degussa Unternehmensarchiv, Frankfurt
HHW	Hessisches Hauptstaatsarchiv, Wiesbaden
LAB	Landesarchiv, Berlin
NWHD	Nordrhein-Westfälisches Hauptstaatsarchiv, Düsseldorf
RA	Archiv der Mahn- und Gedenkstätte Ravensbrück
SSL	Sächsisches Staatsarchiv, Leipzig
SHD	Sächsisches Hauptstaatsarchiv, Dresden
SUAP	Státni ústrední archiv v Praze (State Archives, Prague)

other:

AG	Aktiengesellschaft (= Corporation or Inc.)
DAF	German Labor Front
DPG	Deutsche Pulvermetallurgische GmbH (Degussa subsidiary)
GmbH	Gesellschaft mit beschränkter Haftung (= limited liability company or Co.)
HIAG	Holzverkohlungs-Industrie AG (Degussa division)
KG	Kommanditgesellschaft (= partnership or Co.)
kg	kilogram (= 2.2 U.S. pounds)
MG	Metallgesellschaft
ÖCW	Österreichische Chemische Werke (Degussa subsidiary)
POW	Prisoner of War
RM	Reichsmark (nominal exchange rate, 1935–45 = 2.5:U.S. $1; in relation to U.S. dollar in 1999 = 1:4)
WASAG	Westfälische-Anhaltische Sprengstoff AG (an explosives firm)
ZAV	Zusatzausfuhrverfahren (export promotion procedure, i.e., subsidy)

Preface and Acknowledgments

Readers should know from the outset that this book came into being under unusual circumstances and auspices for a scholarly work. During the 1990s, the end of the Cold War and the completion of German unification removed political impediments to an examination of several issues related to Nazi-era war crimes that had remained incompletely or unsatisfactorily resolved since 1945. As a result, the name of the Degussa corporation of Frankfurt began to appear frequently in news publications worldwide. It surfaced first in connection with revelations concerning the plundered gold, some of it processed by this firm, that the Nazi state had used to pay for vital wartime imports, primarily via Switzerland, and that had remained, for the most part, in that nation's bank vaults ever since. Later, Degussa's American subsidiaries became the object of widely discussed class action suits filed in United States courts. These proceedings sought restitution or compensation payments to the surviving victims of not only the spoliation of precious metals, but also the parent firm's roles in the manufacture of Zyklon B, the infamous pesticide used to massacre hundreds of thousands of Jews at Auschwitz-Birkenau and Majdanek, and in the exploitation of forced laborers, many of them drawn from ghettoes and concentration camps.

Stung by widespread public criticism and eager to demonstrate good faith in establishing a reliable record of Degussa's conduct, the corporation's board of directors resolved in 1997 to follow the example of several other large German enterprises and to charge a recognized scholar in the fields of German, Holocaust, and business history with the task of preparing a detailed study of their firm in the Nazi era.[1] My name apparently came to the directors' attention because I had written a prize-winning book on the IG Farben corporation, had done research in the Degussa archive during the 1980s and published an essay on my findings, and was slated to participate in a panel including Dr. Michael Jansen, then an officer of the corporation, on "Enterprise

---

[1] On the "critical mass" of factors that engendered projects of this sort during the 1990s, see Gerald D. Feldman, "Holocaust Assets and German Business History: Beginning or End?" *German Studies Review* 25 (2002), pp. 26–27.

under National Socialism" at a conference in Frankfurt in early 1998.[2] During the following months, while I was serving as the J. B. and Maurice Shapiro Visiting Senior Scholar-in-Residence at the United States Holocaust Memorial Museum and working on a book on German big business and the Holocaust, Degussa approached me about undertaking the history its leaders envisioned. After a series of verbal and written exchanges, in which the firm renounced any right of review over what I would write, pledged to withhold no extant documentation, promised to keep its archives open to all bona fide researchers upon the completion of the project, and agreed to pay for my expenses and time, I accepted the assignment. From the fall of 1998 through the summer of 2001, as my teaching duties permitted, I worked through the surviving records of the firm in Frankfurt and gathered related material from several other archives, public and private. The publication of this book, the result of that research, stems from independent contracts between me and the English- and German-language publishers, to which the Degussa corporation is not a party.

Accepting a task of this sort entails risks to a scholar's reputation. Suspicion is an almost inevitable and largely understandable reaction to even temporarily preferred access to documents on topical and emotionally charged matters. This is all the more the case when the benefiting scholar is being compensated for his work. A researcher thus privileged must expect to be prejudged, even pilloried, by those who assume that "who pays the piper calls the tune." More specific to this particular subject area is the widespread mistrust that springs from the conviction that everything of importance concerning the implication of German business in the crimes of the Third Reich was established long ago by Allied investigative teams during the run up to the main and subsidiary Nürnberg trials of 1945–48.[3] Although I disagree on that specific point and find many of the charges hurled at "sponsored" histories such as this book quite intemperate, I am grateful for the warnings embedded in such attacks. They have kept me constantly on guard against even subtle forms of conflict of interest. Whether I have succeeded in avoiding them entirely is for readers to judge. I urge them to approach my account with the same sort of simultaneously open-minded and skeptical spirit that they would apply to the work of a conscientious biographer who has studied long and hard, but also come to know the subject's descendants, dined at their table, and intermittently shared in their standard of living. Even as

[2] The essay appeared as "Fritz Roessler and Nazism: The Observations of a German Industrialist, 1930–37," *Central European History* 20 (1987), pp. 58–79; the conference proceedings were published as Lothar Gall and Manfred Pohl (eds.), *Unternehmen im Nationalsozialismus* (Munich: C. H. Beck, 1998).
[3] See, for example, the remarks in the introduction to Christopher Simpson (ed.), *War Crimes of the Deutsche Bank and the Dresdner Bank* (New York: Holmes & Meier, 2002), especially pp. 22–34. My review of this book appears in *German Studies Review* 26 (2003), pp. 667–68.

readers properly allow for these possible seductions of proximity, however, two essential facts should be borne in mind: this book was neither conceived nor written as an "official" history of the Degussa corporation during the Third Reich, and that firm has neither censored nor endorsed the account given here.

In response to the public interest that engendered this work, I have structured it so as to give readers ready access to the means of satisfying their curiosity about the whens, whys, and hows of the following controversial matters: Degussa's relations with the Nazi Party and state; the firm's implication in the dispossession of the European Jews; its part in German military production, hence in enabling the Nazi conquest of much of Europe and the prolongation of World War II; its involvement in the exploitation of involuntary laborers, especially ones drawn from concentration camps; its responsibility for and knowledge of the murderous use of Zyklon B; and its reticence about exposing these matters to public scrutiny prior to now. I have also anticipated that readers will be interested in learning about a far more difficult subject to analyze, namely the degree to which the Degussa AG is still the beneficiary of the policies pursued by its leaders during the Nazi era. In short, this book is designed not as an all-embracing history of the firm under Nazism, but rather as a report on the most sensitive aspects of that history.

The resulting organization mixes thematic and chronological elements, in that I have tried to examine in discrete chapters each of the subjects that are most likely to concern readers, but in an order dictated by both logic and time. Thus, Chapter 1 provides an overview of the firm's history and development so that readers can place the subequent narratives in overall context. Chapter 2 treats Degussa's relationship with the Nazi Party and regime from 1933 to 1945 with the same end in view. Chapter 3 then focuses on the aspect of Degussa's complicity in the persecution of the Jews that arose earliest and continued longest, namely the enterprise's acquisition of Jewish-owned property in Germany and occupied Europe. Chapter 4 turns to the process by which Degussa's commercial interests and the expansionist purposes of the Nazi regime became increasingly enmeshed between 1933 and 1939. Chapter 5 concentrates on a particular aspect of Degussa's business, the operations of its precious metals division, a topic that blends the themes of the preceding chapters but carries over into the time frame covered by the succeeding ones. Chapter 6 resumes the account of Degussa's other productive sectors in 1939 and traces their militarization during the war years. Chapter 7 follows the route by which this transformation entailed implication in the Nazi state's increasingly barbaric labor policies. Chapter 8 lays bare the most infamous aspect of the corporation's wartime activities, the part played by its Degesch subsidiary in the massacre of European Jewry. Finally, Chapter 9 examines the destruction, collapse, denazification, and rebuilding of the enterprise in the years 1944–48, along with the attendant blend of self-protection and amnesia about Degussa's past that survived into the 1990s. Although this organizational scheme requires occasional repetition and some loss of a sense of simultaneity in readers' minds, I have risked these in the hope that readers will have the experience of penetrating not only successive subjects, but also accumulating ever deeper layers of knowledge concerning the firm and the thinking of its leaders.

Naturally, this is a history written from distinct perspectives, not only mine, but also that of its sources, and it therefore has the advantages and faults that go with both. Given the intense and extensive public and legal attention to Degussa in the past decade, I have felt a sense of urgency about making the record of the firm's behavior embedded in its own, rich archive accessible to a wide audience as soon as possible. This has ruled out the sort of meticulous canvass of every conceivably related documentary repository that an assiduous scholar normally wishes to undertake before publishing. Although the footnotes contain references to other sources, I have written largely from Degussa's records while striving not to be confined to their point of view. Only in the most pressing cases did I seek to gain access to the files of the firm's corporate partners, interlocutors, and rivals or to explore potentially relevant holdings in public archives. The papers of Henkel in Düsseldorf were obviously of particular importance, but I was denied access. Those of firms such as Continental Gummiwerke in Hanover or of the military agencies with which Degussa often dealt (in the Bundesarchiv-Militärarchiv in Freiburg), I opted not to explore, lest the completion of this book be greatly delayed. I hope the material presented here will spur other researchers to amplify and contextualize it in illuminating ways.

An earlier version of Chapter 3 appeared in German in the Yearbook 2000 of the Fritz Bauer Institute in Frankfurt, as did an overview in English of some of my provisional findings in volume 5 of the "Lessons and Legacies" conference series.[4] I am grateful to the publishers for allowing me to duplicate some of that material here, but should also point out to close readers that I have made revisions and corrections to these earlier texts. In the event of discrepancies, this book is the authoritative reference.

In order to avoid another sort of possible confusion, I should underline here that the operations of Degussa AG underwent a sweeping transformation through a series of mergers, divestitures, and reorganizations while this book was being researched and written. As a result, the firm's headquarters has moved to Düsseldorf from Frankfurt, where the former central office

[4] Peter Hayes, "Die Arisierungen der Degussa AG: Geschichte und Bilanz," in Peter Hayes and Irmtrud Wojak (eds.), *"Arisierung" im Nationalsozialismus: Volksgemeinschaft, Raub und Gedächtnis* [Jahrbuch 2000 zur Geschichte und Wirkung des Holocaust, Fritz Bauer Institut] (Frankfurt am Main: Campus, 2000), pp. 85–123; and "The Degussa AG and the Holocaust," in Ronald Smelser (ed.), *Lessons and Legacies V: The Holocaust and Justice* (Evanston: Northwestern University Press, 2002), pp. 140–77.

complex is scheduled to be sold in the near future. It is not clear, as of this writing, which of the products that dominate the story told here will still figure in the enterprise's output when readers take up this text. Already, for example, the parent corporation is no longer active in metals separation, the line of business that gave the company its original name and hence the acronym that is its current title. In other words, the subject of this book is the historical Degussa, not the current one.

Finally, many words of thanks. First, to the managers of Degussa AG who decided in 1997–98 to risk this project, knowing that they would have no control over its findings, notably Dr. Uwe-Ernst Bufé, who was then the chairman of the managing board; Dr. Michael Jansen, who has since moved on to the German Stiftungsinitiative for the compensation of former forced laborers; and Dr. Jörg Streitferdt of the firm's legal staff. They took a constant but not intrusive interest in my work and steadily encouraged it. Second, to Frau Dr. Mechthild Wolf, who assumed responsibility in the 1970s for a corporate archive that had been thinned in the final year of World War II by air raids and the destruction of records as Allied troops approached key offices, and perhaps again during the 1950s or early 1960s. She organized the remaining documentation in exemplary fashion, without violating its original provenances, and preserved it with dedication. In the process, as in her dealings with me, she also managed the feat of being loyal simultaneously to the enterprise that entrusted its records to her care and to the historian's obligations to posterity that she learned while completing her doctorate at the University of Vienna. During her long trusteeship of Degussa's archive, moreover, she accumulated a vast interstitial knowledge of the events narrated here, on which I have drawn repeatedly. It is a pleasure for me to express my indebtedness to her work and my thanks to those like her in other enterprises whose daily diligence makes a book of this sort possible. That gratitude extends to her staff, specifically to her successor, Dr. Andrea Hohmeyer, and to Frau Hadersbeck, Frau Polzien, Ms. Whelan, and Herr Beck, who fulfilled many requests speedily and cheerfully and always made me feel at home in Frankfurt. Third, to the distinguished members of the international Academic Advisory Committee for this project, who read drafts of each chapter and made many helpful and stimulating suggestions: Prof. Christoph Buchheim (Mannheim), Prof. David Cesarani (Southampton), Dr. Paul Erker (Munich), Prof. Gerald Feldman (Berkeley), Prof. Carl-Ludwig Holtfrerich (Free University, Berlin), Prof. Christopher Kobrak (ECSP-EAP, European School of Management, Paris), and Dr. Bernhard Lorentz (Hertie-Stiftung, Berlin). Fourth, to Dr. Ralf Banken (Frankfurt), whose own research into Degussa's precious metals operations during the Nazi period has been of great use to me, and to Dr. Daniel Inkelas, my former graduate student, who was particularly helpful in searching Degussa's records concerning the Auergesellschaft. Fifth, to a cohort of friends in Frankfurt: Irmtrud Wojak, Gitta Mohrdieck, Andrea Schneider, and Wolfgang Metternich, as well as an occasional visitor from further south, Stephan Lindner. Their warmth and laughter made spending so much time away from home bearable. Sixth, to a series of administrators at Northwestern University, who have supported me in countless ways: two successive presidents, Arnold Weber and Henry Bienen, Provost Lawrence Dumas, and Dr. Eric Sundquist, Dean of the Weinberg College of Arts and Sciences from 1997 to 2002. And, finally, to my publishers, Frank Smith at Cambridge University Press and Ernst Wieckenburg and Andreas Wirthensohn at Beck Verlag, who never showed how much I tried their patience.

My most personal and happy expressions of gratitude are embedded in the dedication, but I also want to put down in bereavement the name of my friend and colleague at Northwestern, Geza von Molnár, who took a continuous interest in this work and who died suddenly before it was finished. A child of Leipzig, Geza was cut off from his Jewish German mother when she was driven into exile in the United States in 1938, then sent a few years later to his father's Hungarian homeland for safekeeping. After the war, he rejoined his mother and became an American, without ever really ceasing to be a Magyar, a German, and a Jew. He befriended me years ago, traded perspectives on the Germany of the years 1933–45 with me over countless warm and lively evenings, and informed my views in ways paralleled only by another refugee from this dark place and time, Peter Gay. I treasure Geza's memory and thank him still for connecting me with the world I study and with his dear wife, Barbara, from whom I have learned, as in the case of Peter's admirable wife, Ruth, so much over so long about humanity, in both senses of that word.

The responsibility for any errors of fact or interpretation in this work is, of course, exclusively mine.

1

Introduction and Overview

Contradictory as it sounds, in the era of the world wars, Degussa was a rather little big business. Only its lengthy formal name was imposing: the German Gold and Silver Separation Institute, Inc., formerly Roessler (AG Deutsche Gold- und Silber- Scheideanstalt vormals Roessler – it did not begin going by the acronym Degussa until 1943, as a time-saving measure for typists, and did not adopt the abbreviated name officially until 1980).[1] None of even the firm's largest productive installations – those in and around the headquarters city of Frankfurt, at Rheinfelden by the Swiss border, and at Grünau and, after 1933, at Oranienburg, both near Berlin – remotely approached the size of the main works of such industrial giants as IG Farben, United Steelworks, Krupp, and Siemens. Indeed, Degussa's highest *total* labor force prior to 1945 (approximately 30,000 people, including those employed at majority-owned subsidiaries) never exceeded that at several of these corporations' mammoth production sites.[2] Neither was its stock capitalization especially impressive – at 23 million marks in 1927, it came to a fraction of that invested in any of these enterprises or in such other well-known firms as Mannesmann and AEG. By this measure, in fact, Degussa ranked only sixty-fourth out of the

[1] On the use of the acronym, DUA, DL 2/1, Niederschrift über die ausserordentliche Besprechung des Vorstandes am 26. Januar 1943, Anlage I: Scherf's Notiz für Herrn Schlosser. Betr.: Firmenkurzbezeichnung "Degussa," January 19, 1943; on the official adoption of the name, with the suffix AG, see Mechthild Wolf, *Im Zeichen von Sonne und Mond* (Frankfurt am Main: Degussa AG, 1993), p. 46.

[2] Interestingly, Degussa does not appear on a recent set of listings of the 100 largest German corporations, as measured by the size of their domestic workforces, for the years 1907 and 1938 and ranks only eighty-fifth in 1973 and sixty-eighth in 1995; see Martin Fiedler, "Die 100 grössten Unternehmen in Deutschland – nach der Zahl ihrer Beschäftigten – 1907, 1938, 1973 und 1995," *Zeitschrift für Unternehmensgeschichte* 44 (1999), pp. 32–66, and "Die 100 grössten Unternehmen von 1938 – ein Nachtrag," pp. 235–42. Though Fiedler almost certainly has undercounted Degussa's workforce for 1938, his figures for most firms are minimum estimates, so there is no reason to challenge the exclusion of the firm from the list for that year.

100 largest German industrial entities in that year and tenth among the thirteen chemicals firms on the list.[3]

While the firm improved somewhat upon this relative standing during the ensuing two decades, partly through expansion and partly because of the blows events dealt to competitors, Degussa's visibility on the German industrial landscape hardly increased. Certainly the company name was no closer to being a household word in Germany in 1947 than it had been twenty years earlier. Moreover, the firm's administrative apparatus remained strikingly personal and undeveloped. A chairman of the managing board was first named in 1930; regular meetings of that body did not commence until 1938. Even after a modern, divisional, and somewhat bureaucratized management structure began to take shape during World War II, the enterprise continued to be run by a handful of key figures, largely by the exchange of phone calls and memoranda. In short, the Degussa of this book was a far cry from the far-flung multinational that bore that name in the second half of the twentieth century, let alone the one that, following the mergers of 2000, carries that name forward into the twenty-first from a new administrative center in Düsseldorf.

Yet, this inconspicuous and intimate entity left its fingerprints on many of the most dramatic – and, in some cases, criminal – aspects of German history between 1933 and 1945. Much of the gold and silver extorted from Europe's Jews or ripped from their corpses passed through Degussa's refineries, as did some of the far larger quantities of precious metals plundered from the treasuries and citizenries of occupied Europe. Not only was the gold indispensable as a means of paying for the import of vital war materials from Portugal and through Switzerland, but also the silver almost literally gave eyes to the Luftwaffe, since much of it was sold to manufacturers of photographic film. Germany's warplanes also depended on Degussa's cyanide output for the Plexiglas that girded their cockpits, on Degussa's sodium for the tetraethyl lead in their fuel, and on Degussa's rare metal alloys for some of their propellers and engine parts. Later, Degussa's hydrogen peroxide helped propel German torpedoes and U-boats, the V-rockets that Hitler launched against England, and the jets that he hoped would turn the tide of the war. On the ground, German troops rode on tires made with Degussa's carbon black, carried gas masks turned out by Degussa's Auergesellschaft subsidiary, deployed equipment fabricated from Degussa-hardened steel, and fired anti-aircraft shells that contained explosives from Degussa-managed installations. The Zyklon B used to asphyxiate some one million people at Auschwitz and Majdanek was a Degussa product. Had Germany developed a genuine research project for an atomic bomb, Degussa, as the

---

[3] For the comparative data, see Hannes Siegrist, "Deutsche Grossunternehmen vom späten 19. Jahrhundert bis zur Weimarer Republik," *Geschichte und Gesellschaft* 6 (1980), Anhang II, especially p. 97.

nation's principal producer of uranium and other radioactive metals, surely would have played an essential part in it.

That so modest a firm came to be found in so many places at once in the Third Reich – to exercise an importance to the economy, the war effort, and the Holocaust out of all proportion to its size – attests to the particular growth process that had given Degussa its heterogenous form and Degussa's managers their distinct strategic bent by the time Adolf Hitler became Chancellor of Germany on January 30, 1933.[4] Founded sixty years earlier almost to the day, the Scheideanstalt, as it was generally known, was always an exploiter of niches. The firm's precursor, a smeltery for precious metals leased by Friedrich Ernst Roessler from the Free City of Frankfurt, owed its very existence to one such opening, that created by the city's interest in carrying out the resolve of the South German states to standardize their coinages following the German Customs Union of 1834. After establishing its reputation during this currency conversion and adding a laboratory to produce metallic chemicals such as silver nitrate and potassium cyanide, Roessler's little operation was strong enough to make the transition to a flourishing private partnership of his sons, Hector and Heinrich, following the annexation of Frankfurt by Prussia in 1866. Five years later, the unification of Germany offered their company the chance to execute another, even larger monetary transformation, provided adequate financial backing could be found. The incorporation of the enterprise in 1873 satisfied that precondition (while reducing the founding family's holding to 26 percent) and thus secured for the Scheideanstalt a lucrative share of the Reich's business until the reminting process was completed in 1878/79. By then, two other Roessler brothers had opened affiliates in Berlin and Vienna, and Hector and Heinrich, who continued to direct the firm, faced the challenge of finding a replacement for the fulfilled government contracts.

The opportunities Degussa pursued at this juncture set the firm on three separate, though sometimes overlapping, paths of development for most of the period examined in this book. Not surprisingly, immediate salvation came from perfecting and monopolizing a substance closely related to the

---

[4] In general, my summary of Degussa's history rests on Wolf, *Im Zeichen von Sonne und Mond*; idem., *Von Frankfurt in die Welt* (Frankfurt am Main: Degussa, 1983–87), a boxed set of essays on the firm's history at particular key dates; and on DUA: D 2/3, Die Entwicklung der Deutschen Gold- und Silberscheideanstalt vormals Roessler, by Dr. Martin, January 9, 1946; D 2/19, Development and Structure of Degussa, no date; GCH 5/37, U.S. Office of the Military Government of Germany, Division of Investigation of Cartels and External Assets, Partial Report on Examination of External Assets and Activities of Deutsche Gold und Silber Scheideanstalt (Degussa), no date; TLE 1/23, Der Aufbau des Produktionsprogrammes der Degussa, undated [1945–48?] and unsigned; and BU Fritz Roessler, "Zur Geschichte der Scheideanstalt," a remarkable memoir-history written in stages between 1925 and 1937, while the author was chairman of Degussa's supervisory board. I have refrained from citing these sources again below except for specific quotations or statistics.

precious metals processing that remained Degussa's mainstay. This was liquid gold suitable for application to porcelain and enamel. Enormously profitable in the era of Victorian decoration, the innovation led to the founding of a virtually wholly owned American subsidiary, Roessler & Hasslacher, in 1885 and provided much of the capital for further growth in refining gold-bearing silver, lead, and copper ores, out of which came investments, in partnership with the Metallgesellschaft of Frankfurt, in a Belgian plant at Hoboken in 1887 and in the Norddeutsche Affinerie of Hamburg just prior to World War I. A related trend was the firm's increasing engagement in semi-manufactured goods, especially alloys, for the jewelry and dental trades, which entailed the extension of Degussa's precious metals palette to platinum through investment in the G. Siebert firm of Hanau in 1905. But liquid gold also drew Degussa into the fabrication of ceramic dyes, earthenware, and firing ovens, thus beginning the diffusion of the enterprise's activities beyond its traditional base.

Similarly, the second major line of development of the 1880s also pulled Degussa in new directions. Inaugurated by the election of two commercial specialists from outside the Roessler family to the managing board, this consisted of offering the enterprise's services as a sales representative to numerous specialized chemicals manufacturers. As a result, by the 1890s, Degussa was earning profitable commissions not only by speaking for the German participants in numerous international cartels, including those for various acids, cyanides, and quinine, but also by coordinating sales and distribution for many smaller firms. Among these were the two major German makers of charcoal and other wood-based products (e.g., acetic acid, acetone, creosote, methanol, and formaldehyde, which were essential to such diverse products as vinegar, resins and plastics, dyes, solvents, heavy ammunition, and metal alloys and coatings): the Verein für Chemische Industrie and the Holzverkohlungs-Industrie AG (HIAG), the latter of which Degussa helped found in 1902. In conjunction with assorted joint production agreements between the Verein and Roessler & Hasslacher, these arrangements marked Degussa's entree to the sphere of organic chemicals.

The third main line of development, Degussa's own inorganic chemicals manufacturing, remained limited during the 1880s to sodium and potassium cyanides. It was thereafter pushed outward, however, in a fashion typical of the chemical industry, by the quest to cut outlays for raw materials or to find new applications for existing output and byproducts in order to lower unit costs and reduce waste. Thus, once an American plant founded by the [British] Aluminium Company and Roessler & Hasslacher had demonstrated the cost-saving benefits of using hydroelectric power to make sodium, Degussa entered a partnership with the British firm in 1898 to build a comparable German facility at Rheinfelden. Within a decade, the resulting output was serving as the feedstock for not only sodium cyanide, but also sodium peroxide for bleaching and sodium amide as a condensation agent in the production of indigo dye. Most consequentially, the research of a talented young Degussa chemist named Otto Liebknecht, son and brother of the famed Social Democrats Wilhelm and Karl, bred a patent on a process for making sodium perborate, which soon became the active ingredient in the Henkel Company's phenomenally successful detergent, Persil.[5] Along with expanded output came increased ties to firms that used these products, provided intermediates for them, or arrived at them by other means. The results were joint manufacturing ventures with Hoechst AG (indigo), the Chemische Fabrik Weissenstein in Austria (hydrogen peroxide), the Chemische Fabrik Landshoff & Meyer of Grünau (electrolytic fabrication of perborate), and the Dessauer Werke für Zucker und chemische Industrie (hydrogen cyanide from sugar beet plants).

On the eve of the First World War, these semi-diversified operations enabled Degussa to pay regular annual dividends of 30 to 50 percent of nominal capital to its stockholders, but the corporation had neither broken into the ranks of the nation's 100 largest firms nor acquired what today is called name recognition. The latter circumstance changed little during the Weimar and Nazi years, since Degussa largely remained a purveyor of goods and services to other firms not the consumer market. The enterprise's relative standing, however, rose appreciably after 1918, despite the fact that neither the war nor the peace settlement positioned Degussa well for the future. Hector and Heinrich Roessler had retired from the active management in 1901, and though the latter man remained involved in the firm as a member of the supervisory board, his main preoccupations were now idealistic and political: fostering the League for International Understanding and uniting Germany's liberal factions into the Progressive People's Party. Because Alexander Schneider, the headstrong director who became dominant in the Roesslers' absence, had to make good just before the war broke out on one of his periodic threats to resign, another director left with him, a third showed signs of derangement, a fourth died, and two more were called to the colors, leadership of the enterprise fell in 1914 to Heinrich's well-intentioned but halfhearted son, Friedrich (Fritz), a patrician in most of the noble and negative senses of that word.[6] He saw to it that the firm's few suitable capacities were put to the service of the military effort and that the workforce's attachment to the enterprise, which decades earlier had pioneered insurance and bonus programs and the eight-hour day, remained strong. Otherwise, however, he functioned largely as a caretaker, provoking his successor to

---

[5] On Liebknecht (1876–1949) and his career with the firm from 1900 to 1925, see Birgit Bertsch-Frank, "Eine etwas ungewöhnliche Karriere. Otto Liebknecht," in Mechthild Wolf (ed.), *Immer eine Idee besser: Forscher und Erfinder der Degussa* (Frankfurt am Main: Degussa AG, 1998), pp. 54–75.
[6] See Peter Hayes, "Fritz Roessler and Nazism: The Observations of a German Industrialist, 1930–37," *Central European History* 20 (1987), especially pp. 61–64.

1   Fritz Roessler

lament that Degussa "had slept through the war years" and missed the opportunity for expansion that they offered.[7] When they ended adversely for Germany, moreover, the firm was stripped of its lucrative American subsidiary, Roessler & Hasslacher, along with the Hoboken plant and all other foreign shareholdings and patent rights, aside from those in Austria and Hungary. That Degussa retained full title to the Rheinfelden factory – the Reich having seized and sold the British shares at auction in 1918 – seemed small compensation. In 1922, the enterprise's profits came, in real terms, to only one-tenth of their prewar level. The revaluation of Degussa's assets following the collapse of the German currency a year later produced a figure of 25.3 million gold marks, only 43 percent of the total in 1913.[8]

Degussa's remarkable recovery from these losses during the 1920s was due, in part, to the fortuitous extensions of its cyanide operations associated with the names Degesch and Durferrit. Another acronym, Degesch stood for the company name Deutsche Gesellschaft für Schädlingsbekämpfung mbH (German Society for Pest Control, Ltd.). The firm was the successor to the War Ministry's Technical Committee for Pest Control headed by Fritz Haber,

---

[7] Roessler recorded the reproach in his "Zur Geschichte" [1925], Abschrift, p. 35, adding in his own defense that "this hard judgment was delivered without knowledge or consideration of the personal and objective circumstances," p. 36.

[8] On the profits, Wolf, *Im Zeichen von Sonne und Mond*, p. 134; on the balance sheet assets, Heinz Mayer-Wegelin, *Aller Anfang ist Schwer* (Frankfurt am Main: Degussa AG, 1973), p. 167.

which had concentrated on methods of killing lice in trenches, barracks, and submarines. Having been transformed in 1920 into a corporation owned by a consortium of chemical firms, Degesch became Degussa's exclusive property in 1922, the same year that Walter Heerdt, the firm's business manager, perfected a process for packing the volatile hydrogen cyanide in its principal product, a fumigant called Zyklon, in tins filled with absorbent pellets. These stabilized the chemical until the cans were opened, at which point the contents vaporized and blocked the transfer of oxygen to any organism in the vicinity. Known in-house as Zyklon B, the new commodity amounted to a major technological breakthrough and enjoyed immediate success, though more as a source of license fees than direct sales revenue, given the limited demand for it within Germany at the time. Durferrit was a trade name, acquired in 1925, for a process of hardening carbon-poor steel through fixing a powder to the metal's surface. Degussa soon eclipsed this procedure by modifying an American method that involved dipping the metal in a bath of sodium cyanide and charcoal, to which the trade name was also applied. Once more, the licensing of the process, including rights to make the necessary chemical compounds and hardening ovens, began to bring in new and appreciable revenues. Within just over a decade after Germany's defeat, therefore, two new lines of business – pesticides and metal strengtheners – arose to offset some of the damage done to Degussa's fortunes. Moreover, another technical advance was taken over from the now independent Roessler & Hasslacher in this period, the Downs Process for the electrolytic manufacture of sodium, which considerably reduced production costs for this staple. A new installation, built at Knapsack near Cologne in partnership with the American firm, became Degussa's sole property in 1930, as its former U.S. subsidiary disappeared into DuPont.

More important than new technologies to Degussa's postwar revival, however, were the revenue stream provided by perborate sales to Henkel and the ascent of new leadership. Indeed, earnings on perborate remained the lifeblood of the enterprise until well into the Nazi years, and the management team put together following the First World War largely determined the firm's course until well after the Second (for a list of Degussa's board members from 1933 to 1945 and the dates of their terms, see Appendix A). Most of the key figures in that team were competent, steady, and reliable directors of their special spheres, but disinclined to assert themselves beyond them. Three of them, in fact, largely owed their positions to family connections, attesting to how ingrown the enterprise still was. Hans Schneider, the head of Degussa's still profitable but stagnant precious metals sector until early 1941, had his father to thank for his appointments as deputy, then full member of the managing board – indeed, his promotion was negotiated as part of the elder Schneider's severance package when he abruptly resigned from that body in 1913. Hektor Roessler, who was elected in 1921 and handled personnel matters until they drove him to suicide twenty years later, belonged to the founding family. So did his cousin Ernst Baerwind, whose mother was

2   Ernst Baerwind

a Roessler. Trained in chemistry at Munich and Berlin, Baerwind worked at Rheinfelden between 1914 and 1919, aside from a brief period of military service that cost him the sight in one eye, then joined the central administration in Frankfurt and assumed a seat on the managing board in 1926 with responsibility for production at the chemicals and metals plants. He acquitted himself of these responsibilities with literally painstaking devotion and attention to detail, but also with a certain aloofness, all of which qualities attested to his enduring self-doubt. Never convinced that he had risen by virtue of his merits rather than his relatives, always inclined to melancholy, and, after 1933, made still more uncertain because his father's mother had been born a Jew, Baerwind proved the ideal operations man but did not presume to make overall corporate policy. Ernst Bernau also largely tended to his own bailiwick – accounting, taxes, and finance – but he was considerably more assured and urbane than Baerwind. Having been with the firm since 1896, he took charge of Degussa's bookkeeping from 1919 on, though he reached the managing board later than all the other new men, as a deputy member in 1930, then a full one from 1933.

This cohort, including Schneider's assistant and successor, Robert Hirtes, provided Degussa with stable and dependable management virtually throughout the Weimar and Nazi eras, but real direction came from two more galvanic figures: Ernst Busemann and Hermann Schlosser. Forty-three years old in 1919, when he assumed the seat he had been offered three years earlier on Degussa's managing board, Busemann had a doctorate in law,

3   Ernst Bernau

training in finance at a Jewish-owned private bank, and a record of managerial success as head of both the Hoboken unit prior to the war and the War Metals Corporation in Berlin during it. He was sharp, decisive, sure of his own judgment, adept at maneuver and negotiation, and, from the beginning of his tenure, intent on establishing his primacy. He succeeded.

4   Ernst Busemann

5   Hermann Schlosser

By 1923, he had driven Fritz Roessler into the honorific role of supervisory board chairman and emerged as first among equals on the managing board. In 1930, he became its first chairman, which he remained until his death in 1939. The confident and convivial Schlosser was fourteen years younger, a Protestant pastor's son with a talent for English and for negotiating with those who spoke it, which derived from a four-year stint in British India at the beginning of his career. This aptitude served him in good stead as he, fresh from frontline service, sought to rebuild Degussa's export trade from his initial postwar posting in Holland, then, following his elevation to the managing board in 1926, became the enterprise's preferred representative abroad during his climb to the status of Busemann's undisputed successor.

Whereas Busemann carried the stamp of the Imperial educated bourgeoisie in his tastes and bearing – he wore a goatee and a homburg, played piano well and loved music, particularly Bach, admired accomplishment but scorned self-promotion or self-importance, and was more interested in private and professional fulfillment than politics – Schlosser's formative experiences were his regimental duty during World War I and his upbringing in a home that taught patriotism, social obligation, and the dangers of ostentation or pride. As a result, he combined a firm sense of his own worth with a calculatedly modest and accessible demeanor, cosmopolitanism with a strongly national consciousness. Notwithstanding such temperamental and generational differences, the two men had much in common. Both came to

prominence in Degussa from middle-class rather than wealthy backgrounds
and with commercial rather than scientific training. Each saw business as
an arena of practical calculation and compromise, one in which results were
measured by the bottom line but "ruinous competition" should be avoided
through artfully designed and carefully observed intercorporate agreements
and contracts. Their outlook was that of dealmakers, not researchers;
of the boardroom, not the debating hall or academic seminar; and of
"organized" capitalism rather than aggressive profit-chasing. As chairmen,
their styles diverged, Busemann's down-to-earth form of expression and
overt high-handedness giving way to Schlosser's homiletic public utterances
and effort to seem collegial. But pragmatism and ambition characterized
them both. In 1925, when Fritz Roessler concluded that his humanistic education and inherited advantages had hindered him as an executive, since
"he makes faster headway who knows only his own preconceived opinion"
and "people who had to fight their way to a leading position possess greater
ruthlessness and force in business life," he was surely comparing himself to
Busemann, at least in part.[9] But a contrast with Schlosser could have been
drawn almost as pointedly.

Following the Armistice, while Schlosser concentrated on Degussa's chemicals sales, especially on reorganizing the growing Zyklon business and recovering German leadership of the international cyanide cartel, Busemann
applied himself to preserving the stockholders' investments from the inflationary whirlwind of the early 1920s. Whether his methods, which are virtually impossible to recreate from the firm's records, were entirely proper
is open to doubt. Certainly Fritz Roessler took exception to Busemann's
"lax view" of contractual terms and financial reporting requirements.[10] But
the results of their different degrees of punctiliousness toward such matters
were hard to dispute. When the hyperinflation came to a close, Degussa's
stock capital was reissued at real levels nearly identical to those of 1913,
and Busemann could claim that people who had held onto their shares and
stood by his firm had lost nothing.[11] Among those who had sold out at an
inopportune moment, however, were the members of Degussa's founding
family, whose fortune evaporated.

Skilled as Busemann's rescue action proved, his tenure at Degussa got off,
in one respect, to a false start. Several months before he actually joined the
firm, he transmitted the suggestion of the Metallgesellschaft's chief, Alfred
Merton, whose father's private secretary Busemann had been in 1903–04,
that the two firms consider a closer, more mutually reinforcing relationship.
In view of their historic ties (the MG was also headquartered in Frankfurt
and the successor to the Philip Abraham Cohen bank and metals trading
house, which had been among the chief investors at the time of Degussa's

[9] Roessler, "Zur Geschichte" [1925], Abschrift, pp. 17, 19.   [10] *Ibid.*, pp. 39–40.
[11] On the revaluation, Mayer-Wegelin, *Aller Anfang ist Schwer*, p. 167.

incorporation) and the affinities of their businesses (the MG dealt in non-precious metals, Degussa in precious ones, and they were by now equal partners in the Norddeutsche Affinerie, which handled both), the idea was not far-fetched. Opposition within Degussa's managing board initially blocked the proposal, but three years later, Busemann returned to it successfully, this time abetted by the general trend toward corporate concentration encouraged by both the inflation and intense international competition. The result was a community-of-interests agreement under which the two firms would pool their profits and coordinate policy through a committee including representatives of each. Though Busemann and a lawyer from Degussa's supervisory board named Baer generally voted with the MG's representatives, the relationship foundered after only a few years on the divergence between the MG's interests as a metals trader and Degussa's as a manufacturing operation. Even Busemann had to concede that he had miscalculated, and his ties to Alfred Merton and his brother and eventual successor, Richard, for a time suffered.

After the community of interests was dissolved in December 1926, Busemann had to devise an alternative strategy for coping with Degussa's principal problems: its relatively small size and dependence on Henkel's purchases for some 50 percent of its gross profits.[12] At first, his solution was to redouble his pursuit of a relatively common approach to sheltering capital in the early 1920s: the "flight into real values."[13] He concentrated on preserving the receipts from perborate sales and other operations by investing them as much and as rapidly as possible in fixed assets, which could be both depreciated and turned to further productive purpose. The results included expansions of the Rheinfelden and Knapsack plants, as well as a chain reaction of acquisitions, as Busemann plowed revenues into increased stockholdings, then wrote off up to half the face value of each new property during the first year after its purchase, as permitted by German law.[14] For each such possession, the remaining worth on the parent firm's books then equalled the price at which it could sell, if necessary, without incurring either a tax liability or a significant loss, and Degussa meanwhile reinvested the money recovered through depreciation.[15] Many of the applications of this system merely expanded on the enterprise's previous activities, notably the increase in Degussa's holding in the Siebert platinum firm, then its complete acquisition; the purchase of Dr. Richter & Co. of Pforzheim, a producer of precious metals, alloys, and specialized forms of pipe; the buying of controlling blocks of the stock in two long-standing partners, Landshoff & Meyer

---

[12] For the profit share, Roessler, "Zur Geschichte" [1927], p. 60.
[13] See Gerald Feldman, *The Great Disorder* (New York: Oxford University Press, 1993).
[14] Instructive in this connection is DUA, DL 3.Busemann/2, his memo Betr. Finanz-Status, December 28, 1928.
[15] See DUA, DL 3.Busemann/2, his memo Betr. Bilanz Pforzheim, November 23, 1928, for the best illustration of his thinking and practice.

(now renamed the Chemische Fabrik Grünau AG) and the Österreichische Chemische Werke (ÖCW), as well as of 50 percent of L. Roessler & Co. of Vienna; the new investment in a liquid gold factory in Mulhouse (France), a ceramic dyes plant in Teplitz (Czechoslovakia), and a metals trading firm in Amsterdam; and the takeover of HIAG as a wholly owned subsidiary and the enfolding into it of the Verein für Chemische Industrie between 1929 and 1931. A fringe benefit of the last-named transaction was the introduction of new blood to Degussa's managing board, which added two representatives of the charcoalers, Adalbert Fischer and Koloman Róka.

But as Degussa exhausted the possibilities for rounding off its operations or holdings in this fashion, Busemann's asset-sheltering project turned into a program of diversification. One small fruit of this impulse was the purchase of the Deutsche Kunstlederfabrik GmbH of Wolfgang, a maker of imitation leather, in 1933. Far more fateful for Degussa's subsequent development was the decision a year earlier to buy up the August Wegelin AG of Kalscheuren, near Cologne, which had gone bankrupt because of financial mismanagement. Wegelin made a form of lampblack, a sootlike substance that was useful in making printing ink, dyes, and pigments, via the controlled burning off of coal. Though an American gas-based variant of the product, called carbon black, had acquired considerable importance as an additive for automobile tires, Wegelin's output could not compete with it in quality, hence the firm's growth prospects were not particularly good. But because a controlling interest could be had for only 375,000 Reichsmarks (RM), the firm's book value offered enormous possibilities for creative depreciation, and Schlosser thought the company could serve as the entering wedge for making Degussa the sales representative for the entire German carbon black industry, Busemann decided to take his firm into this new sphere of production.[16]

By 1933, in short, Ernst Busemann had reason to feel vindicated in the strategy he had insisted upon as chairman. His financial legerdemain and his eye for favorable takeover opportunities had brought the firm through the inflation, the merger wave of the late 1920s, and the Depression not merely unscathed, but healthier and more broadly based than before. In 1929/30, Degussa's assets reached their pre-Nazi peak of over 85 million marks, and they remained higher throughout the economic crisis than at any time prior to World War I.[17] The enterprise had even begun rationalizing its own splintered chemicals production, notably by shifting all sodium manufacturing to Knapsack, turning Rheinfelden exclusively to making oxygenated chemicals for the bleaching and detergent industries, and dividing most of HIAG's numerous small works into specialized fabricators of the particular end product(s) of wood carbonization to which each site was best suited, rather than letting

---

[16] See Wolf, *Im Zeichen von Sonne und Mond*, p. 164.
[17] Mayer-Wegelin, *Aller Anfang ist Schwer*, p. 167.

each continue to extract all. To be sure, Busemann had designed some of his maneuvers in anticipation of a danger that never materialized, the devaluation of the German currency. But safe had proved better than sorry. Few firms were able to ride out the German economic slump as well as Degussa: unburdened by debts to American creditors, it paid dividends of 9 to 10 percent annually from 1929 to 1932, averted substantial layoffs (though hours and some pay packets were cut, new hirings and all pay raises forbidden, and some early retirements forced), raised its capitalization to 32.4 million Reichsmarks during the crisis, and still showed assets on its balance sheets in 1933 of fully 75.5 million marks, a gain of 46.2 million since the restabilization of the German currency in 1924.[18] Above all, Busemann had reduced, though far from eliminated, his firm's heavy dependence on orders from a single customer (Henkel's contributions to the firm's gross profits fell to an average of 36 percent annually in the period 1930–34) and on the slow-growing precious-metals field.[19]

Of course, Busemann's success was not unbroken. To head off competition in the field of vaporizing pesticides, Degussa had to cut IG Farben and Th. Goldschmidt of Essen into Degesch and reduce its own shareholding to 42.5 percent. But effective leadership of the subsidiary remained with Degussa in the form of Hermann Schlosser as the business manager. Similarly, keeping IG Farben from making hydrogen peroxide in large quantities entailed accepting it as a silent partner when Degussa expanded its shareholding in ÖCW, but this association also had advantages. It led to IG's agreement in 1929 to pay half the costs of an expansion of capacity for the product at Rheinfelden, which greatly reduced Degussa's exposure when demand sagged for a time thereafter.[20] Degussa also neglected its own research efforts during Busemann's buying spree, since it confirmed the chairman in his view that purchasing promising patents and processes was more economically efficient than discovering them.[21] By the early 1930s, Fritz Roessler noted regretfully, the firm lacked a "creative mind" comparable to Liebknecht, who had been stymied to the point of resigning in 1925.[22] Still, the enterprise made some technical advances thereafter, especially concerning heat-resistant oxides of aluminum (Degussit) and of so-called rare metals, including beryllium, thorium, titanium, and zircon, which led to new sales to makers of such diverse products as turbines and flashlights.

[18] *Ibid.*, pp. 167–68; DUA, DL 3.Busemann/3, Busemann's Notiz für die Personalabteilung, January 6, 1932.
[19] See DUA, RFI 4.2/61, 64, 67, Degussa-Jahresabschlüsse, September 30, 1932, 1933, and 1934.
[20] See DUA, D 2/20, Relations between Degussa and former I. G. Farbenindustrie with respect to Hydrogen Peroxide [in English], no date [1946–47].
[21] On this, see DUA, BU Dr. Koloman Róka, Memo by G. Pichler, Betr.: Forschung, February 9, 1968.
[22] DUA, BU Dr. Fritz Roessler, "Zur Geschichte" [1933], Abschrift, pp. 44–45, 62, and (for the quotation) 96.

Nonetheless, Degussa remained vulnerable in a number of respects. The possibility that Henkel might expand its own small facilities for making perborate or find substitutes for it was driving Degussa into price concessions and clouding its prospects. So was the danger that improving processes for synthesizing organic chemicals such as methanol and acetone from coal would render HIAG's traditional fabrication methods via wood carbonization uncompetitive and obsolete. Wherever Degussa turned, except in its core precious metals business, it ran up against the enormous, potentially crushing presence of the IG Farben chemicals concern, whose displeasure had to be avoided at nearly all costs. Meanwhile, even the refineries faced an uncertain future, since one business that had kept them occupied during the Depression – recovering metals from coin issues called in by foreign governments – appeared to be nearing its end. Nor did Busemann's worries about a possible devaluation of the mark disappear with the appointment of Adolf Hitler as Chancellor of Germany.

In consequence, Degussa's commercial calculations and moves after 1933 continued to be aimed at insuring the enterprise against any of these eventualities, primarily by finding new opportunities for expansion. But in the "steered market economy" that the Nazi regime began building, the diversification drive was increasingly channeled toward satisfying three state-imposed goals: so-called Aryanization (the transfer of property owned by Jewish Germans to the hands of non-Jewish ones), autarky (the substitution of products made with domestic raw materials for imports or goods made from them), and armament. As the new regime gradually but systematically blocked the application of resources to other purposes, these became the only avenues of growth available to Degussa, and Busemann's pragmatic sense of his responsibility to the firm assured that he would march down them. Almost equally predictable, and for the same reasons, was that Degussa would accommodate rapidly to the ideology of the self-proclaimed Third Reich and its representatives in positions of influence and power.

All of this Degussa's managers did, despite episodic reservations and reluctance, with considerable success. When an investigator for the decartellization branch of the American occupation administration wrote shortly after World War II that he was "unable to name an industry for which Degussa does not make some key products," he overstated the importance the firm had acquired, but not by much.[23] His remark attests not only to the enterprise's continued surge during the Nazi period, but also to the overcoming of nearly all the dangers that had troubled Busemann at its outset. As early as September 1936, only three and one-half years into the Nazi era, Degussa closed its most profitable business year since the First World War, a fact that indicates the firm's recovery outpaced that of German industry as a whole.[24]

---

[23] DUA, GCH 5/37, Partial Report on Examination of... (Degussa), p. 3.
[24] On, for example, IG Farben's relatively laggard performance, see Peter Hayes, *Industry and Ideology: IG Farben in the Nazi Era* (New York: Cambridge University Press, 1987),

Furthermore, for the first time in Degussa's recent history, gross profits from its precious metals and Rheinfelden operations only narrowly exceeded those flowing in from other departments. What had more than offset the continuing decline in receipts for perborate from Henkel, which now provided less than one-quarter of total profits, were HIAG's swelling sales to many producers that had begun to benefit from the general economic upturn, as well as a fivefold increase since 1933 in annual income from shareholdings in other firms. The latter gain reflected a stunning growth, largely through Aryanization, in the firm's portfolio of participations: their book value on Degussa's balance sheets had risen from 11.2 million to 19.5 million Reichsmarks, despite the simultaneous writing down of their assets by more than 8 million marks.[25] Thereafter, under the aegis of Hitler's (putatively Second) Four Year Plan, which was also announced in September 1936, the rewards of autarky and armament began to exceed those already and not yet reaped via Aryanization.

So ramified and rich had Degussa become by the outbreak of World War II in September 1939 that the enterprise felt compelled and able to embark on a major restructuring. Organizational changes led to the complete absorption into the parent firm of HIAG, the Durferrit and Siebert GmbH, L. Roessler & Co. in Vienna, and several other subsidiaries, and to the elaboration of a framework of committees and technical, sales, and administrative groups, each responsible to a specific director (see Appendix L). More remarkably, Degussa began planning its physical transformation, not only envisioning a new headquarters location (complete with adjoining sports grounds) and a consolidated Central Precious Metals Works for the then outskirts of Frankfurt, but also actually designing and beginning construction on a giant new chemicals plant at Fürstenberg an der Oder, today's Eisenhüttenstadt. At a projected cost that rose rapidly from 15 million to over 41 million Reichsmarks, this factory was supposed eventually to consolidate the production of many of Degussa's approximately fifty scattered and often cramped installations (see Appendix M).[26]

pp. 158–59. For broader comparative data, see Mark Spoerer, *Vom Scheingewinn zum Rüstungsboom: Die Eigenkapitalrentabilität der deutschen Industrieaktiengesellschaften, 1925–1941* (Stuttgart: Franz Steiner, 1996), though neither his sample nor his source base is conclusive.

[25] On the statistics for 1933–36, see DUA, BU Dr. Fritz Roessler, "Zur Geschichte" [1937], Abschrift, pp. 102, 116–20, 125; and RFI 4.2/74, Abschluss vom 30. September 1936.

[26] The organizational changes are summarized in DUA, DL 3.H.Schlosser/1, Innerorganisatorische Massnahmen seit November 1939, March 12, 1942, which is updated by TLE 1/23, Federlin's Notiz. Betr.: Organisation, October 21, 1943, and supplemented by SCH 1/32, Fuchs' Organisation der Forschung, November 4, 1944. On the Fürstenberg project, the basic documents are TA2/72, Róka's Ausbau der Produktionsstätten der Scheideanstalt, October 27, 1939, and his Notiz über die Besprechung der Projektierung des Zentralwerks, January 4, 1940; see also Wolf, *Im Zeichen von Sonne und Mond*, pp. 202–04. On the new installations in Frankfurt, see BU Hermann Schlosser, Pichler's Markante Begebenheiten aus

By the conclusion of the business year 1942/43, just before massive air raids and the retreat of the Wehrmacht began to chip away pieces of what the firm's documents increasingly termed the "Degussa concern," it had become generally recognized as Germany's second or third most important chemicals enterprise.[27] Its stock capital (now 76.5 million Reichsmarks), the worth of its subsidiaries (now 53.6 million marks), and the nominal and taxable value of its total assets (now 181.1 million and 218.1 million, respectively) had more than doubled since 1933 (see Appendix B). As the combined contribution to gross and net profits of the precious metals and Rheinfelden facilities had continued to fall in relative terms (to about 30 percent), the feared erosion of income from the carbonization division had done the very opposite of taking place: rising sales and profits from the production of organic chemicals more than offset declines in the old flagship lines (see Appendices C and D). As a result of steady growth in total sales, gross profits, and net profits after depreciation, which crested in 1942/43 at 230.6 million, 49.3 million, and just over 11 million marks, respectively, the firm by then had accumulated open and hidden reserves of 93.4 million marks, a sum that considerably exceeded its total assets only a decade earlier.[28] The ensuing years brought enormous damage to Degussa's property and inroads on its possessions: Ernst Bernau's more or less final calculation of its losses during and because of the war came to 119.6 million Reichsmarks.[29] Yet he also reckoned that as of September 1946, even after huge deductions for depreciation and damage, the firm's capital assets were still worth nearly three times as much as at the time of the currency stabilization more than twenty years earlier, and the total property on its balance sheets nearly four times as much.[30] Certainly the bulk of these gains – and the ones embedded in Degussa's opening balance sheet value of 116.4 million Deutschmarks following the currency reform of 1948 – are attributable to the Nazi years.[31]

---

der Tätigkeit von Herrn Schlosser, December 23, 1964, and the Ergänzung to this document, April 27, 1965.

[27] See DUA, BU Hermann Schlosser, his draft personal statements of 1945–47, which explain his own rising prominence in the chemical industry with reference to this fact.

[28] See DUA, TLE 1/23, Umsätze und Gewinne der Abteilungen, March 1, 1943, including Übersicht über die Gewinne der einzelnen Abteilung im Verhältnis zum Umsatz 1941/42, DL 3.Bernau/1, Rendite der einzelnen Abteilungen, May 19, 1944, and BET 10/1, Bilanzbericht an den Aufsichtsrat über das Geschäftsjahr 1943/44, May 24, 1945. The figures for sales, gross and net profits, and reserves given here in the text include the results for all of Degussa's wholly owned subsidiaries and are thus higher than the numbers provided in the appendices to this book, which do not.

[29] DUA, DL 11.5/61, Zusammenstellung der Kriegs- und Kriegsfolgeschäden und Vermögenswerte gemäss Gesetz Nr. 53 der Militärregierung bezw. Nr. 5 des Alliierten Kontrollrates per 20. Juni 1948 nach Vermögensarten.

[30] DUA, BET 10/1, Liquiditäts-Übersicht vom 1.10.1923 bis 30.9.1946, April 20, 1948.

[31] Mayer-Wegelin, *Aller Anfang ist Schwer*, p. 169.

There can be, in short, no doubt that the Third Reich was exceedingly –
and lastingly – profitable for Degussa, and equally unmistakable is the degree to which this fact depended on the cultivation of good relations with the
regime and its representatives. By the war years, not only were some of them,
including the prominent Frankfurt Nazis Carl Lüer and Wilhelm Avieny,
ensconced on Degussa's supervisory board and working with Hermann
Schlosser on the parallel groups at Nazified firms such as the Metallgesellschaft and the Dresdner Bank, but these figures were also helping to
promote Schlosser's and his firm's standing. The signs of Schlosser's rising
prominence and political acceptability included his appointment as head
of the Economic Group for Chemistry in January 1943, as well as his accomplishment of a scarcely duplicated feat in the Third Reich: the removal
of a Party representative from Degussa's managing board. In March 1943,
Schlosser persuaded the Gauleiter of Hessen-Nassau to accept the dismissal
of a Nazi stalwart – and member of the Roessler family – on whose appointment he earlier had insisted. So trustworthy and loyal to the Third Reich did
the firm come to appear that some fervent Party figures, as well as officials
in Berlin, toyed at various times during the war with the idea of building
up Degussa – alone or in association with Henkel – as a counterweight to
the power of IG Farben within the chemical industry. At the moral price
of participation in the legalized theft that Aryanization rapidly became and
in the human exploitation that was built into the Nazi system of forced labor, which provided the Degussa concern with the services of some 3,000
concentration camp inmates (about 40 percent of them Jews), the firm had
achieved a scale, significance, and degree of commercial and political security
that Ernst Busemann could scarcely have imagined.

The individual chapters of this book detail the process by which Degussa's
leading figures adapted to then increasingly identified with and/or promoted
the Nazi regime's programs of "racial" persecution, militarization of the German economy, and armed expansion, and finally resisted questioning their
own conduct after it had helped reduce Germany and its reputation to ruins
and laid waste to the lives of millions. Precisely because this story frequently
shows the individuals involved in an unfavorable light – because the times,
sooner or later, brought out the worst more often than the best in them –
a cautionary observation may not be out of place here. The protagonists in
this history generally acted myopically; their tunnel vision, their focus on
immediate and parochial concerns, both patriotic and professional, blinded
most of them to the enormously destructive, sometimes vicious consequences
of their deeds. If contemporary readers similarly fail to think "outside the
box" of their own time and place, they may fall prey to another sort of moral
error, albeit one with far less severe effects. Decency entails not only the ability to evaluate and draw conclusions from past conduct, but also humility
before the human realities it illustrates. One of these is that people lead history forward, that is, without sure or perfect knowledge of its outcomes,

whereas succeeding generations cannot help but read it backward, with the advantage of awareness of where events were heading.

That Degussa's managers could and should have known better and found ways of acting differently is now generally understood; but that does not justify overlooking the impediments to such clarity and courage at the time. Regrettably, Degussa's history suggests that most people, when presented with opportunities or imperatives that they have every imminent or material reason to accept or accede to and only potential or moral grounds to reject, will choose the course of least resistance, internalize the arguments that legitimate it, and balk at admitting that one could or should have done otherwise. In all societies, but especially in dictatorial, arbitrary, and closed ones such as Nazi Germany, power holders rely and capitalize on these inducements to self-centeredness, self-delusion, and self-defense. One difficult but central task of this book is to recover the workings of these impulses (and to cause readers to consider their degree of immunity to them), without seeming to excuse them. However human, the choices made by Degussa's leaders between 1933 and 1945 deserve condemnation. Contempt should be reserved, nonetheless, for the movement that mobilized and manipulated their talents and weaknesses.

2

The Company, the Party, and the Regime

When Adolf Hitler became Chancellor of Germany at the end of January 1933, the nine members of Degussa's managing board included no Nazis. However, two department heads who were later elevated to the board, Helmut Achterath and Hermann Federlin, already had joined the National Socialist German Workers Party (NSDAP) during the previous summer, at the apogee of its electoral success. Their examples highlight the degree to which Nazism – within the firm, as in the nation as a whole – was a movement of the relatively young and restless. Achterath, who had come to Degussa via the merger with HIAG, was a thirty-nine-year-old bachelor when he signed up, already known for an all-or-nothing intellectual disposition that his colleagues still teased him about in his old age; Federlin was thirty-five and a refugee from Alsace, where he had grown up and from which he had fled when the province reverted to France in 1919.[1] Fritz Roessler, from the vantage point of his sixty-two years and his lofty position as head of the supervisory board, knew nothing prior to Hitler's accession of their political affiliation. He was equally oblivious to that of his own secretary, Adolf Hilpert, who had enlisted in the Party in October 1930 at the age of thirty-seven, and of several prominent subordinates in the same generation, such as Friedrich Pressel, an executive at Rheinfelden who later headed the factory; Hans Siebert, the business manager at the Hanau plant; and two of his ranking assistants, Adolf Diebold and Hans Kohlenbusch, all of whom had enrolled in the Party prior to the so-called seizure of power.[2] Still less did Roessler or his senior colleagues on the board take notice of the scattered Party activists in the firm's many other installations and offices, some

---

[1] On the enlistments in the Party, see BAL, NSDAP Mitglieder Kartei, Federlin's membership card, dated August 1, 1932; and HHW, Abt. 483, Akte 10989, Gaupersonalamt, June 13, 1942 (on Achterath). On Achterath's temperament, see DUA, BU Dr. Helmut Achterath, especially the speeches given at his retirement on September 30, 1957 and at his eighty-fifth birthday celebration on October 20, 1987. On Federlin's reasons, see DUA, SCH 01/03, Niederschrift betr. Meine Zugehörigkeit zur Nat. Soz. Arb. Partei, [1947], especially p. 2.

[2] On Roessler's ignorance of the deputy board members' and Hilpert's affiliation, DUA, BU Fritz Roessler, "Zur Geschichte der Scheideanstalt" [1937], Abschrift, p. 137. On Pressel, DUA, SCH 1/04, the documents grouped as Parteibindung Dr. Pressel, 1945–49. On the individuals at Hanau, SCH 1/02, Degussa-Siebert to the Militärregierung Hanau/M., April 11, 1946.

of whom, like Hilpert, were to rise to the status of Local Group Leaders and some of whom, like Pressel and perhaps Achterath, were to fall out with the Party in subsequent years.[3]

To Roessler at the time of Hitler's takeover, Nazism seemed a curious mixture of appealing and repellent elements. He had learned something of its goals and program from his nephew, Hans Menzel, who became Party member number 1830 as a university student in Munich in 1922 and thereafter made no secret of his enthusiasm, despite a period of apostasy between 1927 and 1929.[4] But, as the uncle recalled in a long written attempt "to come to grips with" National Socialism at the end of 1933, he had not taken the movement very seriously. On the one hand, some of its core ideas struck both him and his lifelong liberal father as "quite half-baked," but unexceptionable in principle, "since we had also always felt and thought basically as patriots and worked all our lives for the reconciliation of social clashes." On the other hand,

it was almost impossible to find out anything reliable about the goals and direction of the Party. The standard information that "National Socialism is not a party but a state of mind" was as unsatisfying as Menzel's response "Wait until we are in power, then you will see."...People could not place their confidence in someone who surrounded himself with all sorts of muddle-heads like the economist Feder and the fantastic members of the *Tat*-Circle and who wanted to cure everything with a new consciousness but presented as a practical program only antisemitism and street-fighting with the communists. One heard over and over, of course, of [Hitler's] fascinating speeches and ability to excite the masses, but the slogans that worked in that context said nothing to people who wanted to know how the party planned to relieve the ever more oppressive economic emergency. Pamphlets and books in which one hoped to find enlightenment offered only phrases and utopias. Hitler's own book *Mein Kampf* also disappointed me in this regard.[5]

---

[3] Partial listings of such people are to be found in DUA, BR 1/13, Angestellte, die Aufgrund ihrer politischen Belastung ins Lohnverhältnis übernommen wurden, 4 December 1946; and in SCH 1/02, memo of the Technische Abteilung, 3 May 1945, and Vorentwurf zu einem Schreiben an die zu entlassenden Ortsgruppenleiter unserer Firma, May 28, 1945. For another case of a later falling out, see SCH 1/05, the documents concerning Georg Ungethüm. On Achterath, the evidence is somewhat conflicting; cf. DUA, SCH 01/03, especially Scherf's statement of July 17, 1946, and the complaint in Achterath's postwar denazification process, both of which assert that he turned away from the Party between 1934 and 1937, and HHW 483/10989, the Gaupersonalamt's evaluation of June 13, 1942, which notes no political activity after 1934, but concludes that he can be relied upon "to support the Führer and the state at any time without reservation."

[4] On Menzel's Party membership, see DUA, BU Hans Menzel, Lebenslauf, February 4, 1932, which gives the year of his initial enrollment; and BAL, NSDAP Mitglieder Kartei, Menzel's membership card, which bears the date April 15, 1925, the day of his readmission after the "refounding" of the NSDAP, and shows that he dropped out in late January 1927 and returned to the fold on October 1, 1929.

[5] DUA, BU Fritz Roessler, "Nationalsozialismus" [December 1933], pp. 1–3.

Nor could anyone Roessler respected allay his concerns:

It was striking that within the social and business circles close to me literally no one knew much about the Party. In Frankfurt, the Gutbrod brothers recruited for it, which was certainly no recommendation. It was rumored that the great industrialist Fritz Thyssen, whom people thought an outsider anyway, supported the Party with large funds. Fairly late, we heard that our business associate Engineer [Albert] Pietzsch of Munich was an intimate friend and follower of Hitler. Among my old fraternity brothers, I later discovered only one Nazi, K. Voswinckel.... The Party had as good as no followers among the educated bourgeoisie.... One could go wherever one wanted – to business associates and supervisory board meetings, to fraternity brothers and university professors – everywhere one encountered the same rejection.[6]

Finally, the composition and conduct of the National Socialist delegation in the Frankfurt City Council had done little to elevate Roessler's impression. From 1924 to 1933, twenty Nazis served in that body, nearly all of them lower-ranking white-collar employees; Roessler dismissed them as "completely unknown, little people, who merely made a racket."[7] As far as he could tell, the Nazi Party was a mainly negative coalition of three frustrated groups: young people disgusted by the nation's defeat and shame, its uninspiring politicians, and "the growth of lying and deception in public and private life"; "the many freebooting types brought to the surface by the war," who were ready to fight on alternate days for the Nazis or the Reds; and "the discontented, who...had suffered shipwreck in life [and]...blamed the prevailing 'system' and above all the Jews for their misfortune."[8]

In other words, however acceptable certain of the NSDAP's general positions seemed, only desperation could have driven Roessler and his senior colleagues to affiliate with it, and they were not in a panicky mood at the turn of 1932/33. Neither Degussa's own business, nor the state of the nation's leadership seemed to warrant backing so unpredictable a force as National Socialism. To Roessler's mind, Chancellors "Brüning and Papen knew what Germany needed, they just could not escape certain restrictions, of which the worst was named Hugenberg" – the last remark being a slap at the inflexible leader of the German Nationalist Party (DNVP), who impeded all attempts

---

[6] *Ibid.*, pp. 2, 4. On the Gutbrod brothers and Pietzsch, who later became the head of the National Economic Chamber in the Third Reich, see Peter Hayes, *Industry and Ideology: IG Farben in the Nazi Era* (New York: Cambridge University Press, 1987, 2000), pp. 68, 97, 247.

[7] DUA, BU Fritz Roessler, "Nationalsozialismus," p. 5; Barbara Köhler, "Die Nationalsozialisten in der Frankfurter Stadtverordnetenversammlung 1929 bis 1933," *Archiv Frankfurts Geschichte und Kunst* 59 (1985), pp. 475–83. See also Dieter Rebentisch, "Persönlichkeit und Karriereverlauf der nationalsozialistischen Führungskader in Hessen 1928–1945," *Hessische Jahrbuch für Landesgeschichte* 33 (1983), pp. 293–331.

[8] "Nationalsozialismus," pp. 3–4.

during the Depression years to rally a "Citizens' Bloc" of the parties that stood between the Marxist Left and the Nazi Right.[9] As a result, Roessler wrote in 1937,

> until 1933, the Party had little visibility in the Scheideanstalt. The only person known for years as a member was Hans Menzel, who also served as the Party's county treasurer. He seems to have received contributions to the Party several times from individual directors, but got a stern rebuff from Busemann after the November [1932] elections that were unfavorable to Hitler, when he [Menzel] approached the leaders once more with an appeal for funds that he had signed and that rather tactlessly emphasized the anti-capitalist character of the Party.[10]

It appears, then, that the "fever chart" of support for Nazism among Degussa's elders paralleled that which characterized the older generation of German big businessmen as a whole during the Depression years. Long relatively flat, it spiked upward in mid-1932, then fell anew during the autumn of that year, when signs of economic improvement, maladroit Party propaganda, and corporate satisfaction with the Papen and Schleicher governments combined to stem the momentum Hitler had been gaining in entrepreneurial circles.[11] In retrospect, Fritz Roessler was sure of what an American historian recently has argued to impressive effect: "A really strong and ruthless dictator could have gradually taken the wind from the National Socialists' sails. But the strong man was not there, and so destiny took its course."[12]

When it did, and the "National Revolution" began turning into an unruly and violent groundswell toward one-party dictatorship during the spring of 1933, Degussa's unprepared leaders responded as befit their respective personalities. As always, Fritz Roessler's was the voice of perceptive, high-minded equivocation. On the one hand, he felt compelled from the outset of the Third Reich to admire "the organization and discipline in the Party and the spirit of sacrifice with which so many did the hard political work for years without compensation," along with the regime's initial accomplishments: "With the removal of the parties and the parliamentary system, with the abolition of the state legislatures, with the ever continuing unification of the nation, almost overnight wishes have been fulfilled that every reasonable German, regardless of party persuasion, had long harbored in his breast

---

[9] *Ibid.*, p. 5. On Hugenberg, see John Leopold, *Alfred Hugenberg: The Radical Nationalist Campaign against the Weimar Republic* (New Haven: Yale University Press, 1977); on such efforts on the part of other leaders of the German chemical industry, see Hayes, *Industry and Ideology*, pp. 48–54.

[10] DUA, BU Fritz Roessler, "Zur Geschichte" [1937], Abschrift, p. 137.

[11] See Henry Ashby Turner, Jr., *German Big Business and the Rise of Hitler* (New York: Oxford University Press, 1985).

[12] DUA, BU Dr. Fritz Roessler, "Nationalsozialismus," p. 5 (for the quotation); cf. Henry Ashby Turner, Jr., *Hitler's Thirty Days to Power* (Reading, MA: Addison-Wesley, 1996).

but hardly dared dream of achieving, since the barriers set up by those who profited from these untenable conditions were too great."[13] As time passed, he added other measures to the catalog of those he greeted warmly: "the reintroduction of compulsory military service, the detachment from... the chains of the Versailles Treaty," and the elimination of unemployment. Ever the advocate of improving the lot of his workforce, he could not resist taking sarcastic pleasure in the new government's effect on the behavior of those other employers who "now suddenly discovered their social heart and adopted as a matter of course welfare measures they once laughed off as utopian, such as workers' vacations and profit sharing."[14] Moreover, Hitler pleasantly surprised Roessler. The new Chancellor turned out to be "not only a great demagogue and party organizer, but also a towering, smart, and honest man, a real leader," who delivered speeches "which are masterpieces of simplicity, clarity, and honesty."[15] After so many years of uncharismatic politicians at the helm, the nation seemed finally under the command of an authentic, trustworthy, and inspiring ruler, one unafraid to assert its interests: "Not least, Hitler's manly stance against the comedy of the League of Nations and the swindle of disarmament won him personally all hearts.... The main point is that the nation now stands up to the world in unison on behalf of its honor and prestige."[16]

On the other hand, Roessler thought that the quality of the nation's new masters stopped with Hitler. The speeches of his ministers and the Party bigwigs were "monotonous torrents of phrases;" important state and Party offices were occupied by generally uneducated persons "with whom in their earlier, bourgeois life one would not have liked to traffic;" and "the people one meets in the middle and lower level bureaucratic posts resemble in their behavior, character, and lack of competence almost exactly those one encountered in the same positions after 1918. It is always the same sort of people that a revolution lifts up, only the flag changes."[17] As before, the pettiness, greed, and "delusions of grandeur" of such people were allowed to do much damage to worthier individuals and institutions, this time under the motto "A National Socialist can do no wrong."[18] Fending off "these catalinarian beings..., whom the wave of revolution has raised out of their swamp," from the numerous philanthropic organizations in which Roessler took an interest became one of his principal activities from 1933 to 1936.[19] As for the economic recovery the regime claimed credit for in 1933, here, too, Roessler had his doubts:

---

[13] "Nationalsozialismus," pp. 7–8.
[14] DUA, BU Fritz Roessler, "Nachtrag zur Niederschrift 'Meine öffentliche Tätigkeit'," [1936], p. 1; "Zur Geschichte," [1937], p. 101.
[15] "Nationalsozialismus," p. 6.   [16] *Ibid.*, pp. 9, 11.   [17] *Ibid.*, p. 6; "Nachtrag," p. 14.
[18] "Nationalsozialismus," p. 7.
[19] Roessler's "Nachtrag" details his efforts in this regard; the quoted passage appears on p. 13.

[The government] has tackled work creation with wonderful energy and optimism and without consideration of the costs. But is it not doing exactly that for which municipalities, industry, and private persons were reproached so fiercely in 1928–29? Is it constructing, not stadiums and palatial hospitals, but highways and administrative buildings for the S.A., which are unproductive for the present and likely to have value only in the remote future, and without thinking where the money will come from when the bills fall due? Are we not entering a publicly indebted economy of the worst sort? And another concern is the following: If it is to last, the now definitely developing revival of business can proceed only very slowly and relieve the labor market but gradually. The present forced relief through road and canal construction can be sustained financially for only a few years. Then the hundreds of thousands thus employed will be without jobs once more, probably at a time when business still cannot take them on. That can produce ugly disappointment. What will happen in the meantime if the recovery stalls for reasons outside our control?[20]

Neither distaste for the Party faithful nor scepticism about its economic course explains, however, why Roessler declared himself unwilling ever to join the NSDAP: "To be a genuine National Socialist, one must believe in two things that are the pillars of this world view, first, in the special mission of the Aryans, and particularly the Germans; and second, in the possibility of the total state, that is, of the unity of ideology and state, both terms understood in the broadest sense. I cannot do either."[21]

Roessler was not above certain forms of racist discourse – his disparaging reference to "ambitious Jews" whose presence had alienated him from the German Democratic Party (DDP) in the early 1920s and his description of one Degussa manager as "a clever, somewhat Jewishly and unscrupulously talented salesman," attest to that.[22] Moreover, in 1933, he wrote, "No one can deny that the Jews have played too large a role in German public and economic life for many years and that their influence grew to a frightening degree after 1918 and became a cultural danger. Scarcely anyone would have had any objections to pushing Jewry back strongly, to limiting or even prohibiting access to certain professions."[23] But he drew the line at blanket racial condemnation and despoilment. The notion of pure races and the related glorification of the Aryans struck him as "devoid of any scientific basis." The Party's belief in "the horrible conspiracy of international Jewry with Marxism" he could "only characterize as a fixation." Restrictions on the rising generation of Jews were one thing, but "it is impossible to approve of the ruthless destruction of the livelihoods of thousands of Jewish and half-Jewish fellow citizens, many of whom had done great service to Germany

---

[20] "Nationalsozialismus," pp. 16–17. Cf. Harold James, *The German Slump* (Oxford: Clarendon Press, 1986), Chapter 3, especially pp. 88–90.
[21] "Nationalsozialismus," p. 9.
[22] DUA, BU Dr. Fritz Roessler, "Zur Geschichte," [1933], p. 82.
[23] "Nationalsozialismus," p. 10.

and its science and culture."[24] During the next few years, he temporized over the so-called racial question, laboring to protect individual Jewish associates and to obtain financial support for those driven from their positions, including a half-Jewish nephew, but also participating in the purge of Jews from Degussa's supervisory board and from his old fraternity, acting always, he told himself, "under the terror of the lower and mid-level Party agencies."[25] Only very late in the day, just before he died in 1937, did shame catch up with him and prompt him to admit, at least with regard to his beloved *Corps Suevia*, the correctness of those "who were against all concessions from the beginning and would rather have disbanded than offend their fundamental principles."[26]

The Party's totalitarian aspirations, Roessler believed moreover, were simply pointless, even "laughable," and a sure sign of the usual lack of a sense of history among ideologues. For the moment, he did not begrudge the Nazis their dictatorship, thinking it "probably the only possibility for creating order among us." But he thought that unity achieved by repression could not last. Eventually young people would grow bored with "intellectual tutelage," the middle classes would weary of the endless party meetings and collections, the ever "mentally alive" German people would find the predictable, "prechewed" propaganda intolerable, and the old liberal, conservative, social democratic, and catholic convictions would re-emerge. The Party's hope of banishing such differences of opinion through education in the true ideology seemed to Roessler "just as much an illusion as that of the old democrats, for whose ideal republic the only precondition was that men be angels, who would live in harmony if only they were properly taught and led." Worse, by excusing incompetence and ignorance in the short run, such utopianism created "the danger that we are heading toward chaos."[27] All the more reason, he concluded, for people like him to struggle against "the application of exaggerated or falsely understood Party doctrines" and to ride out the storm, bearing in mind that one "should not stand grumbling on the sidelines, even if one feels momentarily superfluous, but should recognize the good in the movement, ignore the human deficiencies associated with every revolution, and do one's bit so that this wild-grown juice becomes wine."[28]

Just such an attitude suited Ernst Busemann's pragmatic temperament completely, but, as always, he was less willing than Roessler to work out his views in detail, let alone to record them. What Degussa's chairman actually thought of Hitler or the Nazi movement is not clear from any of his surviving comments or writings, and it is hazardous to infer much from the conflicting

---

[24] *Ibid.*, pp. 10–11.
[25] DUA, BU Fritz Roessler, "Nachtrag," especially pp. 13 (for the quotation), 15, and 18. On the removals from the supervisory board, "Zur Geschichte," Abschrift [1937], p. 98.
[26] "Nachtrag," pp. 15–16.   [27] "Nationalsozialismus," pp. 12–14, 16–17.
[28] "Nachtrag," p. 18, and "Nationalsozialismus," p. 18.

body language captured by various extant photos of him in Party-organized settings during 1933 and subsequent years. Certain is only that he learned of the NSDAP's intention to cease accepting new enrollees in May 1933, considered having the entire managing board enlist en bloc before the gates closed, then dropped the idea – and disliked being reminded of it thereafter.[29] By the time the Party resumed accepting applications in May 1937, he had little to gain by joining, and he died two and one-half years later without having done so. Meanwhile, he perfected a rhetoric that suggested support for the new regime, without embracing its most questionable features. Thus, the firm's annual report of late 1933 combined an effusive tone with an *apologia pro vita sua*:

> As we write the report for the sixty-second business year of the Scheideanstalt, the struggle to weld our people together for common work at home and to make good our claim to equality in the counsel of nations is being fought with an enthusiasm not present for centuries. It is an old experience in German history that periods of powerful will in the state leadership coincide with economic upswing. We are all the more justified in expecting this experience to repeat itself because the strong political determination of the national leadership presses externally, not for military glory, but for the creation and maintainance of a healthy peace, and strives internally to give the German economy, and especially the extraordinarily diverse German industry, the stability it needs – an industry that since the end of the war was unhesitatingly kept busy paying the unprecedented domestic and foreign burdens of the state, then criticized as incompetent because of its declining profitability, yet nonetheless still commands respect worldwide.[30]

When the time came to prepare the same document four years later, Busemann was even more subtly ambiguous, noting that he planned "to begin the report more or less as follows: the path of German economic policy is so clearly marked out in the speeches of our Führer and the publications of government and Party offices that general economic remarks are superfluous here."[31]

Mastery of this sort of phraseology, in which the hearer could single out the tone he or she preferred, was emblematic of Busemann's leadership style. Having long since learned to take the world as he found it, he was not one to stake out public positions unless he had to, let alone to break a lance, as the German idiom goes, attempting to change what was beyond his strength. Far better, in his view, to avoid unproductive confrontations, to preserve as much freedom of maneuver as possible, and to concentrate on influencing specific matters of immediate concern to him and his enterprise, preferably from prominent positions but in inconspicuous fashion. Whatever his initial

---

[29] "Zur Geschichte," Abschrift [1937], pp. 137–38.
[30] DUA, Bericht über das 62. Geschäftsjahr 1932/33, prepared for the stockholders' meeting on January 9, 1934, p. 6.
[31] DUA, DL 3.Busemann/5, Aktennotiz, October 22, 1937.

misgivings about the Nazi regime – and his actions establish that he shared the discomfort of many of big business leaders with some of its economic pronouncements and its application of racist precepts to, at least, people like themselves – Busemann was temperamentally and tactically disposed to play along and wait for his chances. Indeed, he was rather representative of the broad band of German industrialists who concluded at the outset of Nazi rule that, as the English adage runs, discretion is the better part of valor. Like so many of them, he instinctively – and, in effect, ruthlessly – prioritized the threats he faced, ranking political chaos and Nazi economic ham-handedness as more dangerous and more easily diverted than the new regime's assault on civil and human rights. He therefore opted to take the time-honored corporate approach to influencing public policy: seeking out responsible figures in political positions and deploying rational arguments to bring them around, without openly challenging the primacy of politics that the new regime proclaimed.

To be sure, Busemann's methods entailed seeming to meet the "New Germany" halfway and amounted to taking the course of least resistance in the face of Nazi zealotry and thuggery. Any other stance, according to the conventional corporate wisdom of the time, would have been both self-indulgent and foolhardy.[32] Thus, in 1933 he concentrated on walking a fine line between aligning himself with the nation's new masters and alienating those they had overwhelmed, whether in his own workforce or in the business world. Representative of the effort – and the compromises it entailed – was his response to the occupation of the Industry and Trade Chamber of Frankfurt by Nazi activists on April 1, 1933, which led promptly to the resignation of its executive committee and the installation as its acting president of Dr. Carl Lüer, a thirty-five-year-old "old fighter" (he had joined the NSDAP in 1927 and held membership number 71,637) and tutor in management and finance at Frankfurt's university. As a member of the Electoral Committee composed to legalize this *Putsch*, Busemann helped assure not only that Lüer would be duly nominated and chosen in a special poll five weeks later, but also that one of the other successful candidates of the Chamber's industrial division would be Hermann Schlosser of Degussa. In so doing, Busemann participated in ratifying both the coordination (*Gleichschaltung*) of Frankfurt's business organizations with the new regime and the purge of their personnel of Jews and other politically unacceptable figures that followed.[33] Equally characteristically, he managed in the ensuing months to

---

[32] See, on the development of this corporate consensus, Peter Hayes, "Industry under the Swastika," in Harold James and Jakob Tanner (eds.), *Enterprise in the Period of Fascism in Europe* (Aldershot, UK: Ashgate, 2002), pp. 28–30, and "Conscience, Knowledge, and 'Secondary Ethics': German Corporate Executives from 'Aryanization' to the Holocaust," in Judith Banki and John Pawlikowski (eds.), *Ethics in the Shadow of the Holocaust* (Minneapolis: Sheed & Ward, 2001), pp. 317–23.

[33] HSW, Spruchkammerakten Lüer, Nr. 646, Bd. 1, the Vernehmungsprotokolle of Josef Flach and Karl Ringel, September 3 and 8, 1948; the excerpt from "Umschaltung an der Frankfurter

navigate the transformation of his industry's independent professional association, the League to Preserve the Interests of the Chemicals Industry, into the nazified Economic Group for Chemistry. As vice president of the former body during the transition, he even succeeded in retaining the friendship and trust of the two men among his oldest business allies most obviously displaced and promoted, respectively, by this development: Carl Bosch of IG Farben and Albert Pietzsch of the Munich Electrochemical Works of Höllriegelskreuth.[34]

Still, neither Busemann's agility nor Achterath's and Federlin's Party memberships seemed quite sufficient in early 1933 as pledges of the firm's goodwill toward the new order taking shape in Germany. At Hans Menzel's instigation, Roessler and Busemann concluded that the enrollment of a full member of the managing board in the Party would lend conviction to Degussa's "state-affirming" stance. As their candidate for the Industry and Trade Chamber's executive committee, Schlosser was the logical choice. After the war, he claimed that these lots fell to him because he was the youngest full member of the managing board and thus most credible as a link to the local Nazi hierarchy.[35] Menzel almost certainly recognized him also as the coming man in the firm, therefore the one the NSDAP would most want and the firm would most need to see wearing a Party badge. But Fritz Roessler recorded a third reason for Schlosser's selection: among the board members, he "had always stood closest to the ideas of the Party."[36] He seemed, in other words, the board member most capable of finding common ground with the Nazi true believers. Theirs was an ideological overlap, however, not an identity, which is not to say that the distinction would matter greatly in practical terms during the subsequent years.

Though not himself notably religious, Schlosser was the son of a pastor, the husband of a woman who responded to the Nazification of German Protestantism in 1933 by joining the dissenting Confessional Church, and the brother of a fervent convert to Quakerism (who, moreover, lost his civil service position in 1933 because of his membership in the Social Democratic

Börse," *Frankfurter Zeitung*, April 4, 1933, p. 4; and the excerpt from "Das Ergebnis der Frankfurter Handelskammerwahlen," *Frankfurter Zeitung*, May 7, 1933, p. 8; Bd. 2, the defense brief by Lüer's lawyers, October 19, 1948, p. 7, which lists Busemann among the members of the Electoral Committee, and the prosecution brief of the Hessisches Ministerium für politische Befreiung, May 30, 1949.
34 See Hayes, *Industry and Ideology*, p. 97; DUA, DL 3.Busemann/4, his Notiz Betr. Verein mit dem Langen Namen, December 20, 1933. Within a year, Busemann had become head of the special subgroup for "other basic chemicals"; DL 3.Busemann/4, his Notiz Besprechung im Verein mit dem Langen Namen bzw. Wirtschaftsgruppe Chemische Industrie, November 11, 1934.
35 For this and the other biographical information that follows, unless otherwise indicated, see DUA, BU Hermann Schlosser, the four versions of his career during the Third Reich, along with his responses to the occupation authorities' *Fragebogen*, that he prepared and his advisors redacted between 1945 and 1947.
36 DUA, BU Dr. Fritz Roessler, "Zur Geschichte" [1937], p. 138.

Party). He did not like the Party's encroachments on the churches, and he had seen the damage its purge of leftists did to individuals. That, at least on occasion, he found its racism difficult to reconcile with Christian charity also soon became apparent. Nonetheless, like countless bourgeois Germans of his day, he felt drawn to the Nazi promise of a "people's community" that would overcome the nation's many internal divisions, particularly along class lines.[37] The attempt to fuse nationalist feeling with a sense of social obligation to one's fellow citizens struck an especially familiar chord, since his father had been a friend of the turn-of-the-century German liberal Friedrich Naumann, who had made his reputation propagating an earlier, far more humane form of National Socialism.[38] Schlosser thus assented to his colleagues' request, applying for admission to the NSDAP as of May 1, 1933. But he neglected to conform to Party policy by resigning immediately from the Freemasons, and his delay of several months in that regard provoked a long argument between local Nazi purists and the regional and national Party bureaucracies over his suitability for enrollment. In late 1934, a Party Court in Frankfurt finally rejected his candidacy. This act seems to have embarassed the Nazi leadership in the city almost as much as it did Schlosser, but no way around the decision could be found until 1938, when the Gauleitung launched an effort to gain him entrance to the Party through the special dispensation of Hitler himself. Following a year of petitioning, the Führer not only assented on December 19, 1939, but also made Schlosser's enlistment retroactive to the date of his original application. Although there is no evidence that the Degussa executive initiated this action, it is unlikely to have occured without his knowledge and solely through the exertions of the firm's Party Foreman Adolf Hilpert, as Schlosser later claimed.[39]

Schlosser accepted joining the Party, both initially and later, as he would accept so much else during the Third Reich, on the basis of the romantic and militarist concepts of duty and solidarity that so many men of his class and age took away from the First World War. Indeed, he exemplified a widespread generational tendency, not only to cultivate the memory of that conflict, but to import its supposed spirit into civilian life.[40] Thus,

[37] See, most recently, on the enormous appeal of this idea, Peter Fritzsche, *Germans into Nazis* (Cambridge, MA: Harvard University Press, 1999).
[38] On Naumann and his efforts, see Gordon Craig, *Germany 1866–1945* (New York: Oxford University Press, 1978), pp. 185 and 276.
[39] BAL, BDC OPG Schlosser, PK Schlosser, and his membership card. Cf. DUA, BU Hermann Schlosser, the responses prepared in 1945–47 to the American denazification questionnaire.
[40] For an interesting examination of a similar tendency on the part of another German industrialist of Schlosser's generation, whose career and worldview show suggestive parallels with his, see Cornelia Rauh-Kühne, "Hans Constantin Paulssen: Sozialpartnerschaft aus dem Geiste der Kriegskameradschaft," in Paul Erker and Toni Pierenkemper (eds.), *Deutsche Unternehmer zwischen Kriegswirtschaft und Wiederaufbau* (München: R. Oldenbourg, 1999), pp. 109–92.

even in 1965, on the occasion of the fiftieth anniversary of his service with Degussa, Schlosser could not help but return to his wartime experience as the touchstone of his professional philosophy and conduct, telling his listeners:

The concept of work-comradeship has never been for me – everyone who knows me knows this – an empty phrase or a means of currying favor or popularity. It corresponds rather to my honest sense of the spirit that should dominate in a plant. . . . This has nothing to do with sentimentality or an unrealistic gushiness. Rather, for me, the indispensable prerequisite for true comradeship, as I understand it, is discipline and readiness for subordination. That is how I experienced and absorbed it in its highest form in the comradeship of the front in the First World War.[41]

And that is how he acted on it before and during the Second. Not otherwise an emotional or selfless man, Schlosser seems to have found an outlet for his feelings – and a psychological legitimation of his own ambition and the gains it brought him – in a melodramatic, almost bathetic glorification of dutiful sacrifice for the national cause, for which his wartime role remained the model. Inclined to represent himself as an old soldier at every passable opportunity, to wax nostalgic at regimental reunions, and to resort reflexively to military analogies when at a loss for words (upon a colleague's death in 1954, Schlosser told Degussa's employees that they "must close ranks to fill the painful gap that Ernst Baerwind leaves behind"), he adopted the self-image of the loyal, if put upon, officer.[42] This made him an easy mark for the Nazis' exploitation of such attitudes, indeed it made him a faithful servant of the regime, and the resulting gap between his moral values and the consequences of his conduct increased from year to year.

Perhaps most revealing of Schlosser's readiness to submit all other considerations to the demands of imposed duty is the address he delivered to the factory assembly on the occasion of his succession to Busemann as company chairman in November 1939:

Dear Comrades, I know that there are matters and questions regarding National Socialism that have been difficult for one or another of us. . . . For myself, I have struggled my way years ago to the conviction that these are all marginal aspects of an immensely great happening that we can neither measure nor evaluate, but that perhaps in a century can be grasped by a historian. . . . We stand in a battle the seriousness of which one cannot depict weightily enough. . . . In such a battle, there can be no half-heartedness. I want there to be no doubt about the fact that I stand behind the Führer, come what may. . . . And [I] expect and demand the same obedient loyalty from you without evasion and quibbling, so that the Scheideanstalt stands as

---

[41] DUA, Hermann Schlosser. Ein halbes Jahrhundert Geschichte der Degussa. Reden zu seinem 50 jährigen Jubiläum, Rede Hermann Schlosser, February 16, 1965.

[42] See DUA, DL 3.Hermann Schlosser/3, Schlosser to Leutnant H. Marx, October 31, 1941; BU Hermann Schlosser, Rede zur Banbana-Feier, December 2, 1959; and Mechthild Wolf, *Im Zeichen von Sonne und Mond* (Frankfurt am Main: Degussa AG, 1993), p. 176 (for the quotation).

a united entity behind the Führer and thus Germany and thereby fulfills its mission in this great struggle, as destiny has prescribed it.[43]

Still more striking, in retrospect, is the closing passage of a speech he delivered in September 1944 to celebrate the raising of a new factory to replace a bombed-out one. Even as the Allies closed in on Germany from both west and east, Schlosser felt moved to tell the assembled workforce that:

...this works has been completed by a National Socialist Plant Community. This concept should be of special importance and immeasurably high value today and in the difficult period which undoubtedly lies before us. The National Socialist Plant Community is built on the comradeship of the front, which we old soldiers brought home from the unhappy course of the last war as the most valuable, perhaps the only, possession. Adolf Hitler, our leader, built his People's Community and his work out of this comradeship of the front, and out of this plant community in these difficult days will emerge a community of fate that must withstand all circumstances in the coming weeks and months. We have seen here, my work comrades, how one can master fate under the most difficult conditions, if [we] only [stand] together unshakeably and [will] it, and my wish today is...that the National Socialist Plant Community will prove itself in all its depth, in its highest value, within this plant as in all of Degussa in the coming weeks and months and years.[44]

Legitimate as it is to relate Schlosser's diction in these speeches to the heat of the respective moments, namely the first and last months of what he considered a "life or death struggle," and to the danger of denunciation for saying anything less slavish, such *Durchhalteparolen* are, nonetheless, the authentic voice of the man. His fixation on the secondary virtues of loyalty and bearing – his addiction to what one contemporary has recalled ruefully as "that damned sense of duty" – disposed him to do what the regime requested, from the beginning to the bitter end, even when he did not agree with all that this required.[45] Given this, the death of his twenty-year-old son on the Russian front in July 1941, and even moreso that of his daughter and grandson in 1945, have the overtones of a classical Greek tragedy. She killed herself and her offspring shortly after her husband fell in the Battle of the Bulge – in fulfillment of a promise to him.[46]

The remaining full members of the managing board who, like Busemann, remained outside the Party in 1933 also acted true to their respective temperaments. Baerwind was excluded, of course, by his Jewish grandmother, but it is hard to imagine he would have joined under other circumstances – he was simply too reserved and aloof. A Party evaluation of him in 1942, which betrayed no knowledge of his heritage, captured something of his stiffness: "In

[43] DUA, Degussa Feldpost Nr. 3, Rede Schlosser, November 23, 1939.
[44] DUA, BU Hermann Schlosser, Ansprache des Herrn Direktor Hermann Schlosser anlässlich des Richtfestes des Degussitbetriebs in Stierstadt, September 5, 1944.
[45] Alexander Stahlberg, *Die verdammte Pflicht* (Berlin: Ullstein, 1987, 1994).
[46] On the daughter's death pact, see DUA D3/2, Ernst Baerwind's diary entry of January 20, 1945.

the plant, he takes the lordly standpoint and is not popular with the work-force. In general, human beings begin to exist for him at the level of academic titles."[47] Bernau also opted permanently against membership, as one might expect from a man of his age and inclination to remain behind the scenes; so did Carl Riefstahl, who was nearing the end of his career (he retired from the board in 1937), and the sensitive Hektor Roessler, who killed himself in 1941, apparently because he could not bear the responsibility of "combing out" workers for military service.[48] Adalbert Fischer's reticence, however, like his abandonment of it after the Party lifted its ban on new members in May 1937, was purely opportunistic. As the sales director chiefly responsible for wood carbonization products, he appears to have acted, both then and earlier, according to momentary calculations of professional advantage. At least the Party thought so: its review of his political reliability some years later concluded that "he has not taken on the national socialist world view as one would expect. . . . He clings to self-interest and petty bourgeois tra-dition."[49] Koloman Róka, the rising star on Degussa's technical side and part of the four-person group (along with Schlosser, Fischer, and Baerwind) that Fritz Roessler considered "the real leadership of the firm" by 1937, did not join the Party until 1940, two years after his exchange of Hungarian citizenship for that of the then-triumphant German Reich removed both a barrier to signing up and an excuse for staying out.[50] Hans Schneider also finally applied for membership in late 1940, but he died a few months later, before being formally admitted.[51]

The following year, seven men were elevated to the board, including the three long-standing Party members (Achterath, Federlin, and Menzel), three who had joined in 1937 and 1940 (Geo Hubert, Robert Hirtes, and Ewald von Retze), and one who never enrolled (August Kolb).[52] Kolb's ability to serve effectively, nonetheless, as Degussa's chief liaison with the government in Berlin demonstrates that obtaining a Party card was not obligatory.[53] The available records also suggest that doing so was not a precise indication of

---

[47] HHW 483/10982, NSDAP Gauleitung Hessen-Nassau an den Sonderbeauftragten für Wirtschaftsführung, January 14, 1942. Baerwind's heritage and manner did not exclude him, however, from the award of the War Service Cross, First Class, late in the Second World War; see DL 2/1, Notizen aus der Vorstandsbesprechung am 27. Oktober 1944, p. 1.

[48] See the undated summary sheet in HSAW, 483/10989. On the causes of Hektor Roessler's suicide, DUA, D 3/2, Baerwind's diary entry for March 23, 1941.

[49] See HHW, 483/10982, Gaupersonalamt to the Gauwirtschaftsberater, May 19, 1943.

[50] See DUA, BU Dr. Fritz Roessler, "Zur Geschichte" [1937], Abschrift, p. 140; and HHW, Gaupersonalamtsleiter to Gauwirtschaftsberater, March 31, 1942.

[51] BAL, NSDAP Mitglieder Kartei, Schneider's membership card, giving his application date as November 18, 1940, and his death date as February 18, 1941.

[52] Heinz Mayer-Wegelin, *Aller Anfang ist Schwer* (Frankfurt am Main: Degussa AG, 1973), p. 165. On Hirtes's, Hubert's, and von Retze's memberships, as well as Kolb's lack of same, see the relevant sections in HHW, 483/10982 and in DUA, SCH 01/004.

[53] On Kolb's lobbying work, see DUA, BU Dr. August Kolb, Degussa to the members of its Aufsichtsrat, December 3, 1941.

6   Hermann Federlin

how each man behaved with respect to Nazi policies. Bernau, a nonmember, descended on at least one occasion to notable viciousness toward Jews who stood in the way of the firm's purposes, and Kolb, another outsider, exhibited a dedication to the German war effort that extended to endorsing "draconian" reprisals, including shooting communists and Jews, for acts of resistance in France.[54] Conversely, among the joiners, only the veteran Party members, especially Menzel and Federlin, appear to have been more than self-interested National Socialists, which explains in part the latter man's inheritance in 1941 of Hektor Roessler's responsibility for personnel policy, a post for which political reliability was an important qualification.[55]

In 1933, however, the urgency of developing these connections with the Nazi Party, not to mention others that were to prove far more significant, was offset by uncertainty concerning how long the new regime would last and how much Germany's elites would have to adapt to it. This perhaps accounts

[54] See Chapter 3 below, regarding Bernau and the takeover of the Margulies family's shares in the ÖCW and Leukon firms; on Kolb, see his remarks concerning Brahn and his nephew, discussed later in this chapter, and DUA, TLE 1/23, Menzel's memo, Die politische und wirtschaftliche Lage in Frankreich, September 20, 1941, reporting on a conversation with Kolb toward the end of his period of service with the occupation administration.

[55] Quite rightly, the judgment in Federlin's denazification case took his withdrawal from the Protestant church as an indication of his degree of identification with the Party; see DUA, SCH 01/003, the text of the judgment, October 3, 1948.

7   Adolf Hilpert

for Busemann's hesitancy about enrolling the managing board as a group. Besides, to neutralize the immediate threats to the firm's operations posed by the Party's factory cells, its so-called racial policies, and its reorganization of economic policy making would require more than adding a few directors to the thousands of "March violets," whom the Nazis often mocked in any case. Success was likely to depend far more on co-opting and mobilizing Party members who were already at hand, namely Adolf Hilpert, Hans Menzel, and Albert Pietzsch.

With Factory Party Cell Foreman Hilpert, Degussa rapidly developed a lasting modus vivendi. The man was, it soon became apparent, a bombastic, bullying racist of the worst Nazi sort. A representative utterance, made to the Plant Assembly of November 1939, denounced the fanciful circumstance that "objectionable Jews at the head of commerce, industry, and all decisive posts in the Reich are doing their criminal work," and witnesses at his denazification proceeding after the war testified to his role in the harassment, arrests, and subsequent deaths of two helpless elderly Jewish women who lived in Frankfurt.[56] But within the firm, he contented himself with

[56] For the quotation, see DUA, BU Hermann Schlosser, Spruchkammerverfahren, Scherf to Offermann, July 13, 1948; on the arrests, see SCH 01/004, Scherf's Notiz über Einsichtnahme in die Spruchkammerakten Hilpert, November 1, 1948.

petty tyrannizing of lower-level personnel on such matters as buying from Jewish shops, hanging Nazi flags, and enrolling in Party fund drives, and rapidly established himself as relatively amenable in the eyes of the senior management.[57] He appears to have recognized that by serving its interests, he would also advance his own, and, indeed, Degussa soon went out of its way to create a position for him commensurate with his rising status as both District Group Leader of the NSDAP and City Councillor. In November 1937, "on political grounds . . . since something had to be done" and over the expressed opposition of both Baerwind and Fischer but with Schlosser and Bernau maintaining discreet silence, Busemann decided to name Hilpert the head of a new office for headquarters administration within the firm.[58] Four years later, he became leader of Degussa's newly created Social Policy Department.[59]

Thus placated with expanded influence over personnel policy, construction, internal propaganda, and other matters affecting the workforce, Hilpert settled into a relatively unobstreperous role in-house, so much so that, at least according to one witness, "the board members . . . often said in my presence that Degussa should be glad that Hilpert and not some other was the Factory Cell Foreman, since another would have . . . in all likelihood helped effectuate the Party's desires much more strongly."[60] Even Ernst Baerwind responded to Hilpert's postwar pleas for help, written from an American internment camp, with the remarks "that I am sorry that you must now pay so heavily for the consequences of your fanaticism. I always had the impression that you behaved overall as decently as was possible for a high officer of this ruined system. Toward me, in any case, you never did anything improper, although I was politically very vulnerable during the Third Reich."[61] Hilpert, in short, quickly proved and remained a Nazi the directors could work with, provided they either humored his pretensions or checked him with his own ideology, as when Schlosser periodically invoked the discipline of the "works community" to justify rejecting one or another Party intrusion on production during the war years.[62] Nazism could live up, as a result, to its totalitarian aspirations by weaving itself into the warp and woof of Degussa factory life. The Party put its political stamp on every sort of workers' recreational activity from river cruises to sports groups, made sure that all employees gathered

[57] Ibid.
[58] DUA, DL 3.Baerwind/21, Baerwind's memo Schaffung eines Referats 'Hausverwaltung' für Herrn Hilpert, November 16, 1937, and his Aktenvermerk betreffend "Referat Hausverwaltung," January 17, 1938.
[59] DUA, DL 2/1, Niederschrift über die Vorstandssitzung am 4. August 1941, p. 198.
[60] DUA, SCH 01/004, Eidesstattliche Erklärung by Hans Scherf, July 14, 1947.
[61] DUA, SCH 01/004, Baerwind to Hilpert, May 21, 1947.
[62] For an example of Hilpert's pliability, see DUA, DL 2/1, Niederschrift über die Vorstandssitzung am 8. Mai 1941, p. 177, which records his withdrawal of a demand that wages be raised as hours were extended during the war.

8   Hans Menzel

to celebrate the Day of Labor on May 1 of each year and around radios on the shop floors and in offices to attend to Hitler's radio addresses, and generally saw to it that the symbols and rhetoric of National Socialism were omnipresent, including after February 1, 1939, the obligatory closing "Heil Hitler!" on all domestic (but not in-house or international) correspondence – but all without direct challenge to the authority of the senior executives.[63] Both they and Hilpert became adept at observing the boundaries of their respective spheres in the National Socialist Works Community.

Hans Menzel, Degussa's self-described "fascist of the first hour," was, however, a looser cannon, not only more difficult to deploy effectively, but also more likely to blow up in the firm's face.[64] Immature, impatient, excitable, overconfident, ambitious, and proud of both his former service in an elite dragoon regiment and a *Freikorps* unit and his marriage to a baroness (Gertrud Freiin von Holzhausen), Menzel had other attributes that strengthened his sense of entitlement and made him all the harder to keep in check: his descent from Degussa's founder and his impressively low Party membership number, combined with his positions as Country Treasurer of the NSDAP and, beginning in 1933, as City Councillor in Frankfurt. Yet, in the early phase of the Third Reich, according to Fritz Roessler, "Menzel made only

---

[63] DUA, BU Fritz Roessler, "Zur Geschichte" [1937], Abschrift, p. 99. On the letter closings, DUA, MEN/29, An alle Abteilungen. Grussformel, February 1, 1939.
[64] DUA, DL 11.5/21, Menzel to Heitjan, July 19, 1933.

loyal use of his status as an 'old fighter.' He could have exploited it more for Degussa had Busemann not explicitly avoided making use of his offices."[65] The mercurial man's demonstrations of fidelity were, in part, tactical – he wished to reduce the resistance that his personality aroused to his claims for accelerated advancement up Degussa's ranks. Busemann's caution, however, reflected not only that resistance, but also his experience on the one occasion when he sought to make use of Menzel's political position, the moment in 1933 when allegations of Degussa's supposed "Jewish character" emerged from Nazi circles in the Rhineland and Hamburg. This imbroglio is worth reviewing in detail, not only because it illustrates the sorts of antisemitic pressure exerted upon Degussa, like many other large firms, almost immediately after Hitler's accession and the ambiguity of the company's response, but also because it introduces the tricky triangular relationship among Degussa's chairmen, Menzel, and the Nazi Party over the succeeding ten years.

Late in March 1933, during the run-up to the national boycott of Jewish-owned businesses that the new regime set for April 1, Degussa's head office in Frankfurt sought to quell questions about the enterprise's "Aryan" status by issuing a notarized announcement to all branches and sales agencies. It proclaimed "that the entire managing board of our enterprise is purely of the Christian faith, that our firm has never employed Jews since its foundation in 1873, and there are also today among its approximately 1,150 workers and about 700 commercial and technical employees and graduates no adherents to the Jewish faith."[66] If true, the policy and the statistics attest to a considerable degree of exclusion on the part of a company headquartered in a city where Jews constituted roughly 5 percent of the population in 1933 and in a country whose constitution had guaranteed equality before the law since 1867. Whatever its practices, the firm would have been loath to trumpet them in this fashion prior to Hitler's ascent. But the Nazis were in the process of transforming the moral valence of discrimination from an unseemly to a patriotic act, so Degussa's chief concern was to distract attention from two suddenly inconvenient facts: individuals whom the NSDAP attacked as Jews – that is, people of Jewish descent, regardless of their faith – occupied six seats on Degussa's supervisory board, including the prominent post of vice chairman, as well as several middle management positions within the enterprise.

Neither zealous racists nor opportunistic competitors were thus diverted for long, however. By May, Nazis in a number of Rhenish chapters of the National Dentists Association and one or more intriguers associated with a rival maker of dental alloys in that region (Clemens Koch) had managed to convince the Nazi-owned *Westdeutscher Beobachter*, based in Cologne, to reject Degussa's advertisements and contemplate warning readers against

---

[65] DUA, BU Dr. Fritz Roessler, "Zur Geschichte" [1937], Abschrift, p. 137.
[66] DUA, DL 11.5/21, An alle Zweigniederlassungen und Verkaufsstellen, March 31, 1933.

its products.[67] Deputized to use his Party contacts to repair the situation, Menzel quickly persuaded an editor of the *Frankfurter Volksblatt*, also a Nazi paper, to set his colleagues in the Rhineland straight. His letter assuring them that the members of the managing board "are all purely German" and that "Director Schlosser is a Party-comrade," had little apparent effect, however.[68] Menzel found himself forced to head north in person, where he encountered a strain of National Socialism resistant to both his reasoning and his Party rank.

After being briefed by Degussa's sales representatives in Düsseldorf and shown a leaflet impugning Degussa that the Clemens Koch firm had sent to its customers, Menzel and these colleagues called upon the Industry and Trade Chambers in that city and Cologne, as well as the regional Economic Commissar to find out whether these offices had received information or inquiries throwing doubt on Degussa's "Aryan" status. Satisfied that they had not, Menzel thought his delegation finally "hit upon the source of the attacks on the Scheideanstalt," when he arrived at the Cologne offices of the Nazi Fighting League of the German Middle Class, where the responsible official nervously denied any role in spreading rumors about Degussa but also repeatedly demanded that it "should demonstrate that it is not a Jewish enterprise and has no personal and financial ties of any sort to Jewry."[69] The irritation provoked by this conversation apparently led the volatile Menzel to overplay his hand badly some minutes later during his visit to A. Heitjan, the advertising editor of the *Westdeutscher Beobachter*. Though that man professed himself to be reassured by the earlier letter from the Nazi editor in Frankfurt, Menzel decided not only to take offense at Heitjan's explicit refusal to pay attention to his visitor's Party membership, but also to spurn what seemed an only grudging willingness to begin accepting Degussa's ads once more. Menzel therefore demanded that the newspaper acknowledge "that we are not to be addressed as a Jewish firm solely on the basis of our few Jewish members of the supervisory board." This merely prompted Heitjan to dig in his heels and deliver a diatribe to the effect that "gold is, anyway, a Jewish invention and anything that trades in gold is a Jewish institution." A few days later, the editor elaborated on his position in writing, thus providing Menzel with a remarkable glimpse into the level of economic sophistication confronting him:

It is for me quite self-evident that a gold and silver separation institute in Frankfurt is a purely Jewish enterprise, even if it has been "coordinated." The Jewish Tietz department store concern, whose leadership has also been "coordinated" is also

[67] DUA, DL 11.5/21, J. Bohn, Degussa Düsseldorf, to Hans Menzel, May 9, 1933.
[68] DUA, DL 11.5/21, Traupel to the *Westdeutscher Beobachter*, May 27, 1933.
[69] For this and the rest of the information in this paragraph, unless otherwise indicated, see DUA, DL 11.5/21, Menzel's Bericht über Besprechungen in Düsseldorf und Köln wegen der in dortigem Bezirk erfolgten Angriffe auf die Scheideanstalt, June 12, 1933.

still excluded from advertising in the *Westdeutscher Beobachter*. The decisive matter is the question of capital, and it is my personal opinion that at the moment no German has enough money to buy a majority of the stock in the Frankfurt Gold and Silver Separation Institute, and even if he did, according to my impressions and my knowledge of economic relations, the previous shareholders, of whom most likely up to 99 percent are Jews, would not sell it readily.... What strengthens my conviction is also the fact that your firm was not to be found before the takeover of power in any National Socialist newspaper.[70]

Having been dispatched northward to win over his fellow Nazis, Menzel only had aggravated them with his tactlessness. Remarkably – and ironically, in view of the lack of respect for civil rights that his Party comrades were showing daily in the streets of Germany – he was reduced to spluttering that, in the editorial rooms of the *Westdeutscher Beobachter*, "it is in no way recognized that accusers or denouncers have the burden of proof for their assertions," and to returning home with no better recommendation than that his firm call in the aid of a "higher authority."[71] Moreover, the practical extent of his failure soon became apparent. In early August, the Düsseldorf office reported that Degussa had been excluded as a supplier to the District Health Insurance System "because it is under the preconception that we are a Jewish firm," and the *Westdeutscher* officially informed Degussa of the intention to reject its ads and to run an announcement of its "incomplete coordination."[72]

Over the ensuing months, Menzel managed to get to the bottom of the Nazi suspicions of Degussa that Clemens Koch merely had exploited. They stemmed from a report on the firm provided by the Information Bureau Henri Kramer of Hamburg. Billing itself as "the first and oldest folkish" organization of this sort in Germany, though it had been founded, in fact, only in 1931, the bureau specialized in investigating whether firms qualified for the award of state contracts and the like by virtue of their freedom from Jewish influence.[73] The version of its report in circulation by early August, of which Degussa obtained a copy, concluded with the following curt and erroneous political summary:

In the supervisory and managing boards of the firm in question, no coordination has been planned; as before, the non-Aryan members of these bodies remain, and the firm in question has no intention of ever undertaking a coordination in keeping with the

[70] DUA, DL 11.5/21, Heitjan to Menzel, June 19, 1933.
[71] The quoted remarks appear, respectively, in DUA, DL 11.5/21, Menzel's report of June 12, 1933, and Menzel to Heitjan, June 15, 1933.
[72] DUA, DL 11.5/21, Bohn to Menzel, August 3, 1933, and Menzel to Koch & Münzberg Annoncen-Expedition, August 7, 1933.
[73] DUA, DL 11.5/21, W. Schmidt, Scheideanstalt-HIAG Verkaufsstelle Hamburg GmbH, to Menzel, October 7, 1933 (on the firm); Auskunftei Henri Kramer, Deutsche Gold- und Silber-Scheideanstalt, vormals Roessler, August 4, 1933 (for the quoted self-description).

national uprising. The firm believes it has satisfied its duty in this regard in that the Workers Council and the Employees Council are each led by a National Socialist.[74]

By November, however, Kramer had amended this document to read that no Jews had ever served on the managing board of Degussa except during the period of the community-of-interests agreement with the Metallgesellschaft, but that five Jews remained on the supervisory board.[75] Since that information was correct at the time of writing, Degussa found itself unable to take legal action against the bureau. Yet the *Westdeutscher* refused to alter its course, indeed it continued into 1934 to circulate its charges of Jewish domination over Degussa.[76] Apparently not until early 1937, more than a year after Heitjan had left the newspaper's service, did it try to put an end to the bad relations between itself and Degussa, only to find the firm itself willing, but Hans Menzel, as the business manager of the Durferrit subsidiary, still starchily insistent on a public declaration of Degussa's pure "Aryan quality."[77]

If the *Westdeutscher Beobachter* affair cemented Busemann's reluctance to rely on Menzel as a political intermediary, it also laid bare the delicate matter of the Jews connected to Degussa. One of the six Jewish members of the supervisory board at the time of Hitler's accession, Paul Hammerschlag, died in June 1933, and another, Georg Schwarz, resigned without apparent pressure from the firm in October.[78] But that left four members of Jewish descent, including the aged Baron Max von Goldschmidt-Rothschild – a member since 1897, the son of one of the firm's original financiers, and currently the vice chairman of the board – at precisely the moment when at least some Nazis were demanding proof of Degussa's freedom from Jewish influence on pain of withholding their business. Faced with this situation, the firm's behavior was neither brave nor craven. On the one hand, Busemann raised the matter with Fritz Roessler and persuaded him to suggest to Goldschmidt-Rothschild that he could ease the enterprise's tasks by resigning. The same hints were probably dropped to Max von der Porten, the distinguished industrialist whom the Nazis had already purged as head of the state-owned United Aluminum Works; he submitted his resignation in December 1933, effective the following month.[79] On the other hand, when

---

[74] *Ibid.*

[75] DUA, DL 11.5/21, Walter Thilo, Nordisches Erzkontor, Lübeck, to Menzel, November 9, 1933.

[76] DUA, DL 11.5/21, Hektor Roessler's memo, Frankfurter Volksblatt – Arier-Eigenschaft der Scheideanstalt, December 11, 1933, and Gollhard's memo, Besuch des Gen. Vertr. Dinkel, February 6, 1934.

[77] DUA, DL 11.5/21, WB to Durferrit GmbH, Frankfurt, February 1, 1937, and reply of February 6, 1937.

[78] DUA, D 8/3, Apr 2, 433. Aufsichtsrat-Sitzung am 17. Oktober 1933, Abschrift, 2, pp. 217–18.

[79] *Ibid.*, 435. Aufsichtsrat-Sitzung am 9. Januar 1934, p. 224.

the old baron proudly refused to go before the upcoming end of his term, Degussa decided not to force the issue in either his or anyone else's case.[80] The firm did seek to avoid public incidents at the stockholders' meetings by not renominating him as the candidate for vice chairman in January 1934 or any of the Jewish members when their terms came up for renewal, but otherwise each was allowed to choose the time of his departure or to serve out the period for which he had been elected.[81] As a result, the Aryanization of that body proceeded gradually: Goldschmidt-Rothschild left in November 1934, Alfred Merton in December 1935, after his emigration, and Ludwig Deutsch in January 1937.[82] Because Merton's brother, Richard, succeeded him as head of the Metallgesellschaft and was still regarded by the Nazis as "politically bearable," and in view of the close relations and interlocking shareholdings of the two firms, he was allowed to assume Alfred's seat and to retain it until the regime revoked his privileged status at the beginning of 1938, then drove him from both his firm and his country. Long before then, however, a not-so-subtle change had taken place in the form of these men's exits: whereas those who retired prior to 1936 were accorded at least warm public expressions of thanks for their services, neither Deutsch's nor Richard Merton's disappearance occasioned any such comment at the pertinent annual meeting. When challenged about this by Deutsch, Busemann excused himself with reference to "the well known reasons," then added the usual formulaic remarks to the private communication.[83]

Less ambiguously considerate, at least for as long as that was possible, was Degussa's stance regarding its Jewish managerial personnel. Of these, the principal figure was Dr. Ernst Eichwald, the head of the firm's patents section in Frankfurt. A convert to Christianity who had returned to his homeland in 1914 from England along with the Jewish woman he had married there then served several years as a German officer and won the Iron Cross, First Class, before joining Degussa, Eichwald was, by all evidence, a much-liked and valued figure at the firm.[84] Indeed, he inspired so much loyalty that both Hermann Leyerzapf, a young Degussa employee, and Hermann Schlosser took considerable risks on his behalf. Leyerzapf's fidelity is all the more remarkable because he was a Nazi of relatively early vintage. He had joined the Party in his late teens in his hometown of Giessen and even met Hitler at the 1927 Party Congress in Nürnberg, but then lapsed in paying dues and had

[80] DUA, BU Max Baron von Goldschmidt-Rothschild, exchange of letters between Busemann and Roessler, July 17–18, 1933, and Roessler to Goldschmidt-Rothschild, December 28, 1933.
[81] *Ibid.*, Busemann to Goldschmidt-Rothschild, December 28 and 30, 1933.
[82] See DUA, BU Fritz Roessler, "Zur Geschichte" [1937], Abschrift, p. 98; D 8/3, 436. Aufsichtsrat-Sitzung, November 6, 1934, Abschrift, Apr 2, pp. 226, 230–31, and D 8/4, 441. Aufsichtsrat-Sitzung, January 8, 1937, p. 4.
[83] DUA, BU Ludwig Deutsch, Busemann to Deutsch, January 11, 1937.
[84] DUA, BU Dr. Ernst Baerwind, Tagebuch, Abschrift, p. 33.

to re-enroll as a student in Marburg in 1930, receiving membership number 286,924. Having been active in the Sturmabteilung (SA or Brownshirts), he went over to the Schutzstaffel (SS or Blackshirts) sometime before beginning work at Degussa's HIAG division in Frankfurt on February 1, 1934. Within only a few more months, however, after witnessing the brutal beating of an SA man caught up in the Röhm Purge, Leyerzapf pled overwork in his new job as an excuse to resign from the SS. But he remained in the Party, continuing to endorse what he took to be its principal goals: the restoration of Germany's international standing and the defeat of Bolshevism.[85] His basic humanity, however, soon created another conflict with the Party's practice, since he had begun walking and riding the train to and from Degussa's offices daily with his suburban neighbor, Ernst Eichwald. When directed by the Nazi District Leader to cease this practice, Leyerzapf refused, with the result that a Party Court was convened, at which "he declared that he also in the future neither could nor would avoid traveling together with the Jew [and] concedes that he is, despite his long membership in the Party, no National Socialist." As a result, Leyerzapf was expelled from the NSDAP for having "offended against Party discipline and the standing of the movement."[86]

Leyerzapf's friendship with Eichwald, and their joint commuting, continued until the pogrom of 1938, when SA rowdies rousted the Eichwalds from their home in the middle of the night, smashing and burning their furniture, and the frightened couple took refuge, first with nearby friends then with the British consulate, which refused sanctuary. Upon finding the damaged house the next morning, Leyerzapf sought and received time off from his office to find the Eichwalds, then arranged safety for them with his mother in Giessen for a week, until a securer hide-out in Frankfurt could be found.[87] That turned out to be with no less a personage than Hermann Schlosser's mother. After the brouhaha died down, Degussa sent Eichwald on a business mission to a British affiliate, the Distillers Company in Hull, and he and his wife were thus able to leave Germany, albeit almost penniless in the sixth decade of their lives. Schlosser paid them a visit while on a business trip a few months later and, as Eichwald recalled after the war, "upon leaving you pressed into my hands in very kind fashion a not inconsiderable gift."[88] In short, Degussa stood by Ernst Eichwald as best it could for as long as possible, though, it must be added, not to a man: Eichwald also remembered after the war that "I had to experience, on the other hand, that colleagues

[85] DUA, BU Dr. Hermann Leyerzapf, Niederschrift über meine Mitgliedschaft in der Partei, SA und SS, October 1988; interview with Herr Leyerzapf, Frankfurt, October 19, 1998.
[86] *Ibid.*, NSDAP, Parteigericht, Beschluss, February 11, 1936.
[87] See DUA, BU Baerwind, Tagebuch, Abschrift, p. 33; BU Leyerzapf, Niederschrift: Meine Erlebnisse am 10. November 1938, October 1988; and SCH 01/004, Eichwald to Leyerzapf, August 28, 1947.
[88] DUA, BU Hermann Schlosser, Eichwald to Schlosser, August 5, 1946.

with whom my wife and I had long been on friendly terms, such as Dr. Federlin,... let us drop completely as soon as they found or recognized their National Socialist hearts."[89]

Eichwald was not the only target of the Nürnberg laws retained by Degussa until the radicalization of Nazi policy in 1938 put an end to that course, nor the only one toward whom Schlosser, in particular, showed sympathy. Theodor Pohl, whose research work had yielded several patents for lightweight building materials, also remained with the firm until the end of 1938. Married to a non-Jew, with whom the Schlossers maintained contact throughout the Nazi period, Pohl survived in seclusion in Frankfurt until February 1945, when he was abruptly shipped to Theresienstadt, from which he returned that June, weighing only 105 pounds.[90] Similar, though less dramatic and sometimes ultimately less fortunate stories can be told of a number of Jewish directors and employees at firms affiliated with Degussa (e.g., Julius Levisohn of the Norddeutsche Affinerie) or that it acquired via Aryanization during the 1930s – notably Erich Nethe and Leo Klopfer of L. C. Marquart, who escaped abroad in 1938 and lived out the war, and Heinrich Ziegler, Alfred Gumperz, Alfred Meyer, Herbert Hirsch, and Karl Wollin of the Auergesellschaft, who did not lose their jobs until 1938 and whose fates are not recorded in Degussa's files.[91]

Still another such episode concerns Curt Brahn, Degussa's Jewish sales representative in Shanghai from August 1932 until January 1940, and his nephew Louis Hannach, who left Germany to take up a position with Brahn in October 1934, after brief training in the Frankfurt offices.[92] Supported by Paul Ungerer, a young "Aryan" sent out from Frankfurt, initially on a temporary basis, Brahn conducted Degussa's interests so satisfactorily that the firm more than doubled his pay between autumn 1932 and spring 1936.[93]

---

[89] DUA, SCH 01/004, Eichwald to Leyerzapf, August 28, 1947.

[90] See DUA, BU Hermann Schlosser, Pohl to Schlosser, January 25, 1946; BU Theodor Pohl, Vereinbarung zwischen der Deutschen Gold- und Silberscheideanstalt vormals Roessler und Dr. Theodor Pohl, April 1, 1946; and BU Ernst Baerwind, Tagebuch, Abschrift, entry for June 28, 1945, p. 55.

[91] Levisohn was ousted from the managing board of the NA sometime between the general meetings of April 1933 and 1934, but he continued to represent the firm in various capacities until at least 1937, and he was not formally dismissed until the end of March 1939; by early 1940, he was in England. DUA, Jahresberichte der Norddeutschen Affinerie, sixty-seventh and sixty-eighth business years; and the summary of the data in his personnel file provided me by the Norddeutsche Affinerie on August 18, 2000. According to the last-named document, the NA settled its outstanding contractual obligations with Levisohn in 1948 and 1950 for what appears to have been a total of approximately 500 Deutschmarks. On the personnel at Marquart and Auer, see Chapter 3.

[92] DUA, DL 12.1/6, Degussa to Brahn, August 9, 1932, and Westpfahl to Brahn, September 17, 1934.

[93] *Ibid.*, re Ungerer, and Niederschrift betr. Bezüge von C. Brahn, no date. See also Hans Menzel's remark that "the activity of Mr. Brahn in China shows that a person stationed

And, when August Kolb, who was sent on a general fact-finding mission for the firm to the Far East in early 1937, reported on the Shanghai operations, he concluded that, even though relations with the local German community and the German military staff in Nanking had to be handled by Ungerer, "Brahn... behaves, for a Jew, with great reserve.... it would be dangerous to remove him at the present time." His nephew, however, struck Kolb as "a disgusting type [who].... possesses really all the defects that one can attribute to a Jew," and therefore a candidate for immediate dismissal or for assignment to functions that would keep him from appearing in the firm's offices entirely.[94] Nothing came of the latter recommendation, but Ungerer stayed on in China, poised to succeed Brahn and Hannach at the inevitable moment, which came during 1939. In January, Hermann Schlosser informed Brahn that Degussa would have to terminate its relationship with him by the end of that year, and by July, Degussa was contracting with Ungerer to take over the Shanghai business and preparing a severance contract calling for the payment to Brahn of 15,000 RM in cash and an equivalent sum in goods – the division having been arrived at as a means of gaining the permission of the Reich Economics Ministry, which was reluctant to approve exports of funds, for any compensation at all – with the understanding that Hannach would be paid a share of this settlement.[95] Brahn eventually received some 22,800 RM in cash and goods and carried on business under his own name in Shanghai through the war. Bearing no grudges, he offered in 1947 to testify to the American occupation authorities on Schlosser's behalf and remarked that "I still appreciate your correct attitude towards myself and my nephew and I can only say that I have no reason to complain of unjust and harsh treatment during all those critical eight years with Degussa. You did your best to hold me in this position as long as you could manage. That I did not consider to have received an adequate settlement... when retiring from my position is another matter for which you cannot be blamed."[96]

In all these instances of considerate and deliberate behavior toward Jews, it must be emphasized, the solidarity shown by Degussa was personal rather than political. If it reflected, on the part of some individuals, a measure of regret about, perhaps even dissent from, the persecution of people known and trusted by the firm, it did not amount to a principled stand against that persecution but, at most, to an attempt to alleviate its effects. Neither was, as Ernst

abroad and familiar with the material in the highly technical Durferrit business can put all earlier successes by exporters or importers in the shade"; DUA, RFI 4.2/74, Menzel's Bericht der Durferrit-Gesellschaft m.b.H, December 20, 1935, p. 2.

[94] DUA, Klb 1/01, Kolb's Bericht über das Büro Degussa Shanghai, February 3, 1937.

[95] DUA, BU Hermann Schlosser, Schlosser to Brahn, January 19, 1939; DL 12.1/6, Originalvertrag zwischen der Scheideanstalt und Paul Ungerer, July 1, 1939; Rau's Aktennotiz. C. Brahn, Shanghai, July 27, 1939; Ungerer's Aktennotiz. China-Geschäft, November 6, 1939.

[96] DUA, BU Hermann Schlosser, Brahn to Schlosser, May 17, 1947 (in English), enclosing Schlosser's letters to Brahn of January 19 and November 6, 1939.

Eichwald's remark about Federlin's behavior toward him indicates, even Degussa's circumscribed form of solidarity universally observed. Moreover, the
effort to shield one's associates, which during the war years continued in the
cases of long-standing employees of one-half or one-quarter Jewish descent
(so-called *Mischlinge*), such as Ernst Baerwind, Leonhard Meyer, and Heinrich Stiege, remained confined to them.[97] By June 1943, it was corporate
policy that "Jewish mixed-breeds must not be hired, even when they are in
the [German] Labor Front."[98] Accordingly, the firm declined a year later to
find a post for the part-Jewish son of a longtime business partner, ostensibly on the grounds that coworkers quickly would "get to the bottom of the
matter" and presumably denounce Degussa to the authorities.[99]

Finally, on one occasion at least, before the consequences of playing the
"racial" card were perhaps fully apparent, it appears that the otherwise conflicted Hermann Schlosser was not above trying to turn Nazi antisemitism
to commercial advantage. In mid-1933, he was irritated that the L. C. Marquart AG of Beuel, a firm owned and led by Jewish Germans, was importing cyanide from a Dutch nonparticipant in the international cartel that he
headed and refusing to place orders, even at preferential prices, for Degussa's
own output. Having failed in an effort to discourage such behavior by obtaining an increase in the relevant German tariff rates, Schlosser approved
an attempt by Menzel to involve the Party's Regional Economic Advisor
for Hessen-Nassau in an "investigation of Marquart's allocations of foreign exchange . . . and a gradual reduction of these." Menzel wrote both the
summary report on the matter and the cover letter, bearing his Party and municipal titles, to the Nazi official, and there is no confirmation that Schlosser
read either. Yet it seems highly unlikely that he did not receive the former and
ask to see the latter, and it explicitly notes that "Mr. Schlosser and I are of the
opinion that we, as Party comrades, should calmly make this matter known
to you and through you to the responsible economic offices of our Party."
In other words, Schlosser was very likely complicit in what amounted to
an antisemitic denunciation, since Menzel's peroration stressed to his fellow
Nazis that, "When one is aware, how bourgeois and liberal circles cry bloody
murder at every opportunity concerning our all too rough antisemitism, it
is also good to know that there are still such impudent Jews as the business
leaders of the firm L. C. Marquart AG."[100]

---

97 See DUA, BU Hermann Schlosser, Anlage 23 zur Verteidigungsschrift für das Spruchkammerverfahren Schlosser, Leonhard Meyer's Erklärung, November 21, 1946, which reports
that Schlosser sent Meyer, who was part Jewish, to manage one of Degussa's interests in
Prague in 1941, in order "to get me out of sight of the Frankfurt Nazis."

98 DUA, TA 2/88, Kühnlein to Personal-Abteilung, Dr. Stumm, June 2, 1943.

99 DUA, DL 13.4/1, Harant to Fischer, August 23, 1944. The person in question was Otto
Röhm, son of the deceased co-owner of Röhm & Haas GmbH.

100 DUA, DL 11.5/21, Menzel to Eckhardt, August 25, 1933, enclosing Menzel's Exposé in
Sachen Degussa gegen Dr. L. C. Marquardt A. G., August 23, 1933.

Whether Menzel's intriguing bore fruit in the Marquart case is undocumented, but his political value to Degussa surely paled in comparison with
that of the firm's most prominent potential entrée to high-level decision making in the new Reich, Albert Pietzsch. This often-overlooked figure was almost prototypical of the sort of industrialist attracted to Nazism prior to
1933 and preferred and promoted by it thereafter. Like more famous figures such as Paul Pleiger (subsequently chief of the Reichswerke Hermann
Göring) from the machine-building sector and Hans Kehrl (later a key figure in the Four Year Plan and the Speer Ministry) from textiles, Pietzsch
had labored to build up his own rather small-scale firm after 1928 with the
financial support of E. Merck of Darmstadt, but always in the shadow of,
and often while at odds with, the dominant producer in his industry.[101] And
like them, he was therefore a vigorous proponent of entrepreneurial will and
initiative, of the energetic, nationally inspired, red tape–cutting independent
manager, as contrasted with the allegedly overcautious and self-centered executives of the nation's lumbering corporate behemoths – in short, he was a
man of "leadership" rather than "administration."[102] His goodwill toward
Degussa rested primarily on their contacts as suppliers of hydrogen peroxide
to Henkel and as partners in a French subsidiary called Soproper, but also
on the fact that Degussa's modest size and highly personal management style
appealed to his ideological predilections.[103] Above all, Degussa represented
an alternative source of advice and assistance to the seemingly ubiquitous
IG Farben concern, toward which Pietzsch harbored a powerful animus.[104]
He could thus be of enormous use in his new functions as head of the Economic Group for Chemistry, of the Bavarian Economic Chamber, and (from
December 1936) of the National Economic Chamber, on many matters of

[101] On these individuals and their type, see Turner, *German Big Business and the Rise of Hitler*,
pp. 191–92, 201–03. On Pietzsch, in particular, who had begun financing the NSDAP in
1923 and joined the Party in 1925, see Fritz Blaich, "Die bayerische Industrie. Elemente
von Gleichschaltung, Konformismus und Selbstbehauptung," in Martin Broszat and Elke
Fröhlich, *Bayern in der NS -Zeit II* (Munich: R. Oldenbourg, 1979), pp. 241–43, 246; on
his partnership with E. Merck, see DUA, GCH 2/11, IG Farben Pharmazeutisches Büro
München to IG Farben pharmaz.-wissensch. Sekretariat Leverkusen, September 11, 1928.
On Kehrl, see his own *Krisenmanager im Dritten Reich* (Düsseldorf: Droste, 1973), and
Rolf-Dieter Müller, *Der Manager der Kriegswirtschaft* (Essen: Klartext, 1999).
[102] On the important ideological distinction between these concepts in the Nazi state, see Dieter
Rebentisch and Karl Teppe (eds.), *Verwaltung contra Menschenführung im Staat Hitlers*
(Göttingen: Vandenhoeck & Ruprecht, 1986).
[103] On Soproper, the full name of which was the Société des Produits Peroxydés, Paris, see
DUA, AW 28.2/1, which contains the founding and profit pooling contracts among the
principal partners, Degussa, ÖCW, Pietzsch's firm, Merck, and a Swiss enterprise.
[104] See DUA, GCH 2/11, Elektrochemische Werke München, Letter to the Amtsgericht, Regis-
tergericht, Gründung und Eintragung der Elektro-chemischen Werke, München AG, June
21, 1928, which justifies the formation of the company as a reaction to IG Farben's support for a competitor in Austria, the ÖCW, without making any reference to Degussa's
relationship with that firm.

importance to Degussa – though dealing with the Jewish question was not one of them, since he was a convinced antisemite himself.

Though there is little direct evidence, almost certainly Ernst Busemann's excellent personal relations with Pietzsch contributed to the firm's success in jockeying for position during the much-feared transition to the Nazi-sponsored Economy of Estates in the period 1933–35. Under this scheme, competing economic interests were supposed to be coordinated and the flow of information to the government and of directives to enterprises was to be assured by the abolition of all previous trade associations and the inclusion of all firms in any productive sphere into a hierarchy of product-based, sectoral, and nationwide groups. All of these were to be tied closely to the relevant ministries and government agencies, which would have considerable influence over the leaders designated for each stratum. By the time the outlines of this system began to assume stable form in the fall of 1934, Busemann had emerged as head of the Specialized Group for Other Chemicals, the largest second-tier grouping within the Economic Group for Chemistry, and as one of the four or five members foreseen for its Leadership Council (later: Advisory Council); his fellow Degussa directors, Riefstahl and Schlosser, had been projected as leaders of the subgroups for detergents and bleaching agents and for cyanide compounds, respectively.[105]

The surviving records give little sign of Busemann playing an assertive role during the development of either this organizational framework or the Economic Group for Chemistry's response to the first major policy challenge posed by the new regime: the inauguration of the Additional Exports Procedure (*Zusatzausfuhrverfahren*) in 1935–36. Rather, while taking private, sarcastic note of the self-interested posturing of many of his colleagues, he intervened at key meetings chiefly in order to moderate industrial counter-proposals that he thought had no chance of being accepted by the government.[106] As always, in other words, he wasted no energy fighting battles he considered unwinnable. Granted, in comparison to the old *Chemie Verein*, the new Economic Group for Chemistry entailed a huge expansion to more than 14,000 members and a near doubling of the assessment per firm per worker in order to belong, exclusive of the 50,000 RM required to pay off the predecessor organization's accumulated budget deficit.[107] Granted that

---

[105] DUA, DL 3.Busemann/4, Busemann's Besprechung im Verein mit dem langen Namen bezw. wie es jetzt heisst: Wirtschaftsgruppe Chemische Industrie der Hauptgruppe V der deutschen Wirtschaft, September 11, 1934.

[106] See his comments in DUA, DL 3.Busemann/5, Busemann's Begräbnis des "Vereins mit dem langen Namen" und erste Sitzung des Beirats der Wirtschaftsgruppe Chemische Industrie, December 15, 1934, p. 3; his Notiz. Besprechung der Wirtschaftsgruppe Chemie, April 3, 1935, p. 1; and his Notiz. Sitzung in der Wirtschaftsgruppe Chemie, April 3, 1935, p. 2.

[107] DUA, DL 3.Busemann/5, Busemann's Begräbnis des "Vereins mit dem langen Namen"..., December 15, 1934; and his Notiz. Besprechung des Beirates der Wirtschaftsgruppe "Chemie," February 6, 1935.

offsetting savings, such as those achieved by folding the former industrial magazine *Die chemische Industrie* into a new publication paid for by the German Labor Front (DAF), came with a significant loss of autonomy, since the DAF assumed control of the political content of the new biweekly, which had a print run of 250,000 copies.[108] And, granted, the new system of export promotion amounted to the imposition of a levy on the domestic sales of *all* German companies in order to enable *some* of them to recoup *part* of their losses from selling in foreign markets that the Reich wished to cultivate instead of at home – in short, it was a tax that practiced, at least by the regime's lights, what the NSDAP had preached: the common good goes before self-interest.[109] But, to Busemann, such matters may have seemed, literally and figuratively, small prices to pay for the overall success of German industry in deflecting the more extreme Nazi visions of economic restructuring that had asserted themselves in the first eighteen months of the regime.[110]

More importantly, Busemann grasped quite quickly during the initial phase of Nazi rule that corporate influence in the new Germany generally would be confined to affecting the implementation not the setting of overall economic policy, and that, even then, such influence would be best exerted subtly, through the appearance of common engagement in achieving national goals, rather than through querulousness about the costs. Whether he would have gone so far as Fritz Roessler, who in 1933 opined that, "At bottom, conditions with us are no different than in Soviet Russia. Here as there, a dictator and a small party clique rules, supported by the Red Army there and the SS and SA here," Degussa's chief executive almost certainly agreed with Roessler's later comment that "the industrial associations have, in truth, no real say and it is therefore a euphemism to refer to the 'self-administration' of the economy."[111] Moreover, Busemann behaved as if he recognized the validity of Roessler's evaluation of the place of business, if not of its earnings prospects, in the economy that had taken shape by January 1937, shortly after the inauguration of the regime's (supposedly second) Four Year Plan:

One must proceed henceforth on the assumption that from investments under the Four Year Plan nothing more than amortization and interest can be earned. That seems to me to be the distinguishing characteristic of future industrial development The times are gone in which profits could be writ large. In agriculture, the farmer

[108] *Ibid.*
[109] On the ZAV and the chemical industry's response, in general, see Hayes, *Industry and Ideology*, pp. 151–54.
[110] On the initial struggle over Nazi conceptions of a "berufständische Wirtschaft," see Avraham Barkai, *Nazi Economics* (New Haven: Yale University Press, 1990); Willi Boelcke, *Die deutsche Wirtschaft 1930–1945* (Düsseldorf: Droste, 1983); and Gerald Feldman's discussion of the tenure of Kurt Schmitt as Economics Minister in *Allianz and the German Insurance Business 1933–1945* (New York: Cambridge University Press, 2001), pp. 60–105.
[111] DUA, BU Fritz Roessler, "Nationalsozialismus," p. 12 (for the first quotation), and "Zur Geschichte" [1937], Abschrift, p. 100.

already has been told what he can produce and how much he can earn from it. In commerce, one is going the same way. Socialization of industry is rejected. The initiative of individual entrepreneurs is not to be restricted and leading people are to be well paid, but the profits of firms themselves will be ever more limited. Via taxes and cartel controls, state officials are looking ever deeper into the books of industry. Over half of the difference between gross receipts and payments to stockholders is already taxed away, not counting the export levy and other "voluntary" payments and deductions. The level of dividends has been restricted by law and, more recently, price increases have been made virtually impossible. The executive will work in the future in the truest sense "for the King of Prussia," only now one says: for the people's community. Once the great private fortunes have all but disappeared and the incomes of the middle classes have undergone a strong leveling effect, the same grading off of industrial profits is to be expected in succeeding years. The Scheideanstalt still possesses good reserves. But who knows whether those very reserves, insofar as they are not consumed by the Four Year Plan, will not become the object of the new tax laws.[112]

Roessler died before the continued ascent of Degussa's profits, despite successive annual increases that doubled the German corporate tax rate between 1936 and 1940, seemed to disprove his forebodings; and Busemann succumbed to cancer in 1939, before government regulations forced the investment of ever larger portions of Degussa's proceeds in Reich bonds and thus partially validated the older man's predictions.[113] But Busemann understood that Roessler was right about who called the economic tune in the Third Reich – and acted accordingly.

In this context, one in which the setting of public priorities increasingly conditioned the pursuit of private ones, finding or placing more and better friends in key positions became a major, continuing concern for Degussa. Only by such means could it hope to avoid unpalatable outcomes and demonstrate its commitment to the national cause, which, in turn, would serve as an implicit justification of such rewards as the firm could obtain. Offering Degussa's managers' time and expertise to the national economic apparatus on a part-time basis proved relatively easy, since the numerous regulatory and planning agencies in Berlin were ever on the lookout for knowledgeable assistance. Thus, as early as 1934, Hans Schneider, the head of Degussa's precious metals refineries, largely took over the administration of the Reich's domestic rationing system for such materials under the auspices of the Reichsbank. And in the final years of the regime, August Kolb led the section for chemicals

[112] "Zur Geschichte," pp. 128–29.
[113] See, for example, DUA, RFI 4.4/7, Eigener Effektenbesitz nach dem Stand vom 30. September 1942, which shows that 46 percent of Degussa's security investments (13.3 million Reichsmarks out of 29.1 million) were invested in government paper. If one takes into consideration the 5 million marks listed as cash in the same volume, Gegenüberstellung zum Finanzstatus per 30. September 1942, the percentage of Degussa's liquid capital in government paper falls to just under 40 percent.

in, first, the Economics Ministry, and then in Albert Speer's Armaments Ministry, without having to resign from Degussa's managing board.[114] By 1944, some thirty-two senior managerial personnel at Degussa were devoting appreciable parts of their time to carrying out similar, quasi-official economic functions.[115] If there are few indications in the sources that these positions could be turned crudely to the firm's advantage, they generally assured, nonetheless, that its interests would not be overlooked.[116] Indeed, on one occasion in 1943, when Kolb appeared to have forgotten where his primary loyalties belonged, Hermann Schlosser did not hesitate "to suggest to him, as a matter of principle, to make important suggestions and proposals to official agencies only after advance contacts with the [Degussa] managing board."[117]

But the seconding of staff to full-time government tasks was more complicated, since the regime thought that such people, as Baerwind discovered in late 1936, when the new Four Year Plan Office for German Raw Materials under Carl Krauch of IG Farben began seeking recruits, "should leave their industrial posts definitively and should become civil servants in the Raw Materials Staff."[118] This meant the loss to Degussa of their experience and the costs of their training, along with the burden of replacing them, which grew ever more difficult as qualified personnel declined in numbers thanks not only to the mounting general labor scarcity, but also to falling university enrollments and rising military inductions under National Socialism. Baerwind gave a discouraging reply to the Krauch office's inquiry, "because of the shortage of available people," and such evasiveness remained corporate policy toward these invitations until the war began, despite the mounting importance of those who accepted them to Degussa's fortunes. Not until 1940, when Krauch personally repeated the request for a Degussa chemist to be appointed to his staff, did Hermann Schlosser decide that "we not only should but must accept this suggestion, if we do not want to expose ourselves to the charge of deficient interest and insufficient readiness." He therefore

[114] On Schneider's role, see Chapter 5, below; on Kolb's appointments, see DUA 2/1, Niederschriften über die Vorstandssitungen am 5. Mai und am 4. Oktober 1943, pp. 310 and 338.
[115] The names are provided in DUA, IW 46.4/1, the Verzeichnis attached to Rundschreiben Betr.: Tätigkeit von Angehörigen des Degussa-Konzerns in der Organisation der gewerblichen Wirtschaft, September 28, 1944.
[116] See, especially, DUA, PCA2/91, Flügge to Schlosser, November 9, 1940, which advises the latter man on how to deal with the office to which the former had been delegated and records his leaking of official correspondence to the firm. On the importance of having Degussa representatives occupying such positions, see DL 2/1, Niederschrift über die Vorstandssitzung am 7. Juli 1941, p. 190, regarding Turowski of the Auergesellschaft and his post in the Air Ministry.
[117] *Ibid.*, am 5. Juli 1943, p. 323.
[118] DUA, DL 3.Baerwind/20, Baerwind's Telefonischer Anruf von Dir. Dr. Wurster – Farben I. G.-Ludwigshafen, December 4, 1936.

directed his colleagues "to free up as suitable a man as possible, even if that means a gap for us at another place."[119] Thereafter, Degussa men occupied no fewer than three positions in the Chemicals Section under Johannes Eckell, formerly of IG Farben, in Krauch's by now renamed National Office for Economic Expansion, with responsibilities for several organic products, sodium and its derivatives, and carbon black.[120]

In the meantime, Degussa relied primarily on its regular personnel's "honorary" governmental assignments and consultations with key officials and on the firm's expanded contacts with prominent Nazis in Frankfurt to assure consideration of its interests. On the political front, Menzel's demonstrated counterproductiveness as an emissary to the NSDAP, along with the desire of the firm's leaders to head off pressures from the Gauleitung to promote him to the managing board, led Degussa as early as 1935 to seek an alternative protector and sign of the firm's loyalty from the Party's ranks. The most acceptable candidate was Dr. Carl Lüer, the veteran Nazi who was by now not only president of Frankfurt's Industry and Trade Chamber but also, among other titles, head of the Economic Chamber of Hessen and of the National Group for Trade, vice chairman of the National Economic Chamber, professor of commerce at the University of Frankfurt, and a member of the Reichstag and of the supervisory board of the Adam Opel AG, General Motors' German subsidiary, which he was later to head as trustee after Germany declared war on the United States.[121] Lüer had distinguished himself in 1933–34 as an aggressive "coordinator" and "Aryanizer" of the Frankfurt Stock Exchange and other commercial entities, on one occasion, for example, even bullying Hans Menzel's way onto the supervisory board of the Frankfurter Hypothekenbank.[122] But by 1935, he had begun to establish

[119] DUA, TLE 1/23, Schlosser's Besuch bei Herrn Prof. Dr. C. Krauch, March 20, 1940.

[120] See DUA, DL 2/1, Niederschrift über die Vorstandssitzung am 2. April 1940, p. 83, which mentions Dr. Flügge as the most replaceable person to send to Krauch, and Anlage 1 zur Niederschrift vom 4. November 1940, Baerwind's memo of the same date, p. 9, which remarks that both Flügge and Dr. Hermann Freudenberg had been delegated to Eckell's staff. DL 3.Baerwind/26, Baerwind's Aktenvermerk betreffend die Organisation der Abteilung Chemie im Reichsamt für Wirtschaftsausbau, February 3, 1943, lists Dr. Flügge as still attached to the organics section, Dr. Harant as in the inorganics one, and Dr. von Sallmann as in the one for synthetic rubber processing. On the subsequent replacement of Sallmann by Harant and Harant by Dr. Kallscheuer, see the same volume, Baerwind's Aktenvermerk betreffend die Entsendung von Dr. Kallscheuer in das Reichsamt, September 9, 1943, and his Aussprache mit Dr. Eckell, September 17, 1943.

[121] See HHW, Spruchkammerakten Lüer, Nr. 646, Bd. 2, the Verteidigungsschrift by Lüer's lawyers, October 19, 1948, and the Klageschrift of the Hessisches Ministerium für politische Befreiung, May 30, 1949.

[122] *Ibid.*, Bd. 1, the Vernehmungsprotokolle of Hans Rammensee and Heinrich Machenheimer, July 20, 1948 (concerning the pressure Lüer exerted on the Torpedo-Werke AG), and Auszug aus dem Vernehmungsprotokoll von Karl Bernard, January 27, 1948 (on Menzel's appointment).

9   Carl Lüer

a reputation as a relative moderate in comparison with the other local Nazi bigwigs, notably Jacob Sprenger, the Gauleiter of Hessen-Nassau, Karl Eckardt, his regional economic advisor, and Wilhelm Avieny, that man's eventual successor, all of whom were among the more loutish figures in a Party replete with such types. Because Lüer was inclined to rank pragmatic considerations ahead of ideological ones in setting policy, he quickly emerged as the Nazi of choice for businessmen in Hessen. In particular, he made, as the vice chairman of Degussa's supervisory board at the time later recalled, "the best conceivable impression" on the vice president of Frankfurt's Chamber, namely Ernst Busemann. He supposedly set out "to make [Lüer's] knowledge and experience useful to the Scheideanstalt in some fashion."[123]

Be that as it may, it was Lüer who actually raised the matter of taking a position at Degussa in February 1935, using as his intermediary Bernhard Pfotenhauer of the E. Merck pharmaceuticals firm, another enthusiastic Nazi who by now had replaced Pietzsch as head of the Economic Group for Chemistry. Apparently the need for a regular salary occasioned Lüer's approach. As he explained to Busemann, the Reich Economics Ministry disliked the exceptional arrangements by which the Chamber President was being paid through donations from several local firms. It had therefore recommended that he seek out a full-time position on the managing board of an enterprise in Frankfurt. Considering himself too busy for that role, Lüer expressed his preference for an appointment to a supervisory board with designated

---

[123] *Ibid.*, Bd. 3, Eidesstattliche Erklärung by Hugo Henkel, May 20, 1948.

responsibility for specific subjects. The obviously well-prepared Busemann replied that ample such opportunities could be found at Degussa, such as representing "our interests in foreign exchange matters and in a series of other things, which concern our work with the Party and Party institutions," and held out the generous prospect, in the event of such an appointment, of the usual directors' fees plus a "fixed compensation" of 18,000 RM per year, which corresponded to the threshold salary for members of the managing board.[124] Within a month, he had his colleagues' agreement to the proffered arrangements and so notified the members of the supervisory board.[125] His letter to Lüer of April 16, 1935, formalized the deal, promising to present his candidacy for that body to the next general meeting of the firm and meanwhile contracting to pay him the agreed upon sum for serving on the Economic Policy Advisory Committee of the managing board for a period of three years, with automatic extensions annually thereafter unless either party gave notice six months prior to the expiration date.[126] While Lüer promptly took up his advisory and lobbying work ("in which," Fritz Roessler averred in early 1937, "he has been of great benefit to us") and his compensation rose to 24,000 RM yearly, his formal election to the supervisory board was delayed for two years, first at his request, then through a miscommunication between him and the firm.[127] Events were shortly to disclose that the completion of the formalities in January 1938 came in the nick of time, for Lüer was about to prove indispensable to Degussa's efforts to navigate the shoals of industrial politics in the Third Reich.

Overlapping and interrelated threats to Degussa's autonomy were emerging from several quarters as Lüer assumed his new appointment. One source of menace was the Nazi leadership in Frankfurt, which harbored two objectives that conflicted with Degussa's commercial interests: taking command of the Metallgesellschaft, the historic partner firm in which Degussa still held slightly more than 10 percent of the stock and vice versa, and forcing Hans Menzel onto Degussa's managing board.[128] Both matters became acute in 1938 in conjunction with the regime's drive to complete the so-called Aryanization of the German economy, which not only entailed the ouster of

[124] DUA, BU Carl Lüer, Busemann's unheaded memo, marked "confidential" ["Vertraulich"], February 19, 1935.

[125] *Ibid.*, Busemann to the members of the Aufsichtsrat, March 5, 1935.

[126] *Ibid.*, Busemann to Lüer, April 16, 1935.

[127] *Ibid.*, Lüer to Degussa, December 30, 1935; Busemann's Besprechung mit Herrn Professor Lüer, February 21, 1936; Hans Schneider's Besprechung mit Herrn Professor Dr. Lüer, September 21, 1936; Busemann and Hektor Roessler to the members of the Aufsichtsrat, January 18, 1937. For the quotation, BU Fritz Roessler, "Zur Geschichte" [1937], Abschrift, p. 138.

[128] On Degussa's shareholdings in the MG, see DUA, Geschäftsberichte for 1937/38 and 1939/40, which give its participation as 4.7 million, then 4.9 million Reichsmarks out of a total stock capital of 42 million. By the end of 1940, as a result of buying several Aryanized portfolios, Degussa's participation rose to over 5.4 million or almost 13 percent; see DL 3.Scherf/1, Notiz für Herrn Scherf, July 17, 1951, as well as Chapter 3.

Richard Merton as head of the MG's supervisory board and of two of its managing board members on "racial" grounds, but also occasioned a new push by the local NSDAP to gain greater representation in Frankfurt's corporate suites.[129] Already in early 1937, at a meeting Lüer arranged in Berlin with Bernhard Köhler, one of Hermann Göring's economic henchmen, Merton had refused to add the Party's future regional economic advisor, Wilhelm Avieny, to the MG's managing board. But the ground was cut out from under Merton between November 1937 and January 1938, during Göring's brief appointment as Acting Economics Minister in place of the somewhat disillusioned and completely outmaneuvered Hjalmar Schacht. Once the Reichsmarschall had used his new post to issue a series of edicts that made the allocation of foreign exchange, raw materials, and government contracts contingent on the elimination of "non-Aryans" from a corporation's management, Merton's position became untenable.[130] His replacement on Degussa's supervisory board followed within a matter of days, his resignation from MG's at the behest of the Economics Ministry within weeks.

Thus, in February 1938, a clash of wills began between the Gauleitung, which now wished to install Avieny as the MG's chief executive, and the businessmen on the firm's supervisory board, especially Carl Bosch of IG Farben, who insisted on a competent and experienced figure from the metals sector. Their candidate was Bosch's son-in-law, Rudolf Kissell, the chairman of the managing board of the Duisburger Kupferhütte. Busemann was caught squarely in the crossfire, not only because he was Merton's successor as chairman of the MG's supervisory board, but because Degussa and IG had a gentleman's agreement by which they would keep their respective participations in that firm at parity and vote them in concert. While a compromise solution was being worked out in the form of a triumvirate composed of Avieny, Kissell, and a veteran MG director to manage the firm, Menzel tried to press his claim to a seat on Degussa's board, but the Gauleiter, perhaps taking into account Busemann's importance to the Party's aspirations regarding the Metallgesellschaft, chose to accept his reasons for opposing the promotion, at least for the present.[131] There the two matters rested for about a year, until the diagnosis of Ernst Busemann's fatal illness on the day Germany invaded Poland.

Meanwhile, power relations in Frankfurt were being complicated by developments concerning another long-standing Degussa partner firm, the Henkel company of Düsseldorf. Though that firm's purchases of perborate still

---

[129] On the events at the MG, see HHW, Spruchkammerakten Lüer 646, Bd. 1, Merton to Peterson, January 7, 1948; as well as Bd. 2, the Klageschrift in Lüer's case, May 30, 1949. Both of the other directors were arrested in September 1938, and one of them, Hermann Schmidt-Fellner, died in Mauthausen concentration camp in January 1940.

[130] See Hayes, *Industry and Ideology*, pp. 169–70.

[131] DUA, BU Ernst Baerwind, diary entries for the first week in and the middle of August, 1938, Abschrift, p. 31.

provided roughly one-fifth of the Scheideanstalt's profits, and Ernst Busemann served as chairman of Henkel's supervisory board and Hugo Henkel as vice-chairman of Degussa's, relations between the two enterprises had been cooling for some years.[132] The problem was Henkel's increasingly obvious intention to insist on major revisions to the perborate sales contract when it came up for renewal in 1940. Both the price Degussa was obtaining (which guaranteed a profit margin of about 25 percent above production costs in compensation for Degussa's investments in manufacturing the product, renunciation of sales to other detergent makers, and grant to Henkel of a license to test an electrolytic process for producing perborate) and the volume Henkel had to buy from Degussa (almost all of the first 9,000 metric tons needed annually) were therefore in jeopardy.[133] As a way of hanging onto as much as possible of a business that was yielding a profit of more than 4 million Reichsmarks yearly in the midthirties, Busemann apparently hit on the clever idea in late 1937, just after Henkel opened its own small-scale perborate manufacturing installation in Düsseldorf, of persuading that firm to increase its shareholding in Degussa. His purpose was to augment the buyer's stake in the seller's profitability, as well as to offer Henkel a greater annual rebate on its perborate purchases via dividends. With the announcement at the stockholders' meeting of January 1938 that Henkel owned more than one-quarter of Degussa's shares and the election of Hugo Henkel to succeed the recently deceased Fritz Roessler as chairman of its supervisory board, Busemann seemed not only to have parried a threat to his firm's proceeds, but also moved a step closer toward a prospect he had apparently been contemplating for some time: the formation of a new German chemicals concern, composed of Henkel and Degussa and, perhaps, the Metallgesellschaft.[134]

[132] See DUA, BU Fritz Roessler, "Zur Geschichte" [1937], Abschrift, p. 119, especially his remark that by 1937, the firms' relations had become "outwardly intimate, inwardly cool, and somewhat condescending on Henkel's part."

[133] DUA, DL 3.Hirtes/1, Schmidt's Die Beziehungen zwischen Henkel & Cie., Düsseldorf, und Degussa, enclosing two memos from the Verkaufsgruppe Chemie/Abt. A, one headed Trio-Vertrag and the other Auszug aus letztem Abkommen mit Henkel & Cie., all three documents dated November 20, 1947. On Henkel's reasons for wanting to revise the contract, see the revealing exchange in DUA, DL 3.Busemann.4, Busemann's Betr. Perborat-Vertrag Henkel, March 28, 1933; and Busemann's Besuch bei den Herren Dr. Henkel und Dr. Bartz, August 27, 1934; DL 3.Baerwind/18, Baerwind's Besuch bei Henkel, September 8, 1934; DL 3.Busemann/5, Busemann's Notizen betr. Persil und was damit zusammenhängt, February 22, 1935; Betr. Persil und Sil, June 1, 1935; and Betr. Perborat/Henkel, December 6, 1935.

[134] See the somewhat differently accented accounts of Busemann's thinking in DUA, TLE 1/23, Menzel's Denkschrift zur Angelegenheit Henkel-Degussa, December 7, 1942, and DL 3.Hirtes/1, Schlosser's Betr. Henkel (marked Confidential!, April 16, 1952), the former emphasizing concern-building as Busemann's main objective, the latter his concerns about the arrangements governing perborate. On Degussa's profits from these arrangements in

If the Party's offensive at the MG introduced a new variable into the latter scheme, a parallel and almost simultaneous "palace revolution" at Henkel had even more unpredictable implications for both of Busemann's objectives.[135] Under pressure from Berlin, exercised through the Gauleitung in Düsseldorf, Hugo Henkel was forced in mid-1938 to withdraw from his firm's supervisory board and to replace several older members of the managing one with his son Jost and his nephews, Carl August Bagel and Werner Lüps, the latter a favorite of Hermann Göring.[136] The new, ambitious, and youthful leadership, closely identified with the Nazi regime and interested in breaking the domination of IG Farben within the German chemical industry, promptly stepped up Henkel's purchases of Degussa's stock. Aided by the availability of shares created by the spoliation of Germany's Jews in the months surrounding the pogrom of November 1938, the shareholding had grown to about 40 percent by the time Busemann fell ill in September 1939, much to the surprise of his heir apparent, Hermann Schlosser.[137]

Schlosser thus found himself in an extremely delicate position precisely at the moment that he, his firm, and his nation were plunged into war: to succeed Busemann, he needed the Frankfurt Gauleitung's endorsement, but he did not want to appoint Menzel to Degussa's managing board or to choose between Avieny and IG with regard to the Metallgesellschaft; Busemann's supervisory posts at both MG and Henkel were now also up for grabs; and, whatever Lüps's intentions, Schlosser could not afford either to alienate the new masters of Henkel or to become prematurely associated with their objectives. The nearly all-purpose, short-range solution to these problems, he seems quickly to have realized, might be Carl Lüer, whose Nazi credentials would satisfy Gauleiter Sprenger and put him beyond challenge by Henkel, but whose reputation for pragmatism would make him acceptable to IG Farben. Late in September 1939, when Schlosser called on Sprenger to reveal Busemann's mortal condition and secure the succession, the Gauleiter's suggestion that Avieny be added to Degussa's supervisory board as chair in place of Hugo Henkel seems to have given Schlosser his opening. He expressed respect for Avieny, but noted that both Henkel himself and Degussa's managing board already had concluded that Lüer's familiarity with the firm

the period 1934–37, DUA, RFI 4.2/70, 74, and 77, Jahresabschlüsse der Rheinfeldener Abteilung.

[135] For the phrase, see DUA, BU Ernst Baerwind, diary entry for October 21, 1938, Abschrift, p. 31.

[136] *Ibid.*, entry for the first week in August 1938, Abschrift, p. 31; Henkel & Cie GmbH, *1876–1976. 100 Jahre Henkel* (Düsseldorf: Henkel & Cie, n.d. [1976]), pp. 126, 130. I should add here that Henkel has refused me – not for the first time – access to its archive in connection with this book.

[137] DUA, TLE 1/23, Menzel's Denkschrift zur Angelegenheit Henkel-Degussa, December 7, 1942; and DL 3.Hirtes/1, Schlosser's Betr. Henkel (marked Confidential! [Vertraulich!], April 16, 1952.

made him the appropriate choice and that he was also ideally equipped to follow Busemann as Avieny's colleague at the Metallgesellschaft. Apparently Sprenger and Schlosser got on well, even allowing for some overstatement in the latter's account a few days later that "I recognized once more with deep satisfaction that understanding and trust can be quickly established between two old front-line soldiers who both honestly keep their eyes on the matter at hand."[138] In any case, because Lüer's multiple advancements strengthened the Party's positions in the Frankfurt business community, Sprenger quickly agreed. A week later, Schlosser invoked more military imagery in his appeal to the apparently somewhat reluctant Lüer to accept the new posts. After declaring that he had taken the Gauleiter's "final decision... naturally as an order" and so informed Hugo Henkel, Schlosser added that "it would seriously impair my authority from the very beginning, if I had to reverse the decision concerning the chairmanship of the Scheideanstalt's supervisory board.... The command to retreat has never been an honorable part of the Prussian military manual; it should also not have a place in the vocabulary of our Gauleiter."[139]

Lüer acceded, becoming chairman of Degussa's supervisory board on November 1, two days after Busemann died, and a month later, IG Farben capitulated as well, clearing the way for Lüer's election to the same post at the Metallgesellschaft.[140] In the meantime, Lüer's tightening connection to Degussa had taken, albeit by an ostensibly independent route, rather ugly symbolic form as well. In the spring of 1939, after the authorities in Wiesbaden refused the neighbor to whom Ernst Eichwald had entrusted his home in Kronberg the right to buy it for a daughter, Lüer presented himself as a prospective buyer, offering the book value for the property. Following the removal of several interior walls to create rooms commensurate with his status, Lüer installed himself in not only a suitable residence, but also a considerably more valuable one, which he remortgaged for a sum 70 percent larger than he had paid.[141]

Schlosser's shrewd deployment of Lüer won him only a breathing spell, however. To be sure, it had cleared his path to office, finessed the Menzel

[138] DUA, BU Hermann Schlosser, Schlosser to Lüer, October 4, 1939, Abschrift aus Akte Dokumente zur Spruchkammersache gegen Wilhelm Avieny.

[139] *Ibid.*

[140] DUA, D8/4, 447. Sitzung [des Aufsichtsrates], November 1, 1939, Abschrift, Apr 3, p. 18; DL 2/1, Anlage 1 zur Niederschrift über die Vorstandssitzung am 2. Dezember 1939, Schlosser's Unterhaltung mit Geheimrat Schmitz, marked "Strictly Confidential!" December 1, 1939.

[141] HHW, Spruchkammerakten Lüer, Nr. 646, Bd. 1, Strott's Ermittlungsbericht, September 7, 1948. According to a statement by building engineer Heinrich Lang, June 15, 1948, in the same file, Lüer used his official positions in 1943 to improve the property, diverting construction materials for damaged houses in the vicinity for the erection of an enclosing wall, then adding a bathing pool, paid for with public funds on the pretext that it would be used to put out fires in the neighborhood.

matter, preserved the tenuous balance of power at MG, and marginalized Henkel's new leadership completely along the way. But both the NSDAP and Degussa's biggest shareholders soon reasserted their claims, and Lüer proved merely a good cover rather than a strong defense during this stage of the infighting. Menzel, for one thing, refused to give up. Late in September, before the succession question had been settled, he tried to take advantage of his opportunity by writing Schlosser to say that he had endorsed the latter man's candidacy to Frankfurt's Nazi leaders, since "Only a genuine front soldier and convinced socialist can guide the fate of such a great firm under the rule of National Socialism. To serve you in the process as a loyal aide and occasionally also as mentor in my capacity as an old Party comrade will be the sole purpose of my civilian life." With typical self-aggrandizement, however, Menzel could not resist appending a clumsy hint concerning the proper reward for his support: "That you perhaps, after testing, will hand over the rudder in the fifties to a grandson of the founder, from whom I obviously have inherited my socialist streak, I consider not entirely impossible."[142] But when he discovered in early November that, despite his objections, the new chairman intended to proceed with the absorption of the Durferrit subsidiary into Degussa and the relegation of Menzel as its former business manager to a mere department head, the insulted aspirant quickly demonstrated what his protestations of loyalty were worth.[143] Immediately following Lüer's designation as supervisory board chair, Menzel wrote directly to his Party comrade to say, "I cannot resign myself to the worsening of my position and believe that it can only be made good when I and some younger men . . . are taken on to the managing board. . . . The Gauleiter, with whom I had the honor of a long conversation fourteen days ago, would welcome and advocate my promotion."[144] Spurned in this attempt, Menzel beset Schlosser with a stream of insistent letters from assorted military postings, both trying to micromanage his office from afar and reiterating that his loss of status justified, now more than ever, his naming to the managing board. This agitation, which drained Schlosser's time and energy during an already hectic period, finally exhausted his patience. On January 19, 1940, he lashed back in no uncertain terms:

I will not be able to withhold from the Gauleiter that your claim to appointment to the managing board rests solely on your Party membership and not, for instance, on your abilities and accomplishments, which, as I have said to you so often, are extraordinarily overestimated by you and, moreover, more than offset by your well known qualities. . . . I have supported you in the past, to be sure, primarily on the basis

---

[142] DUA, BU Hans Menzel, Menzel to Schlosser, September 24, 1939.
[143] On the decision concerning Durferrit, see DUA, D 2/1, Niederschrift über die Vorstandssitzung am 6. November 1939, p. 58, and Anlage 3, Schlosser's Anweisung an Durferrit G.m.b.H., November 3, 1939, which shows that Menzel had been informed of the decision the day before.
[144] DUA, BU Hans Menzel, Menzel to Lüer, November 3, 1939.

of a common attitude toward front-soldiery and in a fashion that has often, in the opinion of my colleagues, exceeded the limits of the defensible. . . . I am in principle ready to engage myself for you further in the future, but on one clear condition: you must finally follow the advice that I have given you so often in vain, and through modest and quiet work over a series of years give proof that you are better than your reputation to date and have acquired the maturity for the sort of cooperative work which you imagine.[145]

So long as Wilhelm Avieny was not yet safely installed as head of the Metallgesellschaft, the Gauleiter heeded Schlosser's and Lüer's objections to Menzel; but the minute Sprenger had that firm in his grasp, he abruptly swept them aside. Lüer's Party status, it turned out, was a double-edged sword. His presence at MG, along with Bosch's degradation to a political outcast and descent into depression following a speech critical of Hitler at the Deutsches Museum in May 1939, then death in April 1940, cut the ground from under Kissell.[146] In November 1940, he was kicked upstairs to the supervisory board, and Avieny took over as General Director of the Metallgesellschaft and claimed the seat on Degussa's supervisory board that went with that post.[147] Simultaneously, Gauleiter Sprenger summoned Lüer and virtually ordered him to arrange Menzel's immediate appointment as a full member of the managing board, thus forcing Degussa to begin the process of expanding the number of seats on that body to make room for him.[148] On May 8, 1941, when he took up his long-sought place at the Degussa directors' table, the Party could count its corporate gains on the Frankfurt scene with some satisfaction: the decisive positions at the MG were in its hands, along with the chairmanship of Degussa's supervisory board and direct access to the firm's highest counsels at what turned out to be a pivotal moment.[149]

One of Menzel's first active involvements as a board member in Degussa's affairs showed how dangerous the Party could be at this juncture for a businessman who misstepped. At the beginning of August 1941, the leaders of Degussa and its subsidiary Degesch learned that the Gauleitung was about to demand the removal of Walter Heerdt, the business manager of the Heerdt-Lingler GmbH, the Frankfurt-based sales agent for Degesch's products in Germany west of the Elbe River and in a number of foreign countries. His wife, unaware that the family had been under Gestapo surveillance since 1936, when Dr. Heerdt became General Consul for Yugoslavia in Frankfurt, just had been arrested for writing a letter that included comments critical of the Wehrmacht, but the Party's complaints against the man himself were

---

[145] DUA, BU Hans Menzel, Schlosser to Menzel, January 24, 1940.
[146] On these events, see Hayes, *Industry and Ideology*, pp. 201–02.
[147] DUA, D 8/4, 450. Sitzung des Aufsichtsrates, December 11, 1940, Abschrift, Apr 3, pp. 23–24.
[148] DUA, BU Ernst Baerwind, diary entry for November 25, 1940, Abschrift, p. 35.
[149] On the date of Menzel's first meeting, *Ibid.*, p. 36.

also numerous. According to what Avieny told Menzel at mid-month, Heerdt "and his family are known for avoiding every contact with the Party," for "ostentatiously" refusing to give "the German greeting," and for maintaining "quite unambiguous" social contacts, as a result of which the Gauleitung some months earlier had declined the Army's request for an assurance of the political reliability of Heerdt-Lingler's management. Menzel quickly concluded "that no possibility exists of stopping the course of events."[150] To just that hopeless purpose, Heerdt had sent his son, Wolfgang, to Hermann Schlosser early in the month, then written directly, excusing his reticence toward the regime as a matter of mere "details" and a product of his skeptical temperament. After saying "as concerns my wife, I can say only that my heart bleeds," Heerdt affirmed his conviction that "the Führer is . . . a genius" and that "I am . . . a thoroughly positive and active member of this state also because I am deeply convinced of the superiority of Germanism."[151] But whatever his personal reaction to this missive, Schlosser decided that he could not afford or did not want to seem sympathetic. On August 14, Dr. Crain of Degussa's legal department set in motion the convening of a meeting of the Heerdt-Lingler partners (Messrs. Heerdt and Lingler with 49 percent, and Degesch with 51 percent) to debate Heerdt's dismissal, and by August 20, Schlosser had sent the targeted man a personal note declining to take up his defense.[152] He resigned the following day.[153] But the Party was not yet finished: it declared the executive who was next in line, one Herr Sänger, as "not wanted" and thus prompted Gerhard Peters, business manager of Degesch and Party member since 1937, to take over the sales agency's leadership as well.[154]

As the NSDAP was winning these battles, the new leadership of Henkel began to exert its clout within Degussa in a manner that pushed Schlosser

---

[150] DUA, IW 57.14/2, Menzel's Bericht über eine Aussprache beim Gauwirtschaftsberater in Sachen Dr. Walter Heerdt, August 18, 1941.

[151] DUA, BU Hans Menzel, Heerdt to Schlosser, August 8, 1941.

[152] DUA, IW 57.14/2, Crain's Bericht. Betr.: Angelegenheit Dr. Heerdt, August 14, 1941; Kaufmann's Aktenvermerk Betr. Dr. Heerdt, August 20, 1941.

[153] *Ibid.*, Heerdt to Heerdt-Lingler GmbH, August 21, 1941. Heerdt, who was hospitalized for heart problems from the time of his wife's arrest until early 1942, was jailed by the Gestapo as soon as he was declared healthy and brought to the same prison that still held his wife. Both were released in March 1942, thanks to the intervention of Winnifred Wagner with Himmler, and ordered to leave Frankfurt. They settled in the Salzkammergut until the end of the war, supported in part by 200 RM per month from Degesch and 600 RM per month from Heerdt-Lingler as well as a guaranteed return of 6,000 RM per year on his shares. On their fates, see Jürgen Kalthoff and Martin Werner, *Die Händler des Zyklon B* (Hamburg: VSA-Verlag, 1998), p. 113; on the financial provisions, DUA, IW 57.14/2, Degesch to Walter Heerdt, July 2, 1943, and Heerdt-Lingler to Walter Heerdt, July 1, 1943.

[154] *Ibid.*, Peters' Persönliche Niederschrift Betr. Geschäftsführerwechsel in der Heli, August 25, 1941. On his Party membership, HHW, 483/10982, Gaupersonalamtsleiter to the Gauwirtschaftsberater, September 4, 1942.

into fresh controversies with both the Sprenger-Avieny-Menzel axis on one side and IG Farben on the other. Having lacked a position from which to influence the succession to Busemann in the fall of 1939, Werner Lüps moved in January 1940 to rectify that situation. He demanded that Henkel's shareholding be given adequate recognition in the form of "one or two additional" seats on Degussa's supervisory board, to be allotted at its impending meeting. Schlosser played for time by pointing out that he would welcome the addition of another Henkel representative, presumably Lüps himself, but that the board was at its statutory maximum number of members and that arrangements for either increasing that number or eliciting resignations could not be made in the few weeks remaining before the session.[155] Within a week, however, Hektor Roessler had provided a plan, adopted by the board on January 16, for including Lüps immediately as a guest at the board's meetings, with a promise to elect him formally at the earliest possible opportunity. This occurred the following January as a result of Bosch's death in the interim, at which point Lüps also replaced his uncle Hugo as vice chairman of the board and was added to the four-man Personnel Committee, with responsibility for managerial salaries and promotions.[156] In the meantime, however, Lüps's influence over Degussa's commercial policies and strategic decisions did not require such formal positions. It rested on Henkel's shareholding, which was still creeping upward; on the regular consultations between the two enterprises concerning common interests (especially regarding hydrogenation, detergents, and hydrogen peroxide); and on the dovetailing of Lüps's aggressive vision of an interdependent future for the two corporations with the objectives of some of Degussa's directors. The last-named is what fostered conflict with both IG Farben and the Gauleitung's man at Degussa, Hans Menzel.

The principal interest of the Lüps coterie in Degussa was to use it (a) defensively, to discourage IG Farben from further encroachments on Henkel's dominance of detergents and the chemistry of fats and oils, and (b) offensively, to broaden Henkel's involvement in other chemicals spheres, in part at IG Farben's expense. These objectives came into the open at a meeting in the fall of 1940, where Henkel's directors "stiffened [Degussa's] spine" against IG Farben's demands that the new "concern factory" Degussa was planning for Fürstenberg an der Oder should not include a manufacturing plant for carbide. This intermediate product had manifold industrial uses, especially in acetylene-based products such as Buna rubber and solvents, that IG was

---

[155] DUA, DL 2/1, Anlage 3a zur Niederschrift über die Vorstandssitzung am 8. January 1940, Schlosser's memo, marked "strictly confidential," January 4, 1940.

[156] *Ibid.*, Anlage 3b, Schlosser to Hektor Roessler, January 10, 1940; D 8/4, 449. Sitzung des Aufsichtsrates, January 16, 1940, Abschrift, Apr 3, pp. 22 and 450. Sitzung des Aufsichtsrates, December 11, 1940, p. 29; and DL 2/1, Niederschrift über die Vorstandssitzung am 3. Juni 1940, p. 95, which records the earmarking of Bosch's seat for Lüps.

particularly keen on controlling. But Lüps and his colleagues were so eager to promote the carbide venture that they pledged, if necessary, to pay half the costs – estimated at 25 million marks for an installation with an annual capacity of 30,000 to 50,000 tons – and to split the managerial responsibilities equally, as well.[157] Degussa's technical leaders, particularly those associated with the firm's carbonization division, needed little encouragement. They were convinced that their operations had no long-range future without beginning the transition from wood to coal as their feedstock, which entailed constructing such a plant.[158] But Schlosser was of another mind. Whereas Ernst Busemann had complained repeatedly during the thirties that "there is no sphere of the Scheideanstalt in which over the years IG Farben has not meddled" or "increasingly got in our way," Schlosser was acutely conscious of how many aspects of Degussa's business involved intricate demarcation pacts with IG Farben regarding patents, markets, research, and more, and he feared endangering them.[159] Though he conceded the logic of Degussa manufacturing its own carbide, he had dragged his feet on the plant for months prior to Henkel's intervention, arguing that Degussa could trade restraint in this field for important guarantees in other ones, notably cyanides and sodium.[160] At the end of 1940, in a last-ditch effort to salvage his strategy, he got his technical colleagues to postpone constructing the carbide plant if Farben provided Fürstenberg with adequate quantities of acetylene at cost, only to be left in the lurch by the giant combine.[161]

[157] *Ibid.*, Anlage 1 zur Niederschrift über die Vorstandssitzung am 4. November 1940, Baerwind's Henkel/Degussa-Tagung auf Elbhöhe bei Hamburg, November 4, 1940, especially p. 4 (for the quoted words). Henkel's offer is recorded in the minutes of the meeting, p. 137.

[158] See, for example, *Ibid.*, Anlage 3 zur Niederschrift über die Vorstandssitzung am 2. September 1940, Achterath's Betr.: Projekt Fürstenberg, August 30, 1940.

[159] For Busemann's comments, see DUA, DL 3.Busemann/6, his Verhältnis Scheideanstalt: I. G., April 23, 1935, p. 3, DL 3.Busemann/5, his Besprechung mit Herrn Dr. Ter Meer, June 14, 1935, p. 1. On Degussa's numerous arrangements with IG Farben, see D 2/20, the summaries by product and subsidiary prepared for the American occupation authorities in 1945–47.

[160] For the best illustration of Schlosser's preferred line in dealing with IG, see DUA, DL 11.5/41, his Verhältnis zur I. G., marked "confidential" [Vertraulich!], March 27, 1940, especially p. 2, where he set forth a willingness to renounce the production of methanol and make concessions regarding uses of chlorine in return for recognition of Degussa's primacy with regard to sodium, oxygenated products, and sodium cyanide, and a partnership regarding hydrogen peroxide; and his follow-up memos with the same title and heading, May 4, June 20, and August 15, 1940. On his temporizing about carbide, see DL 2/1, Niederschrift über die Vorstandssitzung am 2. September 1940, pp. 118–20, and Niederschrift über die Vorstandssitzung am 7. Oktober 1940, pp. 127–30.

[161] DUA, DL 2/1, Niederschrift über die Vorstandssitzung am 7. Oktober 1940, pp. 129–30; Niederschrift über die Vorstandssitzung am 4. November 1940, pp. 135–36, and Anlage 4, Fischer's Betr. Acetylen-Chemie, October 30, 1940; Anlage 1 zur Niederschrift über die Vorstandssitzung am 2. Dezember 1940, Schlosser's Acetylen-Chemie, November 10, 1940; and Niederschrift über die Vorstandssitzung am 3. Februar 1941, pp. 158–59, as well as Anlagen 1–4.

Thus forced to accept the carbide facility, Schlosser still clung to his over-all position regarding relations with IG Farben. His reassertions of it in subsequent months have, however, the sound of a man trying to regain lost authority. Because the costs of provoking reprisals from so large a rival, of which several meetings with Farben executives had reminded him, remained uppermost in his mind, he tried once more to draw a line clearly for the head of Degussa's research division in May 1941:

> Now that I have, to a degree that has been thoroughly recognized by the techni-cal men and with corresponding success, applied myself to the realization of the Fürstenberg project, that is, for the entrance of the Scheideanstalt to the sphere of acetylene chemistry, I consider it now necessary for diverse, very compelling reasons to make an unmistakable declaration at today's managing board meeting that I can-not agree under any circumstances to any sort of further intrusions on the sphere of IG Farben except if either we have a technical breakthrough to present that is convincing to IG or a friendly agreement with it comes into being on the basis of full reciprocity.

He then went on to list a series of products on which he excluded further research work for fear of jeopardizing existing agreements with the giant partner.[162] In the following months, he reiterated his deferential position regarding clashes of interest over ceramic dyes, zircon, and chlorine.[163]

That Schlosser was losing control of events, however, seemed clear not only from his defeat on the single issue of carbide, but from the increasingly manifest interpenetration of Degussa's and Henkel's decision making, sig-nalled by the following agreement between their respective managements in late October 1940:

> Internally applies [the principle] that, in the future regarding all fundamental questions in all spheres of interest to both firms, the closest contact must take place, as between the firms in a concern. Externally, a unified statement about the Henkel/Scheideanstalt relationship is, at least until further notice, not yet possible, and one must – according to the situation – operate with a certain flexibility.[164]

In the context of the obvious imbalance of power between the two enterprises created by Henkel's shareholding and Lüps's ties to Hermann Göring, neither the diplomatic phraseology nor the accompanying invitation for Schlosser to join Henkel's supervisory board concealed the fact that Henkel was now reserving the right to try to shape Degussa's actions to the Düsseldorf

---

[162] DUA, RPW 2.5/4, Schlosser to Otto Fuchs, May 8, 1941. For an illustration of IG's pressure on Schlosser, see DL 11.5/41, Schlosser's Acetylen-Chemie, marked "strictly confidential," October 11, 1940, p. 2.

[163] DUA, DL 11.5/41, Schlosser's Verhältnis I. G./Scheideanstalt, August 8, 1941, and his Chlor/Natrium, August 19, 1941, especially p. 3.

[164] DUA, D 2/1, Anlage 1 zur Niederschrift über die Vorstandssitzung am 4. November 1940, Baerwind's Henkel/Degussa-Tagung auf Elbhöhe bei Hamburg, November 4, 1940.

company's purposes. Neither, one may surmise, was anyone within Degussa deceived by the memo Schlosser appended to the managing board's records in mid-November, which recorded that Henkel's leaders had recognized that "the independence and the characteristic features of the Scheideanstalt are to be in no way infringed upon."[165] Within a year, the two firms were laying plans for a split of Degussa's stock, followed by the issuing of 17 million Reichsmarks worth of new shares, half to be made available to existing shareholders on a ratio of eight old to one new stock certificate. Simply by exercising its option, Henkel could expect its portion of Degussa's total capital to rise from over 43 percent to over 48 percent, and enough other investors would probably be unwilling or unable to pay the issue price of 1,350 RM per share to leave the way clear for a secure majority. But the plan contained a secret feature just in case: Degussa's managing board would retain the other 8.5 million in new stock to use for investment purposes, specifically for the purchase of Henkel's shares in the Metallgesellschaft. In other words, upon the completion of these deals, Henkel would control Degussa, which, in turn, would hold more than 25 percent of the MG, while IG Farben, according to the terms of its now-extended gentleman's agreement with Degussa, would raise its participation in the MG to the same level.[166] On this basis, Henkel would have a stronger hand in negotiating a deal by which it and Farben would renounce, respectively, activities in the dyes and pharmaceuticals and the detergents and cleaning agents fields.[167]

Since these maneuvers threatened to reduce Hermann Schlosser's status in a fashion analogous to Hans Menzel's demotion in 1940, and since this was happening at the hands of the politically well-connected, there are multiple ironies in the fact that Menzel became, virtually upon arriving in Degussa's boardroom, the most outspoken opponent of the takeover by Henkel, yet as much a thorn in Schlosser's side as ever. While Degussa's chairman hardly welcomed Henkel's advance, he consoled himself with the possibility that a later reorganization of the whole concern would leave his still nominally independent enterprise with primacy in chemicals production, and he saw

---

[165] *Ibid.*, Anlage 1a, Schlosser's Henkel/Degussa, November 12, 1940.

[166] A committee of Degussa's managing board convened to consider the stock split and increase in the summer of 1941; see DUA, DL 2/1, Niederschrift über die Vorstandssitzung am 4. August 1941, p. 194. The size of the former was approved two months later, that of the latter, as well as its purpose, the following month; Niederschrift über die Vorstandssitzung am 6 Oktober 1941, p. 203, and Niederschrift über die Vorstandssitzung am 3. November 1941, pp. 209–10. The supervisory board ratified all these decisions, without making explicit reference in its minutes to the shares reserved for the use of management, at its next meeting; Niederschrift über die 452. Sitzung des Aufsichtsrates, April 1, 1942, Abschrift, pp. 30, 33–34. Schlosser informed IG of Degussa's and Henkel's intentions and discussed the shareholding in the MG just before Christmas 1941; see DL 11.5/41, Schlosser's untitled memo of December 29, 1941.

[167] DUA, DL 11.5/41, Schlosser's Verhältnis Henkel/I. G., January 5, 1942.

little to be gained – and perhaps his job to be lost – by open confrontation. Menzel's contrary stance reflected his characteristic mix of personal motives, political calculations, ideological convictions, and temperamental impulses. Assuredly, he imagined Henkel's control of Degussa as damaging to his own ambitions to take over the firm someday, ambitions about which he was none too discreet in the year following his elevation to the board.[168] Quite probably, Avieny was unsettled by the shifting around of shareholdings in a firm he had only recently managed to get in his grasp, regardless of Henkel's good Nazi credentials, and Menzel was eager to be of service to his Party comrade. Although neither man doubted the value of constructing a counterweight to IG Farben in the chemical industry, Menzel could thus vent his sincere disdain for the "purely capitalist considerations" that underlay Henkel's drive and express his preference for bringing the new combine together under National Socialist auspices and on the basis of the primacy of politics over corporate interests.[169] Above all, perhaps, Menzel simply could not help himself. Determined always to be the center of attention, he fomented one dispute after another with Schlosser during 1941–42, each designed to undermine the chairman's authority and make events pivot around his own demands. All of these he presented in the guise of radical patriotism – both to the firm's leaders and to the Party officials in Frankfurt and Berlin with whom he kept up constant, independent contact in defiance of Degussa's rule that only the chairman of the managing board should speak for it to the outside world.

Schlosser was hardly innocent of egging Menzel on. Shortly after his elevation to the board, Schlosser told him that Lüps believed that step had been unnecessary; some months later, the chairman probably took delight in revealing to Menzel that, among some employees, he was being spoken of as "as a National Egoist and not as a National Socialist."[170] But the conflict between the two men was virtually preprogrammed. Menzel's hunger for recognition, his utter lack of subtlety and patience, his recklessness, and his pretentiousness grated on the nerves of a man who prided himself on precisely the opposite qualities – and vice versa. As early as July 1941, they were in open conflict at board meetings, this time probably over Menzel's excessive willingness to enter into development contracts with the Army Ordnance Office, a subject that was thereupon assigned to Róka's jurisdiction.[171] Within weeks and behind Schlosser's back, Menzel was conspiring to take over one

[168] DUA, BU Hans Menzel, Westphal's Aktennotiz, August 14, 1941; and Josef Mayr to Menzel, July 21, 1949, recalling conversations shortly after Menzel's appointment to the managing board.

[169] DUA, BU Hans Menzel (also TLE 1/23), Menzel's Denkschrift zur Angelegenheit Henkel-Degussa, December 7, 1942.

[170] DUA, BU Hans Menzel, Menzel to Schlosser, July 16, 1941; and Menzel to Schlosser, March 17, 1942.

[171] DUA, DL 2/1, Niederschrift über die Vorstandssitzung am 7. Juli 1941, p. 192; see also BU Ernst Baerwind, Tagebuch-Notizen, Heft 2, entry 189, July 28–29, 1941.

director's section from those that reported directly to the chairman.[172] And on September 25, 1941, Menzel went so far as to outline his objections to Henkel's growing influence over Degussa to Economics Minister Walther Funk, who warned him with the reply, "Keep your hands off; do not push further into the Reichsmarschall's neighborhood."[173] Perhaps this admonition explains why Menzel, momentarily backing off, voted in November in favor of the share issue that would have guaranteed Henkel a majority.[174]

Schlosser could do nothing against the Menzel and Henkel problems until fate took a hand, which it did on April 19, 1942, when Werner Lüps's car drove into a bomb crater on a highway during a business trip, killing him. According to company lore, unconfirmed by a written source, the relieved members of Degussa's managing board celebrated the news with champagne. Be that as it may, while Degussa, in Schlosser's typically military description "deliberately stood at ease" during the interregnum that ensued in Düsseldorf, Menzel took it upon himself on June 9 to call on Jost Henkel, who told him that "the quest for a majority had been driven one-sidedly by Herr Lüps."[175] Late in July, after the announcements that Hermann Richter of the Dresdner Bank would take over as chairman of Henkel's managing board and that Hermann Schlosser had been elected to its supervisory body, Schlosser told Degussa's managers that "the possibilities of preserving the Scheideanstalt's independence and of having, in any case, undisputed leadership in the chemicals sector have increased."[176] So cautious a formulation hardly satisfied Menzel, who insisted "that the new era at Henkel should be used to stop any further penetration of the Scheideanstalt by Henkel and, furthermore, when possible, to lower the existing majority of votes in the General Meeting [of the stockholders]."[177] He then went on to report on his conversation with Henkel, of which Schlosser already had learned, which forced the chairman's hand. He felt compelled to demand a vote of the board condemning Menzel's initiative as a "breach of discipline," and this passed without dissent. But when Schlosser pressed his advantage, remarking that Menzel has thus completely isolated himself from his colleagues, at least four of them (Achterath, Baerwind, Hubert, and von Retze), dissented from this assessment, even though they disapproved of what Menzel had done, which provoked Schlosser into demanding a vote of confidence that passed unanimously.[178] So armed, he proceeded that afternoon to a meeting

[172] DUA, BU Hans Menzel, Westphal's Aktennotz, August 14, 1941.

[173] *Ibid.*, Menzel's statement of March 4, 1948.

[174] DUA, DL 2/1, Niederschrift über die Vorstandssitzung am 3. November 1941, which records that all members were present and the vote was unanimous.

[175] DUA, BU Hans Menzel, his Denkschrift zur Angelegenheit Henkel-Degussa, December 7, 1942, pp. 2–3.

[176] DUA, DL 2/1, Niederschrift über die Vorstandssitzung am 3. August 1942, p. 258.

[177] *Ibid.*, p. 259.

[178] Cf. *Ibid.*, p. 259–60; DUA, BU Hans Menzel, the draft version of the minutes prepared by Schlosser, August 4, 1942, which lists the dissenters by name; and Menzel's statement of

with Avieny and Gauleiter Sprenger, from which he emerged with a ringing endorsement of his authority, a prohibition on independent communications by Menzel with Avieny and Lüer, and a declaration that "if he nonetheless makes further difficulties and thus endangers industrial peace, then he must go," but not with the complete disavowal that Schlosser perhaps sought.[179]

Though not beyond repair, Menzel's position was badly eroded by this episode and by the turn of events at Henkel. That Schlosser and Richter soon reached an agreement essentially halting both Henkel's stock purchases and the transfer of the MG shares not only deprived Menzel of an issue, but also made him dispensable to Wilhelm Avieny, who now began to jettison his outspoken ally.[180] Heedless of what was happening, Menzel completed his own demolition. In December 1942, he made a vain – in both senses of the word – attempt to get Degussa to create a new special Office for Planning and Organization. On the very day that the managing board rejected that idea unanimously, he wrote and began widely circulating two memoranda, one gratuitously restating his case regarding the Henkel-Degussa combination and the other calling for the drafting of almost every German male born in the years 1908–22, including from the industrial workforce, which would have to find replacements "from conscripted foreigners, from prisoners and, above all, from rationalization."[181] He followed up on the former document in February 1943 with a specific scheme for reducing Henkel's shareholding, only to be rebuffed unanimously once more by the managing board, but the second memorandum is what brought him down.[182] It infuriated the Gauleiter, provoked von Retze and Avieny to break openly with Menzel, and caused Lüer to begin assembling a case on paper against him to present to the Personnel Commission of Degussa's supervisory board.[183] His fate

March 4, 1948, which claims he had five allies on the matter of his isolation, hence the vote stood at six to six. This is possible only if Stiege, who attended meanings of the managing board as a guest, was eligible to vote.

[179] Cf. DUA, BU Hans Menzel, Schlosser's Besprechung beim Gauleiter, August 4, 1942, and his letter to the Minister für politische Befreiung, Kammer Frankfurt am Main, January 13, 1947, which recalls the "negative result" of this meeting.

[180] On the agreement with Richter, see DUA, DL 2/1, Niederschrift über die Vorstandssitzung am 7. September 1942, p. 265; and DL 3.Hirtes/1, Schlosser's Betr. Henkel, April 16, 1952. For Menzel's recognition, in retrospect, that Avieny dropped him when he could no longer be useful, see BU Hans Menzel, his statement of March 4, 1948, p. 4.

[181] DUA, DL 2/1, Niederschrift über die Vorstandssitzung am 7. Dezember 1942, p. 288, and BU Hans Menzel, Denkschrift zur Angelegenheit Henkel-Degussa, and Denkschrift zum militärischen Erfassungswesen, both dated December 7, 1942.

[182] See DUA, DL 2/1, Niederschrift über die Vorstandssitzung am 1. Februar 1943, pp. 301–02.

[183] DUA, BU Hans Menzel, Auszug aus Notiz Schlosser vom 16. Dez. 1942 betr. Besuch Dr. Richter/Schlosser bei Gauleiter Sprenger am 14. Dezember 1942; Schlosser to Lüer, December 17, 1942; Retze to Menzel, January 5, 1943; Retze's Bemerkungen zur Denkschrift Menzel, January 13, 1943; Lüer to Sprenger and Lüer to Menzel, February 4, 1943; and DL 2/1, Niederschrift über die Vorstandssitzung am 11. Januar 1943, pp. 291–92, including Anlage I, Lüer to Schlosser, December 28, 1942.

was sealed in March, when it became apparent that he had circumvented Schlosser once more by meeting clandestinely concerning his conscription program with Walter Schieber, the official in Berlin responsible for the allocation of prisoners to industrial sites.[184] Lüer promptly suspended Menzel from the managing board and polled the members of the supervisory one by mail on the question of his removal.[185] Having already been told that the Gauleiter refused even to meet with him, let alone to protect him, Menzel was informed on April 2 of his dismissal by unanimous vote and given the option of resigning to save face, which he accepted after making minor adjustments to the financial terms of his separation.[186] These provided him some 200,000 RM over the next two and one-half years as he searched in vain for a new industrial position, went back into the army, and suffered an accident that left his left leg severely damaged.[187]

The final phase of the drawn-out Henkel and Menzel affairs stabilized Schlosser's commanding position within Degussa, won him the respect of Frankfurt's Nazi paladins, and smoothed the way for his rise to the leadership of the Economic Group for Chemistry in January 1943. At the moment of truth in March, he thus could play the threat to resign from that post as a trump card with the Gauleiter. But these developments did not quite put an end to his difficulties with the NSDAP. To be sure, he had little trouble thereafter enforcing his conciliatory policy toward IG Farben within Degussa.[188]

---

[184] DUA, BU Hans Menzel, Menzel to Stefan and Menzel to Schieber, March 4, 1943.

[185] DUA, BU Hans Menzel, Lüer to Menzel and Lüer to the members of the Aufsichtsrat, March 29, 1943, the latter accompanied by Begründung zu der vom Vorsitzer ... vorgeschlagenen Beschlussfassung über den Widerruf der Bestellung des ordentlichen Vorstandsmitgliedes der Degussa Hans Menzel.

[186] DUA, BU Hans Menzel, Schlosser's Notiz, March 11, 1943 (on the Gauleiter's statement), Lüer to Menzel, April 2, 1943 (the dismissal), Schlosser's Betr. Ausscheiden von Herrn Menzel aus dem Vorstand, April 3, 1943 (on the offer and Menzel's conditions), and Vereinbarung, April 3, 1943, signed by Menzel and Lüer (sealing the terms). DL 2/1, Niederschrift über die Vorstandssitzung am 5. April 1943, pp. 309–10, records the board's unanimous conclusion that "another solution than that of recalling Herr Menzel from the managing board was no longer possible."

[187] DUA, BU Hans Menzel, Scherf to the members of the supervisory board, May 5, 1949, and Schlosser to Charlotte Menzel, Hans' mother, September 13, 1950. After the war, as these documents record, Menzel intrigued against Schlosser's reinstatement as chairman of the managing board, underwent a divorce as his wife transferred her affections to an American officer, and saw his pension nearly obliterated by the effects of the war and the currency reform. Degussa agreed "in memory of your ancestors and in consideration of your children" to pay him a monthly allowance of 250 Deutschmarks, which – allowing for the firm's experience with the man – was revocable at any time; Altwein and Scherf to Menzel, October 2, 1950. See Chapter 9.

[188] See, for example, DUA, D 2/1, Niederschrift über die Vorstandssitzung am 5 Juli 1943, pp. 322–23, where Schlosser rejected the Speer Ministry's suggestion that Degussa enter into Buna production; and DL 3.Schlosser/1, Schlosser's Hydrierung, November 4, 1943, which characteristically concluded "I am of the opinion that we must seek a thoroughly friendly compromise with IG, which probably can only be found through our withdrawal

And both Henkel and the local NSDAP ceased to be serious problems. Indeed, all-around harmony seems to have been established by the time the supervisory board convened in March 1944, when Lüer, who by now had run afoul of Sprenger and begun retreating from prominent posts, both announced his intention to relinquish the chairmanship to a Henkel representative and proposed the election of Aviony to the board's Personnel Committee.[189] Of course, even to the bitter end, the Party kept sticking its hand out. Officially, Degussa and other big businesses were exempted from Nazi fund drives by virtue of payments to the *Adolf Hitler Spende der deutschen Wirtschaft*, a compulsory system of donations that generally amounted to .5 percent of each firm's total wage and salary expenditures. Degussa thus paid the Party 651,000 RM between 1933 and 1944 via this program, along with over 1.5 million marks to the Nazi Winterhilfswerk charitable organization (see Appendix B). Recurrent additional requests for money, only a few of which can be ascertained from the surviving records, nevertheless had continued to flow in, and not all of them could be deflected with reference to the *Spende*.[190] Thus, in April 1939, Busemann saw no way of evading the Party's request for 40,000 RM toward the building of a new Regional Party Administration Building.[191] Even as the Western allies stood on the Rhine and the Russians on the Oder in January 1945, Schlosser politely complied with Aviony's request that Degussa contribute 22,500 RM for a donation to Obergruppenführer Hildebrandt of the SS, for reasons unspecified in their correspondence.[192] Irritating as these tribute payments were, however, they were neither large nor, from the point of view of Degussa's leaders, altogether different from all sorts of small appropriations by which firms in most times and places win friends and influence people. More serious was the enduring pressure from Party radicals in Berlin, notably Martin Bormann, on such general issues as increases in the corporate tax rate and the abolition or at least severe regulation of supervisory boards, which served as a constant reminder that the anticapitalist strain of Nazism for which Menzel sometimes had spoken remained alive and well.[193]

from this sphere." Also pertinent are the documents concerning relations in the ceramic dyes sector in GKF 2/1, Hübner's Gedanken zur Frage Keramisches Geschäft I. G. Farben-Degussa, August 31, 1944; Degussa to I. G. Farben, Leverkusen, September 18, 1944; and Schlosser's Aktennotiz Keramische Farben – Verständigung mit der I. G., September 27, 1944.
[189] DUA, D 8/4, 455. Sitzung des Aufsichtsrates ... am 13. März 1944, Abschrift, Apr 3, pp. 48–49.
[190] That some could be so handled is indicated by DUA, DL 3.Busemann/5, Busemann's Betr.: Spenden der Wirtschaft, March 26, 1938.
[191] DUA, DL 3.Busemann/5, Busemann's Betr. Spende für das neue Gebäude der Gau-Verwaltung, April 4, 1939.
[192] DUA, DL 3.Schlosser/1, Aviony to Schlosser, January 11, 1945, and reply of January 24, 1945.
[193] DUA, TLE 1/23, Scherf's unheaded memo for the Vorstand, November 21, 1942.

Indeed, Schlosser's last tussle with the NSDAP before the collapse of the Third Reich was with just this sort of character and a microcosm of the behind-the-scenes fight for control of the war economy and the economic soul of the Nazi state that filled its last year. His antagonist was C3 89s Ungewitter, the National Delegate for Chemistry and a dedicated convert to Nazism, and behind him stood Walter Schieber, once an employee of IG Farben, then a strong promoter of German synthetics production during the 1930s, and by now the man responsible for the industrial application of prisoner labor.[194] Though Schieber headed the Armaments Delivery Office in the Armaments Ministry of Albert Speer, both he and Ungewitter had grave doubts about the willingness of big business to subordinate self-interest to the demands of total war as posited by the program of "self-responsibility of the economy" under the aegis of Speer and the head of his Raw Materials Office, Hans Kehrl. From the time Schlosser succeeded Johannes Hess of Wacker-Chemie as head of the Economic Group for Chemistry in early 1943, Ungewitter and Schieber sniped at his reorganization of that entity, which built up the power of a board composed of senior figures from major corporations and trimmed that of functionaries such as Ungewitter, who long had combined a series of quasi-official supervisory posts over the chemical industry with the status of Chief Business Manager of the Group. By January 1944, when Kehrl summoned Ungewitter and stripped him of his "previous competence and responsibility for directing production and shifting assignments," he already had lost his earlier roles in securing labor, coal, and electricity for the industry to August Kolb, in his capacity as leader of the chemicals section in Speer's ministry.[195] Dejected, Ungewitter now observed that there was "no room left for the activity of a Chief Business Manager in its previous form."[196]

As Ungewitter's resentment grew, Schlosser held most of the cards, notably the backing of the bullish Hans Kehrl, so the measured way in which Degussa's chairman proceeded is particularly revealing of his political shrewdness. When Ungewitter's frustration bubbled over in August 1944, and he wrote and widely distributed a long memorandum criticizing the proliferation of coordinating bodies and alleging a loss of organizational clarity and administrative ability to coordinate production under Schlosser's leadership, then asked to be relieved of his duties, Schlosser opted for conciliation over confrontation.[197] Though Kehrl was furious, seeing Ungewitter as a stalking horse for Schieber's plans to disband the Economic Group for Chemistry

---

[194] On Schieber and his offices, see Walter Naasner, *Neue Machtzentren in der deutschen Kriegswirtschaft 1942–1945* (Boppard am Rhein: Harald Boldt, 1994), pp. 300–01, 308–09.

[195] DUA, D 14/1, Ungewitter to Schlosser, no date, but marked "received 17 January 1944."

[196] For Ungewitter's depiction of developments and the quotation, see D 14/1, his lengthy letter to Schlosser, January 5, 1944.

[197] DUA, D 14/1, Ungewitter to Schlosser, August 10, 1944.

and replace it with a new Main Committee under his direction, Schlosser maneuvered – behind a smoke screen of verbal agreement on the need for greater consultation between Ungewitter and Speer's Ministry – to get the angry Chief Business Manager to go on "a several-month-long health leave" in order to repair the effects of overwork and stress.[198] Even after both Speer and the board of the Economic Group took sides clearly against Ungewitter's criticisms in early October, and Schlosser in the meantime had allowed himself the satisfaction of refuting them in writing, he was willing to keep Ungewitter on at the Group in return for a declaration of loyalty, which the latter man gave at mid-month.[199] Indeed, Schlosser went so far as to make clear to the relevant officials that any harder stance would result in his own resignation.[200] No illusions guided this unusually forbearing course. As Schlosser told one of his industrial colleagues on the Economic Group's board, Ungewitter's "attitude...in many demonstrable cases was not any longer appreciably distinguishable from sabotage."[201] But the man had to be mollified and sent on vacation, Schlosser argued to another peer, since he was not removable as Delegate for Chemistry, a position controlled by the Economics Ministry, and therefore could have remained troublesome.[202] Early in November, Ungewitter apologized to Kehrl in person for his conduct and promised Schlosser to take the proferred leave.[203] The patience and consideration of Degussa's chairman appeared to have paid off once more, and he was freed to devote himself without further bureaucratic distraction to the intractable problems created as his firm and nation were being overrun.

This sort of tactical foresight on both Busemann's and Schlosser's parts – along with the impetuousity of their opponents, the absence of Jewish managing board members whose places Nazis could usurp, and the luck of the bomb crater that swallowed Werner Lüps – explain how and why Degussa escaped direct domination by the NSDAP during the Third Reich. But, there was, as the contents of this and succeeding chapters suggest, another reason. Direct control became superfluous in Degussa's case – at least prior

---

[198] DUA, D 14/1, Schlosser's Notiz für Personalakte Dr. Ungewitter, August 21, 1944; Kolb to Schlosser and his three replies, September 7, 1944; and (regarding Kehrl's anger), Kehrl to Hayler of the Economics Ministry, September 11, 1944; Kehrl to Ungewitter, September 11, 1944; Auszug aus Brief Dr. Kolb an Schlosser, September 14, 1944; Kehrl's nine-page Stellungnahme zum Schreiben Dr. Ungewitter, September 26, 1944; Kehrl to Ungewitter, September 27, 1944; and Kolb to Schlosser, October 4, 1944.

[199] DUA, D 14/1, Kolb to Schlosser, October 7, 1944; Schlosser's Betr. Denkschrift von Herrn Dr. Ungewitter vom 10. August 1944, October 9, 1944; Ausserordentliche Sitzung des Präsidiums der Wirtschaftsgruppe Chemie, October 12, 1944; and Schlosser to Kolb, October 14, 1944.

[200] DUA, D 14/1, Schlosser to Kolb, October 18, 1944.

[201] DUA, D 14/1, Schlosser to Kluftinger, October 24, 1944.

[202] DUA, D 14/1, Schlosser to Dörr, October 24, 1944.

[203] DUA, D 14/1, Excerpt of Kolb to Schlosser, October 25, 1944; Ungewitter to Schlosser, November 3, 1944; and Schlosser to Dörr, November 9, 1944.

to the great ideological reorganization of the nation that the Party faithful expected to follow the "Final Victory." In a revealing passage of his letter defending his stewardship of the Economic Group for Chemistry from Unge-witter's charges, Schlosser unwittingly had illuminated why this was so. He recalled that "the establishment of self-responsibility in the economy was an order from above.... Personally I felt ill at ease with this directive and behaved only pursuant to command. I have in the meantime come to the conclusion, however, that the establishment... not only has proved itself in excellent fashion, but that without this institution the mastery of the present difficulties would not be conceivable."[204] Hermann Schlosser showed a re-current and remarkable capacity to adjust to instructions from on high, then to convince himself of their correctness. One of the secrets of his success, this leitmotiv of his leadership also characterized the conduct of his firm during the Third Reich – with advantageous results for the enterprise but terrible consequences for countless Germans, as well as for those "inferiors" the Nazi regime brutalized.

[204] DUA, D 14/1, Schlosser's Betr. Denkschrift von Herrn Dr. Ungewitter vom 10. August 1944, October 9, 1944, pp. 2–3.

3

Aryanization

Between 1933 and 1944, Degussa expended approximately 18 million Reichsmarks, a sum equal to about half of the firm's total capitalization at the outset of the Third Reich, on the acquisition of formerly Jewish-owned property – that is, on what the Nazi regime dubbed "Aryanization." Fully or jointly owned subsidiaries spent at least another 645,000 RM to the same end.[1] Among the objects obtained were no fewer than ten firms, seven of them in Germany and three in the so-called Protectorate, one of which was bought by a corporation Degussa had Aryanized earlier. In addition, the concern augmented its holdings in three other enterprises by buying up four substantial stock packets from emigrating families; took over ten pieces of real estate in Frankfurt, Cologne, Hamburg, Berlin, Vienna, and Prague (two of these also were serial Aryanizations, i.e., takeovers by earlier targets of the same procedure); and capped the process of expansion at Jews' expense with the purchase of a confiscated patent in August 1944.[2]

Although it is extremely difficult to specify how much these purchases improved Degussa's balance sheets and profitability both during the Nazi

---

[1] An earlier, shorter version of this chapter appeared as "Die Arisierungen der Degussa AG: Geschichte und Bilanz," in Irmtrud Wojak and Peter Hayes (eds.), *"Arisierung" im Nationalsozialismus: Volksgemeinschaft, Raub und Gedächtnis*, Jahrbuch 2000 des Fritz-Bauer-Instituts (Frankfurt: Campus Verlag, 2000), pp. 85–123. Readers should note that I have found two additional Aryanizations on Degussa's part since that article was written, and hence the figures presented in this book for the total number of cases and the sums involved are different from those in that essay.

[2] The firms, stock packets, and three of the real estate parcels are discussed in turn below. Most of the other properties are listed in DUA, D 2/6, Mayer-Wegelin to Scherf, August 24, 1949, and in UV 1/48, Steuer-Abtg. to Zentral-Abteilung, January 20, 1948. They included Boyenstrasse 8–10 and Vogelweidstr. 7 in Frankfurt; Rothenbaumchaussee 40 in Hamburg; Siegburgerstr. 110 in Cologne; and the Speyer & Grund parcel in Berlin-Weissensee. On the takeover of the former Adler clothing factory in Frankfurt's Boyenstrasse, see DL 3. Baerwind/ 20, Aktenverm. btr. Schaffung eines Lagerhauses, June 8, 1937; and UV 1/48, Haus – und Grundstuecksverwaltung to Lenz, January 15, 1948. On the acquisition of the house formerly owned by Albert and Sally Stern in July 1940 from the Reichsversicherungsanstalt, which had bought it at auction, see HHW, Bestand 519/V Nr. 3107/1, Rückerstattungsklage vor dem Amtsgericht Frankfurt, 29 June 1951, and Anlage zum Vergleichsprotokoll, of the same date. For a complete list of the property acquired and the compensations payments made after the war to the previous owners or their heirs, see Appendix F, below.

period and later, there can be no doubt that Aryanization contributed appreciably to the corporation's short- and long-term success.[3] All but two of the enterprises taken over returned substantial profits during the 1930s and 1940s; most of them remained in Degussa's possession through the 1950s, and three of them, along with at least one of the stock packets, still did at the end of the twentieth century. Perhaps the best way of expressing the importance of Aryanization to Degussa, both then and now, is to take note of a symbolic fact: the buildings that served until very recently as the firm's headquarters complex in Frankfurt stand, in part, on land acquired from two Jewish families in 1934–35.[4]

Tracing the story of these acquisitions (see Appendix F for a list and a tabulation of the sums involved) strikingly illustrates, however, the double-edged nature of the ugly process of exploitation in which Degussa became a participant. On the one hand, the surviving records make clear that there was almost no such thing in Germany after 1933 as a "voluntary" Aryanization. Of the twenty-five transactions to which Degussa or a wholly owned subsidiary was a party, it is true that fewer than half (eleven) of them were compulsory in the sense that they occurred after April 1938 pursuant to the confiscatory procedures laid down by Nazi decrees. Nonetheless, all of

---

[3] Detailed findings concerning the involvement of other large German firms in Aryanization, which would reveal the degree to which Degussa's conduct and gains were typical or exceptional, are scarce. That the major German banks engaged extensively in takeovers of Jewish property is, however, well documented. See Christopher Kopper, *Zwischen Marktwirtschaft und Dirigismus: Bankenpolitik im "Dritten Reich" 1933–1939* (Bonn: Bouvier Verlag, 1995), Harold James, "The Deutsche Bank and the Dictatorship 1933–1945," in Lothar Gall, Gerald Feldman, Harold James, Carl-Ludwig Holtfrerich, and Hans E. Büschgen, *The Deutsche Bank 1870–1995* (London: Weidenfeld & Nicolson, 1995), pp. 301–08; Harold James, *The Deutsche Bank and the Nazi Economic War Against the Jews* (New York: Cambridge University Press, 2001); Peter Hayes, "The Deutsche Bank and the Holocaust," in Peter Hayes (ed.), *Lessons and Legacies III: Memory, Memorialization, and Denial* (Evanston, IL: Northwestern University Press, 1999), pp. 71–89, 265–70; and Bernhard Lorentz, "Die Commerzbank und die 'Arisierung' im Altreich," *Vierteljahrshefte für Zeitgeschichte*, 50 (2002), pp. 237–68. With regard to manufacturing firms, see L. M. Stallbaumer, "Big Business and the Persecution of the Jews: The Flick Concern and the 'Aryanization' of Jewish Property before the War," *Holocaust and Genocide Studies* 13 (1999), pp. 1–27; Peter Hayes, "Big Business and 'Aryanization' in Germany, 1933–1939," *Jahrbuch für Antisemitismusforschung* 3 (1994), pp. 254–81; Peter Hayes, "State Policy and Corporate Involvement in the Holocaust," in Michael Berenbaum and Abraham J. Peck (eds.), *The Holocaust and History* (Bloomington: Indiana University Press, 1998), pp. 197–218; Joachim Scholtyseck, *Robert Bosch und der liberale Widerstand gegen Hitler 1933–1945* (Munich: C. H. Beck, 1999), pp. 269–74; and Wilfried Feldenkirchen, *Siemens 1918–1945* (Munich: Piper Verlag, 1995), though the obfuscating organization of this book makes tracking down the Siemens concern's involvement in Aryanization almost impossible for a reader.

[4] These real estate transactions are treated in detail below. The properties still in Degussa's possession as of 1999 were Homburg, Wyhlen, and Marquart. Its 50 percent share of Kulzer was not sold until 1987; see Mechthild Wolf, *Im Zeichen von Sonne und Mond* (Frankfurt am Main: Degussa AG, 1993), p. 315.

the sales involved an element of duress – the differences among them concern either the intensity or the source of the pressure exerted on the Jewish owners, not its existence. In one instance, that pressure was homemade, a consequence of the owner's own managerial failings, and in two other cases, it was circumstantial and slight. But otherwise it mounted to the point of being in some cases terrifyingly immediate and strong. Although Degussa's managers usually played little part in creating that pressure, they were its beneficiaries *nolens volens*, and they became increasingly prepared to use official agencies, even the Gestapo on one occasion, to get the corporation's way.

On the other hand, neither Degussa's quickness to capitalize on the vulnerability of German Jewish businessmen prior to 1938, nor its willingness to employ both theft and extortion thereafter reflected political or racist zeal on the part of the firm's upper echelons. In the earlier phase, Degussa's prominence as an Aryanizer resulted from the confluence of an ongoing corporate strategy, namely Busemann's diversification drive, with the opportunities that Nazi persecution created. The resulting convenience, as well as an absence of civic courage and the presence of Roessler's patrician sort of irresolution on the "Jewish question," assured that the prevailing spirit among Degussa's leaders regarding Aryanization became that to which Ernst Busemann – in, for him, quite characteristic fashion – gave words in July 1937: "It is pointless to swim against the stream."[5] But the enterprise tried neither to roil the waters further nor to breach the dikes Jewish businessmen set up around their companies – at least for a time. Prior to January 1938, while the antisemitic current in the corporate sphere was being driven by extralegal Party intimidation and harassment, Degussa played a generally reactive and decent role, usually making acquisitions after being approached by the threatened sellers, who often were long-standing business partners, and paying commercially fair prices that were arrived at by normal business processes of evaluation. In the later phase, however, after a flood of official decrees in early 1938 turned the stream of dispossession into a torrent that threatened to sweep away some of Degussa's own interests as well, the firm stopped throwing lifelines. Indeed, its remaining annexations proceeded in heartlessly self-interested fashion. The best one can say concerning Degussa's participation in Aryanization after 1938 is that it could have been more extensive.

That, at least prior to the radicalization of official Aryanization policy at the turn of 1937/38, Degussa's managers behaved with a measure of sensitivity and consideration toward the Jews whose property was at stake was due, in significant part, to Ernst Busemann. Trained at the outset of his career at the Bankhaus Seligmann and as Wilhelm Merton's secretary, Busemann was assuredly no antisemite in the pseudoscientific, which is to say all-encompassing, Nazi sense. Whether he shared the prejudice widespread

[5] DUA, IW 22.5/4–5, Busemann to Herzog, July 30, 1937.

among his peers that Jews were disproportionately active on the Left and in cultural quarters often critical of private enterprise, notably the journalistic and artistic worlds, is undocumented. But, whatever his general attitudes toward Jews as a category, his stance toward the Jewish individuals with whom he came into professional contact was – so long as he thought he had any choice in the matter – almost invariably sympathetic, humane, and marked by respect for their business accomplishments. This pattern emerges quite clearly from the negotiations and the terms arrived at between Degussa and the Jewish owners of enterprises targeted by the new regime during the initial wave of Aryanization cases in 1933–34.

The first such case concerned the Chemisch-Pharmazeutische Werke AG, Bad Homburg, a manufacturer of medicinal preparations that had been founded in 1920 then moved its headquarters to Frankfurt in 1927.[6] Created, led, and financially controlled in 1933 by Arthur Abelmann, the enterprise came under attack almost immediately after the so-called seizure of power. In the final two weeks of March, after the Doctors League of Greater Berlin and the Association of Doctors and Public Health Insurers declared a boycott of Homburg's supposedly "Jewish" products, the company's sales dropped by 30 to 40 percent. Abelmann immediately bowed to the pressure by resigning from the managing board and as business manager of his firm, turning the latter job over to an Aryan subordinate named Karl Beister, who promptly joined the NSDAP. Moreover, in an obvious attempt to appeal to the Party's sense of the national interest, the shrunken board now declared that Abelmann would confine his activities henceforth to promoting the firm's exports, primarily from an office in Basel.[7] These concessions brought the boycott to an end, but Abelmann probably knew that it was only a matter of time until the NSDAP discovered that his family owned the Swiss firm that had held most of Homburg's stock since 1920.[8] He therefore decided to try to interest an Aryan investor in taking 51 percent of the shares and turned in early May to Degussa because it had long been one of his principal suppliers.[9]

---

[6] See BUA, Sig. 6/14, Betr.: Chemisch-Pharmazeutische A. G. Bad Homburg, June 30, 1933.

[7] See DUA, IW 46.5/3, Chemiewerk Homburg AG, Aufsichtsrat-Protokoll, Sitzung von 6. April 1933. On Beister, compare the material regarding his denazification in DUA, SCH 1/03, with HHW, Abt. 483, Akte 10982, Gaupersonalamtsleiter to Avieny, June 12, 1942.

[8] On the end of the boycott, see BAL, R 8119 F, Deutsche Bank, Fich 2372/Akte 14732, Bl. 33, an undated document filed amid others from April 1933, which is headed "Attention! Concerning the boycott of pharmaceutical preparations under Jewish control" and has the following text: "Now that the Chem.-Pharmazeutische AG Bad Homburg has proved convincingly that its managing board and leadership are in German-conscious hands, particularly [that] the well-known Jewish director, Pharmacist Arthur Abelmann, has resigned, we request that the preparations [a listing follows] be stricken from the boycott list." Signed by "The Provisional Managing Board of the Doctors League of Greater Berlin, Dr. Claus, Dr. Quandt, Dr. Villain."

[9] See DUA, IW 46.4/1, Weickel's Betr.: Chemisch-Pharmazeutische AG Bad Homburg (Chemiewerk), May 9, 1933.

Since Abelmann's offer dovetailed nicely with Busemann's determination to turn cash into real values, he quickly paid a visit to the Homburg plant. Its facilities and finances impressed him, but he also came away convinced, as Hermann Schlosser put it a few weeks later, that Abelmann "is a main asset of the business," whose "complete freedom of action and initiative" had to be preserved under any new ownership arrangements. Furthermore, Degussa dared not enter the pharmaceuticals sphere without the approval or joint participation of IG Farben's Bayer division, all the more so since Degussa's unusually lucrative contract to supply sodium to the giant concern was coming up for renewal.[10] At the end of June, therefore, Busemann and Schlosser had separate meetings with Farben officials, foremost among them Wilhelm Rudolf Mann, Jr., the sales director of Bayer and the only member of IG's managing board to have joined the NSDAP prior to Hitler's accession.[11] Mann instantly began throwing both his commercial and political weight around. He informed the Degussa executives that his firm, of course, would have to be cut in on the purchase of at least half the stock Abelmann sold, that this should come to a secure majority (i.e., around 60 percent) of Homburg's shares, and that IG should be able to name the principal business manager. Moreover, Mann pointedly noted that he had just become chairman of the Pharmaceuticals Association, which was carrying out "coordination according to very strict standards," hence he would have to make inquiries about Abelmann. Mann also made Schlosser promise to investigate whether Homburg "falls under the corruption clauses as a result of its earlier machinations while introducing preparations to the health insurance system," thus suggesting a way to force the selling price down.[12]

These maneuvers on Mann's part came to nothing over the ensuing months. Equally unsuccessful were his obvious attempts more or less to absorb Homburg into IG Farben, regardless of the distribution of shares, and to get Degussa to reduce the price it considered fair, which included an allowance for the owners' lost earnings over the next five years and came to between seven and eight times the face value of the stock.[13] But in two respects,

[10] DUA, DL 3.Busemann/4, Busemann's Notiz Betr. Homburg, May 27, 1933. On the importance of the Natrium-Vertrag to Degussa's dealings with Farben at this time, see the retrospective accounts in DL 11.5/41, Schlosser's Notiz Betr. Chlor/Natrium, August 19, 1941, and DL 3.H. Schlosser/1, Doc. 824, Schlosser's Notiz Betr. Pharmazeutika, September 26, 1941. For the quoted remarks, IW 46.4/1, Betr. Chemisch-Pharmazeutische Werke Homburg, June 30, 1933, p. 3.

[11] See Peter Hayes, *Industry and Ideology: IG Farben in the Nazi Era* (New York: Cambridge University Press, 1987), pp. 62 and 101.

[12] See DUA, DL 3.Busemann/4, Besprechung mit Herrn Direktor Mann von der I. G. am 22.6.33 in Düsseldorf; IW 46.4/1, Schlosser's Notiz. Chemisch-Pharmazeutische Werke Homburg GmbH, June 30, 1933; and BUA, Sig. 6/14, Notiz betr. Besprechung zwischen Schlosser von der Scheideanstalt und Mann und Dr. Peiser, June 30, 1933.

[13] On Degussa's efforts to preserve Homburg's independence, see DUA, DL 3.Busemann/4, Busemann's Notiz Betr. Besprechung mit Herrn Generalkonsul Mann, June 23, 1933; his Notiz Betr. Besprechung mit Herrn Professor Bosch in Heidelberg, July 13, 1933; his Notiz

Mann got his way. In early August, arguing that the Pharmaceuticals Association was about to require all state health insurers, which accounted for some 60 to 70 percent of Homburg's sales, to purchase only from purely German firms, Mann persuaded Degussa that it and IG would have to take over 76 percent of Abelmann's company, and that Abelmann could not be kept on in any capacity at the factory, lest Degussa and IG be accused of camouflaging Jewish influence.[14]

IG Farben's nervousness about Abelmann – whether feigned or genuine – put an end to that man's hopes of continuing his life's work and to Degussa's theretofore repeatedly expressed interest in retaining his expertise. "Visibly upset" by the terms Mann and Schlosser dictated to him on August 1, Abelmann apparently decided within days to sell out completely and emigrate to Switzerland. By the end of the following year, he was dead. At least, however, he could still get out of Germany in 1933 and take the fruits of his acumen with him to pass on to his relatives. For 95 percent of the shares with a face value of 237,240 RM, Degussa and IG paid him and his family's Swiss firm the full audited value of Bad Homburg, including an allowance for forgone earnings. The price came to 1,860,703 RM; of this, the equivalent of 1.2 million marks was paid over in Swiss francs at the full international rate of exchange, and the remainder came in the form of stock in Degussa and Farben. Abelmann was not only exempted from the National Flight Tax, thanks to Degussa's lobbying, but also hired as Homburg's sales agent for western and southern Europe, Egypt, and Palestine, under salary and pension terms that called for payments to him and his heirs of another 427,000 Swiss francs through 1948.[15] Generous as these terms were, they proved thoroughly justified to Degussa, which now held 43 percent of the shares in Bad Homburg. Not only did the deal enable Degussa to shelter capital as Busemann wished, but it also probably produced sufficient dividends and profits by 1943 to cover Degussa's expenditures on the purchase, though not the lost interest on their outlay, which was recouped only after the war.[16]

The second of Degussa's major Aryanizations began rather similarly to the Homburg case, but a bit later, and its evolution showed that the amounts Jewish owners could save from the wreckage of their fortunes were already

---

Betr. Abelmann. Besprechung mit Herrn Prof. Bosch in Heidelberg, October 26, 1933; his Notiz Betr. Abelmann, October 30, 1933. On this matter, as well as the price, see DUA, IW 46.4/1, Bernau's Notizen, Betr.: Homburg, July 7 and 14, 1933.

[14] DUA, IW 46.4/1, Schlosser's Notiz Betr. Homburg, July 26, 1933; and Bernau's Notiz Betr. Homburg, August 1, 1933.

[15] BUA, Sig. 6/14, Niederschrift über die Besprechung vom 10. August 1933 in Leverkusen, and Vertrag, October 27, 1933; DUA, IW 46.4/1, Niederschrift über die am 3. August in Koblenz... stattgehabte Besprechung, among Abelmann, Mann and Brüggemann of IG, and Schlosser, Bernau, and Weickel of Degussa.

[16] Calculated from the statistical data in BUA, Sig. 6/14. Actual management of the firm fell increasingly into the hands of IG Farben during the war years; see DL 2/1, Niederschrift über die Vorstandssitzung am 2. März 1942, pp. 236–37.

declining. At issue was the Degea AG (earlier and later again known as the Auergesellschaft) of Berlin, a manufacturer of heating and lighting equipment, assorted – especially radioactive – chemicals, and gas masks. In early 1933, the firm was suffering from the collapse of lightbulb sales during the Depression and resting its hopes on government, especially military, contracts.[17] Once more, it was the Nazi boycott campaign, now supplemented by agitation on the part of Nazis in the company's workforce, that impelled the "racially" Jewish owner, a convert to Protestantism named Alfred Koppel, to try to gain Aryan status for his enterprise.[18] In August, he transformed the Deutsche Gasglühlicht GmbH, which had been owned by his family's bank, into the Degea AG by supposedly selling it to a consortium led by the Commerzbank and by simultaneously reducing the capitalization of the firm from 10 million to 7 million marks.[19] Koppel's move was extraordinarily maladroit, explicable only by the fact that he had inherited the firm just a few months earlier and had little experience with either business or politics. The very reason for the choice of the Commerzbank as the front for his continuing ownership of the shares, namely that the bank had excellent connections to the Nazi Party via its two board chairmen, assured that the gambit would be exposed even before it was announced.[20] Thus, Koppel found himself, like Abelmann, searching for an Aryan buyer of enough of his stock to mollify the Nazis. That quest led him, on the advice of his lawyer, to the Mendelssohn Bank in Berlin, which turned, for reasons that remain unclear, to the leaders of the Henkel company. In July 1933, they apparently suggested the takeover to Degussa, largely as compensation for the fact that they wished to reserve for themselves another Jewish-owned firm, Böhme Fettchemie, in which Degussa was interested.[21]

The businesses of Degussa and the Auergesellschaft had few points of contact: Degussa's HIAG division supplied charcoal for Auer's gas masks; Auer provided Degussa with rare, often radioactive, metals, ores, and derivatives

---

[17] See DUA, DL 3.Busemann/4, Busemann's Das Glühkörper-Geschäft der Auer-Gesellschaft, November 9, 1933. In addition to its plants in Germany, the Auergesellschaft owned a subsidiary in Prague and one-third of a Polish factory in Neutomischel. Evasive but somewhat informative on the history of the firm is Friedrich Klauer (ed.), *Geschichte der Auergesellschaft von der Gründung im Jahre 1892 bis zum Jahre 1958* (Berlin: Auergesellschaft, 1962).

[18] DUA, IW 24.4/4, Busemann, Besprechung wegen Auer am 4. Sept. 1933.

[19] DUA, IW 24.4/4, Zeitungsausschnitte, August 1933. The reorganization entailed, among other things, detaching Deutsche Glasglühlicht's shares in Osram GmbH from the new firm; see IW 24.18/1, Bericht betr. Entwicklung der Auerges., April 29, 1955.

[20] DUA, IW 24.4/1, Busemann's report "Betr. Auer-Gesellschaft," September 18, 1933, relating his conversation with Koppel two days earlier.

[21] DUA, IW 24.4/4, Busemann to Baerwind, July 31, 1933, enclosing Busemann to Henkel of the same date; Henkel to Busemann, August 1, 1933. On Henkel's takeover of Böhme in 1935–36, see Henkel & Cie GmbH (ed.), *1876–1976. 100 Jahre Henkel* (Düsseldorf: Henkel & Cie, n.d. [1976]), p. 106.

of them; and the two firms had made a handful of agreements demarcating their respective interests in certain products.[22] Furthermore, Auer's plants in and around Berlin were far from the Frankfurt firm's center of gravity in western Germany. For these reasons, Fritz Roessler opposed the purchase, and even Busemann had initial reservations, commenting that "the main thing is that, if we do this at all, we do it cheaply."[23] After he visited Auer's Oranienburg plant in mid-September, however, his usual investment calculations won out in his mind – Auer offered a truly enormous opportunity to shelter capital – buttressed by the prospect of lucrative government orders, since Busemann now saw firsthand "how extraordinarily favorable the relationship of the [plant manager] to the military authorities is."[24]

As a result, Busemann and Koppel began negotiations, rapidly reaching agreement that Degussa would buy 51 percent of the shares, would promise to purchase the remainder at the same price in real terms if Koppel chose to sell during the two years following the contract, and would allow Koppel to remain active in the enterprise. The sticking points concerned control of the corporation and the price. Koppel wanted a veto right over policy, especially an assurance that he could block the firm from ever producing poison gas. He also sought a price of 130 to 150 percent of par, whereas Busemann hoped to pay no more than 100 to 110 percent.[25] In October, Busemann gave enough ground on all these matters to secure an agreement. In particular, he guaranteed Koppel's position with the firm until 1953, unless he sold his remaining shares, and agreed to pay 4.6 million marks for the nominal 3.6 million being sold, which is to say 130 percent.[26] Two weeks before the deal was concluded, Busemann wrote in a memo for his files that he had already decided to agree to that price, if necessary, "so that cooperation with Mr. Koppel, whom I also this time have come to know as an uncommonly appealing and distinguished person, will not begin in unfriendly fashion."[27]

Though cooperation between Degussa and Koppel did, in fact, get off to a good start in November 1933, Busemann's first meeting with army

[22] On these agreements, see DUA, IW 24.10/1, Vertrag, January 8, 1931, concerning Zirkonoxyd; and PCA 1/214, Degea to Degussa, June 13, 1932, and Baerwind to Quasebart, June 15, 1932.
[23] DUA, BU Dr. Fritz Roessler, "Zur Geschichte der Scheideanstalt" [1937], Abschrift, pp. 121–25; IW 24.4./4, Busemann to Baerwind, August 2, 1933.
[24] DUA, IW 24.4/4, Busemann's report Betr. Auer-Gesellschaft, September 18, 1933. The plant leader was Prof. Quasebart.
[25] *Ibid.* Koppel's stipulation regarding poison gas was a reversal of his predecessors' policy. On Auer's production of preliminary products for mustard gas since 1928, see Bernhard Lorentz, *Industrieelite und Wirtschaftspolitik 1928–1950: Heinrich Dräger und das Drägerwerk* (Paderborn: Ferdinand Schöningh, 2001), p. 154.
[26] DUA, IW 24.4/4, Busemann to Koppel, October 7, 1933; IW 24.4/7, Koppel to Degussa, October 17, 1933; Koppel to Busemann, October 20, 1933; two letters from Koppel to Degussa, October 20, 1933.
[27] DUA, IW 24.4/4, Busemann's Betr. Auer-Gesellschaft, October 5, 1933.

representatives caused him to note that "it is astonishing how strong the desire is, even from the Defense Ministry, to ascertain the Aryan quality of Degea and its principal stockholder."[28] The documentary record does not disclose what influence this interest had – especially in conjunction with Auer's eagerness to cash in on the military's prospective order for 1 million to 1.3 million gas masks – on Alfred Koppel's rapidly growing sense that his position was becoming untenable.[29] But in February 1934, he raised the issue of selling his remaining shares to Degussa, if it was willing to pay a higher price in view of Degea's improving prospects.[30] By May, he had resolved to leave Germany and began bargaining, only to discover that Busemann was prepared to play poker. When Koppel tried to get Degussa to increase its offer per share by implying that he might sell his 49 percent to IG Farben, Busemann calmly expressed disinterest and wished him luck.[31] The standoff did not last long. In June, Koppel signaled his willingness to settle for the agreed-upon price, and in July, Degussa bought his remaining 3.4 million marks of stock for 4,624,000 marks, giving him a rate, after deducting his share of the stock transaction tax, of about 136 percent.[32] In view of the military's concern for "Aryan quality," it is surprising that Koppel's departure did not set off a general purge of Auer's staff. To be sure, Busemann soon agreed to terminate the contract of Dr. Hörnes, the plant manager at the Oranienburg installation, because he had a Jewish wife, "and that is held against him and cannot be defended to the Defense Ministry in the long run."[33] But at least four Jewish directors remained until forced out by Nazi decrees in early 1938, as did Heinrich Ziegler as a member of Auer's managing board, though his ancestry was in dispute, and his wife and both his stepsons were Jews.[34]

---

[28] DUA, DL 3.Busemann/4, Busemann's two memos Betr. Degea, November 29, 1933.

[29] On the military's order, see DUA, DL 3.Busemann/4, Notiz Bespr. mit der Herren der Auer-Ges. u. Herrn Koppel, January 31, 1934.

[30] DUA, IW 24.4/1, Busemann's Notiz, February 1, 1934.

[31] DUA, DL 3.Busemann/4 (also IW 24.4/7), Notiz. Bespr. mit Prof. Quasebarth, May 4, 1934; IW 24.4/7, Busemann to Koppel, June 9, 1934. DL 3.Busemann/4 (also IW 24.4/7), Notiz betr. Auer-Ges., May 8, 1934, indicates that Auer had recently been denounced once more to the Gestapo as a "Jewish" firm, which may have been the last straw for Koppel. Interestingly, Busemann chose to play for time on this occasion. He pacified Claus Ungewitter, a zealous supporter of the new regime, by passing on the rumor that banks had bought Koppel's 49 percent for cash, which Busemann, of course, knew was false.

[32] DUA, IW 24.4/1, Koppel to Busemann, June 13, 1934; Koppel to Busemann, July 27, 1934.

[33] DUA, IW 24.5/2, Busemann's Notiz. Personalverhältnisse/Auer-Ges., November 14, 1934. Hörnes got a one-time severance payment of 30,000 RM, but appears to have been kept on in a lesser research capacity at Oranienburg, where he was "hidden" on the staff of Nikolaus Riehl; see Nikolaus Riehl and Frederick Seitz, *Stalin's Captive: Nikolaus Riehl and the Soviet Race for the Bomb* ([Washington, DC]: American Chemical Society and the Chemical Heritage Foundation, 1996), p. 90.

[34] DUA, IW 24.4/6, Walter Loerbroks to Mayer-Wegelin, August 27, 1951; DL 3/17 and IW 24.5/2, announcement in the *Reichsanzeiger*, February 15, 1938, and Federlin's Notiz für Herrn Dr. Busemann, April 7, 1938.

All in all, Alfred Koppel got almost 9.3 million marks, the full market rate, for 7 million marks in stock, but the deal was not quite as favorable as it sounds – for either party.[35] No official record has yet surfaced of how much money he actually could take with him to England when he emigrated later that year before going on to the United States. It seems likely that he emerged with only 60 to 75 percent of the proceeds on the sale.[36] Moreover, in one nonmaterial respect, Koppel lost badly. Within only a few months of his departure from Germany, Degea became one of the cofounders of the Orgacid AG for the manufacture of poison gases.[37] For its part, Degussa, according to Fritz Roessler's estimate, got assets worth some 14 million marks for its money.[38] One million of this was in precious foreign exchange, which Busemann quickly transferred to Degussa's accounts.[39] However, though Auer's business grew rapidly during the following years – so much so, in fact, that the firm was by some measures soon a bigger enterprise than Degussa itself – most of the rising revenues went into the reinvestment required to meet escalating military demand. Indeed, the subsidiary's repeated resort to borrowing was a constant source of concern in Frankfurt and one of the reasons why, by the end of the business year 1942/43, Degussa had recovered in dividends only about half (i.e., almost 4.8 million Reichsmarks) of the initial purchase price.[40]

With the conclusion of the Auer takeover eighteen months after Hitler's accession, Degussa already had spent some 58 percent of its total outlays on Aryanization during the Third Reich. There is little sign in the surviving records of an active search at this time for additional Jewish property to snap up, except in conjunction with the firm's efforts to obtain real estate surrounding its cramped offices in Frankfurt. Here Degussa made two acquisitions in 1934–35. The first, of the Neptunhaus at the corner of the Weissfrauen- and Neue Mainzerstrasse, provided the occasion for a nasty slur by Degussa's Adalbert Fischer, who derided the previous owners as "these racial Jews" when he could not break their insistence on a price of

[35] That this was the stock market rate at the time is confirmed by DUA, RFI 4.8/5, Körperschaftsteuer Bericht 1934, which records the rejection of an attempt by Degussa to report a lower value for the firm's shares.

[36] In DUA, IW 24.4/6, Walter Loerbroks to Mayer-Wegelin, August 27, 1951, the former Syndicus at Auer recollects that Koppel's fortune upon emigration came to 64 million marks, hence that his tax bill was 16 million, part of which he paid from the proceeds of the Degea sale.

[37] DUA, IW 24.5./2, Quasebart to Busemann, November 23, 1934; Busemann's Aktennotiz, November 29, 1934; Quasebart to Busemann, April 25, 1935.

[38] DUA, BU Dr. Fritz Roessler, "Zur Geschichte" [1937] Abschrift, p. 125.

[39] DUA, DL 3.Busemann/4, Notiz. Besuch bei der Auer-Ges., 10 August 1934; Notiz Betr. Auerges., September 13, 1934. The firm's export proceeds, however, began vanishing rapidly; see Notiz Besuch bei der Auer-Ges., November 1, 1934.

[40] DUA, IW 24.4/1, Degussa to G. Lancelle, May 15, 1952. Auer's annual profits peaked at 700,000 RM in 1938/39, at which time its debt load exceeded 8 million marks; IW 24.9/1, Gewinn- und Verlustrechnung, September 30, 1939.

600,000 RM, including the assumption by Degussa of an outstanding mortgage from a Swiss bank.[41] In truth, Max and Ludwig Lorch probably did not want to sell at all; they came to the bargaining table only as a result of the urgings of their broker and the steadily worsening prospects in Germany for their children, nearly all of whom already had been sent abroad. Sensing that the men's mood might change at any moment, Degussa also agreed to cover all taxes and fees as part of the deal, which eventually cost it some 712,000 RM and netted the Lorchs more than three times what they had paid for the property a decade earlier.[42] Ludwig Lorch may have managed to take some of the proceeds with him when he later followed his children abroad, but the Nazi state seized whatever remained to Max and his wife Frumet after they were deported from Frankfurt to the East in October 1941, never to be heard from again.[43] Degussa turned the building into the main offices of its HIAG division – until they were almost completely bombed out in March 1944.[44]

The second real estate case, at another corner of the Neue Mainzerstrasse, unfolded under quite different circumstances and yielded the Jewish titleholders far less money, but they ultimately survived both Nazi Germany and their place of refuge, Vichy France. Adolf and Irma Wolf were already virtually bankrupt before the Nazi takeover, in part as a result of embezzlement by a former partner. Since they therefore had ceased to pay taxes, upkeep, and mortgage interest on their double parcel of land in 1931, Degussa was able to work hand in glove with the creditors to bring the adjoining plots to public auction, then to buy them up in return for settling the substantial debts the Wolfs had run up on the properties. Only at the last minute, as Degussa was about to obtain the larger part of the site in late 1935 for less than half what the now-fugitive Adolf Wolf had paid prior to World War I, did the enterprise extend 1,800 Reichsmarks to the destitute members of his family still in Frankfurt so that they would stop trying to obstruct the sale in court.[45] The firm later constructed a new laboratory building on the spot.

Until the second wave of Degussa's industrial Aryanizations gathered in 1936, the firm's only other involvement in the process of dispossession

---

[41] DUA, IW 1.2/3, Besprechung mit den Herrn Gebrüder Lorch in Gegenwart von Herrn Baer, am 17. Februar 1934, dated February 19, 1934.

[42] See DUA, IW 1.2/3, Memo by Josef Baer, January 25, 1934, Betr.: Wiessfrauenstr. 11, Fischer's Besprechung mit den Herrn Gebrüder Lorch in Gegenwart von Herrn Baer, February 19, 1934, and Baer to Degussa, February 21, 1934; UV 4/44, eidesstaatliche Erklärung von Ruth Fleischer, the daughter of Max Lorch, March 2, 1949, and Degussa to Nelken, May 21, 1949.

[43] DUA, UV 4/44, Nelken to Zentral-Anmeldeamt, Bad Nauheim December 22, 1948.

[44] DUA, UV 4/44, Degussa to Zentralmeldeamt Bad Nauheim, April 28, 1948.

[45] IW 1.2/3, exchange of letters between Rosenburg and Barz, lawyers for the two parties, October 3–12, 1933; and UV 4/44, especially Urkunden-Verwaltung to Mayer-Wegelin, July 18, 1949, unsigned memo to H. Roessler, Bernau, and Munding, March 23, 1935, and Frankfurter Hypothekenbank to Degussa, December 23, 1949.

occurred almost as a matter of professional and personal courtesy, out of place as that term sounds. When Alfred Merton, a member of the founding family of the Metallgesellschaft and of Degussa's supervisory board, decided to emigrate in 1934, Degussa purchased 435,000 RM of his shares at the market rate of 85 percent, and Merton applied most of the proceeds to paying the Flight Tax of 325,000 RM that had been imposed on him.[46] Degussa, as noted in Chapter 2, promptly elected his brother, Richard, to fill the vacant seat on its supervisory board.

Like the Merton case, the three Aryanizations that took place in 1936 demonstrated that Degussa was ready to grasp opportunities presented by Nazi persecution, but not to extract every last advantage from the situation. The first of these new takeovers and the third of Degussa's industrial Aryanizations was not, strictly speaking, a product of the Nazi assault on the Jews at all. In question was the Carbidfabrik Wyhlen, which had been owned by Beer Sondheimer, a holding company that had gone bankrupt in 1929 and still owed its creditors some 8 million marks in October 1932, when they began trying to sell the property to Degussa.[47] The contribution that official antisemitism made to the transaction was in causing the liquidators, which were mostly banks outside of Germany, to fear that the property would lose value, hence in increasing their eagerness to sell.[48] Their problem was that the plant was burdened with a demanding long-term contract for its electricity supply, which outweighed in the eyes of buyers Wyhlen's principal assets, a guaranteed share of 5 percent in the sales of the German carbide syndicate and solid rates of profit per ton of output, especially when the factory was able to operate at capacity.[49] In early 1934, however, the revival of the German economy began to make Wyhlen more, not less, saleable, and both IG Farben and Degussa seriously considered the acquisition, in Degussa's case because it saw an opportunity to save on purchasing and transport costs of an intermediate product for its own chemicals output.[50] Still, it was not until September 1935, when the Lonza company made a bid on the property, that Degussa finally took action. It made an initial offer of 1.2 million marks for the factory and its inventory, which it raised to 1.3 million a few weeks later, by which time the carbide syndicate was itself trying to obtain the installation

---

[46] DUA, RFI 4.3/1, especially Baer to Merton, May 26, 1934, and Baer to Busemann, May 29, 1934, which lay out the terms of the transaction. It was carried out in mid-September 1934.

[47] DUA, DL 3.Busemann/4, Aktennotiz Betr. Karbidfabrik Wylen [sic], October 21, 1932.

[48] DUA, IW 38.4/1, Carbidfabrik Wyhlen, report by Lampe, November 20, 1945.

[49] DUA, DL 3.Baerwind/17, Bespr. über die Karbidfabr. Wyhlen, December 13, 1933; Besuch in der Karbidfabr. Wyhlen, January 2, 1934; Karbidfabr. Wyhlen GmbH und deutches Karbidsyndikat, January 2, 1934; Stromverträge der Karbidfabrik Wyhlen GmbH, January 2, 1934.

[50] DUA, DL 3.Baerwind/17, Allgemeines betr. das Projekt Karbidfabr. Wyhlen, January 2, 1934, and Karbidverbrauch im Werk der Farben-I. G. Rheinfelden, January 3, 1934; and DL 3.Busemann/4, Aktennotiz Betr. Wyhlen, April 27, 1934.

in order to shut it down.[51] There followed a series of delays occasioned by Reichsbank regulations and by a brief controversy with IG Farben that almost made Busemann abandon the initiative, but in March 1936, Degussa sealed the deal.[52] For 1.55 million Reichsmarks – 1.3 million to the creditors and 255,000 to the Swiss estate of the deceased owner – Degussa added to its holdings a firm that yielded a net profit from 1936 to 1948 of 2.4 million marks.[53]

As this transaction was being completed, events presented Degussa with the chance to make still another industrial Aryanization, its fourth, when Ignaz and Justin Hirsch decided – not least because the former man was being subjected to police harassment – to sell their vinegar and preserves operations in Düsseldorf and Schweinfurt (but not those in Leipzig), along with two associated companies and their offices.[54] Degussa's HIAG division negotiated the sales contract, acting on behalf of a consortium of Degussa, IG Farben, Lonza, Wacker, and the Essigsäure GmbH, which were to become the shareholders in the new owner, a firm dubbed Fränkische Weinessig- und Konservenfabriken, in which Degussa took 36 percent of the stock.[55] The Hirschs appear to have received 149,250 RM for the offices, equipment, recipes, and sales contracts, and another 304,700 for the principal factory site, out of which they had to pay all outstanding obligations and debts.[56] In this instance, Degussa's motives related to control of the market for acetic acid, a major end product of carbonization, but Busemann's investment strategy also played a part. By 1945, the firm's capitalization had increased from 500,000 RM to almost 1.8 million, and Degussa's holding had risen to 41 percent.[57] Whether Justin Hirsch, who emigrated, was able to take any of the

[51] DUA, DL 3.Busemann/5, Notiz Betr. Wyhlen, September 13, 1935, and Notiz Betr. Wyhlen, September 21, 1935; IW 38.4/1, Busemann and Bernau to Ludwig Scherbel, Basel, September 17, 1935 and October 7, 1935.

[52] DUA, IW 38.4/1, Correspondance between Reichsbank Abt. f. Auslandsschulden and S. Japhet & Co., London, January 21–29, 1936. On the clash with IG Farben, DL 3.Busemann/5, Busemann to Degussa Direktion, Betr. Wyhlen, January 22, 1936.

[53] DUA, IW 38.4/1, Scherbel to Degussa, January 30, 1936; Elektro-Metallurgie AG, Basel to Degussa, March 23, 1936; Degussa to Scherbel, May 15, 1936; Fragebogen für arisierte Unternehmen, signed by Bernau, February 14, 1946; Bernau and Scherf to Ernst Dobler, June 9, 1948; Entwicklung der Carbidfabr. Wyhlen, signed by Lampe, March 15, 1950.

[54] On the harassment, NWHD, RW 58–11288, Gestapo-Akte Ignaz Hirsch, Stichwortartige Darstellung des politischen Lebenslaufes, May 31, 1941, and Bayerische politische Polizei to the Staatspolizeistelle Düsseldorf, April 14, 1936.

[55] DUA, IW 41.4/1, Contract of April 20, 1936 between Ignaz and Justin Hirsch and HIAG-Verein, representing IG, Wacker, Lonza, and the Essigsäure GmbH; Notarized contract of May 6, 1936 founding Fränkische Weinessig. Another copy of the Gesellschaftsvertrag is in BUA, Sig. 6/14. IG Farben took 32 percent of the shares, Wacker and Lonza 16 percent each.

[56] DUA, IW 41.4/1 Verkaufsvertrag, May 26, 1936; Urkunde, September 1, 1936.

[57] DUA, IW 41.4/1, Vollmacht, October 12, 1937; Vertrag, September 25, 1941; and Vertrag, December 10, 1941; D 2/18, decartellization report re Fränk. Weinessig- u. Konservenfabr. How much of this increase can be traced to the takeover of the remnant of the Hirschs'

sales price away with him is not documented, but is doubtful. Certain, how-
ever, is that Ignaz lost everything; he was deported from Düsseldorf to the
Lodz ghetto at the end of 1941 and his property confiscated by the Reich.[58]
He never returned.

Degussa's fifth industrial Aryanization, also concluded in 1936, showed
that the firm was still concerned to observe the normal business proprieties
in such transactions. The entity at stake was L.C. Marquart AG of Beuel,
which had been the object of Hans Menzel's machinations in 1933. Owned
by Meno Lissauer & Cie. of Cologne, the enterprise was a reprocessor of
metallic by-products into marketable compounds and, as such, a major consumer of cyanides. Instead of paying dividends during the preceding ten
years, it had plowed its profits back into equipment and operations, which
were therefore in excellent condition.[59] At the end of 1935, Leo Klopfer,
Marquart's chief technical specialist, told a Degussa executive that the company might be obtainable "considering the existing, special circumstances,"
if the prospective purchaser could pay cash and offer reasonable guarantees
of keeping the enterprise going. Since the current annual profit was about
250,000 RM and the stock had a value of 800,000, Klopfer thought a price
of 2 million marks would be appropriate and indicated that payment in German currency would suit Marquart's interests. A few days later, he called at
Degussa's offices in Frankfurt, discussed the price with Hermann Schlosser,
and pointed out that the three principal figures at Marquart, himself, the
chief chemist, and the head salesman, were all Jews but willing to stay on to
facilitate the transition to Degussa's ownership.[60]

Ernst Busemann did not wish to appear too eager to pursue the sale, even
though a visit to the factory in February 1936 left him impressed and convinced that it could be had for some 3 million marks, half of that sum
for the plant itself and the rest in payment of its debts, mostly also to
Lissauer & Cie. He was also unsure what to do about the fact that the
firm had twelve to thirteen "non-Aryans" in key positions.[61] As a result,
nothing further happened until June, when the advent of two other con-
tenders for the property prompted Schlosser to endorse the acquisition and
forced Busemann's hand.[62] He therefore directed Ernst Bernau, Degussa's

operations in Leipzig on August 9, 1938, and how much Fränkische Weinessig paid on that
occasion are matters that await clarification.

[58] See SSL, Amtsgericht Leipzig, HRA 70, Ignaz and Theodor Hirsch to Amtsgericht in Leipzig,
December 30, 1938, and IHK Leipzig to Amtsgericht Leipzig, December 19, 1939; and
NWHD, RW 58–11288, Exchange of correspondance between the Vorsteher des Finanz-
amtes in Eisenach and the Gestapoleitstelle Düsseldorf, September 17–October 11, 1942.

[59] DUA, IW 21.2/1, Busemann's Notiz betr. Marquart, February 27, 1936.

[60] DUA, IW 21.2/1, Graseck to Abtg. Keram. Farben, Frankfurt, December 4, 1935.

[61] DUA, IW 21.2/1, Busemann's Notiz Betr. Marquart, December 30, 1935; and Busemann's
Notiz betr. Marquart, February 27, 1936.

[62] DUA, IW 21.2/1, Schlosser's Notiz betr. Marquart, June 22, 1936.

financial expert, and Ernst Baerwind, its technical leader, to prepare analyses of the property, both of which were favorable. Bernau endorsed the project with particular force, noting that it promised not only to bring steady annual returns, but also important immediate ones. As he put it, "the purchase of M[arquart], even at a small annual rate of return, is thoroughly defensible, since the plant and the today much sought-after metals extracted there seem to me more valuable as inventory than the comparable worth in cash."[63] In August, the deal was concluded on the terms Busemann had anticipated; Lissauer was paid 1.5 million Reichsmarks in cash for the shares – 187.5 percent of par and about 100,000 RM more than the total worth of Marquart's assets according to its profit-and-loss statement – and the acquired firm later fulfilled its financial obligations to him.[64] Degussa immediately took a huge tax write-off, primarily on the raw materials, then began reaping annual dividends of 5 to 6 percent in the ensuing years while the assets of the firm more than doubled.[65] As for the Jewish members of Marquart's managing board, Klopfer and Erich Nethe, agitation by the DAF branch at the factory forced them out in February 1938, when they received half their total contractual salaries through the end of July 1941, with a promise of the remaining half at a time they determined, providing they did not emigrate. They wisely did so, however, following the pogrom in November, with the result that the Reich collected most of what they had received, and the second installment became moot.[66] Both men outlived the Nazi regime, as did Meno Lissauer.

The sixth of Degussa's industrial Aryanizations signaled the onset of a new phase in the corporation's involvement in the dispossession of Jews, a phase characterized by a transition to increasingly raw behavior on the firm's part as it reacted defensively to a radicalization of Nazi persecution that seemed to endanger its own interests, along with those of the people the regime targeted. The Chemische Fabrik Grünau AG specialized in the electrolytic manufacture of intermediates for detergents and of pest- and weather-resistant materials (*Bautenschutz*) for agricultural buildings. Earlier called Landshoff & Meyer, the firm's non-Aryan owners had sold a majority of their stock to Degussa during the 1920s, but they still held 12 percent of

[63] DUA, PCA 1/244, Bernau's financial analysis of Marquart, June 25, 1936, from which the quotation comes, and his follow-up report of July 9, 1936; DL 3.Baerwind/20, Besichtigung der Fabrik der Dr. L. C. Marquart, July 9, 1936.

[64] DUA, IW 21.2/1: exchange of letters between Degussa and Marquart/Lissauer, August 27–28, 1936; IW 21.5/1, Gewinn- und Verlustrechnung, 1932/33–1934/35.

[65] DUA, IW 21.5/1, Aufsichtsratprotokolle, especially March 16, 1942 and April 8, 1943; RFI 4.8/5: Körperschaftsteuer, 1934–41, cover letter for the tax return for 1936; and D 2/18, decartellization report re Marquart, giving its balance sheet value as of September 30, 1946 as 3.1 million Reichsmarks.

[66] DUA, DL 3.Busemann/5, Notiz Betr. Marquart, May 7, 1937; Notiz einer Besprechung mit den Herren Klopfer und Pfister, February 4, 1938; IW 21.2/1, especially Schlosser to Klopfer, February 16, 1938.

the shares in 1937, and three members of the Meyer family remained on the managing and supervisory boards.[67] Long before 1937, their presence had resulted in difficulties for the firm, but Ernst Busemann had stood by them, agreeing in late 1934, for instance, not to carry out a proposed fusion of Grünau with Degussa because the Meyers thought they could better maintain their positions in a legally separate, smaller, and less noticeable enterprise.[68] A few months later, when the idea of promoting an Aryan over the head of one of the Meyers was raised, he pleaded with Busemann not to undermine him in this fashion, and Busemann's response is worth quoting at length as an indication of his human sympathy for the family's position and willingness to act accordingly:

I must confess that, considering our long association with these thoroughly decent people, it will be hard for me now to make the rest of their lives unbearable, and I do not really know what I should do in this conflict between what is fundamentally correct and sentimental considerations. We are obligated to these men for certain things, and therefore I come finally to the result that we should try to let matters go on as they are.[69]

In consequence, the appointment was not made. The following month, Busemann overrode fears that another new appointee to the managing board would be unacceptable because he had a Jewish wife, and decided that two departing Jews on the supervisory body, Ernst Meyer and Max Warburg, should continue to receive their profit shares.[70]

By July 1937, however, when a new crisis over the Meyers erupted, Busemann thought he had little room left for "sentimental considerations." What brought matters to a head appears to have been the conjunction of a whispering campaign instigated by the Party against Grünau's products and the desire of the German Labor Front chapter in the plant to apply for designation as a National Socialist Model Factory, an initiative that had no chance of approval as long as Jews were prominent in the firm.[71] Reporting on all of this to Degussa, the Aryan business manager of Grünau took care to stress that the damage done to sales and operations thus far had been limited, but he feared the worst. As a result, and in spite of the fact that the Nazi Regional Foreman had made quite clear that the presence of Jews on the managing board constituted the real problem, Grünau's manager and both Bernau and Baerwind at Degussa began trying to persuade the Meyers to sell their remaining stock. Indeed, Grünau's manager argued to them and

[67] DUA, IW 22.5/4–5, Herzog's Aktennotiz, July 21, 1937; Feldmann to Wüstney, June 1, 1945.
[68] DUA, IW 22.5/5, Notiz. Besprechung mit Herrn Dr. Theo Meyer, November 14, 1934.
[69] DUA, IW 22.5/5, Busemann's Notiz. Personalangelegenheiten Grünau, April 26, 1935.
[70] DUA, IW 22.5/5, Busemann to Th. Meyer, May 14, 1935; Busemann's Notiz betr. Personal-Angelegenheiten Grünau, May 23, 1935.
[71] DUA, IW 22.5/4–5, Herzog's Aktennotiz, July 21, 1937; Herzog's Aktennotz Betr. Gauobmann, July 21, 1937; Herzog to Baerwind, July 22, 1937, with enclosures.

their patron Busemann, either duplicitously or with astounding naivete, that doing so would be the best way to assure "that Dr. Meyer's position with us is assured for the long term." The Meyers, however, refused to play along until they could talk with their old friend Busemann, which prompted the business manager to appeal for authority to speak in the Degussa leader's name.[72] That request precipitated a reply from Busemann on July 30, 1937, that says much about the man and the situation in which he found himself:

> Your letter touches me greatly, since I know the Messrs. Meyer, including their father, as able, thoroughly fair businessmen. The gentlemen have stood by the Scheideanstalt and ... by me and showed us loyalty before the revision of political conditions set in. They have placed their fate in our hands through the sale of their stock, and now comes a moment in which I have to negotiate with them over a further, substantial reduction in their influence. These negotiations will be hard for me because two equal partners will not appear, but rather for the most diverse reasons there will be nothing that can be done about my decision. Your letter shows with complete clarity that much must happen concerning Aryanization. It is pointless to swim against the stream. Our effort must be directed, both in the interest of the firm and of the Meyer family, at preserving for our plant the Messrs. Theo and Viktor Meyer. The way you suggest seems the right one to me. But I think it is also right to speak openly about this to the Messrs. Meyer. I hope that they place enough confidence in you and me to arrange matters as well as possible. I will strive to justify the confidence that they have shown me for many years.[73]

Busemann's efforts to justify their confidence appear to have taken about six months, but did not end with their retention. The Meyer brothers left Grünau's managing board and their father its supervisory one in late January 1938. They sold their remaining common and preferred shares with a nominal value of 262,500 RM to Degussa in three stages over the next three months for common stock in IG Farben with a nominal value of 364,600 RM, or an overall rate of 139 percent. Since the market value of IG stock was much higher than Grünau's, however, the real rate was close to 200 percent at a time when Grünau's stock was trading at 160 percent of par. That price was sufficiently generous to provoke challenge during the regime's Audit of Dejewification Transactions of 1942, but Degussa was not fined for having overpaid.[74] In the interim, the Reich almost certainly confiscated most of the proceeds, but the father and at least one of the sons survived the war.

[72] DUA, IW 22.5/4–5, Baerwind to Victor Meyer, July 23, 1937; Herzog to Dr. [presumably Baerwind], July 25, 1937; Baerwind to Herzog, July 27, 1937; Herzog to Busemann, July 29, 1937; Herzog to Baerwind, July 29, 1937.

[73] DUA, IW 22.5/4–5, Busemann to Herzog, July 30, 1937.

[74] DUA, IW 22.5/5, Herzog to Busemann, January 26, 1938; Entwurf, Vorstand von Grünau to IHK Berlin, September 22, 1942, Betr.: Nachprüfung von Entjudungsgeschäften, enclosing a copy of Degussa Bank-Abtlg, Bernau and Nagel, February 15, 1938; Schlosser and Scherf to Grünau, October 13, 1942, enclosing Entwurf. Betr.: Nachprüfung von Entjudungsgeschäften.

Although Degussa's seventh industrial Aryanization, that of the Hydrocarbon KG, involved an extension of the Frankfurt firm's production palette, the acquisition also was, as in the Grünau case, defensive in inspiration, motivated by the desire to head off intruders on Degussa's emerging virtual monopoly over German carbon black production. Hydrocarbon belonged to Philipp Burger, an Austrian Jew, and manufactured the substance from acetylene at a rather decrepit plant in Blankenburg near Berlin. Degussa had been the little firm's sales agent to the rubber and printing industries from November 1933 until July 1935, thus masking it against the usual pressures on purchasing from non-Aryan enterprises.[75] But the larger firm's mounting involvement in carbon black production led Burger to resume marketing his own output to the rubber industry, and this was not the only sign for the aging proprietor that the field was growing too crowded and capital intensive for a small producer like himself.[76] Thus, in the fall of 1937, after one firm approached him about selling, he began exploring some form of "support" from his Frankfurt partner, suggesting that it might want to buy half of the company's nominally 99,000 RM in shares for 200,000 RM, half to be paid to him and half to be invested in the enterprise, while he remained technical director of the plant.[77]

Though Bernau found the firm unappealing from a financial point of view and Baerwind considered the productive installations "miserable," Degussa decided in December to offer Burger 198,000 RM for all his shares, motivated, as Schlosser later wrote, by the desire "to close a gap in our carbon black position, namely with regard to that made from acetylene, without having to expend much money on experimentation."[78] That the price came to only about 73 percent of the firm's official balance sheet value was offset by the fact that it was twice what Hydrocarbon's own assets were worth once obligations were deducted and 138 percent of the company's taxable value.[79] Moreover, the arrangements were sweetened (for both sides) during

[75] DUA, DL 3.Baerwind/16, Aktenvermerk betr. Russ, January 19, 1933; 2/14, Besuch bei Philipp Burger bezw. Hydrocarbon AG, April 18, 1933; DL 3.Baerwind/17, Besuch bei der Hydrocarbon AG, October 14, 1933; Besuch bei der Hydrocarbon AG, November 14, 1933; Besuch bei der Hydrocarbon, June 8, 1934; and GPT 4/1, Vertrag, November 15, 1933.

[76] DUA, DL 3.Baerwind/17, Besuch bei der Hydrocarbon, January 18, 1934; Besuch bei der Hydrocarbon, June 8, 1934; GPT 4./1, Degussa to Hydrocarbon, July 25, 1935.

[77] DUA, DL 3.Baerwind/21, Aktenverm. betr. Hydrocarbon KG, September 18, 1937; Zweite Aussprache mit Philipp Burger, September 24, 1937; Gespräch mit Hn. Ph. Burger, September 29, 1937.

[78] DUA, DL 3.Baerwind/21, Besprechung mit Hrn. Burger, December 6, 1937; Notizen von dem Besuch der Acetylenrussfabr. der Hydrocarbon, December 17, 1937; PCA 2/13, Baerwind to Burger, December 20, 1937; DL 3.H.Schlosser/1, Dok. 850, Notiz, December 18, 1941, enclosing a memo for Dr. Achterath betr. Russ, December 2, 1941.

[79] These calculations are based on DUA, PCA 2/13, Bilanzen, November 30, 1937; PCA 2/14, Bernau to Ph. Burger, July 12, 1938; and UV 2/32, Sumera and Feldman, Degussa, to Stadt Frankfurt, October 4, 1971.

the next few months by the terms of separate contracts that granted Burger 30 percent of the gross income earned from his foreign patents and 120,000 RM for his services over the following five years, subject to certain reductions if sales fell below a specified volume.[80] On April 1, 1938, the deal was concluded, just before a series of decrees subjected Aryanizations to state control and made retaining Burger impossible. Degussa then set about dismissing the last Jewish employee, melding the patent rights into the firm's assets (which shot up to almost double what Degussa had paid), and coming to terms with the fact that the factory was on the verge of collapse.[81]

Having bought Hydrocarbon for its processes rather than its facilities, Degussa refused to put its name on the Blankenburg installation and immediately began trying to transfer output to Cologne or Kalscheuren.[82] Because the move turned out to be more costly than anticipated, however, the site continued to operate on a small scale throughout the Second World War, earning enough of a profit to recover Degussa's investment.[83] Always short of labor, it filled out its workforce until February 1943 with a compulsory work batallion of some twelve to twenty-five, often elderly German Jews, who were given, as Degussa's Nazi Plant Foreman Adolf Hilpert noted with satisfaction, "the most unpleasant work." After their unit was "completely dissolved," these men were replaced by Poles and prisoners of war. Meanwhile, Degussa resolved to shut Blankenburg down as soon as the new "concern factory" at Fürstenberg an der Oder was completed.[84] As for Philipp Burger, he is last mentioned in the documents in early May 1938.[85] No record has surfaced of him or his heirs having survived the Third Reich to raise a claim for restitution on the basis of the probable nonfulfillment of his patents and consulting contracts with Degussa, if he succeeded in emigrating, or the seizure of the proceeds on them by the Nazi state, if he did not. Degussa,

---

[80] DUA, PCA 2/13 Federlin's Richtlinien für den Entwurf eines Abkommens, January 22, 1938; Federlin to Burger, January 28, 1938; Scherf's Abgeänderte Fassung des von Herrn Burger eingereichten Entwurfs, February 21, 1938.

[81] DUA, BET 10/014, Eröffnungsbilanz der Hydrocarbon Ges. f. chem. Produkte mbH, May 15, 1938.

[82] DUA, DL 3.Baerwind/21, Aussprache mit den Herren Burger u. Simanowsky, March 10, 1938; Notiz betr. Hydrocarbon, March 25, 1938; Übernahme der Hydrocarbon, April 9, 1938; PCA 2/13, Acetylenruss, Hydrocarbon, Vertrag, April 1, 1938; DL 3.Baerwind/21, Besuch bei der Hydrocarbon, June 30, 1938; PCA 2/14, Federlin's Notiz betr. Hydrocarbon GmbH, Berlin, October 18, 1938, Baerwind's Notiz, Acetylen-Russ, November 7, 1938; and Nagel's Bericht. Besuch bei der Hydrocarbon, October 11, 1938. Degussa did not buy the land on which the plant was located, which went to the Reichspost.

[83] DUA, DL 3.Schlosser/1, Dok. Nr. 882, Schlosser's Notiz betr. Russ, April 15, 1942.

[84] DUA, PCA 2/15, Hilpert's Akten-Notiz Betr. Besuch der Hydrocarbon GmbH, July 1, 1939; DL 3.H.Schlosser/1, Dok. 850, Schlosser's Notiz, December 18, 1941, enclosing Notiz für Herrn Dr. Achterath betr. Russ, December 2, 1941; PCA 2/18, Monatsberichte, 1939–43.

[85] DUA, DL 3.Baerwind/21, Nochmals: Karbidbedarf der Hydrocarbon, May 9, 1938.

however, initiated its own request for compensation in 1971 for the seizure of the plants by the German Democratic Republic, but then withdrew the application on the grounds that "even if we had retained this plant after the war, it would have been worthless."[86]

The last of Degussa's primarily defensive industrial Aryanizations, its eighth overall, revealed how fundamentally the firm's conduct was transformed by the Reich's mounting onslaught on the Jewish economic presence in early 1938, for in the cases of the Jews associated with the Österreichische Chemische Werke (ÖCW), Degussa showed no trace of the consideration it had extended the Meyers and Philipp Burger only weeks earlier. Having first bought into this producer of hydrogen peroxide in 1910, Degussa had raised its holding in 1927 to 74 percent, divided equally with IG Farben as a silent partner, through purchases from the Creditanstalt Bankverein and Hugo Fürth, the head of one of the two Jewish families that had founded the firm years earlier. Descendants of the other founder, Benedikt Margulies, retained the remaining 26 percent of the stock, and two of them, along with Adolf Fürth, were among the firm's principal managers when the *Anschluss* took place.[87] That event, therefore, made not only their positions suddenly precarious, but also the position of the whole firm, for the ÖCW was now in danger of being declared non-Aryan by virtue of the fact that the Jewish share of its capital exceeded, however slightly, the threshold of 25 percent established by the recent round of government decrees. Moreover, since the Margulieses held exactly 26 percent of the shares in Leukon AG, Degussa's sales firm in Switzerland, that enterprise, too, appeared exposed to unwanted Nazi attention.[88]

Though alarmed by this situation, Degussa's managers at first rested their hopes on the circumstance that Erwin Margulies, the owner of 6.45 percent of the shares, had only one Jewish parent and lived in Paris. It seemed likely that he would be declared a "foreigner with reference to foreign exchange," and thus that the "Jewish" capital share would fall below the danger level. In any case, Degussa did not expect any difficulties with the Margulieses, who immediately promised to sell.[89] So the first order of business in Vienna was to purge the offices of the Jewish personnel, a process that was completed late in May 1938.[90] But by then disputes had arisen over the price for the Margulies

[86] DUA, UV 2/32, Sumera and Feldman, Degussa, to Stadt Frankfurt, October 4, 1971.
[87] DUA, AW 5.2/1, Erinnerungen von W. Josef Skowronek, Wien 1962, especially pp. 14, 35; AW 5.2/3, ÖCW to Degussa, August 8 and 19, 1927, with enclosures.
[88] DUA, AW 5.2/3, Degussa (Bernau and Feldmann) to IG Frankfurt, Betr. Spezialbuchhaltung, February 22, 1939.
[89] DUA, AW 5.2/3, unheaded document signed by Haim, the business manager of ÖCW, Marianne Margulies and Erwin Margulies, March 23, 1938.
[90] DUA, AW 5.2/3, Busemann to Hans Kühne, IG Leverkusen, May 16, 1938, which reports on the events at ÖCW, mentions that much of the management was Jewish, and adds "We

shares in the Austrian enterprise, which had a face value of 576,096 RM, but which the business manager at the firm thought were worth some 2 million. When he informed Busemann of this, the latter man exploded. After declaring that he would rather liquidate the company and use the proceeds to build a brand new hydrogen peroxide installation in Germany, Busemann added blunt remarks that cast him in a much less humane light than those he had made about the Meyers only a few months before:

> For the Scheideanstalt, there is a much simpler arithmetic: even after making all possible allowance for sentiment and tradition, we can pay for the Margulies shares only what they are worth to us. That is very little.... The Scheideanstalt is quite comfortable with 37 percent, plus IG's 37 percent, of the ÖCW, and it is of no business significance whether we have 50 percent instead of 37 percent with the same equal partner. On the contrary, under some circumstances it could be quite pleasant to have a third investor. But the Margulies Group will scarcely find a third investor, given two such [existing] partners.

Nor was Busemann ready to come up with even the 1 million marks that Bernau initially thought justified for the purchase. Instead, he made clear to his representatives in Vienna, Degussa would prepare an affordable offer, and the Margulieses would have to take it or leave it.[91] That offer, it became apparent at the end of May, would be no more than 800,000 RM for all of the Margulies shares in the Österreichische Chemische Werke *and* Leukon, despite the fact that Bernau's financial analysis meanwhile had convinced

---

have immediately completely rectified this error." The letters to Paul Margulies and Adolf Fürth, May 24, 1938, explained that the firm was terminating their contracts "in adaptation to the situation created by the changed conditions." A few days later, Bernau's Notiz. Betr. Personalia Wien, May 27, 1938, added that "Herr Haim has not succeeded in presenting proof of his half-Aryan quality, so he must also definitively leave," and advised Busemann to notify Dr. Baum of the termination of his contract before the renewal deadline of June 15. Adolf Fürth got a one-time payment of 10,000 RM for his patent rights; ÖCW to Schlosser and Bernau, July 26, 1938. Though Haim ultimately succeeded in having himself declared a *Mischling 1. Grades*, his retirement became final at the end of 1938; Haim to Bernau, November 15, 1938 and Busemann to Haim, January 2, 1939. Haim received a pension of 18,000 RM per year and a consulting contract paying another 18,000 for the next three years; Gedächtnisprotokoll of January 31, 1939. It ran out and was replaced by an annual letter of agreement in December 1941; AW 5.2/3, Bernau to Robert Haim, December 16, 1941. Haim was still representing ÖCW in conversations with Degussa as late as May 1942; PCA 1/139aII, Bernau's Betr.: ÖCW, May 26, 1942. Later, "he was drafted for unaccustomed manual labor" and "died in 1944 of heart ailments in a Vienna hospital as a result of physical and psychological strain"; AW 5.2/1, Erinnerungen von W. Josef Skowronek, Wien 1962, p. 43. Baum emigrated to England and Fürth and Paul Margulies to America; all three survived the war; see BU Hermann Schlosser, Baum to Schlosser August 25, 1946, and Skowronek's Erinnerungen, pp. 43–44.

91 DUA, AW 5.2/3, Busemann's Notiz Betr. Kauf der Anteile der Gruppe Margulies, May 13, 1938 (also in DL 3.Busemann/5).

him that the fair figure would be 911,856 RM, or 150 percent of their collective par value, somewhat less if the authorities would permit some part of the payment in foreign exchange.[92] This they flatly refused to do in July, even though the ever more fearful Margulieses meanwhile had declared their readiness to sell the Swiss shares for 35.65 percent of par, merely in return for not having their bank deposits in Switzerland and their dividend from Leukon confiscated by the Reich, and to let the Austrian shares go at about 75 percent of their face value, an offer they quickly slashed to 25 percent.[93]

At this point, the desperateness of the family's situation broke its ranks. While Marianne, Franz, and Peter Margulies apparently decided not to sell anything for mere Reichsmarks, which would be largely useless abroad, Paul Margulies announced his willingness to part with his 3.2 percent in the Austrian firm and 2.5 percent in Leukon for a mere 55,000 in German currency, about half of which was to go to paying his Flight Tax and the remainder to a blocked-mark account.[94] Degussa snapped up the offer, since after adding fees for lawyers, accountants, and the Property Transfer Office in Vienna, the cost of the purchase still would total to less than the nominal value of the shares.[95] With Paul Margulies's departure for New York in late 1938, Degussa's incentive to negotiate further with his siblings over the Austrian shares disappeared. Their holding had now fallen below one-quarter of the stock, and the settlement with Paul had set a precedent capping the share price at 75 percent of the face value.[96] It became, for the moment, far more important to attend to the matter of the Margulies mansion on the Karlsplatz in Vienna, which Degussa bought in February 1939 for 129,000 RM, net of the mortgage payment, almost certainly a fraction of the building's worth.[97]

---

[92] DUA, AW 5.2/3, Bernau's Notiz. Anteile Margulies, May 28, 1938.

[93] DUA, AW 5.2/3, Niederschrift über Verhandlungen mit Margulies, Wien, June 10–12, 1938, with multiple enclosures; Bernau's Notiz. Anteile Margulies, June 13, 1938; Unsigned letter to Devisenstelle, Wien, June 23, 1938; AW 6.4/1, Gedächtnisprotokoll, June 23, 1938; Devisenstelle Wien to Degussa, August 31, 1938.

[94] DUA, AW 6.4/1, Bernau's Notiz Betr. Leukon/Margulies, August 13, 1938; AW 5.2/3, Karl Feldmann to Bernau, August 20, 1938; Unterredung mit Dr. Julius Jeannée, August 26, 1938; Paul Margulies to E. Bernau, September 24, 1938; certification of tax payment, Finanzamt f. d. I. Bezirk Wien, September 24, 1938; Vermögensverkehrsstelle to Degussa, Fft., November 7, 1938; Notariatsakt, January 11, 1939; Notariatsakt, January 14, 1939; Degussa to IG Farben, March 11, 1939.

[95] DUA, Bernau and Feldmann to IG Frankfurt, Betr. Spezialbuchhaltung, Febuary 22, 1939; Degussa to IG, April 21, 1939. Moreover, the stock dividend for 1938 was assigned to the new owners.

[96] DUA, AW 5.2/3, Busemann to Kühne, February 22, 1939; Degussa to IG Frankfurt, Betr. Spezialbuchhaltung, February 22, 1939.

[97] DUA, AW 5.2/3, Kaufvertrag, Technikerstr. 5, February 11, 1939; AW 5.2/1, Erinnerungen von W. Josef Skowronek, p. 45.

10   Adolf Fürth   11   Paul Margulies

12   The Margulies-Haus am Karlsplatz

One of the most striking consequences of the situation as of early 1939 was the way in which it corrupted Degussa's financial expert Ernst Bernau. Having obtained for Degussa everything the Margulieses had in Vienna that the firm also needed, he appears simply to have waited for the Revenue Office to seize and sell the rest of their assets within the Reich in order to collect trumped-up charges for back taxes. But the shares in Leukon in Switzerland were another matter, and to get them, Bernau was willing not just to profit from theft, but to instigate it. Sometime around the turn of 1938/39, he suggested to the Reichsbank that it should, "on the basis of the regulations concerning Jewish property, seize the shares," and the robbery would have taken place if an official of the Creditanstalt branch in Zurich had not failed to bring to Vienna the stock certificates the family had deposited with him. Thus stymied, Bernau was caught between the refusal of the Foreign Exchange Office to part with francs and the determination of the Margulieses, all of whom had by now managed to escape Germany, to accept nothing else. Not until October 1939 was a satisfactory compromise found by which Leukon appeared to buy the shares back for Swiss francs out of its own reserves, and then Degussa paid the firm for them.[98]

Meanwhile, however, Bernau's waiting game in Vienna paid off. Since Erwin Margulies had been accorded his nonresident classification, his 6 percent of the stock was no longer in play, only the 16 percent still owned by Marianne, Peter, and Franz Margulies. Although the face value of this packet was 374,660 RM and Bernau calculated its worth as a share of ÖCW's assets as 472,000 RM, he told his lawyer in Vienna to spend no more than 273,000, including all related fees, for the stock. If that was not enough for the government agencies that were bound to confiscate it, Bernau noted cooly, then they should try to auction it off. In taking this stance, Bernau could be reasonably sure that no investor would commit a larger sum, since it would not have been recoverable at the current dividend rate in less than fifteen years, and he or she would acquire virtually no influence on the firm's decisions in the meantime.[99] Degussa thus was able to obtain the remaining shares in question from the Nazi state in two stages during 1940 and 1943 for an all-inclusive sum (284,000 RM) that only slightly exceeded Bernau's

---

[98] DUA, AW 6.4/1, Bernau memo, Erwerb von weiteren Leukon-Anteilen der Gruppe Margulies, July 8, 1939, from which the quotation comes; Devisenstelle Wien to Jeannée, August 8, 1939; Oberfinanzpräs. Kassel to Degussa, March 7, 1939; BET 10/42, Leukon, Bernau's Notiz. Leukon AG, Zurich, August 9, 1945; and a handwritten table titled Kapitalmässige Entwicklung, undated, which shows that Degussa paid in RM 52,734.50 for the Sw.Fr. 91,000 shares that Leukon bought from Margulies group; BET 9/136, Degussa to IG Farben, Spezial-Buchhaltung, October 18, 1939.

[99] DUA, AW 5.9/3, Jahresabschlüsse, Bernau's Notiz Betr.: Wiener Niederlassungen, December 12, 1939.

maximum, while the Margulieses got nothing.[100] But whether the purchase was worth the expenditure is another matter, since neither ÖCW nor Leukon gave off appreciably larger income for the parent company in the subsequent years as a result.[101] It appears that Degussa ended up purchasing protection for itself more than anything else.

The Margulies Aryanization case was the first in which Degussa actually worked to obtain what can only be called legally stolen property, but it was neither the last nor the crudest. The strenuously pursued acquisition of Kulzer & Co. of Frankfurt, Degussa's ninth takeover of Jewish-owned industrial assets, constituted a "compulsory Aryanization" in an even more extreme sense, in that the Gauleiter of Hessen adjudicated the sale, and the three Jews (the Messrs. Frank, Fuld, and Isaacson) among the four owners played almost no role in the negotiations whatsoever. Kulzer manufactured high-quality dental prosthetics and related items, primarily from a resin-based material called Paladon, which had been elaborated by the fourth partner, an Aryan Swiss citizen named Gottfried Roth, on the basis of patents held by the Röhm & Haas AG of Darmstadt, as well as from precious metals provided by various smelters and refiners, including Degussa. Because the Economics Ministry had begun pressuring Röhm & Haas to shift its deliveries to an Aryan firm; the metals components were rationed, therefore denied to Jewish companies by the Nazi decrees of early 1938; and much of Kulzer's output was sold abroad for badly needed foreign exchange, Kulzer's swift Aryanization was a matter of importance to the local and national economy and a cause of rivalry between Degussa and other metals refining firms that saw a chance to expand their businesses vertically.[102] All this helps explain

---

[100] DUA, AW 5.2/3, Urkunden, May 28, 1940, regarding the compulsory sale of Franz and Marianne Margulies' shares; ÖCW to Bernau, June 5, 1940; Degussa to ÖCW, June 11, 1940; Notariatsakt, June 26, 1943, regarding the compulsory sale of Peter Margulies' shares. Included in the payment for Peter's shares was a special additional "honorarium" for the assessor who, while reviewing the purchase for the Oberfinanzpräsident, had been willing to overlook a possible undervaluation of ÖCW's reserves in determining the price for all the Margulies shares, "in order not to complicate the matter"; Jeannée to ÖCW, June 3, 1943; ÖCW to Bernau, June 8, 1943; ÖCW to Bernau, July 22, 1943. In paying this thinly disguised bribe, Degussa was explicitly greasing the wheels for a later purchase of Erwin Margulies' shares, which had by now been seized by the Gestapo. But they appear never to have been sold; AW 5.2/1, Erinnerungen von W. Josef Skowronek, pp. 80–81.

[101] See, in particular, DUA, BET 10/42, handwritten, undated, table of Erträgnisse from Leukon.

[102] On the history of the firm, which had been founded in 1934 as a sales agency, then combined with a manufacturing operation in 1936 after the departure of its Aryan and Nazi namesake, see DUA, DL 11.5/48, Notiz für Herrn Dr. Müller, Heraeus, signed by Roth, enclosing Unterlage für die Klage Kulzer-Rock, August 8, 1941. On the relationship between Kulzer's patents and those of Röhm & Haas, GEH 3.Hirtes/11, Furler's Notiz... betreffs Kunstharze für Zahnersatz, August 20, 1938, and Degussa's Notiz, August 23, 1938, which also describes the Economics Ministry's intervention.

the Gauleitung's intervention in the case by the summer of 1938 and the rapidity with which it came to insist on a partition of the firm's stock as a compromise between ideological reservations about a takeover by a large corporation and a recognition of the advantages of employing Degussa's well-developed sales organization.[103]

By December, the competing parties had worked out a solution. It divided the shares and net profits between Degussa and the Heraeus platinum firm, and made Roth the business manager in return for an annual salary and a license fee on all sales. To the Party's Regional Economic Advisor was left the task of determining the price.[104] He had done so by February 1939, when two of the Jewish owners each got 70,000 RM for their shares – that is, about two-thirds of their commercial value – most of which was subsequently confiscated. The third partner, who had emigrated to the United States, was paid with rights to an American patent and profits from an American firm that had belonged to Kulzer.[105] Degussa does not appear to have instigated what by now amounted to a forced sale; the firm became involved only after the failure of an attempt by Roth to buy out his Jewish colleagues put Kulzer up for grabs. Neither did Degussa apparently play any part in fixing the unfair total payment of 268,000 RM to the owners, plus an "equalization payment" of 18,600 RM to the state, since the regime now required these sums to be set by a Nazi-appointed auditor.[106] But in this instance, as in the Margulies case, the corporation became, for the first time, deeply implicated in acts of naked plunder. Insofar as Degussa's leaders had misgivings about this – and there is no record to this effect – they no doubt consoled themselves with the thoughts that competitors would have taken what they did not and that the resulting loss of revenue would have been enormous. In 1939 alone,

[103] DUA, GEH 3.Hirtes/11, Furler's Notiz. Vorsprache bei der IHK Frankfurt a.M. betreffs Arisierung der Firma Kulzer & Co.-Paladon, August 16, 1938, and his Aktennotizen Paladon, September 15 and 26, 1938; and GBE 1/119, Degussa to Gauwirtschaftsberater Eckardt, August 23 and 27, 1938; Decker (IHK Rhein-Main) to Degussa, September 29, 1938; and Decker to Hirtes, October 21, 1938.
[104] DUA, GBE 1/119, Vereinbarung zwischen Degussa und Heraeus betr. Kulzer, October 28, 1938; and Niederschrift über die Besprechung vom December 14, 1938; and GEH 3.Hirtes/11, Furler's Aktennotizen Betr. Paladon, October 25 and 31, 1938.
[105] DUA, GBE 1/119, Vollmacht, signed by Jakob Frank, February 6, 1939; Urkunde, signed by lawyer Carl Hans Barz, February 8, 1939; Oberfinanzpräsident Kassel, Genehmigungsbescheid, April 3, 1939.
[106] DUA, GBE 1/119, Höhne's Bericht über die Ermittlung der Ausgleichsabgabe, March 28, 1939, which reckoned Kulzer's Substanzwert (and sales price) at 268,000 RM, its Rentabilitätswert (based on the average profit of the preceding three years) at 330,000, hence its Verkehrswert at 299,000, and therefore die Ausgleichsabgabe (60 percent of the difference between the Substanz- and the Verkehrswerten) at 18,600; Regierungspräsident Wiesbaden, Genehmigungsbescheid, signed by Faust, May 25, 1939. See also GEH 3.Hirtes/11, his Notiz Betr. Übernahme der Firma Kulzer & Co. GmbH, June 7, 1939.

Degussa recovered its share of the purchase price from Kulzer's sales profits; although the statistics for later years are incomplete, they suggest annualized returns for Degussa of at least 700,000 RM in the early 1940s.[107]

Equally blinding was the rate at which Degussa completed its tenth expansion at the expense of Jews, the increase in its shareholding in the Metallgesellschaft in 1939–40. At a price of 115 percent of par (compared with the rate of roughly 160 percent at which the stock was trading), Degussa acquired some 705,000 Jewish-owned shares in this enterprise, most of which Richard Merton had been forced to relinquish as he was expelled from Germany, from the Prussian State Bank. This worked out to a windfall of some 317,000 RM, and Degussa thus strengthened its position within this longtime partner firm at a discount of almost 26 percent.[108]

The mounting ruthlessness of Degussa's behavior in the ÖCW, Kulzer, and Merton cases was exceeded after 1940 by the enterprise's conduct in its final three industrial Aryanizations, its eleventh to thirteenth overall, which were concentrated in the occupied Protectorate of Bohemia and Moravia. The first of these concerned the Aurora Nasch & Co. precious metals refinery of Brünn (Brno). The installation itself was, from Degussa's point of view, so run down as to be virtually worthless, and the value of its assets barely covered its obligations. Aurora, however, had inventories of precious metals valued at about 100,000 RM in May 1939, and it was entitled to annual allotments of gold, platinum, and other metals from the National Bank of Prague, which continued throughout the German occupation.[109] Though two of the Jewish owners, Sidonie Nasch and Samuel Frankfurter, quickly indicated their willingness to sell, their initial terms were unacceptable to Degussa, hence the leader of the metals division in Frankfurt opted to put off negotiations until "the non-Aryan owners have become somewhat more pliant."[110]

In June 1939, Degussa had to step up the pace, however. Erwin Scheinost, the ethnic German and Nazi Party member in Brünn who had been made provisional business manager of the Aurora firm, had been seeking a job

---

[107] DUA, GBE 1/120, Degussa and Heraeus to Kulzer, March 14, 1940; GBE 1/119, Lizenz Roth, August 25, 1942. See also RFI 4.2/89, Jahresabschluss per 30. September 1940, Anlage 5a, which gives the acquisition costs of Degussa's shares in Kulzer as 196,000 RM and the first year's dividend payment as 200,000 RM.

[108] DUA, DL 11.5./41, Betr. Metall-Ges., November 14, 1939, Unterhaltung mit Geheimrat Schmitz, December 1, 1939, and Metallges. AG Aktien, January 6, 1942, show that Degussa and IG Farben divided the "shares held by Jews" that became available in this period. On the 5,000 other such shares that belonged to Wally Liebman, see UV 1/46. I have estimated Degussa's windfall from the figures in DL 3.Scherf/1, Notiz für Herrn Scherf, n.d. [June/July 1951].

[109] DUA, GEH 6./11, Walter Roessler's Bericht über Besuche in Brünn vom 23.–24. Mai 1939. The metals on hand came to 13.5 kilograms of gold, 2.25 kilograms of platinum, .5 kilogram of palladium, 32 kilograms of silver, and 100 grams of rhodium.

[110] DUA, GEH 6./11, Hirtes' Notiz Betr. Aurora-Brünn, June 7, 1939.

with Degussa since prior to the German occupation of the Sudetenland, let alone of Bohemia and Moravia. When that event occurred, he had drawn Frankfurt's attention to the little enterprise, more or less offering to deliver it in return for the transfer he so coveted. Now he found that he could not get permission to leave the Protectorate and had to bring Aurora back into operation immediately in order to support his family.[111] Thus, he and Degussa quickly contrived a new plan by which he would buy the enterprise with the German firm's money, then either run it on behalf of or resell it to Frankfurt, depending on whether he was allowed to change his residence. To assure that this would be the case, Degussa's leaders decided to dispatch Hans Menzel, their "old fighter," to work on Dr. Jury, the relevant Gauleiter.[112]

Degussa's tactics succeeded rapidly, but not its strategy. By August 1939, the corporation had allayed the local NSDAP's objections to both the "concern-building" entailed in Degussa's expansion and the loss of German blood in the region through the departure of Scheinost and his family.[113] The takeover, via Degussa's wholly owned subsidiary in Vienna, Louis Roessler & Co., seemed on the verge of completion for a sum of only about 60,000 RM. Frankfurt already was counting on shutting down the smelting facilities immediately, reducing the firm to a sales outlet, and transferring the metals allotments to Vienna.[114] During the winter, however, the local lawyer for Bruno Elsner, the third Jewish partner, who had fled abroad, took such an adroitly dilatory approach to all proposals for winding up the deal that Walter Roessler, the manager of the Vienna branch, decided to invoke higher powers. He called at the Gestapo office in Brünn to point out that Elsner was, in fact, a Polish citizen of a town that Germany had annexed, hence was now subject to German laws, including the one that permitted the seizure of property belonging to German subjects who had fled to enemy territory. In short, "his citizenship has to be revoked and his property confiscated by the state," as the manager rather proudly reported to Frankfurt on April 5, 1940.[115]

[111] DUA, GEH 6./11, Scheinost to Walter Roessler, June 28, 1939. Scheinost applied for a post at Degussa on April 4, 1938, and in early May 1939, apparently in hopes of speeding his transfer to Frankfurt, he broached the subject of the takeover to Ernst Baerwind of Degussa; see DL 3.Baerwind/42, Baerwind's memo, Aussprache mit Dr. Scheinost in Prag, May 6, 1939.
[112] DUA, GEH 6./11, Bericht über die Angelegenheit Dr. Sceinost [sic] u. "Aurora" Nasch & Co., Brünn, July 10, 1939.
[113] DUA, DL 3.Baerwind/42 (also GEH 6/11), Scheinost to Baerwind, July 12, 1939; Menzel's Bericht über den Besuch bei der Affinerie Aurora Nash & Co, July 31, 1939; and Menzel to Gauleiter Jury, August 1, 1939.
[114] DUA, DL 3.Baerwind/42, Walter Roessler, Bericht über die Angelegenheit Affinerie Aurora Nash & Comp. – Dr. Scheinost, August 4, 1939; and Walter Roessler to Baerwind, October 10, 1939.
[115] DUA, DL 3.Baerwind/42, Roessler's Bericht über Besuch in Brünn und Prag in Angelegenheit der Arisierung der Firma Aurora, April 5, 1940.

Seven years after embarking on the course of Aryanization, Degussa had completed its descent from taking advantage of Nazi pressure on Jews to instructing the Gestapo on how to exert it. Nonetheless, all sorts of legal and bureaucratic technicalities consumed another eighteen months until the broad terms of the takeover were in place and almost another year after that before the new firm was officially registered as the Aurora Edelmetallscheide-anstalt GmbH, co-owned by Degussa, L. Roessler & Co., and Karl Endres, the former business manager of the latter firm, who now assumed the same title at Aurora.[116] Wearisome as the process proved, Degussa's representatives thought in 1943 that they had reason to be grateful for the delays. Because the takeover price was pegged to Aurora's worth in September 1939, it now could be paid almost entirely out of the reserves that had been accumulated since then and were acquired at the moment of sale. Degussa therefore ended up pocketing Aurora's metals inventory and quota allotments essentially for free, while the Reich siphoned off the recent earnings. Three-quarters of the nominal price paid went into blocked accounts at the regime's disposal in the names of the former owners, and one-quarter went directly to the Reichsprotektor in the form of an "equalization payment."[117] But Degussa gained nothing else from the transaction. Its Vienna branch finally had obtained title to the profits just before they ceased to come in, and Endres found his time and energy being consumed by such matters as getting his lawyer released after he was caught trying "to establish a relationship with an interned Jewish woman," struggling unsuccessfully to get a telephone connected, and coping with the local Nazi Party's efforts to take over his offices and reconvert them to a dwelling. He sold his small shareholding to Degussa in June 1944, and the firm appears to have suspended operations

[116] DUA, DL 3.Baerwind/42, Degussa Wien to Degussa Frankfurt, October 31, 1941; GEH 6/11, Genehmigung, Oberlandrat in Brünn, June 10, 1942, and Landespräsident in Mähren to Degussa Wien, January 11, 1943, which superseded the earlier approval. The firm was not recorded in the Brünn Handelsregister, however, until October 1, 1943; GEH 6/11, Degussa, Wien to Bernau and Hirtes, October 4, 1943.

[117] DUA, DL 3.Baerwind/42, Degussa Wien to Degussa Frankfurt, October 31, 1941; GEH 6/11, Degussa Wien to Degussa Metall-Abt., Fft., October 31, 1941; W. Roessler to R. Hirtes, July 27, 1942; Genehmigung, Oberlandrat in Brünn, June 10, 1942, Entwurf zum Gesellschaftsvertrag, September 15, 1942; Entwurf zum Ges.-Vertrag der neuen Aurora GmbH, n.d.; Landespräsident in Mähren to Degussa Wien, January 11, 1943; Endres, Ruecksprachen in Brünn wegen Aurora, February 1, 1943; and AW 2.4./1, Aurora to Endres, December 1, 1943. On the basis of the sometimes contradictory figures and calculations in these documents, it appears that the buyers expended some 1.5 million Czech crowns for the firm, including the equalization payment and a later additional one demanded by the Gestapo, and that Aurora's profits from 1939 to 1943 more than covered the costs. At most, L. Roessler may have had to provide some 20,000 crowns for a short period. On the dispute over the extra payment, see GEH 6/11, Endres's Notiz Betr.: Aurora, December 31, 1943, and Endres's memo, Kaufvertrag Aurora Brünn, August 7, 1944.

altogether in November, when it was moderately damaged in an air raid.[118] Bruno Elsner meanwhile had made it to England; Degussa's files say nothing of the fates of Sidonie Nasch and Samuel Frankfurter.[119] While the Aurora takeover was being completed, Degussa began pursuing control of the Fröhlich, Ing. Jermár & Co. of Prague, a glazing firm that the managing board in Frankfurt considered "a very desirable extension of the program of our ceramic dyes section."[120] At first, in late 1940, when Bernau sought the help of officials at both the Economics Ministry in Berlin and the Trade Ministry in Prague for this initiative, the move had the form of a partial Aryanization, in that Degussa thought that 25 percent of the shares were owned by a Jew and 24 perecnt were in "half-Aryan posses- sion," while the majority holding was not, at least in its entirety, for sale.[121] By June 1941, however, when Karl Feldmann was dispatched to Prague to conduct the takeover, it had become apparent that the two vulnerable part- ners each held 26.575 percent of the shares and that an option could be had on the remainder owned by Eugen Fröhlich in the event that Degussa got title to the others.[122] Though the extant records throw little light on how the Jewish owner, Dr. Josef Pick, and the part-Jewish one, Dr. Georg Brumlik, were induced to sell, it is clear that the purchase price for each holding came to almost 1.6 million Czech crowns, exclusive of outstanding claims against customers in nations at war with Germany, which each original owner re- mained entitled to collect according to his percentage share, after deductions of taxes and administrative fees. While Brumlik also could continue to claim his proportion of the firm's annual profit, payable along with the price for his shares into an account at Degussa that he could call in at any time, Pick's proceeds were placed at the disposal of the Reichsprotektor's office in Prague, and he received nothing.[123] His only role in the negotiations over his

---

[118] DUA, GEH 6/11, Endres's Notizen, May 24, and July 26, 1943 (on the lawyer); exchange of letters, Degussa and Endres, April–June 1944; Endres's Notiz Aurora GmbH-Brün, June 6, 1944; Endres's memo, December 8, 1944.

[119] On Elsner's whereabouts, DUA, DL 3.Baerwind/42, Roessler's Bericht über Besuch in Brünn und Prag, April 5, 1940.

[120] On the goal of total control, see DUA, DL 2/1, Niederschrift über die Vorstandssitzung am 2. Dezember 1940, pp. 145–46; for the quotation, Niederschrift über die Vorstandssitzung am 9. Juni 1941, p. 183.

[121] DUA, DL 2/1, Niederschrift über die Vorstandssitzung am 2. Dezember 1940, pp. 145–46; and Anhang 9, Bernau's Betr. Erwerb der Firma Fröhlich in Raudnitz, November 28, 1940.

[122] DUA, GKF 2/5, Spezial-Generalvollmacht, June 3, 1941, from Degussa to Karl Feldmann; Gesellschaftsvertrag, June 9, 1941, between Feldmann and Fröhlich.

[123] DUA, GKF 2/5, Willy Magerstein, Brumlik's lawyer, to Degussa, June 18, 1941, enclosing Abtretungsvereinbarung dated June 9, 1941, and the reply from Feldmann and Bernau of July 2, 1941; exchange of letters between Degussa and Pick, June 12–19, 1941, enclosing Abtretungsvereinbarung dated June 9, 1941; and Degussa to Josef Mandi, Pick's lawyer, May 16, 1942.

property appears to have been to sign the contract selling it to Degussa. The occupation administration later refunded some 12 percent of the share price to Degussa, which thus emerged with not only a majority packet (valued at 318,900 RM) at a total cost, including fees, of 335,039 RM, but also the right to buy the remainder for about 281,000 RM whenever Fröhlich either died or chose to withdraw from the firm, but in no case later than the end of 1952.[124] Degussa promptly delegated Leonhard Meyer to take over the sales department of the firm, in which capacity he increased its receipts by over 60 percent between 1941 and 1944, and began collecting annual license and technical support fees that came to almost 26,000 RM in 1942.[125] On the respective fates of Pick and Brumlik, the firm's files are silent.

Although the takeover of the Fröhlich firm's shares constituted the last of Degussa's own industrial Aryanizations, it also benefited from another acquisition made by the Auergesellschaft in Prague, which brought the concern's total number of such takeovers from Jews to thirteen. In March 1942, Auer obtained the Ing. Robert Müller firm, a manufacturer of heating and ventilation equipment in Prag-Dewitz (Praha-Dejvice). Once more, the price paid (280,000 RM) was so far below the company's assessed value that Auer had to transfer an equalization payment to the *Reichsprotektor* of an additional 100,000 RM, later reduced by 27,000 to allow for the firm's losses in 1941–42.[126] Later that year, Auer also bought the premises of a non-Aryan shoe polish manufacturer in Prague for 45,000 RM in order to transfer the production of lightbulbs to the site. The deal amounted to a temporary Aryanization of a piece of real estate, however, since the contract included a promise to resell the property to an ethnic German at the end of the war.[127]

---

[124] DUA, DL 2/1, Niederschrift über die Vorstandssitzung am 3. November 1941, p. 211; RFI 4.8/1, Beteiligungs-Konto nach dem Stand vom 30. September 1942; GKF 2/5, Fick and Winarsky of the Reichsprotektor's office to Degussa, May 22, 1943 (recording the payment of the rebate); and BET 10/39, Feldmann's Notiz betr. Fröhlich, November 6, 1942 (on the total cost).

[125] DUA, BU Hermann Schlosser, Anlage 23 zur Verteidigungsschrift für das Spruchkammerverfahren, Erklärung von Leonhard Meyer, November 21, 1946; DL 3/17, the documents formalizing Degussa's takeover on January 12 and 17, 1942; GKF 2/5, Degussa to Fröhlich, February 17, 1942 and March 11, and May 3, 1943; and GKF 2/9, Bernau's Betr.: Firma Fröhlich, July 6, 1944, and Fröhlich's Geschäftsbericht 1944, January 4, 1945.

[126] DUA, IW 24.9/12, Auergesellschaft Monatsbericht Nr. 6 für März-Geschäftsjahr 1941/42, April 29, 1942. On the subsequent reduction, SUAP, URP, Karton 178, Entjudungsreferat to Oberkasse, January 19, 1943. Auer may have carried out still another Aryanization in the Protectorate, this time via Gasma AG of Prague, a subsidiary owned jointly with Continental Rubber of Hanover. The files of the Staatssekretär des Reichsprotektors in Prague, SUAP, Bestand 109–4, Akte 1259, list the "Optimit" Gummi- und Textilwerke AG, in Liquidation, as acquired by Gasma via the Böhmische Escompte Bank, the Dresdner Bank's outpost in Prague, but give no date for the transaction or any other details.

[127] DUA, IW 24.5/5, Bericht des Vorstandes für das Geschäftsjahr 1940/41, January 27, 1942, p. 6. On another dimension of Aryanization by Degussa in the Protectorate, namely the

If Degussa's involvement in Aryanization was infrequent after 1939 and confined to the Greater German Reich, including the Protectorate, that record of abstinence only makes the last of the firm's Aryanizations stand out as all the more crass. In August 1944, as the Russians were on the Vistula and the Western Allies beginning to advance through France, Degussa's Austrian branch availed itself of the limited time remaining to acquire legal title to formerly Jewish property. At issue was a patent to a process of gold-plating lead and making dental inserts from the resulting product, which was held by Heinrich Kammer but being sold by a Nazi-appointed trustee on behalf of the Liquidation Section of the Property Transfer Office in Vienna. For 6,500 RM, paid to a blocked mark account, plus costs, Degussa bought the rights before it was too late.[128] Whether in doing so the local representatives of the firm were expressing confidence in the Final Victory of the Third Reich or in the death of the previous owner (or even in both) is not indicated by the few extant papers concerning the transaction.

Clearly, both Degussa's motives in carrying out Aryanizations and its conduct toward those victimized by the process shifted during the period 1933–43. Initially interested primarily in seizing opportunities to shelter capital (e.g., Homburg and Auer), the firm gradually began capitalizing on the dispossession of the Jews as a means of securing or extending key market positions – either in Degussa's familiar, core areas, such as the metals, cyanide, and liquid gold fields (Marquart, Kulzer, the Metallgesellschaft, Aurora, and Fröhlich) and, perforce, at its endangered subsidiaries (Grünau and ÖCW), or in the newer growth sector of the firm, the carbonization sphere (Wyhlen, Hirsch, and Hydrocarbon). Conversely, Degussa appears to have considered and turned away numerous potential acquisitions, usually because their operations would have carried the firm too far away from its traditional bases.[129]

---

removal of Jews from the boards and staff of the Kaliwerke AG of Kolin, in which Degussa controlled 13.35 percent of the shares, between 1939 and 1942, see Chapter 6, below.

[128] DUA, AW 2.6/1, Martin to Dickert, February 13, 1945, enclosing Vertrag, 22/29. August 1944. The surviving documents do not indicate whether Kammer had managed to escape Austria, had been deported, or was still in the country for some reason at the time of the sale, but no records of a restitution proceeding have come to light.

[129] See, for example, DUA, IW 24.4/7, Busemann's Notiz Betr. Radium, January 5, 1934, and Degea to Busemann, January 15, 1934, concerning the Deutsche Radiogen-Gesellschaft, which apparently held exclusive German rights to the sale of radium; and DL 3.Busemann/ 5: unsigned Akten-Vermerk betreffend Philipp Mühsam Akt. Ges., November 12, 1935, a wholesaler of gasoline and oil; (also IW 22.5/5), Busemann's Notiz Betr. Pharmazeutische Fabrik Rosenberg in Freiburg, December 1, 1937, in which the Grünau subsidiary was interested; and Busemann's Finanzlage der Auergesellschaft, April 4, 1938, in which he "very cooly treated" Auer's zeal to take over the Kreidl, Heller & Co. of Vienna, a maker of sweeteners, synthetic resin, pesticides, and darkening agents, the latter especially important in the manufacture of enamels and ceramics. Degussa, however, wanted only the owner's patents, and the two parties could not agree on the terms of a contract by the time a local

If its objectives remained relatively circumscribed, however, Degussa's behavior toward its opposite numbers in Aryanization proceedings quite obviously degenerated. Seen prior to 1938 as people of standing and accomplishment, the sellers became in the eyes of the enterprise's leaders mere problems to sweep aside at minimum expense. Their firms were treated as no more than the largest items among the many formerly Jewish goods that the regime routinely auctioned off to German citizens or gave away to bombed-out householders, from art objects to bed sets, from watches and jewelry to personal clothing and kitchen utensils.[130]

The ethical hardening that increasingly characterized Degussa's conduct toward Jewish owners was reversed after 1945 no more rapidly than it had developed prior to 1938. Rather than being moved by the uprooting and personal destruction that the erstwhile sellers had experienced, Degussa's representatives used every legal possibility during the restitution wrangle that followed the war to keep, once more at the lowest achievable cost, what the enterprise had obtained. In this, they were aided by the fact that the Nazi regime's program of expulsion and murder had made Aryanization largely irreversible, since few Jews wanted to return to the scene of the crimes or to try to resell their former property from afar and/or in the prevailing postwar economic climate. A brief review of the outcomes of these postwar negotiations is therefore appropriate here, as an indication of not only how slowly the corporation recognized the nature of what it had done, but also of the extent (and the imperfection) of the justice nonetheless achieved. Appendix F provides a tabulation of the Degussa concern's total outlays for acquisition and restitution in each of the twenty-five Aryanization cases to which the firm or a wholly or jointly owned subsidiary was a party.

With regard to Homburg, Degussa contested the Abelmann heirs' claim after 1945 that the sale had occurred under duress and at an unfair price, arguing that (a) he had not really had to sell in 1933 because of his Swiss holding company, and that (b) the family had actually gotten almost 1.5 million marks of the sales price in Swiss francs and still owned both the Degussa stock it had been paid and 5 percent of Homburg. However, perhaps because, in the rather uncharitable view of Degussa's lawyers, "the restitution law gives every emigrant a hunting license, and when he cannot shoot a stag, the courts try to give him at least a rabbit," Degussa accepted the suggestion of the first restitution chamber to hear the case that the parties should

National Socialist, perhaps bankrolled by IG Farben, succeeded in taking control of the firm; see DUA, GKF 5/5, Degussa to Reichsstatthalterei, Abt. Staatskommissar für Wirtschaft, April 30, 1938, and Federlin's Besprechung bei der Auergesellschaft, August 3, 1938. Finally, see GEH 3.Hirtes/12, his Notiz betreffend Zahnfabrik Hoddes, Bad Nauheim, February 1, 1939, in which Hirtes said Degussa's Metall-Abteilung was not interested in the acquisition because "the field of work of this firm is foreign to us."

[130] See Frank Bajohr, "The Beneficiaries of 'Aryanization': Hamburg as a Case Study," *Yad Vashem Studies* 26 (1998), especially pp. 198–201.

work out a settlement.[131] The court proposed an amount of about 200,000 Deutschmarks, but the final agreement of July 1952 called for payments to the Abelmanns of 350,000 Deutschmarks, 150,000 each from Degussa and IG Farben, and 50,000 from Homburg. Degussa also agreed to pay another 90,000 Deutschmarks for the family's remaining shares in their father's former firm.[132]

Concerning the Auergesellschaft, Alfred Koppel declined to agree with Degussa's contention that the sale had taken place without coercion and insisted that the price had been unfair because he had felt forced to sell at a time when the market value of the stock was atypically low. The case dragged on for four years, reaching a low point when one of Degussa's lawyers argued that Alfred Koppel had not been under any real threat, since he was married to a non-Jew.[133] The final settlement called for Degussa to pay Koppel 385,000 Deutschmarks, plus court costs, which was just over half the sum he had sought, but almost four times what Degussa initially had offered.[134] In 1958, Degussa sold almost all of the firm to an American enterprise, retaining only the operations at Gandersheim in the form of the Auer-Glaswerke GmbH.[135]

In the matter of the Weinessigfabrik L. Hirsch, the settlement of 1954 ordered the Gritto-Werke, the successor firm to Fränkische Weinessig, and its owners to pay Hans Hirsch and other family members 245,000 Deutschmarks, plus court costs and most of the plaintiffs' legal fees. Degussa's direct share of the restitution payment came to 18,495 Deutschmarks.[136] In 1962, Degussa's holding in the Gritto-Werke was sold.

[131] DUA, D 2/6, Dekartellisierung (IG Farbenindustrie) – Mayer-Wegelin, Rechts-Abtl. to Scherf, August 19, 1949, quoting Dr. Boesebeck and enclosing a draft settlement offer worked out in consultation with him, and Niederschrift, Achterath and Mayer-Wegelin, August 22, 1949; IW 46.4/1, Akten-Notiz, Betr. Chemiewerk Homburg AG/ Rückerstattungsprozess Abelmann, March 24, 1952, and Cahn (lawyer for the Abelmanns) to Landgericht Frankfurt a.M., April 23, 1952.

[132] DUA, IW 46.4/1, decision of the Landgericht, June 25, 1952.

[133] DUA, IW 24.4/6, Lancelle to Degussa, January 6, 1953.

[134] DUA, IW 24.4/1, Degussa to Koppel in New York, October 20, 1949, enclosing an earlier letter from Degussa to Koppel in Toronto, June 4, 1948; Degussa to Hermann Simon, Koppel's lawyer in New York, August 18, 1950, enclosing the Koppel family's restitution claim to the Magistrat von Gross-Berlin; Degussa to Magistrat, August 17, 1950; Senator für Justiz, Berlin, to Degussa, July 17, 1951; Degussa to Hermann Simon, October 3, 1951; Degussa to Lancelle, May 15, 1952; decision of the 143. Zivilkammer, Landgericht Berlin, September 25, 1954. For a good summary of the unrealistic demands each side made during the process, see IW 24.18/1, Pulch's Bericht über die Entwicklung der Auergesellschaft, April 29, 1955.

[135] Klauer (ed.), Geschichte der Auergesellschaft, pp. 47–48.

[136] DUA, IW 41.4./1, Gritto-Werke GmbH, Schweinfurt, Vergleich, May 6, 1954. I have not yet clarified the terms of the settlements regarding two smaller enterprises that had been absorbed into Fränkische at the time of its takeover. As of 1949, Degussa was trying to retain them by offering to return their owners a parcel of real estate as compensation; see D2/6, Meyer-Wegelin's Notiz für Herrn Scherf, August 24, 1949.

Regarding Marquart, Meno Lissauer asserted in 1948 that he would never have sold the firm but for Nazi persecution, hence sought restitution, but preferred a continuing business arrangement with his old firm and the return of Leo Klopfer as its chief manager to a cash payment. In October 1949, Lissauer's assorted companies became the principal supplier of raw materials to Marquart, with the right to have them processed for export at cost; Klopfer recovered his old job; and the case was dropped.[137] Two years later, Klopfer ascended to Marquart's supervisory board, Degussa having meanwhile agreed to pay the half of its contractual obligations that had been voided by Klopfer's emigration, plus 4 percent annual interest.[138]

In settlement of the claims of Theodor Meyer arising from the events at Grünau, Degussa agreed in 1950 to pay him a one-time sum of 18,000 Deutschmarks; an annual pension of 6,000 Deutschmarks, including to his heirs until the seventh year after his death; and license fees on the proceeds of Grünau's basic products of 1.5 percent per year from 1948 to 1958 and .75 percent per year thereafter, but in no case less than 90,000 Deutschmarks during the earlier period and 30,000 during the later one.[139]

In June 1953, the Federal Ministry of Finance in Austria instructed Degussa to restore the shares that "were taken away" from the Margulies family, including those that Paul had sold, and to pay each family member the corresponding share of all net profits that had been earned since March 1, 1947. In 1955, the Margulieses sold all their shares in ÖCW to Leukon AG, which still belonged to Degussa and which expanded the holding into a majority in the Austrian firm the following year, thus restoring it to Degussa's portfolio.[140]

The final arrangements with regard to Kulzer are not entirely clear from the surviving records. Jacob Frank, the partner who had been paid with American property, appears never to have filed a restitution claim. The heirs of Arthur Fuld got a minimum of 245,000 Deutschmarks from Degussa and Hereaus in 1950, which was converted to U.S. $30,000 by an elaborate

---

[137] DUA, IW 21.2/1, correspondence with Meno Lissauer, January 1948–October 1949. Nethe, the former sales director, chose not to return to Germany, and became the firm's commercial leader in Holland.

[138] DUA, IW 21.2/1, assorted documents, September 24, 1948–March 9, 1951.

[139] DUA, IW 22.2/1, Amt f. Vermögenskontrolle u. Wiedergutmachung, Frankfurt, June 2, 1950. In addition, Grünau signed a consulting contract with Th. Meyer in 1957 that paid him another 2,000 Deutschmarks per year until his death in 1961; UV 2/12, Urkundenverwaltung.

[140] DUA, AW 5.2/3, Bundesministerium f. Finanzen an Herrn Dr. Julius Jeannée, Wien, June 15, 1953. In the meantime, Erwin Margulies had died in Paris in 1949, so his heirs collected his portion of the settlement. Peter, Marianne, and Paul, who was by then working at a hydrogen peroxide plant in Buffalo, NY, were the other beneficiaries. The Margulies family home on the Karlsplatz was seized by the Austrian state in 1946, and I have not traced its legal status thereafter. See, on all of this, AW 5.2/1, Erinnerungen von W. Josef Skowronek, pp. 44, 80–82, 99.

banking process that occasioned an inquiry from the state financial authorities in Wiesbaden. Degussa defended the procedure successfully by pointing out that it had saved German ownership of Kulzer, which would have been lost if the heirs had reclaimed their 75 percent of the stock. Arthur Fuld's descendants may have received up to another 100,000 Deutschmarks, depending on the behavior of other claimants, which is not documented. In a separate settlement, Arthur Isaacson (who by now had changed his name to Saxon) received the equivalent of 370,000 Deutschmarks, some of it from the convertible profits of Kulzer's Brazilian subsidiary. Finally, Arthur Engel, a former partner and half-Jew whose patent rights had been infringed by Kulzer, was awarded 220,000 Deutschmarks.[141]

No claims for compensation appear to have been made regarding the Carbidfabrik in Wyhlen or the Austrian patent. When Communist regimes came to power in East Germany and Czechoslovakia, Degussa lost title to Hydrocarbon, Aurora, and the factories in Prague, and hence could no longer be sued for restitution. Similarly, the home on Vienna's Karlsplatz that had been bought from the Margulieses was seized by the Austrian state after the war.

Finally, Alfred Merton does not appear to have claimed compensation for his sale of stock in the Metallgesellschaft in 1934, and Richard Merton had to seek restitution from the Prussian State Bank for the shares he signed over in 1938, so Degussa retained title to all of these acquisitions. As part of the American decartellization program, however, Degussa agreed to sell its entire 13.56 percent holding in the Metallgesellschaft via the Rhein-Main Bank, one of the entities into which the Deutsche Bank was temporarily divided during the 1950s, and to share some of the proceeds with it. After being converted from Reichsmarks to Deutschmarks on a ratio of 5:4, the shares were sold at an average rate of return for Degussa of 181.7 percent.[142] In other words, the 1,140,000 RM in shares taken from the Mertons and other Jews in 1934 and in 1939–40 (for which Degussa had paid about 1,181,000 RM) were converted to 912,000 Deutschmarks, then sold for 1,657,104

---

[141] DUA, D 2/21, Ergänzung zur Notiz Dekartellisierung Degussa, August 12, 1949, by Mayer-Wegelin; UV 1/43, settlement of June 23, 1950 with heirs of Arthur Fuld; Degussa to Oberfinanzdir. Wiesbaden, Dr. Jahn, March 2, 1953; HHW, 519/V, 3107/1, Wirtschaftsprüfungsbericht für das Jahr 1948 (on Frank), Vergleich, August 23, 1950 (on Saxon), and Vergleichsprotokoll, June 15, 1951 (on Engel). According to DL 11.5./48, Heinz Mayer-Wegelin to Dr. Schramm, IG Leverkusen, May 3, 1948, the heirs claimed that Degussa's deal with the Gauleiter had short-circuited an offer from IG Farben to buy the shares with foreign exchange, but the Leverkusen plant of the giant concern claimed after the war to have no record of such an offer.

[142] DUA, DL 3.Scherf/1, Ludwig Erhard to the Allied High Commission, January 29, 1952; Degussa to Oberfinanzdirektion Frankfurt, March 21, 1956. BU Hermann Schlosser, Pichler's unheaded note of April 25, 1967, indicates that Schlosser told her he was glad of the American order to sell, since "the proceeds of it were badly needed for reconstruction."

Deutschmarks, thus yielding Degussa a striking profit. By any process of computation that allows for the difference in the worth of the currencies, the return on this package of Aryanizations went far toward offsetting the restitution paid for all the others.

In sum, by 1962, the Aryanized properties that remained part of Degussa's industrial realm came down to most of the real estate parcels, the minorities in ÖCW and Grünau, and four flourishing productive units: Homburg, Wyhlen, Marquart, and Kulzer. Allowing for all the expenses of acquiring and maintaining these entities – even allowing for any nonrecovered investments (after government payment for war damage and loss of property in East Germany and the territory annexed by Poland) in the plants that were nationalized – as well as for the proceeds on the sale of the firms Degussa parted with (e.g., Auer, and the Gritto-Werke), there can be little doubt that the balance sheet of Aryanization remained positive for Degussa long into the postwar era.

4

Autarky and Armament

On January 9, 1934, Degussa's managing board reported to its stockholders on the first business year completed under National Socialism. Calling sales "normal" and "fairly satisfactory" in the period from October 1932 through September 1933, since "in the course of the year worsening export difficulties were somewhat offset by a certain improvement in the domestic market mentioned already in the last report," the directors nevertheless sounded a cautionary note:

We cannot conceal that the export conditions for most of our fields [of production] are continuously and considerably worsening. In this, the boycott movement abroad plays a much smaller role than the great and in the most recent past growing drive in almost all countries to produce as much as possible of some of our products at home. We consider it our duty to note that we see in this movement a danger for the future profitability of the Scheideanstalt.[1]

Almost four years later, as Ernst Busemann began drafting the final report on the business year 1936/37, the air had long since gone out of "the boycott movement abroad" in reaction to the brutalities that followed the Nazi takeover.[2] Yet, the foreign trade situation remained troubling, and he planned to emphasize once more that "we place the greatest weight on the cultivation of exports (foreign business)."[3]

The similar preoccupation of these comments was – and is – profoundly misleading. To be sure, they reflected a constant concern that went with doing business in a relatively resource-poor country such as Germany. But this structural continuity also masked fundamental transformations that took place during the interval between the two statements, both in Degussa's own business and in the role of corporations in the German economy. Whereas at the end of 1933, the firm's concerns about foreign trade were microeconomic (that is, they frankly reflected worries about the future health of

---

[1] DUA, Bericht über das 62. Geschäftsjahr 1932/33, prepared for the general meeting of the stockholders on January 9, 1934, pp. 6–7.

[2] Edwin Black vastly overstates the effects of the movement to boycott German exports in the United States in *The Transfer Agreement* (New York: Macmillan, 1984) and *IBM and the Holocaust* (New York: Crown, 2001).

[3] DUA, DL 3.Busemann/5, his memo Betr. Jahresbericht, October 22, 1937.

Degussa's own balance sheets), by late 1937, the situation was somewhat different. Doubts about the ability of an individual firm, even in the once highly export-dependent chemical industry, to rely predominantly on domestic demand had not disappeared from the Frankfurt headquarters in the interim, but they had declined in urgency. After all, the enterprise's workforce had more than doubled since September 1933, and the total worth and net profits recorded on Degussa's published balance sheets and confidential tax returns had climbed to unprecedented levels (see Appendix B), yet export proceeds had played an annually falling part in these results (see Appendix E). Even before the share of foreign sales in the corporation's total turnover hit its peacetime low of 15 percent in the business year 1938/39, income from both marketing and manufacturing operations abroad almost had ceased to matter as a direct source of revenue to Degussa or most major German companies. For one thing, they generally could not retain foreign-denominated proceeds on activities abroad, but had to place these at the service of the German state by swapping them for Reichsmarks at the National Bank.[4] In addition, the sums obtained overseas usually were, as a result of prevailing exchange rates and price levels and despite the subsidies provided through the German Export Promotion Procedure (ZAV), less than those that selling the same goods at home would have yielded. Only a desire to preserve market positions abroad as insurance against a future domestic downturn gave firms such as Degussa a continuing commercial interest in sustaining exports as of 1937.

But exports still mattered immediately – and vitally – to Degussa because the German Reich needed them to keep domestic demand rising. That upward thrust, initially propelled by highway and other forms of government-fostered construction, drew momentum after 1935 largely from the twin Nazi programs of armament and autarky, that is, boosting German military power and reducing German dependence on foreign goods to levels that would serve Hitler's expansionist objectives.[5] Without proceeds from overseas, the Reich could not pay for certain materials obtainable only abroad

---

[4] See, for example, DUA, BET 9/136, Degussa to I.G. Farbenindustrie A.G., January 21, 1937, which records the liquidation of the hidden reserves of the Österreichische Chemische Werke, pursuant to an order of October 23, 1936 from the Reichsstelle für Devisenbewirtschaftung. After the conversion of Degussa's and Farben's joint share of these into 335,569 Swiss francs, the sum was furnished to the Reichsbank in return for 191,140 RM, split evenly between the German partners. Also relevant is IW 3.6/1, Siebert GmbH to Reichsbankdirektorium, April 20, 1937, which reports on the delivery to the Reichsbank of a blocked account in Swiss francs that Degussa had held at the Bankhaus Greutert & Co. in Basel.

[5] See, and compare the accounts of, R. J. Overy, *The Nazi Economic Recovery 1932–1938* (London: Macmillan, 1982) and *War and Economy in the Third Reich* (Oxford: Clarendon Press, 1994); Fritz Blaich, *Wirtschaft und Rüstung im "Dritten Reich"* (Düsseldorf: Schwann, 1987); Harold James, *The German Slump* (Oxford: Clarendon Press, 1986); and Dan P. Silverman, *Hitler's Economy* (Cambridge: Harvard University Press, 1998).

and indispensable to either the manufacture of weapons or the construction of factories to produce import substitutes.[6] Without generating the necessary earnings, therefore, private firms not only faced the prospect of an economic implosion, but also opened themselves to the charge of being inadequate to the Fatherland's geopolitical challenges and hence, as Hitler menacingly remarked in his confidential memorandum of August 1936 on the Four Year Plan, of being "unfit for survival in this modern age."[7]

Thus, when Busemann renewed Degussa's commitment to international commerce in 1937, he was no longer speaking the liberal capitalist language of economic interdependence or referring primarily to the need for his firm to remain competitive in world markets, as his managing board had four years earlier – much as he may have wished to be doing so. Instead, he was responding to the macroeconomic imperatives of the Reich's balance of payments and thus confirming Fritz Roessler's recent prophecy concerning the cameralist economic system he saw being recreated in Nazi Germany: "The executive will work in the future in the truest sense 'for the King of Prussia,' only now one says: for the people's community."[8]

Busemann's announcement of the renewed export drive, in fact, opened the business year that marked Degussa's virtual conscription into the Nazi economic system – the year in which the firm's leaders not only ceased being able to behave with consideration toward Jewish employees and property owners, as described in Chapter 3, but also largely lost control, without comprehending it yet, over the direction of their own enterprise. During the first four years of Nazi rule, as the regime concentrated on reviving employment and production in Germany by means that intruded only marginally – and allegedly temporarily – on corporations' autonomy, Degussa could remain focused on Busemann's diversification program. Thus, the firm's annual investments in new buildings or machinery never exceeded yearly levels of depreciation during this period, and most of the fruits of economic recovery could be directed toward acquisitions and retained earnings (see Appendix B for the development of Degussa's sales, fixed capital, portfolio of subsidiaries, and surplus of assets over liabilities). But in 1937–38, the Reich's cumulative success in creating a "carrot and stick" economy, one in which a militantly expansionist government alternately could lure and lash corporations in the directions it preferred, began to get the better of Degussa's chairman.[9] His corporate strategy – indeed, any independently defined

[6] The most up-to-date study of this problem is Albrecht Ritschl, "Die deutsche Zahlungsbilanz 1936–41 und das Problem des Devisenmangels vor dem Kriegsausbruch," *Vierteljahrshefte für Zeitgeschichte* 39 (1991), pp. 103–23.
[7] Quoted in Wilhelm Treue, "Hitlers Denkschrift zum Vierjahresplan 1936," *Vierteljahreshefte für Zeitgeschichte* 3 (1955), p. 209.
[8] DUA, BU Fritz Roessler, "Zur Geschichte der Scheideanstalt" [1937], Abschrift, p. 100.
[9] For a description of this process, see Peter Hayes, *Industry and Ideology: IG Farben in the Nazi Era* (New York: Cambridge University Press, second edition, 2001), as well as the same

one – henceforth took a backseat to coping with incentives and pressures from Berlin that increasingly dictated the enterprise's financial decisions and reconfigured its activities. For the rest of the Nazi era, Degussa's managers would struggle to regain control of events, deluded by their operational responsibilities and swelling earnings into thinking that they were laboring to retain it. But in truth, to modify Richard Grunbergers memorable metaphor, they already had been demoted from drivers of the corporate bus to mere fare collectors.[10] The Primacy of Politics proclaimed by the Third Reich increasingly determined not only where the firm was headed, but also the speed and conditions of the journey.

This remaking of Degussa's business into an instrument of National Socialist objectives proceeded with most eventually criminal consequences in the firm's traditional, core sectors of precious metals and cyanide-based fumigants, which are treated separately in Chapters 5 and 8. But the rest of Degussa's operations also underwent this metamorphosis, especially three of the fields opened up and out during Busemann's diversification drive: carbon black; air purification devices, including gas masks; and the organic chemicals produced by the HIAG division. It was the Nazi regime's promotion of production in these fields, its use of state power to generate markets for them and to funnel resources to them, that signaled Degussa's transformation, like that of most German manufacturers during the 1930s, from a purely private enterprise, though it remained nominally so, into a quasi-public one, a servant of "national interests" as defined in Berlin. Sealed by the proclamation of the Four Year Plan in 1936, the "indirect socialization" that industrialists had exaggeratedly bewailed as the hallmark of economic policy in the Weimar Republic became a scarcely contested reality under Nazism. Only now the state itself, not wage or salary earners, was to be the chief beneficiary, and now the demand for firms' output, as well as the proceeds from it, was to be channeled toward government-sanctioned ends.

The history of Degussa's involvement with the manufacture of gas-based (later styled: active) carbon black provides an almost prototypical demonstration of how the Nazi regime's priorities molded the firm's commercial development during the 1930s – and of how decisive the year 1937/38 proved in this process. As a key component of durable rubber tires, the granular, sootlike product engaged the attention of Hitler's new government almost immediately. It wanted to foster German motorization but faced the problem

author's "Polycracy and Policy in the Third Reich: The Case of the Economy," in Thomas Childers and Jane Caplan (eds.), *Re-evaluating the Third Reich* (New York: Holmes & Meier, 1993), pp. 190–210, and "Industry under the Swastika," in Harold James and Jakob Tanner (eds.), *Enterprise in the Period of Fascism in Europe* (London: Ashgate, 2002), pp. 26–37. Also essential in this regard is Avraham Barkai, *Nazi Economics* (New Haven: Yale University Press, 1990).

[10] Richard Grunberger, *The 12-Year Reich* (New York: Holt, Rinehart and Winston, 1971), p. 184.

that the Reich imported most of the additive from the United States, thanks largely to the price and quality advantages conferred on American manufacturers by their ample supplies of cheap natural gas, a raw material that would-be rivals in Germany lacked. Among those rivals was Degussa, which just before the Nazi takeover had acquired its own reasons for wanting to break the American hold on the German market. In November 1932, Busemann's search for investment opportunities and Hermann Schlosser's quest to extend Degussa's marketing program led to the purchase of the August Wegelin AG, which controlled about half of the existing, but largely obsolescent and unused German capacity to make carbon black from coal.[11] Operating at only 15 percent of its potential, the new subsidiary could offer Degussa little more than a slightly better return on its sales apparatus and short-term tax benefits unless the main plant at Kalscheuren near Cologne could be converted to turning out a substance that challenged the American one effectively. Accordingly, while Schlosser bought time during 1933 by assembling the other German manufacturers into a new cartel and getting Kalscheuren's production quota raised, Degussa responded to prodding from the German Economics Ministry and launched a feverish research effort in Frankfurt.[12] At a cost of some 370,000 RM, a team led by Dr. Harry Kloepfer overcame the main hurdle, identifying a domestically available raw material to substitute for natural gas, and solved the principal manufacturing problems in remarkably short order. By June 1934, Degussa had a mass-producible form of carbon black, dubbed CK3, that equalled the American product in quality but resulted from gassifying naphthalene, a distillate of coal tar.

Kloepfer's technical virtuosity (he accomplished in less than a year what a division of IG Farben had been trying unsuccessfully to achieve since 1928) presented Degussa, however, with new difficulties. His discovery was not yet price competitive, had no track record with potential buyers, and would require substantial new plant investment. Unless the Economics Ministry was prepared to put its money where its mouth had been, the task of turning Degussa's potential contribution to "national self-sufficiency" into a profitable venture remained intimidating. Consequently, during the summer of 1934, the enterprise lobbied the Nazi regime for assistance and won it, after hard bargaining, in two rather circumscribed forms. First, Acting Economics

---

[11] This and the following paragraph rest, unless otherwise indicated, on DUA, DL 13.3/1, K. Bonath, "Russ. Geschichte der Verfahren, der Produktion, der Entwicklung und der Forschungsarbeiten," dated July 1969, especially pp. 13–14, 17–21, and 40–44; as well as DL 3.H.Schlosser/3, Schlosser's memo Russgeschäft Degussa, December 18, 1941, enclosing Federlin's Notiz für Herrn. Dr. Achterath betr. Russ, December 2, 1941. For Schlosser's reasons for favoring the purchase of Wegelin, see DL 5/35, Schlosser's Notiz betr. Wegelin, September 10, 1932.

[12] DUA, DL 3.Baerwind/17, Baerwind's Aktenvermerk betreffend Aktivruss, November 2, 1933, records the decision to undertake the research effort.

Minister Schacht issued an order prohibiting the reactivation, construction, and expansion of any German carbon black plant unless specifically authorized by him, thus partially insulating an attempt to actualize Degussa's invention from additional domestic competition.[13] Second, the Economics Ministry guaranteed a price of 1 RM per kilogram for the first 2,400 metric tons of output under Degussa's new process for the first two years, which would cover the costs of going over to large-scale production and thus relieve the firm of immediate risk. These undertakings smoothed the way for Degussa's decision to authorize work in October 1934 on a suitable installation at Kalscheuren, with an initial capacity of 600 tons per year but a built-in possibility of quick expansion to twice that level.

But in return for insuring Degussa's growth, the government demanded the right to determine its pace, extent, and form: not only had Kalscheuren to be operational within six months, but also still another plant, this one capable of 3,000 tons per year and located in a less militarily exposed region east of the Rhine, had to be completed by October 1935.[14] Nor were these the only ways in which the Nazi Reich proved an uncongenial partner. Degussa's designated contacts at the Economics Ministry constantly changed their projections of German demand for carbon black and the appropriate ways of meeting it, toyed with other possible suppliers, dallied over imposing tariffs on American imports, displayed favoritism toward a parallel, ultimately impracticable pilot project by Degussa's HIAG division to make the substance from methane, and even on one occasion called Degussa "punishable" for its failure to apply for construction permits by the government-established deadlines.[15]

As a result, within only six months of Kloepfer's triumph, even Hermann Schlosser, ever the believer that "one can make something out of anything," was inclined to restrict Degussa's carbon black venture to Kalscheuren while waiting to see how the market developed, though for tactical reasons, he assured the Economics Ministry that the firm would "immediately seriously investigate" four named sites in central Germany for a second plant.[16] Ernst Busemann, moreover, had grown downright pessimistic. In January 1935, he concluded that "the CK3 process looks simply hopeless in the long run," since the supply and price of naphthalene were uncertain, the prospects of attaining price parity with American carbon black doubtful, and, in that event,

[13] DUA, GPT 4/1, Schacht's Anordnung über das Verbot zur Errichtung von Anlagen zur Herstellung von Russ, August 17, 1934.

[14] DUA, DL 3.Baerwind/18, Baerwind's memo on Grossfabrikatorische Herstellung von Gasruss ab April 1935 beziehungsweise ab Oktober 1935, August 24, 1934.

[15] DUA, GPT 4/1, Schlosser's Aktennotiz. Betr. Russ, October 18, 1934.

[16] *Ibid.*, and Schlosser's Besprechung im Reichswirtschaftsministerium über Russ, January 26, 1935; his optimistic remark is quoted in DUA, DL 13.3/1, Pichler's undated memo on Übertragung unserer Russinteressen auf die Auergesellschaft 1935 und Rückübertragung 1938.

the Economics Ministry's commitments unreliable. Frustrated, as well, that his firm had expended some 2 million marks on carbon black to date (including for HIAG's pilot program), without achieving a sure return, he moved to shift part of the accumulated and all of the future costs of development onto Degussa's newly acquired and momentarily cash-rich subsidiary, Degea AG (the Auergesellschaft). As the month came to a close, he sold Frankfurt's stock in Wegelin, along with all production responsibilities for carbon black, to Auer at 70 percent of par plus reimbursement for the research and development expenditures to date on CK3, and he billed Wegelin for the first 200,000 RM in new construction costs at Kalscheuren. Degussa retained responsibility for selling the output, which shortly began to pile up in warehouses because the tire makers proved slow to place orders.[17] Meanwhile, at the end of February, Degussa and Auer pled raw material shortages as an excuse for declining to pursue further the idea of building a second CK3 plant.[18]

For a time, the second thoughts of Wegelin's old and new owners seemed to make an impression on the economic authorities in Berlin. Having repeatedly refused to authorize Kalscheuren's expansion to 1,200 tons annually unless Degussa/Auer broke ground on a second plant, they backtracked so far during 1935 that yearly production at the initial site rose to 1,800 tons.[19] To be sure, mounting inventories drove Degussa in April 1936 into price concessions that reduced prospective income on this output: in return for assurance that the tire makers would buy at least 1,400 tons per year, Kalscheuren agreed to charge only seventy-five pfennigs per kilogram.[20] Even so, Busemann's financial worries eased. If the long-term outlook for CK3 remained uncertain, the product appeared on the verge of at least paying for itself and for Degussa's acquisition of the Wegelin firm, after which it would be returning a profit, however insecure. But, the respite from official pressure to sink more resources into the substance did not occur in deference to

---

[17] Busemann's reservations are listed in DUA, IW 24.5/2, Busemann to Schlosser, January 28, 1935. The sale to Auer, formalized the following day, is detailed in the same volume; see especially Bernau's memo on the Auergesellschaft, January 21, 1935; Busemann and Bernau to the Direktion der Degea AG (Auergesellschaft), January 23, 1935; Schlosser's Übergang des Aktienbesitzes . . . , January 23, 1935; and Busemann's Aufsichtsratsitzung der Degea am 29. Januar 1935, dated February 1, and enclosing the memo from Auer's management to the members of its supervisory board, January 24, 1935. On the HIAG project, conducted in cooperation with the Hibernia mine, see GPT 4/1, Róka's Stand der Russversuche bei der Scheideanstalt, November 13, 1934. On the accumulation of inventory in 1934, DL 3.H.Schlosser/3, Federlin's Notiz für Herrn Dr. Achterath betr. Russ, December 2, 1941, p. 6.
[18] DUA, IW 24.5/2, Schlosser's Russ. Aussprache mit der DEGEA in Berlin, February 26, 1935.
[19] See DUA, GPT 4/1, Hagemann of the Economics Ministry to the Scheideanstalt, February 1, 1935, for the final refusal to authorize expansion at Kalscheuren.
[20] See DUA, DL 13.3/1, Bonath's Russ report, p. 24; and DL 3.H.Schlosser/3, Federlin's memo of December 2, 1941, p. 6.

such private commercial considerations. It stemmed rather from temporary circumstances, primarily the Economics Ministry's continuing inability to gauge Germany's likely carbon black needs or to bet on one or all of several possible production processes for the gas-based variant of the product: CK3; IG Farben's similar procedure, which came on line at Ludwigshafen in 1936; and a method being developed by the Continental Rubber Co. of Hanover in cooperation with Krupp to obtain carbon black from residues of anthracene, another distillate of coal tar.[21]

With the inauguration of the Four Year Plan in September 1936 and the appointment of an apparatus to direct it that included an Office for German Raw Materials, this impasse was broken. Both Air Force Lieutenant Colonel Fritz Löb, the new head of the Office, and Johannes Eckell, a former employee of IG Farben who now led the Chemicals Section within it, brought considerable fervor to their new duties, which developments with regard to active carbon black gave them occasion to demonstrate within only weeks of assuming their posts. The impetus came from the maturation of the Continental-Krupp pilot project. By October 1936, it had recorded sufficient success that the rubber company was offering Krupp a six-figure amount for complete control of the production rights and had put together a consortium of tire makers (Ideuka) to build a corresponding plant on the outskirts of Dortmund, on the east bank of the Rhine, for which the land and the gas supply already had been purchased. The partners' need for an exemption from the standing prohibition on new carbon black plants – which would amount to an authorization to enter into competition with Degussa – now presented Eckell with a dilemma that he turned into an opportunity. Though eager to enlist industry behind his goal of producing enough additional tons of gas-based carbon black from German resources annually to emancipate the domestic rubber industry from American imports, Eckell had contradictory information about the available production processes. The Ideuka procedure enjoyed the advantage of being based on a cheaper, slightly more plentiful raw material than Degussa's CK3, but the latter's machinery was less liable to break down, indeed had been thoroughly tested over months of smooth operation.[22] Given this, Eckell applied what became virtually standard practice under the Four Year Plan: he coupled his approval for the new factory with peremptory stipulations – the owners would have to provide the full 6,000 tons that he currently wanted, and they would have to mix or merge their processes so as to do so in the promptest and cheapest feasible manner. In short, the consortium of tire makers got enough of a green light to threaten Degussa with exclusion from a burgeoning market unless the Frankfurt firm entered into some sort of partnership with them, while

---

[21] On the competing processes, see DL 13.3/1, Bonath's Russ report, pp. 22 and 41.

[22] *Ibid.*, pp. 22–24; on the raw material supplies, see also DL 3.Baerwind/20, Aktenvermerk betreffend Russbesprechung beim "Rohstoff- und Devisenstab" . . . , October 20, 1936.

the maker of CK3 got the chance to limit its losses by demonstrating the superiority of its production method, even when applied to a different raw material.

The result, worked out in intense negotiations during November 1936, was a three-part agreement between Degussa and the rubber firms.[23] First, the Auergesellschaft, as the nominal owner of Wegelin's Kalscheuren plant, agreed to assume half the stock capital of a new carbon black firm, the Russwerke Dortmund, and the consortium members divided the remaining 2 million Reichsmarks worth of shares, with Continental taking 29 percent of the total, German Dunlop 7 percent, and seven other companies (Deka, Englebert, Phoenix, Fulda, Vorwerk, Metzler, and the German branch of Michelin) 1 to 3 percent each. Degussa got the right to name the new entity's business manager for operations (Dr. Backe), and the tire firms the one for sales (Dr. Hermann); whereas the ten voting seats on the supervisory board were split evenly, with the nonvoting chairman, a lawyer named Georg Kemnitz, regarded as neutral. Second, the tire makers promised to abide by the earlier agreement of April 1936 and to purchase the first 1,400 tons of carbon black needed annually from Kalscheuren. Third, Degussa licensed its CK3 process to the new enterprise at a fee of two pfennigs per kilogram of output, and the Russwerke contracted to furnish the rubber firms directly with up to 6,000 more tons per year at a price that reflected only manufacturing costs plus an allowance for full amortization of any new installations within ten years and 5 percent annual interest on the invested capital. Once the facilities were paid off, the tire manufacturers were free of further obligation to buy from the new firm; meanwhile, any output beyond what they needed would be sold by Degussa on commission.[24] In other words, by exploiting its head start in the production of carbon black, Degussa managed to coopt a competing technology, gain access to the proceeds on growing demand (via both license fees and dividends from the new firm), and limit its exposure to possible changes in international market conditions or national economic policy (through the pricing scheme).

The agreements of November 1936 were later the source of some controversy within Degussa. Charges that its managers had unnecessarily "given away" the chance to control all production of gas-based carbon black in

---

[23] See DUA, DL 11.5/40, Schlosser to Kemnitz, November 19, 1936, in which the Degussa manager argues that the new firm being discussed "for us...seen from a private economic perspective not only is completely unattractive, but also constitutes in many respects a substantial burden" and goes on say "that we even today would be completely ready...to leave the field to the tire makers alone."

[24] DUA, D 2/20, Summary of the carbon black agreement for the American occupation authorities, 1947; DL 13.3/1, Bonath's Russ report, pp. 24–26; DL 11.5/40, Schlosser to Degea AG, November 21, 1936; and PCA 2/10, Federlin's Vertrauliche Notiz betr. Russwerke Dortmund GmbH, November 30, 1936, and Kemnitz to Amt für deutsche Roh- und Werkstoffe, November 27, 1936.

Germany became sufficiently audible after World War II that both Schlosser and Ernst Baerwind, who had judged the Continental-Krupp project viable "even without our cooperation," wrote memoranda in 1952 defending their decision to ally with the rubber consortium.[25] As late as 1969, one Degussa expert concluded, however, after reviewing Continental's own records of the negotiations, that the tire maker had "mightily bluffed."[26] But the critics were being wise after the fact – and missing the historical point. Schlosser and Baerwind had to react quickly in 1936 to events that took them by surprise. Indeed, Baerwind seems scarcely to have known what hit him that October, when Eckell summoned him with only two days' notice to a "dictatorially" scheduled meeting in Berlin to deal with the carbon black situation.[27] Measured by market position, the two Degussa executives probably salvaged as much as was possible, if not more, during the ensuing month. The arrangements they secured, after all, both proved lucrative for Degussa until the end of the Nazi era (see Appendices C–E) and laid the foundation of the firm's status fifty-five years later as the second-largest producer of carbon black worldwide, with an international market share of about 15 percent.[28]

The chief costs to the firm of what happened, which went unmentioned apparently in the postwar internal discussion, concerned its autonomy, and they became ultimately, as a result, moral rather than material. Degussa now became inescapably enmeshed in a governmental decision-making process that paid scant regard to commercial considerations because the product involved was essential to the Nazi regime's expansionist course. Carbon black production henceforth had to increase continuously in order to feed the Wehrmacht's growing appetite for tires, an appetite that powered the foreign policy of the Third Reich – and came to be powered by its barbaric exploitation of human beings. That a contingent of concentration camp inmates drawn from in and around Auschwitz was put to work in 1942–45 at a carbon black factory owned by the (by then renamed) Russwerke (see Chapter 7) symbolizes the close connection of this product, and thus of the firm, with the terrible toll Nazi aggression would exact.

At its inception, however, the fateful outcome of Degussa's new partnership was all but beyond anticipation; more immediately and obviously

[25] DUA, DL 11.5/40, Schlosser's Betr. Deutsche Gasrusswerke Dortmund, July 29, 1952 (in which the first quoted remark appears), and Baerwind's Notiz betreffend die Entstehungsgeschichte der Deutschen Gasrusswerke Dortmund, July 31, 1952 (which is the source of the second quoted passage).

[26] DUA, DL 13.3/1, Bonath's Russ report, p. 24.

[27] DUA, DL 3.Baerwind/20, Aktenvermerk betreffend Russbesprechung beim "Rohstoff- und Devisenstab," Berlin..., October 20, 1936.

[28] On Degussa's postwar expansion of carbon black production, see Mechthild Wolf, *Im Zeichen von Sonne und Mond* (Frankfurt am Main: Degussa AG, 1993), pp. 170 and 292. For the firm's international market share and ranking at the end of the twentieth century, see *Verschmelzung Degussa AG und Hüls AG künftig Degussa-Hüls AG* [1999], Teil B: Verschmelzungsbericht, p. 53.

troublesome were its financial requirements, at which Busemann bridled, and the tensions that arose from working with the tire makers and the Four Year Plan administration. The nub of both problems was that Degussa was laboring to apply its carbon black production process to a new raw material (anthracene residues). This worked quickly in small-scale tests but took time to translate into industrial practice. In order to perfect the relevant machinery so as to assure an uninterrupted, cost-efficient flow of the output (labeled CK4 in order to distinguish it from Kalscheuren's), Degussa's builders envisioned erecting a factory consisting of four freestanding production halls, each fabricating 1,500 tons. These were to be constructed in sequence, with each new hall designed to improve upon experience gained in operating the previous one, thus saving on outlays and simultaneously reducing unit costs and widening profit margins. Though logical to an enterprise worried about recovering its investments in what was still an uncompetitive product under open-market conditions, such planning was bound to run afoul of the considerations that dominated in Eckell's office. There speed was of the essence, and one thing alone mattered: getting the Dortmund factory fully operational in tandem with IG Farben's synthetic rubber (Buna) plant at Schkopau, started a year earlier.[29] Moreover, while this goal made Eckell a constant source of pressure to build quickly rather than prudently, Colonel Löb's insistence on design changes to render the new installation impervious to air attack also pushed the cost estimates for the Russwerke plant upward.[30] This made Degussa's managers, who were exclusively responsible for constructing the new factory, all the more intent on wringing every possible saving from a deliberate building tempo.

Thus, for a full year after the founding of the Russwerke, the Raw Materials Office and Ernst Baerwind of Degussa wrangled over the construction timetable until their mutual frustration erupted into an open test of wills.[31] Eckell's patience had been stretched to the limit by his Office's reckoning that the Reich's annual carbon black needs had grown to 20,000 tons, Baerwind's by his staff's arithmetic that the total expense for the new installation had swollen to 9 million Reichsmarks, a sum vastly exceeding the rather arbitrarily set figure of 4 million marks that the partners had invested a year earlier. Thus, the former man insisted on the immediate completion of all four manufacturing halls, whereas the latter countered with a "rough, commercially reasonable (naturally nonbinding) program – in contrast to the precipitate one of the Raw Materials Office" that foresaw starting up

---

[29] On the struggle between IG Farben and the Four Year Plan administration over this plant, which paralleled Degussa's experience with carbon black, see Hayes, *Industry and Ideology*, pp. 148–51, 188–91.

[30] See, on both Eckell's adamance concerning the building tempo and the costs of air defense, DUA, DL 3.Baerwind/20, Aussprache beim Rohstoffstab über die Errichtung der Dortmunder Russfabrik, January 23, 1937.

[31] For example, see DUA, DL 3.Baerwind/20, Besuch beim Rohstoffstab..., March 15, 1937.

the first hall in the middle of 1938 and the second one toward the end of the year, at which time final decisions would be made about the design and equipment of the remaining two.[32] At a meeting with four representatives of the Russwerke on November 19, 1937, Eckell reiterated his conviction that the Reich's needs demanded that "even commercially fully justified considerations must be consciously suspended" and declared that he could not countenance a delay in reaching full production until the end of 1939 or the beginning of 1940. He, therefore, moved to break Baerwind's resistance by threatening to reallocate supplies of iron and steel to the expansion of IG Farben's acetylene-based carbon black output and away from Dortmund, thus endangering the completion of that installation and with it the recovery of its owners' investments.[33]

This gambit adroitly opened a split between Degussa and its tire-making partners. Even after Baerwind's sounding of IG Farben revealed that firm's lack of interest in increasing its carbon black production, they found other reasons, above all an interest in Eckell's later cooperation with regard to pricing, to justify concessions to his sense of urgency.[34] Baerwind grudgingly consented, but Degussa and the Auergesellschaft now selected a new ground on which to take their stand: the issue of financing the Russwerke beyond the 4 million marks at which it had been capitalized.[35] They flatly rejected the tire firms' suggestions that the investors double their respective shareholdings or back a bank loan of comparable size to pay for the accelerated completion of the plant. Instead, arguing that the commercial viability of the installation could not be assumed, the Degussa/Auer members of the Russwerke supervisory board took the position that "if the Raw Materials Office forces the construction of the factory against commercial considerations, then it must effect a governmentally guaranteed loan" to fund the plant.[36]

The upshot was perhaps the most decisive of the Pyrrhic victories that punctuated the history of Degussa's carbon black operations during the Nazi period. In July 1938, the Russwerke got a Reich-guaranteed loan of 5.5

---

[32] DUA, DL 3.Baerwind/21, Aussprache im Kreise des Aufsichtsrates der Russwerke, November 18, 1937.

[33] DUA, DL 3.Baerwind/21, Verhandlung über die Weiterentwicklung der Dortmunder Russfabrik beim Rohstoffstab, November 20, 1937.

[34] DUA, DL 3.Baerwind/21, Aussprache mit der Farben-I. G. über das Russgebiet, November 30, 1937, and Sitzung des Ausschusses der R.D., of the same date.

[35] DUA, DL 3.Baerwind/21, Aufsichtsratssitzung und Gesellschafterversammlung der Russwerke Dortmund, December 4, 1937, enclosing his Für den Aufsichtsrat bestimmter Kommentar, December 3, 1937.

[36] DUA, DL 11.5/40, Protokoll der Aufsichtsratssitzung der Russwerke Dortmund GmbH, December 3, 1937. For the terms governing such loans, see DL 11.5/40, Finance Minister Schwerin von Krosigk's Bürgschaftserklärung, March 8, 1935, his Zusatzerklärung zu der Bürgschaft, January 5, 1937, and his Zweite Zusatzerklärung zu der Bürgschaft, April 4, 1938.

million Reichsmarks from a consortium led by the Dresdner Bank, repayable at six-month intervals between 1940 and the end of 1948, with an annual charge for interest and administration equal to the prevailing Reichsbank discount rate plus 2 percent.[37] But the stringent conditions attached virtually transformed the company into an agency of the German state, reducing Degussa's role, in effect, to an advisory and administrative one. Not only did the loan contract stipulate that "the firm has primarily to serve the public good for the entire duration of its existence and without regard to its legal form or its owners" and that it "is obligated to execute at any time the measures that the Reich considers necessary to the purpose of the contract," but also the terms gave the government ample means of enforcing these provisions: it could audit the firm at any time, alter the management on four weeks' notice, lay claim to the sales income as security, and appoint two members to the supervisory board (one of whom turned out to be Johannes Eckell). Perhaps most tellingly, the regime chained the corporate owners of the Russwerke to its fate; they were forbidden to dispose of their shareholdings without the government's consent. In return for all this, Degussa gained only momentary release from having to bankroll the Russwerke's initially underestimated building costs and a precedent for seeking outside funding, in case Eckell's hunger for carbon black mounted.

That hunger, indeed, had shown no signs of slackening following the clash of November 1937. Briefly around the end of the year, Eckell held open the possibility of relenting about completing the fourth production hall at Dortmund, providing the Russwerke could present proof that stepped-up operations at the other three would bring forth the targeted 6,000 tons annually.[38] But he soon reneged, and by March 1938, Degussa's managers at the site had committed themselves to both full completion of the works and an elevated output of 9,000 tons, as well as to the growth of Kalscheuren's production to 3,000 tons annually, only to be told that they were chasing the horizon: after 1939, German needs for domestic carbon black would approach 30,000 tons because of the Volkswagen program and the realization that synthetic rubber tires required a 25 percent larger admixture of the substance than did ones made from natural rubber.[39] While Eckell developed plans to narrow the impending shortfall by encouraging an additional

[37] For these and the other terms, see DUA, DL 11.5/40, Vertrag zwischen der Deutschen Revisions- und Treuhand AG, namens und im Auftrag des Deutschen Reiches,... und der Russwerke Dortmund GmbH, July 8, 1938 (with a notation that Bernau, one of Degussa's representatives on the Russwerke supervisory board, had approved it on June 13), and Dresdner Bank to the Russwerke, July 19, 1938.

[38] DUA, DL 3.Baerwind/21, Besuch im Rohstoffstab, January 13, 1938, enclosing Kemnitz to the members of the supervisory board of the Russwerke, January 12, 1938.

[39] DUA, DL 3.Baerwind/21, Besuch beim Rohstoffstab, March 7, 1938. For the authorization raising Kalscheuren's capacity to 3,840 tons per year, see GPT 4/1, Hoffmann of the Economics Ministry to Degussa, November 29, 1937.

entrant into the carbon black field (he wooed the Bayerische Stickstoff-
werke to assemble a new plant that would operate on the basis of acetylene
and carbide in conjunction with another synthetic rubber factory destined
for Fürstenberg an der Oder), and shortly after the tire makers delivered
a pessimistic projection that Dortmund would not return an annual profit
until 1942 and work off its accumulated losses until 1947, Degussa found itself compelled to relieve the financially overextended Auergesellschaft of the
Russwerke and Kalscheuren.[40] For just over 4.4 million marks, Frankfurt
eased its subsidiary's cash flow problems, spared it several impending tax
payments, and resumed full responsibility for the Degussa concern's carbon
black interests (indeed, the parent company promptly dissolved the Wegelin
AG and absorbed the now profitable Kalscheuren works) – all just in time
for Eckell to up the ante once more.[41]

On July 5, 1938, Eckell dropped the first hint to Degussa that "he had in
mind" the construction of a third CK3/4 plant, either in central Germany or
the vicinity of Berlin, with a capacity of 3,000 or 6,000 tons. To Baerwind's
objection that not enough anthracene residues were available to generate
such output, Eckell could only reply that he was looking into the matter. But
to the Degussa manager's response that his firm had no funds left to put into
such a project, Eckell had a sharper, bullying retort: "industry will surely have
the money, if [Field Marshall] Göring personally converses with the chairmen
of the supervisory or managing boards."[42] Ten weeks later, Eckell thought he
had found the appropriate location, one that underlined the personal interest
of the head of the entire Four Year Plan, namely Salzgitter, where the newly
founded Hermann-Göring-Werke would generate the necessary coal tar and
provide half the capital for a new plant for 4,000 to 5,000 tons of active
carbon black, with Degussa putting up the other 50 percent. Having only
hours before secured an increase in the set price of CK4 to eighty-five pfennigs
per kilogram, thus hastening the day when the Dortmund plant finally would
break even, the Frankfurt firm now was being asked to advance still more
money in the name of autarky.[43] Schlosser thought he had no choice but to
try to strangle this notion at birth: he emphatically told Eckell "that we – as
a result of the extraordinary demands on our concern for other projects of
the Four Year Plan – could in no case for the foreseeable future take part in

[40] DUA, DL 3.Baerwind/21, Gespräch mit Dr. Eckell ... über die Pläne ... für die Vergrösserung
der Fabrikationskapazität in deutschem Aktivruss, May 7, 1938; and Russwerke Dortmund –
Kalkulation, May 9, 1938.
[41] DUA, DL 11.5/40, Auszug aus Protokoll ... über eine Besprechung bei der Auergesellschaft, June 26, 1938; IW 24.5/5, Feldman's Betr.: Steuerliche Auswirkungen eine evtl.
Rückübertragung der Russinteressen an die Degussa, June 29, 1938. On the integration of
Kalscheuren into Degussa, DL 13.3/1, Bonath's Russ report, p. 21.
[42] DUA, DL 3.Baerwind/22, Besuch von Herrn Dr. Eckell in Frankfurt, July 9, 1938.
[43] See DUA, DL 3.Baerwind/22, Sitzungen des Ausschusses und des Aufsichtsrates der R. D.,
September 17, 1938, on the pricing agreement.

financing a new carbon black factory," though the firm would be willing to investigate the feasibility of the Salzgitter project as a courtesy.[44] This may have been the occasion when the ever impatient Eckell, as Schlosser later recalled, "threatened me with the charge of economic sabotage."[45] But, if so, the crisis soon passed. By October, Eckell's interest in the Salzgitter project was declining because it would take far too long to realize – his calculations meanwhile had revealed that Buna output would begin to outstrip inventories and production of carbon black in July 1939, so stopgap solutions had to be found.[46]

For once, Eckell's sense of urgency made him more cooperative with the Russwerke's owners, especially with Degussa, rather than less. Desperate for the quickest possible increase in output, he rapidly went along with their proposals simply to expand both Kalscheuren and Dortmund by 1,500 and 5,000 tons per year, respectively, despite the intensified concentration of carbon black production in the exposed western parts of Germany that this entailed.[47] As earlier, however, the sticking point was financing, with the tire makers again willing to provide half the necessary capital and Degussa not.[48] Because Eckell had the rubber firms cowed by his threat to press for more carbon black from acetylene, which would raise their raw materials costs, if they did not pay for the new CK3/4 facilities, he could afford to take Degussa's side in a series of disputes with the consortium in early 1939 as a means of leveraging Frankfurt into opening its wallet. Thus, when the tire producers tried to argue, for example, that Degussa was not entitled to license fees on output over the Russwerke's original 6,000 tons, since it embodied no additional inputs of know-how, Eckell threw his weight behind Degussa, and the compromise formula arrived at gave Frankfurt two pfennigs per kilogram for each of the first 6,000 tons produced in Dortmund, 1.66 pfennigs for the next 6,000, 1.5 for the next, and .75 for any additional tons.[49] These and other financial arrangements paved the way for another government loan, this time of 4 million Reichsmarks, but also for an increase in the Russwerke's capital by 2 million, half from Degussa and half from the tire consortium, to

[44] DUA, DL 3.Baerwind/22, Gespräch mit Herrn Dr. Eckell über eine eventuelle dritte CK3-Gasrussfabrik..., September 19, 1938.
[45] DUA, DL 11.5/40, Schlosser's Betr. Deutsche Gasrusswerke Dortmund, July 29, 1952.
[46] DUA, DL 3.Baerwind/22, Aussprache bei der Reichsstelle für Wirtschaftsausbau, October 21, 1938.
[47] DUA, DL 3.Baerwind/22, Russbesprechungen in der Reichsstelle...und im Reichs-wirtschaftsministerium, January 27, 1939; and DL 3.Baerwind/23, Besuch bei der Reichs-stelle, May 2, 1939.
[48] DUA, DL 11.5/40, Konecke and Assbroicher of Continental Gummi-Werke to the Schei-deanstalt, March 28, 1939, and Busemann and Federlin of Degussa to Continental, April 12, 1939.
[49] DUA, DL 3.Baerwind/23, Besuch bei der Reichsstelle, May 2, 1939; DL 11.5/40, Nieder-schrift über die Sitzung der Kommission für die Erweiterung der Russwerke Dortmund, May 15, 1939.

which Semperit-Gummi-Werke of Vienna and the Veith-Werke of Frankfurt were added as replacements for the German branch of Michelin, which had withdrawn during the preceding year.[50] Eckell's maneuvering thus enticed Degussa into a further commitment of capital, even though various financial restrictions were simultaneously reducing the annual expected interest rate on Degussa's existing investment to 4.25 percent in 1939–40, rather than the 5 percent provided for in the founding contract of 1936.[51]

Ironically, however, Eckell's partiality toward Frankfurt also may have contributed to driving the rubber firms finally into sympathy with Degussa's relatively slow-paced approach to expansion, thus underlining the enduring gap between the thought processes of business leaders and those of the Nazi regime's economic policy makers. In August 1939, only three weeks before Hitler launched the Second World War, one of Continental Rubber's delegates to the Russwerke's supervisory board outlined to Baerwind a series of practical grounds for turning against the rapid expansion of Dortmund, including lagging Buna production, delayed building materials, and the high local cost of gas, and argued for a pause in the work, during which a different site should be reconsidered, after all.[52] It was as if the speaker had slept through the preceding three years, during which the government had swept aside virtually every commercially motivated reason for caution, then pushed and pulled the producers into augmenting their output targets to levels (from 1,200 tons in early 1935 to 7,800 in 1936 to 22,000 in 1939) that became more rather than less financially risky than their predecessors, by virtue of being all the more remote from any conceivable estimate of "normal" demand. That Continental's director still thought he could inject even a measure of commercial rationality into this spiral, even as it was about to be accelerated by war, reflected a surprisingly widespread delusion of the German business elite. Hermann Schlosser certainly shared this delusion, and even the temperamentally less sanguine Ernst Baerwind could not shake it. The emotional and professional consequences of doing so would have been paralyzing. Yet, the history of Degussa's role in carbon black production from 1933 to 1939 reveals nothing more strikingly than how thoroughly the role of most German businesses and businessmen had been reduced in the interim to a narrowly reactive one. Having embarked on producing the gas-based product in order to cash in on the Nazi regime's desires, the manufacturers were now largely prisoners of them.

Even more pronounced than the evolution of Degussa's carbon black venture from an instrument of autarky into one of armament was the

[50] *Ibid.*; also Rossel's Kapital-Beteiligung Russwerke Dortmund GmbH, June 22, 1939; and, on Michelin's withdrawal, DL 13.3/1, Bonath's Russ Report, p. 24.
[51] DUA, DL 11.5/40, Russwerke Dortmund GmbH, June 9, 1939, p. 2.
[52] DUA, DL 3.Baerwind/23, Sitzung des Aufsichtsrats-Ausschusses, der Geschäftsführung und der Bauleitung der R.D., August 7, 1939.

simultaneous and virtually complete mutation of the Degea AG (Auergesellschaft), the firm Degussa acquired from Alfred Koppel in 1933–34, into a purveyor to the German military. Primarily a producer of incandescent mantles for lightbulbs prior to 1933, this enterprise had three other main pillars: the manufacture of radioactive substances, among them mesothorium, radium, and a toothpaste; of so-called rare earths (scarce metallic oxides) derived from monazite sand; and of air renewal and "breathing protection" equipment, including gas masks. These businesses intersected with Degussa's, since it converted many of Auer's oxides into rare metals (e.g., thorium) in Frankfurt and also made air filtration materials, including activated charcoal and a sodium peroxide–based granular substance called Proxylen, which absorbed carbon monoxide and emitted oxygen. It was not Degussa's interest in these fields that made them into the mainstays of the Auergesellschaft during the 1930s, however, but the simultaneous stagnation of the lightbulb market and appearance of large-scale military orders.

Auer's gas mask production had begun during the First World War, then had been converted under the direction of Karl Quasebart, a specialist in the field who joined the managing board in 1922, to the service of peacetime, industrial demand, especially from mining firms.[53] But ties to the German military had continued. The enterprise not only delivered a new model mask (GM 24) to the army in the mid-1920s, but also entered into secret contracts with it that violated the Treaty of Versailles by establishing a proving ground for gas defense and a facility to manufacture preliminary products for mustard gas at Auer's principal plant in Oranienburg, just north of Berlin. At the end of 1929, the firm and its main competitor in the field, the Drägerwerk of Lübeck, made sure to include military demand in the sweeping market division program they negotiated. Henceforth, government orders were to be split between them on ratios of 65:35 for gas masks, 50:50 for other gas defense products, and 35:65 for oxygen-generating equipment, with medical demand wholly reserved for Dräger. As the Depression drove other sales down sharply, these arrangements conferred essential offsetting income: the military contracts issued in 1928 called for the purchase of some 170,000 gas masks by 1932 at a cost of 1.5 million Reichsmarks, the lion's share of that going to Auer.

Following the Nazi seizure of power, Auer's business became ever more concentrated around satisfying the German Defense Ministry's burgeoning appetite for air renewal equipment (see Appendix G). To be sure, the firm made considerable advances in producing the chemical coatings for

---

53 On the history of Auer's gas mask operations prior to 1933, see Bernhard Lorentz, *Industrieelite und Wirtschaftspolitik 1928–1950: Heinrich Dräger und das Drägerwerk* (Paderborn: Ferdinand Schöningh, 2001), pp. 149–56; and Friedrich Klauer (ed.), *Geschichte der Auergesellschaft von der Gründung im Jahre 1892 bis zum Jahre 1958* (Berlin: Auergesellschaft, n.d.), pp. 20–22.

flourescent lights, and its incandescent lamp division managed, despite intense competition, to sustain sales of roughly 3 million marks per year in the late 1930s and to hang onto much of Auer's external market, partially with the help of the Reich's ZAV. Research at Oranienburg on rare earths also led to several lucrative innovations, notably Neophanglas, which became the preferred German material for sunglass lenses, and metal alloys that could substitute as catalysts and in heat-conducting wiring for more expensive, often imported metals, such as chrome and nickel.[54] Auer's thorium oxide also found a market as a catalyst in the production of gasoline from coal via the Fischer-Tropsch process.[55] The proceeds of these developments were dwarfed, however, by the explosive growth of the gas defense sector. It came to account for a steadily rising proportion of Auer's skyrocketing annual sales totals, reaching in 1938/39 the extraordinary figure of 90 percent. An indication of the enormity of the military demand for this output is provided by the following statistic: at 64 million marks in that business year, Auer's receipts from respiration equipment alone would have increased the net turnover of its parent, Degussa, by almost 50 percent, had they been included.[56] A measuring stick of the artificiality of this demand – and, therefore, of the perilous commercial position into which the Auergesellschaft increasingly maneuvered itself – is suggested by another ratio: in July 1940, when the sudden Nazi victories in Western Europe created the possibility of an abrupt return to peacetime conditions, the firm estimated future annual sales at only 20 million marks, that is, at a mere 21 percent of its actual turnover during the current business year.[57]

Although Auer's mounting dependence on government orders was inevitable in the economic context of the Third Reich, the extent of the firm's addiction was not. Faced with the same temptations and pressures, the rival Drägerwerk remained sensitive to the danger of overexpanding capacity in order to serve a rearmament boom that might someday go bust. By laboring to preserve its technological and patent leads over Auer, especially with regard to compressed air devices that had numerous medical and industrial applications, the Lübeck company managed to avoid ever becoming so lopsidedly oriented around official contracts, let alone during the prewar years.[58] Unable to keep pace inventively, however, Auer's leaders consciously

[54] *Ibid.*, pp. 30–32; on the struggle to retain foreign markets for incandescent mantles and the ZAV, see DUA, IW 24.9/1, Berichte des Vorstandes, November 1934, October 30, 1935, and November 15, 1938.
[55] See DUA, DL 3.Busemann/5, his Besprechung mit der Auer-Gesellschaft, November 14, 1934, and IW 24.5/2, Quasebart to Busemann, June 25, 1938.
[56] See DUA, IW 24.9/1, Bericht des Vorstandes für das Geschäftsjahr 1938/39, October 21, 1939. Cf. the figures on Degussa's turnover in Appendix B.
[57] DUA, IW 24.5/5, Niederschrift zur Aufsichtsratsitzung am 10. Juli 1940, p. 2.
[58] Compare the figures in Lorentz, *Industrieelite und Wirtschaftspolitik*, p. 194, with those in Appendix G of this book. Armament contracts averaged out to 62 percent of Dräger's total sales in the period 1933–44 and reached their highest level (71 percent) in 1934. A major

opted to exploit their advantages of geography and scale – their firm's closer proximity to government agencies in Berlin and its larger production runs, which won it advantageous prices from suppliers, notably Continental Rubber – to secure the greatest possible share of the Reich's business. The result was an almost exclusively volume-centered business strategy on Auer's part during the 1930s, one that dovetailed neatly with the military's drive for the quickest possible expansion of output and required little imagination on the part of the company's managers. But this course also consumed mounting capital investments to keep pace with escalating orders and returned declining proceeds per unit as the military restricted profit margins. Thus, tension gathered between the subsidiary's leaders in Oranienburg and its owners in Frankfurt.

Despite having acquired all the shares in the Auergesellschaft in 1934, Degussa largely refrained from altering the company's management or its internal practices in the ensuing years. General Director Heinrich Ziegler continued to preside over the enterprise until 1938, when his problematic "racial" status led to his replacement by the veteran Quasebart, and Robert Vorbau, who had been with the firm since before World War I, then assumed the post of plant manager at Oranienburg, where he had the enthusiastic support of the regional Gauleiter and the branch of the German Labor Front (DAF). Given Degussa's limited stock of managerial personnel and lack of experience with Auer's main products, there seemed little reason for the parent company to exert more than general oversight over these executives. Moreover, unless a direct collision of interests arose between Frankfurt and Oranienburg, the latter's cozy relationship with both Party and state agencies suggested additional reasons for a hands-off course. The circumstance, however, that Auer's managers were both physically nearer to and more concerned with satisfying their military customers than their corporate proprietors soon assured that exactly such intramural clashes would emerge. From 1935 on, Degussa was drawn with increasing frequency but only marginal effect into trying to rein in its subsidiary.

Some of Degussa's interventions were primarily formal and disciplinary, a matter of holding Auer's independent-minded leadership to the general lines of policy laid down in Frankfurt. Thus, Busemann flatly rejected Ziegler's claim in 1936 that contracts entered into by one of the firms were not necessarily binding on the other and, two years later, informed his successor that he could not as chairman overrule the majority vote of his colleagues on the managing board.[59] Other assertions of Frankfurt's authority went further, reminding Auer's managers that they had to subordinate their commercial

---

contributor to Dräger's relative success in retaining diversified sales was its victory over Auer in a patent dispute concerning oxygen-supply machinery; see IW 24.5/2, Aktennotiz über die Besprechung mit der Direktion der Auergesellschaft, February 14, 1936.
[59] DUA, IW 24.5/2, Busemann's Besprechung mit der Direktion der Auergesellschaft, July 2, 1936; and Busemann to Quasebart, August 24, 1938.

interests to those of other parts of Degussa's realm, as when Busemann directed Quasebart to drop a demand for license payments that conflicted with the HIAG division's purposes.[60] Similar in tenor were Ernst Baerwind's demands that Auer make a greater effort to promote one of his pet projects, the Proxylen air exchange system, to the naval authorities in Berlin, after he began to suspect that the desire to wrest a share of the contracts for U-boat air renewal from the Drägerwerk had led Oranienburg to accept the compressed air processes with which the authorities were familiar rather than to plump for Degussa's not-yet-established alternative.[61] But in this instance, Degussa ended up having to beat a retreat, and the experience may have reinforced Frankfurt's reluctance to second-guess Auer's leaders on technical matters. A lengthy and elaborate testing program carried out during 1936 at both Oranienburg and the Degussa plant at Rheinfelden that manufactured Proxylen indeed established the chemical's efficacy, but foundered on the fact that the canisters of it required to achieve the same results as compressed oxygen took up twice as much space in cramped U-boats.[62]

The most serious strain on Degussa's willingness to let the Auergesellschaft manage its own affairs proved, however, to be the costs of doing so. To the subsidiary's leaders, expansion was the only answer to every new government request or competitive move on the part of the Drägerwerk, and the resulting expenses grew exponentially. As early as February 1934, Degussa's chief financial officer had wondered at the Auergesellschaft's peculiar internal accounting practices, as a result of which the firm had no stable definition of what it should be earning on each gas mask it produced and no capacity to reckon its profits and losses on a monthly basis. Moreover, he worried about the uncertainty that went with heavy dependence on government orders, arguing that "despite the considerable profits that are to be expected in this field, great emphasis will have to be placed on keeping in reserve as much as possible of the proceeds at any time, since it cannot be foreseen how long the business will proceed on the current basis."[63] But he had little success in imposing either better bookkeeping or greater saving on his nominal subordinates. By both necessity and choice, they sank all their energy into mastering the avalanche of official commissions that rolled with ever greater force, beginning with orders for the armed services in 1933–34 of 10 million Reichsmarks (more than three times the total gas mask sales of the preceding

---

[60] DUA, IW 24.5/2, Busemann's Betr. Streitfall der Auergesellschaft: Lizenzvertrag mit Röhm & Haas, Philadelphia, December 20, 1938.

[61] See DUA, DL 3.Baerwind/19, Gespräch mit Prof. Quasebart über Proxylen für U-Boote, September 25, 1935; on Baerwind's personal attachment to the product, see PCA 2/130, his letter to Ulrich Müller, September 10, 1935.

[62] DUA, PCA 2/130–31 contain the relevant documentation; see especially Degea to Baerwind, April 8, 1936, enclosing Versuch mit Proxylen Patronen; Quasebart to Baerwind, June 3, 1936, enclosing Degea to the Reichskriegsministerium, May 4, 1936, and an 11-page report comparing the alternative air renewal systems tested.

[63] DUA, IW 24.5/2, Bernau's Betr.: Degea, February 5, 1934, pp. 8–9.

year and possibly corresponding to an annual output of 400,000 to 500,000 masks) and culminating in 1937–38 with the added demand for some 2.8 million simplified, cheap (and far less profitable) "People's Gas Masks" per year.[64] Long after the war began, Degussa was still lamenting Auer's failure to develop adequate cost accounting for its output.[65] Meanwhile, the firm's cash flow situation steadily worsened, in part because the costs of meeting escalating demand had to be met in advance via investments in new construction and machinery, and in part because, even once deliveries had been made, the military authorities tended to pay slowly, sometimes only after conducting audits that resulted in deductions for "excess profits," and in part with tax rebate certificates that could be redeemed only after further delay.

The resulting gap between expenditures and receipts opened during 1937 and assumed extreme dimensions during the ensuing, fateful year. In the course of 1937 alone, the relationship between the firm's liquid resources and its bank and other loans dropped from a positive figure of 1.9 million Reichsmarks to a negative one of 2.5 million, as it sold off more than a million marks in stocks and government bonds and not only borrowed another million from Degussa, but also began taking short-term credits from the Berliner Handels-Gesellschaft (BHG) and, at Busemann's suggestion, from the Henkel firm of Düsseldorf. After tabulating the Auergesellschaft's pending outlays on modernizing and expanding the factory grounds at Oranienburg, repaying the Reich for a converted installation there, and building and outfitting a new administration building in Berlin, the total costs of which came to 2.8 million marks, Busemann concluded that "we will have to wrack our brains about how we will raise these sums."[66] His first round of ratiocination led to a reduction of Auer's annual dividend to 6 percent, the addition of Hermann Schlosser to Auer's supervisory board, where he could begin helping to bring the subsidiary under tighter control, and the stepping up of Auer's rates of depreciation, so that the firm began writing off the full expenses of new machinery, as well as those for tools and inventory, in the year they were made.[67]

---

[64] DUA, DL 3.Baerwind/17, Besuch bei der Auergesellschaft, March 16, 1934 (on the orders for 1933–34); IW 24.4/2, unsigned Exposé Deutsche Gasglühlicht-Auer-Gesellschaft m.b.H, July 3, 1933, p. 5 (on gas mask sales in 1932–33); IW 24.5/2, Quasebart to Busemann, January 9, 1937; and Lorentz, *Industrieelite und Wirtschaftspolitik*, pp. 156, 198–200.

[65] See DUA, IW 24.6/1, Schlosser to Kolb, October 4, 1944.

[66] DUA, IW 24.5/2, Busemann's Notiz für die Herren Baerwind, Fischer, Schlosser, Bernau betr. Degea, September 20, 1937. On the sales of stocks and bonds and the loans, see IW 24.5/2, Busemann to the Degea Direktion, March 25, 1937, and DL 3.Busemann/5, Notiz betr. Geldbedarf der Auer-Gesellschaft, April 23, 1937.

[67] DUA, IW 24.5/2, Busemann to Direktion der Degea, September 28, 1937 (on the dividend reduction), and Busemann's Notiz... betr. Degea, September 20, 1937 (on Schlosser's election); and IW 24.9/7, Degea AG Bericht über das dritte Geschäftsjahr 1935/36 and Ziegler to Busemann, October 14, 1937, including the financial report for the following year, as well

By the end of March 1938, nonetheless, the Auergesellschaft owed assorted lenders (Degussa, Henkel, the BHG, the Dresdner Bank, and the Reichs-Kredit-Gesellschaft) some 7 million Reichsmarks and had accumulated, by Busemann's calculations, an excess of obligations to creditors and suppliers over liquid assets of almost 9.7 million marks, compared with less than one-half million some four years earlier.[68] Though Busemann saw no grounds for panic as yet, since his repurchase of the carbon black sector would shortly ameliorate the situation, Auer's cash flow continued to worsen. When Henkel refused to renew its loan beyond the autumn of 1939, it could easily be replaced by the Dresdner Bank, so Auer's actual indebtedness held roughly constant during that year.[69] But its anticipated need for outside funds, over and above receipts, climbed to more than 13 million marks.[70] Had Auer's spendthrift managers had their way, the figure would have been still greater. Degussa blocked the subsidiary's eager managers from throwing money after properties in Austria and the Protectorate of Bohemia and Moravia in at least two cases just before the war began, and in two more, one involving a factory near Dresden, shortly thereafter.[71]

On only one occasion during the late 1930s, this time "at the behest of the Reich Economics Ministry," did Busemann relax his resistance to acquisitions by Auer. He permitted it to expend 50,000 RM on a one-third holding in the St. Joachimsthaler Bergbau-GmbH, a firm formed to operate a radium and uranium mine in the annexed Sudetenland under a lease from the Reich, which took ownership of the property.[72] The importance of the installation had risen significantly in December 1938, when Otto Hahn used material

as IW 24.9/1, Bericht des Vorstandes zur Bilanz für das Geschäftsjahr 1937/38, November 15, 1938, especially p. 2 (on the accelerated depreciation).

[68] DUA, IW 24.5/2 (also DL 3.Busemann/5), Busemann's Finanzlage der Auergesellschaft, April 4, 1938 (on the debts), and Busemann's Betr. Auergesellschaft, May 28, 1938 (on the liquidity situation).

[69] DUA, IW 24.5/2, Henkel to Busemann and Henkel to Auergesellschaft, June 16, 1939, and Quasebart to Busemann, July 1, 1939 (on the loans); DL 3.Busemann/5, Busemann's Betr. Auergesellschaft, July 1, 1939 (on the total indebtedness, then figured at 9.4 million marks).

[70] DUA, IW 24.4/7 (also DL 3.Busemann/5), Busemann's Betr. Auergesellschaft, April 1, 1939.

[71] On the prospective takeover of Kreidl, Heller & Co. in Vienna, see DL 3.Busemann/5, Finanzlage der Auergesellschaft, April 4, 1938, as well as Chapter 3; on Auer's interest in the smallest of three Czech gas mask factories, see IW 24.5/2, Busemann's Besprechung bei der Auergesellschaft, August 7, 1939; on its ambitions regarding the Eschebach-Werke in Radeberg and the Treibacher Chemische Werke, IW 24.5/5, Bernau's Betr.: Auergesellschaft, February 2, 1940, and Schlosser's Auergesellschaft AG, February 26, 1940.

[72] DUA, IW 24.9/1, Bericht des Vorstandes für das Geschäftsjahr 1938/39, October 21, 1939, p. 6 (including for the quoted phrase); Klauer (ed.), *Geschichte der Auergesellschaft*, p. 33. The background to the formation of the company, which Auer initially sought to avoid by suggesting that the Reich take over the mining itself, can be traced in IW 24.5/2, especially Quasebart to Chininfabrik Braunschweig Buchler & Co. and others, January 24, 1939, and Quasebart to Busemann, January 31, 1939.

from it in the first successful splitting of the atom.[73] But the implications of this were not yet fully apparent, and Degussa's main interest may have been in the long-standing use of uranium pitchblende in the manufacture of ceramic colorings. Either way, however, Busemann surely authorized the exception because the ores were simultaneously important to Degussa's rare metals operations, Auer's production of oxides, and the government.

Just such an overlap of interests had animated the only extension of Auer that Degussa had approved in the preceding years (aside from the temporary transfer of Degussa's carbon black holdings), namely the formation in November 1934 of the Orgacid AG, an equal partnership with the Chemische Fabrik Buckau, a subsidiary of Th. Goldschmidt. Created to lease and operate Reich-owned plants for mustard gas and diglycol, a component of explosives, on Buckau's property in Ammendorf, Orgacid initially amounted to a cost-free tie-up between the provider of the key raw materials (ethylene and chlorine) and the firm most closely engaged, again under contract with the Defense Ministry, with testing and defending against the projected output.[74] Not until three years later, when Goldschmidt's decision to contribute half of Orgacid's operating capital prompted Auer to seek the remaining 300,000 to 400,000 RM from Degussa, did the partnership actually start entailing new outlays by the parent firm, but it had found by now ample reason to honor the request.[75] Ammendorf had begun not only ordering 125 tons of chlorine per month from Degussa's Knapsack plant, but also exploring the possibility of still greater quantities, all of which might be purchased at the artificially high government price that Goldschmidt had negotiated earlier.[76] Though IG Farben resisted this intrusion on its control of German chlorine sales, long contention over the subject eventually brought Degussa an extremely advantageous outcome: guaranteed orders from Orgacid of some 200 tons per month, as long as its current needs continued, half of that amount being purchased at the above-market rate and half at the prevailing one.[77]

---

[73] Gine Elsner and Karl-Heinz Karbe, *Von Jáchymov nach Haigerloch* (Hamburg: VSA Verlag, 1999), pp. 27–28.

[74] DUA, IW 24.5/2, Quasebart to Busemann, November 23, 1934, reports the founding of the firm, Busemann's Notiz, November 29, 1934, the arrangements governing it, and Quasebart to Busemann, April 25, 1935, Auer's involvement in the research work for the Defense Ministry. See also DL 3.Baerwind/20, Notizen betreffend die Chemische Fabrik Buckau, March 22, 1937. On the background to the Orgacid plant, which was built on commission by IG Farben and operated, in part, on the basis of its patents, see Hayes, *Industry and Ideology*, p. 137.

[75] DUA, IW 24.5/2, Quasebart to Busemann, May 28, 1937.

[76] DUA, DL 3.Baerwind/21, Gespräch mit Dr. Theo Goldschmidt über unsere Chlorflüssiglieferungen nach Ammendorf, July 6, 1937, and Chlorflüssig Ammendorf, July 8, 1937.

[77] See DUA, DL 3.Baerwind/21, especially Einspruch der Farben-I.G., July 10, 1937, Telefongespräch mit Prof. Quasebart, September 16, 1937, and Aktenvermerk betreffend

Despite such spillover gains from the acquisition of the Auergesellschaft, it had become by 1937/38 a very long-term, even questionable investment for Degussa. The parent company could hope to recover its initial outlays but slowly, and chances for ever exceeding them depended on victory in the war for which Auer and its new offshoots were increasingly devoted to equipping Germany.

By the late 1930s, in fact, the financial overextension of both the Russwerke and Auer subsidiaries was but an extreme version of Degussa's own. Ernst Bernau reported in February 1938 that Frankfurt's reserves of cash, stocks, and bonds, which had risen by 7 million marks between October 1934 and October 1937, had plummeted in the four months since by more than 9 million. About two-thirds of Degussa's remaining securities holdings, moreover, would be needed to cover the obligations that the Auergesellschaft had incurred. As a result, he considered "it unavoidable that measures be taken with immediate effect to prevent a further sinking of our cash resources," including "a prohibition on construction and purchasing" and a "hiring ban."[78] The building and buying stop was not implemented, but the firm promptly tightened its internal budgeting and supervision of outstanding accounts. Degussa also introduced the practice of holding "obligatory" managing board meetings on the first Monday of each month in order to assure better coordination of the members' actions. At the inaugural session in October, the board resolved that "considering the current business position of the company, increases in salaries, efficiency premiums, and previously granted bonuses should be refrained from in the current [business] year... [and] additional hirings should be avoided absolutely."[79] Because "cases may arise in which it will be necessary for the Scheideanstalt to restrict its activities," Busemann already had informed his colleagues that he was appointing two commissions to review the research and commercial sides of the firm's operations with an eye to identifying "what one can cut back if necessary."[80] Significantly, IG Farben arrived virtually simultaneously at similar conclusions and procedures with regard to its own

---

Chlorflüssig für die Orgacid, October 18, 1937; DL 3.Baerwind/23, Verhandlung Goldschmidt A.G./Auergesellschaft/Degussa, April 17, 1939; and GCH 2/3, Auseinandersetzung über die zukünftige Belieferung der Orgacid, September 28, 1937, and Baerwind to Cordes, May 20, 1939.

[78] DUA, TLE 1/23, Bernau's Finanzen, February 26, 1938, especially p. 5, where the quoted words appear.

[79] DUA, DL 2/1, Niederschrift über die Vorstandssitzung am 4. Oktober 1938, pp. 2–3. The initial plan was to convene on the second Monday of the even-numbered months, but this quickly gave way to the monthly, first Monday schedule; see Niederschrift über die Vorstandssitzung am 18 Januar 1939, p. 19.

[80] DUA, DL 3.Busemann/5, Notiz für Vorstand/SchA, September 6, 1938.

operations – according to the smaller firm's analysis of the two enterprises' financial resources a few months later, with even greater cause.[81]

This overstretching of corporations' reserves mirrored that of the Reich's, and the reasons were almost identical. On both the macro- and microeconomic levels, the months covered by Degussa's business year 1937/38 marked a delicate passage in the Nazi remaking of the German economy, the moment when the regime's demands for investments that would serve arms and autarky outstripped the level that either the country or many corporations could finance prudently. The resulting tension between commercial and political interests precipitated both Hjalmar Schacht's resignation as Economics Minister and the adoption in Berlin of a blatantly intimidating tone toward the business world. Not only were allegations of "sabotage" deployed to break the resistance of the German iron and steel industry to the foundation of the Reichswerke Hermann Göring just as the business year began, but that precedent was then repeatedly invoked during subsequent months as a means of silencing objections to the regime's impositions.[82] Johannes Eckell's high-handedness toward Baerwind and Schlosser concerning a third carbon black plant was hardly atypical of business–state contacts in this period.

Such saber rattling seemed necessary because of the toll the transition from a competitive market economy to a cameralist one seemed about to begin taking on the financial positions of firms such as Degussa. The Reich's export promotion system already had cost the firm just under 4 million Reichsmarks in the business years 1934–37, some 6 percent of total earnings. Such outlays, tolerable as long as Degussa was either reactivating formerly idle capacity or holding new investments more or less even with depreciation, were bound to press on the firm more heavily as the government insisted on adding new production facilities. Equally troubling were the immediate burden and incipient effects on long-term profitability that seemed likely to flow from Berlin's selective fostering of particular forms of output. From Degussa's point of view, even the moderate aggregate investment in new plant and machinery undertaken in 1934–37 (11.5 million marks) still came to more than twice the surplus that remained after deducting net expenditures (aside from those on stockholdings and other securities; 61.4 million marks) from total earnings during that period (66.6 million).[83] Against the backdrop of the "deeply deformed growth" of the Nazi years, of the "strip-mining

---

[81] On Farben's retrenchment program, see Hayes, *Industry and Ideology*, pp. 205–06; for the comparison of the two firms' financial positions, see DUA, DL 3.Busemann/6, Bernau's I.G.-Scheideanstalt-Bilanz, July 5, 1939.

[82] For examples, see Hayes, *Industry and Ideology*, pp. 169–72. On the establishment of the Reichswerke, see Overy, *War and Economy in the Third Reich*, pp. 93–118.

[83] DUA, TLE 1/23, Bernau's Finanzen, February 26, 1938, p. 2, provides the breakdown of Degussa's earnings and expenditures during these three business years.

of the economy" by which the regime encouraged neglect of commercially promising in favor of militarily useful products, Degussa's managers had to wonder whether much of their new plant would have to be written off in the future.[84] This made the sudden erosion of their reserves in 1938 all the more alarming.

Yet during the final year prior to World War II, the distorting impact of Nazi policy on Degussa's core operations became even more pronounced. In the heady atmosphere surrounding the uncontested takeovers of Austria, the Sudetenland, and Bohemia-Moravia, which quelled many doubts about the staying power of Hitlerian economics and the genius of the Führer, Degussa's leaders proved no more capable than IG Farben's of slowing the spiraling process by which the regime baited and bullied them into committing ever larger portions of their unprecedentedly high receipts to ever burgeoning building plans, each of them propelled by swelling government-induced or -inspired purchases. In the mere eight months between December 1938 and August 1939, Degussa's managing board authorized appropriations for land and construction of almost 16 million Reichsmarks, which was nearly equal to the total amount so earmarked during the preceding four business years.[85] At the end of June, even before this figure had been reached, Bernau tabulated the sum for approved capital outlays that were not covered by liquid assets and operating revenues in the current business year at 21.4 million marks, a number that had ballooned from only 8.5 million during the previous four months. Busemann therefore concluded that Degussa probably would have to follow in the tracks of the Auergesellschaft and Russwerke subsidiaries by resorting to its longtime "house bank," the Dresdner, for financing.[86]

If relatively few of the products into which Degussa increasingly poured its money had exclusively or primarily military value, that was a consequence of their versatility and not, contrary to what the firm's leaders often claimed after the war, because Degussa eschewed opportunities to capitalize on the rearmament drive prior to World War II.[87] As early as April 1933,

---

[84] See Christoph Buchheim, "Die Wirtschaftsentwicklung im Dritten Reich–Mehr Desaster als Wunder," *Vierteljahrshefte für Zeitgeschichte* 49 (2001), pp. 653–64, especially p. 662, from which the first quoted phrase is taken, as well as the same author's "The Nazi Boom: An Economic Cul-de-Sac," in Hans Mommsen (ed.), *The Third Reich between Vision and Reality* (Oxford: Berg, 2001), pp. 79–94. For the second quotation, see Joachim Fest, *Hitler* (New York: Vintage, 1975), p. 538.

[85] Calculated from the individual appropriations recorded in DUA, DL 2/1, Vorstands-Niederschriften, December 12, 1938 to August 7, 1939. Significantly, Degussa's investment total in 1938/39 outstripped that for depreciation for the first time during the Third Reich.

[86] DUA, DL 2/1, Niederschrift über die Vorstandssitzung am 3. Juli 1939, p. 35. That the Dresdner would be the source of the funds is indicated by the minutes of the preceding meeting on June 5, p. 32.

[87] For examples of such claims, see BU Unterlagen Hermann Schlosser, the successive drafts of his response to the postwar denazification questionnaire, and BR 01/0012, several of

Ernst Baerwind noted the advisability "that we tighten the still very loose contact that we have with the Army Ordnance Office... through occasional visits during stays in Berlin."[88] Such efforts began paying off modestly in 1935, when the expansion of the German Air Force yielded a sudden jump in orders for beryllium metal and compounds for spark plugs and propellers; but thereafter sales of these materials appear to have leveled off at around 100,000 RM per year.[89] Shortly thereafter, Degussa complied with the Air Ministry's request for an experimental quantity of a sodium–potassium mixture for use in a sort of aerial flamethrower, then agreed to supply some three metric tons of the substance between August 1936 and March 1937 and to consider large-scale manufacture of not only that ingredient, but also the emulsive final product at the Grünau plant.[90] Though nothing seems to have come of the project, Degussa's stance toward it hardly bespoke a rejection of armaments contracts in principle. Indeed, much of the research and development work in the firm's rare metals sector during the 1930s related to potential military applications of its output. Thorium was tested in compounds with cerium for self-igniting or pyrophoric metals and with aluminum for nonburning and noncorroding ones, and zirconium was alloyed with steel to strengthen it, particularly in automotive or airplane parts that came into contact with tetraethyl lead, with nickel and chrome to reduce inflammability, and with aluminum to increase durability, especially against the effects of sea water.[91] Here too, however, prewar sales remained small, though profitable (see Appendix D).[92]

the declarations concerning Schlosser collected by Zirkelbach, especially those of Fuchs and Schulenburg.

[88] DUA, DL 3.Baerwind/16, Gespräch mit Oberregierungsrat Dr. Zahn, April 18, 1933.

[89] See DUA, PCA 2/84, Jaeger's Beryllium-Präparate, April 29, 1936, on the quantities sold to that date; PCA 2/83, the chart headed Erlös für Be-Metall, BeO, reinst., Be-Salze [1932–35], on the sales proceeds; and DL 3.Baerwind/18, Baerwind's Aktenvermerk betreffend eventuelle Verwendung von Berylliumoxyd, December 3, 1934, and DL 3.Baerwind/19, his Besuch von Reichsbahnrat Otto wegen Beryllium, August 31, 1935, and his Besuch beim Reichsluftfahrtministerium, January 21, 1936, on the uses of the output. Degussa's financial closing statements list no gross profits on beryllium for the years 1932–36, 167,000 RM in 1936/37, 7,000 in 1937/38, and 72,000 in 1938/39; see DUA, RFI 4.2/64, 70, 74, 77, 80, and 85, Jahresabschlüsse, 1933, 1935–39.

[90] DUA, DL 3.Baerwind/19, his Besuch beim Luftfahrtministerium, January 21, 1936, and Kalium-Natrium-Legierung für das Reichsluftfahrtministerium, June 22, 1936.

[91] See, especially, DUA, IW 24.17/1, Baerwind's Besprechungen bei der Auergesellschaft über zunderfeste thoriumhaltige Legierungen, April 12, 1935; DL 3.Baerwind/19, his Aussprache in der Rotherstrasse, January 20, 1936; DL 3.Baerwind/23, Thorium-Metall, June 24, 1939; and IW 24.17/1, Ruppert's Verwendungsmöglichkeiten des Zirkoniums und seiner Verbindungen, January 14, 1943.

[92] See DUA, PCA 1/211, Thoriummetall-Produktion und Verkäufe, 1.10.1938–1.5.1939, which shows that Degussa sold during this period less than half of its average monthly output (34.5 kilograms) and only 17 percent of the productive capacity (ninety-six kilograms) reported in PCA 1/214, Schulenburg to Auergesellschaft, May 23, 1938; and DL

Most major earners (and expense producers) among Degussa's militarily significant products served German armament at one remove – that is, they were sold to other firms for assembly into the goods finally delivered to the Defense Ministry or to aid in their manufacture. One such material was sodium, which Degussa made at Knapsack, near Cologne, and generally used internally to fabricate metal hardeners and other cyanide products, along with bleaching agents. Annual proceeds on external sales of metallic sodium more than doubled between 1934 and 1939 (to more than 1.25 million Reichsmarks) and the gross profits derived from its production nearly quadrupled (to 463,000 RM), as the discovery of the substance's importance to the manufacture of tetraethyl lead, an essential component of high-performance, especially aircraft, fuels, counteracted declining orders from IG Farben for use in synthesizing indigo dye.[93] Whereas the German maker of the gasoline additive, a joint subsidiary of IG Farben and Standard Oil called Ethyl GmbH, ordered only 100 to 200 metric tons of metallic sodium during its entire initial year of operation in 1936, that figure escalated to ninety tons per month by the first half of 1939 and was expected to reach 140 monthly tons a year later.[94] Because previously idle capacity soon would no longer suffice to meet the demand, Degussa now budgeted one-half million Reichsmarks to expand its facilities at Knapsack, hoping that its earlier appropriation to create a 120-ton stockpile of the metal at Grünau in central Germany would placate the military agencies worried about exposure to air attack.[95] But the project encountered obstruction from another quarter, that of Johannes Eckell of the Four Year Plan, who declined to issue the necessary building permits until IG Farben activated the backup sodium factory it had

3.Baerwind/22, his Bemerkung zu der Notiz von Herrn H. Menzel, August 17, 1938, which remarks "that our zirconium metal business is indeed small but in no sense suffering." Degussa's financial closing statements for 1933–39 list no gross profits on thorium, 6,000 RM on titanium and 32,000 on uranium in 1938/39, and a total of 81,000 RM on zirconium in 1934–39; RFI 4.2/4.2/64, 70, 74, 77, 80, and 85, Jahresabschlüsse, 1933, 1935–39.

[93] On the firm's base external sales in 1934–35 of seventy-five tons of sodium per year to IG Farben for about 550,000 RM, see DUA, DL 3.Baerwind/17, his Natriumlieferung an die Farben I.G., May 22, 1934, p. 3, and DL 3.Busemann/6, his Verhältnis Scheideanstalt:I.G., April 23, 1935. On the discovery of the product's new importance, see DL 3.Busemann/5, his Betr. Tetraaethylblei, May 15, 1935, and DL 3.Busemann/6, his Besprechung mit Herrn Dr. Ter Meer, June 14, 1935, and Reifstahl's Besuch des Herrn von Heider, June 22, 1935. On the gross profits, RFI 4.2/70 and 85, Jahresabschlüsse per 30. September 1935 and 1939.

[94] DUA, GCH 2/9, Degussa to Ethyl GmbH, January 24, 1936, records the first year volume, and Schmidt's Niederschrift über die Verhandlung mit I. G. . . . über Natriummetall für Tetraäthylblei, May 25, 1939, the most recent and projected figures.

[95] See, on the creation of the reserve at Grünau, DUA, PCA 2/98, Degussa to IG Farben, November 11, 1938, and Oberkommando Wehrmacht to IG of the same date. On the appropriation for Knapsack's expansion, see DL 3.Baerwind/23, his Derzeitige Leistungsfähigkeit unserer Natriumfabrik. . . . , May 19, 1939.

built at Gersthofen in order to cover its own needs beyond what Knapsack could furnish.[96]

Similarly striking growth characterized Degussa's output of a compound of sodium cyanide, acetone cyanohydrin, that was the basic component of a new hard and clear acrylic called Plexiglas, which the Röhm & Haas firm of Darmstadt had developed in the late twenties.[97] Particularly suitable for the portholes and bridges of ships and the windows of airplane cockpits and gun turrets, the product experienced a prompt increase in demand following Hitler's accession – so much so, in fact, that Degussa was producing the preliminary material in lots of ten metric tons by March 1934, and Röhm & Haas was buying equivalent quantities per month by mid-1936.[98] In November of that year, the two companies arrived at an exclusive price-and-purchase contract by which Degussa pledged to supply twenty-eight tons of acetone cyanohydrin per month until March 1937 and thereafter to meet the requirements of an expanded Röhm & Haas factory for up to eighty tons monthly, all at a price of 1,750 RM per ton.[99] In fact, though monthly orders came to only thirty-five tons throughout 1937–38, this amount stretched the productive capacity of Degussa's plant at Mombach to the limit and required more sodium cyanide than Degussa could allot to acetone cyanohydrin from its own output, thus driving the firm to purchase additional, less highly concentrated quantities of the former chemical from IG Farben and cutting into the profit margin.[100] By various expedients, including the diversion of apparatus and personnel toward acetone cyanohydrin production at the Wildau plant, Degussa managed not only to catch up with Röhm & Haas's needs in mid-1939, which had reached ninety tons per month (corresponding to payments to Degussa of 2 million Reichsmarks per year), but also to anticipate satisfying the demand for 130 monthly tons projected from October 1939 on, when another Plexiglas plant would come on line.[101] Between 1933 and 1939, Degussa's gross profits on the new product came to almost 600,000 RM.[102]

[96] DUA, DL 3.Baerwind/23, his Besprechungen mit der Reichsstelle für Wirtschaftsausbau, June 12, 1939, and his Besuch bei der Reichsstelle für Wirtschaftsausbau, June 21, 1939.

[97] On the invention of the product, but Degussa's inability to overcome Röhm & Haas' continuing efforts to keep its nature secret, see DUA, GCH 9/21, Menzel's Notiz betr. eines neuen Verwendungszweckes von Cyan bei der Röhm & Haas A.G., March 1, 1928; Westphal's Besuch bei der Firma Röhm & Haas, March 19, 1929; and Westphal's Cyanverhandlungen mit Röhm & Haas, May 7, 1930.

[98] DUA, GCH 9/21, Fuchs' Verrechnung des Cyannatriums für die Acetoncyanhydrin-Lieferungen an Röhm & Haas, March 13, 1934; Finck's Röhm & Haas A.G./ Acetoncyanhydrin, July 2, 1936.

[99] DUA, GCH 9/21, Finck to Röhm & Haas, November 30, 1936.

[100] DUA, GCH 9/21, Akten-Notiz. Betr. Acetoncyanhydrinbetrieb, November 9, 1937.

[101] DUA, GCH 9/21, Anruf von Fa. Röhm & Haas, August 30, 1939.

[102] Tabulated from the annual figures in DUA, RFI 4.2/70, 74, 77, 80, and 85, Jahresabschlüsse 1935–39.

In related fashion, demand for Degussa's steel hardening processes and equipment underwent after 1933 "a very steep climb, which was primarily determined by the then beginning armaments production."[103] Indeed, when reporting on the Durferrit subsidiary's striking increases in sales and gross and net profits during the business year 1934/35 (up by 80 percent, 70 percent, and 95 percent, respectively, over the preceding year), the firm's head proudly noted that "we have thus participated in Germany's rearmament to a quite special degree.... a large part of the manufacturing plants for infantry and artillery munitions work almost exclusively with our process. Ties to the Army Ordnance Office therefore were cultivated correspondingly."[104] Such efforts helped to push the company's production of sodium cyanide to more than five times the pre-Hitler level of 1,000 metric tons per year by 1939, prompting Degussa to transfer fabrication of the hardening salts from Frankfurt to Grünau in 1937 just to free up manufacturing space for the preliminary product.[105] That the rising sales continued to be driven by military needs emerges clearly from the refusal of the Four Year Plan administration to take this transfer under its wing. Instead, the relevant agency referred Degussa's request for allocations of building materials and other supplies to the Army Ordnance Office, since the matter "does not concern the fabrication of products that save foreign exchange, but products whose manufacture is in the interest of the army."[106] Between 1933 and 1939, Durferrit's annual dividend payments to Degussa climbed from 15,000 to 850,000 RM and totaled more than 2.1 million.[107]

Even Degussa's traditional mainstays, the Rheinfelden plant and the metals division, shared in the benefits and burdens of the Reich's pursuit of armaments and autarky after 1936. Having been rather neglected during Busemann's diversification drive, Rheinfelden enjoyed a resurgence as a result of waxing demand for hydrogen peroxide, primarily from the makers of synthetic fibers and for internal use as a basic component of a substitute form of perborate whenever imports of borax became unavailable, but also as a propellant of U-boats and torpedoes. Output multiplied fourfold between 1933 and 1938 (see Appendix I), and in the spring of 1939, faced with the fact that "it is now no longer possible to cover the urgent need," the managing board overcame long hesitation and appropriated 2.5 million Reichsmarks to double Rheinfelden's capacity to 160 monthly tons of the

---

[103] DUA, DL 13.3/1, Report by K. Bonath, "Natriumcyanid. Geschichte der Verfahren, der Produktion, der Entwicklung und der Forschungsarbeiten," November 1967, p. 24.

[104] DUA, RFI 4.2/74, Hans Menzel's Bericht der Durferrit-Gesellschaft m.b.H., December 20, 1935, p. 1.

[105] DUA, DL 13.3/1, Bonath's "Natriumcyanid" report, November 1967, p. 20, and the graph of NaCN Produktion between pp. 40–41.

[106] DUA, DL 3.Baerwind/20, his Kontrollnummern für die Vergrösserung der Cyanid-Betriebes, Gutleutstrasse und für die Durferritsalz-Bereitschaftsanlage, Grünau, April 23, 1937.

[107] DUA, RFI 4.2/64, 70, 74, 77, 80, and 85, Jahresabschlüsse 1933–39.

product at 100 percent purity.[108] Though Baerwind assigned the project "commercial priority...ahead of *all* our other current building projects," shortages of building materials held up support for the plan from Eckell's office until after the war began.[109] The precious metals sector meanwhile had developed new alloys suited to the special capillary tubing required to spin synthetic fibers and in catalysts for the oxidation of ammonia, an essential intermediate in the production of munitions.[110] By 1939, moreover, research in cooperation with the Norddeutsche Affinerie on pressed metal powders of copper, iron, and lead that might substitute for more expensive or imported materials for industrial soldering, bearings, and cannon or rifle shells had progressed far enough to seem to warrant the founding of a new jointly owned firm to develop the products.[111]

Last but the very opposite of least among the Degussa product lines that gained from the militarization of the German economy between 1933 and 1939 were those grouped in the HIAG wood carbonization and distillation division, whose products figured vitally in the manufacture of gas masks, munitions, industrial solvents, metal hardeners, and synthetic resins, and had a host of other applications to the quests for autarky and armament (see Appendix H). The division's output not only grew at phenomenal rates between 1933 and 1938 (doubling or more for charcoal, activated charcoal, wood tar, tar oils, formaldehyde, and acetates at many of its plants; see Appendix I), but also spinning off even more imposing profit rates, thanks to the relatively non–capital-intensive nature of its production processes. As early as September 1936, HIAG's gross profits reached 8.3 million Reichsmarks, nearly three times their level in 1929/30 and almost exactly as much as was yielded by Degussa's precious metals and perborate operations, heretofore the corporation's principal breadwinners.[112] That figure reached 10.5 million marks three years later, when it accounted for more than 31 percent of Degussa's total gross profits, up from the 25 percent it had generated in the early 1930s (see Appendices C and D).

[108] DUA, PCA 1/139bIII, Degussa to Reichsstelle für Wirtschaftsausbau, August 10, 1939, in which the quoted words appear; and DL 2.1, Niederschriften über die Vorstandssitzungen am 6. März und am 8. Mai 1939, pp. 23 and 28, on the appropriations.
[109] DUA, DL 3.Baerwind/23, his Besprechung in der Reichsstelle für Wirtschaftsausbau, May 11, 1939, opens with the quoted words.
[110] On the latter discovery, see DUA, TME 1/19, Schneider of Degussa to Schneider of the Reichswirtschafts-Ministerium, October 25, 1939, which reports the discovery of a rhodium-free platinum catalyst that will save the Reich some $150,000–200,000 in previous expenses for imports and licenses; and Erner's memo on his conversations with the Heereswaffenamt, November 27, 1939.
[111] DUA, DL 2/1, Niederschriften über die Vorstandssitzung am 18. Januar 1939 und am 3. Juli 1939, pp. 17–18 and 36.
[112] See DUA, BU Fritz Roessler, "Zur Geschichte der Scheideanstalt" [1937], pp. 116, 119; and RFI 4.2/74, Abschluss zum 30. September 1936.

14 Bodenfelde

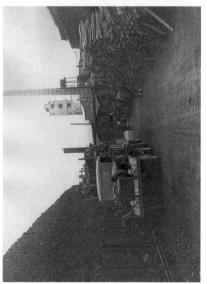

13 Wood carbonization plants

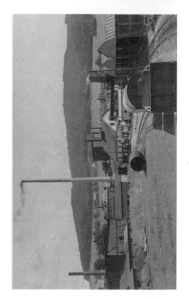

16 Konstanz

15 Oeventrop

142

Here too, however, such rapid expansion bumped up against the ceilings of existing capacity in 1938, and thus HIAG installations were the sites of more than a quarter of the 16 million marks Degussa appropriated for capital expenditures during the following business year. But alone among Degussa's operating divisions, the carbonization and distillation section had enough cash on hand to cover the projected expenditures; its account at Degussa contained fully 5.5 million out of the 6 million Reichsmarks that the corporation possessed in unencumbered liquid funds in the last summer of peace.[113] Even so, such spending begged the increasingly pressing question of HIAG's dependence on wood as a raw material, which was both economically uncompetitive with chemically synthesized methanol (a danger Degussa had checked for the time being through cartel arrangements with IG Farben) and in too-limited supply, thanks to the proliferation of synthetic fiber production from cellulose, to feed the growing appetites for acetone and similar derivatives of wood vinegar.[114] In consequence, Degussa's leaders began weighing the massive investments that would be required to shift HIAG's raw material basis to acetylene and ethylene, without being able, however, to assemble the will or the money to take the plunge prior to the war's outbreak.[115]

Meanwhile, Degussa's most lucrative direct connection with the Third Reich's preparations for war had emerged in the form of a derivative of HIAG's formaldehyde. Called pentaerythrite or Hexalol and code-named Zeins or Holzmehl, the substance was an important preliminary product for explosives and munitions turned out by companies such as the Westfälische-Anhaltische Sprengstoff AG (WASAG) and Dynamit AG of Troisdorf.[116] Beginning in the autumn of 1936, HIAG undertook to build and pay for an extension on its factory at Wildau to make the substance in return for a commitment from the Army Ordnance Office to buy 1.9 million Reichsmarks worth of the output at a price of some 4,300 RM per metric ton.[117] But within a year, the project took on much greater dimensions, entailing HIAG's erection and operation on commission of "preparedness plants . . . at four

---

[113] See, on the appropriations (4,247,000 RM), DUA, DL 2/1, Vorstands-Niederschriften, December 12, 1938 to August 7, 1939; and on the credit balance, DL 2/1, Bernau's report at the meeting of July 3, p. 35, and Fischer's at the meeting of August 7, p 41.

[114] On the cartel arrangements, which reserved most German methanol production to IG Farben, but alloted its sale, along with priority in making and selling formaldehyde, to the wood charcoaling firms, see DUA, DL 3.Fischer/1 (also: IW 50.11/1), Schmitthenner's Der Methanolvertrag mit der I.G. Farbenindustrie A.G., May 15, 1945.

[115] See DUA, KLB 1/01, Kolb's Studie über die Erweiterung unserer Rohstoffgrundlage, March 14, 1938.

[116] On the code names, see IW 50.11/1, Pichler's Notiz, May 29, 1964; and HIA 1/84, HIAG to Frisia Bau- und Verwaltungs-GmbH, October 18, 1937.

[117] DUA, HIA 1/84, Zahn of the Oberkommando des Heeres to Hiag-Verein, Berlin, September 12, 1936, and von Retze to Zahn, October 28, 1936.

widely separated locations in Germany" for the Reich. Along with Wildau, Bodenfelde and two otherwise unspecified Bavarian sites already had been chosen by the company, and it had estimated total building costs at approximately 28 million marks, plus its commission of just over 1.2 million. Only the percentage of the final bill that was to constitute the construction contractor's fee remained unresolved.[118] As the work commenced and the cost projections rose to 41.5 million marks over the next few months, however, the relevant military and governmental agencies balked at HIAG's method of calculating its compensation, so no formal agreement was completed – and no funds transferred, aside from the payment of actual construction costs by the government.[119] Moreover, in December 1938, the Army not only stepped up the timetable for completing the plants, calling for two to come on line in the summer of 1939 and the others by the beginning of 1940, but also indicated a desire for two additional ones, each with a productive capacity of 125 tons of pentaerythrite per month.[120]

These developments prompted Degussa to pursue a new arrangement by which the Wildau and Bodenfelde installations would remain its property, but the four Reich-owned plants would be grouped into a new subsidiary, the Paraxol GmbH. It would construct them at cost plus a small fee on behalf of the government's Verwertungsgesellschaft für Montanindustrie GmbH, a holding company for factories of purely military use, and operate them in return for the annual profit minus a leasing charge as long as military interests required. The corresponding general contract was signed in May 1939.[121] By the time the four plants were completed during the war in rural spots near Welden and Schrobenhausen in Bavaria, Niederlehme west of Frankfurt an der Oder, and Lippoldsberg in northern Hessen, Degussa's reward for supervising the planning and construction appears to have come to fewer than 600,000 RM.[122] Meanwhile, Degussa's books recorded virtually no profits on pentaerythrite production through September 1939. But the

[118] DUA, HIA 1/84, von Retze's Betrifft: Vertrag Frisia-Hiag, October 18, 1937.

[119] On the wrangling over the commission, see HIA 1/84, HIAG's Verlauf der Verhandlungen mit der Frisia, September 20, 1938, Fischer and von Retze to Oberkommando des Heeres, September 20, 1938, von Retze's Notiz betr. Vergütung für unsere Leistungen beim Bau von Anlagen für das Heereswaffenamt, November 4, 1938, his Notiz betr. Vergütung für den Bau der G-Kohle-Bereitschafts-Fabriken, December 3, 1938, and his Notiz über Besprechung gemeinsam mit der I.G. beim Heereswaffenamt, December 17, 1938.

[120] DUA, HIA 1/84, von Retze's Notiz über eine Besprechung beim Heereswaffenamt, December 19, 1938.

[121] DUA, HIA 1/84, von Retze's Betr. Bereitschafts-Anlagen, December 19, 1938, records the inception of the idea of an operating subsidiary; IW 50.2/1 contains the Mantelvertrag between the Reich and Degussa, dated May 6, 1939. On the Montan system, see Barbara Hoppmann, *Von der Montan zur Industrieverwaltungsgesellschaft (IVG) 1916–1951* (Stuttgart: Franz Steiner, 1996), pp. 29–136.

[122] DUA, HIA 1/84, von Retze's Verhandlungen beim Oberkommando des Heeres, July 16, 1941. On the remote locations of the plants, see the colored maps in HIA 1/63.

foundation for the ultimate value to the corporation – the proceeds on sales of pentaerythrite by its own plants and of formaldehyde as a raw material to the Paraxol ones – had been laid before the war broke out.[123]

For Degussa, as for Germany as a whole, the material balance sheet of Nazi rule appeared a great deal more favorable in 1939 than it was in reality. Just as the nation had virtually eliminated unemployment, erected monumental buildings and highways, and expanded both its boundaries and the gross national product, Degussa's workforce, infrastructure, extent, and total worth had increased enormously. Indeed, the liquidity crisis of 1938 now looked, in retrospect, like a mere hiccup. The enterprise's roster of workers and salaried personnel, in all likelihood, had at least quadrupled since 1933 (precise figures have not survived). It had added numerous new productive installations and, in Frankfurt, both constructed a modern, "quite monumental new laboratory building," opened in the fall of 1937, and embarked on the process of extending its overcrowded headquarters, at a cost of 2.8 million Reichsmarks.[124] And the corporation's tax returns reported a total worth of 124.9 million Reichsmarks and a net profit of some 10.1 million in 1938/39, increases of 29 percent and 140 percent since 1932/33, respectively, as well as an excess of assets over liabilities of 34 million, more than twice the level of five years earlier.[125] Though the export promotion procedure was costing the firm endless paperwork, the net payments under it were more than offset by the rising level of domestic sales, and meanwhile the system helped Degussa to hang onto such important international positions as its sales quota under the international cyanide convention.[126] The enterprise, in fact, managed to hold its annual export earnings roughly constant in the latter half of the 1930s at around 25.4 million Reichsmarks, plus or minus 5 percent, and

---

[123] On the prewar sales of pentaerythrite produced at Degussa's Wildau and Mombach plants, see DUA, HIA 1/84, Notiz betr. Hexalol, January 16, 1939.

[124] See, on the new laboratory, Wolf, *Zeichen von Sonne und Mond*, p. 162, and on it and the expansion of especially the Frankfurt plant in the Gutleutstrasse, DUA, BU Fritz Roessler, "Zur Geschichte" [1937], pp. 109–10, and 142 (where the quoted words appear). On the construction of the new headquarters building, DL 2/1, Niederschriften über die Vorstandssitzungen am May 8, June 5, August 7, and September 4, 1939, pp. 28, 31, 39, and 43, and DL 3.Baerwind/23, his Beschlossene Geländekäufe, September 5, 1939.

[125] See, on the net profits, DUA, RFI 4.8/5, Bilanz per 30. September 1934, Anlage 2, and Bilanzen per 30. September 1939, Anlage 2; and, on the balance sheet worth, Appendix B of this book.

[126] See, DUA, GCH 2/4, Mann's Rest-Antrag Z.A.V. Cyan Frankfurt für 1938, September 15, 1939, which includes a table indicating that Degussa was selling sodium cyanide overseas at about 40 percent of its domestic price and receiving in return 30 percent of the total foreign proceeds through the export promotion procedure. This means that Degussa's receipts per kilogram of exported sodium cyanide ultimately equalled about half of what the firm earned from domestic sales. On Schlosser's success in assuring Degussa a fixed portion of world cyanide consumption under the international cartel agreement of 1936, see BU Fritz Roessler, "Zur Geschichte" [1937], p. 117.

their composition hardly changed (except for a sharp drop in Rheinfelden's already low foreign sales), even as their contribution to the firm's profits dropped by one-quarter (see Appendix I).

Even the difficulties brought on by mounting international tension in August 1939 seemed manageable. By then, Hektor Roessler had coordinated the firm's mobilization planning in such a way as to protect many of the most essential workers from call-ups in the event of hostilities, and the enterprise had set in motion the camouflaging or "cloaking" of its patent rights and stockholdings in the U.S. and Britain.[127] To be sure, these arrangements were not secure against legal challenge if war erupted, since they involved seeming to transfer Degussa's American possessions to the Chemical Marketing Co., Inc., a firm owned by Degussa's longtime U.S. representative, the recently naturalized Fred Kertess, and its British ones to a Dutch firm, the Allgemeene Norit Maatschappy, in which Degussa had a minority shareholding. Essentially trustee agreements effected by sham payments, the deals plainly assumed that the value of Degussa's future business to the supposed new owners would guarantee the return of its property at the end of any potential conflict. But Frankfurt had achieved at least a measure of legal safety in timely fashion.[128] Only in the case of the British Industrial Solvents, Inc., Ltd., a company formed in 1929 as a partnership with the Distillers Co., Ltd. of Hull to produce acetone, acetic acid, and water-free alcohol, among other products, did Degussa fail to move quickly enough to protect its HIAG division's stake.[129] Finally, quick action by the firm's precious metals division had enabled it to convert the sterling balances made available by the Reich for international transactions to 82.3 kilograms of gold, which Degussa spirited to Frankfurt just before fighting broke out.[130]

But just as the Third Reich also had created an economy that could neither raise its people's standard of living nor sustain itself without territorial expansion, which ultimately meant conquest, had neglected fitting Germany for the long-range demands of international competitiveness in favor of achieving

[127] See PCA 2/144, the chart headed "1939. Stand Anfang August," which records the mobilization assignments of fourteen Degussa plants and the degree to which each's workforce had been "secured." Also Roessler's report to the managing board, DUA, DL 2/1, Niederschrift über die Vorstandssitzung am 5. Juni 1939, p. 33.

[128] On the American transactions, see DUA, DL 2/1, Niederschrift über die Vorstandssitzung am 6. Mai 1940, p. 86 and Anlage 3; and GCH 5/37, Division of Investigation of Cartels and External Assets, Partial Report on Examination of External Assets and Activities of Deutsche Gold- und Silber-Scheideanstalt (Degussa), [1945], pp. 9–13. On the Dutch trusteeships, see DL 2/1, Niederschrift über die Vorstandssitzung am 3. Juli 1939, p. 36; DL 11.5/41, Roediger's Betrifft: Shares der BCU, Ltd., August 10, 1939; and HIA 1/28, Scherf's British Carbo Union Ltd., London, April 17, 1942.

[129] On the firm, see Wolf, *Im Zeichen von Sonne und Mond*, p. 163; on the failure regarding Bisol, see DL 2/1, Niederschriften über die Vorstandssitzungen am 7. August and am 4. September 1939, pp. 41, 43.

[130] DUA, GEH 11/13, Schneider and Deppe to Reichsbankdirektor Treue, September 13, 1939.

the short-term output goals of armaments and autarky, and had built up an extraordinarily complicated and internally incoherent economic bureaucracy, Degussa also had accumulated problems for the future by adapting reflexively to these trends. During the first six years of Nazi rule, in Fritz Roessler's opinion, the enterprise's management had been so preoccupied with responding to opportunities and pressures "that no time and energy are available for organizational questions," such as the consolidation and rationalization of the company's scattered plants, their modernization around commercially promising products, and the elaboration of a formalized, well-articulated managerial structure.[131] Consequently, the experience of Degussa's Grünau factory was not unusual. Military priorities increasingly reoriented its production palette toward camouflage colorings, disinfectants, and metal hardeners, so that one Degussa official wrote after the war, "The result was certainly temporary profits, but the healthy extension of the plant for long-range, peacetime production did not occur."[132]

Moreover, the subordination of Degussa's development to the dictates of Nazi economic policy, which became complete in the business years 1937–39, prepared the way for the transition from cooperation to complicity to which the title of this book refers. Whether in fields of operation initially disadvantaged by the regime's course, such as the precious metals division discussed in the next chapter, or in those fostered by the Reich's ambitions, which are the subjects of the ensuing ones, the end result was identical: implication in pillage and murder.

---

[131] See, DUA, BU Fritz Roessler, "Zur Geschichte" [1937], pp. 142–43.
[132] DUA, RFI 4.8/6, Degussa to Finanzamt Frankfurt, February 27, 1951.

5

Precious Metals for the Reich

Although the German Gold and Silver Separation Institute had outgrown its name long before 1933, the smelting and processing of precious metals remained vital contributors to the firm's prosperity during the Nazi period. Having yielded, on average, one-fifth of annual gross profits in the decade leading up to Hitler's accession, Degussa's metals section and its associated operations (ceramic colors and the dental instruments produced by the Weber & Hempel subsidiary in Berlin) performed at virtually the same relative level over the ensuing eleven years. Keeping up in this fashion entailed more than doubling the division's profits between 1933 and 1944 (see Appendix D), a remarkable and improbable feat in view of the simultaneous decline of Degussa's gold production by 87 percent and its silver output by 51 percent (see Appendix J). Achievements of this sort generally came at a high moral cost in the Third Reich, however, and Degussa's precious metals operations proved no exception. Their history provides an almost textbook illustration of how Nazi goals dictated the parameters of commercial activity, challenged bureaucrats and executives to improvise means of doing their perceived jobs within these, and thus increasingly channeled corporate ambitions into the service of the regime's exploitative purposes.

What earmarked Degussa's precious metals division for politicization during the 1930s was its leading, indeed linchpin position in an essential but heavily import-dependent industry – that is, in a productive sector predestined for prompt "coordination" with the new regime's economic priorities.[1] Because of Germany's limited mineral deposits, virtually all of the platinum and gold and a majority of the silver produced or consumed annually within the country had to be brought in from outside, preferably in either raw or recyclable form so that the nation's refineries could derive work and income from the processing. As of 1933, the greater part of the resulting fine metals

---

[1] Unless otherwise or more specifically indicated below, my discussion of Degussa's precious metals business, its market position, and the environment in which it operated rests on the thorough and groundbreaking research of Ralf Banken, *Die Entwicklung des Edelmetallsektors im "Dritten Reich" 1933–1945* (forthcoming), Chapter 2, though our interpretations are not always identical. Banken's work is also the source of all statistical information, unless otherwise referenced.

that remained at home went to the consumer-oriented jewelry, tableware, and hammered metal industries, which mattered to Hitler's government primarily because they provided livelihoods for tens of thousands of Germans, especially in such manufacturing centers as Pforzheim and Nürnberg. But precious metals also had numerous industrial applications in electrodes, solders, alloys, photographic and X-ray films, sophisticated measuring instruments, and specialty piping and catalysts for the production of synthetics, not to mention as a medium of international exchange in the case of gold. Their indispensability to the goals of armament and autarky thus assured that precious metals supplies would be a matter of intense and long-term importance, not only to Degussa as the nation's principal purchaser and purveyor of these goods, but also to the administrators of the Third Reich.

Degussa's preeminence in the German precious metals business rested in the early 1930s on its semi-monopolistic control over inflows. The platinum sector deviated from the norm, in that Degussa's Siebert subsidiary divided it at every level – from purchasing, through smelting and processing into semi-finished materials for the dental, jewelry, electrical, and instrument industries, to even manufacturing of some sophisticated end products – with the W. C. Heraeus GmbH of Hanau and lesser firms on a ratio of roughly 43:49:8. With regard to gold and silver, however, the Frankfurt firm held uncontested pride of place, especially concerning supplies to commercial and industrial users. As both cause and effect of this status, Degussa was the only German precious metals firm with foreign subsidiaries that traded on its behalf (L. Roessler & Co. in Vienna, Leukon AG in Zurich, and Schöne & Co. in Amsterdam) and the only one with sufficient standing to reach market-division and -sharing contracts with the other major European silver dealers and refiners (Johnson, Matthey & Co. in England and the Comptoir Lyon Allemand in France) that kept them from selling in Germany or to most other German enterprises. To be sure, the National Bank (Reichsbank) and a few of the major incorporated banks, such as the Deutsche and Dresdner, also engaged in international gold transactions, but not for domestic resale in quantity under normal conditions. Furthermore, only three of the twenty-odd German precious metals refineries other than Degussa also possessed the capacity to separate gold or silver from ores or alloys on a large scale, and they encroached but marginally on Frankfurt's control over imports. Instead, the state-owned Sächsische Hütten- und Blaufarbenwerke Freiberg and the Allgemeine Gold- und Silber-Scheideanstalt of Pforzheim (in which Degussa held 13 percent of the stock in 1933) concentrated on processing domestic metals-bearing materials. Although the gold and silver refined by the Norddeutsche Affinerie of Hamburg (where Degussa possessed 37 percent of the shares) came primarily from foreign suppliers, it either reexported the output or passed it on in semi-purified lots to Degussa for final processing. Through a series of agreements with individual German smelters of imported heavy, nonferrous metal ores, Degussa also received most of their silver-containing by-products.

The enterprise's grip on the precious metals, mostly silver, extracted from domestic sources (ores, coins, and recycled decorative objects or industrial materials) was nearly as tight. Degussa not only had an exclusive price-and-purchase contract with the Mansfelder Kupferschieferbergbau AG of Eisleben, the largest German miner of silver-bearing ores, but also led and carried out all sales for the German silver convention. That cartel tied the remaining extractors of 95 percent of German output (the Preussische Bergwerks- und Hüttenwerke AG or Preussag and AG für Bergbau, Blei- und Zinkfabrikation zu Stolberg) to the four refineries that, along with Mansfeld itself, controlled 96 percent of the nation's silver-purifying capacity (Degussa, Freiberg, Allgemeine, and Norddeutsche) through preferential purchase prices and smelting rates, then apportioned the proceeds of the fine metal yield among the refiners according to periodically adjusted quotas. Finally, the terms of the German smelting convention, over which Degussa also presided, cemented its market dominance. By setting uniform national prices for most forms of rendering and purifying precious metals, this agreement insulated smaller refiners from competition, but also, in effect, confined them to their regional markets. None could build up sufficient capital to maintain a nationwide web of metals selling and buying agents like Degussa's.

Predominance in the trading and refining of gold and silver in Germany was, however, only the foundation of the profitability of Degussa's precious metals operations, not necessarily its chief source. Indeed, the firm's status as the producer of well over half the respective amounts of fine gold and fine silver that emanated from German smelteries in 1933 (exact percentages are impossible to establish because of double counting and other defects in the surviving tabulations) gave it primacy only in the phases of the precious metals business where profit margins were narrowest and capital requirements greatest. International competition and domestic cartel negotiations kept trading commissions and smelting fees down to usually 1 percent or less of the value of the fine metals involved. Although operating expenses were correspondingly low, since foreign offices and precious metals refineries cost little to establish or maintain, transactional risks and domestic overhead charges were other matters. Not only did Degussa have to support the numerous representatives who linked it to individual customers in the dental profession, the jewelry trade, and industry, but also the time lags inherent in precious metals production required the enterprise to tie up substantial funds in inventory, which both imposed costs on the firm and exposed it to price fluctuations. These lags stemmed from a central, easy-to-overlook fact: precious metals inputs and outputs were almost never physically identical.

In order to utilize its refineries efficiently (see Appendix K for a diagram of the processes involved), Degussa needed to collect heterogeneous inputs until their composition or volume was suited to turning out the momentarily most desirable end product. But in order to attract these inputs and to serve its clientele while they aggregated, Degussa had to be able to pay vendors in cash or refined goods immediately following delivery and to fulfill orders from customers quickly. That meant always having a reserve of pure metals on hand, which cost the firm, in accounting terms, an interest charge equivalent to what Degussa would have earned by otherwise investing the capital thus engaged (estimated at 4 percent per annum). At the end of the business year 1932/33, for example, when Degussa's metals stock of 2,390 kilograms of gold, 120,767 kilograms of silver, and seventy kilograms of platinum had a combined worth of 10.4 million Reichsmarks on the firm's balance sheets and 11.4 million on its tax returns, the annual overhead burden came to over 400,000 RM. Moreover, the acquisition cost of the specific inventory being released at any given time could differ considerably from that of the fine metal content of the new materials being obtained. As a result, the profitability of trading and refining varied directly with the quantities of precious metals involved and the tempo of the business. Unless volumes were abnormally high and turnover of reserves unusually rapid, the enterprise's likely sole gain on mere smelting commissions (*Lohnscheidungen* or deals in which Degussa · furnished pure metals to the suppliers of refinable materials) emerged from the residues they left behind for recovery from the company's apparatus and further processing, and the refineries' only high-margin form of immediate output was silver nitrate for films, demand for which was rising even though the largest consumer (IG Farben) covered the bulk of its own needs.

The reliably lucrative stages of Degussa's metals operations thus lay further along the production chain, in the processing and preparation of retained pure platinum, gold, and silver into semi-finished goods – that is, sheets, foils, wires, alloys, solders, amalgams, and compounds for thermal equipment – that were sold at significant markups over the prevailing prices of the metallic content. This is where competition within the industry was most intense, albeit in highly cartellized form, and where Degussa took increasing pains to translate its dominance of supplies into high returns.[2] Though overall statistics are available only for the war years, the pattern they convey already pertained in 1933: Degussa's metals smelting, refining, and processing units in Frankfurt, Hanau, Pforzheim, and Berlin-Reinickendorf accounted for some 82 percent of the gold salts and 33 percent of the gold alloys produced in Germany (within the borders of 1937); 63 percent of the silver

[2] The relative contributions of trading, refining, and semi-finished or finished goods to the annual profits of Degussa's precious metals sector cannot be disentangled precisely from the firm's records. However, the yearly closing statements (*Jahresabschlüsse*) group gross profits by metals accounts, materials for separation (*Scheide- und Gekrätz-Konto*), and particular products, and these can serve as rough proxies for earnings from the respective forms of operation. The figures indicate that trading and refining brought in over one-half of the division's profits only between 1932 and 1935, after which their share dropped to 30 to 40 percent annually.

semi-finished goods, 62 percent of the silver salts, 51 percent of the silver solders, and 41 percent of the silver alloys; 43 percent of the platinum and 36 percent of the platinum alloys; and 47 percent of all the dental alloys. Even in a field where Degussa's market share was relatively low, dental amalgams at 29 percent, the corporation was the nation's largest producer. Only in special forms of gold and silver plating (*Double*) did Degussa play an insignificant role. Not surprisingly, therefore, the firm had formal leadership of every major cartel agreement governing German precious metallic input and semi-finished output and thus valuable knowledge of the other signatories' businesses and considerable experience in dealing with their leaders.[3]

Degussa therefore stood in the initial years of Nazi rule at the apex of a rewarding but delicately balanced industry, one that depended on a substantial, smooth, swift, and internally regulated flow of inputs and outputs, many of which were bought and sold abroad. At first, the advent of the Third Reich seemed to pose no danger to these arrangements. To be sure, German firms' precious metals needs in 1934–35 – approximately 2.5 kilograms of platinum, twelve to thirteen metric tons of gold, and 500 metric tons of silver (350 of them imported) per year – corresponded to a theoretical annual outlay of 55 million to 58 million Reichsmarks in foreign exchange, whereas regulations introduced by the Weimar Republic had limited expenditures of convertible funds abroad on precious metals to the equivalent of 30 million Reichsmarks per year.[4] But a series of special circumstances had prevented supply problems from arising. Degussa's refineries continued to function at near capacity throughout the Depression thanks to, first, an unusually large number of commissions from foreign governments to reprocess their coinages and, later, a roughly 20 percent share in the Reich's own reminting program.[5] Even more helpful, however, was the willingness of the Soviet Union in the period 1931–34 to exchange hundreds of metric tons of gold, silver, and platinum for some 880 million Reichsmarks with which to buy German goods. This influx of Soviet precious metals not only sustained Degussa's metals division and the nation's processers and consumers of gold and silver in the early 1930s, but also kept the Reich solvent internationally. Without the resulting additions to its foreign exchange reserves, Germany's

[3] For a listing of the cartel agreements in force and their members as of March 10, 1938, see DUA, GEH 3.Hirtes/10, Konventionen auf dem Edelmetallgebiet.

[4] On the pattern of "normal consumption," see DUA, GEH 3.Schneider/15, Schneider's Akten-Notiz über die gestrige Aussprache mit Herrn Reichsbankdirektor Blessing, April 5, 1935, Schneider's Niederschrift über die Frage der deutschen Metallversorgung, April 24, 1935, Schneider's Die deutsche Goldversorgung, June 19, 1935, and Schneider's Edelmetall-Kontingente für Russengeschäfte für 1936, December 9, 1935.

[5] See DUA, GEH 11/15, especially the unsigned and undated listing of allocations headed Betr. Reichsmünzensilber-Geschäft, Pfister's Notiz, January 8, 1936, and Range's Notizen, April 13, and May 4, 1937, which indicate that Degussa was alloted and received 915 out of 5,153.5 metric tons of the coins smelted in the course of this operation.

worsening balance of payments situation would have left the nation unable to pay its import bills during the first two years of Hitler's rule.[6]

In 1934, however, relations between the Nazi and Communist regimes deteriorated, Moscow demanded surcharges on precious metals purchases to compensate it for the declining relative purchasing power of Reichsmarks, and the inflow began to narrow to a trickle. Both the German government and the country's precious metals industry faced a crisis, the harbinger of which was a gold shortage. While the National Bank's foreign exchange reserves plummeted by three-quarters to less than 100 million Reichsmarks during the first half of the year, Acting Economics Minister Hjalmar Schacht resorted to a series of expedients, which he eventually bundled together as the New Plan of September 1934, in order to preserve access to foreign goods and sustain the ongoing economic recovery without devaluing the currency. The central feature of Schacht's program was the creation of twenty-five Oversight Offices empowered to prioritize German imports according to their importance to autarky and armament and to reorient them toward countries that would barter goods with the Reich or with which it enjoyed export surpluses. But this system quickly proved of little help to the German precious metals business, since few such states possessed the relevant resources. Authority over purchases of gold, silver, and platinum from abroad therefore rapidly reverted to the National Bank, where some officials already had begun wondering whether the inventories maintained by Degussa and the other refineries ought to be drawn down in order to meet domestic needs. Meanwhile, in response to a parallel crisis regarding nonprecious metals, the Nazi regime introduced full-scale, government rationing of that industry's inputs and production within Germany.

All of these developments alarmed Hans Schneider, the industrious but rather naive and blinkered Degussa managing board member responsible for the metals division.[7] He reacted as most other German industrialists did in 1933–34, regardless of the specific issue involved, and as Ernst Busemann generally advised. Instead of challenging the regime's course, which Schneider thought maladroit, at least toward the Russians, he volunteered his expertise in order to manage the consequences. Since, as his aides assured Schacht's, Degussa had "always viewed itself more or less as the trustee of the [German] National Bank Directorate" in managing precious metals flows, Schneider put himself forward in Berlin as the logical person to handle the task of adjusting the industry's demand to supply, working in conjunction with the other producers and under the direction of the bank.[8] In this fashion, he hoped to head off rationing or any other form of direct government

---

[6] See the figures provided by Banken, *Entwicklung des Edelmetallsektors*, Chapter 2, Table 10.
[7] For the description, DUA, BU Fritz Roessler, "Zur Geschichte der Scheideanstalt 1933 bis 1936," pp. 132–33.
[8] DUA, GEH 3.Schneider/13, Hirtes and Durchardt to Reichsbankdirektor Wilhelm, July 1934.

17   Hans Schneider

interference in the agreements and practices that underpinned his firm's position, thus preserving them and it until normal conditions returned.[9]

Schneider might have achieved his purpose, had there been any real
prospect of such a day coming. That there was none, however, probably
should have dawned on him in April 1935, when, with a silver shortfall now
also looming, the German negotiators of a hard-fought new trade treaty with
the Soviet Union turned out to have made no provision for imports of precious metals, aside from a small quantity of platinum. The omission reflected
a reality that constrained Degussa's gold and silver business for the rest of the
decade: the Reich needed too many other goods more pressingly. In effect,
as soon became apparent, the Nazi regime had decided to limit gold imports
from Russia to those to which it was otherwise already obligated (worth
100 million Reichsmarks). These, along with any other quantities acquired
overseas, were commited to three purposes: paying for other essential commodities obtainable only with foreign exchange, building up a secret gold
reserve at the National Bank, and allotting small quantities to makers of exports that would return more than the value of their content in convertible

---

[9] DUA, GEH 3.Schneider/15, Schneider's Akten-Notiz über die heutigen Verhandlungen mit der
I. G. wegen Überlassung weiterer Silbermengen, November 8, 1934, in which he intervened
against a particular initiative on the part of Farben, for fear that it would bring on "exactly
that...which we have been working with much effort to avoid, namely the rationing of
precious metals."

funds and thus further promote the first two objectives. As for silver, the German negotiating stance amounted to leaving the nation's producers to rely on domestic supplies, supplemented by periodic allocations from ample government coinage stocks and/or official assistance in financing occasional purchases outside the country.

Consequently, Schneider's success in acquiring authority to administer precious metals allocations within Germany proved hollow, as well as time consuming and – in the short run – somewhat thankless. Having obtained this responsibility, first, with regard to the 500 kilograms per month of gold that the National Bank began providing in August 1934 to sustain exports, then in mid-1935 concerning the initially 600 but soon 500 additional kilograms monthly that it felt compelled to release for the domestic market, he learned in November 1935 that "it now has been decided on high that silver distribution, like that for gold, should be entrusted to Degussa." But the expanding competence came at a price and with a catch. Degussa had to sacrifice 20,000 kilograms of its silver reserve (one-sixth of the whole) to tide German firms over the upcoming Christmas season.[10] Meanwhile, the Economics Ministry had created a new Oversight Office for Precious Metals (*Edelwache*) under former National Bank Director von Schaewen, to whom at least one of his ranking erstwhile colleagues favored transferring Schneider's duties. Nor was that the only quarter from which he had to contend with bureaucratic warfare from then on. Since the regime's precious metals policy came down to maintaining exports from and jobs in the industry, diverting small quantities of gold and larger ones of silver for the purposes of arms and autarky, and alloting only what remained from shrinking supplies for the domestic consumer market, Schneider found himself fending off all sorts of special pleading from metals-hungry individual producers, sometimes backed by Nazi Party functionaries, and often having to give way.

All in all, Degussa's precious metals division and its leader invested countless hours from 1934 to 1939 in brokering the needs of the government and individual firms, collecting supply and production data, filing reports with the National Bank and the Oversight Office, persuading the regime not to encroach too far on inventories, and alerting officialdom to ways of stretching the nation's gold and silver supplies or laying hands on quantities in private possession. Yet this diligence did not assuage the enduring mistrust that assorted agencies expressed through repeated audits and spot checks of the enterprise's activities. Nor did it earn Schneider sufficient credit in Berlin to assure a reliably favorable reception for his policy recommendations, which prevailed on more than one occasion only after Degussa deployed Carl Lüer's political influence. Most tellingly, at the turn of 1936/37 and despite

---

[10] DUA, GEH 3.Schneider/15, Schneider's memo on Meine verschiedenen Unterredungen mit Reichsbankdirektor Dr. Blessing...am 29. und 30. November 1935, December 2, 1935, p. 2 (for both the quotation and the statistic).

Schneider's exertions, the official rationing of gold and silver that he had sought to prevent came to pass (it followed for platinum, whose military importance had made the Reich willing to finance expanding imports, in mid-1938). And in the final months of 1938, the Oversight Office largely succeeded in reducing Degussa to an executor of its orders. The company's initial assignment to spread broad allotments among firms and subsectors of the industry gradually had devolved into merely disbursing preset amounts of gold or silver to designated recipients according to the instructions of the state bureaucracy.

The explanation for this trend might best be termed regulatory momentum. Capping imports of gold and silver led to distribution quotas – first between production for export and for the home market, then by categories of domestic usage (e.g., military, industrial, pharmaceutical, photographic, dental), and finally by specific enterprise. The steady tightening of these quotas, in turn, encouraged strict accounting for amounts dispensed, reclaiming of unused portions, call-ins of metals-bearing items (e.g., coins), price controls, prohibitions on the possession or manufacture of certain goods, and the establishment or expansion of mechanisms and agencies to enforce all these measures. At every stage, both the government and sometimes even Degussa as its agent found additional restrictions necessary in order to effectuate earlier ones and thus slid further toward the outcome each had shied away from initially: the substitution of all-encompassing state administration for corporate self-rule. Haphazard and halting as the process seemed, it was not a happenstance. It derived almost inexorably from its point of departure: the foreign trade situation of a Germany determined to prioritize armaments and autarky. That program precluded a return to the conditions of international exchange on which the nation's precious metals industry historically had depended and virtually dictated an increasingly state-directed allocations system. Whether Schneider ever grasped the root of his industry's problems, however, seems doubtful. Certainly, when he reported to Degussa's managing board on March 6, 1939, regarding "the continuing great difficulties for precious metals supply and distribution that result especially from the fact that too many agencies and offices are involved and work in part against each other," he mistook effect for cause.[11]

Despite such administrative confusion, the rationing of precious metals served the Nazi regime well. By 1938, it had reduced total annual fine gold consumption in Germany (including for exports) to approximately six metric tons (down from thirteen in 1935 and twenty-six in 1928), slashed the share of domestic usage dependent on direct imports to only 12 percent, and assumed the role of providing nearly all of the rest from the National Bank's various stockpiles, which continued to rise nonetheless, even before the booty

[11] DUA, DL 2/1, Niederschrift über die Vorstandssitzung am 6. März 1939, p. 21.

from the annexation of Austria and the occupation of Prague flowed in.[12] In the course of this quasi-nationalization of the nation's gold industry, preferential allocations, especially to labor-intensive sectors of production, prevented layoffs and bankruptcies, and the burden of the supply squeeze was shifted unobtrusively onto German consumers in the forms of the declining availability and precious metals content of jewelry and decorative or serving pieces. Total output and domestic sales of fine silver also dropped sharply – the former from 1,478 metric tons in 1934 to 664 in 1938, the latter from some 500 metric tons in 1935/36 to 290 in 1938/39 – but without the state ever having to become more than a supplementary supplier, thanks to native ores and Degussa's international position. Once again, consumer goods for the home market were pinched most, while manufacturing of priority products (solders, amalgams, X-ray materials, pharmaceuticals, and Christmas decorations) or for preferred end-users (the Army, the Four Year Plan, the electro-technical industry) was fully provided for. Indeed, so effective did the rationing program prove that it preserved the precious metals industry's status as a foreign exchange profit maker for the Third Reich. In 1938, the average monthly net convertible income on German silver-bearing products sold abroad exceeded the total cost of purchasing silver outside the nation's borders during the entire year; the aggregate surplus over twelve months came to more than enough to pay for all the Reich's gold and platinum imports in that period as well.

Ironically, the rationing system also did far less damage to Degussa's business than the firm had feared. In 1938/39, the precious metals division's turnover was 10 percent less than in the peak year of 1933/34 and one-fourth smaller as a share of the firm's total sales. Production of fine gold and silver had fallen since 1933 by almost 67 percent and more than 50 percent, respectively, reserves of these metals by 15 percent and 20 percent (see Appendix J). Yet the division had managed to hold its domestic market share roughly constant and, despite erosion of its international market position, to keep both the proportion of its sales reaped abroad and their relative contribution to Degussa's total exports from declining (see Appendix E). Most importantly, the metals sector's gross profits had stabilized in the late 1930s at an average level 40 percent higher than in 1932/33 and thus nearly kept up with the growth rate of 46 percent for the firm as a whole (see Appendix D). In other words, the overall shrinkage of the enterprise's precious metals business had not translated into lower returns, but higher ones – indeed, Degussa's precious metals operations earned greater gross profits than in 1932/33 in all but one subsequent prewar year, despite the precipitous drops in quantities processed. As the low-margin activities of trading and smelting had contracted, growing demand for high-margin products such as solders,

[12] See Ralf Banken, "Die deutsche Goldreserven- und Devisenpolitik 1933–1939, *Jahrbuch für Wirtschaftsgeschichte* 43 (2003), pp. 49–78.

silver nitrate, and non–gold-bearing dental alloys had more than taken up the slack. And Siebert, Degussa's platinum-making subsidiary, flourished on the basis of the armaments boom; its annual dividend payments to Degussa increased from 200,000 RM in 1934 to 500,000 in 1938. Finally, the rationing system that had evolved by 1939 had one other, less quantifiable but equally satisfactory consequence from Degussa's point of view: it respected the cartel relationships that Hans Schneider had labored to protect, freezing the number of participants and their respective roles more or less in place.

Nonetheless, the effect of events on Degussa's primary smeltery in Frankfurt disturbed the leaders of the enterprise's precious metals division. The source of 3.2 million Reichsmarks in gross profits in the business year 1935/36, that plant gave off only 1.9 million in 1938/39, by which time the processing branches and sales agencies in Berlin, Pforzheim, and Düsseldorf collectively had overtaken it as money makers for the division. As a result of the steadily declining inflows of smeltable materials, Fritz Roessler had worried as early as January 1937 that he might soon run out of arguments against simply closing the installation and subcontracting for all metals separation and refining with the Norddeutsche Affinerie's works in Hamburg.[13] By 1938/39, the situation had surpassed even his dire expectations. The Frankfurt unit's fine metal yield from its principal categories of raw material dropped during that year to 58 percent of the 1935/36 level for silver, 66 percent for gold, and 80 percent of that for platinum (see Appendix J); the decline for the last two metals had been still deeper during the preceding business year (to 61 percent and 70 percent, respectively), with the result that from May 1938 on, "the employment of the plant was...but insufficient."[14] In short, however healthy the overall profitability of Degussa's precious metals operations remained in the context of rationing, the heart of the corporation's standing in the industry was ailing. Although a transfer of raw smelting to the Affinerie offered a potentially acceptable solution to the problem in financial terms, as well as an escape from cramped confines and pollution problems in Frankfurt, the prospect alarmed Degussa's metals leaders on other grounds. Adamant that "the metals department and the refinery belong indissolubly together," these executives knew that the Norddeutsche's hard-nosed managing director, Felix Warlimont, had a long record of asserting its interests against Degussa's, despite its 37 percent shareholding in his firm, and hardly relished having to wrangle with him over decisions that always had been taken in-house.[15]

---

[13] DUA, BU Fritz Roessler, "Zur Geschichte," p. 107.

[14] DUA, GEH 5/5, Degussa to the Reichskommissar für die Preisbildung, February 10, 1939, p. 2, which contains the quotation, and December 1, 1939.

[15] For the quotation as well as the general position, see DUA, GEH 2/1, Die technische Reorganisation der Metall-Abteilung, by H. Houben, February 14, 1941, p. 25.

Thus, at least three considerations – the vulnerable position of the Frankfurt refinery, Hans Schneider's desire to preserve what was left of his company's role as distributor of precious metals within Germany, and the firm's general interest in augmenting the supplies available to it and its customers – combined in early 1939 to propel Degussa's pursuit of a fateful business opportunity. At issue were the gold, silver, and platinum possessions of Jews in the Greater German Reich, which the regime, stimulated by the example of rampant Nazi pillaging in Vienna after the *Anschluss*, had been eyeing since the preceding spring and now set out to transform into revenue. In the wake of the so-called Crystal Night pogrom of November 9–10, 1938, the government first authorized the use of such objects to pay the Orwellian "atonement levy" imposed on the Jewish population, then forbade any other disposal of them, and finally ordered their surrender during March 1939 to the state-run pawnshops that were conveniently scattered about the country, equipped with adequate storage capacity, and experienced in turning precious metals–bearing items into cash.[16]

From the outset, it was plain that this "Jew Metal" or "Pawnshop Action" was a cruelly confiscatory operation. A rapidly improvised system of sham compensation to the former owners hardly concealed the openly and widely publicized intent of the regime: to drive Jews from the Reich and meanwhile to shear them of their supposedly ill-gotten gains at the expense of the Volk. Payments to the victimized individuals and representatives of communal institutions, who were directed to turn in all precious metals–bearing objects other than their own or their deceased spouse's wedding rings, their silver wrist or pocket watches, their dental prostheses, and two used four-piece place settings of silver per person, were pegged initially at the international wholesale price of the estimated fine metal content of the objects delivered, with no allowance for antiquity or workmanship, from which the pawnshops then deducted 10 percent as their service fee. And that marked only the beginning of the chicanery. Because appraisals had to be made quickly, were subject to little supervision, and could not be appealed, the pawnshops often saved time and effort by arbitrarily crediting owners with 40 percent of the amount their property might fetch at auction or 10 to 15 percent of its original cost. In many cases, people received as little as 18 RM per kilogram of silver and 1 RM per gram of gold contained in the pieces submitted, which is to say just over one-half and one-third of the respective official German prices of these metals.[17] Generally deposited directly and in stages

[16] On the origins and development of this phase of Nazi plundering and for references to the relevant literature, see Banken, *Entwicklung des Edelmetallsektors*, Chapter 4. Unless otherwise indicated, my account rests on the evidence provided in this work.

[17] LAB, Rep. 39, Restitution Court decision 3W2683/62, February 20, 1963, and testimony of Hartmann, former director of the Pfandleihanstalt Frankfurt, January 10, 1955, in case

to blocked bank accounts that the nominal recipients could barely access, the resulting sums were destined to be skimmed by Nazi-appointed trustees, then pocketed by the regime under one regulation or another when the Jews emigrated or were deported.[18]

Since these measures proceeded under the cover of law, capped a year-long campaign of dispossession in which Degussa's leaders already had joined (see Chapter 3), and impinged directly on the firm's current and prospective standing in the precious metals industry, the surviving documents give no sign of any corporate reaction other than a reflexive and eager pursuit of gain from the situation. Sadly unsurprising as that fact seems in context, however, the way in which Degussa and other firms initially hoped to benefit looks astonishingly delusional against the backdrop of the quasi-nationalization of their industry during the preceding years. In their need and greed for the commodities being expropriated, the precious metals producers and processors chose to believe that the loot would swell their existing allocations, alleviating the prevailing underutilization of the refineries and undersupply of consumers, and that the entire operation would be over within six months. To be sure, the precedent of events in Austria following the *Anschluss*, when some of the enormous quantities of precious metals plundered from Jews quickly began passing through the Dorotheum, Vienna's principal pawnshop, and into the hands of processors and jewelers, encouraged this credulity. But in succumbing to it, the would-be beneficiaries from the Pawnshop Action overlooked more than just the emergent determination of the authorities in Berlin to prevent anything like the dissipation of Jewish wealth that had occured in the so-called Ostmark. Also ignored was the regime's by now well-established practice of tailoring German precious metals policy to the Reich's strapped foreign exchange budget, not the industry's wishes.

Between February and May 1939, Degussa executives hastily conferred with the relevant governmental bodies (the Reichsbank, the Oversight Office, which was soon restyled the National Agency for Precious Metals, the National Commissioner for Pricing, and the Jewish Office of the Economics Ministry), the professional associations of the manufacturers and artisan shops that most needed the "Jew metals," and the other precious metals refineries. The objective was to establish the basis on which some or all of the last named would be authorized to relieve the pawnshops of most of the objects handed in, isolate the fine metal content and resell its equivalent on commission to designated producers, and remit the net income to the Third Reich. That the resulting arrangements involved discounting the cartellized smelting rates by 6 to 10 percent, reducing the usual sales markup that

ORG/A/3317. These documents provide no indications of the prices paid by the pawnshops for platinum-bearing objects.

[18] See DUA, DL 11.5/53, Hans Strauss to the Schlichter für Wiedergutmachung, Stuttgart, undated [December 1950] and the enclosed documents for an illustration of the procedures.

refineries could keep, and restricting Degussa's share of what its documents began to call "Jew silver" to an artifically low level seemed acceptable prices to pay for a rapid influx of materials that would ease prevailing shortages and bring in additional, albeit limited, earnings.[19]

But, as these provisions got hammered out, the relevant official agencies started to change their minds concerning the most appropriate usage of the booty. As they had done repeatedly in the preceding years, the decisive officials put their own balance sheets, especially with regard to foreign exchange, ahead of the industry's profit and loss calculations. In May 1939, only a month after the first caches of "Jew silver" arrived at the refineries, the Reich declared that corresponding amounts of fine metal would be allocated henceforth in lieu of, not in addition to, the yield from raw or recyclable metal previously purchased abroad; in June, the regime placed the distribution of all silver obtained from Jews under the authority of the Oversight Office and voided Degussa's agreement with the users' associations. After the German invasion of Poland precipitated general war and slashed export prospects, policy tightened again, as the government opted to hold the metals extorted from the Jews in reserve. In November, the flow of all gold to German fabricators was cut off; decrees followed later that month and in January 1940 terminating deliveries of "Jew silver" to manufacturers for the domestic market, then for the foreign one.

Midway through the "Jew Metal Action" the refiners thus were left literally holding the bag. Having agreed to buy, process, and sell the extorted silver and gold on relatively unrewarding terms because the materials represented a windfall, the contractors saw the regime renege on them. Not only was the new inflow now cancelled out by reductions from other sources on which the companies had earned more for refining and reselling, but also the firms were turned into cost-free storage facilities for the government. The latter circumstance meant that the funds the refineries had expended in the purchase of the metals were now "unproductive" as long as these were to be held as a reserve. The inferred interest charges on this capital (4 percent of the sum invested per annum) began adding up, to the point that they threatened to exceed the limited smelting fees and trading margins that the agreements with the Reich provided for at the eventual moment of sale.

The economics of the Pawnshop Action differed between silver and gold in ways that may startle contemporary readers. Because the cheaper metal was more plentiful and had wider industrial applications, it was more contested and ultimately almost as lucrative to both the refiners and the regime. But in each case, the system developed in 1939 rebounded on the precious metals firms and redounded to the benefit of the Reich. With regard to gold objects,

---

[19] GEH 6/11, memos by R. Hirtes, June 9 and 15, 1939, summarize the arrangements. GEH 4/1, Betr. Judensilber, June 30, 1939, signed by Dr. Eitel, lays out the silver quotas awarded to the various refiners in Germany proper.

from March 1939 until January 1940, the pawnshops were forbidden to resell any obtained from Jews except for useable pocket watches. All other gold-bearing goods were dispatched to the Central Pawn Office in Berlin, where they were screened for artistic value or possible foreign sale. Those not set aside on these grounds then were bundled or pressed together and made available for any interested refinery to pick up and purify upon making a payment that eventually was fixed at 3,400 RM per kilogram of fine gold content (about 22 percent higher than the official German gold price), minus a refining charge of 15.9 RM per kilogram of gross weight. In order to break the bottlenecks that resulted from this centralization, local pawnshops were freed at the beginning of 1940 to isolate the most valuable gold items for shipping to Berlin and to amalgamate the rest for on-the-spot collection at the same rates by the refineries. While these rendered the fine gold, they could sell equivalent quantities only to processors designated by the National Agency for Precious Metals and only when and in the amounts it determined, at a price that varied between 3,530 to 3,600 RM per kilogram, according to the industry involved.[20] The refineries thus ultimately pocketed the smelting fee and a margin of 4 to 6 percent, which was designed to cover their distribution and interest costs, over their payments to the pawnshops.[21] These meanwhile recouped their expenses (the payments to the former Jewish owners plus the 10 percent service fee) and passed on the surplus (often at least an equal amount, that is a minimum profit rate of 100 percent) to the Reich Finance Ministry.

With regard to "Jew silver," procedures were more complicated, in part because of the larger number of refineries and processors competing for it, but the net result was identical. Early in the action, the local pawnshops could conduct their own auctions of useable items with values of up to initially 300, then 150 RM, but this loophole was closed in June 1939. All other silver objects before that date, and all of them after it, were handled as gold ones eventually were: the most curatorially or commercially significant items went to Berlin and the rest were bagged for on-the-spot collection by precious metals refineries. In this case, however, only eight such companies had the right to participate and then only in accordance with specially fixed quotas (Degussa's came to 40 percent of the "Jew silver" obtained in Germany and L. Roessler's to 67 percent of that in the Ostmark). Moreover, the pricing regulations differed somewhat from those regarding gold. The

---

[20] On the smelting fees and the resale prices, see DL 11.5/58, Mayer-Wegelin's Gutachten, April 13, 1948. Although platinum-bearing objects were generally subject to the same procedures as gold-bearing ones, the surviving sources convey almost no information on their handling beyond the notation that the acquisition price from the pawnshops was 3.3 RM per gram. The refining rate and permitted resale margin are not noted.

[21] On the purpose of price spread, see *Ibid.*, Auszug aus der Aktennotiz über die Besprechung mit den Herren des Edelmetallreferats, June 28, 1940.

refineries bought the silver at the lower standard Berlin price (for materials that required refining) per kilogram of fine content on the day of transfer (34 to 36 RM), minus a smelting fee of 2 RM per kilogram. When authorized by the National Agency for Precious Metals, they sold corresponding amounts of fine silver to industrial customers at the upper standard Berlin price (for ready-to-process product) on the appropriate day (38 to 40 RM per kilogram), pocketed the smelting fee and a handling charge of 1 RM per kilogram (again intended to cover interest and distribution costs), and remitted the remaining difference between the lower (acquisition) and upper (sales) standard price to the Reich. The Nazi regime once more frequently netted, in this case from both the pawnshops' surpluses and the refineries' proceeds, an amount roughly equal to what had been paid out in pseudo-compensation for the formerly Jewish-owned silver – that is, a revenue profit of 100 percent.

The Reich had reaped some 9 million to 10 million Reichsmarks in these fashions by the time the refineries' last sales of the silver and gold credited to the "Jew Metal Action" occurred in 1941 and 1943, respectively. But Nazi Germany's overall proceeds were much higher, including in addition not only the pawnshops' nearly equivalent initial outlays, which the regime reclaimed as it drove Jews from the Greater German Reich, but also the value of the foreign exchange that no longer needed to be spent on formerly imported precious metals–bearing materials. Altogether, then, this round of pillaging must have generated some 20 million Reichsmarks in disposable income for the German state, exclusive of the returns on the sale of gold and silver objects abroad and of jewels that were also obtained.

The scale of the profits may have contributed during 1940 to loosening the regime's resistance to the refineries', especially Degussa's, mounting pleas for relief from the gathering interest burden imposed by the accumulating stocks of "Jew metals." Regarding silver, the first request of this sort occurred on June 29, 1939, immediately after the abrogation of Degussa's plan for the rapid distribution of that metal to the principal producers' associations, and was dismissed out of hand.[22] Fifteen months later, the firm had no better luck. Its petition for a doubling of the silver handling fee in view of the fact that the metals now were being held for much longer than the originally foreseen duration of six months merely elicited the Economic Ministry's reply that "the general opinion here in house is that certain sacrifices must be expected of the industry during wartime."[23] Simultaneously, however, the National Agency for Precious Metals agreed to Degussa's last-ditch proposal to sell the backlogged "Jew silver" to IG Farben for its manufacture of militarily

[22] DUA, GEH 4/1, Eitel's memo titled Manipulationsgebühr für Silber, June 30, 1939.
[23] DUA, DL 11.5/58, Degussa to the Economics Ministry, October 29, 1940; Economics Ministry to Degussa, November 25, 1940; and Notiz über die Aussprache mit dem Edelmetallreferenten im RWM, November 29, 1940, in which the remark quoted appears.

important silver nitrate and as an addition to the regular monthly metals allocations. This expedited consumption and put an end by mid-1941 to the financial drain caused by idled capital. With regard to the burgeoning gold stocks, the National Bank behaved more cooperatively and explored various means of lightening the firm's load from the fall of 1939 on, after Degussa raised the issue of its interest expense in this connection. Not until a year later, however, did the two parties settle on a procedure by which the bank bought from the corporation 1,200 kilograms of gold of non-Jewish origin for its relatively low acquisition price per kilogram, thereby paring Degussa's total carrying charges, but with the proviso that the enterprise could repurchase the metal whenever domestic demand so justified.[24] By way of further assistance, the bank also paid Degussa an extra 71,994 RM to cover its incurred interest charges through January 1941, since the interest allowance originally built into the permitted resale price margins for gold had been based on an eight-month maximum period of possession, which was sure to be exceeded yet again.

How much did Degussa, in the end, earn from this process of governmentally sanctioned plundering? The question is difficult to answer definitively, since the proceeds are not listed separately in the firm's financial accounts, the entries in its refinery books identify only some of the relevant deliveries as "Jew silver" or "Jew gold," and the potentially informative files of the branch office in Berlin, which picked up objects weekly from the Central Pawn Office, were destroyed intentionally in February 1945.[25] One must therefore reconstruct the quantities involved from incomplete and not entirely consistent surviving tabulations, then calculate the probable net receipts. The available documentation suggests that the German precious metals refineries turned the formerly Jewish-owned goods provided by the pawnshops into 130 metric tons of pure silver (143 U.S. tons), most of which went to industrial consumers (IG Farben's film-making factories alone used up more than seventy-six metric tons), and some 1.5 metric tons of fine gold (about 1.65 U.S. tons), most of which went to firms manufacturing for export.[26]

[24] DL 11.5/51, Schneider's Akten-Notiz über die heutige Aussprache mit Herrn Reichsbankdirektor Joost, November 8, 1939; GEH 11/13, Schneider's Akten-Notiz über die heutige Aussprache mit Herrn Reichsbankdirektor Jost [sic], November 21, 1939; Schneider's Akten-Notiz über unseren heutigen Besuch bei Herrn Reichsbankdirektor Pirr, December 20, 1939; Schneider's Akten-Notiz über die Aussprache mit der Reichsbank wegen Goldfinanzierung, August 1, 1940, enclosing Degussa to the Reichsbankdirektorium of the same date; and DL 11.5/58, Aktennotiz über die Besprechung in Gold- und Silberangelegenheiten, August 28, 1940.
[25] See DL 3.H.Schlosser/1, Deppe to Hirtes, February 8, 1945. Even less is clear regarding Degussa's intake of platinum. The surviving records note only that the firm got 279.9 grams of the metal via the Dorotheum in the course of 1940.
[26] For slightly different total figures, see Ralf Banken, "Der Edelmetallsektor und die Verwertung konfiszierten jüdischen Vermögens im 'Dritten Reich,'" *Jahrbuch für Wirtschaftsgeschichte* 39 (1999), pp. 152 and 155; Peter Hayes, "The Degussa AG and the Holocaust,"

The extant data also indicate that Degussa and its Viennese subsidiary actually processed somewhat larger proportions of these metals than predicted by either the quota allotments for silver or the prevailing market shares for gold. In the case of silver, the pattern was as follows, according to Degussa's own records:

As of	Total collected (kg)	To Degussa and L. Roessler (kg)	D/R ÷ T = %
December 1939	79,321.9	40,046.5	50.5[27]
September 1940	120,190.4	65,095.9	54.2[28]
February 1941	126,028.0	68,674.3	54.5[29]
August 1941	129,988.0	72,231.0	55.6[30]

These tallies are not exhaustive, since at least one Degussa document gives 130,401 kilograms as the total intake, but they are probably nearly so.[31] In any case, two points are clear: (a) as Degussa admitted in at least one postwar restitution case concerning silver taken during the Pawnshop Action, "our

in Ronald Smelser (ed.), *Lessons and Legacies V: The Holocaust and Justice* (Evanston, IL: Northwestern University Press, 2002), p. 154. As a result of further research since these articles appeared, both Banken and I have refined our statistics and analyses, and the divergence between our earlier findings has all but disappeared.

[27] DUA, DL 11.5/51, Degussa to the Reich Economics Ministry, February 16, 1940, with enclosed tabulations for each refinery as of December 31, 1939.

[28] Computed from the data in *Ibid.* and in DUA, DL 11.5/42, Notiz. Betr.: Silber-Zuteilung an die I. G. aus Leihhaussilber, signed by Benz, October 19, 1940. These provide figures for the quantities of "Judensilber" on hand at Degussa, L. Roessler, and the other refineries, either individually or collectively, as of the end of 1939 and the end of September 1940. Since virtually no outflows of silver taken from Jews were permitted between these dates, I have subtracted the inventory figures at the end of 1939 from the later ones to arrive at the total inflows during the period, then added that figure to the corresponding one for 1939 in order to reach the numbers presented here.

[29] Calculated from the data in DUA, DL 11.5/42, Leihhaus-Silber Stand vom 25. Februar 1941, signed by Benz, February 25, 1941, which gives the total intake as of that date. This indicates an inflow of 5,837.6 kilograms since October 1, 1940. My figure assumes that Degussa took in the same proportion of silver in this period as during the preceding nine months, that is, 61.3 percent or 3,578.4 kilograms.

[30] DUA, GEH 3/Schneider 1, Degussa to the Reichskommissar für die Preisbildung, August 27, 1941 (for a total intake of 129,231 kg as of the end of June), and GEH 5/5, Degussa to the Reichskommissar für die Preisbildung, August 27, 1941 (for the amount that "has passed through our plant"). These letters are not identical, though their headings and dates are. DL 2.1, Niederschrift über die Vorstandssitzung am 1.9.1941, p. 202, records that Degussa held 761 kilograms of "Judensilber" on that date, whereas the preceding managing board meeting on August 7 had been told that none remained. This therefore represents a new inflow during August, raising the total received in the Pawnshop Action to 129,988 kilograms. Though it is not absolutely clear that this sum was included in the total amount processed by Degussa reported to the Preiskommissar four days earlier, that is likely to be the case, since all the figures mentioned in Degussa's letter were end-of-the-calendar-year projections.

[31] Banken, *Entwicklung des Edelmetallsektors*, Chapter 4.

share must altogether have been between 50 and 60 percent"; and (b) that share rose in the course of the action as the other refineries concluded that the low profit margins provided were inadequate recompense for the bother of collecting the metals from the pawnshops and of holding them until the government instructed their release.[32] With regard to gold, the story was similar, but with more extreme effects. By the fall of 1940, Degussa held at least 825.7 kilograms obtained through the action and was "the only refinery that was still ready to accept any more Jew gold at all."[33] In August 1941, the corporation informed the German Commissioner for Pricing that 1,113 kilograms of pure metal had been produced at Degussa's facilities in consequence of the "Jew Metal Action," and a postwar estimate raised that figure to approximately 1,200 kilograms.[34] The latter tally, which is consistent with the scattered indications presented in the metals section's periodic reports to meetings of the firm's managing board, corresponds to 80 percent of the probable total amount of fine gold taken in by the pawnshops.

Given the refining and handling fees outlined above, Degussa probably collected about 217,000 RM on silver taken from the Jews of Germany and Austria, along with some 25,000 RM for purifying the gold, 180,000 for selling it at an average markup of 150 RM per kilogram, and almost 72,000 in the form of the interest subsidy from the Reichsbank – altogether, approximately 494,000 RM. But most of these sums are uncertain for several reasons. Degussa had to grant a commission of 20 percent from the silver handling fee to middlemen and retailers in an indeterminate number of cases.[35] The enterprise also could not always keep the full fee on the silver assumed and sold when other refiners declined to exercise their quotas (roughly the 20,630 kilograms that Frankfurt processed over and above its original 40 percent share). For example, Degussa rebated to Freiberg 20 percent of the handling fee on the 7,833 kilograms of pure silver refined on its behalf, a sum of almost 1,567 RM.[36] Conversely, Degussa's silver deliveries to IG Farben appear to have involved an extra one-half mark in distribution fees, which would have aggregated to more than 16,000 RM.[37] All told,

[32] LAB, Rep. 039-01, Bd. 28, Nr. 334, Bl. 229–32, Degussa to the Kammergericht 3. Zivilsenat Berlin-Charlottenburg, July 7, 1960, p. 3.

[33] DUA, GEH 11/13, Stand der Goldfonds der Reichsstelle für Edelmetalle per 28. September 1940, unsigned; and DL 11.5/58, Deppe's Notiz vom 2.11.40 betr. Zinsvergütung für Judensilber.

[34] See GEH 5/5, Degussa to the Reichskommissar für die Preisbildung, August 27, 1941; and DUA, DL 11.5/58, Mayer-Wegelin to Scherf, April 13, 1948, and DL 11.5/44, Baerwind and Hirtes to Leiter des Amtes für Vermögenskontrolle, June 15, 1948.

[35] DUA, GEH 6/16, Schneider and Hirtes to Freiberg, December 15, 1939.

[36] DUA, GEH 6/16, Degussa to Freiberg, August 1, 1941.

[37] DUA, DL 11.5/42, IG Einkaufsabteilung to Degussa, October 21, 1940. For further information on the rates charged to Farben, see GEH 3.Schneider/9, Degussa to I. G. Farbenindustrie, January 9, 1942.

therefore, Frankfurt's revenues on silver from the Pawnshop Action probably fell between 200,000 and 225,000 RM. With regard to gold, the chief imponderable results from the fact that the refining fees were based on the gross weight of the intake, but the surviving data record only the fine metal yield. A refining income of 25,000 RM presupposes that the goods submitted had an average content of eighteen karats (i.e., were 75 percent pure); if that figure was lower, the gross weight required to yield 1,200 kilograms and thus the fees would have been higher. Similarly, the average resale margin on gold may have been slightly greater or less than 150 RM per kilogram, depending on how much of the metal went to specific industries, on which the surviving sources are inconclusive. Assuming that these variables evened out at an income for Degussa of roughly 490,000 RM, that sum corresponded to almost 2 million American dollars at the end of the twentieth century.[38]

Yet the company was probably correct in regarding the Pawnshop Action as an almost profitless undertaking.[39] Because of the preferential fees offered the Reich, the negative net capital charges that remained even after the National Bank's supplementary payment for some of the gold, and the regime's practice of substituting "Jew metals" for other inputs that Degussa would have received in due course, neither the firm's balance sheets nor the problems of underutilization at the Frankfurt refinery were much improved by the extortion to which the Jews of Greater Germany were subjected.[40] In fact, the most positive evaluation of the entire operation in the firm's surviving records is Hermann Schlosser's wan remark to the managing board in August 1941 that "a change for the better has set in concerning the Reich's habit of exploiting us in this sphere."[41] In the end, loot from the action accounted for 5 percent of Degussa's gold output and about 9 percent of its silver production between April 1939 and September 1941, but for only about .5 percent (60,000 RM) of the metals sector's gross profits (12.9 million Reichsmarks), assuming that these were generated from the proceeds (490,000 RM) at the rate of 12 percent that characterized the division during this period (see Appendices C and D). All that said, the salient points about Degussa's participation in the "Jew Metal Action" appear to be that (a) it

---

[38] In converting the currencies and estimating present values, I have divided the number of Reichsmarks by 2.5 (according to the official exchange rate of the Nazi era), then followed the generally accepted current practice of multiplying the resulting number of dollars by ten. Cf. Banken, *Entwicklung des Edelmetallsektors*, Chapter 4.

[39] See, for example, DUA, GEH 3.Schneider/9, Deppe's Notiz Betr. Feinsilberpreis für I. G.-Käufe, December 23, 1941, which notes regarding Jew silver that "no profit remains to us on these transactions anyway."

[40] On the underutilization, see Appendix J to this book and DUA, GEH 5/5, Degussa to the Reichskommissar für die Preisbildung, February 10, 1939, November 19, 1940, and August 27, 1941. All three documents report to the effect that, as the third one says, "also in this reporting year our plant capacity could not be fully used."

[41] DUA, DL 2/1, Niederschrift über die Vorstandssitzung am 4. August 1941, p. 198.

did not add to the supply of precious metals or the earnings on them that Degussa would have obtained in 1939–41 had the action not occurred; but (b) the firm eagerly entered into it on the opposite expectation and persisted for other self-interested reasons.

On the eve of his death from a sinus infection in February 1941, before a final balance sheet of the Pawnshop Action could be drawn up, Hans Schneider could have anticipated its disappointing bottom line and felt vindicated nonetheless. Immediate profit had not been his or Degussa's chief objective, especially after the Reich decided to reduce other inflows, then the war began. Preserving the firm's pivotal place in the precious metals industry was the paramount purpose, now reinforced by ideals of national service. As Schneider put the matter in April 1940, "our policy... absolutely must be set, in order not to lose our key position, on doing our utmost to have the available silver... go through us."[42] By this standard, he had largely succeeded. He had managed during the development of precious metals rationing and the Pawnshop Action to prove that private business could meet the Reich's needs and that Degussa could do so better than its smaller competitors, yet also to show sufficient consideration for them to blunt charges of monopolizing. Thus he had brought his firm through the tricky transition from a market to a state-directed economy, from one in which commercial agreements and acumen determined access to supplies and relative standing to one in which political influence and intelligence were decisive. In the process, he had assured that Degussa's loss of control over inflows to its industry had not led to loss of primacy within it. If this was largely a record of defensive victories, it still positioned his enterprise favorably for the future.

Moreover, at the apogee of Nazi power in February 1941, the future seemed to have arrived. While participation in the Pawnshop Action was bringing few net profits to the firm, the preservation of its leading role in the precious metals industry had begun to pay off noticeably. The business year 1940/41 saw the first appreciable jumps in the sales and gross profits of the precious metals section since 1935/36. They climbed by 39 percent and 55 percent, respectively, over the totals for 1939/40, reaching 43.4 million and 5.9 million Reichsmarks (see Appendices C and D). Even more striking were the leaps in net profits by 126 percent (from 1.45 million to 3.27 million Reichsmarks) and in their ratio to gross profits from 1:3 to better than 1:2. That ratio became yet more favorable during the succeeding business years, as gross and net profits vaulted again in 1941/42 by another 41 percent and 46 percent (to 8.3 million and 4.77 million Reichsmarks) on the way to peaking in 1943/44 at 8.8 million and 5.33 million, respectively. Between 1938/39, the last peacetime business year, and 1943/44, the gross profits of the precious metals section grew by 62 percent, outpacing the figure of 50 percent

---

[42] DUA, GEH 6/18, Schneider's Notiz über eine kurze Aussprache mit Herrn Dr. Reinhard Heraeus, April 2, 1940, p. 3.

for Degussa as a whole. This surge in profitability is all the more remarkable because the average annual quantities of silver and gold flowing in and out of Degussa's refineries during the calendar years 1941–44 were lower than even the already depressed norms for the preceding four-year period.

Small wonder, then, that neither Schneider nor his colleagues showed any sign of thinking twice about the feature of his policy that seemed most axiomatic at the time but looks most reprehensible in retrospect: Degussa's indifference to the origins of increasingly large portions, beginning with the Pawnshop Action, of the metals the firm pursued. This is not to say that the corporation took no interest in such matters or was blind to delicate issues raised by them. On the contrary, Degussa often inquired in the early 1940s about the provenance of metals Frankfurt received and sought to tread carefully in sensitive cases. In April 1943, for instance, presumably because the enterprise's employees knew of widespread looting in Nazi-controlled Europe, they sought and received official guidance concerning which submissions of "used gold . . . from military departments, civil agencies in occupied lands, and army personnel" the concern should refine and return.[43] But such requests expressed a desire for covering authority, not moral qualms. As long as the Nazi state sanctioned specific conduct, Degussa demonstrated no collective or corporate reservations about engaging in it.

Such indifference functioned as the necessary condition of the precious metals sector's rising fortunes during Hitler's war, but not the sufficient one. While willingness to use or launder stolen property underpinned the division's success between 1940 and 1945, several other causes also contributed to this result. Despite the large gaps in the documentary record created by the purposeful destruction of files near the end of World War II (and perhaps again later), four overarching trends stand out in this regard: the regularization of Degussa's supplies, the militarization of its output, the rationalization of its operations, and the consolidation of its industry. Each development attested to the way wartime urgencies worked to the advantage of the largest and richest firm in the business, serving to streamline its operations and make them more rewarding at reduced aggregate levels of inputs.

First, although inflows of gold, silver, and platinum proved less than desirable during the war, they were more than adequate – and more dependable, as well as easier to obtain and process, than in previous years. Thanks to prewar constriction of demand, wartime conservation, and the conquests of 1940–41, the German domestic economy never experienced a serious shortage of precious metals after the first year of fighting, although intermittent scares arose. With gold usage down to one metric ton annually (one-third of it mined in Germany), silver consumption back up to the prerationing rate of about 550 tons (140 to 180 of them from domestic ores), and platinum

[43] DUA, GEH 11/4, Burchard's Zirkularnotiz Betr. Ausführungen von Aufträgen auf Umtausch von Altgold in Zahngold, April 22, 1943.

metals needs running at some 2.5 tons (virtually none of them obtainable internally), the shortfalls were made up easily from occupied Europe and the reserves that the Reich had built prior to 1939 and, in the case of platinum, via purchases from the Soviet Union in 1939–41.[44] After October 1941, with the exception of five months during 1943, the Reich Finance Ministry made coin silver from its mints available for German production at an average rate of twenty-five metric tons per month, and, in order to keep the operation secret, exclusively through Degussa.[45] These deliveries covered about 40 percent of German requirements in 1942–44, yet both the nation and the corporation ended the war with considerable stockpiles of not only silver, but also gold and platinum, on hand. In fact, the Reich's gold reserves actually increased slightly from September 1, 1939 to June 30, 1945.[46] So unimperiled were Degussa's own "iron reserves" that it locked away 145 kilograms of platinum and 224.6 kilograms of palladium in the cellars of the old National Bank building in Berlin in August 1942 and 445 kilograms of gold in the vaults of the Länderbank in Vienna the following December and left both caches untouched until early 1945, when the platinum was evacuated to Frankfurt and the gold presumably to hiding places in the Tyrol.[47] For much of the war, the firm's chief concern about inventories was to keep them in check so as to rein in the capital expenses.[48]

---

[44] On the German domestic output of gold, DUA, Einzelakten, Degussa Metallwerk Betriebs- berichte 40a, Nr. 210, 20 December 1941. On the arrangements with the Russians, which called for imports of some 3.4 metric tons of platinum metals by August 1941, see DUA, IW 3.6/1, especially Siebert and Hereaus G.m.b.H. to UdSSR Allunionistische Vereinigung für den Export von Industriewaren, 7 September 1939, and Hans Siebert's Unterredung auf dem Russland-Ausschuss der Deutschen Wirtschaft, March 14, 1940. On one flurry of concern regarding silver supplies, brought on by the increase of military consumption from six to fourteen tons per month on average, see GEH 3.Hirtes/4, Fröhlich's Sparmassnahmen auf dem Silbergebiet, October 2, 1942.

[45] DUA, GEH 6/10, Hirtes to Warlimont, October 11, 1941; on the supplies from the state, DL 2/1, Niederschriften über die Vorstandssitzungen am 5. Januar 1942, p. 228, 7. Dezember 1942, p. 290, 1. Februar 1943, p. 301, 5. April 1943, p. 313, 3. Mai 1943, pp. 317–18, and 4. Oktober 1943, p. 340; GEH 11/11, Reichsfinanzminister to Degussa, October 28, 1943; and GEH 3.Hirtes/4, Schleicher to Deppe, January 26, 1945, on the sources of German silver supplies in 1944. Degussa bought coin silver from the Reich at 36.50 RM per kilogram, minus 80 RM per kilogram for refining charges, so the firm's usual income on reselling the fine output was 2.80 RM per kilogram; see GEH 11/11, Reichsfinanzminister to Degussa, August 12, 1943.

[46] Independent Commission of Experts on Switzerland and the Second World War [Bergier Commission], *Switzerland and Gold Transactions in the Second World War: Interim Report* (Bern, 1998), Table I, p. 38, which gives the value of German reserves at the outbreak of the war as U.S. $256.7 million and in June 1945 (exclusive of the reserves of the Hungarian National Bank) as $265.6 million, which translates approximately into an increase from 228 to 236 metric tons.

[47] See the relevant records in DUA, GEH 11/27.

[48] See DUA, DL 2.1, Niederschrift über die Vorstandssitzung am 14. August 1940, pp. 115– 17, at which the fundamental policy line was laid down; 3. August 1942, pp. 263–64; and

Adequate supplies greatly reduced the time and energy Degussa spent on costly foreign transactions and the uncertainties of arbitrage. The surviving sources allude to short-lived efforts by Degussa's Swiss subsidiary, Leukon, to arrange imports of silver and platinum from the United States via Italy in late 1939, longer-running purchases of gold in Switzerland by that firm, and continuous work by the Vienna branch (L. Roessler & Co. until 1940) to buy up refinable materials and conclude reminting contracts in the Southeastern Europe states allied to the Axis during the war years.[49] Degussa also purified metals provided by Swiss, Italian, Scandinavian, and Hungarian customers on commission throughout the war.[50] But the firm's predominant international interest from 1941 to 1945, as well as the Reich's, was in selling, not purchasing, precious metals–bearing materials. By late 1942, in fact, Degussa largely ceased acquiring platinum or silver via Switzerland or from Vichy France unless the objective was to hamper competitors there in third markets.[51] Instead, the enterprise concentrated on retaining or adding to its customers in – or (via Leukon) through – the few export markets that remained to it, and the German National Bank was pleased to collect the resulting earnings in foreign currency in exchange for Reichsmarks. From Leukon alone, including through its nominal purchase of Degussa's Dutch subsidiaries in 1944 as a means of transferring funds, this income came to at least 1.1 million Swiss francs between 1940 and the end of the war, even as the precious metals sector's total exports declined.[52]

5. Oktober 1942, p. 280. This did not prevent Degussa, however, from reacquiring most of the gold it had sold to the National Bank in 1940 during 1942–43; see the minutes of the meetings of December 7, 1942, p. 290; March 1, 1943, pp. 306–07; April 5, 1943, pp. 312–13; and May 3, 1943, pp. 317–18.

[49] On Leukon's activities, see DUA, GEH 3.Hirtes/12, Furler's Notiz Betr. Palladiumbeschaffung über Italien, September 19, 1939; IW 3.6/1, Siebert to Schneider, October 6, 1939; and AW 6.8/1, Hirtes's Notiz Betr. Besprechung mit der Leukon A. G., October 12, 1939, and his Notiz Betr. Leukon A. G., August 31, 1940. On Vienna's, see GEH 6/14, Walter Roessler's Bericht über das abgelaufene erste Halbjahr des Geschäftsjahres 1943/44, June 2, 1944, Beilage 2.

[50] See DUA, GKF 2/9, Thoma to Hirtes, August 7, 1944, enclosing a list of current projects of this sort.

[51] See DUA, GEH 6/10, Hirtes to Poncet, October 10, 1942, Degussa to Reichsstelle für Edelmetalle, October 12, 1942, and Hirtes's Notiz Betr. Französicher Exportsilberhandel, December 14, 1943. Degussa made an exception to this policy in the case of a purchase of five kilograms of platinum from Leukon for the National Agency for Precious Metals in mid-1943 as a partial substitute to having to pay over foreign exchange earned by that firm to the German National Bank; see AW 6.8/1, Bernau's Leukon A. G., April 19, 1943, and Reichsstelle für Edelmetalle to Degussa, May 25, 1943.

[52] On Leukon's use as a sales agency and its earnings, see DUA, BET 10/42, Degussa to Leukon, December 12, 1940, contract between Siebert and Leukon, May 27, 1941, Leukon to Siebert, May 28, 1941; BET 10/43, Bernau's Leukon A. G., October 3, 1941; AW 6.8/1, Hirtes's Notiz Betr. Leukon A. G., August 31, 1940, Bernau's Abschluss der Leukon A. G., February 23, 1942, Bernau's Betr.: Leukon A. G., June 13, 1942, Bernau's Betr.: Unterredung mit

Second, the militarization of Degussa's output made it virtually self-marketing, and at prices and quantities that were as predictable as those for inputs. A concise illustration of the effects came from the unlikely quarter of Degussa's ceramic colors department, which concentrated in peacetime on making metallic applications and enamels for porcelain and glass objects and became more closely tied to the metals division proper in the course of the war. Though the department's sales averaged 20 percent less annually during the war years than during the last peacetime ones, its gross profits held constant, largely because the collapse of the consumer market for a variety of products was more than offset by the growth of the military appetite for a narrow array of preparations, especially silver ones, that even a thinned workforce could produce profusely for high-frequency communications apparatus and radios.[53] Similar consequences were all the more apparent in already arms-related productive sections of the precious metals division, such as the manufacture of silver nitrate, and largely explain Degussa's ability to sustain output and increase earnings despite the steady attrition of the firm's skilled workforce during the war.

Third, as military needs channeled Degussa's production, initiatives to rationalize it – that is, to maximize yields from finite human and material resources – also contributed heavily to the precious metals sector's improving balance sheets. While technical personnel were encouraged to devise new alloys that stretched available quantities of gold, silver, and platinum over more units of output, organizational changes cut wasteful redundancies.[54] Early in 1941, Dr. Houbens, a veteran manager in the division, capitalized on the urgency of wartime conditions to win the managing board's general support for his long frustrated desire to rearrange production among Degussa's five main precious metals processing installations so as to streamline the flow of materials to them, optimize their use of space, raise technical quality, and curtail overhead through specialization. His "immediate program," which called for concentrating the manufacture of platinum-based or high-quality finished goods, including rivets and contacts, at the Siebert subsidiary's Hanau plant, semi-finished silver products at the Reinickendorf works in Berlin, and gold-based, jewelry, and dental preparations at Pforzheim, while leaving

---

Reichsbankrat Goerling wegen der Leukon A. G., February 19, 1943, and Bernau's Leukon A. G., April 19, 1943, AW 6.8/1, Zusammenstellung der Gewinne an freien Devisen aus dem Jahr 1943 mit Hilfe der Fa. Leukon AG, Zürich, abgewickelten Edelmetall-Auslandsgeschäfte, January 24, 1944; BET 10/22, Bernau's Notiz Betr. N. V. United Metal and Chemical Co., Amsterdam, August 7, 1945, and Bernau to Reichsbankhauptstelle, May 30, 1944; BET 10/43, Bernau's Betr.: Leukon A. G., January 27, 1944; and GKF 2/9, Hübner's Notiz über Reise in die Schweiz, April 20, 1944.

[53] DUA, GKF 2/9, Kollmar's Der Glanzgoldbetrieb im Krieg, December 10, 1942.

[54] On the materials-saving initiatives, see GEH 6/6, K. W. Fröhlich, Der technische Einsatz der Edelmetalle in Deutschland in den Jahren 1939–1945, undated; and GEH 3.Hirtes/12, Protokoll über die...Konzernbesprechung der Metall-Abteilung, April 3, 1940.

Frankfurt to conduct refining and reducing Vienna to a primarily marketing role, was partially carried out over the ensuing two years and achieved
noteworthy economies.[55] Even more effective in cutting costs were Degussa's
intense efforts in early 1942 to slash the array of alloys and semi-finished
products the firm made, often in time-consuming small batches. As a result,
silver solder compounds were reduced from 120 types to only fifteen, silver
alloys for the jewelry and tableware industries from fifteen kinds to three,
gold alloys for jewelers from more than sixty sorts to three and for the dental trade from ten to fifteen to three, amalgams to five, then two mixtures,
and grades of purity for fine gold or silver sold to other manufacturers to
two levels each. Further abridgements in Degussa's assortment of laboratory
equipment, electrodes, nettings, and capillary tubings followed.[56] Finally in
this connection, the national labor shortage imposed another sort of unit-
cost-reducing action: the extension of the work week at the metals plants to
generally fifty-four to sixty hours (for women and men, respectively).[57]

Fourth, wartime inroads on competition also benefited Degussa's precious
metals business. By late 1942, the state's drive to free up workers for the arms
industry had led to full or partial shutdowns of all but twelve of thirty-one
precious metals manufacturing firms in Germany, thus funneling business
toward the enterprise with the greatest capacity.[58] The same motive underlay
the Reich's sweeping decision in early 1943 to prohibit German production of
semi-finished silver articles except at Degussa's plants, a move that naturally
had the identical effect but more strongly.[59] Meanwhile, a deal with the
Norddeutsche Affinerie finally had achieved a fairly precise delimitation of
its and Degussa's claims to precious metals–bearing materials. This reserved
the processing of most ores to the Norddeutsche Affinerie and that of most
German coin silver and virtually all recyclable or semi-purified materials,
along with the sale of all refined output, to Frankfurt. One of the chief
consequences of the settlement was to cut the fraction of government coin

---

[55] See DUA, GEH 2/1, H. Houben's Die technische Reorganisation der Metall-Abteilung, February 14, 1941; DL 2/1, Niederschrift über die Vorstandssitzung am 3. März 1941, p. 167;
GEH 3.Hirtes/1, Degussa to Fachgruppe Metallhalbzeug-Industrie, 11.iv.42 (on the concentration of the production of semi-finished silver goods in Berlin during 1941), and TLE
1/23, Krebs' Bericht über das III. Geschäftsvierteljahr 1942/43, December 8, 1943 (on the
termination of most semi-finished production in Vienna by order of the National Agency for
Precious Metals in the spring of that year).

[56] See DUA, GEH 3.Hirtes/1, especially Schleicher's Niederschrift über die vierte Zusam-
menkunft des Beirats der Metall-Abteilung, January 30, 1942.

[57] The 48-hour work week was set formally by the managing board meeting of April 7, 1941
(DL 2/1, p. 169), but actual working hours generally were longer; see DUA, GEH 3.Hirtes/10,
the four reports of the Hanau plant to the Geschäftsführer der Wirtschaftsgruppe Metall-
waren, February 26, 1942.

[58] DUA GEH 3.Hirtes/6, Schleicher's Kurzer Bericht über die Lage beim Sonderring Edelmetalle,
November 27, 1942, and Tätigkeitsbericht Hauptring Metalle, December 1942.

[59] DUA, DL 2/1, Niederschrift über die Vorstandssitzung am 5. April 1943, p. 313.

silver that Degussa earlier had agreed to share with the Norddeutsche from one-half to one-quarter, a large enough gain to more than outweigh Freiberg's success in inserting itself into this business late in the war.[60]

Interestingly, however, very few of the precious metals division's gains from 1941 to 1945 appear to be attributable to direct exploitation of Nazi victories in order to dispossess or weaken rivals on the European continent. Aside from the Aurora refinery in Brno discussed in Chapter 3, Degussa's metals sector took over no competing sales or productive outlets in the German sphere during World War II. The single documented attempt of this sort, an effort that Hans Schneider promoted shortly before his death as a "surely one-time opportunity" to take "the Dutch precious metals industry completely in hand," foundered on the refusal of Degussa's French counterpart and cartel partner, the Comptoir Lyon Allemand, to sell all of its shares in the H. Drijfhout & Zoons Edelmetaalbedrijven of Amsterdam. Though Degussa at one point hinted that the Comptoir's continued presence in what was becoming part of the internal German market could become a justification for intruding on the French one, that turned out to be no more than a bargaining ploy, and Frankfurt let the matter drop in November 1941.[61] Even less seems to have come of a contemplated parallel project to take over the Comptoir's 100 percent holding in the Annibale Columbi S. A. of Milan.[62] Similarly, Degussa's precious metals sector persisted in its long-standing policy of declining to engage in mining, despite several proffered takeovers, and displayed caution about expanding its operations in Poland and Denmark.[63] At least briefly in the summer of 1941, the division's leaders

[60] On this agreement and the long wrangling that preceded it, see DUA, GEH 6/11, Hirtes's Notiz Betr. Verständigung Affinerie/Degussa auf dem Edelmetallgebiet, November 14, 1940; and GEH 4/1, Schlosser's Betr. Norddeutsche Affinerie, August 28, 1942, Heide's Silberabkommen Scheideanstalt, September 17, 1942, and Vereinbarung Degussa/Affinerie, November 6–10, 1942. On Freiberg's offensive, see GEH 6/16, Benz's Notiz Betr.: Reichsmünzsilber-Geschäft/Freiberg, August 1, 1944.

[61] DUA, DL 2/1, Niederschrift über die Vorstandssitzung am 6. Januar 1941, p. 151, and Anlagen 1–2, Hirtes's Notiz Betr. J. Drijfhout & Zoon's, December 28, 1940, and Schneider's Notiz with the same title, January 3, 1941 (from which the quoted words come); GEH 6/10, Hirtes's Notiz Betr.: H. Drijfhout & Zoons, February 1, 1941, Degussa to Jean Le Bec, July 15, 1941, and Degussa to Comptoir Lyon-Allemand, November 18, 1941.

[62] DUA, DL 2/1, Niederschrift über die Vorstandssitzung am 2. Dezember 1940, p. 145, and Anlage 8, Hirtes's Notiz Betr. unsere Stellung im italienischen Edelmetallgeschäft, November 29, 1940. However, Degussa did take advantage of wartime conditions to strengthen its position in the German precious metals industry at the expense of property owners in an enemy country. When the Norddeutsche Affinerie increased its stock capital by 20 percent in 1940, Degussa and the Metallgesellschaft acquired not only the shares to which their existing stockholdings entitled them, but also those to which British investors could not exercise their rights; see DL 2/1, Niederschrift über die Vorstandssitzung am 7. Oktober 1940, p. 134.

[63] For examples of Degussa's rejection of proferred investments in mining enterprises, see DUA, DL 2.1, Niederschriften über die Vortstandssitzungen am 6. März 1939, p. 21 and Anlage 2 (regarding a one-third holding in an Austrian gold mining firm), and 8. Januar 1940,

harbored larger long-term ambitions, as indicated by the remark of Robert Hirtes, Schneider's successor, that "we now indeed hope after the war to be able to pull to us a large part of the European silver trade, insofar as it previously took place with London, and thus to bring about a considerable increase in our sales."[64] But this sort of fantasizing rapidly gave way to preoccupation with more immediate tasks.

Although the rising profitability of Degussa's precious metals division was, thus, partly an artifact of wartime economic conditions, most of the firm's gold inflows from 1941 to 1945, nearly half its silver ones, and (in contrast to the Pawnshop Action) a substantial share of the earnings from both stemmed from the Nazi state's plundering of occupied Europe, including of its Jews. As in the case of another vicious form of Hitlerian policy, the exploitation of forced labor (see Chapter 7), the horrors of the Holocaust have tended in recent decades to obscure a central reality concerning the Third Reich's pillaging: the quantities extracted from non-Jews vastly exceeded those taken from Jews. For example, one authoritative recent analysis concludes that the Nazi regime seized gold in occupied Europe worth some U.S. $532 million (in 1945 dollars) during World War II, of which $450 million (85 percent) came from the vaults of the National and state-owned banks in occupied countries. Within the $82 million (15 percent) confiscated from individual persons or commercial entities, the amount extracted from Jews is impossible to specify.[65] It can have been, in my view, no less than $5 million and may have been much more, but even an expansive accounting is unlikely to produce a final number that composes more than 20 to 25 percent of this subset or 3 to 4 percent of the whole. Nonetheless, the barbarism to which Jews were subjected was both unspeakable and distinct in its comprehensiveness, and Degussa became deeply implicated in not only benefiting from it and the other forms of Nazi looting, but also in making such viciousness rewarding for the Third Reich. Given the fragmentary nature of the surviving sources, one can provide only exemplary and global indications, but not an itemized breakdown, of the amounts of stolen gold and silver that passed through Degussa's operations and the firm's likely income as a result. Even so, the sums are appreciable, and they weigh heavily in any assessment of the enterprise's historical conduct.

pp. 69–70 (concerning a gold mine in the Protectorate). On Poland, see GEH 3.Schneider/5, Brauer's Notiz über das frühere Silbergeschäft der Zweigniederlassung Berlin in Polen, July 24, 1941; on Denmark, GEH 3.Schneider/4, Deppe's Notiz Degussa-Kopenhagen, June 17, 1941, and BET 10/1, Bernau's Betr.: A/S Degussa Kopenhagen–Jahresabschluss 1943, June 7, 1944.

[64] DUA, GEH 6/11, Hirtes's Notiz. Betr.: Ausdehnung von Mansfeld und Preussag auf dem Balkan, July 31, 1941.

[65] Independent Commission of Experts, *Interim Report*, Table I, p. 38. My calculations exclude the reserves of the Hungarian National Bank, which were only briefly in German possession. At seventy-three metric tons, the total amount of gold seized from individuals was just a bit more than what the Nazis took from the National Bank of Italy alone.

The great preponderance of precious metals routed to Degussa from Nazi-occupied Europe appears to have been unrelated to the Holocaust and to have emanated from Poland, France, Belgium, Serbia, the Czech lands, Greece, and Holland. The paper trail varies greatly in quality, however, among the points of origin and the metals concerned. About inflows from Poland, Degussa's files provide only scattered indications of what must have been substantial volumes. The company sought to control the disposition of "Cracow silver" – that is, material from the seat of the German administration in the unannexed portion of the country – as early as April 1940 and later cited an unspecified intake – perhaps amounting to fifteen to twenty metric tons – of "Polish coin silver" as one cause of the slight resurgence in Frankfurt's silver output during the first wartime business year.[66] Multiple subsequent deliveries likely were on a similar scale, with the exception of the 432 bars of "looted silver, in fact from Poland" that Degussa's Berlin branch inspected at the Reich Treasury in April 1943 and then shipped to Frankfurt and to the Norddeutsche Affinerie in Hamburg; these probably weighed five to eight metric tons.[67] Two months later, Degussa anticipated the arrival of another fifteen metric tons of silver from the General Government and some fifteen to eighteen more tons from Lithuania.[68] And in the months surrounding the turn of 1943/44, the Vienna office "further pursued the government coin silver business with the General Government, which can now be regarded as completed," with the result that "the lack of material at our refinery could... be remedied."[69] Though Degussa's documents say nothing of the quantities involved in this instance, bank records in Warsaw suggest that they exceeded twenty metric tons.[70]

---

[66] DUA, GEH 6/18, Hirtes's Akten-Notiz über eine kurze Aussprache mit Herrn Dr. Reinhard Heraeus, April 2, 1940; GEH 11/13, Deppe's Akten-Notiz mit den Herren der Edelwache, August 30, 1940; and GEH 5/5, Degussa to the Reichskommissar für die Preisbildung, November 19, 1940, p. 2.

[67] On this material, which apparently came to Berlin via Romania, see DUA, GEH 11/11, Zweigniederlassung Berlin to Sales Group Frankfurt, April 29 and May 5, 1943.

[68] DUA, DL 2/1, Niederschrift über die Vorstandssitzung am 7. Juni 1943, p. 321.

[69] DUA, GEH 6/14, Roessler's Bericht über das abgelaufene erste Halbjahr des Geschäftsjahres 1943/44 der Zweigniederlassung Wien, June 2, 1944, p. 4 (for the first quotation); and DL 2/1, Niederschrift über die Vorstandssitzung am 5. Februar 1944, p. 358 (where the second quotation appears).

[70] Archivum Akt Nowych, Warsaw, Bank Emisyjny w Likwidacji, Tabulation of "Metall-sendung im Reich," Copy, July 9, 1946, lists four payments by Degussa to that bank between April and June 1944 totaling 1.8 million zloty. Three of these are clearly marked as being made in return for deliveries of Polish coin silver. Only one notation, however, that for a payment of 445,510 zloty on April 9, 1944, indicates the quantities involved, which came to a gross weight of 10,115 kilograms, or 44 zloty per kilogram. At that rate, the two remaining marked shipments would have contained 15,437 kilograms. If the unmarked shipment also referred to coin silver, the contents would have been 15,555 kilograms. Altogether, then, the possible gross weight of the final round of Polish coin silver deliveries would have been 41.1 metric tons. Assuming that the normal alloy ratio of 50 percent fine silver obtained, the yield

With regard to France, the extant documents convey more information, but only for a short period of time. In October 1940, the National Agency for Precious Metals granted Degussa's request for permission to buy precious metals in the area governed by the Military Commander in Belgium and Northern France and set purchase prices at 2 to 5 percent below the official German rates. All gold so obtained was to be sold to the German National Bank at cost plus a commission of one-half percent and reimbursement for the transportation expenses. For platinum, palladium, and silver, which were intended for German industrial customers, Degussa's reward was embedded in the difference between the officially determined acquisition and resale prices.[71] By Bastille Day of 1941, the enterprise had purchased 61,052 kilograms of probably confiscated French silver from the Reich-owned Raw Materials Trading Company (Roges) for just over 2 million Reichsmarks. Since the rate per kilogram was 5.30 RM less than the likely price at which Degussa sold the material while closing the gap between German production and needs between May and October of that year, the firm's markup approximated 323,575 RM, and even more was earned on the indeterminate portion of the metal that went toward Degussa's own output of semi-finished goods.[72] No similar details on other transactions involving French property turn up in the firm's files.

By far, the most complete records of Degussa's precious metals acquisitions from an occupied country deal with Belgium, since its Military Mission in Frankfurt made repeated inquiries on the subject in 1945–47. Immediately following the German conquest of the country, Degussa cooperated with the efforts of the Metallgesellschaft's Wilhelm Avieny to reassert joint control over the major precious and base metals refinery in Hoboken, near Antwerp, that the two firms had founded in 1887 and owned until 1918.[73] Their plan for the Société Générale Metallurgique struck the German military authorities, however, as premature. They opted instead to reinstall the Belgian managers under German oversight; to revive the output of lead, copper, zinc, and cobalt; and to reserve the question of eventual ownership for later settlement – but to divert all the plant's semi-purified precious metals by-products beyond those required by Belgian industry (primarily by the Gevaert photographic firm) to Degussa for ultimate refining and distribution.[74] Because

to Degussa would have been 20.5 metric tons. I am indebted to the late Sybil Milton for drawing this information to my attention.
[71] DUA, GEH 11/3, Reichsstelle für Edelmetalle to Degussa, October 3, 1940.
[72] DUA, GEH 6/11, Deppe to Hirtes, February 6, and July 14, 1941. See also DL 2/1, Niederschrift über die Vorstandssitzung am 3. März 1941, p. 167, and Anlage 2, memo by Benz, July 4, 1941, to the minutes of the meeting of July 7, 1941.
[73] DUA, DL 2/1, Niederschrift über die Vorstandssitzung am 1. Juli 1940, p. 99; GEH 6/20, Schlosser's Hoboken, July 6, 1940.
[74] DUA, GEH 6/20, Menzel's Bericht über meine Reise nach Belgien, July 30, 1940, and Hirtes's Notiz Betr. Hoboken, August 16, 1940; DL 2/1, Niederschrift über die Vorstandssitzung am 5. August 1940, p. 102.

Hoboken operated largely on the basis of imported materials, British command of the sea lanes made this concession a waning asset, but it proved
quite valuable between November 1940 and August 1941, when deliveries
were concentrated. The fifty-five metric tons of fine silver, two metric tons of
fine gold, and seventeen kilograms of fine platinum that Degussa obtained
in that interval from Belgian inputs (which represented 67 percent, 100 percent, and 95 percent of the firm's final respective production totals from
this source for the entire period 1941–45) contributed 15 percent, 30 percent, and 25 percent, respectively, to Degussa's yields from refinable inflows
during its 1940/41 business year.[75]
Few of these materials were, strictly speaking, plundered, since Degussa
purchased all the Belgian precious metals it obtained, and at prices that
corresponded to prevailing international, though not German rates. In all
probability, however, neither the firm nor the Reich would have gained access
to these metals without conquest. The gold, as in northern France, was
of much more interest to the Nazi state than to Degussa, which earned
little from "functioning only as a transfer office for the [German] National
Bank." Corporate receipts came to a mere 20,897 RM as a commission
for buying and conveying 1,633 kilograms fine from the Emissionsbank in
Brussels and 27,203 RM for paying for, purifying, and passing on 2,000 more
fine kilograms from Hoboken and three lesser Belgian providers. Various
import fees may have reduced the eventual total compensation to only about
45,000 RM, and possibly less, over a period of almost five years.[76] But the
silver Degussa acquired from the country or processed for and returned
to Belgian firms (30,795 kilograms and 52,995 kilograms, respectively, in
1941–45) and the platinum, palladium, and rhodium that either went to
Frankfurt or there and back to Belgium (altogether 42.9 and 5.3 kilograms,
respectively) gave off greater returns because of the associated smelting fees
and resale markups. By my calculations, for example, Degussa earned at least
237,000 RM on the Belgian fine silver that emerged from its refineries during
World War II, exclusive of any profit on the transformation of some of the
metal into semi-finished goods.[77] And the benefits of military occupation did

[75] Computed from DUA, GEH 5/5, Degussa to the Reichskommissar für die Preisbildung,
August 27, 1941; and GEH 6/20, Ochs's Betr.: Mission Belge Militaire, Frankfurt/Main,
November 29, 1947.
[76] Computed on the basis of *Ibid.* and the price schedule set forth in GEH 6/20, unsigned memo
headed Edelmetalle, undated [November 1940]. On the fees, see GEH 6/20, Ochs's Notiz
Betr. Gebühren auf belgische Edelmetalleinfuhren, April 3, 1941, and Deppe's Notiz Gebühr
auf belgisches Gold, May 30, 1941, where the quoted words appear. In all probability,
Degussa also made incidental reformatting fees on some of the gold, such as the 770 kilograms
that the National Bank ordered cast into plates and bars suitable for international exchange;
see GEH 11/13, Schneider's Notiz Besprechung mit der Reichsbank wegen Goldfinanzierung,
November 29, 1940.
[77] Calculated from the data in GEH 3.Hirtes/12, his Notiz Betr. Hoboken, October 24, 1940;
GEH 6/20, unsigned memo headed Edelmetalle, undated [November 1940]; GEH 6/10,

not stop there. The mounting transfer of film-making contracts to Belgium after 1942 increased its demand for silver nitrate to the point that, in effect, more fine silver (the equivalent of almost 69,000 kilograms) flowed into the country's economy from Degussa's refineries during the war than out to them. The enterprise, as a result, made almost equal amounts of money from the occupation both coming and going – just as the Nazi regime gained war material either way.[78]

Degussa's intakes from Serbia were of two sorts. One consisted of shipments of former Yugoslavian coin silver via the German Finance Ministry, of which some forty metric tons that arrived in the first half of 1942 and twenty metric tons processed in 1944 are documented.[79] The second comprised deliveries of silver- and gold-bearing by-products from the copper mines at Bor and Trepca that a consortium of state-subsidized or -owned German firms took over from French and Anglo-American shareholders in 1941. From this source, another twenty-seven and thirteen metric tons of fine silver are known to have resulted in late 1941 and early 1943, respectively, and 912 kilograms of fine gold in 1943–44.[80] The figure for gold may be complete, aside from another thirty kilograms that Degussa perhaps received in late 1941, because the firm avoided acquisitions of that metal during 1942 while negotiating a new agreement with the Reich concerning the interest burden of carrying large inventories.[81] But the silver quantities probably represent only portions of the ultimate inflows, especially from Bor-Trepca, since Degussa had exclusive rights after September 1941 to process the precious metals materials given off by these installations.[82] At 2,850 RM per kilogram of

Bernau and Furler to Mission Belge Militaire, January 16, 1946; and GEH 6/20, Ochs's Betr.: Mission Belge Militaire, Frankfurt/Main, November 29, 1947. The figures tabulated in Degussa's postwar memoranda are confirmed by contemporary documents, notably GEH 6/20, Ochs's Notiz Betr.: Edelmetalle aus Belgien, November 22, 1940, and Ochs's Bericht Nr. 4 Betr. Belgien, February 27, 1941.

[78] See GEH 6/20, Ochs's Betr.: Mission Belge Militaire, Frankfurt/Main, November 29, 1947.

[79] DUA, DL 2/1, Niederschriften über die Vorstandssitzungen am 2. Februar 1942 (p. 235) and 1. Juni 1942 (p. 253); and GEH 3.Hirtes/4, Schleicher to Deppe, January 26, 1945.

[80] See, on the silver intakes, DUA, DL 2/1, Niederschriften über die Vorstandssitzungen am 3. November 1941 (p. 214) and 11. Januar 1943 (p. 295). On the gold, the managing board minutes make reference to specific quantities totaling 912 kilograms on March 1, April 5, May 3, June 7, July 5, August 3, and December 6, 1943, and on January 4, February 5, March 6, and September 4, 1944.

[81] See GEH 6/16, Deppe's Übernahmebedingungen für Edelmetalle aus Bor/Trepca-Produktionen, November 26, 1941. On the agreement with the Reich that led Degussa to resume gold intakes, see DUA, DL 2/1, Niederschrift über die Vorstandssitzung am 5. Oktober 1942, p. 280.

[82] DUA, GEH 6/16, Hirtes's Notiz Betr.: Edelmetalle aus Bor/Trepca-Produktion, September 20, 1941. On the precondition for this deal, a sale by Degussa and the Metallgesellschaft of 300,000 RM worth of shares each in the Norddeutsche Affinerie to the Mansfeld mining firm, one of the Bor-Trepca partners, and the promise to support its eventual acquisition of the almost 22 percent of Norddeutsche stock held by the British Metal Corporation, see

fine gold and 3,470 RM per kilogram of fine silver, the purchase prices eventually arranged were somewhat less advantageous than those established for Belgium. The former amount had little relevance to Degussa, however, since it retained only the refining fees when transferring the gold to the German National Bank; and the latter sum was net of the freight and import charges paid by the providers and did not apply to certain categories of intermediate materials, for which Degussa had to pay only 3,270 RM per kilogram.[83] As a result, the effective markup on pure silver that Degussa produced from Bor-Trepca came to 4.30 to 5.80 RM per kilogram, which translates in the case of the forty documented tons to some 200,000 RM in income, again exclusive of that made from specialized semi-finished goods.

Coin silver constituted the main inflows to Degussa's refineries from the Protectorate of Bohemia and Moravia (eleven metric fine tons) and Greece (30.5 metric fine tons) in 1942–43, but 1943–44 brought the firm into a direct relationship with the principal Czech precious metals firm, the Prager Berg- und Hüttenwerke, and its mines at Pribram.[84] That enterprise generated about twenty-four metric tons of fine silver yearly from domestic mines, all of it consumed within the Czech lands prior to their occupation.[85] Thereafter, most of the silver-bearing residues from the Prague works went for refining in Freiberg, just across the former international border in Saxony, and as pure metal either back to the Protectorate for internal consumption or on to the Reich's Raw Materials Trading Company for sale to Degussa and introduction into the German distribution system.[86] During 1943, however, Degussa began receiving direct deliveries from Pribram and compensating Freiberg accordingly. By October, 15,753 kilograms of fine silver had resulted, and 2,100 more were generated from these shipments during the first half of 1944.[87] Under the fee structure the parties arranged, Degussa earned 2 RM per kilogram for the refining and 1.60 RM per kilogram as a resale

---

GEH 4/1, Schlosser's Norddeutsche Affinerie/Mansfeld, July 26, 1941; GEH 6/11, Hirtes's Notiz. Betr.: Ausdehnung von Mansfeld und Preussag auf dem Balkan, July 31, 1941; DL 2/1, Niederschrift über die Vorstandssitzung am 3. November 1941, p. 210; and D 2/18, The Relations between Degussa, Frankfurt/Main and the Norddeutsche Affinerie, Hamburg, unsigned, undated [1946/47].

[83] DUA, GEH 6/16, Deppe's Übernahmebedingungen für Edelmetalle aus Bor/Trepca-Produktionen, November 26, 1941.

[84] On the Czech coin silver, DUA, GEH 11/12, Zweigniederlassung Berlin to Verkaufsgruppe 1, Frankfurt, January 25, 1943; and as background, GEH 11/4, Zweigniederlassung Berlin to Frankfurt, January 21, 1943. On the deliveries from Greece, DL 2/1, Niederschriften über die Vorstandssitzungen am 2. Februar 1942, p. 235, and am 1. Februar 1943, p. 301.

[85] DUA, GEH 3.Hirtes/12, Furler's Bericht über meine Besprechungen in Prag, October 30, 1939.

[86] DUA, GEH 6/16, Degussa to Freiberg, July 6, 1942.

[87] DUA, GEH 6/16, Degussa to Freiberg, July 17, 1944. The shipments through October are also referenced in DL 2/1, Niederschrift über die Vorstandssitzung am 6. Dezember 1939, p. 349.

margin – a total of roughly 64,271 RM on this Pribram silver, in addition to the approximately 207,500 RM brought in by the allotments of Greek and Czech coin silver.

Finally, in the waning months of the war, Degussa took over, apparently to process for the Reich's accounts, substantial shares of 200 tons of coin silver taken from Holland, indeterminate stocks of gold and silver that belonged to the Falconbridge Nickel Works of Norway, and some 200 kilograms of gold that Mussolini's Republic of Salo in Italy agreed to loan to the German Armaments Ministry.[88] The surviving records do not make clear, however, whether any of these materials ever were refined.

Over and above all these amounts, Degussa also received, refined, and resold significant quantities of precious metals that the Nazi regime stripped from the Jews of Europe in the course of immiserating, torturing, and slaughtering them from 1939 to 1945. Although the remaining data on such intakes are even more predictably partial than those summarized above, there can be no doubt that Degussa contributed more than any other German refinery to turning these bloodily stolen goods to the Reich's purposes. Equally clear is that the overall pattern established during the Pawnshop Action held throughout this more ferocious and naked program of robbery. Once more, the chief beneficiary was the German Treasury. And, as before, Degussa's leaders showed no scruples about the provenance of inputs that the firm wanted to obtain.

The most sensational instance of Degussa's trafficking in the proceeds of the Holocaust occurred in connection with the infamous Melmer deliveries of loot from concentration camps in Poland.[89] Brought personally to the German National Bank by SS-Hauptsturmführer Bruno Melmer on seventy-six occasions between August 1942 and the end of 1944, these shipments consisted of valuables and dental work taken from deportees or their corpses. The bank, in effect, bought these materials from the SS, liquidated them, and eventually deposited their worth in Reichsmarks to a special account under the cover name of Max Heiliger. In the course of monetizing the precious metals so received, the bank retained negotiable gold coins, sent already purified gold to the Prussian Mint for melting into bars, and reserved the remaining objects for pickup by a refinery – in practice, this meant by Degussa's Berlin branch – either directly from the bank or after further sorting at the Central Pawn Office. The branch, in turn, forwarded these materials to Frankfurt for recycling, and the refinery there either dispatched equivalent amounts of pure metals to the National Bank or added them to the quantities being

[88] See DUA, DL 3/20, Postzettel Nr. 101, October 14, 1944; Postzettel Nr. 115, October 31, 1944, p. 2; and Postzettel Nr. 129, November 21, 1944.

[89] My account of Degussa's involvement with the Melmer deliveries follows, unless otherwise indicated, that of Ralf Banken's as yet unpublished paper, "Melmer Gold," presented at Bielefeld University in June 1998.

held for it or the National Agency for Precious Metals at Degussa's facilities. In fact, however, the metals content of only forty-three Melmer deliveries underwent this entire process; the last thirty-three caches apparently did not leave the bank's premises until evacuated in labeled bags and boxes to a salt mine in Thuringia, where the United States Army captured them intact in 1945.

Even this reduced number of Melmer shipments is impossible to trace through Degussa's records, since its assay books do not distinguish among payments due to the National Bank, the refinery books identify sources only when a specific lot of metal was to be purified or reformatted and returned to the provider, and the delivery book contains but brief and scarcely decipherable indications of destinations. But Ralf Banken's painstaking analysis of the bank's ledgers indicates that it got at least 1,015 kilograms of fine gold from Degussa in return for Melmer deliveries and that another 359 kilograms of "Melmer gold" received by the bank almost surely came from Frankfurt. In addition to this total of 1,374 kilograms, most of the remaining 588 kilograms of fine gold that Degussa delivered to the bank between October 1942 and September 1944 was in payment for plundered metal, much of which probably came from Melmer shipments. All told, then, the death camps of Poland yielded the Nazi Reich via Degussa somewhere between one and two metric tons of fine gold during World War II, but in all probability an amount far closer to the latter than the former number.[90] At the

---

[90] The likelihood of the larger figure – indeed, of even its insufficiency – is strengthened by the fragmentary surviving information concerning the probable total gold content of the Melmer shipments. According to the Swiss Commission of Experts' estimate, based on the records of the German National Agency for Precious Metals, that amount came to almost 2,578 kilograms fine, exclusive of dental gold, watches, rings, eyeglass frames, and the like from Auschwitz; *Interim Report*, pp. 31, 35–36, and 43. By my own very rough calculation, however, that camp may have yielded some 588 kilograms of gold from dental work alone; see Peter Hayes, "Auschwitz, Capital of the Holocaust," *Holocaust and Genocide Studies* 17 (2003), p. 338. Moreover, the only known contemporaneous indication of the size of deliveries from Poland suggests that the Swiss Commission may understate even the quantities its total encompasses. In a letter of January 5, 1944, Otto Globocnik submitted to Heinrich Himmler an itemization of the valuables taken from Jews in Poland during Operation Reinhard, including what had been collected at Belzec, Sobibor, and Treblinka prior to their closings, and stated that 2,910 kilograms of gold bars were among the booty; see Yitzhak Arad, *Belzec, Sobibor, Treblinka* (Bloomington: Indiana University Press, 1987), pp. 160–61. If these bars were only 90 percent pure, which is possible, then the Commission's fine gold estimate would appear nearly accurate, but the Commission's own text also points out that gold from Auschwitz was not included in the bars fabricated in Lublin from Operation Reinhard loot. Instead, that gold went unprocessed and by a different route into the Melmer deliveries, which means that they may have been larger than the National Agency's records reveal. Ralf Banken's essay on "Melmer Gold" concludes that the probable maximum quantity of fine gold delivered to the National Bank via this conduit was 2,642 kilograms (1,962 in possible wartime production, plus 680 kilograms derived after 1945 from the unprocessed Melmer shipments), and that is probably the soundest conclusion the surviving documentation allows. But the circumstantial evidence strongly suggests that much additional Melmer gold is just not yet identifiable in the available documentation.

official German gold price during the war, two metric tons would have been worth some 5.5 million Reichsmarks to the Nazi regime, which translates to 22 million U.S. dollars at the end of the twentieth century.

Degussa's income from these shipments is difficult to establish with precision. According to the fee structure laid down in the refining conventions that were renewed annually during the war and, by Banken's reckoning, produced average charges of 17.2 RM per kilogram of gross weight, and assuming an overall level of purity of 62.5 percent (i.e., 15 karats), quantities of 1,015, 1,374, and 1,962 kilograms would have given off assaying, refining, and delivery fees that totalled to 27,933 RM, 37,840 RM, and 54,008 RM, respectively (the recent U.S. dollar equivalents would be $111,732 to $216,032).[91] Moreover, Degussa acquired title to twenty-eight kilograms of the Melmer gold, which it presumably devoted to the production of high-profit semi-finished or finished goods. And the firm enjoyed resale fees of 130 to 200 RM per kilogram on that portion of the formerly Jewish-owned gold allocated for distribution in Germany by the National Agency for Precious Metals from the Fund E that Degussa held for it, which was the normal destination of gold obtained via the Central Pawn Office in 1942–44. The minutes of Degussa's monthly managing board meetings indicate that at least 343 kilograms of fine gold entered that fund during these years, only 14 of which remained on deposit at Degussa in August 1944. If one supposes the sale of 330 kilograms at an average markup of 150 RM each, the firm's additional revenue comes to 49,500 RM, exclusive of income derived from turning any of this metal into semi-finished or final products. On the other hand, Degussa made no markup on the 119.5 kilograms of Melmer gold with which the German National Bank paid Swiss creditors or the at least 1,018 kilograms that it sold for foreign exchange to the Dresdner and Deutsche banks in 1942–43 so that they could market the metal at a substantial profit to Turks seeking a hedge against inflation.[92] The latter transaction had its

---

[91] The surviving sources provide no sure basis for estimating the gross weight of the Melmer shipments or their average level of fine metal content. After the war, however, when Degussa was directed to process the raw metals in the 33 Melmer deliveries that had not reached it earlier, 1,278 kilograms of "old and broken gold" yielded 631.6 kilograms of fine gold, which suggests an average purity of 50 percent, and thus the possibility of higher gross weights and refining fees from the wartime shipments than I have estimated in the text. However, the average fine gold yield of the earlier deliveries was at least 32 kilograms each (1,374 kilograms divided by forty-three shipments), compared to only 20.6 for the thirty-three postwar batches, and this may have been due to the fact that the share of "tooth gold" in the latter group, some 60 percent, was unusually high. My estimate of 62.5 percent purity in the wartime deliveries is an attempt to take all of these data into account. See DUA, DL 11.5/44, Notiz by Ochs, June 16, 1948. On the complicated refining fee structure, see GEH 5/5, Degussa's Betr. Rohsilber-Konvention und Scheidgut-Konvention, April 9, 1942, with enclosures.

[92] See Swiss Commission of Experts [Bergier Commission], *Interim Report*, pp. 48–49; and Jonathan Steinberg, *Die Deutsche Bank und ihre Goldtransaktionen während des Zweiten Weltkrieges* (Munich: Beck Verlag, 1999), especially p. 45; and Johannes Bähr, *Der*

own rewards, however, since the banks generally needed the gold reformatted from 12.5 kilogram bars to more saleable plates of .5 to 1.0 kilograms, which led to a second round of refining fees on the same metal.

Even after taking all these fees into account, Degussa is likely to have netted relatively little profit from the gold that the SS ripped from Jews in 1942–44 – certainly it earned only fractions of what the National, Dresdner, and Deutsche banks did. But, as in the case of the Pawnshop Action, the monetary rewards were less important to Degussa's refineries – and certainly to the German war effort – than the volumes that flowed in. At 1,374 kilograms, the intake came to almost 7 percent of the 20,292 kilograms of fine gold produced by Degussa in these years (see Appendix J); at 1,962 kilograms, the share would have been nearly 10 percent; and, when one takes the reprocessing into consideration, the proportion rises still further to almost 15 percent.

Furthermore, the concentration camp loot also contained silver, though in amounts one can estimate only by extrapolating from the contents of the 33 Melmer shipments that the National Bank held onto during the war. In 1947, and rather ironically, the recyclable components of these too came to Degussa's refineries, this time for purification on behalf of the International Refugee Organization. The ratio between the gross weights of silver- and gold-bearing materials in these deliveries was 13:1 (16,400 to 1,278 kilograms) and that of the fine silver and gold that resulted 12:1 (7,939.5 to 631.6 kilograms).[93] If these ratios characterized the 43 wartime shipments, Degussa's intake of "Melmer silver" would have been sixteen to twenty-four metric tons fine, on which the enterprise would have made 3 RM per kilogram from the refining fees and sales margin, as in the Pawnshop Action, or 48,000 to 72,000 RM, exclusive of markups on any resulting semi-finished products. Nonetheless, neither the receipts nor the quantities involved approached those that the gold in the Melmer deliveries brought in: at most, Degussa earned half as much on the commoner metal; and sixteen to twenty-four metric tons comes to about 2 percent of the total silver tonnage (1,026.5) that the firm produced in 1942–44 (see Appendix J).

Far more substantial than the Melmer deliveries were the quantities of precious metals that the Nazi regime extracted from Jews outside of concentration camps. To take one illustration, in July 1942, just before Bruno Melmer began his visits to the National Bank, the Warsaw Office of the SS informed Heinrich Himmler that two metric tons of gold, presumably extorted from the ghetto in that city and its environs, already had been sent to Lublin and another 629 kilograms collected.[94] If the latter quantity may

---

Goldhandel der Dresdner Bank im Zweiten Weltkrieg (Dresden: Gustav Kiepenheuer Verlag, 1999), especially p. 64.

[93] DUA, DL 11.5/44, Notiz by Ochs, June 16, 1948.

[94] See Steinberg, *Deutsche Bank und ihre Goldtransaktionen*, p. 43.

have ended up as part of the Melmer deposits, the former one is much too large to have done so. It probably arrived at the National Bank and possibly at Degussa's refineries under other, as yet undeciphered labels, like the 3.2 kilograms of gold delivered from the National Loan and Credit Office (Reichskreditkasse) in Stanislau, Poland, in March 1942, then processed by Degussa and sold to the Deutsche Bank in July, which Jonathan Steinberg has connected to a massacre of 10,000 to 12,000 Jews in that town the preceding October.[95] One could make similar suppositions about the ninety-six kilograms that the Army High Command sent to the National Bank between March and May 1942, possibly from the Soviet Union; that metal also went to Degussa's refineries before becoming the Deutsche Bank's property in August.[96] But sums of this sort have left few indelible tracks in Degussa's records, partly because the files on the Berlin branch's direct dealings with agencies such as the Lodz ghetto administration, the Army, or the SS were burned in 1945, and partly because the Reich routed much of the Eastern European loot through the Dorotheum in Vienna or the Central Pawn Office in Berlin, where it became mixed with other intakes that seldom aroused any special comment in Degussa's documents.[97]

A rare and illuminating exception to the latter rule occurred in the autumn of 1943, when the efforts of Karl Endres to get the Aurora subsidiary that he headed cut in on refining "Jew silver and gold from the Protectorate" led Degussa to examine its intakes more closely and to conclude that Endres's activity was superfluous.[98] The Berlin branch realized that at least some of the 128 kilograms of gold and 6,569 kilograms of silver in "enemy material" that it had collected from the Central Pawn Office between January 1942 and October 1943 already included metals from Czech Jews.[99] A few days later, direct inquiries at the Pawn Office produced confirmation that "in general shipments of the most diverse sort flow into the Berlin Pawn Office, such that we [Degussa] have just received a larger quantity of silver and gold that supposedly stems from similar sources in Latvia."[100] Endres's discoveries concerning the mechanisms in the Protectorate for turning Jewish property into pure metals unravelled two other mysteries for

---

[95] *Ibid.*, pp. 37–38.   [96] *Ibid.*, pp. 104–05.

[97] That Degussa's Berlin branch received deliveries directly from the Lodz ghetto administration and remitted the postcommission proceeds to accounts in its name at the Reichsbank is demonstrated by the documents from 1943–44 in *Dokumenty i Materialy, Tom III, Getto Lodzkie* (Warsaw: 1946), pp. 156–57, 163. On the deliveries to the Dorotheum, see LAB, Rep. 39, Bd. 19, Bl. 76–77, Degussa to Landgericht Berlin, Wiedergutmachungskammer, April 16, 1962.

[98] See DUA, GEH 11/4, Endres's Bericht über Scheidung bzw. Verwertung von Judensilber und -gold im Protektorat Böhmen und Mähren, October 21–27, 1943.

[99] DUA, GEH 11/4, Benz to Zweigniederlassung Wien, November 16, 1943.

[100] DUA, GEH 11/4, Zweigniederlassung Berlin to Verkaufsgruppe I Edelmetalle, November 19, 1943.

Degussa. The first concerned the unusually large deliveries of silver that the Freiberg refinery had contributed to the national distribution system between August 1942 and March 1943. It soon became clear that at least sixteen fine metric tons stemmed from "Jew-silver from the Protectorate," along with some forty kilograms of fine gold that Freiberg had refined and returned to Prague.[101] The second puzzle was why these flows had dropped off since March, which Endres resolved by informing headquarters that the SS and the Finance Ministry in Berlin were squabbling over which organization had title to the proceeds from formerly Jewish-owned metals, with the result that "for the moment everything is stuck and one can make no progress."[102] This controversy and the resulting paralysis apparently lasted until April 1944, when the accumulated materials began being sent to Freiberg once more, but no data on the quantities involved have surfaced in Degussa's records.[103] One may question, however, how much of the plundered metals actually got to the Saxon site, in light of the postwar testimony of a former manager in the Scheidische Affinerie in Prague, who recounted his firm's involvement in the smelting of metals from the Jewish Emigration Fund in the Protectorate. He recalled that his company was asked at the end of 1944 to separate the remaining items in the fund, that these came to eighty kilograms of gold and 9.2 metric tons of silver, and that the local facilities could not render these metals sufficiently pure, so that they were sent on to the only installations in Germany that could, those of Degussa in Frankfurt and the Norddeutsche Affinerie in Hamburg.[104] In response, Degussa could neither rule out nor document that it had received the metals in question.[105] The most recent and thorough study of the surviving Czech documents concludes that the total quantity of gold seized from Jews in the Protectorate during the German occupation came to about 615 kilograms, of which almost 414 went to the Czech National Bank for its reserves or distribution to domestic firms.[106] Thus, at most, some 200 kilograms ended up in Berlin (and potentially in Frankfurt) via one or another route. But similar limiting data on silver flows have not surfaced.

[101] For the quoted words, DUA, GEH 11/4, Benz's Notiz für Herrn Dir. Otto Deppe, November 3, 1943; for the amounts, Endres's Notiz Betr. Vorsprache in Prag wegen Scheidung bzw. Verwertung von Judensilber und -gold aus dem Protektorat, November 10, 1943.

[102] *Ibid.*

[103] DUA, GEH 11/13, Endres to Hirtes, February 18, 1944, and Endres's Bericht, April 22, 1944.

[104] LAB, Rep. 39, Bd. 19, Bl. 568–70, letter by Viktor Odslon, January 5, 1963.

[105] LAB, Rep. 39, Bd. 19, Bl. 578, Degussa to Kammergericht, Berlin-Charlottenburg, January 5, 1967.

[106] Drahomir Jančik, Eduard Kubů, Jiři Novotny, and Jiři Šouša, "Der Mechanismus der Enteignung jüdischen Goldes im 'Protektorat Böhmen und Mähren' und seine Funktionsweise (1939–1945)," *Zeitschrift für Unternehmensgeschichte* 46 (2001), pp. 73–76.

The portion of metals pillaged from Czech Jews that arrived at Degussa's refineries in 1944–45 is as uncertain as the quantities forwarded by the Main Trusteeship Office East, the main German plundering agency in Poland, after they finally were released for processing in mid-1944.[107] It is unlikely, however, that much gold taken from Jews in occupied countries reached Berlin or Frankfurt even in earlier years. For a variety of reasons to do with containing the inflationary pressures brought on by wartime shortages of goods combined with generous German payments to occupation forces in local currencies, most of the gold probably was channeled into local precious metals markets and national banks.[108] In any case, the only other recorded intakes of formerly Jewish-owned metals by Degussa come from Holland and register one purchase of 1.7 kilograms of fine gold and three purchases totaling 225 kilograms of fine silver from the Lippmann, Rosenthal Bank branch in the Sarphatistraat, Amsterdam, the main Nazi collecting point for the financial assets of Dutch Jews. All these transactions occurred in 1944 and via Degussa's Schoene subsidiary, which appears to have done the initial refining, and all of the metals went into the National Agency for Precious Metal's accounts at Degussa, becoming its property only in the event of a later allocation of the metal to the firm.[109] Neither Schöne nor Degussa is likely to have made anything other than service fees on the gold, since the National Agency bought it at the lowest German price level, that for fine metal obtained from mines, and had it deposited to Fund H in Frankfurt, from which the gold is more likely to have been sent abroad than sold domestically.[110]

If one adds the quantities described above (exclusive of the Pawnshop Action), Degussa's documented minimum intake of plundered gold from 1940 to 1945 exceeds five metric tons. Including the 2.1 tons that had been stolen from Jews, the total comes to 15 percent of the thirty-three metric tons the firm refined in this period. For silver, the pillaged amount is 412 to 420 metric tons (43 to 51 of them from Jews), constituting 22 percent of Degussa's silver production of 1,856 metric tons. The smelting fees alone on

---

[107] On the HTO's deposits, see Banken, *Jahrbuch für Wirtschaftsgeschichte* 39 (1999), p. 139, note 13.

[108] See Christian Gerlach and Götz Aly, *Das letzte Kapitel: Der Mord an der ungarischen Juden* (Stuttgart: Deutsche Verlags-Anstalt, 2002), pp. 212–39. I am drawing here as well, thanks to the generosity of the author, on Aly's as yet unpublished article on the expropriation of the Jews of Salonika. See also the fascinating account of Ronald W. Zweig, *The Gold Train* (New York: William Morrow, 2002), which shows how little of the valuables confiscated from the Jews of Budapest is likely to have reached Germany.

[109] See DUA, DL 11.5/53, Degussa to the Treuhänder der Bank Lippmann, Rosenthal & Co., February 16, and March 2, 1944; Degussa to Firma Lippmann, Rosenthal & Co., August 23, 1944, and Degussa to the Reichsstelle für Edelmetalle of the same date.

[110] DUA, DL 11.5/53, Degussa to the Reichsstelle für Edelmetalle, March 13, 1944, and Betr.: Fonds "H," April 19, 1944.

these quantities probably worked out to around 800,000 RM, and the resale markups to 1.6 million Reichsmarks, resulting in total minimal revenues for Degussa from looted materials of 2.4 million Reichsmarks (U.S. $9.6 million in contemporary currency), of which approximately 350,000 RM derived from metals formerly owned by Jews (i.e., U.S. $1.4 million today).

But proceeding in this fashion only highlights the numerous gaps in Degussa's records. To be sure, the one surviving contemporary analysis of the origins of Germany's fine silver output during a war year states that 76 percent of the 548 metric tons produced in 1944 came from domestic mines and reserves, 21 percent from materials obtained in occupied countries, and 3 percent from "confiscated material," and these amounts suggest that a plundered proportion of 22 percent is plausible.[111] But, the overall statistical record indicates that German sources provided only one-half of the roughly 2,750 metric tons of fine silver that the nation consumed between 1940 and 1945, about two-thirds of them produced by Degussa. Thus, the plundered component of Degussa's output is likely to have been over 900 metric tons, the quantity taken from Jews to have surpassed 100 tons, and the respective proportions of the whole to have equaled 48 percent and 5 percent. With regard to gold, the probable understatement that results from merely aggregating the firm's proven intakes is even greater. According to the best currently available estimates, in excess of 65 percent of the gold at the disposal of the German National Bank from 1939 to 1945 and 95 percent of the gold it acquired during that period was plundered, including over 15 percent of the latter figure (almost seventy-three metric tons) that was taken by the Nazi regime from private persons or firms.[112] As the only firm in Germany capable of purifying gold to international standards and the fabricator of some 60 to 90 percent of German fine gold by 1943, Degussa was the predestined way station for much of this metal – certainly for nearly all of that whose origins had to be disguised. Given the enormous volumes involved, which came to seventeen times Degussa's total wartime output, and the paucity of other possible sources, the inference is inescapable that almost all of the gold that entered Degussa's refineries during the war years was stolen property.

Harder to assess, however, is the amount of this metal derived from the persecution and murder of the Jews. Given the scarcity of figures concerning

---

[111] DUA, GEH 3.Hirtes/4, Schleicher to Deppe, January 26, 1945.

[112] Swiss Commission of Experts [Bergier Commission], *Interim Report*, Table I, p. 39, excluding the Hungarian National Bank reserves, which Germany held only briefly, and the gold transfers from the Soviet Union, which appear not to have become German property. Cf. Bähr, *Goldhandel der Dresdner Bank*, p. 23, who counts the Austrian and Czech gold reserves as plundered and thus arrives at the figure of 80 percent for the share of the Reich's gold, 1939–45, derived in this fashion.

Degussa's total intake via the Central Pawn Office in Berlin during the war, the discrepancies among the available data on what was extracted at concentration camps, and the fact that the 1,500 kilograms of fine gold yielded by the German Pawnshop Action, to which several hundred thousand Jews were subjected, is likely to have been dwarfed by that from the Holocaust, to which millions were, it is not far-fetched to suggest that the total quantity of fine gold that Degussa's refineries derived from these later victims alone may have gone as high as five metric tons (15 percent of Degussa's gold production from 1939 to 1945), even after allowing for the fact that much (indeed, probably most) of the loot from the Holocaust never reached Frankfurt. Such suspicions are strengthened by the pattern of Degussa's gold output during the war years. Whereas the peak period of the firm's silver production came in 1941, when it shot up by 33 percent as the French and Belgian booty flowed in, Frankfurt's fine gold yields rose by only 8 percent in that year, but then by 17 percent in 1942 and another 18 percent in 1943, the most murderous years of the Holocaust (see Appendix J). The records of the Frankfurt refinery alone show that the spike in output there was concentrated between October 1942 and August 1943, an especially deadly time for Poland's Jews.[113] Bor-Trepca's output and the known Melmer deliveries were not sufficient to account for these surges, and the National Bank's requirements probably do not either.

Once more, the problems of quantification are compounded when one tries to calculate Degussa's earnings from all this plunder. For refining and smelting fees, the most easily, albeit imperfectly calculable part of the firm's proceeds, represented the least rewarding segment of the metals production process. In the four business years between October 1, 1940, and September 30, 1944, refining generated only 1.8 million Reichsmarks in gross profits for Degussa, a mere 6 percent of the metals division's total of 31.5 million. Roughly one-seventh of this income (261,000 RM) would have resulted from gold inputs and the rest from silver, given the quantities of each that the firm produced in 1940–44 and the prevailing refining fees. The firm's gold and silver accounts, which probably tally the returns on selling purified metals, another relatively unlucrative activity, produced 1.8 million Reichsmarks and 5.9 million Reichsmarks, respectively, or 24 percent of the whole.[114] The largest earnings came from processing retained precious metals into marketable products. Thus, those derived primarily from gold yielded 7.2 million Reichsmarks and those from silver at least 4.1 million, or 36 percent of the division's gross profits. The remaining one-third of these either cannot be disaggregated by metal or stemmed from platinum and products made from it.

[113] DUA, ZVS 1/10, Betr.: Produktionszahlen im Werk I, July 9, 1945.
[114] DUA, RFI 4.2/93, 98, 104, and 108, Jahresabschlüsse.

If one posits that 95 percent of Degussa's gold intakes and 50 percent of its silver ones from 1940 to 1944 represented plundered materials and 15 percent of the fine gold and 5 percent of the fine silver that Degussa retained, like that which it produced, stemmed from once-Jewish property, then the corresponding shares of the gross profits ascribable to these sources, as best one can reconstruct them from the internal financial statements for the business years ending in 1941–44, are as follows (in thousands of Reichsmarks):

	From all plunder		From Jews	
	Gold	Silver	Gold	Silver
Refining	248	770	39	77
Trading	1,729	2,960	273	296
Manufacturing	6,840	2,050	1,080	205
Totals	8,817	5,780 = 14,597	1,392	578 = 1,970

Of course, these are uncertain estimates, since the plundered percentages have been arrived at by deduction, the profit figures do not encompass the last eight months of the war, and the portions of the earnings of the ceramic colors department that derived from precious metals have not been considered. Moreover, here as elsewhere in this chapter, the calculations do not take platinum intakes and outputs into account, on which the surviving records are too sparse to permit even this sort of analysis. Still, it would appear that Degussa's gross profits from the plundering of the Jews from 1939 to 1945 come to a minimum of around 2 million Reichsmarks (U.S. $8 million in recent values), including the Pawnshop Action.

In the end, however, these computations are only slightly better than nothing. It is almost impossible to stipulate the proportion or amount of Degussa's income or profits from precious metals operations during World War II that stemmed from the Holocaust. That virtually all the division's gold earnings and half of its silver ones after 1940 rested on Nazi conquests is relatively clear. But one will never know with certainty how much of the enterprise's fortunes depended on Auschwitz or Treblinka beyond the sadly obvious point that the tally is far greater than one would wish.

Moreover, war damage and postwar losses complicate the analysis, since what Degussa received or reaped is not the same as what it retained. The destruction of many of its plants and the confiscation of many of its precious metals in 1945 certainly eroded what the corporation had gained from Nazi plunder. These developments were, in effect, forms of retribution for the enterprise's complicity in the Nazi war and murder efforts. Although Degussa's numerous compilations in 1945–48 of gold and silver taken from it are not altogether consistent, American, British, French, and Soviet forces appear to have managed to ferret out and expropriate most of the firm's silver reserves (at least 104 metric tons) and about one-tenth of its gold holdings (155.4 kilograms) in the months surrounding the German capitulation, quantities that were valued at the time at 4 million to 5 million Reichsmarks (U.S. $16 million to 20 million at the end of the twentieth century).[115] Neither Degussa nor Germans in general walked away from the Third Reich altogether unpunished for having participated in it.

Whether the corporation had been adequately punished and the actual victims of its actions properly compensated was the issue at the heart of a class action suit against Degussa decided in the United States District Court of New Jersey in 1999. By dismissing the case on the grounds that such questions are matters for intergovernmental determination, were settled legally by a series of postwar international agreements, and thus could not be subjected to American judicial review, the ruling probably closed an over fifty-year period in which the possibility of adversarial proceedings and material penalties distorted public discussion of Degussa's implication in Nazi crimes.[116] The consequences are likely to prove ironic and the firm's victory perhaps even Pyrrhic, at least in the court of public opinion. For, if the judgment disappointed the plaintiffs, rendering moot any attempt to tally the profits from persecution that Degussa ought to "disgorge," the court's decision also lifted the interpretation of Degussa's conduct out of the blind alley created by the judicial demand for mens rea, criminal intent, as a prerequisite for a finding of guilt.

As with regard to the general topic of German industry's actions under the Third Reich, far too much of the analysis of Degussa's role in the processing of precious metals has centered since World War II on efforts to demonstrate or disprove that the relevant corporate officers understood and therefore intended what they in fact were doing: making stolen goods, many acquired through murder, not only financially rewarding to their firm, but also fungible and productive for the Nazi state. Thus, even in the early postwar years, when the officials involved knew better from personal experience, they exercised their memories selectively, denying any awareness of metals confiscations in occupied countries or the procedures by which such material

[115] The figures provided in GEH 6/10, Bernau and Furler to Mission Belge Militaire, January 16, 1946, for the quantities seized by the Allies to date are surely wildly high for silver (181,776 kilograms) and low for gold (fifty-nine kilograms). The numbers presented here come from the most apparently reliable compilation, DUA, DL 11.5/61, Aufstellung über Kriegs- und Kriegsfolgeschäden und Vermögenswerte gemäss Gesetz Nr. 53 der Militärregierung bezw. Nr. 5 des Alliierten Kontrollrates per 20. Juni 1948.

[116] *Alice Burger-Fischer et al. v. Degussa AG and Degussa Corporation*, Civil Action No. 98-3958 (DRD), and *Michael Vogel et al. v. Degussa AG and Degussa Corporation*, Civil Action No. 98-5019, United States District Court, District of New Jersey, judgment by Dickinson R. Debevoise, September 10, 1999.

might have reached Frankfurt. Consider, for example this letter responding to a restitution application from Holland:

We do not know whether a compulsory handing in of precious metals took place in Holland during the war as in Germany. In any case, we did not take delivery of this sort of precious metals or negotiate with German agencies concerning reworking such metals. The applicant ... apparently gave his things to the Lippmann Rosenthal & Co. bank in the course of an isolated operation. ... During the war, we received ... a small quantity of silver from Lippmann Rosenthal & Co. ... According to the memory of our personnel, this consisted of fine silver, that is of already purified precious metal, not of used silver objects. It is therefore impossible in our opinion that the ... objects taken came to us.[117]

Above all, Degussa took pains to refute charges that it had received or processed deliveries from concentration camps. In 1948, both Ernst Baerwind, who may have been ignorant in this regard, and Robert Hirtes, who is quite unlikely to have been, replied as follows to an inquiry on this matter from the Property Control Office in Frankfurt:

The separation of old and broken dental gold (crowns, bridges, inlays, pins, etc.) has always belonged to the normal business of all refineries and so to our operations. Never, however, have such materials been delivered to us from concentration camps or other SS departments. In all the years of National Socialist rule, we also never received such material under circumstances that could have given rise to suspicion. As far as we know, witness testimony in the Wilhelmstrasse Trial has shown that the SS delivered broken and thus also dental gold that it had appropriated to the National Bank in Berlin. This, however, handed over this broken and dental gold exclusively to the Prussian State Mint for melting down and neither to us or other refineries.[118]

This remained the firm's position, repeated more compactly in the assurance to a subsequent restitution panel that "the private German refineries, we included, fortunately did not deal during the war with precious metals that came from concentration camps."[119]

In short, rather than offer the historically tenable but legally vulnerable defense that Degussa's leaders had entered into complicity with Nazi brutality out of myopia and self-centeredness and realized only gradually the depths of what they were abetting, the firm took the steadfast position that it had not been complicit at all. As perhaps during the events in question themselves, Degussa's stance conformed to the sarcastic German expression that "what must not be cannot be." But the Aurora subsidiary's leader explicitly

---

[117] DUA, DL 11.5/53, Degussa to Ernst Boesebeck, March 13, 1951.

[118] DUA, DL 11.5/44, Baerwind and Hirtes to Leiter des Amtes für Vermögenskontrolle, Frankfurt, June 15, 1948.

[119] DUA, DL 11.5/43, Degussa to Landgericht Frankfurt, 8. Zivilkammer (Wiedergutmachung), November 30, 1961.

pursued "Jew metals" from Czechoslovakia; the Berlin branch's managers both knew they were receiving shipments directly from the Lodz ghetto and learned that they were taking in "Jew metals" from the Protectorate; and the wholesale destruction of documents by the branch's chief in 1945 suggests awareness of having a great deal to hide. With regard to the articles that office received via the National Bank or the Prussian Mint from the Gestapo or the SS, including metals extracted from the mouths of corpses, illusions about the origins were possible for a time. The shipments generally arrived in compressed form that rendered the components no longer immediately recognizable, and reprocessing dental gold was, indeed, a common activity in the refining business. But on some occasions, an intern in the Reinick-endorf smeltery from 1941–45 later recalled, deliveries came in a condition that made drawing conclusions hard to avoid. According to Erna Spiewack's rather understated written account,

It was rumored clandestinely that the jewelry came from Poland, where it had been taken from the Jews and so to speak confiscated from them. Gold teeth, which, as one later knew, probably were from concentration camps, also came to the refinery by the crateload. At the time, such suppositions were not expressed. We girls did not think about that anyway. We had other concerns.[120]

In 1998, however, when she was interviewed for German television, her memories about the dental gold were more vivid – and ghastly:

the crowns and the bridges, there were those where the teeth were still attached.... That was the most depressing, the fact that everything was still there. It was probably just like it had been when broken out of a mouth. The teeth were still there and sometimes still bloody and with pieces of gum on them.[121]

To be sure, the documentary record does not confirm that this information flowed up the chain of command in the firm, and little, if any, of the plundered material was still identifiable as such by the time it reached Frankfurt, as opposed to Reinickendorf. Nonetheless, the conclusion appears justified that Degussa's management knew as much as it wanted or considered necessary to know, and it exhibited no compunction about doing business as usual. It is simply not credible, in view of Degussa's pivotal position in the purification of gold for the National Bank, to maintain that the precious metals division's leaders, and perhaps even the firm's, were unaware that they were receiving large quantities of plundered metals, including from Jews.

But laboring to establish such specific knowledge conclusively seems – from a historian's point of view if perhaps not a lawyer's – almost beside the point. One simply has no reason to believe that the firm's leaders would

---

[120] DUA, BU Erna Spiewack, Erinnerungen, p. 128.
[121] ARD, "Report," October 12, 1998, Eric Fielder and Oliver Merz, "Zeugen des Grauens–Teil 2: Der SS-Buchhalter Melmer."

have rejected these intakes even if fully informed of the circumstances of their origin, perhaps even if openly confronted with them.[122] Degussa took part in the plundering of the Jews, not just or primarily to gain immediate profits from it, but rather for the sake of larger ones that might follow and in order to avoid the penalties that noncooperation might have entailed. Knowledge of the gruesome process by which these metals were extracted would not have altered the calculations that motivated the firm's behavior. After 1939, Degussa had nothing to gain (but honor, and that only in the long run and if Germany lost the war) from refusing to carry out tasks that the Nazi state was bound to request of the predominant firm in the industry. The enterprise had, however, something to lose, namely that very standing, if the regime had to look elsewhere. Meanwhile, Degussa could bet that its usefulness would translate into the sorts of consideration regarding prices, supplies, and production that, in fact, the corporation received when granted virtual monopolies over processing government coin silver in the fall of 1941 and over German production of semi-finished silver products in 1943.

Can one imagine that, against these advantages and in a context of war and dictatorship, a sense of morality and feelings of shame and disgust would have arisen, let alone prevailed? Not, one has to say, within a refinery staffed by a young Erna Spiewack, a corporate division shaped by Hans Schneider's tunnel vision, and a firm guided by Ernst Busemann's pragmatism and Hermann Schlosser's dedication to soldierly virtues.

---

[122] I am echoing here the trenchant observation of Jonathan Steinberg, *Deutsche Bank und ihre Goldtransaktionen*, p. 86.

6

War Production and Spoliation

If, as the preceding chapters have argued, Degussa's decisions and development had become irreversibly oriented toward serving state-determined markets by 1937–39 and the morally corrupting effects on corporate conduct already had begun to emerge, the onset of World War II clearly intensified both trends. Even at the height of Hitler's military success in July 1940, when peace seemed at hand, the terms of doing business in the Third Reich remained tightly prescribed. As Hermann Schlosser informed his colleagues, the future would resemble the past, only now on a larger geographical scale:

the "Great European Economic Sphere" must embrace almost the entire continent, which should confront the other economic blocs as a solid unit. The clear result is that the foundation of autarky will...be extended to the whole Sphere....Certainly one has to reckon with a considerable reduction in armament, even with the maintenance of a very strong military....Peacetime economic prospects are assessed so favorably, however, that further accelerated expansion is to be expected in the vast majority of fields....This creates for industry the extraordinarily important and equally difficult task of keeping pace through private-sector initiative without abandoning private-sector caution and responsibility. It will not always be easy to do both, for if, rightly or wrongly, the initiative and tempo of expansion on a private economic basis become viewed as inadequate, then the danger of not only a planned but also a state-imposed system will be strengthened....[T]he tendency expressed by the Hermann-Göring-Works will be reinforced yet again if business does not exploit its chances sufficiently.[1]

In other words, whether the immediate priority of Nazi government policy was to maximize the nation's military power or economic autonomy, German corporations somehow had to combine serving that purpose with satisfying their own commercial interests, lest the state impose new forms of control, compulsion, and competition. This was Degussa's central dilemma during the war years. The firm's efforts to ride both horses at once, so to speak, proved both contentious and profitable – and led to mounting entanglement in the spoliation of occupied Europe and the barbarism of Nazi labor policy.

That the Reich's economic objectives and Degussa's would continue both to coincide and clash during wartime became apparent in the very first

---

[1] DUA, TLE 1/23, Schlosser's Grosswirtschaftsraum Deutschland, July 6, 1940, pp. 1–3.

months of the conflict. To be sure, the outbreak of hostilities, along with Schlosser's succession to Busemann two months later, triggered actions from which both the state and the firm would benefit. Centralization and tightened coordination of Degussa's rather ramshackle organizational structure began in earnest (the result, finalized during 1943, appears in Appendix L); the processes of meshing the parent corporation's Austrian properties and absorbing previously semi-independent productive units (e.g., HIAG, Durferrit, and Siebert) accelerated; and the firm compiled its first systematic census of the degree to which each manufacturing sector served armaments-related purposes.[2] Mobilization proceeded fairly smoothly, moreover, despite the shift of some 20 to 25 percent of Degussa's workforce into the Wehrmacht in 1939–40.[3] Although a much-needed extension of the headquarters building obviously would have to be put off for the duration, the company saw no reason to suspend planning for the project and meanwhile pursued expedient solutions to its shortage of administrative space.[4] Even the first abrupt changes in production runs provoked but passing difficulties for Degussa's managers. They rearranged machinery in order to turn out more hexalol and formaldehyde for munitions, went over to manufacturing substitutes for Henkel's perborate so as to reserve sodium supplies for the war effort, and even largely acquiesced when briefly confronted with the "somewhat grotesque situation" that carbon black yields (which the regime had driven skyward over Ernst Baerwind's objections) would have to be halved, since they had accumulated faster than rubber supplies.[5] But real differences soon arose, as they would recurrently during the war, over Degussa's interrelated efforts (a) to maintain its fully or partially monopolistic position in fields that were central to its commercial strength – above all, hydrogen peroxide, sodium and cyanides, formaldehyde and organic distillates of wood, carbon

[2] On the corporate reorganization and the absorptions, DUA, DL 2/1, Niederschriften über die Vorstandssitzungen am 6. November 1939, pp. 57–58 (and Anlagen 2–4); 8. Januar 1940, pp. 67–68, 70–71 (and Anlage 1); 6. Mai 1940, pp. 86, 89 (and Anlagen 4–5); 3. Juni 1940, p. 95; and 7. April 1941, pp. 170–71. The results of the census are to be found in PCA 2/143.
[3] See Appendix M on the call-ups at Kalscheuren and Rheinfelden; DUA, IW 2.8/8, Jahresbericht Werk Gutleutstrasse 1940, August 8, 1941, p. 2, on those at Werk II in Frankfurt; and DL 2/1, Niederschrift über die Vorstandssitzung am 2. September 1940, p. 122, where the figure given for the initial call-up (424 men) applies to Degussa's Frankfurt operations alone and corresponds to about 20 percent of their personnel.
[4] For the continuing discussions of an eventual new headquarters building, see ibid., 6. November 1939, p. 61; 4. März 1940, p. 79; 2. April 1940, p. 84; 6. Mai 1940, p. 90; 3. Juni 1940, p. 93; 5 August 1940, p. 107; 3. März 1941, pp. 165–66; 9. Juni 1941, p. 182; 7. Juli 1941, p. 190 and Anlage 1; 6. Oktober 1941, p. 204; and 7. September 1942, p. 269.
[5] Ibid., 11. September 1939, p. 46, on perborate; 2. Oktober 1939, p. 56, on the carbon black reduction; and 2. Dezember 1939, p. 66 (and Anlage 2) on hexalol and formaldehyde. Also pertinent concerning carbon black are DL 3.Baerwind/23, Aussprache bei der Reichsstelle für Wirtschaftsausbau, September 23, 1939, where the words quoted appear, and PCA 2/10, Baerwind's Russwerke Dortmund-Sitzungen, November 20, 1939.

black, and rare metals – but at the same time (b) to draw a line between making or processing militarily valuable commodities and getting too deeply engaged in producing goods directly for the Wehrmacht and (c) to bring its runaway Auer subsidiary under control.

It is only a slight exaggeration to say that, by and large, the Second World War brought Degussa greatest expansion where the company's leaders were least interested in it and lowest growth where they sought it most intently. Behind this outcome lay a series of mismatches between the time horizons of the firm and the regime, their respective standards of success, and the power of each to impose its view. Whereas Degussa sought durable returns on investment over the long term, the Reich desired large quantities of essential goods as soon as feasible. Whereas the former worried about future market shares and prospects, the latter cared primarily for immediate contributions to the war effort. Of course, such differences were frequently bridgeable in a state as financially profligate as Nazi Germany. The potential monetary costs to the enterprise of fulfilling the government's demands almost always could be met from the public purse or private loans that it guaranteed and thus brushed aside as a barrier to complying. But the company's opportunity costs were another matter. Command over the allocation of labor, raw materials, and most capital enabled the regime to override such considerations but not to abolish them. Consequently, chances curtailed or forgone as a result of official policy created considerable frustration within Degussa between 1939 and 1944, despite the enormous expansion of the firm and its profits in these years.

Cases in point are the three projects to which Degussa assigned highest priority as the war commenced: the doubling of the company's hydrogen peroxide capacity, preferably through additions to the Rheinfelden installation; the construction of a new factory for sodium at a less vulnerable location than Knapsack; and the erection of a giant central works (Konzernwerk or Zentralwerk) somewhere near coal deposits in the eastern half of the Reich. The first two of these projects were primarily demand driven. In 1939, Degussa's own hydrogen peroxide installations produced at 98 percent of capacity (3,400 tons per year at a concentration of 30 percent) and those of its Austrian subsidiary (ÖCW) at Weissenstein at 70 percent of what available supplies of hydroelectric power would allow (3,000 tons). The resulting output covered not only all of Degussa's and most of IG Farben's needs, but also 33 percent of cartel sales within Germany, more than any other manufacturer provided.[6] More than two-thirds of production went to the synthetic fiber and textile processing industries, whose appetite had quadrupled since 1937 and was on its way to doing so again by 1942. Meanwhile, replacing sodium perborate would entail increasing supplies of hydrogen peroxide to make the

---

[6] DUA, GCH 5/38, Degussa to Generalbevollmächtige für Sonderfragen der chem. Erzeugung, September 17, 1942.

substitutes, and two new applications of the "universally useful" substance promised to push orders still higher: porous concrete, for which two factories set to open in 1939–40 were about to raise demand from 2 to 200 tons annually; and "a still-unknown W[ehrmacht] purpose," for which Albert Pietzsch's Munich Electrochemical Works (EWM) of Höllriegelskreuth already was buying 10 percent of Degussa's output and forecasting a huge surge in subsequent needs.[7] With large-scale additions to the Reich's hydrogen peroxide capacity inevitable, Degussa would have to keep up or watch one of its mainstay market positions erode.

The same prospect loomed regarding sodium, especially under wartime conditions. As of October 1939, the combined monthly production of Degussa's Knapsack and IG Farben's Gersthofen factories (650 and 160 tons, respectively) already was 26.5 tons less than projected demand, 88 percent of which pertained to the armaments program, since metallic sodium was an essential intermediate in the production of cyanides, metal hardeners, and tetraethyl lead, as well as in the hydrogenation of fuel.[8] Hermann Schlosser thus concluded that not only the immediate outlook for sales, but also the needs to head off potential competitors and control all additional capacity after the war, dictated that "we must retain under all circumstances exclusive initiative concerning the construction of a new sodium plant in Germany, even if it costs us much money."[9] That sodium peroxide, not to mention sodium perborate, was vital to detergent making, and thus to Degussa's long-term relationship with Henkel, no doubt contributed to the unequivocal nature of Schlosser's commitment.

Arguments for the Konzernwerk, however, rested on somewhat broader calculations, ones involving both demand and supply issues. For Koloman Róka, the major proponent of the project on the managing board, recognized that Degussa's fabrication of many chemicals was not only reaching the limits of current capacity but also laboring under expensive inefficiencies. Some of these derived from the age of Degussa's main plants, but the chief cause was their odd geographical configuration (see Appendix M). Long distances between the sites that made sodium and its derivatives, for example, ran up transportation charges and impeded the productive use of by-products. The remoteness of most of the firm's installations from coal deposits also bred

---

[7] DUA, PCA 1/139bIII, Wasserstoffsuperoxyd Verkauf, 20. September 1939; GCH 5/38, Ullmann's Entwicklung der H2-O2 Bezüge der Zellwolle-Industrie, August 31, 1945. The first set of words quoted appear in GCH 2/11, Schmidt's Niederschrift über die Besprechung betr. Erweiterung der Rheinfeldener H2O2-Anlage, March 18, 1942. On the military purpose, see DL 2/1, Niederschrift über die ausserplanmässige Vorstandssitzung am 11. September 1939, from which the second set of quoted words come, and PCA 1/139bIII, Schmidt's Bericht. Reise nach Berlin, September 25, 1939.

[8] DUA, DL 3.Baerwind/23, Aussprache in der Reichsstelle für Wirtschaftsausbau, October 19, 1939, especially Anlage 2.

[9] DUA, DL 2/1, Vorstandssitzung am 6. November 1939, Anlage 5, Schlosser's Neue Natriumfabrik, October 20, 1939, p. 3.

18   Koloman Róka

costs, while the proximity of many factories to Germany's borders increased pressure to appropriate funds for backup facilities in securer locations. Lest "inability to deliver on orders or higher prices" someday force Degussa "either to lose whole product lines or at least considerably scale back their proceeds," Róka appealed to his colleagues in October 1939 to break once and for all with their enterprise's tradition of piecemeal, ad hoc growth. Instead, he called on them to formulate a "long-term production plan" that would govern all future construction projects concerning chemicals and to designate a single, expansive, coal-rich location where these would be realized as funds permitted and conditions warranted. If correctly conceived and executed, such a program would enable Degussa to modernize, integrate, and consolidate its operations, thus assuring that "we really have the best and cheapest that there is at any given time."[10]

Róka took care to couch this proposal in terms of Degussa's collective interests, but as a veteran of HIAG carbonization sector. Already in 1938, August Kolb had pointed out that "the raw material base of HIAG is restricted and increasingly endangered, so that an expansion of production on the basis of wood appears scarcely possible, but rather a reduction of output is to be expected." He therefore explored the possibility of launching Degussa into the synthesis of organic chemicals on the basis of acetylene obtained from calcium carbide, a process that required massive quantities of electric power, and hence depended on having at hand large supplies of coal or the gases given off by hydrogenation.[11] No concrete steps to this end had been taken by the autumn of 1939, however, and Róka knew that his firm

[10] *Ibid.*, Anlage 6, Róka's Ausbau der Produktionsstätten der Scheideanstalt, October 27, 1939.
[11] DUA, KLB 1/01, Kolb's Studie über die Erweiterung unserer Rohstoffgrundlage, March 14, 1938.

was running out of time, all the more so as he foresaw great increases in formaldehyde sales, which Degussa monopolized in Germany, for resins and plastics. In fact, the relative contribution of HIAG's plants to Degussa's total gross profits was about to crest at 35.6 percent in 1939/40, then to fall back below the pre-Nazi level in 1941/42 and thereafter (see Appendix D). The chief causes of this turnabout were the increasing scarcity, declining quality, and rising price of the wood on which the carbonization plants relied, as indicated by the facts that the quantity Degussa processed also peaked in 1939/40 and that the production costs per cubic meter of input, which had risen from 74 to 86 RM since 1932/33, shot up to 125 RM in 1941/42.[12] Róka's advocacy of the Konzernwerk thus came not a moment too soon from HIAG's perspective. On the contrary, as one of his colleagues in Degussa's organic chemicals sector noted a few months later, "the most favorable time to build was approximately ten years ago."[13] But at least now, with Germany at war, Róka could remind anyone intimidated by the enormous price tag of his conception that "the government surely also will set great store by the transfer of our plants," and thus be inclined to help with the financing.[14]

Although Degussa's managing board swiftly endorsed these projects, all three fell prey to the stop-and-go decision making that characterized the "steered economy" under Nazism. By January 1940, the concern had settled on Rheinfelden as the location for the hydrogen peroxide plant and Fürstenberg an der Oder for the full-fledged Central Works, including the sodium installation with a capacity of 325 monthly tons (as well as units for formaldehyde and hexalol in the first construction phase).[15] But both inorganics factories succumbed during the "Phony War" to downward revisions of the nation's needs – for hydrogen peroxide because "the militarily important special purpose will not require such large quantities as originally expected," and for sodium as a result of IG Farben's sudden claim that the substance soon would be unnecessary to the manufacture of tetraethyl lead.[16]

---

[12] DUA, RFI 4.2/104, Bericht über die Tätigkeit und Leistung der Werke im Geschäftsjahr 1942/43, Technische Abteilung II, Anlage B, March 1944.

[13] DUA, DL 2/1, Vorstandssitzung am 2. September 1940, Anlage 3, Achterath's Betr. Projekt Fürstenberg, August 30, 1940.

[14] *Ibid.*, 6. November 1939, Anlage 6, Ausbau der Produktionsstätten, October 27, 1939, p. 6.

[15] *Ibid.*, Niederschriften über die Vorstandssitzungen am 6. November 1939, p. 59; 8. Januar 1940, pp. 68–69, and Anlage 2, Róka's Notiz über die Besprechung der Projektierung des Zentralwerks, January 4, 1940. On the background to the choice of Fürstenberg, see DL 3.Baerwind/23, Besprechungen in Berlin, November 18, 1939; Fürstenberg/Oder als eventueller Standort, December 4, 1939; and Besuche in Fürstenberg/Oder und Aussig, December 22, 1939.

[16] DUA, PCA 1/139bIII, Baerwind's Telefongespräch... betreffend die eventuelle Vergrösserung unserer Wasserstoffsuperoxydkapazität, December 23, 1939, from which the quotation is drawn; DL 3.Baerwind/23, Aussprache... über eine neue Natrium-Fabrik, October 19, 1939, and Telefongespräch mit Direktor Müller-Cunradi, October 21, 1939, as well

That Farben also offered to supply Degussa with sodium cyanide at favorable prices from the giant firm's Breslau plant meanwhile undercut the need for Frankfurt to add to its capacities, as did the readiness of the Reich to pay the interest costs on stockpiling at several secure reserves in central Germany.[17] Degussa's managers pressed on with the rest of the initial program for Fürstenberg, however, completing the purchase of the site for 975,000 RM and a contract governing its electricity supply during April 1940, then appropriating in July 1.3 million Reichsmarks for the boiler plant.[18] But the project bogged down over the summer, as the eagerness of economic planners in Berlin and Degussa's technical leaders to substitute a carbide plant for the abandoned sodium one provoked vehement opposition from IG Farben and a case of cold feet on Schlosser's part as a result (see Chapter 2).[19] With the cost estimates for the carbide and formaldehyde factories rising rapidly from 9 million to 10 million Reichsmarks to 20 million to 23 million, uncertainty about economic conditions in the wake of Germany's conquests in Scandinavia, the Low Countries, and France provided an excuse in September for the managing board to defer further decisions for six months.[20]

The hydrogen peroxide expansion project got a new lease on life in early 1942 and official sanction at midyear, but by the time the new facilities came on line in the summer of 1944, Degussa's relative standing in the field had declined appreciably.[21] During the long interval prior to construction, as the needs of the still secret military purpose (which turned out to be fuel for ramp-launched or takeoff-assisted rockets and aircraft) rose exponentially after all, Degussa's erstwhile ally Albert Pietzsch managed to exclude the firm completely from that market.[22] Exploiting his excellent political connections, he obtained a virtual monopoly over making the volatile and highly concentrated hydrogen peroxide (80 to 90 percent pure) required as a propellant, some of it at his own firm, but principally at two huge government-owned factories in Thuringia that a subsidiary of his managed for the Reich. Simultaneously, IG Farben developed a new production process

as the retrospective remarks in DL 3.Baerwind/26, Besprechungen im WiRü-Amt und im Reichsamt, September 28, 1942.

[17] DUA, DL 2/1, Niederschrift über die Vorstandssitzung am 2. April 1940, p. 82, and Anlage 1, Schlosser's Verhältnis zur I. G., March 27, 1940; DL 3.Baerwind/23, Besuch bei dem Wehrwirtschaftsstab, December 4, 1939.

[18] DUA, DL 2/1, Niederschriften über die Vorstandssitzungen am 2. April 1940, p. 81; am 6. Mai 1940, pp. 90–91, and Anlagen 10–13; and am 1. Juli 1940, p. 99.

[19] DUA, DL 2/1, Niederschrift über die Vorstandssitzung am 5. August 1940, pp. 103–05.

[20] *Ibid.*, pp. 105–07, and Anlage 1–2; am 14. August 1940, pp. 111–13, and Anlage 1; and am 2. September 1940, pp. 118–21, and Anlagen 1–4.

[21] For the time sequence, see *ibid.*, am 5. Januar 1942, p. 226; am 6. Juli 1942, p. 254; am 5. Juni 1944, n.p.; and am 4. September 1944, p. 394.

[22] On the technology of hydrogen peroxide propulsion, see Michael J. Neufeld, *The Rocket and the Reich: Peenemünde and the Coming of the Ballistic Missile Era* (New York: The Free Press, 1995), pp. 60–61.

and began building a vast facility at Heydebreck in Upper Silesia, chiefly to serve its own fabrication of synthetic fibers.[23] By 1942, the parts of these installations completed or under construction could turn out 88,000 tons per year at a 30 percent concentration, and plans called for total outputs of 200,000 yearly tons. Only the realization in Berlin that even these capacities were insufficient led the regime's economic and military planners to reverse themselves regarding Rheinfelden. In typical fashion, they suddenly urged not merely a doubling of that plant's existing yield of 3,400 yearly tons, but a tripling, and called upon Degussa to devise its own means of achieving higher concentrations.[24] The latter task proved difficult for the firm's technicians – though not for their colleagues at ÖCW – and this failure, along with problems with the purity of Degussa's output, prompted official backtracking to the original scale of Rheinfelden's expansion, a development that now drove Ernst Baerwind almost to despair.[25] In June 1942, he summarized the "catastrophic shift in the power relationships in the activated oxygen field" by saying that Degussa had so "lost our previous decades-long position . . . to the greatly expanded Höllriegelskreuth and to the Reich-owned plants," that Henkel might be tempted to transfer its business to them after the war unless Rheinfelden grew to the maximum degree possible.[26]

Although Baerwind got the plan to triple Rheinfelden's size restored in the fall of 1942, that additional round of growth remained unfinished when the Allied occupiers arrived in 1945.[27] Neither did Degussa ever begin producing concentrated hydrogen peroxide; Rheinfelden's role in military applications of the product remained confined to selling normal hydrogen peroxide to Pietzsch for upgrading.[28] Had Germany won the Second World War, Degussa's long struggle to preserve its leadership position regarding this product would have seemed, at best, a draw. The firm managed to arrest the slides in its relative shares of cartel sales and production during the first years

---

[23] See, as background, DUA, S/3404, W. G. Gormley, "Hydrogen Peroxide Electro Chemische Werke, Höllriegelskreuth," Combined Intelligence Objectives Sub-Committee Report, June 1945.

[24] DUA, GCH 2/11, Kolb to Degussa's managing board, March 7, 1942, and Schmidt's Besprechung betr. Erweiterung der Rheinfeldener H₂O₂-Anlage, March 18, 1942; TLE 1/23, Auszug aus dem streng geheimen Schreiben des Herrn Dr. Kolb an Herrn Direktor Schlosser, April 21, 1942; capacity figures calculated from the data in PCA 1/139aII, Baerwind's Aussprache mit Pietzsch, September 12, 1942.

[25] On Rheinfelden's problems producing high-test hydrogen peroxide and Weissenstein's success, see DUA, PCA 1/139aII, Martin's Betrifft: Herstellung von hochkonzentrietem H₂O₂, June 16, 1942; Baerwind's Besprechungen in Berlin, June 17, 1942; and Harant's Besuch in Weissenstein, June 26, 1942.

[26] *Ibid.*, Baerwind's Aussprache im Reichsamt . . . über unsere Wasserstoffsuperoxydbauvorhaben, June 30, 1942, p. 3.

[27] DUA, DL 2/1, Niederschriften über die Vorstandssitzungen am 2. November 1942, p. 282; 5. Juni 1944, n.p.; 21. November 1944, n.p.

[28] DUA, S/3404, W. G. Gormley, "Hydrogen Peroxide," CIOS Report, June 1945, pp. 16–17.

of the conflict, but Degussa's gross profits from hydrogen peroxide never recovered their level of 1938/39, its technical preeminence disappeared, and its manufacturing capacities shrank in relation to those that IG Farben and the German state amassed.[29]

With regard to Degussa's standing in the field of sodium and its derivatives, the course of events after 1939 proved even less satisfactory. Though the Reich's military and economic planners belatedly embraced the idea of a second Degussa factory for the metal in September 1942, the project could not be completed by 1945.[30] Only in March 1943, after Farben's Gersthofen plant had been fully activated and Degussa's Knapsack installation badly damaged in an air raid, did the regime even promise the necessary building materials so that work could begin. Thereafter, shortages of labor and equipment plagued the effort, even though it had been cut back slightly to a target output of 315 tons per month and relocated to Rheinfelden, where building supposedly could proceed most rapidly.[31] Degussa also made little headway with its petition for the government to assume the construction costs (estimated at 7.35 million Reichsmarks), ultimately settling for a guarantee under the "war risk clause" by which the regime promised to take over the amortization and interest charges on any unused capacity in peacetime at either of the corporation's sodium facilities.[32] In the event of a Nazi victory, that insurance would have cushioned Degussa against the fact that IG Farben finally made good in 1944 on its claim to have a useable process that dispensed with the metal in making tetraethyl lead. But the Reich's financial

---

[29] On the cartel sales and production, see the somewhat inconsistent statistics provided in DUA, GCH 5/38, Martin to Beauftragte für den Vierjahresplan, September 17, 1942; Absatz der H2O2-Konvention, December 1, 1942; H2O2-Produktionszahlen der Erzeuger 1943 und Vorausschätzung 1944, February 26, 1944; and Ullmann's H2 O2-Produktions-Kapazitäten, August 31, 1945. On the loss of technical leadership, see PCA 1/139aII, Baerwind's Aussprache mit Pietzsch, September 12, 1942, p. 7.

[30] See DUA, DL 3.Baerwind/26, Besprechung im WiRü-Amt und im Reichsamt für Wirtschaftsausbau, September 28, 1942, and Natriumplanung in Berlin, January 25, 1943.

[31] DUA, GCH 2/9, Inhaltsverzeichnis zu Lippe 3, records the pace of events regarding Gersthofen. On the damage to Knapsack and its consequences, DL 3.Baerwind/26, Besuch im Werk Knapsack, March 10, 1943, and Gespräch mit Herrn Dr. Eckell, March 18, 1943. On the firm's and government's decisions to build, DUA, DL 2/1, Niederschriften über die Vorstandssitzungen am 5. April 1943, pp. 311–12; 7. Juni 1943, p. 319; 5. Juli 1943, p. 325; and 3. August 1943, p. 330. The final official approvals are recorded in BET 10/2, Krauch to Kehrl, July 6, 1943, and Eckell to Kehrl, July 29, 1943. On the labor and materials shortages that impeded completion, DL 2/1, Niederschriften über die Vorstandssitzungen am 5. Juni 1944, n.p.; am 3. Juli 1944, n.p.; am 25. Juli 1944, p. 1; and am 4. September 1944, p. 394.

[32] DUA, DL 2/1, Niederschrift über die Vorstandssitzung am 1. November 1943, p. 343. See also BET 10/2, Bernau and Baerwind to Ministerialrat Dr. Römer, September 7, 1943; Bernau's Betr.: Reichskredit für die in Rheinfelden zu erstellende Natriumfabrik, September 17, 1943; Mureck's Aktenvermerk, November 11, 1943; and Bernau's Betr.: Auslegung der Kriegsrisikoklausel für die Natriumanlage, February 23, 1944.

assistance would not have alleviated a second respect in which Frankfurt's position in the sodium field meanwhile had deteriorated.[33]

Along with sodium perborate, sodium cyanide was a cornerstone of Degussa's chemicals business, not only as the key component of acetonecyanohydrin for Plexiglas, the metal hardeners of the Durferrit division, and the insecticides of the Degesch subsidiary, but also because the corporation functioned as the sales agent for all German output of the product. Yet in this essential sphere, Degussa also proved powerless to prevent an erosion of its standing during the war years. As concerning hydrogen peroxide, the problem was not that Degussa lost substantial ground in the cartellized market. Even though the firm's own production of sodium cyanide (including hydrocyanic acid or *Blausäure*, the liquid form of the product) topped out both by volume (at 5,500 metric tons) and as a share of all continental European sales (at 34 percent) in 1939, the figures for subsequent years did not change greatly until 1944, when air raid damage began to have a distorting effect.[34] Rather, what hurt the firm was that overall demand kept ballooning, IG Farben's internal needs and capacities (as well as those it operated for the state at Dyhernfurth) soared, Degussa's technological lead vanished in the process, and the yield obtained by the processors of desugared beet plants (*Schlempe*) actually dropped by about one-half from the 1939 level (about 4,300 yearly tons) as the raw material increasingly was diverted for use as animal feed and in making yeast.[35] With Frankfurt therefore falling ever further behind in its deliveries, Röhm & Haas, the manufacturer of

[33] DUA, DL 2/1, Notizen aus dem Vorstandscolloquium am 20. Juni 1944, p. 1.

[34] DUA, DL 13.3/1, Bericht Nr. 2, K. Bonath, "Natriumcyanid. Geschichte der Verfahren, der Produktion, der Entwicklung und der Forschungsarbeiten," November 1967, pp. 40–42, with graphs, and Anlage 4.

[35] On IG Farben's mounting production and technical lead, along with the overall increase in consumption, see DUA, GCH 5/1, Westphal's Cyan-Situation-1943, September 8, 1942; his Cyannatrium, September 11, 1942; and DL 3.Baerwind/26, Aussprache in Ludwigshafen, May 10, 1943; and Besprechung mit Dr. Holl/OKH . . . über den Cyanidbedarf des Werkes "Dy," May 15, 1943; as well as PCA 2/143, Baerwind's Derzeitiger Stand der von Deutschland kontrollierten Produktionskapazitäten in Natriumcyanid und Blausäure und Vorschlag für die Erweiterung derselben, June 3, 1943, which shows Farben's share of German productive capacity about to rise from 49 percent to 56 percent and envisions a further increase to almost 65 percent. On the decline in *Schlempe*-based output, see GCH 5/1, Westphal's Cyan-Konvention, June 5, 1942; Dreyer and Kluge's Melasse-Schlempe für die deutsche Cyaniderzeugung, March 11, 1943; and Der Melasse-Bedarf der chemischen Industrie im Wirtschaftsjahr 1943/44, May 17, 1943, unsigned; as well as GCH 5/2, Effektive Lieferungen der Kontinentalen Werke, May 6, 1939, and Westphal's Cyan-Besprechung in Dessau, August 15, 1942; and DL 13.3/1, Bonath's Natriumcyanid-Bericht, pp. 40–41. In 1942–44, Degussa made several efforts to induce the Swiss firm Ciba to provide Germany with sodium cyanide and thus narrow the gap between demand and supply, apparently with only minor success; see DL 3.H.Schlosser/1, Doc. 911, Ciba, Basel, September 21, 1942, and Doc. 964, Ciba-Basel, September 25, 1943, as well as Lukas Straumann and Daniel Wildmann, *Schweizer Chemieunternehmen im "Dritten Reich"* (Zurich: Chronos, 2001), pp. 52–54.

Plexiglas, felt driven to take up production of the intermediate in late 1944, despite continued willingness to purchase whatever Degussa could provide under previous contracts.[36] In other words, had the war ended victoriously for Germany, Degussa would have bulked much smaller in the field overall and found its lucrative sales to two previously vital customers, Farben and Röhm & Haas, effectively capped. After recording rising profits through 1941, mostly because unrewarding exports had been replaced by internal demand, Degussa's sodium cyanide business faced relegation to secondary significance.[37]

The delays that also left the Zentralwerk at Fürstenberg unfinished in 1945 stemmed initially from Degussa's own hesitation, but they also evolved into an expensive demonstration of the gap between the firm's and the state's economic priorities. From the beginning, the plant's problem was that it was not regarded in Berlin as "decisive for the war effort."[38] Admittedly, the centerpiece carbide and formaldehyde factories had enough long-term military-economic importance for the regime to favor their construction, but when it came to actually allocating such scarce commodities as building materials, machinery, and laborers to assemble them, more urgent needs almost always took precedence. Thus, very little happened on the site until 1942, long after Degussa's managing board (prodded by Henkel – see Chapter 2) overcame Schlosser's reluctance to antagonize IG Farben and Bernau's reservations about the costs and reaffirmed its commitment to Róka's brainchild. The group voted again in December 1940 to build the formaldehyde unit (with a capacity of 12,000 metric tons per year), in February 1941 to attach sections for carbide (30,000 to 50,000 tons) and solvents (14,400 tons of alcohols, acetic acid, and its derivatives), and in June 1941 to decide "unanimously and finally in favor of carrying out the project," even though the huge expense entailed the recognition that the "financial program of the Scheideanstalt also is now settled for years to come."[39] Nonetheless, shortly after that last vote occurred, the exasperated construction manager on the

---

[36] DUA, TLE 1/23, Schlosser's Betr. Röhm & Haas, Darmstadt, September 16, 1943; GCH 9/21, Hubert's Besuch von Dir. Dr. Mueller, December 17, 1943; and DL 13.4/1, Hubert's Notiz für Prof. Dr. Fuchs, August 16, 1944, and Riesenhuber's Notiz für Dr. Fischer, September 13, 1944. These documents also indicate that the increasing threat posed by IG Farben in the field of acrylics contributed to Röhm & Hass's decision.

[37] See DUA, GCH 5/1, Westphal's Cyan-Konvention, May 22, 1942.

[38] DUA, TLE 2/75, Schulz's Niederschrift über Besprechung betr. Baustelle "F," March 25, 1941.

[39] On the development of opinion within the board, see DUA, DL 2/1, Niederschriften über die Vorstandssitzungen am 7. October 1940, pp. 125–30, and Anlagen 2–3; November 4, 1940, pp. 135–38, and Anlagen 1–7; December 2, 1940, pp. 142–43, and Anlagen 1–3; February 3, 1941, pp. 157–60, and Anlagen 1–4; March 3, 1941, pp. 162–63; and June 9, 1941, p. 181, where the quoted words appear. Along the way, Degussa had to fend off Johannes Eckell's desire to transfer the site to his favorite industrial region, Eastern Upper Silesia; see Vorstandssitung am April 7, 1941, p. 168, and Anlagen 1–3.

19   The Zentralwerk at Fürstenberg an der Oder, 194?

site succinctly summarized the course of events to date: "we have been working on F[ürstenberg] for more than $1\frac{1}{4}$ years, without even having begun a
building."[40] By the end of the year, little more had been done, since the
blueprints for the boiler house authorized seventeen months earlier had only
just arrived.[41]

Seeking to gain the official support that alone could speed Fürstenberg's
pace, Degussa increasingly focused the project on providing militarily vital
organics. Not only would such facilities become the nucleus of later expansion, but the firm could hope along the way to apply possible surplus supplies
for these undertakings on other sectors of the site. Thus, in May 1942, total
appropriations for the Zentralwerk reached almost 34 million Reichsmarks,
the latest round of increases being a result of decisions to double the size of
the formaldehyde plant, revive the original intention to build one for hexalol (at 1000 tons per month), and add an ammonia-making unit, all "in
order to secure Fürstenberg in the reduced Speer building program." Although Schlosser also took this occasion to declare that he could not answer
for any further expenditures of this sort, the firm had passed the point of

[40] DUA, TLE 2/72, Schulz's Aktennotiz betr. Baustelle "F," June 24, 1941.
[41] DUA, TLE 2/75, Schulz's Niederschrift über die Besprechung betr. Baustelle "F," December
4, 1941.

no return.[42] In response to the regime's demands for 36,000 yearly tons of formaldehyde production and 1,500 monthly tons of hexalol, Degussa had raised by November its projected outlays to almost 37 million Reichsmarks, a sum that exceeded the corporation's total capitalization prior to 1941.[43] All of this just sufficed to keep construction going. In December 1943, the formaldehyde plant began producing, eighteen to twenty-four months after Róka originally had projected and at a rate that the firm feared would outstrip postwar demand.[44] No other segment of the Konzernwerk came on line prior to the evacuation of the site in March 1945, by which time Degussa managed to carry off much of the inventory and some of the machinery, almost the only material returns to the firm on actual outlays of 23.6 million Reichsmarks (out of a total appropriation of 41.6 million) over the preceding four years.[45]

While the expansion projects Degussa most desired came largely to naught between 1939 and 1945, those the Reich most wanted enjoyed a different fate. Once more, as in the late 1930s, carbon black provided the starkest illustration of the regime's ability to impose growth where it wished. Even before the fall of Poland, Johannes Eckell of the National Office for Economic Expansion not only resurrected the idea of a third factory to supplement Degussa's output at Kalscheuren and that of the Russwerke subsidiary at Dortmund – a notion that Schlosser and Baerwind had fought off the year before – but also expressed in "extraordinarily sharp" terms a desire for an Upper Silesian location.[46] Because current carbon black production now seemed likely, by the government's own calculations, to exceed the absorptive capacity of the German rubber industry until at least mid-1941, the

[42] DUA, DL 2/1, Niederschrift über die Vorstandssitzung am 4. Mai 1942, pp. 246–48 (the words quoted appear on p. 247). See also, PCA 2/91, Fischer's Aussprache mit der I. G. über Wirtschaftsplanung, May 7, 1942.
[43] On the creeping growth and shifting production targets for the site, see *ibid.*, am 7. September 1942, pp. 270–71; am 5. Oktober 1942, p. 274; am 2. November 1942, pp. 282–83, and Anlage 2; and am 1. Februar 1943, p. 300.
[44] See *ibid.*, am 6. Dezember 1943, p. 346, on the fear of postwar overcapacity; and TA2/73, Degussa to Gebechem, December 14, 1943, on the onset of production. For Róka's prediction of the completion of the formaldehyde plant "in the first half of 1942," Anlage 2 zur Niederschrift über die Vorstandssitzung am 2. September 1940, p. 3. In the meantime, shortages of labor and building materials dictated the cancellation of several other components of the plant; see Niederschrift über die Vorstandssitzung am 3. April 1944.
[45] DUA, TA 2/86, Genehmigte Investitionen. Anlage Fürstenberg/O., February 21, 1945, for the figures on appropriations and expenditures. See also DL 2/1, Notizen aus der Vorstandsbesprechung am 20. Februar 1945, p. 2, on the evacuation of inventories; and am 20. März 1945, p. 2, on efforts to ship machinery up the Elbe to some storage point. TA 2/87, Kühnlein's Bericht Betr.: Anlage F, Fürstenberg/Oder, March 15, 1945, provides an itemization of the quantities of materials on hand and removed to date.
[46] DUA, PCA 2/3, Baerwind's Gespräch mit Dr. Kemnitz...betreffend Aufforderung der Reichsstelle, September 11, 1939, and his Notizen betreffend...das Projekt einer dritten CK3-/CK4-Fabrik, September 18, 1939, where the quoted words appear on p. 3.

undertaking struck Baerwind as "from a commercial point of view some-what absurd." But Eckell pressed on. He insisted that "for military reasons, the project...must be so worked out that it can be pulled ready from the drawer at any time," and directed Baerwind in November 1939 to present such a plan in the latter half of the coming January.[47] After Eckell reiterated this demand a month later, Baerwind resignedly noted that "we will not be able to get out of an inspection of locations in Upper Silesia" early in the new year, only to be rescued briefly by other developments.[48] Until tests showed the value and time revealed the useable quantity of the carbon black that IG Farben's second synthetic rubber (Buna) factory at Hüls was to give off as a by-product – indeed, until events clarified whether the German victories in the West had made further growth in Buna output unnecessary (and thus that of carbon black), Eckell had to relent.[49]

The failure of the Reich to bring Britain to terms over the summer of 1940 indicated that a long war was in the offing and enabled Eckell to resume his offensive. In September, he openly threatened Degussa and Russwerke that, in the event of further foot dragging, "then the National Office will have to call upon other carbon black makers, for example Rütgers in Mährisch-Ostrau, to provide for the expansion of capacity."[50] As usual in the Third Reich, this gambit worked. The managing board in Frankfurt promptly de-duced that "in order to preserve its leading position in the carbon black field, Degussa must take an active part" via Russwerke, even though, as Baerwind pointed out, the anthracene derivatives that an Upper Silesian plant would depend on were both twice as expensive as feedstocks in western Germany and heavily contested by other claimants.[51] While Degussa appropriated one-half million marks to squeeze another 1,000 yearly tons of carbon black out of Kalscheuren, Baerwind and Georg Kemnitz of Russwerke gradually agreed that the best available eastern site was one offered by Borsig Coking Works (Kokswerke) adjoining its factory in Gleiwitz, the former border town

[47] See, on the relative overproduction of carbon black, DUA, DL 3.Baerwind/23, Aussprache bei der Reichsstelle für Wirtschaftsausbau, September 23, 1939; and PCA 2/10, Baerwind's Russwerke Dortmund-Sitzungen in Berlin, November 20, 1939. The two quoted passages appear in the latter document, p. 3.
[48] DUA, PCA 2/3, Baerwind's Aussprache...über das Projekt einer dritten CK3-/CK4-Fabrik, December 27, 1939.
[49] *Ibid.*, Baerwind's Aktenvermerk betreffend die Aussprache beim Reichsamt, July 18, 1940, and Auszug aus dem Bericht des Herrn Dr. Kemnitz vom 10. Juli 1940. On the pause in IG Farben's Buna expansion program, which Eckell opposed, see also PCA 2/3, Freudenberg's Notiz, July 25, 1940, and Peter Hayes, *Industry and Ideology: IG Farben in the Nazi Era* (New York: Cambridge University Press, 2001), pp. 347–48.
[50] DUA, DL 2/1, Niederschrift über die Vorstandssitzung am 7. Oktober 1940, Anlage 1, Baerwind's Besprechung mit Dr. Eckell, September 23, 1940, p. 1. For the background to this meeting, see PCA 2/3, Auszug aus Bericht Dr. Baerwind, September 19, 1940, and Baerwind's Aktennotiz. Besprechung vom 20. September 1940 im Reichsamt.
[51] DUA, DL 2/1, Niederschrift über die Vorstandssitzung am 7. Oktober 1940, p. 125, for the quotation, and Anlage 1, p. 3, on the raw materials situation.

where World War II had begun.[52] Their attention apparently had been drawn to the spot already in the preceding year because of the usefulness of the gas given off by the existing plant to the operations of a new facility.[53]

Once again, as in the 1930s, the unwanted expansion required the owners of the now renamed Deutsche Gasrusswerke GmbH (DGW) – Degussa and the consortium of rubber manufacturers – to put up considerable capital. The initial cost estimates for a plant at Gleiwitz that could fabricate 6,000 tons of active carbon black annually came to 12 million to 13 million Reichsmarks. Just under half the total was to be raised immediately from the investors (6.2 million Reichsmarks: 1 million in final payments on a previous capital increase, 3 million in purchases of new shares, and 2.2 million in expenditures funded by depreciation of the Dortmund installation), and the balance (6.8 million) from mortgages and bank loans.[54] But Eckell remained sure that Buna output soon would outstrip carbon black production, and in the autumn of 1941 an explosion at Kalscheuren and an air raid near the Dortmund plant presented him with another rationale for even greater growth: the urgent need to have replacement capacity in the German East in case of "accidents in the West."[55] Though DGW's leaders still doubted the reliability of raw materials supplies, they knuckled under in November and approved an increase in Gleiwitz's capacity to some 14,000 yearly tons at a cost of a further 10.7 million Reichsmarks, 2 million from another stock issue and the rest from additional borrowing, which brought the firm's total indebtedness to 21.2 million Reichsmarks.[56]

This time, however, the company demanded that the Reich lighten the burden somewhat. Because the first round of construction at Gleiwitz already had cost twice as much as Dortmund's entire development, while generating

---

[52] *Ibid.*, am 4. November 1940, p. 140, and Anlage 8, concerning the expansion at Kalscheuren; am 2. Dezember 1940, p. 147, on the probable choice of Gleiwitz. As background, see PCA 2/3, Baerwind's Verhandlungen in Berlin...über die zweite R. D. Fabrik, November 11, 1940, and his Berliner Besprechungen, November 25, 1940.

[53] *Ibid.*, Baerwind's Aussprache bei der Reichsstelle, December 27, 1939.

[54] DUA, DL 11.5/40, a collection of the loan agreements between July and October 1941, which also outlines the overall financing, pp. 17–25 and 35–46. The plans included 500,000 RM for further expansions at Dortmund, which I have factored out of the figures presented here. DL 2/1, Niederschrift über die Vorstandssitzung am 7. April 1941, pp. 172–73, records the appropriation of 1.5 million Reichsmarks to purchase Degussa's share of the new stock issue. Anlage 4, Bernau's Russwerke Dortmund, March 29, 1941, calculates that Degussa could expect to earn almost 585,000 RM annually or 13 percent of its investment in DGW once the Gleiwitz plant began operating.

[55] DUA, BET 9/46, Baerwind's Verhandlung im Reichsamt, October 20, 1941, and his Sitzung der Erweiterten Arbeitsausschusses der Deutschen Gasrusswerke, December 1, 1941, which is the source of the quotation.

[56] *Ibid.*, Bernau's Deutsche Gasrusswerke GmbH, Dortmund, November 14, 1941, in which he also calculated that Degussa could continue to expect an eventual return of almost 13 percent on its investment, provided demand remained high long enough to pay off the debts. DL 2/1, Niederschrift über die Vorstandssitzung am 2. Februar 1942, p. 232, records Degussa's agreement to the capital increase at DGW.

20   The Deutsche Gasrusswerke plant at Gleiwitz, 1944

only half the capacity, DGW claimed it would be unable to carry out further expansion unless the regime renounced the taxes on up to 3 million marks in annual, postdepreciation profits at the older plant so that they could be applied to augmenting the newer one and covered it under the protections against superfluity afforded by the "war risk clause." Unwilling to assume the building costs itself or to chance further delays, the Finance Ministry agreed and arranged supplemental relief from local taxes.[57] But even this go-ahead did not satisfy Eckell. In May 1942, with Gleiwitz now projected to equal Dortmund in size, he sought still more output of carbon black in Upper Silesia. By once again indicating readiness to turn to a competitor, he won DGW's agreement to an eventual capacity of 17,000 tons per year.[58] As

---

[57] DUA, BET 9/46, Kemnitz to the Reich Finance Ministry, November 25, 1941; Kemnitz to Bernau, December 22, 1941; Kemnitz to the Reich's Finance Minister, December 22, 1941; and Kemnitz to Römer (RWM) and Mundt (RFM), December 22, 1941, with Anlagen. The exemption applied originally to 1941–42 only, but was extended through 1944, by the end of which it had enabled Dortmund to transfer 11.4 million Reichsmarks to the building of Gleiwitz; see BET 9/51, Treuhand- und Wirtschaftsprüfungs-Gesellschaft mbH, Bericht über die Prüfung der Bilanz nebst Gewinn- und Verlustrechnung per 31. Dezember 1944 der Deutsche Gasrusswerke GmbH.

[58] DUA, PCA 2/4, Baerwind to Eckell, May 27, 1942.

a result, by the turn of 1942/43, DGW and Degussa foresaw the final cost of Gleiwitz as between 27 million and 30 million Reichsmarks.[59] Technological breakthroughs abruptly rendered much of this expenditure unnecessary in the course of 1943, just as Gleiwitz began to produce. Degussa researchers discovered that employing hydrogen rather than coke-oven gas in the making of carbon black increased yields by 75 percent and that alterations to improve air flow to the burners produced a further gain of 15 to 20 percent.[60] In short order, the capacity of all existing installations doubled to a level far in excess of even Eckell's predictions of what the German rubber and tire industries needed. This prospect did not deter him from demanding that DGW capitalize immediately on the new technology by building a pipeline between IG Farben's hydrogenation plant at Heydebreck and Gleiwitz, thus raising its future output to at least 25,000 yearly tons, and he grew more insistent after an air raid heavily damaged the Dortmund plant in late May.[61] But Degussa and DGW preferred a cheaper and closer supplier of hydrogen, the Hermann-Göring-Werke facility at Knurow, and refused to accept the link to Heydebreck unless the Reich paid for it.[62] When it became apparent in December 1943 that current carbon black output surpassed demand by some 25 percent and would continue to do so in the coming year, the firms lost interest in paying for either connection.[63] By early 1944, with their calculations showing that they could produce almost twice as much carbon black as Germany's rubber manufacturers conceivably could absorb, DGW's executive committee seized the chance to cut Gleiwitz loose. It ordered a reduction of the company's total production to 15,600 tons per year, the winding down of further construction at Gleiwitz, and the classification of that plant as a "backup factory," for which the Reich, not DGW, henceforth was financially responsible.[64]

Events now conspired to vindicate Eckell after all, at least partially. The halt in Upper Silesia, which reflected the gathering perception that "after the war, we will have trouble keeping Dortmund and Gleiwitz afloat," soon

---

[59] DUA, BET 9/48, Kemnitz to Gesellschafter der Deutschen Gasrusswerke, December 1, 1942, Anlage 1 (for the higher figure, as of September 1942); and DL 3.Baerwind/26, Deutsche Gasrusswerke GmbH, January 22, 1943 (for the lower total).

[60] DUA, PCA 2/144, Baerwind and Bonath to Forschungsführung des Reichsministers der Luftfahrt, October 8, 1943.

[61] DUA, DL 3.Baerwind/26, Aussprache zwischen dem Arbeitsausschuss der DGW und dem Reichsamt für Wirtschaftsausbau, May 15, 1943, and Wiederaufbau bei den D. G. W. in Dortmund, May 31, 1943.

[62] *Ibid.*, Aussprache mit Dr. Eckell und Dr. Kemnitz, July 19, 1943; BET 9/49, Kemnitz to Römer (RWM), September 29, 1943; and DL 3.Baerwind/27 (also BET 9/50), Russ-Besprechung in Oberschlesien, October 20, 1943.

[63] DUA, BET 9/50, Kemnitz to Baerwind, December 9, 1943.

[64] DUA, PCA 2/143, Oelmann's Besprechung über Russfragen, February 2, 1944 (on the supply-to-demand ratio), and BET 9/50, Herrmann's Niederschrift über die Besprechung des Arbeitsausschusses, March 29, 1944 (on the decisions regarding Gleiwitz).

was countermanded by the mounting threat of the complete destruction of the Kalscheuren and Dortmund plants from the air.[65] With the first phase of construction at Gleiwitz complete in June 1944 and the facility beginning to show an operating profit, the management resumed work on the second phase in hopes of insuring output for the moment and salvaging something for the future.[66] In consequence, Degussa's and DGW's aggregate production actually rose slightly in 1944, and Gleiwitz's contribution increased from 23 percent to 47 percent of the whole.[67] Eckell was positioned to boast that he had prevented carbon black from ever becoming one of the bottlenecks that restricted German industry during the war, though his obsessiveness also had led to considerable overcapacity in the long run.

Nor was this Eckell's sole imposition regarding carbon black. In 1943–44, he also overrode Degussa's objections to a new facility in the East for lampblack, the old-fashioned, inactive form of the product that he wanted for the manufacture of pigments and as a supplementary additive to tires. Though opposed to both the location and capacity Eckell favored (Gleiwitz and 6,000 tons per year) and to pouring energy and material into an essentially outmoded substance, Degussa once more gave in to Eckell's usual form of blackmail, namely the threat to entrust the task to the German rubber producers and thus dilute Frankfurt's market share.[68] The result in the summer of 1943 took the form of a new Flammruss GmbH, a consortium of lampblack makers led by Degussa, which promised, in the event that the members could not meet demand from existing installations, to lease a backup factory for 3,000 annual tons that the Reich would build at Degussa's Vosswalde plant in Upper Silesia.[69] By the time the need became

---

[65] *Ibid.*, Achterath's Betr.: Russ, June 20, 1944 (for the quotation), and Kemnitz to the Gesellschafter der Deutschen Gasrusswerke GmbH, June 27, 1944.

[66] Gleiwitz began producing in April 1943 and made a profit over its unit costs briefly in June to July of 1944, then steadily from October, which led to an operating profit for the year of 1.2 million marks. All things considered, however, the plant was still 3 million Reichsmarks in the red when it was overrun by the Soviet army. See DUA, PCA 2/1, Endabrechnung der Bauarbeiten, Stichtag 31. Dezember 1944, July 26, 1945; PRO 1/12, Schlussabrechnung DGW Gleiwitz, October 8, 1945; PCA 2/2, Gegenüberstellung von Gestehungskosten und Erlösen [1943], and Bisherige Betriebsergebnisse des Werkes Gleiwitz, August 14, 1944; and BET 9/5, Bericht über die Prüfung der Bilanz nebst Gewinn- und Verlustrechnung per 31. Dezember 1944, November 5, 1945.

[67] DUA, DL 13.3/1, K. Bonath, "Russ," 1969, graph of production between pp. 45 and 46; PCA 1/338, Hupe's Notiz betr. Leistungssteigerung, May 6, 1944. Degussa contrived to turn the excess production to advantage by selling it to Hungary in order to increase rubber production there and "to prevent as much as possible the construction of a carbon black factory" there; see DL 2/1, Niederschrift über die Sitzung des Ausschusses für Verkaufsorganisation, August 9, 1944, p. 2.

[68] DUA, DL 3.Baerwind/26, Stand der Russplanung im January 1943, January 22, 1943; and BET 9/49, Achterath's Betr.: Neue Flammrussfabrik, January 30, 1943. See also DL 2/1, Niederschrift über die Vorstandssitzung am 26. Januar 1943, pp. 296–97.

[69] DUA, BET 9/43, Protokoll über die Arbeitsausschuss-Sitzung der Deutschen Gasrusswerke GmbH am 4. März 1943; Achterath's Betr.: Neue Flammruss-Fabrik, March 5, 1943; IW

acute in October 1944, however, Vosswalde's proximity to the front line in the East ruled out building there, and the entire project was transferred to Degussa's factory at Bodenfelde in the Weserland, where it never came into operation despite frantic efforts in the final months of the war.[70] Naturally, not every instance in which the state frustrated or forced Degussa's output proved disadvantageous to the firm. The Reich's appetite for the inactive form of carbon black, to cite a small-scale and short-term example, intermittently generated license, sales, and dividend income from the financially precarious Kaliwerke Kolin in the Protectorate, which Degussa dominated, since the carbon residues in *Schlempe* could be burned off to make the substance.[71] More importantly in the long run, Degussa's aspirations in the hydrogen peroxide field prompted the corporation to expand its holding in the Chemische Fabrik Wesseling AG from 12.5 percent to 51 percent early in the war at a cost of some 564,000 RM. Though the initial purpose, securing an adequate internal capacity for sulfuric acid, proved relatively insignificant prior to 1945, the plant became a centerpiece of Degussa's postwar revival.[72] Meanwhile, the continuing emphasis on deriving new materials from domestic resources inspired Harry Kloepfer to replicate his earlier inventiveness in the carbon black sphere. This time he devised a process for making a colorless, colloidal variant of the product, so-called *Weissruss*, from silicic acid. Dubbed K3 within the firm and marketed under the name Aerosil, the substance had numerous applications as an additive for rubbers, plastics, and lacquers and as a thickening agent, including for certain explosives.[73] Actual output, which began at Rheinfelden in 1944 at

28.2/1, Satzung der Flammruss GmbH, June 11, 1943; and DL 2/1, Niederschrift über die Vorstandssitzung am 7. Juni 1943, pp. 319–20, which also establish that Degussa controlled a majority in the firm indirectly and would provide the chief managers.

70 DUA, IW 28.2/1, Achterath's Betr. Flammruss GmbH, October 20, 1944; and DL 2/1, Niederschriften über die Vorstandssitzungen am 2. Oktober 1944, n.p.; am 13. Oktober 1944, p. 2; am 31 Oktober 1944, p. 1; am 19. Dezember 1944, p. 2; am 23 Januar 1945, p. 2; and am 20. März 1945, p. 1.

71 DUA, TLE 1/83, Baerwind's Ausserordentliche Hauptversammlung des Syndikats der Kaliwerke Kolin, June 28, 1941; AW 33.15/1, Kaliwerke to Rüstungsinspektion-Prag, July 26, 1941; PCA 2/11, Baerwind's Besprechung mit den Herren Dr. Stoecker und Direktor Lutz, December 8, 1941, and Achterath to Stoecker, December 16, 1941, with enclosed contract; PCA 2/142, Degussa to Kaliwerke, December 2, 1942, and February 4 and 12, 1943, and Baerwind to Stoecker, September 30, 1943.

72 DUA, DL 2/1, Niederschriften über die Vorstandssitzungen am 5. Februar 1940, p. 72, and am 6. Januar 1941, p. 150; IW 23.5/7, Wesseling AG an die Herren des Aufsichtsrats, September 11, 1943, which indicates that the firm operated at a loss in the early 1940s, despite rising sales; and Mechthild Wolf, *Im Zeichen von Sonne und Mond* (Frankfurt am Main: Degussa AG, 1993), pp. 243–46.

73 DUA, Geschichte-Produkte, Kloepfer's Der Weg zur Kieselsäure K3, August 20, 1942, and Bonath's Aktennotiz betreffend Aerosil, January 15, 1946; PCA 2/144, Baerwind's Gespräch mit Dr. Ambros ... über die Anwendung von K3 auf dem Sprengstoff-Gebiet, December 10, 1943; and GPT 2/12, Bojunga's Anwendungsmöglichkeiten von Kieselsäure K 3, December 8, 1944.

the rate of 10 tons per month, was limited during the war, but the product emerged as a major profit source for Degussa in subsequent decades.[74]

Similarly, Degussa's wartime entrance into the manufacture of uranium metal laid the basis for the corporation's involvement with nuclear energy after 1955, even if the immediate returns (some 250,000 RM in gross profits from 1939 to 1944) were small.[75] Though the firm first recorded earnings on the product in the business year 1938/39, output on a serious scale commenced pursuant to an urgent request by the Auergesellschaft in May 1940, about a year after that subsidiary had stepped up its research on the separation of radioactive isotopes and begun turning ore into uranium oxide for the Army Ordnance Office.[76] From the outset, Auer insisted that "outwardly the strictest silence is to be maintained concerning the matter," and Degussa's leaders seem to have learned gradually, and possibly incompletely, about the reasons for the sudden interest.[77] That a typescript of a Swiss scientist's article on "The American Superexplosive U-235" circulated among Degussa's principal researchers in the fall of 1940 suggests greater curiosity than knowledge as of that date, and as late as October 1941, one official noted that "Auer sells special metal [uranium metal] directly to the Wehrmacht.... What the Wehrmacht needs the metal for is unknown."[78] Ernst Baerwind apparently solved that riddle to his own satisfaction only in August 1942, and he then emphasized to his colleagues that "considering the

[74] See DL 2/1, Niederschrift über die Vorstandssitzung am 4. September 1944, p. 394; and Wolf, *Zeichen von Sonne und Mond*, pp. 251–53.

[75] Tallied from DUA, RFI 4.2/85, 89, 93, 98, 104, and 108, Jahresabschlüsse 1938/39–1943/44.

[76] On the contentious history of German atomic research during the Second World War, the most reliable accounts are Bernard Kroener, Rolf-Dieter Müller, and Hans Umbreit, *Germany and the Second World War*, vol. V/2 (Oxford: Clarendon Press, 2003), pp. 783–801; Gine Elsner and Karl-Heinz Karbe, *Von Jáchymov nach Haigerloch* (Hamburg: VSA Verlag, 1999), pp. 27–35 and 94–103; Kristie Macrakis, *Surviving the Swastika: Scientific Research in Nazi Germany* (New York: Oxford University Press, 1993), pp. 162–86; Thomas Powers, *Heisenberg's War* (New York: Alfred A. Knopf, 1993); Paul Lawrence Rose, *Heisenberg and the Nazi Atomic Bomb Project* (Berkeley: University of California Press, 1998); Mark Walker, *German National Socialism and the Quest for Nuclear Power 1939–1949* (Cambridge: Cambridge University Press, 1989); and Rainer Karlsch and Zbynek Zeman, *"Urangeheimnisse." Das Erzgebirge im Brennpunkt der Weltpolitik 1900–1960* (Berlin: Ch. Links, 2003), which expands upon Rainer Karlsch, "Der Uranwettlauf 1939 bis 1949," *Der Anschnitt*, 50 (1998), pp. 46–58. An indispensable primary source is *Operation Epsilon: The Farm Hall Transcripts* (Berkeley: University of California Press, 1993). Interestingly, Degussa's role in the manufacture of uranium metal is scarcely mentioned in most of these works, Elsner's and Karbe's being the notable exception. Particularly valuable on the role of the Auergesellschaft is Frederick Seitz and Nikolaus Riehl, *Stalin's Captive: Nikolaus Riehl and the Soviet Race for the Bomb* (Washington, DC: American Chemical Society, 1996).

[77] DUA, PCA 1/559, Auergesellschaft to Scheideanstalt, May 14, 1940.

[78] DUA, PCA 1/559, Dr. Alfred Stettbacher, "Der amerikanische Super-Sprengstoff 'U-235,'" *Nitrocellulose*, 11 (1940); Klänhardt's Spezialmetall-Projekt. 1. Bericht, October 10, 1941 (for the quotation).

confidentiality of the main sphere of application . . . all negotiations with the authorities must be conducted exclusively by the Auergesellschaft, and the role [of Degussa's factories] is to be solely that of subcontractors."[79] In any case, by then Degussa had turned out more than 3.8 tons of the substance in Frankfurt and agreed to license additional production by its Grünau subsidiary, as usual because the military pressed for a relatively secure installation and the desire to preempt competition argued for going along.[80] Construction delays on that plant soon added, however, to the labor, supply, and air raid problems that repeatedly interrupted output in Frankfurt, so the total quantity ultimately produced at both locations was well below their nominal capacities of 1,000 and 600 kilograms per month, respectively.[81] Frankfurt certainly fabricated at least 5.5 tons of uranium metal by 1945, but the total output of both plants probably fell well short of ten tons.[82] Many of these were smelted either in Frankfurt or at Auer's plant in Berlin into the small cubes or plates required by the multiple German research teams that tried, sporadically and unsuccessfully, to generate a nuclear chain reaction

---

[79] DUA, DL 3.Baerwind/26, Aussprache mit Herrn Dr. Zimmer/Auergesellschaft über Spezialmetall, August 10, 1942.

[80] On Auer's pleas for increased output and the elaboration of the production facilities in Frankfurt, see especially DUA, PCA 1/211, Quasebart and Riehl to Baerwind, February 14, 1941, and Schuppert's Stand der Vereinbarungen mit der Auergesellschaft betreffend . . . Uranmetall, February 27, 1941, pp. 4–5. For the production figure, which covers 1940–41, PCA 1/211, Völkel's Aktennotiz betr. Mangel an Kalzium, March 22, 1941; and GEH3.Hirtes/1, Völkel's Produktionen für den Verkauf vom 1. Jan. bis 31. Dez. 1941, May 30, 1942. On the decision for Grünau, PCA 1/559, Baerwind's Aussprache bei der Auergesellschaft . . . über Uranmetall, September 2, 1941; and on the license agreement, PCA 1/559, Baerwind to Herzog, September 18, 1941, and Klänhardt's Spezialmetall-Projekt. 3. Bericht, October 18, 1941.

[81] I have not been able to establish exactly when Grünau began to turn out uranium metal; DL 3.Baerwind/26, Besprechung bei der Auergesellschaft . . . betreffend Spezialmetall, July 19, 1943, states that "it is likely that the Grünau installation will be operational by the end of the year," but a postwar account by Dr. Völkel, cited by Karlsch, indicates that it did not begin producing until the end of 1944. On the shortages of labor and calcium metal, an essential component in the manufacturing process for uranium metal, see PCA 1/559, Degussa to Riehl, July 11 and 16, 1941; Auer to Degussa, October 24, 1941; and Degussa to Auer, December 4 and 13, 1941. On the respective production capacities, PCA 1/559, Klänhardt's Spezialmetall-Projekt. 1. Bericht, October 10, 1941 (regarding Grünau), and PCA 2/144, Erzeugungsbericht für die Reichsstelle Chemie, Ms-4-Betrieb, December 14, 1943, Bl. 1 (regarding Frankfurt).

[82] Frankfurt's total production calculated from the sources cited in note 80, as well as DUA, PCA 1/205, Völkel's Vorrats- und Verbrauchsaufstellungen Ms-4-Betrieb, February 1944 to January 1945, and Klänhardt's M-s Betrieb Grünau 5 March 1945. Karl Heinz Roth, "Ein Spezialunternehmen für Verbrennungskreisläufe: Konzernskizze Degussa," *1999*, 3 (1988), p. 25, states that Degussa delivered 14.3 tons of uranium metal, 13.6 of them from Frankfurt, by 1945, apparently on the basis of postwar American sources, but I have been unable to confirm this figure. Nikolaus Riehl recalls that "we had produced only a few tons of uranium fuel elements by the end of the war"; Seitz and Riehl, *Stalin's Captive*, p. 90.

during the war, but other batches went monthly to steel producers such as Krupp and Röchling for use in special alloys.[83] In the end, the Reich derived few benefits from the entire effort, but the corporation acquired considerable valuable know-how, especially regarding the vacuum ovens for smelting the metal that constituted a key aspect of the firm's postwar technical edge.[84]

Neither these false starts nor Degussa's disappointments regarding hydrogen peroxide, sodium, the Zentralwerk, and carbon black prevented the firm from profiting handsomely during World War II. Between September 1939 and their respective wartime peaks, Degussa's capitalization rose by 115 percent, its aggregate worth on the published balance sheets by 116 percent and on the corporation's tax returns by 87 percent, its declared surplus of assets over liabilities by 42 percent, the value of its stockholdings by 73 percent, its sales by 45 percent, its gross profits by 50 percent, and its pre-tax proceeds by 113 percent (see Appendices B–D). Even more than was already the case in the 1930s, however, this growth reflected Degussa's militarization. Virtually all of the net increase in sales between the outbreak of the war and September 1943 (71.8 million Reichsmarks) came from three productive sectors that were vital to the war effort: organic chemicals, including carbon black (23.9 million), metals treating (22.6 million), and the artificial leathers, adhesives, and water-resistant cloths of the Wolfgang group of factories (21.9 million). Consequently, these productive sectors now overtook precious metals and inorganic chemicals as Degussa's mainstays. Whereas the gross profits of the former group of products skyrocketed by 132 percent between 1932/33 and the outbreak of the war, then another 73 percent during it, those of the latter inched up by only 15 percent and 7 percent in the two intervals. The relative contributions to gross profits therefore changed from 27 to 64 percent in 1932/33 to 43 to 51 percent in 1938/39 to 49 to 36 percent in 1943/44 (the remainder in each year came from investment income). No observer could accuse Degussa of having slept through this war, as Busemann lamented about its forerunner, or doubt that his diversification program was paying off – at least in the short run.

But many of the firm's leaders recognized that adaptability could be overdone, leaving them no better prepared for peacetime conditions than their predecessors had been. Such worries apparently animated Degussa's persistent attempts to confine itself to intermediate production for the German war machine. For Schlosser and most of his colleagues, the model relationship

---

[83] On the manufacturing format, DUA, PCA 1/559, Völkel's Aktennotiz betr. Besprechung über Spezialmetall, April 7, 1941, and Bauer's betrifft: Spezialmetall, July 16, 1941; as well as DL 3.Baerwind/26, Aussprache mit Herrn Dr. Zimmer, August 10, 1942, which also dates the decision to establish a smelter at Auer's site. On the sales to Krupp and Röchling, PCA 2/144, Ausgeführte Aufträge im September 1943, October 4, 1943, and Ausgeführte Aufträge im Oktober 1943, November 9, 1943.

[84] See Wolf, *Zeichen von Sonne und Mond*, pp. 262–63.

between the firm and the military market was the production chain for Plexiglas, which Röhm & Haas made and sold on the basis of the acetone cyanohydrin that Degussa provided. A distant second choice was the arrangement typified by Paraxol GmbH, from which Degussa earned some 300,000 RM in 1940–45, namely the formation of a special subsidiary to lease and operate plants that Frankfurt declined to own because it doubted their long-term profitability.[85] Each system insulated Degussa somewhat from abrupt changes in demand on the part of authorities that neither understood nor sympathized with private commercial considerations, and both pushed the financial risks of dependence on official orders off on other enterprises or the government itself. Thus, most of Degussa's military output during the war years was sold to other firms for final fabrication into armaments or their components: not only acetone cyanohydrin to Röhm & Haas (on which Degussa earned gross profits of 2.4 million Reichsmarks during the business years 1939/40–1943/44), carbon black to IG Farben and assorted rubber makers (gross profits of 11 million marks in the same period), and uranium to Auer (219,000 RM), but also Proxylen to that firm, beryllium (284,000 RM) to Heraeus Vacuumschmelze or IG Farben for fabrication into adjustable propellers and other machine parts, and zirconium (273,000 RM) to Gekawerke, Gustloffwerke, and various metals and textiles firms for flares, bomb fuses, corrosion-resistant alloys, and water- and fire-retardant cloth, including that for uniforms.[86] Thus, too, one of Degussa's most contentious and difficult internal administrative issues during the war became overseeing and controlling the relationship between individual departments and determined military agencies, whose contacts perpetually threatened to beget obligations that the enterprise wished to restrain.[87]

[85] DUA, IW 50.9/1, Deutsche Revisions- und Treuhand AG, Übernahme Bericht des Treuhänders, Paraxol GmbH, April 12, 1948, gives total payments to Degussa of just over 360,000 RM between 1940 and 1944, the last profitable year. But 75,000 of these were applied to the firm's capitalization, according to IW 50.2/1, Protokoll über die zweite Aufsichtsratssitzung der Paraxol GmbH, September 22, 1941, p. 3.

[86] On Degussa's adamant refusal to prepare Proxylen canisters for the army directly, see DL 2/1, Niederschrift über die Vorstandssitzung am 6. Mai 1940, pp. 86–87, and Anlage 7; on the beryllium arrangements with IG Farben, Vorstandssitzung am 2. März 1942, p. 239; on the purpose of the sales to Heraeus, DL 3.Baerwind/23, Berylliummetall für Verstellpropeller, September 4, 1939; on the volume of mineral sales to Heraeus and Gustloff, among others, PCA 2/144, Ausgeführte Aufträge im August-Dezember 1943, September 2, 1943 to January 12, 1944; and on the sales and uses of zirconium metal, PCA 1/559, Völkel's Betr.: Besuch des Herrn Direktor Krebs von den Geka-Werken, April 24, 1940, and Schenk's Betrifft: Verkauf von Zirkon-Metall, August 20, 1940; as well as IW 24.17/1, Ruppert's Verwendungsmöglichkeiten des Zirkoniums und seiner Verbindungen, January 14, 1943. For the gross profits, RFI 4.2/85, 89, 93, 98, 104, and 108, Jahresabschlüsse 1938/39–1943/44.

[87] See DUA 2/1, Niederschrift über die Vorstandssitzung am 7. July 1941, p. 192, on the assignment to Róka of centralized authority to decide what development contracts the firm's offices would accept from the Army Ordnance Office; am 4. August 1941, pp. 195–96, on Menzel's appointment to direct a central office to keep track of relations with the Air

The policy of being a military wholesaler rather than retailer did not rule out cultivating the armaments market. On the contrary, Degussa took care "to strengthen personal contact" with important generals and other officers, especially in the Frankfurt vicinity, by hosting lecture programs at which board members, including Hermann Schlosser, expatiated on the firm's many contributions to the war effort.[88] More importantly, the firm repeatedly demonstrated its eagerness to research and test potential new compounds and processes for the armed services.[89] In a few instances, notably those concerning uses for long-standing and commercially rewarding Degussa products such as Degussit and synthetic resins, the enterprise went so far as to set up new manufacturing facilities, but usually it sought to assign the task of following through on any purely military applications of its discoveries to another company, even if only, in the worst case, to a subsidiary.[90]

In 1941–43, for example, corporate research teams busied themselves with numerous experiments concerning the possible use of zirconium, sodium alone or in combination with potassium, and several silicides in the manufacture of firebombs.[91] None of these projects led to assembly-line production of weapons by Degussa, however, and in the cases of sodium- and silicide-based firebombs, the reason was the firm's flat refusal to take on that task. Despite success by the fall of 1942 in developing a sodium firebomb that appeared superior to those currently in use, Degussa argued early in the following year against the Air Ministry's zeal for the product on several self-interested grounds – namely that diversion of sodium metal for bombs would undercut the corporation's production of metal hardeners and acetone cyanohydrin, as well as for tetraethyl lead, and that the use of such ordnance would attract the attention of British bombers to Knapsack.[92] At minimum, Ernst Baerwind advised the Ministry, "one should not apply such a firebomb so long as it

Ministry; and am 1. September 1941, pp. 201–02, on Menzel's responsibility for coordinating Frankfurt's relationship with the Army Ordnance Office.

[88] DUA, TLE 1/23, Federlin's Notiz Betr.: Unterrichtung der Rüstungs- und Wehrersatzbehörden, September 19, 1941; DUA 2/1, Niederschrift über die Vorstandssitzung am 1. Dezember 1941, p. 217, and Anlage 1; and Men/Bd. 29, memo from Bugge, Krebs, and Schimmelbusch headed Betrifft: Vortrag von Herrn Schlosser, July 10, 1942.

[89] For a list of thirty-three Degussa patents with important military applications at the war's midpoint, see DUA, PCA 2/144, Patentabteilung, Betr.: Geheimzuhaltende Erfindungen, September 15, 1942.

[90] See DUA, DL 2/1, Niederschriften über die Vorstandssitzungen am 8. Januar 1940, p. 71 (on a new section to produce "Degussit-Werkzeuge"); am 5. August 1940, p. 109, and am 4 August 1941, p. 195 (on pilot plants for nonglare windshields and a substitute for Plexiglas).

[91] On the attempt to use zirconium for delay fuses on these bombs, see PCA 1/559, Kern's Aktennotiz über Berliner Besuche, March 31, 1941, p. 5; Menzel's Besuche und Telefonate wegen Zirkonmetall, July 3, 1941; and Völkel's Versuche und Untersuchungen zur Zirkonfabrikation, May 19, 1945; as well as PCA 2/144, Schmidt's Betr. Besprechung mit Major Prof. Lachewsky, August 15, 1942.

[92] DUA, PCA 2/143, Martin's Besuch in Rheinfelden … betreffend Brandbombversuche, October 27, 1942, and Baerwind's Aussprache im Reichsluftfahrtministerium, April 5, 1943.

is not used by the enemy side, at least certainly not before one has another sodium factory at his disposal in addition to Knapsack and Gersthofen."[93] By August 1943, the firm had retreated from this position enough to concede readiness "in case the Air Ministry wishes large-scale manufacturing of the B4Na [the model number for the firebomb], to deliver the necessary quantities of sodium metal and sodium peroxide, to provide all formulas and Herr Dr. Rath as an expert, and to support eventual production with extensive advice," but Degussa still pled shortages of labor and space to explain why it could not possibly do the manufacturing itself.[94] The 1,000 bombs that Degussa furnished to the Air Ministry's testing grounds at Rechlin by early 1944 apparently marked the end of the firm's participation in this line of activity.[95] Meanwhile, Baerwind did his best to quash any idea of translating a parallel research project on silicide bombs into actual production, telling his colleagues bluntly at the end of 1943 that the Rheinfelden plant already had squandered too much time and energy on projects "which as far as anyone can judge cannot any longer attain large-scale production during the war."[96]

Of course, Germany's declining military prospects contributed to the firmness with which Degussa fended off making firebombs, but the wartime histories of several subsidiaries attest to the consistency of the concern's efforts to keep weapons-building and purely conflict-related lines of output at arm's length. That Orgacid GmbH, the chlorine gas manufacturer co-owned by the Auergesellschaft since the midthirties, was superseded during the war by deadlier installations that IG Farben owned or operated seems to have occasioned no countermeasures in either Frankfurt or Oranienburg.[97] When the regime insisted on the establishment of a pilot plant for the production of watch stones (*Uhrensteine*), which Degussa thought had little commercial value, the firm managed to get the project assumed by a separate new

[93] DUA, PCA 2/143, Baerwind's Besprechung im RLM, April 27, 1943. On Degussa's simultaneous exploration and rejection of a project to make bombs from a sodium-potassium mixture, see this document, as well as PCA 2/143, Martin's Besuch im RLM, November 16, 1942, and Harant's Besuch ... im RLM, January 25, 1943.
[94] *Ibid.*, Baerwind's Besprechung in Rheinfelden, August 4, 1943. For a repetition of Degussa's position, see DUA 2/144, Besuch der Herren Fl. Ing. Müller und Fl. Haupt-Ing. Luster vom RLM, September 29, 1943.
[95] *Ibid.*, Degussa Rheinfelden to Müller of the Air Ministry, January 31, 1944.
[96] *Ibid.*, Baerwind's Akten-Vermerk betreffend den von der Forschungsführung des RLM in Aussicht gestellten Forschungsauftrag über Natriumsilicid und Kaliumsilicid, December 30, 1943.
[97] TLE 1/23, Retze's Aktennotiz, July 23, 1941, comments on the situation and says it bears watching, but I have found no indication of further concern. GCH 2/13, Mietvertrag zwischen der Firma Orgacid GmbH und der Firma Deutsche Gold- und Silber-Scheideanstalt, 6/11 August 1943, records the latter's rental of some 82,000 RM worth of equipment from the former, an indication of its declining operations. In 1941, Orgacid paid a dividend of 314,000 RM, but only 78,689 RM in 1942; IW 24.9/1, Bericht des Vorstandes [der Auergesellschaft] für das Geschäftsjahr 1942/43, April 5, 1944, pp. 15 and 27.

company, in which Frankfurt's stake came to only 25 percent.[98] Two and one-half years later, as the Reich pressed for the development and stockpiling of solid fuels to substitute for gasoline, Degussa reluctantly agreed "to make a further contribution to the war" by authorizing the expenditure of up to 500,000 RM on a new partnership with the Generatorkraft AG. In reality, the principal motivation was to defend the firm's position in the production and sale of charcoal.[99] Not even that sort of interest, however, could persuade Degussa to give up its general aversion to engaging, either directly or via subsidiaries, in the direct extraction of minerals. In 1942 and 1944, the corporation turned down officially sponsored opportunities to take over beryllium mines on the Iberian peninsula and in South Tyrol.[100]

Prototypical of Degussa's approach to military sales – and the difficulty of sustaining it – was a subsidiary that grew out of the firm's own metals research laboratories and developed by mid-1943, after several false starts, into a partnership with the Metallgesellschaft.[101] The German Powder Metallurgical Company (Deutsche Pulvermetallurgische GmbH or DPG) concentrated on developing powdered and rollable or pressable forms of aluminum and base or ferrous metals for use instead of scarcer imported components in sintering; bearings; the guide rings and shell cores of ammunition; incendiary grenades, bombs, and shrapnel; and rifle, machine gun, cannon, and torpedo parts.[102] Those products and processes with broad industrial applications, especially concerning sinter blocks, were to be retained and exercised by the enterprise or its owners, and the others, including the manufacture of the powders themselves, licensed to other manufacturers, among them arms makers.[103] In practice, however, DPG generally undertook to furnish these with the metals, with the result that income from licenses made up less than

[98] DUA, DL 2/1, Niederschriften über die Vorstandssitzungen am 6. Mai und 3. Juni 1940, pp. 91–92 and 95–96.

[99] *Ibid.*, January 11, 1943, pp. 293–94.

[100] *Ibid.*, Niederschrift über die Vorstandssitzung am 2. März 1942, pp. 238–39; Notizen aus dem Vorstandscolloquium vom 30. Mai 1944, p. 3; and Niederschrift über die Vorstandssitzung am 5. Juni 1944, n.p. (Point 6).

[101] DUA, DL 2/1, Niederschriften über die Vorstandssitzungen am 8. Januar 1940, p. 70; am 5. Februar 1940, pp. 73–74; am 9. Juni 1941, p. 183; am 7. Juli 1941, pp. 188–89; am 5. April 1943, pp. 310–11; 3. Mai 1943, pp. 315–16; and 3. August 1943, p. 329, mit Anlagen.

[102] See DUA, TA 2/124, the following reports by Dr. Oxenius, the director of research on powder metals within Degussa: Aktennotiz Arbeitsprogramm Dr. Oxenius, December 4, 1939; Bericht über die Besuche in Berlin beim Heereswaffenamt und der DVL, January 24, 1940; Besuch bei der Arbeitsgemeinschaft Cornelius, Berlin (Torpedierungsausschuss), December 10, 1940; Besuch bei der D. W. M. Lübeck-Schlutup, November 22, 1941; Besuch im Unterlüss, November 22, 1941; Besuch beim DWM, Lübeck, January 19, 1942; Bericht über den Besuch von Herrn Dr. Weidle von D. W. M., October 28, 1942; Besuch bei D. W. M. Lübeck, January 6, 1943; and Besuch bei DWM-Lübeck, February 16, 1943.

[103] DUA, DL 3.H.Schlosser/1, Document 951, D.P.G., July 10, 1943; PCA 2/72, Kaufmann's Bericht der DPG über das I. Quartal (Okt.-Dez.) des Geschäftsjahres 1943/1944, January 20, 1944.

10 percent of the firm's turnover in the business years 1941–43, while sales of aluminum powder to Westfälisch-Anhaltische Sprengstoff AG for explosives composed some 40 percent. DPG's gross profits during the period totaled almost 240,000 RM.[104] Moreover, experimental success with the manufacture of rifle parts out of pressed metals led in 1943 to official requests for DPG to embark on manufacturing them, which it began doing, first in Frankfurt then during the latter half of 1944, in Neurod.[105] By the end of the year, that plant was producing some 15,000 bolts per month for Mauser rifles.[106]

Degussa's preference for an intermediate role in the war economy owed much to the object lesson presented by the troublesome Auer subsidiary, whose nearly complete dependence on the military market remained a constant source of concern in Frankfurt from 1940 to 1945. Already heavily indebted when the fighting began and suddenly faced with a 46 percent jump in military orders for respiratory equipment, Auer ran up its obligations to creditors and banks to almost 22 million Reichsmarks by the time France capitulated, a sum that came to more than three times the firm's capitalization and alarmed Degussa.[107] In mid-1940, the parent corporation's managing board resolved first, that it "should be made emphatically clear to the managing board of Auer that the Scheideanstalt must limit its risk and reject responsibility for further expansion," then weighed "the oft-considered idea of selling off the shareholding in Auer in order to use the proceeds to fulfill other industrial tasks," and finally decided, over the opposition of the subsidiary's leaders, to insist on receiving monthly projections and justifications of likely investment needs, so as "to be included in the future financial control" of the firm.[108] But this assertion of authority – and its grudging acceptance – made scant lasting difference to the relationship between Frankfurt and Oranienburg. Far from creating a system by which Degussa, as its leaders prematurely concluded, "in the future can reject extensions that seem inappropriate to us," the new arrangements were virtually powerless against the adverse dynamic of Auer's business.[109]

[104] DUA, Kaufmann's Bericht der DPG über das 1.Quartal (Okt.-Dez.) des Geschäftsjahres 1943/1944, January 20, 1944, p. 8.
[105] Ibid., pp. 12–14; and DUA, PCA 2/72, Bernstorff's Monatsbericht für Juni 1944. D.P.G. Betrieb Neurod.
[106] Ibid., Monatsberichte für September/Oktober, November, Dezember 1944, and Januar 1945, October 31, 1944 to February 15, 1945.
[107] DUA, IW 24.5/5, Bernau's betr.: Auergesellschaft, June 10, 1940, p. 5; and, as background, Bernau's Auergesellschaft, April 5, 1940. On the increase in military orders from 48 million to 70 million Reichsmarks, IW 24.9/1, Berich des Vorstandes für das Geschäftsjahr 1939/40, January 28, 1941, p. 2.
[108] DUA, DL 2/1, Niederschrift über die Vorstandssitzung am 6. Mai 1940, pp. 87–88 (for the first two quoted passages), and am 1. Juli 1940, Anlage 1, Bernau's Auergesellschaft, June 14, 1940, p. 2 (for the third quotation). See also DUA, IW 24.5/5, Schlosser's Auergesellschaft A. G., May 11, 1940.
[109] Ibid., am 1. Juli 1940, Anlage 1, Bernau's Auergesellschaft, June 14, 1940, p. 6.

That dynamic amounted to an almost Sisyphean cycle, in which the state demanded continuous increases in the output of breathing protection equipment (especially gas masks), backed by allocations of additional labor, and the firm complied, purchased the necessary components, and repeatedly fell behind its production timetables, thus compounding its cash flow problems. These were aggravated by periodically mandated price reductions and the Reich's practice of paying only 75 percent of invoices upon receipt and withholding 25 percent until subsequent audits established whether Auer's profit margins conformed to official guidelines. As a result, the gaps between outlays and receipts, orders and delivery dates, continuously widened, no matter how rapidly Auer's workforce grew (from just over 3,000 in 1939 to almost 11,000 in 1944), how many assembly lines the firm added (either at Oranienburg, when other branches of production were transfered to the Protectorate, or at the new plants set up at Guben and Danzig in 1939/40) or how much its sales expanded (they rose by 48 percent during the war – see Appendix G).[110] By October 1942, the backlog of gas mask orders came to 80 million Reichsmarks, the equivalent of just less than a year's production; a year later, it was 165 million Reichsmarks, or almost twice the annual output.[111]

All of this meant that Degussa could do little during most of the war except constantly warn Auer against the burden of additional capacity, then acquiesce in it. In March 1941, for example, Hermann Schlosser wrote the chairman of the subsidiary's managing board to say flatly that "expansion ... is in the future simply impossible. ... even when that means that one must reject new and additional tasks, even when they come from official agencies."[112] But only four months later, he agreed to new investments in 1941/42 totaling 4.5 million Reichsmarks, and in 1942/43, another 1.3 million Reichsmarks were spent.[113] Blocking corporate acquisitions fell within the parent company's reach, so Degussa meanwhile prevented Oranienburg from purchasing a minority share in the neighboring Byk-Gulden Werke chemicals

---

[110] On the workforce, Friedrich Klauer (ed.), *Geschichte der Auergesellschaft von der Gründung im Jahre 1892 bis zum Jahre 1958* (Berlin: Auergesellschaft, n.d.), p. 33, and Appendix O to this book. On the Reich's payment system, IW 24.5/5, Bernau's Auergesellschaft, April 5, 1940, p. 2. On the new plants at Guben and Danzig, IW 24.9/1, Bericht des Vorstandes für das Geschäftsjahr 1939/40, 28 January 1941. On the transfer of lightbulb production to the Protectorate, IW 24.8/5, Wiese's Monatsbericht Nr. 6 für März-Geschäftsjahr 1941/42, April 29, 1942, p. 2.

[111] DUA, IW 24.9/1, Bericht des Vorstandes für das Geschäftsjahr 1942/43, April 5, 1944, p. 4. See also the same document, p. 3, and IW 24.8/5, Monatsbericht Nr. 1–3 für Oktober-Dezember 1943, April 19, 1944, for the information that Auer proved unable in the fall of 1943, for the first time since the war began, to raise its output of gas masks or even to operate the relevant facilities at capacity.

[112] DUA, IW 24.5/5, Schlosser to Quasebart, March 21, 1941.

[113] DUA, IW 24.5/2, Schlosser's Investionsplan Auergesellschaft, July 24, 1941; IW 24.9/1, Bericht des [Auer] Vorstandes für das Geschäftsjahr 1942/43, April 5, 1944, p. 5.

firm.[114] But even that sort of limitation rarely occurred, as indicated by Auer's Aryanizations in the Protectorate (see Chapter 3); its purchase of 50 percent of the shares in Gasma AG of Prague, the owner of a gas mask factory in Zubern, for 110,000 RM in 1940; its assumption of a trusteeship over the Rare Earths Company (Société des Terres Rares) in Alsace and pursuit of rights to rare earth ores on the Kola Peninsula in Russia during 1941; the attainment of such rights over zircon ores in Stretenka (Ukraine) from 1942 to 1943; and the takeover of the Glassworks Götzenbrück in Lorraine for 497,000 RM between October 1942 and June 1943.[115] With regard to operations within Germany, the parent managing board in Frankfurt quickly found that monthly reports constituted an "unsatisfactory" substitute for the fact "that we still do not have at Auer our own man of the Degussa school...in order to exercise more influence from here on the development of the Auergesellschaft."[116] Yet that, too, could not be changed overnight. In the autumn of 1942, Hermann Schlosser persuaded – of course, "in comradely fashion" – Robert Vorbau and his patrons in the regional Nazi Party organization to accept that man's retirement as plant leader in Oranienburg in return for elevation to Auer's supervisory board and a lucrative consulting contract, but only after a two-year delay to allow for the training of Friedrich Zürcher as the successor.[117] Consequently, Auer's profits as a percent of sales remained decidedly below the average for Degussa during the war years (in 1941/42, the respective figures were 7.75 percent vs. 10.74 percent), and a financial review in 1944 concluded that the subsidiary's liquid funds actually had declined by more than 188,000 RM between July 1933 and September 1943 because its debts had increased faster than its capital and reserves. In other words, virtually everything the Auergesellschaft earned during the

[114] DUA, DL 2/1, Niederschrift über die Vorstandssitzung am 3. März 1941, p. 163, and Anlage 1.

[115] *Ibid.*, am 7. Oktober 1940, p. 125 (on the Alsatian installation); DUA, IW 24.8/5, Monatsbericht Nr. 7 für die Zeit vom 1. August–30. September 1941, p. 3 (on the Russian ores); IW 24.5/5, Bericht des Vorstandes für das Geschäftsjahr 1941/42, February 22, 1943, p. 6, and IW 24.9/1, Berichte des Vorstandes für die Geschäftsjahre 1939/40, January 28, 1941, p. 9 (on Gasma AG) und 1942/43, April 5, 1944, p. 8 (on the gain and loss of Stretenka); and IW 24.9/12, Monatsberichte Nr. 1 für Oktober 1942, p. 2, and Nr. 8 für Mai 1943, pp. 2–3 (on Lorraine).

[116] DUA, DL 2/1, Niederschrift über die Vorstandssitzung am 7. April 1941, p. 170.

[117] See DUA, DL 3.H.Schlosser/1, Doc. 920, Unterhaltung mit Pg. Wohlleben, Gauobmann des Gaues Mark Brandenburg der D. A. F., October 19, 1942, where the quoted words appear; and IW 24.6/1, Scherf's Niederschrift über eine Besprechung in Wächtersbach, November 30, 1944, p. 2. Zürcher's appointment as deputy member of Auer's managing board took effect on January 1, 1943; IW 24.5/5, Niederschrift über die Aufsichtsratsitzung am 25. Februar 1943, p. 4. Concerning the large and damaging influence of the local branch of the DAF on Auer's operations, see Bernhard Lorentz, *Industrieelite und Wirtschaftspolitik 1928–1950* (Paderborn: Schöningh, 2001), p. 256.

decade had been sunk into buildings, equipment, and inventories – all of which became increasingly vulnerable to obliteration from the air.[118]

The issues of overdependence on the military market (80 to 90 percent of sales during the war years – see Appendix G) and overaccumulation of supplies and incomplete or undelivered goods (their value rose from 9.6 million Reichsmarks at the beginning of the war to just under 20 million Reichsmarks in September 1941 to about 38 million in early 1945, despite a doubling of the annual depreciation rate to 10 percent in 1941/42) became truly acute after Germany was thrown on the defensive by the battles of El Alamein and Stalingrad.[119] Of course, the interaction of wartime imperatives with Auer's corporate culture had continued to overwhelm thoughts of refitting the company for an eventual return to peacetime operations. As the managing board's annual report for 1940/41 understatedly noted, "the development of new industrial appliances, which are of importance for the future, suffers under the prevailing conditions."[120] A year later, the same document underlined the point by remarking that "the work of our research offices is concentrated during the war exclusively on the products needed by the armed services."[121] Thus, the firm's own estimates of its likely postwar sales volume were but 2 million Reichsmarks higher in April 1944 than in July 1940; the increase by only 10 percent meant that Auer's projections of how far its turnover would drop when fighting ceased had risen from 79 percent to 83 percent.[122]

In response, Degussa tried to prevent the situation from growing worse. This meant (a) approving expenditures designed to save Auer's existing output of consumer goods, especially lightbulbs and toothpaste, by transferring it to Prague and Brünn in the Protectorate or buying out competitors and (b) emboldening the subsidiary to evade military demands for new mass production of gas masks for civilian use.[123] Late in 1943, therefore, for the first time

---

[118] DUA, IW 24.9/11, Bericht zum Monatsstatus per 31. August 1942, p. 1 (on Auer's profit rate in 1941/42), and TLE 1/23, Übersicht über die Gewinne der einzelnen Abteilungen im Verhältnis zum Umsatz 1941/42, March 1, 1943 (on Degussa's).

[119] On the value of supplies, DUA, IW 24.5/5, Bericht des Vorstandes für das Geschäftsjahr 1940/1941, January 27, 1942, p. 11; IW 24.9/11, Bericht zum Monatsstatus per 31. August 1942, p. 4; and IW 24.5/3, Bernau's Betr.: Auergesellschaft, February 14, 1945, p. 2. On the increase in the rate of depreciation, IW 24.5/5, Bericht des Vorstandes für das Geschäftsjahr 1941/42, February 22, 1943, p. 13.

[120] *Ibid.*, Bericht des Vorstandes, January 27, 1942, p. 3.

[121] *Ibid.*, für das Geschäftsjahr 1941/42, February 22, 1943, p. 8.

[122] Cf. *ibid.*, Niederschrift zur Aufsichtsratssitzung am 10. Juli 1940, p. 2, and DUA, IW 24.9/1, Bernau's Aktennotiz Betr.: Auergesellschaft, April 25, 1944, p. 5.

[123] See DUA, IW 24.9/12, Monatsbericht Nr. 5 für Februar 1943, p. 2, on the purchase of the lightbulb operations of Zar AG of Neutomischel in the Warthegau. On the consolidation of Oranienburg's civilian-oriented production in the Protectorate under Auer GmbH of Prague, see IW 24.9/1, Bericht des Vorstandes für das Geschäftsjahr 1942/43, April 5, 1944, pp. 18–20.

since the beginning of the war, Auer declined to accept the burden of such an assignment, which in this case would have entailed borrowing 30 million Reichsmarks. Instead, Oranienburg agreed only to invest 260,000 RM in and provide two managers to a new Voga Gerätebau GmbH, which would be funded primarily by the German Air Ministry's financial arm (the Bank der Deutschen Luftfahrt AG) in cooperation with the Dresdner Bank.[124] The plan was virtually stillborn, however, and the new firm dissolved at the end of June 1944, so Auer escaped the obligation, though at an alarming moral and political cost discussed in Chapter 7.[125] As for the inventory problem, it became Degussa's chief worry from late 1943 on, all the more so as it was financed increasingly by bank loans, which shot up by 16.9 million Reichsmarks during 1942/43.[126] The combined physical and financial exposure occasioned renewed and repeated expressions of concern, but to no avail.[127] Because neither a dispersal nor emptying of Auer's storehouses took place, a single air raid on Oranienburg in March 1944 wiped out 7 million to 8 million Reichsmarks worth of goods.[128] The remaining inventories, which continued to mount as a result of a series of massive cancellations of military, export, and industrial orders during 1944, were "completely destroyed" in another attack almost exactly a year later.[129]

All in all, then, the Auergesellschaft remained Degussa's overdeveloped problem child during the war, and its gas mask business reinforced the parent firm's reticence concerning direct production for the German military effort. The evolution of even Auer's more versatile lines of production, notably that of Neophanglas for sunglasses, which also was buffeted by the combination of urgency and erraticism that characterized army contracts, only confirmed the commercial danger of relying on them and underlined the advantages of letting other producers serve as buffers between Degussa's factories and the High Command's procurement offices.[130] Nonethless, in a host of fields,

---

[124] DUA, IW 24.9/1, Bericht des Vorstandes für das Geschäftsjahr 1942/43, April 5, 1944, pp. 4–5; DL 2/1, Niederschrift über die [Degussa] Vorstandssitzung am 1. November 1943, p. 1.

[125] DUA, IW 24.8/5, Monatsberichte No. 6, 7, und 8 für März, April, und Mai 1944, p. 2, on the dissolution.

[126] DUA, IW 24.9/1, Bericht des Vorstandes, April 5, 1944, p. 24.

[127] For example, DUA, IW 24.5/5, Bernau's Betr.: Auergesellschaft, October 2, 1943, p. 2; and IW 24.9/1, Bernau's Aktennotiz Betr.: Auergesellschaft, April 25, 1944, p. 6.

[128] DUA, IW 24.8/5, Monatsbericht Nr. 4–5 für Januar und Februar 1944, April 19, 1944, p. 1.

[129] On the cancellations, which came to 86 million Reichsmarks worth of orders, DUA, IW 24.8/5, Monatsberichte No. 6, 7, und 8 für März, April, und Mai 1944, n.d., pp. 1–2, and Monatsberichte Nr. 11 und 12, für August und September des Geschäftsjahres 1943/44, November 17, 1944, p. 1. On the second air attack and for the quoted words, IW 24.5/3, Bernau's Betr.: Auergesellschaft, July 24, 1945, p. 2.

[130] On the roller coaster history of Neophanglas production, see IW 24.5/5, Bericht des Vorstandes für das Geschäftsjahr 1940/41, 27 January 1942, p. 6; IW 24.8/5, Monatsbericht

Degussa did its part, often eagerly albeit generally at one remove, in helping Nazism expand and maintain its murderous power. Moreover, in the process, the corporation became implicated in two of the Third Reich's greatest crimes: the spoliation of occupied Europe and the exploitation of its citizens' labor.

Profitable as Degussa's expansion was from 1939 to 1945, it also stretched the enterprise's finances nearly to the breaking point. As early as November 1939, when Ernst Bernau's projections of wartime capital needs came to only 11 million Reichsmarks (at most, some 15 percent of what Degussa ultimately envisioned spending on land, buildings, and equipment during the war), he warned his colleagues that "our means suffice for already planned expenditures, but no longer for newly considered projects," and the managing board therefore began canvassing various ways to raise or borrow additional funds.[131] Within a year, Hermann Schlosser laid down the rule that, in view of the enormous outlays that Fürstenberg would require, "the greatest thrift must be practiced in all other spheres in the near future," and the board accordingly resolved "that new industrial projects should not be 'sought out,' even when they appear ever so tempting."[132] But neither these calls to self-restraint nor later decisions that largely froze promotions for the duration, made all major hirings dependent on Schlosser's personal approval, and suspended anniversary bonuses for board members greatly improved the corporation's liquidity.[133] A stock split in early 1942 in effect raised Degussa's reserves, and the sale of new shares shortly thereafter brought in almost 11.5 million Reichsmarks.[134] But even the firm's new total capitalization of 76.5 million Reichsmarks and rising sales proceeds were

Nr. 9 für Juni–Geschäftsjahr 1941/42, July 21, 1942, pp. 2–3; and IW 24.9/1, Bericht des Vorstandes für das Geschäftsjahr 1942/43, pp. 7–8.

[131] DL 2/1, Niederschrift über die Vorstandssitzung am 6. November 1939, p. 61, where the words quoted appear, and Anlage 8. I have estimated Degussa's actual wartime investment in plant at 50 million Reichsmarks on the basis of BET 10/1, Bernau's Liquiditäts-Uebersicht vom 1.10.1923 bis 30.9.1944, July 20, 1945, Anlage 1, which gives almost 90 million Reichsmarks as Degussa's total figure for land, buildings, and equipment, exclusive of subsidiaries, from 1923 to 1944. In addition, Degussa had appropriated but not yet awarded contracts on another 23.6 million Reichsmarks worth of such expenditures as of January 1944; see RFI 4.2/104, Bilanzbericht an den Aufsichtsrat über das Geschäftsjahr 1942/43, March 3, 1944, p. 14.

[132] *Ibid.*, am 14. August 1940, pp. 113–14.

[133] *Ibid.*, am 3. November und am 1. Dezember 1941, pp. 215 and 219, and on 3. August 1943, p. 330 (on the moratorium on promotions), but am 5. Oktober 1942, pp. 274–75, for the sole round of wartime exceptions; am 3. August 1942, p. 261 (on hirings); and am 7. September 1943, p. 334 and Anlage 2 (on the bonuses).

[134] On the evolution of the stock split and issue, see *ibid.*, am 4 August 1941, p. 194; am 6. Oktober 1941, p. 203; am 3. November 1941, pp. 208–10; am 2. März 1942, p. 236; and am 7. September 1942, p. 270, as well as Niederschrift über die gemeinschaftliche Sitzung des Aufsichtsrats und des Vorstands der Deutschen Gold- und Silber-Scheidanstalt, April 1, 1942. On the proceeds from the sale of new shares, RFI 4.4/7, Gegenüberstellung zum Finanzstatus per 30. September 1942, October 13, 1942, p. 4.

not enough to carry the weight of the Zentralwerk, Gleiwitz, multiple additions to Rheinfelden, numerous backup plants and production transfers (especially to Grünau), improvements to the increasingly lucrative Wolfgang group of factories, expansion of the metal hardening operations and the related Industrial Oven Building division, the mounting cost of fortifying installations against air raid damage, and a host of lesser claimants on corporate funds.

Thus, in early 1943, for the first time in Degussa's history, the enterprise bowed to "pressing necessity," brought on by the fact "that we cannot expect to finance our construction projects from profits in the foreseeable future," and sold a bank consortium 30 million Reichsmarks of promissory notes carrying an annual interest rate of 4 percent.[135] Yet, the funds seemed to evaporate as fast as they flowed in. A year later, Bernau calculated that the gap between Degussa's current resources and projected outlays had narrowed only from 34.4 million Reichsmarks to 24.8 million since the loan.[136] The managing board already had drawn the inescapable conclusion that it could "take on further investments only when they are absolutely necessary because of the war situation."[137]

All this helps explain why Degussa, which long had been a niche firm in Germany, remained largely that in occupied Europe. The demands on the corporation at home made sparing money and personnel for takeovers elsewhere a daunting prospect, unless some overriding feature of a particular opportunity made it irresistable. In the first two years of the fighting, therefore, Degussa acquired no properties in Nazi-conquered territory, aside from those Aryanized in Prague (see Chapter 3), despite repeated invitations to do so.[138] Only three of the proferred projects, all of them wood carbonization facilities, turned out to be of enough interest to merit further exploration, namely the existing factories at Likier and Smolenice in Slovakia and a site in the San region of Poland, where the Reich wanted a new plant built to exploit the local forests.[139] Nothing came of the first two possibilities, since

---

[135] On the resort to this financing and the background to it, *ibid.*, am 2. September 1940, Anlage 1, Bernau's Betr.: Projekt Fuerstenberg, August 16, 1940, which first predicted that a loan would have to be sought; am 26. Januar 1943, p. 296; am 1. Februar 1943, p. 298; and Bericht des Vorstandes über das 72. Geschäftsjahr 1942/43, March 6, 1944, p. 7, which dates the sale to March 31, 1943. For the quoted words, which are Bernau's, *ibid.*, am 7. September 1943, p. 332.

[136] DUA, RFI 4.2/104, Bilanzbericht an den Aufsichtsrat über das Geschäftsjahr 1942/43, March 3, 1944, especially pp. 13–14.

[137] DUA, DL 2/1, Niederschrift über die Vorstandssitzung am 5. Februar 1944, p. 356.

[138] Degussa's Degesch subsidiary did expand its holding in the Sofumi company of Paris from 25 percent to 49 percent, however, and did take over technical leadership of the firm; Hervé Joly, "L'implication de l'industrie chimique allemande dans la Shoah: Le cas du Zyklon B," *Revue d'histoire moderne et contemporaine* 47 (2000), p. 386.

[139] See DUA, DL 2/1, Niederschriften über die Vorstandssitzungen am 11. September 1939, p. 48, and Anlage 1; am 25. September 1939, p. 52; am 2. Oktober 1939, pp. 54–55; am 5. Februar 1940, p. 73; am 4. März 1940, pp. 77–78, and Anlagen 1–3; am 2.

the principal shareholder – the Böhmische Union Bank in Prague, which the Deutsche Bank controlled – refused to sell, and Degussa grew increasingly reluctant to expend funds on a declining technology that the Fürstenberg plant was intended to supersede.[140] But the San project proved impossible to pass up entirely, given the emerging wood shortage, the military importance of the potential output, and the pressure exerted by the Reich Forest Administration, the Economics Ministry, and the officialdom of the General Government. Early in 1941, Degussa committed 250,000 RM to secure the region's wood supply and make it accessible, then followed up on this in May 1942 by authorizing an expenditure of up to 1.25 million Reichsmarks on a factory – chiefly, however, in order to gain enough influence "to slow down the implementation."[141] Whether Frankfurt accomplished this purpose is not clear from the firm's files. At a small nominal value, Degussa continued to carry the subsidiary on its books (the Hiag Holzverwertung GmbH, Cisna) that had been founded in mid-1941 to process wood from the region, and in mid-1943, the parent managing board took note "of a possible expansion of the San project in the direction of solvents and yeast," but the records provide no indication of large-scale investment in the undertaking.[142]

Throughout occupied Europe until 1945, Degussa appears to have consummated only two outright takeovers of non-Jewish-owned factories, both of them in regions the Reich had annexed. In 1940/41, Frankfurt spent 25,000 RM to acquire 50 percent of the shares in the Elsässische Sauerstoff-und Acetylen-Werke KG, Schöberl & Co., a partnership with Heinrich and Hermann Schöberl formed to obtain and manage an oxygen and acetylene plant in Mulhouse that the Air Liquide company of Strasbourg had owned.[143] And, as of January 1, 1942, Degussa assumed a two-year lease, renewable on an annual basis with an option to buy, on a charcoaling factory formerly owned by the Russian state at Hainowka in the vicinity of Bialystok. In return for the right to sell all output, Degussa was to purchase the considerable existing inventory, to pay the German Reich a fee of 1 RM

September 1940, pp. 119–20; am 7. Oktober 1940, pp. 131–32; am 4. November 1940, p. 139; am 2. Dezember 1940, pp. 143–45, and Anlagen 4–7. The regime had sought to interest Degussa in the Smolenice factory, and Degussa had begun considering buying both it and Likier, as early as the autumn of 1938; see *ibid.*, am 12. Dezember 1938, pp. 6–7.

[140] *Ibid.*, am 6. Januar 1941, p. 155.

[141] *Ibid.*, p. 154, and am 4. Mai 1942, p. 248 and Anlage 2, Fischer and Schmitthenner's Projekt Sanverkohlung, April 24, 1942, from which the quotation comes.

[142] On the formation of Cisna, *ibid.*, am 9. Juni 1941, p. 187 and Anlage 1; and for the quotation, am 7. Juni 1943, p. 320. For the company's continuation, see DUA, RFI 4.8/5, Körperschaftssteuerberichte, 1942–44, Beteiligungskontos.

[143] See *ibid.*, Körperschaftssteuerbericht 1941, Anlage I2a, Beteiligungskonto nach dem Stande vom 30. September 1941, p. 3; and D 2/3, Elsässische Sauerstoff- und Acetylen-Werke Kom.Ges. Schöberl & Co.

per meter of wood processed, but at least 70,000 RM in the first two years, and to cover all set-up costs, insurance, and taxes.[144]

Neither venture proved especially profitable. In fact, when Allied armies reconquered Mulhouse in 1944, Degussa's managing board noted that "the loss of... Schöberl & Co... will have almost no financial effect."[145] At Hainowka, initial operating losses and the apparent sufficiency of the local wood supply until only mid-1943 prompted Degussa to declare its intention in August 1942 to terminate the lease as of the following June.[146] But the situation righted itself in the meantime, raising sales from 663,000 RM in 1941/42 to almost 1.5 million Reichsmarks in 1942/43 and the workforce to 352 people, so Degussa reversed its position and continued to manage the plant until its evacuation on July 15, 1944, as the Soviet army approached.[147] Though preparations had been made for dismantling the installation and transporting most of it to Germany, these were carried out only partially, with the result that Degussa applied to the Reich in December 1944 for reimbursement of war damages attendant on the loss of the plant in the amount of almost 540,000 RM.[148] In all probability, that payment left Frankfurt with a comfortable return on its services.

This is not to say that Degussa harbored no further ambitions in the lands under German domination. The corporation, for instance, gladly would have completed its ownership of the Chemische Fabrik Czichow at Sosnowitz in Eastern Upper Silesia by acquiring the half interest that Degussa did not possess already when the war began. But the Main Trusteeship Office East, which controlled property seized from Poles and Jews in the region, insisted on selling shares there only to "a physical person," namely one Friedrich Hartwich, a chemist at Schering AG, and Degussa therefore opted to let him have its stockholding as well for 30,000 RM and a pledge to end the firm's production of acetic acid.[149] When the German acetic acid syndicate

[144] DUA, IW 35.2/10, Vertrag zwischen dem Deutschen Reich... und der Deutsche Gold- und Silber-Scheideanstalt, 16/23 December 1941; and Aufnahme der Warenbestände im Hiagwerk Hainowka... Zusammenstellung, February 5, 1942.

[145] DUA, DL 2/1, Niederschrift über die Sitzung des Ausschusses für Verkaufsorganisation, December 6, 1944, p. 2.

[146] DUA, IW 35.2/10, Degussa to Reichsjägermeister, August 21, 1942.

[147] Ibid., Degussa to Reichsjägermeister, May 10, 1943, and Nachtrag zu dem Pachtvertrag vom 16./23. Dezember 1941, December 20, 1943/ January19, 1944, as well as DL 2/1, Niederschrift über die Vorstandssitzung am 11. Januar 1943, p. 295 (on the improving situation and the renewal); IW 35.8/1, Hiagwerk Greifenhagen to Fischer, July 20, 1944 (on the evacuation); and RFI 4.2/104, Technische Abteilung II, Bericht über die Tätigkeit und Leistung der Werke im Geschäftsjahr 1942–43, pp. 1 and 56 (on the workforce and output).

[148] DUA, DL 2/1, Niederschrift über die Vorstandssitzung am 6. März 1944, p. 361 (on the preparations); DL 11.5/61, Degussa to Chef der Zivilverwaltung für den Bezirk Bialystock, December 21, 1944 (on the war damage claim).

[149] DUA, HIA 1/28, Schmitthenner's Abschliessender Bericht über die Liquidation unserer Beteiligung an der Chemischen Fabrik Gzichow [sic] A. G., Sosnowitz/OS, February 24, 1943.

meanwhile moved to take over a plant at Warthenau in the annexed portion of Poland, Frankfurt quickly agreed to pay in its cartel quota share (41 percent) of the purchase price of 150,000 RM.[150]

And in the conquered sections of the Soviet Union, Degussa officials scouted several factories during 1941–42 with an eye to seeking trusteeships over them. Those for carbon black at Kalusz and Daszawa eventually fell to the Beskiden-Erdölgesellschaft, and those for sodium cyanide from *Schlempe* at Stalinskaya in Ukraine seemed better suited for dismantling and shipping to Germany, where the machinery ended up in the hands of Röhm & Haas, than for revival.[151] But the organic chemicals and explosives facilities at Kamenskoje in Ukraine looked more attractive, and Degussa briefly explored the possibility of operating them in partnership with WASAG, though the reversal of German military fortunes at Stalingrad appears to have killed the idea.[152] Certainly, the hostility of the Nazi occupation administration to large corporations, on which Hans Menzel remarked as the head of Degussa's Eastern Committee in early 1943, also played a part in stymieing initiatives of this sort, including a scheme involving Degussa's hard fuels subsidiary, Festkraftstoff AG, to exploit peat fields in the former Baltic states.[153]

For obvious reasons, however, 1943 constituted the high-water mark of even Degussa's limited expansionist efforts, both actual and projected, in Europe. Early in the year, the firm obtained official permissions to found offices in the Reichskommissariate Ostland and Ukraine, and Hermann Schlosser enjoyed the satisfaction of describing to an IG Farben director "our measures for the East . . . with which we incidentally are ahead of IG by several horse lengths."[154] In June, the managing board appropriated 150,000 RM for the establishment of a Durferrit metals-hardening facility in Warsaw,

---

[150] DUA, DL 2/1, Niederschrift über die Vorstandssitzung am 1. Februar 1943, p. 300.

[151] DUA, BET 9/46, Baerwind to Kemnitz, September 15, 1941; Baerwind's Besuch bei Regierungsrat Wille . . . betreffend "Russherstellungs-G.m.b.H-Ost," October 20, 1941; Baerwind's Verhandlung im Reichsamt, October 20, 1941; and Kemnitz's Aktennotiz, 13 November 1941; as well as DL 3.Baerwind/26, Aktenvermerk betreffend Karpathen-Oel-A.G./Beskiden-Gesellschaft, November 6, 1942 (on the carbon black plants); PCA 2/61, Degussa to Wirtschaftsstab Ost, September 1, 1942; Bonath to Kolb, November 7, 1942; and Baerwind and Bonath to Reichsministerium für die besetzten Ostgebiete, November 7, 1942 (on Stalinskaya); and TLE 1/23, Schlosser's Betr. Röhm & Haas, September 16, 1943 (on the eventual destination of the equipment).

[152] DUA, DL 2/1, Niederschrift über die Vorstandssitzung am 2. November 1942, pp. 281–82 and Anlage 1 (on Kamenskoje); am 1. März 1943, p. 306, reports the return of Goecke, who had been designated to run this factory, from the East, and am 5. April 1943, p. 313, refers to his report to the board on his experiences.

[153] *Ibid.*, am 2. November 1942, p. 282 (on Menzel's report); and am 7. Juni 1943, p. 320 (on the peat project). Menzel assumed responsibility for "the execution of our Eastern interests" in the summer of 1942; see *ibid.*, am 3. August 1942, p. 264.

[154] See HHW, Reichskommissar für das Ostland to Gauleitung Frankfurt/Main, December 17, 1942, and reply of December 31 (on the establishment of a Riga office); AW 33.4/1, Degussa to Reichskommissar für die Ukraine, February 22, 1943 (on the office in Kiev);

and during the fall, Degussa apparently founded a new firm to embrace all of its French interests, the Procima S.r.l. Produits Chimiques pour toutes Industries, with a capital of one million French francs, or 50,000 RM.[155] But within months, Frankfurt had written off the entire operation and signified how rapidly the tide had turned by refusing to expend 200,000 to 250,000 RM on a proferred sulfuric (or ethyl) ether installation in France.[156] That interval also saw the cancellation of Degussa's plans, which had been developing since late 1941, to build carbon black plants in France and Italy in partnership with native firms and license its manufacturing processes to them.[157]

In the meantime, however, two instances of Degussa's efforts to consolidate its interests in Nazi-dominated Europe led to greater extension of the Reich's vicious racism than of the firm's real property. The first of these involved the possible absorption by the Bantlin'sche Chem. Fabriken of Perecin, which was located in the part of Slovakia that Hungary had annexed, of another organic chemicals and acetic acid producer called Clotilde that the Salgo-Tarjaner coal mining corporation of Budapest controlled. For Frankfurt, whose relative shareholding in Perecin (40 percent) would decline by virtue of the merger, the principal attractions appear to have been the managerial and marketing influence that Degussa would acquire over Clotilde's plant, the capital infusion that its owners would provide, and the foundation for further cooperation with them in Hungary that would be laid.[158] But there was a catch: Clotilde's board and senior officials included a considerable number of "to us undesirable... non-Aryan elements." On condition that the former situation would be "cleared up" and the offensive personnel

and DL 3.H.Schlosser/1, Doc. 936, Notiz für das Ostreferat, January 14, 1943 (for the quotation).
[155] DUA, DL 2/1, Niederschrift über die Vorstandssitzung am 7. Juni 1943, p. 320 (re Warsaw); and RFI 4.8/5, Körperschaftssteuerbericht 1944, Anlage 2c, p. 5 (on the new firm in Paris).
[156] *Ibid*; and DL 2/1, am 5. Februar 1944, p. 356.
[157] *Ibid*., am 3. November 1941, p. 211; the documents collected in GCH 2/13, especially Baerwind to François Gall, May 28, 1942, Vertrag zwischen Deutsche Gold- und Silber-Scheideanstalt vorm. Roessler und Société d'Electro-Chimie, Société Bruay-Progil... Société des Usines Chimiques Rhône, February 12, 1943; and Bonath and Flasskamp's Französische Aktivrussfabrik, April 22, 1943; DL 3.Baerwind/26, Besprechungen in Paris, July 13, 1942; Aussprache mit der Société d'Electro-Chimie, July 13, 1942; Gespräch mit Herrn Dr. Eckell, August 10, 1942; Verhandlungen in Paris, September 1, 1942; Aussprache in Paris, September 2, 1942; Notizen aus Gesprächen... über schwebende Fragen auf dem Russgebiet, September 30, 1942; Abschluss des französischen CK3-/CK4-Lizenzverträge, February 15, 1943; and Pariser Besprechungen, July 7, 1943; BET 9/49, Riesenhuber's Notiz für Herrn Feldmann, May 17, 1943; and DL 3.Baerwind/27, Russ-Besprechungen in Oberschlesien, October 20, 1943, which reports decisions neither to complete the Italian plant in S. Guiseppe del Cairo nor to begin the French factory in Bruay because the "labor... can no longer bring any military-economic benefit."
[158] On Degussa's shareholding, see RFI 4.8/5, Körperschaftssteuerberichte 1941, Anlage I2a, p. 3; 1943, Anlage 2c, p. 4; and 1944, Anlage 2c, p. 4.

"eliminated," Degussa's executives authorized the deal in August 1942.[159] It was, however, never concluded, for reasons that Degussa's files do not elucidate. Although the nasty phraseology in this connection issued from Hermann Federlin, who vied with Hans Menzel for the dubious honor of being the most fervent Nazi on Degussa's board, the unfolding of a related story at the Kaliwerke Kolin in the Protectorate makes clear that the words represented corporate policy.

Degussa controlled only 13.135 percent of the shares in Kolin at the outbreak of the war and that indirectly, via Frankfurt's 51.67 percent holding in the Chemische Fabrik Schlempe GmbH. The bulk of the stock (almost three-fourths) belonged individually to several German- and Czech-based member firms of the ethyl alcohol syndicate. But nearly all of Kolin's products had been based since prior to the First World War on licenses from Degussa and therefore marketed almost exclusively by it for decades before the German occupation of the Czech lands in 1939.[160] Accordingly, Hermann Schlosser succeeded to Frankfurt's seat on the little company's administrative board in 1932, then became its vice president in mid-1938, several months prior to the Sudeten crisis.[161] But he took a dark view of the long-term outlook for the firm. He therefore repeatedly resisted the efforts of Max Stoecker, the executive director of Kolin, to get Degussa to increase its shareholding, including by buying up the 12.6 percent of the stock that two Jewish co-owners, Messrs. Bauer and Fischl, were forced to turn over to the Böhmische Escompte Bank (BEB) following the Allied abandonment of Czechoslovakia, as that institution became an arm of the Dresdner Bank and they were driven from Kolin's board.[162] There matters rested until mid-1941, when Stoecker, probably trying to strengthen his enterprise's reputation with key Nazi officials in Prague, moved to put an end to the Czech majority on that body and thus to highlight "the German character of the Kaliwerke."[163] He also quickly terminated the consulting contract on which Bauer's and Fischl's livelihoods had been depending since 1939, then invited Schlosser to become the president of the new, smaller, and German-dominated board.[164]

[159] DUA, TLE 1/23, Federlin's Besprechung mit den Herren der Salgo-Tarjaner Steinkohlenbergau Aktiengesellschaft, Budapest, April 30, 1942 (for the first quotation); and DL 2/1, Niederschrift über die Vorstandssitzung am 3 August 1942, p. 262 (for the other quoted words and the rationale). As background, see *ibid.*, am 18. Januar 1939, p. 15, and ad 3. Juni 1940, p. 96.
[160] On the historical background of relations between the two firms, see DUA, AW 33.2/1, especially Lizenzvertrag, May 30, 1907; Fritz Roessler's Niederschriften, December 7, 1927 and August 13, 1928; and Chem. Fabr. Schlempe to its Gesellschafter, June 17, 1926.
[161] DUA, AW 33.6/1, Verwaltungsratprotokolle, June 4, 1932 and June 24, 1938.
[162] DUA, TLE 1/83, Westphal to Stoecker, March 24, 1939; Beteiligungsverhältnisse bei der Kaliwerke AG, April 19, 1939; Schlosser's Kaliwerke AG, June 14, 1939; and Dostal to Schlosser, December 11, 1939.
[163] *Ibid.*, Baerwind's Notiz betr. die Besitzverhältnissen der Kaliwerken Kolin, June 30, 1941.
[164] *Ibid.*, Protokoll über die…Sitzung des Exekutiv-Kommittees, July 15, 1941; DUA, DL 3.H.Schlosser/14, Stoecker to Schlosser, October 29, 1941.

Schlosser may have accepted out of a sense of obligation to see if Kolin could be made into a sound and enduring enterprise, which is how he, more or less as always, presented his decision.[165] But Kolin's increasing significance to Degussa was becoming obvious. Not only did Frankfurt need the firm's output of sodium cyanide, Zyklon, and, most recently, carbon black, however limited by declining raw material supplies, but also Kolin's location was of mounting importance as a possible destination for transferred or augmented manufacturing units, especially for metal hardeners. Thus, within days of Schlosser's formal election in early March 1942, a meeting of several Degussa board members and directors, Stoecker, and Gerhard Peters of the Degesch subsidiary came "more or less inevitably to the conclusion that the purchase of a majority stockholding in Kolin, against which so many reasons spoke earlier, is today absolutely appropriate." To achieve that end, those present foresaw the purchase of the shares being administered by the BEB, followed by a stock issue that Degussa would buy up entirely for, at most, 250,000 RM.[166] The scheme miscarried almost immediately, however, because the BEB, backed by the Dresdner, declined to sell, on the grounds that most of the proceeds would be taxed away and it could imagine no better investment for any that remained.[167] Degussa thereafter made do with the bank's voting support, but for this there was a price. In July 1942, the BEB's representative on the administrative board brought up the matter of two Jewish chemists who still held important managerial positions in the company's production of cyanide and Zyklon and insisted on their dismissal, which followed immediately.[168] Kolin managed to hold onto two of the three department leaders who later experienced "continuous difficulties because of their non-Aryan wives," and Stoecker apparently experienced no difficulties on account of having a Jewish grandmother.[169] But once more Degussa had become complicit in Nazi persecution.

Far and away, Degussa's largest role in the spoliation of occupied Europe was as the recipient of machinery or raw materials plundered by or at the behest of the Reich, then sold or given to the firm. In the first category fell the payment to the Army High Command of 450,000 RM in May 1941 for machinery to increase production of paraformaldyde; the purchase of a seized Yugoslav ammonia plant for 1.2 million Reichsmarks at the turn of 1942/43 in order to remove it to Fürstenberg; and the dismantling and

---

[165] *Ibid.*, Kaliwerke AG, January 26, 1942; as background to Schlosser's thinking, see DUA, TLE1/83, Schlosser to Dostal, June 17, 1941.

[166] *Ibid.*, Westphal's Kaliwerke AG, March 9, 1942; see also DUA, DL 2/1, Niederschrift über die Vorstandssitzung am 30 März 1942, pp. 243–44.

[167] DUA, TLE 1/83, Feldmann's Aktennotiz Betr.: Kaliwerke AG, April 1, 1942.

[168] *Ibid.*, Baerwind's Aktenvermerk betreffend Personalia Kaliwerke Kolin, July 7, 1942. I have found no documentation of the fates of the two individuals affected, Drs. Grossmann and Graf.

[169] On Stoecker's heritage, see Jürgen Kalthoff and Martin Werner, *Die Händler des Zyklon B* (Hamburg: VSA-Verlag, 1998), p. 218.

shipping of an acetone installation from Italy at the end of 1943, again for the benefit of the Zentralwerk.[170] The Auergesellschaft also expended 500,000 RM in the summer of 1941 so as to gain title to the equipment being cannibalized from a confiscated, formerly state-owned gas mask factory in Serbia, and there were no doubt countless additional incidents of this sort involving lesser amounts of money.[171]

As for Degussa's receipts of largely stolen raw materials, mostly rare earths, these were voluminous and usually comparable in etiology and form to the enterprise's activities in the Third Reich's precious metals economy. Because Degussa held a virtual monopoly of beryllium ore processing in Germany, for example, Frankfurt was the inescapable destination for 9.4 tons of that substance, clearly labeled "looted goods Le Havre," that arrived in April 1941.[172] But by 1943, the firm's personnel were willing to take an active part in the stealing. Shortly after Italy tried to withdraw from the war, Dr. Völkel of Degussa's Frankfurt plant drew official attention to the beryllium factory in Chivasso owned by the Industria del Berillio, then enthusiastically accepted the assignment to supervise its seizure and shutdown. He relented on the last point and ultimately left enough materials on the site for it to continue operating for some months. But, before returning to Frankfurt in late October 1943, he saw to the confiscation of 470 metric tons of beryllium metal, 8.2 tons of beryllium oxide, 14.4 tons of beryllium alloys, 19.6 tons of aluminum and copper, and 6.3 tons of magnesium, lead, and cobalt. His report on the endeavor says nothing of compensation and reveals that he disregarded attempts by Swiss investors to place the factory under the protection of the Swiss consulate. Indeed, he arranged for the goods to reach Degussa's plant in Hanau via Genoa and France explicitly so as to avoid the resulting risk of impoundment that might have gone with shipping through Switzerland.[173] Meanwhile, Degussa may also have participated in pillaging Soviet borax deposits in 1941/42 and buying uranium from the Reich's Roges GmbH, which that organization probably had acquired on exploitative terms from the Union Minière of Brussels.[174]

The preponderance of the concern's actions of this sort occurred, however, via the Auergesellschaft and concerned uranium, zircon sand, and the

[170] DUA, DL 2/1, Niederschrift über die Vorstandssitzung am 8. Mai 1941, p. 175 (paraformaldehyde); am 7. Dezember 1942, p. 290a (ammonia); and am 6. Dezember 1943, p. 348 (acetone). The ammonia plant ultimately cost only 450,000 RM, 70 percent of its original price; see TA 2/73, Degussa to Reichsamt für Wirtschaftsausbau, December 1, 1942; telegram from Wifo Berlin to Frankfurt, May 27, 1943; Degusa to Wifo, May 28, June 26, and August 12, 1943.

[171] DUA, IW 24.8/5, Monatsbericht Nr. 7 für die Zeit vom 1. August–30. September 1941, p. 2.

[172] DUA, IW 2.8/8, Betriebsbericht Werk Gutleutstrasse, May 12, 1941.

[173] PCA 2/143, Völkel's Reise nach Italien, November 22, 1943.

[174] See Roth, "Konzernskizze Degussa," 1999, 3 (1988), p. 19 (on the borax); and Karlsch and Zeman, "Urangeheimnisse," Chapter 1 (on the Roges purchases).

monazite sand from which Auer derived assorted rare metallic oxides. Having quickly secured thousands of tons of both sands from France in the latter half of 1940, Auer's grasp widened thereafter. As it proudly reported in January 1941, "all the monazite sand within reach in Europe has been placed at our disposal with the help of official German agencies."[175] Two years later, the firm noted that it had purchased during 1941/42 some 250,000 RM worth of monazite sand, derivatives, and residues that the Reich had seized in France, and that "a considerable profit resulted."[176] These gains augmented the modest ones that continued to flow from Auer's one-third share in St. Joachimsthaler Bergbau GmbH, whose output of radium doubled to 3.3 grams per year between 1939/40 and 1943/44, and which paid dividends of 5 to 6 percent annually from 1941 to 1944.[177]

Altogether, then, Degussa played a largely reactive role in the Nazi war economy and a modest part in the New Order in Europe. But it derived appreciable advantages from both, all the same, and in the process, as the next two chapters demonstrate, became caught up in the most vicious of the regime's crimes: the exploitation of labor from across Europe and, in particular, the torture and murder of the European Jews.

---

[175] On the acquisitions in mid- to late 1940, see DUA, IW 24.5/5, Besondere Daten 1939/1940, n.d., and Menzel's Notiz betr. Unterredung mit Herrn Direktor Meier-Oswaldt von der Auergesellschaft, November 25, 1940. The quotation appears in IW 24.9/1, Bericht des Vorstandes für das Geschäftsjahr 1939/40, January 28, 1941, p. 5.

[176] DUA, IW 24.5/5, Bericht des Vorstandes für das Geschäftsjahr 1941/42, February 22, 1943, p. 6.

[177] DUA, IW 24.9/1, Bericht des Vorstandes, April 5, 44, p. 16. Auer earned, however, no returns on its 27 percent holding in Radium-Bergbau GmbH of Berlin, which in 1941–43, further developed mines in Portugal and did preliminary work on a uranium mine in Bulgaria, but paid no dividends; *ibid.*, pp. 12, 17.

7

Forced Labor

As regarding Aryanization, the best that can be said of Degussa's roles in war production and the spoliation of occupied Europe is that they could have been worse, and the same applies to the firm's implication in the exploitation of foreign and forced labor. Moreover, as with the corporation's readiness to reap benefits from the Nazi state's extortion of companies and precious metals from Jews, complicity in its compulsory labor policies began, not in defeated enemy countries and under pressure of war, but within Germany and before the fighting commenced – in fact, in the summer of 1939 and on the outskirts of the nation's capital. The occasion was a series of labor problems at Degussa's run-down carbon black factory at Blankenburg, where the managers had proved unable to keep workers from decamping for jobs elsewhere and become embroiled in disputes with the local chapter of the German Labor Front (DAF). Frankfurt therefore sent its Nazi Plant Foreman, Adolf Hilpert, in late June to rectify the situation, and he and his Party comrades quickly agreed on several minor concessions concerning working conditions and decided to capitalize on new regulations by which the regime, after stripping most German Jews of their livelihoods, had begun assigning them to labor battalions.[1] After pledging that "the Jews requested by the plant will be kept separate from the rest of the workforce ... applied to the most unpleasant work, and supervised by a reliable Aryan work comrade," Hilpert proudly reported that "the labor supply is guaranteed and the previous constant objections of the DAF will stop."[2] This upshot meant, in practice, that about half of Hydrocarbon's workforce for the next three and one-half years consisted of initially about a dozen but later some twenty-five mostly elderly Jewish men, who were paid at officially prescribed and

---

[1] On the problems at Blankenburg, DUA, PCA 2/15, Baerwind's Aussprache in der Zweigniederlassung Berlin ... über die Produktionsverhältnisse bei der Hydrocarbon, June 13, 1939. On the forced labor program for German Jews, see Wolf Gruner, *Der Geschlossene Arbeitseinsatz deutscher Juden* (Berlin: Metropol Verlag, 1997), especially pp. 55–106, as well as Dieter Maier, *Arbeitseinsatz und Deportation* (Berlin: Edition Hentrich, 1994), especially pp. 15–67, and the pioneering study of H. G. Adler, *Der verwaltete Mensch* (Tübingen: Mohr, 1974), pp. 207–15.

[2] DUA, PCA 2/15, Hilpert's Akten-Notiz Betr. Besuch der Hydrocarbon Gesellschaft für Chemische Produkte GmbH, July 1, 1939.

discriminatory wage rates and often worked to the point that they were dismissed and replaced by others. In February 1943, the remnant of this group was "dissolved completely" and at least some of its members presumably deported, as part of the "Factory Action" by which the regime sought to make the Reich, including the labor force within it, as "Jew-free" as possible.[3]

From the point of view of Degussa's leaders, the employment of aged men, largely unsuited for industrial labor, was not a desirable or durable outcome at Blankenburg, but a temporary necessity produced by the tightness of the German labor market and, in this case, the enterprise's reluctance to invest in improving a factory that was slated for abandonment as soon as circumstances permitted. This completely expedient attitude also characterized the firm's reaction to the subsequent metastasis of Nazi labor exploitation during wartime. Over the ensuing five years, Degussa and its subsidiaries came to employ thousands of European civilians and prisoners of war under varying degrees of duress and discomfort and at often discriminatory rates of compensation. Even worse, the concern undertook to lease somewhat lesser numbers of inmates from ghettoes and concentration camps to labor on much harsher terms in return for payments per head and per day, not to these victims, but to the agencies that furnished them. In every case, whether Degussa's managers sought the allotment of foreign or forced labor from pools the Reich had established or merely accepted the proposals of relevant government agencies (e.g., local Labor Offices or the National Office for Economic Expansion or the General Plenipotentiary for Chemical Production), the main motivation was straightforward, practical, and, to the executives involved, unarguable: the absence of an adequate alternative source of workers.

At existing plants within Germany, Degussa's readiness to take almost any workers it could get from 1940 to 1945 stemmed from the impasse created by the military's simultaneous and mounting needs for soldiers and goods. While the Wehrmacht withdrew ever more men from the firm's shop floors and offices and soaked up most of the potential replacements, the war economy required ever larger volumes of output. Illustrative of the resulting situation was what happened to the workforce at Degussa's Rheinfelden factory, even as its ample supplies of hydroelectricity and close proximity to the Swiss border (which deterred Allied air raids) attracted the numerous additional facilities referred to in Chapter 6. Of the 622 workers there on

[3] On the numbers and turnover of this workforce, DUA, PCA 2/18, Betriebsberichte Werk Blankenburg, especially November 12, 1941, p. 2; December 20, 1941, p. 2; April 20, 1942, p. 3; January 20, 1943, p. 3; February 18, 1943, p. 3; and March 22, 1943, p. 3. On the extent – and the limits – of this effort by the regime to purge the nation's workforce of Jews, see Wolf Gruner, "The Factory Action and the Events at the Rosenstrasse in Berlin: Fact and Fictions about 27 February 1943," *Central European History* 36 (2003), pp. 184–94, and 205–08.

August 31, 1939, only 270 (43.4 percent) remained in early November 1943; in the meantime, 144 had resigned or retired (23.2 percent), and 208 had been called to military or other national service (33.4 percent).[4] During the same period, the plant succeeded in adding a net total of only 103 German men to its ranks, which meant that their number fell by 36 percent (from 584 to 373 – see Appendix N).

Equally comprehensive and comparable figures are not available for other factories or Degussa as a whole, but a few examples convey a sense of the firm's labor problem. The Gutleutstrasse plant in Frankfurt lost 118 of approximately 490 wage and salary earners (24 percent) to national service during the first year of the fighting, and by the end of April 1942, 509 of the 1,687 German men on Degussa's entire roster in Frankfurt had been called up (i.e., 30 percent of those working in the headquarters staff, Werk I in the Weissfrauenstrasse, and Werk II in the Gutleutstrasse), and 130 more were about to be.[5] Kalscheuren's German workforce fell by over one-half, from 279 to 137, between mid-1940 and mid-1944, with 60 percent of the loss (eighty-four men) accounted for by mobilization. A few plants managed to fare better. At Brilon-Wald, a charcoaling site in Westphalia, the net attrition came to only 26 percent from May 1940 to September 1944 (229 to 169), by which time such plants had come "to enjoy special protection against further call-ups."[6] The vital factories for sodium and acetone at Knapsack apparently held the net decline of German male workers below 20 percent during roughly the same interval (for detailed data on these installations as well, see Appendix N). And, of course, nothing could stop the breakneck, army-supported expansion of the Auergesellschaft, not even its loss of 1,282 wage or salary earners to the services and another ninety-two to death at the fronts by the end of September 1943.[7] Over the entire Degussa concern, including Auer, however, the call-ups alone had claimed roughly 40 percent of prewar personnel by the beginning of that month, judging by the managing board's computation that 4,179 employees and workers were in national service as of then.[8]

---

[4] DUA, PCA 2/144, Bewegung der vor dem Krieg im Werk tätigen Arbeitskräfte (ohne Angestellte) bis November 1943, November 5, 1943.
[5] See DUA, IW 2.8/8, Jahresbericht Werk Gutleutstrasse 1940, August 8, 1941, p. 2; DL 2/1, Niederschrift über die Vorstandssitzung am 1. Juni 1942, p. 252.
[6] DUA, DL 3.Baerwind/35, Federlin and Goecke's Rundschreiben Betr.: Freimachung von Arbeitsplätzen für deutsche Frauen und Intensivierung der Arbeiten ausländischer Arbeitskräfte, October 24, 1944.
[7] DUA, IW 24.9/1, Bericht des Vorstandes für das Geschäftsjahr 1942/43, April 5, 1944, p. 2.
[8] DUA, DL 2/1, Niederschrift über die Vorstandssitzung am 7. September 1943, p. 334. This percentage coincides almost exactly with that for all German working men who had been mobilized by May 31, 1943, according to Bernhard R. Kroener, Rolf-Dieter Müller, and Hans Umbreit, *Germany and the Second World War*, vol. V, Part I (Oxford: Clarendon Press, 2000), p. 927.

The losses could be offset only partially by hiring German women. In Frankfurt, Degussa added 521 "mostly female" (and German) personnel between the summer of 1939 and February 1942.[9] Rheinfelden raised the number of its native women employees from 15 in August 1939 to 107 four years later. But for both practical and political reasons, there was little elasticity in this segment of the labor market. More than half of all German women between the ages of fourteen and sixty-five already were employed in May 1939 (a higher share than ever reached in the United States or Great Britain during the war), including 36 percent of all married women and 89 percent of single women aged fifteen to sixty.[10] Both the regime and the army were reluctant to push these figures upwards for fear of damaging morale at home and on the front lines, but even in the absence of such concerns, domestic female labor could not have answered Degussa's production needs without a considerable relaxation in the German safety and health regulations that barred assigning women to many forms of hazardous or dirty work.[11] Neither would many more men have been freed up for assembly line duty if the government had driven women into office employment to a greater extent, since nearly all Degussa's desk personnel by 1943 consisted of men disqualified for military service, and thus for significant factory labor, on grounds of age, health, or indispensable experience.[12]

The extant sources suggest that the enterprise and its subsidiaries made considerable efforts to recruit and apply women wherever possible, including on a part-time basis, but that the supply proved inadequate to Degussa's overall needs and often inappropriate to its specific ones.[13] Only in exceptional locations and the early stages of the war (e.g., those 521 women hired in Frankfurt by early 1942) could hirings of German women keep pace with the attrition of the homegrown male workforce or answer to the needs of new factories (as at Auer's two new gas mask installations at Guben and Danzig, where German females made up 686 out of 737 and 480 out of

---

[9] *Ibid.*, am 2. März 1942, p. 239.

[10] Kroener et al., *Germany and the Second World War*, V/ I, pp. 860, 883–89; and R. J. Overy, *War and Economy in the Third Reich* (Oxford: Clarendon Press, 1994), pp. 303–11.

[11] See, for example, the prohibition on women working in the beryllium, aminopyridine, and cyanide sections of the Gutleutstrasse plant, DUA, IW 2.8/9, Betriebsbericht März 1943, April 12, 1943, p. 1.

[12] Indeed, in late 1943, the managing board resolved to begin releasing the last of its able-bodied "leading personnel" for induction in order to head off further inroads in "key figures in production"; DL 2/1, Niederschrift über die Vorstandssitzung am 1. November 1943, p. 344.

[13] See, for example, DUA, PCA 2/141, Federlin's Notiz Betr.: Einsatz weiblicher Arbeitskräfte, March 11, 1943; DL 2/1, Niederschrift über die Vorstandssitzung am 3. Mai 1943, p. 316; and DL 3.Baerwind/35, Federlin and Goecke's Rundschreiben Betr.: Freimachung von Arbeitsplätzen für deutsche Frauen und Intensivierung der Arbeiten ausländischer Arbeitskräfte, October 24, 1944.

546 laborers, respectively, by September 1941).[14] Apparently more representative of the general pattern are the statistics for the Gutleutstrasse and Rheinfelden factories. At the former the number of German women rose by about 116 between July 1941 and September 1943 and about 130 from the earlier date through early 1945, but the fall in the number of German men was 201 and 269 over the two intervals. At Rheinfelden, the women's increase by 92 between the war's outbreak and August 1943 amounted to only one-third of the men's decline by 277, and for the period 1939 to mid-1944 the gap widened, since the overall net gains and losses came to 69 and 293, respectively.

The labor reallocation committees that Degussa established in February 1942 and the successive "combing out" commissions that the Reich set in motion also failed to satisfy the firm's labor requirements.[15] Although these groups managed to arrest or slow the decline in the raw number of Germans working at places such as Knapsack and Rheinfelden from 1941 on and even to raise it slightly at Werk II in Frankfurt, the clamor for output from and hence laborers at all these sites grew faster than redistribution could accommodate. Thus, neither hiring more German women, nor better apportioning German male workers closed the gap between the supply and demand curves for labor at Degussa's plants. Moreover, such achievements masked the problem of declining quality. The 373 remaining German men at Rheinfelden in November 1943 included 21 teenagers, 20 severely disabled, and 42 persons "functioning at less than 60 percent"; altogether, these people composed 22 percent of the German males on the site and 12.4 percent of its total workforce.[16] As early as 1941, even the spoiled Auergesellschaft complained on this score, noting that among the clerical staff being sent to it by the regional Labor Offices "a large number do not satisfy even remotely the requirements we must reasonably pose." The consequences included steep rises in overtime charges, and these were not the only additional financial burdens that came with "conscripted" German workers – others were moving allowances, rent subsidies, travel assistance for home visits, and the construction of a barracks for women.[17]

In this context, Degussa's decision to avail itself of any supplementary source of labor the Reich offered appeared as a stark choice between meeting manufacturing targets or not, between doing the firm's perceived economic duty or failing the nation. The cost of the available workers was a secondary element in the enterprise's pursuit of them, especially since the first groups involved – French and Polish prisoners of war and civilians from

[14] DUA, IW 24.8/5, Monatsbericht Nr. 7 für die Zeit vom 1. August–30. September 1941, p. 2.
[15] DUA, DL 2/1, Niederschrift über die Vorstandssitzung am 2. Februar 1943, p. 234.
[16] DUA, PCA 2/144, Gesamtgefolgschaft am 1.XI.1943, November 5, 1943.
[17] DUA, IW 24.9/1, Bericht des Vorstandes für das Geschäftsjahr 1939/40, January 28, 1941, pp. 1–2.

Western Europe and Scandinavia supplied by subcontractors or recruited, later increasingly just rounded up, by the Reich – were not much cheaper than the Germans being replaced. Charges for such POWs, for example, came to 60 to 80 percent of comparable domestic wage rates for the jobs involved, plus 10 percent for taxes and minus capped rebates for food and any necessary lodging (and that of the required guards). The set-up charges for barracks, bedding, and the like were the employers' responsibility and often not covered fully by the wage differential or the permitted deductions.[18] Since working hours were pegged to those of Germans in the same plant, the major advantage concerning compensation came in the realm of benefits, including pay increments for dependents, which companies seldom had to extend to captured soldiers or foreign contract workers. As a result, people in these virtually all-male groups cost Degussa somewhat less per day than German men (though usually not less than German women under the prevailing wage and benefit schedules). For each Belgian assembly worker the Vanderhaegen firm of Brussels provided to Knapsack from 1941 to 1944, for instance, Degussa spent 5.25 to 5.50 RM daily, which corresponded to a German male counterpart's base earnings, but only those.[19] Benefits accounted for two-thirds of the difference between Degussa's outlays per domestic worker per hour (1.39 RM) and those per prisoner of war (.63 RM) at Kalscheuren in December 1941 and 116 percent of the meanwhile much reduced gap in June 1944 (1.42 vs. 1.11 RM per hour).[20]

But European civilians and even prisoners of war often were difficult to obtain and retain in the right quantities. For one thing, the latter had to be ordered in groups of twenty to twenty-five, worked as units under guard, and adequately housed in or around a factory, and all these conditions raised problems or created delays. For another, Degussa's preference for the role of intermediate supplier to the German military made its requests often seem less pressing than those of more immediately "war deciding" enterprises. By August 1941, about a year after Degussa's first applications for such workers, a comprehensive internal survey of forty-four of the firm's branches and factories indicated that they had managed to receive only 244 captured soldiers and enlist thirty-eight foreign civilians, while requests for at least 137 more people in both categories remained pending.[21] Other sources suggest

---

[18] For typical contracts, see DUA, PCA 1/244, L. C. Marquart AG to Baerwind, August 3, 1940, with enclosures; and IW 40.10/1, Vertrag zwischen dem Deutschen Reich... und der Fa.... in Brilon-Wald, July 29, 1940.
[19] DUA, IW 33.8/7, Betriebsbericht für Juli 1941, August 7, 1941, p. 25.
[20] DUA, IW 34.8/2-23, Erläuterungen zu den Kalkulationen Dezember 1941, February 17, 1942, p. 6, and June 1944, September 21, 1944, p. 3. As background to the breakdown of wage payments between categories, IW 34.8/1, September 1940, October 29, 1940, p. 6.
[21] DUA, PCA 2/144, Einstufung der Betriebe nach Kriegswichtigkeit, August 15, 1941. The first reference to requests for POW labor appears in the managing board's minutes for September 1940; DL 2/1, Niederschrift über die Vorstandssitzung am 2. September 1940, p. 123.

that this tabulation was not quite up to date (twenty uncounted POWs already were at Kalscheuren, to mention one inaccuracy), and it omits the Auergesellschaft, which had "proportionately very few" former soldiers on its grounds at roughly the same time, thanks to the firm's role in military production, but approximately 220 foreigners.[22] In any case, the total of perhaps 500 to 600 auxiliary laborers of these sorts by the turn of 1941/42 hardly met the Degussa concern's needs. Those acquired until then and later, moreover, often departed on one ground or another fairly promptly, including the many French prisoners who declined to convert to civilian employment when they were released in 1943 and the Belgian contract workers at Knapsack who "repeatedly refuse work in our difficult plant and must be sent back."[23] Here the pattern at Rheinfelden is again telling. Of 182 foreign laborers who signed on there in 1942–43, over half (95) had left by the end of the latter year, including three-quarters of those enrolled during it, which meant a net gain of only 87 laborers for a factory that had given up over 250 men to the Wehrmacht.[24]

Numbers again, therefore, rather than relative costs, drove Degussa's receptiveness to the second wave of the Third Reich's program of importing foreign laborers, this one commencing in 1942 and encompassing former Soviet soldiers and civilians. Indeed, the firm's records on the matter repeatedly speak a language of perceived compulsion. In June, the managing board concluded that, as a result of new call-ups in Frankfurt, "we are forced to prepare to take on for now fifty Russian civilian workers," and two months later, the executives at Knapsack reported that "the prospects of being allocated suitable Belgian workers are extremely slight, so that we must attend to the question of deploying Russian civilians."[25] To be sure, the regime contrived even more clearly than before to induce German firms to request such laborers by curtailing their basic wage rates and to divert a large share of the payments to the German treasury. Thus, the "savings" to employers increased (by June 1944, when the hourly cost of POWs at Kalscheuren was 78 percent of that of a German worker, the figure for so-called Eastern Workers, or *Ostarbeiter*, was 59 percent), and whereas the *Stalag*s generally pocketed one-half of what prisoners of war earned, a special "Eastern worker levy" saw to the direct transfer of an even larger portion of the new group's income to the Reich.[26] Even in this context, however, there is evidence that

---

[22] Appendix N and IW 24.5/5, Bericht des Vorstandes für das Geschäftsjahr 1940/1941, January 27, 1942, p. 2, apparently referring to September 1941.

[23] DUA, IW 33.8/8, Betriebsbericht für September 1942, October 12, 1942, p. 27.

[24] Tabulated from DOK 1/5, Fremdarbeiter während des Zweiten Weltkriegs [Rheinfelden], January 13, 1992, a computer listing of the employment and departure dates of the 494 foreign laborers at that plant from 1942 to 1945.

[25] DUA, DL 2/1, Niederschrift über die Vorstandssitzung am 1 Juni 1942, p. 284; IW 33.8/8, Betriebsbericht für Juli 1942, August 7, 1942, p. 19.

[26] DUA, IW 34.8/3, Erläuterungen zu den Kalkulationen Juni 1944, September 21, 1944, p. 3. Indicative of the Reich's profits on POW labor are the totals for Knapsack's outlays from

the cost advantage to Degussa was not uniform from place to place or as great as the regulations would suggest. At Knapsack in 1944, when the 100 POWs employed were exclusively Russian, Degussa's payments per person were almost twice what they had been for an entirely Polish block of fifteen captured soldiers in 1941.[27] In one documented case of an Eastern worker at the Gutleutstrasse plant, his gross pay per week corresponded to that of a native unskilled worker, exclusive of benefits.[28]

Not even local pride could withstand the pressure to import Eastern workers, though it could restrict their application, as the course of events at Auer's part-owned uranium and radium mining firm, St. Joachimsthaler Bergbau, demonstrates. A contingent of French POWs was sent to that site in 1940, then its dwindling numbers were replaced in June 1942 by captured Soviet soldiers, of whom some 100 were in place by the middle of the following year, perhaps more by 1944. Although the German miners and managers accepted using the captives underground, they balked at the insistence of the chief medical advisor to Konrad Henlein, the Gauleiter of the Sudetenland, that the high incidence of lung cancer among the native miners argued for replacing them completely with "foreigners or prisoners... whose premature death would be no loss to the German people." Arguing that such interchangeability would degrade the honor of mining and discourage the next generation from entering the trade, Nazi labor representatives and the firm's executives closed ranks against the proposal and accepted a compromise, backed by no less a figure than the director of the Kaiser Wilhelm Institute for Biophysics in Frankfurt. That allowed for the removal of individual miners from the pits upon completion of fifteen years of service there and the temporary substitution of Eastern workers, but preserved the possibility of restoring the prewar status quo when times allowed.[29]

Thus, as the war continued, Degussa's workforce became increasingly non-German. The following table indicates the degree of dependence on foreign

mid-September 1940 until the end of August 1943. Out of total expenses of 121,952 RM, 58,261 RM (48 percent) was paid to the *Stalag* and the remainder went to pay for food and lodging and to the prisoners themselves. On the pay regulations governing Eastern workers, see DUA, Druckschriften, *Lohnsteuer-Berechnungstafel...und Entgelttabelle für Ostarbeiter* (Darmstadt: Ludwig Kichler Verlag, [1943]); and k06098, J. Oermann, *Die arbeitsrechtliche und die steuerliche Behandlung der Ostarbeiter* (Berlin: Verlag für Wirtschaft und Arbeit, 1944). On the regulations governing expenditures for their provisions, see IW 40.10/1, Hilfstabellen für die Berechnung des Bedarfs an Lebenmitteln für sowjetische Arbeiter in der Rüstungsindustrie bzw. Gewerblichen Wirtschaft, June 26 to September 17, 1944.

[27] Calculated from DUA, IW 33.10/1, Hauptabrechnung Nr. 9 vom 1.9. bis 30.9.1941, and Aufstellung für sowj. Kriegsgefangene aus Monat Oktober 1944, November 20, 1944.

[28] DUA, DL 11.5/43, correspondence between Degussa and the United Nations High Commissioner for Refugees and the Bundesverwaltungsamt, November 17, 1965 to October 27, 1967, concerning Jozef Przystrom, with contemporary documents.

[29] See Elsner and Karbe, *Von Jáchymov nach Haigerloch*, pp. 61–70, 76–81, and 88–93. The quoted remarks appear on p. 64.

workers that key Degussa installations acquired and compares that to the national averages for German industry, armaments producers, and several notorious enterprises.

Facility	1943	1944
Auergesellschaft	19% (September)	?
Brilon-Wald	23% (October)	47% (September)
Gutleutstrasse	26% (August)	30% (September)
Rheinfelden	26% (August)	38% (July)
Reinickendorf (laborers only)	37% (October)	35% (September)
Knapsack	43% (August)	52% (September)
Kalscheuren	?	62% (August)
Average at 16 charcoaling plants	53% (October)	?
All German industry	26% (June)	29% (June)
All German armaments firms	30% (June)	35% (June)
IG Farben	40% (August)	46% (October)
Hermann Göring Works	51% (June)	59% (June)[30]

Even these statistics do not tell the whole story. At the Welden and Schrobenhausen factories of Paraxol GmbH, Degussa's munitions subsidiary, the relatively low share of non-Germans among all employees (26 percent and 34 percent, respectively) in June 1944 concealed their extremely high proportion among those actually on the production lines (68 percent and 76 percent), which provoked two visiting officials to speak of "these almost horrifying foreignization numbers."[31] All in all, the fragmentary data suggest that Degussa's largest plants came to rely on non-German labor to about the same extent as most German industrial firms, and the corporation's smaller installations rather more so. If one assumes conservatively that foreigners made up one-quarter of the Degussa concern's total active workforce in September 1943 (20,718) and one-third of it in September 1944 (about 27,000, exclusive of concentration camp inmates and allowing for the plants in Appendix O for which statistics are unavailable), then their numbers came to at least 5,180 and 9,000 in the respective months.[32]

---

[30] See Appendix N, as well as IW 24.9/1, Bericht des Vorstandes für das Geschäftsjahr 1942/43, April 5, 1944, p. 2 (on Auer); DOK 1/5, Wolf's Beschäftigung von Fremdarbeitern im Zweiten Weltkrieg, March 12, 1986, p. 2 (on Reinickendorf and the charcoaling plants in 1943); PERS 02/0016, Degussa Berlin to Degussa Frankfurt, November 4, 1944 (on Reinickendorf in 1944); and Edward L. Homze, *Foreign Labor in Nazi Germany* (Princeton: Princeton University Press, 1967), p. 235–36 and 239 (for the comparative data).

[31] DUA, IW 50.11/2, Pernice and Bender's Die Lage der Pulver, Sprengstoff u. Vorproduktions-Betriebe im Bereich der Rü JN VII, June 23, 1944.

[32] DUA, DL 2/1, Niederschrift über die Vorstandssitzung am 7. September 1943, p. 334, for the total workforce as of that date.

Yet it was never enough. Labor shortages remained the most tenacious impediment to the firm's business until the great air raids of 1944, notwithstanding Hermann Federlin's occasional bursts of optimism on the subject.[33] Not even repeated extensions of the normal workweek, which reached fifty-one hours in early 1943 and fifty-six hours in September 1944 in Frankfurt and up to sixty at other factories, could compensate for the effects.[34] The substantive ones included long delays in beginning uranium production in Frankfurt in 1941, twelve-hour shifts in other shorthanded sectors there later, and constant trade-offs of staff between various production lines or building projects almost everywhere, especially in 1944.[35] Among the less consequential but nevertheless revealing results was a relaxation of the firm's habitual security measures. Though troubled by the increasing access of foreign workers to technical and trade secrets, Degussa's managers had to concede early in 1943 that "we have consciously to put aside private commercial reservations in order even to approach achieving the main goal, namely the maintenance of militarily important production." Therefore, "foreigners in the future of necessity must be appointed to posts that entail the danger of a later spreading of important company secrets."[36]

Of course, the principal reason that the supply of non-German labor never proved sufficient was the decline in the Reich's military fortunes, which reduced both the Nazis' ability to sweep up new workers and the inclination of those already on hand to aid the German cause, but the working and living conditions to which foreign civilians or POWs were subjected also played a role. Although often not as noxious as generally imagined since, the environment was seldom good enough to make those who had experience with anything better and a choice in the matter – that is, primarily Western Europeans, especially those working at plants near their homelands – feel loyalty to their workplaces. Thus the records of the Knapsack and Rheinfelden installations near the western borders of the Reich are replete

[33] For one such, see *ibid.*, am 1. März 1943, pp. 304–05.
[34] *Ibid.*, and Notizen aus der Vorstandsbesprechung am 15. September 1944, p. 1 (on the increases in Frankfurt), PCA 1/536, Anlage zum Schreiben an Bez. Obm. der Wigru. Chem. Ind., July 22, 1944 (on hours at Rheinfelden); and IW 33.8/9, Betriebsbericht für August 1944, September 8, 1944, p. 15 (on hours at Knapsack).
[35] DUA, IW 2.8/8, Betriebsberichte Juli 1941, August 12, 1941, p. 1, and December 1941, January 18, 1942, p. 2, and PCA 1/559, Auergesellschaft to Degussa, October 24, 1941 (re uranium and extended shifts); PCA 1/536, Baerwind's Aktenvermerk zu der Notiz des Herrn Goecke ... betreffend Rückführung landwirtschaftlicher Arbeitskräfte, May 19, 1944, as well as DL 2/1, Notizen aus der Vorstandsbesprechung am ... 9. Mai 1944, concerning the trade-offs among output of cyanide, Degussit, dyes, beryllium, and ****aminopyridine as a result of the return of some borrowed foreign workers to agricultural tasks; and DL 2/1, Niederschrift über die Vorstandssitzung am 5. Juni 1944, n.p., on the same problem at Rheinfelden.
[36] DUA, DL 3.Baerwind/26, Aktenvermerk betreffend Beschäftigung von ausländischen Arbeitern im Degussit-Betrieb, March 2, 1943.

with reports of foreigners who had failed to return from furloughs or otherwise fled; and thus the number of imported workers crossed off the roster at Rheinfelden by the end of 1944 (212) surpassed the total of those the factory had brought in during 1942–43 (182).[37] *Ostarbeiter* and other foreigners laboring at more remote locations had fewer options, but neither were the arrangements and regulations that confronted these workers likely to stimulate high performance.

Conditions for Degussa's foreign workers clearly varied somewhat from place to place and year to year, as well as according to their nationalities' rank in the Nazi racial hierarchy. In general, it appears that accommodations, provisioning, and attentiveness to cultural needs, such as newspapers and entertainment, were makeshift and minimal almost everywhere in 1941–42. All then improved in 1943–44 – especially at plants in urban areas, as one would expect from a company that was learning to try to reduce desertion, cut down on sick days, and inspire effort – before deteriorating considerably during the collapse of the Reich in 1945. Whereas at first Degussa tended simply to contract local inns or guest houses to house and feed foreign workers, it gradually fitted out barracks, some in existing brick or stone buildings and some of the wooden ones with plastered and/or painted interiors, and sought to hold down the infestations of lice that such quarters attracted.[38] A few extant prisoner rosters for scattered plants in the western parts of Germany indicate only isolated deaths among foreign workers from 1942 to 1945, although it is not possible to say which, if any, of these are traceable to mishandling, and the evidence is too scant to permit generalization in this regard. What does seem clear is that physical punishments on factory grounds occurred rarely or not at all, as indicated by the many recorded instances in which managers engaged in extensive correspondence with local POW camps or labor officials in order to persuade them to remove individuals perceived as troublesome or otherwise correct their behavior. Yet if the amenities generally grew somewhat better over time, supervision, suspicion, and attempts to exert discipline all mounted in the post-Stalingrad phase of the war, which made the situation of even foreign civilian workers, and all the more so of *Ostarbeiter*, increasingly resemble that of convicts.

[37] On the AWOL workers at Knapsack, see IW 33.8/8, Betriebsbericht für November 1943, December 11, 1943, p. 15, für März 1944, April 6, 44, p. 15, and für Juli 1944, August 8, 1944, p. 15. On those at Rheinfelden, see especially IW 29.10/1, unsigned note to Chef der Werbestelle für den Arbeitseinsatz in Deutschland, Brüssel, July 28, 1943, which complains that "unfortunately the cases are increasing in which people do not return on time from their vacations" and seeks assistance in tracking down seven individuals. Overall figures for Rheinfelden calculated from the list of Rheinfelden's foreign workers in DOK 1/5, Fremdarbeiter während des Zweiten Weltkriegs, January 13, 1992.

[38] For examples of such efforts, see IW 34.8/3, Erläuterungen zu den Kalkulationen Juni 1944, September 21, 1944, p. 4, which notes Kalscheuren's expenditures on "interior painting of the Eastern workers' barracks and other related outlays."

21   The HIAG plant at Brilon-Wald

These general trends are apparent in the nevertheless contrasting experiences of forced laborers at the rural Brilon-Wald plant in Westphalia and at Degussa's main works in the city of Frankfurt. At the former, prisoners of war worked mostly barefoot in the summer of 1940 because the plant managers claimed to lack permits to buy rationed nails and yarn with which to repair worn-out shoes.[39] In March 1941, when the commander of the responsible *Stalag* complained that the prisoners' mattress straw had not been changed since their arrival the preceding July, the executives took more than another month to arrange delivery of fresh material from a nearby village.[40] Despite such passivity and indifference, I have found a record of only one death among the first twenty-five French POWs sent to the site – and that of typhus two days after the man arrived – and of none among the roughly fifty-five who served there from October 1942 until December 1944, though the

---

[39] DUA, IW 40.10/1, Brilon-Wald to Kreiswirtschaftsamt Brilon, August 22, 1940; Brilon-Wald to Stalag VI/A, Hemer, August 19, 1940, and reply of August 21, 1940. See also the follow-up pleas for warm clothing and replacement footwear from the *Stalag* in Brilon-Wald to the Kreiskommando Olsberg, December 9, 1940.
[40] *Ibid.*, Arb[eit] K[omman]do Führer to Lagerverwaltung...Brilon-Wald, March 31, 1941; Kreiskommandoführer Brilon to Werk Brilon-Wald, April 23, 1941, and reply of April 26, 1941.

incidence of hospitalization increased markedly in 1944.[41] By then, when the factory's workforce contained more than twice as many *Ostarbeiter* (most of them female) and other foreigners than captured soldiers, the management appears to have recognized that at least some forms of better treatment were in its own interests. The plant partook of a traveling troupe of singers and musicians that the regional German Labor Front had arranged for the resident *Ostarbeiter*, though the costs of 350 RM were assessed to the workers; paid for some (but not all) of the foreign-language newspapers and magazines the workforce ordered; launched still another round of fumigation for the three residence barracks; and complied with the Party's insistence on the provision of air raid shelters, however modest, for even non-Germans.[42]

Greater attentiveness was accompanied, however, by mounting restrictions on the workers' freedom of movement and harsher responses to perceived malingering or challenges to authority. By September 1944, the curfew, also imposed by the Labor Front, was at 8:00 P.M.[43] Early in the year, company officials saw to it that two French prisoners were subjected to four weeks of hard labor for defying a foreman, and an Eastern European was arrested for three days for making claims about her health that the jail's physician and the city health office then found justified.[44] Perhaps one may best infer the atmosphere at Brilon-Wald from a handwritten listing of in- and outflows at the "Russian camp" from February 24, 1943 to March 11, 1945. Of the ninety-nine people ever assigned to the barracks, sixty-three were still there when the table leaves off, twenty-two had been transferred to other sites, two had gone home, one woman had died, six men and one woman had escaped, and a net of four had been taken away by the police (two others returned after brief arrests).[45]

In Frankfurt, foreign and forced laborers experienced the pros and cons of assignment to work in a large German city and the immediate vicinity of Degussa's headquarters, which is to say, under the direct oversight of the firm's managing board member for personnel, the Nazi Hermann Federlin. It appears that these workers resided in four different places: a set of barracks on

[41] *Ibid.*, Brilon-Wald to Stalag VIA, Hemer, August 19, 1940; Brilon-Wald, summary listing of 25 Hilfs- und Platzarbeiter, November 27, 1940; handwritten undated roster headed "Franzosen."
[42] *Ibid.*, Brilon-Wald to Firma Egenolf, July 18, 1944; Kreiswart of DAF's KDF [Kraft durch Freude] organization to Brilon-Wald, July 5, 1944; July 26, 1944, Hauptgemeinschaftsleiter der NSDAP, Olsberg to Brilon-Wald, July 26, 1944; and Lagerführer to DAF Kreiswaltung Olsberg, January 8, 1945.
[43] *Ibid.*, Korf of DAF Kreiswaltung to Brilon-Wald, September 24, 1944.
[44] *Ibid.*, Brilon-Wald to Kriegsgefangenenarbeitskommando 2928, March 27, 1944, and Notiz für Herrn Mürköster, March 31, 1944 (on the French prisoners); as well as Brilon-Wald to Staatliches Gesundheitsamt Brilon, July 5, 1944, and Amtsarzt to Brilon-Wald, Betrifft: Ostarbeiterin Mistschenko, July 6, 1944.
[45] *Ibid.*, Russenlager, no date [February 1943 to March 45].

Degussa's property in the Boyenstrasse that were erected initially for French POWs, then occupied by Eastern women; the Plow Inn in Ginnheim (also called the camp "am Hochwehr") to which seventy Eastern women were brought between 1942 and 1944; the third story of Degussa's Adler building until Degussit's operations displaced the Polish men billeted there; and the Galluslager, a cooperative venture that multiple firms paid the Telefonbau und Normalzeit company to operate and that eventually became reserved for Western European and Polish males. In May 1943, Degussa's Frankfurt operations had 206 foreign personnel (151 of them men, including 47 French POWs), but at least 65 arrived at later dates (25 of them Polish males and the rest Eastern women), so the total foreign contingent seems to have come to at least 271 people, 176 men and 95 women, between 1943 and 1945.[46]

Very little is documented about the living conditions of these people. Two points are clear concerning the women, however: Federlin went out of his way to make sure they received the hardest labor assignments, arguing that "otherwise we run the risk that the Russian women will be taken away from us and put to more difficult work elsewhere," and this notwithstanding, none of them appear to have died during their tenure at Degussa.[47] At least, there is no record of such an occurrence, and the roster books of the Hochwehr/Ginnheim facility indicate that, of the seventy women consigned to it, one fled, eleven were transferred, and the rest were present on March 25, 1945, when their overseer, Frau Bliste, mustered them at the Frankfurt University sports grounds for transport out of the city. In the meantime, we know only that they ranged in age at that moment from fourteen to forty-seven, that the sick among them were regularly treated at the municipal hospital, and that in the final winter of the war they had so few blankets that, as Frau Bliste noted, "the girls freeze at night."[48] As for the men housed in the Galluslager, their beds cost Degussa an investment of 30,000 RM, plus 950 RM for every resident over the firm's initial reservation for thirty-three, and a proportionate share in the 6,500 RM required annually to pay the staff.[49] Whether the facility was as habitable as such amounts might suggest is open to doubt, judging from the often squalid conditions at Frankfurt's

---

[46] See DUA, DL 2/1, Niederschrift über die Vorstandssitzung am 3. Mai 1943, p. 316, on the total as of that date. On the accommodations and the other arrivals, DOK 1/5, Wolf's Beschäftigung von Fremdarbeitern, March 12, 1986; PCA 2/141, Kohl's Notiz. Betrifft: Arbeitseinsatz, December 3, 1943; and the entries in D 4/1, Hausstandbuch..., Rüssin. Lager am Hochwehr 1, September 16, 1942, to September 20, 1944.

[47] DUA, PCA 2/141, Federlin's Notiz Betr.: Einsatz weiblicher Arbeitskraefte, March 11, 1943.

[48] DUA, D 4/1, Hausstandbuch..., Rüssin. Lager am Hochwehr 1, September 16, 1942, to September 20, 1944; and Biste's Notizbuch über Einsatz von Ostarbeiterinnen aus dem Lager Ginnheim im Werk I und II sowie Stierstadt, September 19, 1944, to March 29, 1945 (where the quoted words appear in an entry for January 29, 1945).

[49] See DUA, DL 2/1, Niederschrift über die Vorstandssitzung am 6. Juli 1942, pp. 255–56 (on Degussa's upfront costs); and RFI 4.8/6, Krebs and Albrecht's Notiz Betr.: Gemeinschaftslager "Gallus," June 29, 1943 (on the conversion of the barracks from Russian to Western

other, better-documented consortial accommodations for foreign workers.[50] Whatever the material situation, however, the harassment to which the inhabitants were regularly exposed is suggested by Federlin's memorandum of March 15, 1943, recommending the following in the aftermath of Goebbels's declaration of "total war":

> strict oversight of all foreigners and their behavior with one another. . . . The accommodations and lockers of all foreigners are to be subject to surprise inspections by the plant police and examined for sabotage-related material. The time off of the Eastern workers must be monitored with an eye to whether and where they get together. Private lodgings for foreigners are to be stopped as much as possible and common accommodations promoted for the purpose of better surveillance.*****[51]

Severe as the conditions for prisoners of war and civilian workers were, they generally did not approach the level of misery experienced by the ghetto and concentration camp inmates who came to be used at four installations of the Degussa concern: the Zentralwerk at Fürstenberg an der Oder, the plants of the Auergesellschaft at Oranienburg and Guben, and the Deutsche Gasrusswerke factory at Gleiwitz. Significantly, two of these were construction projects, three had considerable military significance, and all were in the eastern half of the Reich, circumstances that contributed to the particular intensity of the labor situation at each and the solutions adopted. The story at Fürstenburg is briefly told, because but for a seven-month period in 1942, developments there regarding forced labor appear to have proceeded along the same lines as at Degussa's other factories, with some adjustment for the special pressures that went with being a building site, rather than an existing facility. The forced employment of inmates at Oranienburg and Guben lasted slightly longer – ten months at the former, from July 1944 to April 1945, and perhaps eight months, beginning in September 1944, at the latter – but also receives short treatment here because very few records survive to throw light on how events unfolded. Documentation on the lengthier Gleiwitz case permits fuller analysis, however, and reveals the extent to which Degussa became seriously implicated in the Nazi persecution and murder of Jews.

A form of forced labor figured in Degussa's thinking about the Fürstenberg site from the moment of its initial inspection. As the committee that visited the place in December 1939 reported, albeit speculatively: "During the construction, the circumstance could be very favorable that in the first months

---

European inhabitants, the other charges, and Degussa's intention of expanding the number of its workers there from thirty-three to fifty).
[50] See Lutz Becht, "Arbeitseinsatz in Frankfurt am Main 1938–1945. Ein Aufriss," manuscript prepared in cooperation with the Institut für Stadtgeschichte, Frankfurt am Main. I am grateful to the author and to Prof. Dr. Dieter Rebentisch, the head of the Institute, for sharing this study with me.
[51] DUA, TLE 1/23, Notiz, March 15, 1943, circulated to Schlosser, Baerwind, von Retze, Bauer, Rühl, Hilpert, and Krebs.

of 1940 a prisoner camp designed for 10,000 Poles will be ready close by, from which laborers apparently can be obtained for 3 RM per day."[52] That price represented a welcome savings over the local wage rates for unskilled construction workers, which Ewald von Retze, the Degussa board member assigned primary responsibility for building the plant, shortly thereafter recorded as .48 RM per hour, or 3.84 RM for an eight-hour day (apparently not counting benefits).[53] But, once again, cost was not the main attraction. The chief appeal of POW labor resulted from the general difficulty of finding workers for the project, given that its limited military relevance elicited a low "urgency rank" from the Reich's economic planners until Degussa foregrounded the formaldehyde installation in 1942. However, the new factory's builders soon found, as one of them later noted, "that the prisoners of war are just as scarce as the other workers," and for the same reason.[54]

As a result, in March 1941, one official of the National Office for Economic Expansion bluntly advised Degussa against even beginning the work, "since you will get no people and, even if you do, these will have to be taken away at the first opportunity; prisoners also will have to be withdrawn in order to further more pressing building projects."[55] The firm pressed ahead anyway, despite having managed to scrape together only seventy-eight local laborers by the end of that month and only about 200 of the 500 needed by December, when the builders resolved to work straight through the winter "because in six months a review of performance will take place and a shutdown of the entire project has to be reckoned with in case of deficient progress."[56] That outcome became increasingly likely following the German reversals before Moscow, which led the regional Labor Office to start stripping local construction companies of laborers for "Eastern deployment" (*Osteinsatz*) in January 1942.[57]

Frustration and desperation on the building site thus provide the background to the sudden appearance of preparations for "accommodating 150 Polish Jews" in the surviving records of the Zentralwerk a month later.[58] Whence the idea of using these people came or how contact was established with their source, the German Ghetto Administration in Litzmannstadt (Łodz), some 200 miles to the east, remains unclear. It is certain, however, that the arrangements were authorized by von Retze in Frankfurt, who sanctioned

[52] DUA, DL 3.Baerwind/23, Fürstenberg/Oder als eventueller Standort der neuen Fabrik, December 4, 1939, pp. 3–4.

[53] DUA, TA 2/72, Notiz. Werk F, February 8, 1940.

[54] DUA, TA 2/75, Schulz's Niederschrift über die "F"-Besprechung, October 20, 1942, p. 3.

[55] *Ibid.*, Schulz's Niederschrift betr. Fürstenberg/Oder–Anlage "F," March 13, 1941, p. 5.

[56] *Ibid.*, Schulz's Niederschrift über Besprechung betr. Baustelle "F," March 25, 1941, p. 1 (on the number of workers); Niederschrift über die Besprechung ... betr. Baustelle "F," December 4, 1941, p. 1 (including for the quotation).

[57] *Ibid.*, Schulz's Niederschrift der F-Besprechung, January 13, 1942, p. 3.

[58] *Ibid.*, Niederschrift über die "F"-Besprechung, February 10, 1942, p. 1.

a contract to lease an inactive glass-making works adjacent to the building site as a means of creating immediate housing for the ghetto inmates, and that the deal, calling for their arrival on March 15, was sealed on February 19.[59] Each worker was to cost Degussa .30 RM per hour, from which the enterprise could apply 1.50 RM per day to the costs of room, board, and guards (any remainder, minus a tax payment at the unmarried person rate, was to be divided between the ghetto administration and the laborer on a ratio of 80:20). Though Degussa was relieved explicitly of furnishing sheets for the inmates, it was nominally required to make shoe and clothing repair facilities available, along with hot water, showers, and a laundry room.[60] These stipulations, along with an estimated charge of some 44,000 RM annually from the Wach- und Schliessgesellschaft of Breslau, "which had assumed the guarding of Jew-camps for the Reichsautobahnen until now," seem to have concerned the building staff at Fürstenberg. It foresaw "extraordinary final figures for additional expenses per year."[61] Moreover, Degussa was soon complaining that the work of 150 Jewish laborers, who now constituted 41 percent of the 362 personnel on site, was comparable to "at most ninety workers," especially because so many were ill.[62] Apparently to offset this deficiency, fifty more Jews arrived on April 20.[63] Here the relevant extant records abruptly trail off. They mention Jews as present only once more, on September 1, and provide no indication of their condition or the date of their departure.[64] Presumably they were still there in early October, when the installation reported an effective workforce of 665, an impossibly high number without them.[65] But they were gone without a trace by the time later in the month when eighty-eight Eastern workers and sixty-two Soviet POWs arrived, and the latter group was assigned lodgings in the glass factory where the Jews had been.[66] As at Hydrocarbon, the cause probably was the incipient purge of all remaining Jews, aside from those married to so-called Aryans, from the Reich.

The frantic remainder of the labor history of Fürstenberg is fairly typical of Degussa's in the last stage of the war and would merit little more than

---

[59] DUA, TA 2/73, Schmidt to Bauleitung Fürstenberg, Betr. Lager für polnische Juden, February 20, 1942. See also TA 2/78, Deck's Aktennotiz Betr. Fürstenberg/Mietvertrag betr. Judenlager, April 21, 1942, with von Retze's handwritten comments justifying the lease as faster and cheaper than building barracks.

[60] DUA, TA 2/78, Schulz's Aktennotiz, February 23, 1942.

[61] DUA, TA 2/73, Schmidt to Bauleitung Fürstenberg, February 20, 1942 (on the Breslau firm); TA 2/75, Schulz's Niederschrift über die "F"-Besprechung, April 1, 1942 (on the costs).

[62] DUA, TA 2/73, Degussa to Gebechem, April 14, 1942.

[63] DUA, TA 2/75, Niederschrift über die "F"-Besprechung, April 21, 1942, p. 2.

[64] *Ibid.*, Niederschrift über "F"-Sitzung, September 1, 1942, p. 2.

[65] DUA, TA 2/78, Schulz's Baustellenbegehung am 5./6. Oktober 1942 in Fürstenberg/Oder, p. 2.

[66] DUA, DOK 1/5, Wolf's Beschäftigung von Fremdarbeitern im Zweiten Weltkrieg, March 12, 1986.

22   Ewald von Retze

summary comment were it not for an illuminating altercation with the local German Labor Front (DAF) organization, which the corporation had subcontracted to manage the barracks lodgings and the provisioning of most of the German and all of the foreign laborers on the site. Until early 1944, a majority of the latter (at least 245 people at one time or another) consisted of Eastern workers or Soviet POWs, since the French construction firms Degussa tried to attract to Fürstenberg declined to come "because the local wages are too low." Therafter, at least 268 Italian military internees and civilian workers arrived, but the influx was offset by withdrawals of some 275 workers for emergency projects elsewhere.[67] By late February 1945, shortly before the evacuation of the plant, its workforce came to 450 people, 113 German men (25 percent of the total), 44 German women (10 percent), and 293 foreigners (65 percent).[68]

Long before such instability might have made Degussa skeptical about expending energy and money on motivating the workers at Fürstenberg, Ewald von Retze made clear that the enterprise intended to keep its distance from responsibility for their living conditions. As he explained in October 1942 in

[67] DUA, TA 2/75, Niederschrift über die "F"-Besprechung, October 20, 1942, p. 2 (on the French firms and for the quotation); and TA 2/87, Deneke to von Retze, March 18, 1943; Deneke to Usinger, May 5, 1944; and Deneke to Gebechem, July 21, 1944 (on the other nationalities).

[68] DUA, TA 2/79, unsigned Aktennotiz Betr. Werk Fürstenberg/Oder, February 27, 1945.

response to complaints about their food, then reiterated to Dr. Deneke, the
plant leader, during a crisis over the management of their room and board
in mid-1943:

We have worked from the beginning to avoid having to take on caring for the
[barracks] camp, but rather to push this onto an official agency, preferably the DAF.
If we had the administration in our own hands, complaints would not cease.... We
would be pressured continuously by the DAF. If it, however, manages the camp itself,
we are rid of this concern.[69]

Indeed, Retze was so determined to preserve these arrangements, which had
been threatened by the DAF's sudden – and in the sources unexplained –
decision to terminate them, that he was willing to overlook the organization's
veiled admission that it had been pocketing surpluses of 5,000 to 7,000 RM
monthly from the funds Degussa paid for food, heat, and upkeep of the
barracks.[70] By September 1943, the status quo had been restored at the
expense of the workforce, which remained undernourished despite Deneke's
illegal additions to the official monthly maximum rations. It also continued to
be so badly housed that the German assembly workers periodically stationed
at the site flatly refused to set foot in the barracks or contemplate resting on
the standard-issue, sawdust-filled sleeping bags. Fearing that their defiance
soon would force him to make an example by having someone sent to a
Work Education Camp (*Arbeitserziehungslager*) for eight to fourteen days,
Deneke pleaded with Retze to head this off by authorizing expansion of a
well-built administrative barracks and its conversion into a residential one
for the transient skilled German laborers.[71] In short: Fürstenberg was an
uncomfortable posting for Germans, let alone for foreign workers; this was
so even during 1943, the year the site was best supplied and making its most
rapid progress; and the local management's attempts to improve the situation
appear to have gotten little support from Frankfurt, where Retze was more
interested in avoiding political problems than seeing to the welfare of the
workforce.

Though almost as brief as the Zentralwerke's, the Auergesellschaft's exploitation of laborers delivered by the SS involved far more people. But it
did not result from a shortage of workers at the firm. Auer's military importance assured that its active workforce grew throughout the war (from
8,845 people in September 1941 to 10,614 in September 1944), despite the

---

[69] DUA, TA 2/78, von Retze's Notiz. Betr. Fürstenberg: Verpflegungsfrage, October 28, 1942;
and TA 2/87, von Retze to Deneke, July 12, 1943, where the quoted words appear.
[70] DUA, TQ 2/79, von Retze's Notiz. Betr. Fürstenberg/Verwaltung des Arbeiter-Lagers,
September 3, 1943; and, on the surpluses, TA 2/87, Deneke's Betr.: Gemeinschaftslager, July
13, 1943, and TA 2/79, Deck's Aktennotz. Betr.: Fürstenberg–Lagervertrag DAF, September
21, 1943.
[71] DUA, TA 2/87, Deneke to von Retze, October 7, 1943; as background, see also Deneke to
von Retze, September 7, 1943.

toll taken by military service. In the process, the enterprise received enough German women to keep its share of foreign laborers unusually low (2 percent in September 1941, 17 percent a year later, and 19 percent in September 1943).[72] The problem in early 1944 was not the number of workers from the point of view of the company but the way those present were being applied, according to a key figure in Albert Speer's Armaments Ministry, Walter Schieber. His role as deputy to Dr. Karl Brandt, whom Hitler put in charge of "all issues of chemical warfare" in March, brought Schieber into contact with Auer's production backlog and new-found reluctance, encouraged by Degussa, to accept further contracts for gas masks.[73] Incensed at both, he promptly demanded a governmental investigation of the firm's management and meanwhile appointed a special commissioner to run the relevant plants. To that post, he initially named Director Jahn of the Eschebachwerke in Radeberg, but Schieber seems eventually to have had in mind his clandestine collaborator during this attempted *Putsch*, Auer's government liaison officer, Heinrich Paetsch.[74] In preparation for their success, the two men apparently already had begun exploiting Schieber's power over the distribution of concentration camp inmates so as to stock the company with personnel who could be driven to meet his demands.

Most of Schieber's plan miscarried. By November 1944, he had lost his post in the Speer ministry, and Brandt had been dismissed. Heinrich Küppenbender, the investigator Speer named in September, had filed a report recommending various internal reforms and accelerating the process by which Degussa now completed the scheduled retirement of Robert Vorbau as plant manager and his replacement by Friedrich Zürcher. And both Schlosser and Quasebart, the respective leaders of the parent company and the subsidiary, had seen through Paetsch's role in the entire affair and decided to dismiss him at the conclusion of his current contract toward the end of 1945.[75] But there seems to have been no question at Auer or Degussa of not

---

[72] DUA, IW 24.5/5, Berichte des Vorstandes für die Geschäftsjahre 1940/41, January 27, 1942, p. 2, and 1941/42, February 22, 1943, pp. 1–2; and IW 24.9/1, Bericht des Vorstandes für das Geschäftsjahr 1942/43, April 5, 1944, p. 2.

[73] On Schieber's role in Brandt's assignment, see BAL, R 3/1932, Bl. 150, an organizational table for Brandt's office. For a good account of Schieber's actions in the following months, see Bernhard Lorentz, *Industrieelite und Wirtschaftspolitik 1928–1950* (Paderborn: Schöningh, 2001), pp. 284–95 and 309–35, though our interpretations differ at minor points. On Degussa's refusal to provide funds to meet the goals of the Brandt program and support for a plan to form a government-dominated gas mask firm, see IW 24.5/3, unheaded and unsigned report of the meeting of Auer's supervisory board, April 22, 1944, and Schlosser's Auergesellschaft, July 29, 1944.

[74] See DUA, DL 3.H.Schlosser/1, Dok. 997, Auergesellschaft Berlin, August 30, 1944; and IW 24.6/1, Kolb to Schlosser, September 21, 1944.

[75] On the settlement of the crisis, see DUA, IW 24.6/1, Kolb to Schlosser, September 29, 1944, reply of October 4, 1944, and Kolb's response of the same date; DL 3.H.Schlosser, Auergesellschaft, October 14, 1944; IW 24.6/1, Aktennotiz über eine Besprechung im Büro des

using the roughly 2,000 female inmates received from the Ravensbrück concentration camp from July 1944 on.[76] By October, they already had helped bring about increases by one- to two-thirds in the firm's output of military and civilian gas masks, filters, uniforms, and cots since the preceding May.[77] Surprisingly few, if any, of these inmates were Jews. Rather, like most of Ravensbrück's denizens in the final phase of the war, they consisted largely of Eastern Europeans.[78] Virtually all records concerning them or their time at Auer, however, appear to have been destroyed just before or after Soviet troops arrived in 1945, either by the enormous American air raids that leveled Oranienburg in mid-March or by the actions of German or Russian officials. Reasonably certain is that Auer paid the camp four Reichsmarks per laborer per day, minus a charge for the inadequate rations; that the women worked twelve-hour shifts at least six days per week; and that at least thirty of them died on the site and some 247 in the air raids before they were taken away on aimless death marches as the Soviet armies closed in.[79]

If the use of inmate labor was brief at Fürstenberg and not entirely the Auergesellschaft's own doing at Oranienburg and Guben, neither of these mildly extenuating circumstances applies to the history of the Deutsche Gasrusswerke factory in Gleiwitz that Degussa assumed responsibility to build and equip after the site was chosen at the end of 1940. To be sure, the initial allocation of Jewish prisoners to the site, which occurred in April 1942 and consisted of some 200 men from Annaberg and other forced labor camps in Upper Silesia, apparently was not Degussa's idea.[80] Throughout

Herrn Werner, November 22, 1944, and that man's Bericht über die Untersuchungen bei der Firma Auergesellschaft A.-G., November 29, 1944; and Scherf's Niederschrift über eine Besprechung in Wächtersbach, November 30, 1944.

[76] On the numbers of inmates sent to Auer, see the reference to "1700 female inmates" at Oranienburg in DUA, DL 3.H.Schlosser/1, Quasebart to Schlosser, February 17, 1945. The records at Ravensbrück establish that the first transports from there to the "Auer-Werke Oranienburg," occurred in the summer of 1944 (e.g., RA IV, Nr. 11a, Sign. 22, Liste der 5. Überstellung, July 20, 1944), and that the number of women provided quickly reached 900 to 1,200 (RA Bd. 22, Bericht 211, Affidavit by Fritz Suhren, Commandant at Ravensbrück from 1942 to 1945, June 17, 1946) and then 1,500 (RA Bd. 11, Witness Report of Renée Duchaille, January 13, 1959). The arrival of probably another 300 such workers at Guben may be inferred from the authorization to construct two new barracks conveyed in IW 24.5/5, exchange of letters between Quasebart and Schlosser, September 11 and 16, 1944.

[77] Calculated from the graph enclosed with DUA, IW 24.6/1, Quasebart to Schieber, November 13, 1944.

[78] See Jack G. Morrison, *Ravensbrück: Everyday Life in a Women's Concentration Camp* (Princeton: Marcus Wiener Publishers, 2000), pp. 70–71 and 86–87.

[79] On the wages and deaths, RA Bd. 11, Berichte 67a, 538, and 610, and the account concerning Auer's competitor, the Drägerwerk, in Lorentz, *Industrieelite und Wirtschaftspolitik*, pp. 329–30.

[80] The arrival of the Jews at Gleiwitz is recorded in DUA, PCA 2/4, Ziegler's memo of April 21, 1942.

1941, the firm planned on constructing the plant with some 300 laborers, roughly 200 of them foreigners, and by September, three months after the ground breaking, a workforce of 280 men had been arduously pulled together. The non-Germans came primarily from Bulgaria and Italy, received the prevailing local wages for Germans of the same skill classifications, and were housed temporarily nearby in a well-outfitted former camp of the National Labor Service (Arbeitsdienst) pending the completion of on-site barracks.[81]

But the ever impatient Johannes Eckell was unimpressed. Having angrily pronounced in July that "no other building project . . . is going so wrong," he insisted at the end of the year on a tripling of Gleiwitz's workforce during the following spring, not least because he had just forced through an increase in the originally planned production capacity by 133 percent.[82] To this end, his aides told Degussa's architect that "it is unavoidable that Russian prisoners of war also be used on the project," and countered his fears of possible sabotage with reassurances "concerning the quality of this human material." Degussa's man reluctantly gave in, concluding that "we therefore will have no choice but to cover a portion of the labor requirements with Russians."[83] By late January 1942, however, Soviet POWs no longer were sufficiently available to reach Eckell's target of 900 workers. Accordingly, at a meeting he attended in Gleiwitz, along with nine additional government officials, architect Ziegler and one other Degussa representative, Georg Kemnitz of DGW, and Robert Pross, the man already destined to take over the plant in July, "the use of Jews was suggested and accepted in principle by the building supervisors."[84] Though such phrasing is purposefully vague, both

---

[81] On the projected workforce, see DUA, PCA 2/3, Nagel's Besuch bei den Borsig-Kokswerken in Oberschlesien, December 12, 1940, p. 3, which also sets the average wages at fifty to sixty pfennigs per hour; Herrmann's Bericht über die Verhandlungen in Gleiwitz, Kattowitz und Breslau, March 17, 1941, p. 4; Ziegler's Notiz betreffend Russwerke Dortmund G.m.b.H., Werk Gleiwitz, Barackenlager, March 25, 1941, p. 2. On the accommodations, PCA 2/4, Ziegler's Deutsche Gasrusswerke . . . Notiz über die Besprechung beim Stadtbauamt, May 21, 1941; and Mühlschwein's Notiz Betrifft: R.-OS., Werk Gleiwtiz, August 21, 1941. That the minimum wage for Italian workers was sixty-seven pfennigs per hour is established in PCA 2/4, Mühlschwein's Notiz Betreffend: R.-OS. Werk Gleiwitz. Einsatz ital. Arbeitskräfte, July 21, 1941. On the workforce in September, PCA 2/4, DGW Bauleitung to Arbeitsamt Gleiwitz, September 2, 1941; Mühlschwein's Notiz. Betrifft: R.-OS., Werk Gleiwitz, Arbeitereinsatz, September 10, 1941; and Ziegler's Notiz . . . über meinen Besuch in Gleiwitz, September 20, 1941.

[82] DUA, PCA 2/4, Ziegler's Betrifft: Deutsche Gasrusswerke G.m.b.H., Werk Gleiwitz, July 7, 1941, for the quotation.

[83] *Ibid.*, Ziegler's Betrifft: Deutsche Gassrusswerke G.m.b.H., Werk Gleiwitz, December 7, 1941.

[84] *Ibid.*, Pross's Besprechung über Material- und Arbeitseinsatzfragen in Gleiwitz am 27. January 1942, undated.

it and Eckell's zeal regarding the factory imply that the management was on the receiving end of the idea.

Be that as it may, at almost exactly the same time as the Zentralwerk contracted with the Lodz ghetto for Jews, the Degussa/DGW carbon black factory at Gleiwitz thus embarked on what became a three-year-long, ever expanding, and highly ambiguous linkage to the Holocaust. For it turned out that the 200 Jewish construction workers constituted only the first wave of a widening flow of inmates to the site. Moreover, in this case, the sources clearly indicate that, on the one hand, numerous people were killed while or as a result of working there and the plant came to operate hand in glove with the SS, but that, on the other hand, the prevailing conditions for the victims of this process were somewhat better than at many nearby installations, among them the infamous Monowitz works of IG Farben, only twenty-five miles to the southeast.[85]

One survivor of the first shipment of Jews recalls that "the food was catastrophic," the clothing insufficient during winter, the footwear made of wood, and the labor both hard – largely because it consisted of excavating deep foundations for a subcontractor (the Allgemeine Hochkonstruktions-Ingenieure firm of Düsseldorf) with only shovels – and, on occasion, murderous.[86] In addition, the housing appears to have been overcrowded during most of 1942 (as it would be again later) and sometimes flimsy, since barracks were delivered slowly and partially recycled from other building sites.[87] By the time Coen Rood, a Dutch Jewish tailor who also managed to outlive the factory, arrived in November, only the accommodations, which included showers and adequate toilet and washing facilities, had improved. They were still lice infested, however, and the rations consisted of pumpkin and cabbage soup, along with bread adulterated with sawdust. Put to work without gloves moving ice-cold iron and steel containers, Rood soon had reason to

[85] Regarding the dreadful course of events at Monowitz (on whose disputed origins, incidentally, the early history of DGW's plant at Gleiwitz casts much light), see Peter Hayes, *Industry and Ideology: IG Farben in the Nazi Era* (New York: Cambridge University Press, 2001), pp. xii–xv and 348–68, and the excellent work of Bernd C. Wagner, *IG Auschwitz: Zwangsarbeit und Vernichtung von Häftlingen des Lagers Monowitz 1941–1945* (Munich: K. G. Saur, 2000).

[86] Interview with Martin Sojka, Frankfurt, October 22, 1998.

[87] By the end of 1942, there were twenty-four structures in the barracks camp, twelve residential, each built for 100 people, and twelve ancillary structures for supplies, washing, and toilets. On this and the repeated delays in obtaining them, see DUA, BET 9/48, Jahresbericht 1942 über den Aufbau Werk Gleiwitz, undated [after April 27, 1943), p. 2, as well as PCA 2/3, Ziegler's Notiz betreffend... Barackenlager, March 25, 1941 (which reports the cost of the first three residential and first five support barracks as 131,490 RM); PCA 2/4, Ziegler's Notiz über die Besprechung mit der Abteilung Rüstungsausbau, April 21, 1942, pp. 2–3; his Notiz über mein Besuch beim Reichsamt für Wirschaftsausbau, May 18, 1942; and his Besprechung mit Herrn Direktor Pross, July 31, 1942.

discover that the infirmary possessed only the most basic of medicines and bandages and that bartering whatever he could for extra food would be indispensable to survival. By the end of January 1943, eight of the men who had accompanied him from Holland were dead, two from beatings; a month later, six others were among the twenty-two men in the infirmary who were taken away in a truck, supposedly for work elsewhere.[88] Altogether, at least 246 Jews arrived at the Gleiwitz factory camp in 1942, and the number may have gone as high as 400; only 166 remained on February 26, 1943.[89] In the factory management's records, one finds but faint echoes of this reality, as when Pross remarked in his annual report for 1942 that, "special concern was directed at . . . the implementation of effective means to call lazy foreigners or those who have fled to account. The educational effect of the methods applied has resulted in a notable decline in loafing."[90]

Although DGW's managers clearly viewed their foreign and especially their first round of Jewish laborers as a handicap to be overcome, the firm initially shirked responsibility for the conditions that helped make such people relatively unproductive.[91] In keeping with von Retze's general line, Degussa apparently made arrangements at one time or another in 1941–43 with the Todt Organization, the National Labor Service, and the German

[88] Coen Rood, *"Wenn ich es nicht erzählen kann, muss ich weinen": Als Zwangsarbeiter in der Rüstungsindustrie* (Frankfurt am Main: Fischer Taschenbuch Verlag, 2002), pp. 46–70. Rood wrote down his recollections in 1945–49, but they have been considerably edited and shortened for publication. His memory concerning the clearing of the infirmary seems corroborated by Robert Pross's handwritten contemporary record of the camp population from February 5, 1943, to March 1, 1944, which notes that the number of Jews on site dropped from 196 to 166 between February 19 and 26, 1943, that is, at roughly the time Rood remembers the infirmary being emptied; see DUA, BU Robert Pross, Russ-Tagebuch, final, unnumbered pages [June 10, 1938, to January 10, 1945].

[89] On the final count, *ibid.* Two hundred forty-six is the sum of the 200 initially reported and forty-six Dutch Jews accounted for by Rood (eight dead, six sent from the infirmary, and thirty-two still present in March 1943), but Rood's is not likely to have been the only group of Jews to reach Gleiwitz during these months, especially since the workforce totals given in DGW's Monatsberichte for the latter half of 1942 do not disaggregate the category of "foreigners" while rising by some 300. The supposition draws some strength from the comment of an official in the Breslau branch of the Department for Armaments Expansion to Degussa's architect that "skilled workers cannot be provided, just 300 to 400 Jews, who are to be used as unskilled workers"; PCA 2/4, Ziegler's Notiz über die Besprechungen am 25.3.42, March 29, 1942, pp. 1–2.

[90] DUA, BET 9/48, Jahresbericht 1942 über den Aufbau Werk Gleiwitz, undated [after April 27, 1943] p. 2.

[91] For a litany of complaints about the "underperformance of the foreign workers," which climax with the condescending remark that "concerning the performance of the Jews we wish to refrain from reporting here," see DUA, PCA 2/1, Monatsbericht Nr. 18 für September 1942, October 21, 1942. Also Ziegler's comment that "unfortunately the representatives of foreign nations on our building site are not acquainted with the German concept of a daily work quota"; BET 9/48, Monatsbericht Nr. 16, August 26, 1942.

Labor Front to supervise the workers' room and board, oversee their labor, and guard the barracks in return for monthly and/or daily fees.[92] The executives then left the matter at that, even though they suspected or knew that the deals provided considerable room for chicanery, especially with regard to food purchasing. Moreover, at the end of October 1942, DGW's leaders acquired still another reason not to expend any thought on improving the Jewish prisoners' situation. According to Ziegler's summary of his and Pross's conversations with officials of the Armaments Ministry branch in Breslau,

> at the moment a transfer of Western [European] Jews to the East is in process. Among them are quite useable skilled workers, who can achieve even better performance with further, intensive direction. Before the allocation of these Jews, however, the present Eastern Jew camp is to be dissolved. Since we already have been contemplating giving the Eastern Jews back soon, this exchange corresponds closely to our way of thinking and fits into our plan. It was therefore agreed that DGW in combination with the local building office immediately will make the labor requirements known to the Department for Armaments Expansion in Breslau.... Director Pross already has telegraphed this information to Gleiwitz, Dr. Shenk, and given instructions that the necessary steps are to be taken immediately.[93]

Having been maneuvered into including Jews among their workers only seven months before, DGW's leaders no longer needed coaxing. Despite having a workforce on the site during the last quarter of 1942 that averaged 1,343 people (310 *more* than the need projected during the preceding April), they now jumped at the chance to obtain additional such unfortunates, while dispensing with the ones who had been worn down in the interim.[94]

The anticipated exchange took place in March 1943 and brought a second, augmented round of Jewish deportations to the Gleiwitz factory camp, but not according to the plan formulated in October 1942. Most of the 130 Jews shipped out were Western Europeans, of whom only 32 Dutch seemed

---

[92] On the initial arrangements with the DAF for foreign workers, see DUA, PCA 2/3, Herrmann's Bericht über Verhandlungen in Gleiwitz, Kattowitz und Breslau, March 17, 1941, pp. 7–8; but I have found no document recording subsequent agreements. Survivors recall being guarded in 1942–43 by men in a succession of uniforms, first brown, then blue, then green.

[93] DUA, PCA 2/4, Ziegler's Notiz über den Besuch bei der Abteilung Rüstungs-ausbau... Aussenstelle Breslau, November 2, 1942.

[94] See PCA 2/4, Ziegler's Notiz über die Besprechung mit der Abteilung Rüstungsausbau, April 21, 1942, which projects the labor need at 1,034 people; and, on the labor force in September to December 1942, BET 9/48, Pross and Dreske's Verwaltungsbericht und Personalstandsmeldung, October 1, 1942 (1,367 on site), and Monatsbericht Nr. 19, November 1, 1942 (1,329); and PCA 2/1, Personalstandsmeldung zum 31. Dezember 1942 (1,334). That Eckell had obtained another increase in the eventual capacity (this time from 14,000 to 17,000 annual tons) in May does not alter the fact that there was no longer a labor shortage on the site.

to have remained. Their replacements, whose number provided for "a considerable expansion of the Jewish labor force," consisted almost entirely of Yiddish speakers from Eastern Upper Silesia, many from the last ghetto liquidated there in Sosnowitz.[95] Gleiwitz now received 379 workers, at least 330 but probably almost all of them Jews, in return for 335 laborers transferred away, primarily to armaments projects.[96] A month later, 209 foreign women, almost certainly all of them Jews also from Eastern Upper Silesia, appeared on the plant's roster. There the total number of Jews at the end of the month came to 535, 46 percent of the 1,152 foreign personnel and 38 percent of the total workforce, including Germans, of 1,393.[97] In preparation for these changes, the inmate labor camp was extended to include several of the barracks formerly for foreign workers and a twelve-foot-high barbed wire fence erected both around the compound and between the sectors henceforth reserved for men and women.[98]

Robert Pross later maintained that the Gleiwitz Labor Office suggested the use of Jewish women, but affirmed nonetheless that "the responsibility for this decision lay on my shoulders alone."[99] There is no reason to doubt him on either count. His retrospective version of the rationale for his actions is surely incomplete, however. Given the consideration that he (and his secretary) later demonstrated for the workforce, it may be true that he "saw...the possibility...of perhaps saving these people from worse," but his overriding thought at the time was assuredly more practical.[100] As he wrote shortly after the first section of the plant commenced producing at the end of April 1943, "Only because of the success in obtaining female Jewish forced laborers through the good offices of the Plenipotentiary for Building was the chief prerequisite for the start-up even present."[101] Not yet forty years old, Pross was both under enormous pressure to reach the spiraling production targets at Gleiwitz and conscious of the potential rewards of doing so (in 1944, as the second part of the plant was being finished, he received

[95] On the number transferred out, see DUA, PCA 2/1, Monatsbericht Nr. 24 für März 1943, April 12, 1943; on those remaining and their replacements, Rood, "*Wenn ich nicht erzählen kann,*" p. 75. For the quotation, DUA, BET 9/43, Protokoll über die Arbeitsausschuss-Sitzung der Deutschen Gasrusswerke GmbH am 4. März 1943, p. 4.
[96] DUA, PCA 2/1, Monatsbericht Nr. 24 für März 1943, April 12, 1943.
[97] *Ibid.*, Personenstandsmeldung zum 30. April 1943, May 6, 1943; and BU Robert Pross, Russ-Tagebuch, entry for 30.4.43.
[98] Rood, "*Wenn ich nicht erzählen kann,*" p. 74.
[99] On the role of the Labor Office, DUA, PRO 01/0012, Pross's Erinnerungen an die Zeit meiner Tätigkeit bei den DGW Gleiwitz 1941–1945, July 25, 1963, p. 1; and BU Robert Pross, Betr. DGW – Werk Gleiwitz–Einsatz von Häftlingen, January 23, 1996. For the quotation, see the latter document, p. 2.
[100] *Ibid.*, for the quotation. On his kindness and that of his secretary, Fräulein Mittas, see Rood, "*Wenn ich nicht erzählen kann,*" pp. 84–85 (where his name is remembered erroneously as Prost and hers as Marx) and 115.
[101] PCA 2/2, Betriebsbericht Nr. 1 für Mai 1943, June 5, 1943, p. 6.

the War Service Cross, First Class).[102] His reputation as a "vertical starter" within the Degussa concern was at stake, and he could only benefit from his colleagues' appreciation of "what it means to the plant leaders to start a factory with a workforce that consists, aside from a few German craftsmen and foremen, exclusively of Polish Jewesses."[103] In this context, and since he already had acquiesced without recorded comment in the decision more than a year earlier to use Jewish male laborers on building the plant, the idea of rescuing Jewish women through putting them into the production line probably functioned, if it occurred to him at the time, more as a rationalization than a reason for his decision.

Whatever the mix of Pross's motives, the cost of Jewish labor is unlikely to have been one of them. He took Jewish women because they were the only workers he could get, not because they came cheap. On the contrary, DGW's leaders always listed their dependence on low-performing foreign or forced labor as an – admittedly convenient – part of the explanation for the "excess expense" of building at Gleiwitz. And experience during the first year, as recorded in the Profit and Loss Statement for 1943, largely bore them out. This document, the only surviving one that throws appreciable light on the overall and relative charges incurred for forced labor at Gleiwitz, includes statistics covering the nonsalaried workforce during that calendar year, when the average number of non-Jews actually working on the site came to 611 and the average total of Jews to 480, as well as data for the month of December in particular.[104] The comprehensive figures show that during 1943, the non-Jewish workforce received 716,205 RM including an annual supplement, and that 117,574 RM went to subcontractors' presumably non-Jewish laborers, for a total of 833,779 RM. For the Jews, DGW paid 584,159 RM, plus a charge for management of their barracks of 124,878 RM, which yields a sum of 709,037 RM.[105] It appears, then, that the non-Jews, who made up on average 56 percent of the wage force, received 54 percent of the firm's disbursements for labor, but the Jews who constituted on average 44 percent of the workers cost DGW 46 percent of the bill. If one takes into

[102] See DUA, BU Unterlagen Robert Pross, which gives his birthday as June 27, 1906 and contains a copy of the award of the medal, dated September 1, 1944. See also his Russ-Tagebuch, p. 64, where the entry for November 4, 1944 reads, "Honored by the workforce on the occasion of the award of the KVKI."

[103] This is the stunningly self-absorbed comment of Ernst Baerwind; DL 3.Baerwind/26, Besuch im Werk Gleiwitz der DGW, April 21, 1943, p. 2.

[104] For the labor force figures, see DUA, PCA 2/1, Monatsbericht für Januar 1943, February 11, 1943, and BU Unterlagen Robert Pross, Russ-Tagebuch, workforce entries for February 5, 1943, to January 1, 1944. All such figures in this and subsequent paragraphs exclude workers absent for any reason or ill (and the figures for January 1943 have been estimated accordingly).

[105] DUA, PCA 2/2, Gewinn- und Verlustrechnung, Deutsche Gasrusswerke GmbH, Gleiwitz, December 31, 1943.

consideration the 66,480 RM expended during the year on "legally required and other voluntary social welfare contributions," which went exclusively to non-Jews, the percentages come almost into alignment. Thus, the per capita costs of workers from Degussa's point of view work out for 1943 to 113.67 RM per month for non-Jews without benefits and 122.73 RM with benefits and, rather astoundingly, 123.20 RM for Jews.[106] From the company's perspective, this amounted to a theoretical relative *disadvantage* of using Jewish forced labor for two reasons: (a) the productivity difference, since Jewish men, in particular, were generally thought to contribute less work product per hour than non-Jews, even foreigners (and were, of course, worked and fed in such a way that this was likely to be so); and (b) the gender gap, since the non-Jewish labor force was almost universally male, while the Jewish one was about 40 percent female, which meant that the base wages for each group were not comparable, that is, if non-Jewish women had been available, they might have been less expensive than Jewish ones.

Upon closer examination, however, this startling pattern turns out to be characteristic only of the construction phase at Gleiwitz, when the prevailing wages of civilian unskilled building workers, German and foreign, were relatively close to those that the SS demanded of companies for Jews (generally 3 to 6 RM per day, depending on sex and skill level, minus allowances for food and housing). In February, construction workers constituted 82 percent of all workers on the site; by June, the figure was 47 percent, and in December it came to only 41 percent. As the share of skilled workers bulked larger among the Germans (and the non-Jewish foreigners), their average hourly wage diverged increasingly from the costs of each Jewish forced laborer. The trend was reinforced by the gradual and related increase of the share of women among the Jews during the year. Thus, by December, when non-Jews barely outnumbered Jews on the Gleiwitz site on average (468 to 463), the relative shares of the outlays for wages, benefits, and barracks were 65 percent and 35 percent, the relative monthly costs per capita 192 RM to 104 RM, and the relative daily ones 6.86 RM to 3.71 RM. On an hourly basis, the discrepancy stood out still more sharply: whereas the cost to the company of non-Jews, including benefits, averaged out to between .80 and .86 RM per hour in December 1943 (it is not clear whether they were working sixty- or fifty-six-hour weeks at this point), that for Jewish men came to only .33 RM per hour, given their twelve-hour workdays, and that for Jewish women was only slightly higher at .38 RM per hour, despite the fact

---

[106] DGW's Profit and Loss Statement for 1943 also includes a reference to an additional amount of 119,904 RM paid out in "manufacturing wages," but there is no telling how these were divided. The line entry for "Jews' wages" includes the notation "without manufacturing wages," an addition that would be superfluous if they were excluded altogether from them. In view of the uncertainty about the allocation, I have left this category of compensation out of my calculations here.

that their shifts on the production lines were limited to eight hours.[107] In other words, the purely financial benefit of Jewish labor to DGW emerged only as the plant matured.

Of course, arithmetic of this sort is uncertain and cold, and it ought not divert attention from the ghastly realities of inmate labor, including the fact that its victims saw none of the income, which went partially to those who confined and underfed them and primarily to the SS and thus ultimately the Reich Treasury. But such statistical analysis does highlight the inaccuracy, at least in this instance, of two aspects of popular opinion concerning "slave" labor, namely that its attraction was its cheapness, and that its cheapness made German employers spendthrift regarding it. For the factory managers at Gleiwitz, the use of inmate labor was not at the outset a considered decision based on or buttressed by cost calculations; it was an act of selfish and desperate improvisation, a reflex response to the desire "to do what had to be done," as American usage would put the matter today, in a context that afforded few other means to that end. Moreover, and ironically, this sort of idealized egocentrism also had much to do with a perceptible shift in the Gleiwitz management's attitude toward the installation's Jews during 1944. Though they had not been sought after because they were cheap (indeed, the fact that they were not may have prompted resentment that strengthened DGW's indifference to their plight in 1942–43), the fact that they obviously were becoming so enhanced their value to the firm.

Robert Pross, in particular, appears to have grown increasingly attentive to the ways that the administration of the inmate labor camp on the factory grounds undermined his own efforts to complete and operate it. In November 1943, "100 Jews had to be given up in the construction sector," allegedly owing to a lack of guards, and there were other signs of increasing mismanagement by the DAF.[108] Survivors report a decline in the already poor quality of the food around the turn of the year and, consequently, a mounting incidence of illness and the trucking away of inmates from the infirmary to Auschwitz. Pross later attested that his growing suspicion that "much was going into the wrong channels" prompted him to remonstrate with the relevant officials.[109] In mid-January 1944, Gauleiter Bracht of Upper Silesia, Colonel Hueter of the regional Armaments Inspection Office, and two officials of the DAF visited the factory and held a discussion with Pross "of all the difficulties concerning personnel, especially the longer stay of the Jewesses," which had been threatened by a short-lived general order

---

[107] On the length of the women's workday, interview with Manya Friedman and Helen Luksenberrg, August 14, 1998; and DUA, DOK 1/05, Sándorné Orosz and Judit Varga to Direktion der Deutschen Gasrusswerke GmbH, November 7, 1990.

[108] DUA, PCA 2/2, Betriebsbericht Nr. 7 für November 1943, December 9, 1943, p. 8.

[109] Rood, "*Wenn ich nicht erzählen kann*," p. 84; DUA, PRO 01/0012, Pross's Erinnerungen an die Zeit meiner Tätigkeit bei den DGW Gleiwitz 1941–1945, July 25, 1963, p. 1.

for the removal of Jews from the region toward the end of the preceding year.[110] With his works only half complete, and Jews composing 44 percent of his total personnel and just over 50 percent of his effective workforce at the time, Pross no doubt underlined the importance of their labor – and of ensuring that they, in fact, could perform it. Whether humanity played as large a role as pragmatism in his stance is impossible to say on the basis of the records that have come to light.

Either way, Pross's dependence on Jewish labor provides an explanation for the pleasure with which he greeted the sudden takeover of DGW's factory camp by the SS on May 3, 1944, and its incorporation into Auschwitz's network of branches.[111] The extant sources contain no indication that he sought this development; he claimed later that "one day we were surprised by the announcement"; and it occurred amid a general extension of the Auschwitz subcamp system in early 1944 and a sharp increase in the number of forced laborers at the neighboring Borsig Kokswerke, part of the Schering concern, who were also housed in DGW's barracks.[112] Yet one cannot exclude the possibility that Pross's dissatisfaction with the previous operation of the labor camp in some way helped precipitate the changeover. It was surely welcome to him, providing a virtual guarantee of the supply of inmates to the site. And, hard as this is to credit in retrospect, the transfer of authority seemed to promise an amelioration of conditions for the workers. Along with the "considerably reinforced guard force (Waffen-SS)" and the electric fences that the SS ordered erected around the prisoners' compound and the factory grounds came at first, even survivors attest, much better food, clothing, and bedding and much greater attention to the cleanliness of the barracks. The improved diet reflected, in part, DGW's agreement with the SS to assume direct responsibility for provisioning the inmates, which led to an immediate increase in the firm's budget for that purpose by 10,000 RM.[113] There were,

---

[110] DUA, PCA 2/2, Betriebsbericht Nr. 9 für January 1944, February 5, 1944; on the short-lived directive, BET 9/50, Kemnitz to Baerwind, December 9, 1943, which concluded that, despite the reversal of the order, "I hardly believe that we can count on the possibility of being able to keep the Jewish workers for very long." For background to the directive, which apparently coincided with the "clearing" of the last Upper Silesian ghettoes, see Sybille Steinbacher, *"Musterstadt" Auschwitz: Germanisierungspolitik und Judenmord in Ostoberschlesien* (Munich: K. G. Saur, 2000).

[111] For the date of the takeover, DUA, Geschichte Werke, Bescheinigung (Zur Vorlage beim Wirtschaftsamt), signed by SS-Hauptsturmführer Schwarz, May 15, 1943.

[112] For the quotation, DUA, PRO 01/0012, Pross's Erinnerungen . . . Gleiwitz 1941–1945, July 25, 1963, p. 2. On the sequence of subcamp foundings or takeovers by the Auschwitz administration in early 1944, see Aleksander Lasik, Franciszek Piper, Piotr Setkiewicz, and Irena Strzelecka, *Auschwitz 1940–1945*, vol. I (Oświęcim: Auschwitz-Birkenau State Museum, 2000), pp. 122–26.

[113] DUA, PCA 2/2, unsigned and undated Kommentar zur Zwischenbilanz des Werkes Gleiwitz per 31.5.1944; and, for the quotation, Betriebsbericht Nr. 13 für Mai 1944, June 5, 1944. On the building of the fence and the initial improvement of conditions, Rood, *"Wenn ich*

however, ominous signs: the prompt tattooing of the prisoners and shaving of their heads, the requirements that they put on striped inmate uniforms and attach stars of David to the jackets and legs, and the suicide of two terrified women, whose memory of previous encounters with the SS drove them to despair.[114] But these events did not dent the near euphoria of DGW's managers. They were so delighted with the new situation that they reported at the beginning of June 1944, a day before Auschwitz Commandant Rudolf Höss paid them a visit, "we are striving little by little to replace the foreigners entirely with Jewish inmates."[115] Indeed, already by the end of that month, the number of Jews working on the site had risen to 724 from 506 when the SS took over, their proportion from 50 percent to 67 percent. And both figures kept climbing: the raw number peaked in November 1944 at 813, the percentage a month later at 76 percent.[116]

Pross thus secured his flow of labor, but at a troubling human cost. That does not appear to have been his chief preoccupation amid the excitement of completing the plant, bringing it into full operation, and beginning to turn a regular, indeed widening, operating profit – all of which occurred in October 1944.[117] But neither could the worsening treatment of the prisoners by the SS altogether escape his attention. Nor could what awaited them at Auschwitz, with which DGW's intensified relationship pulled Pross into direct contact. He went at least twice in the second half of 1944 to choose laborers from the concentration camp, and he learned either there and then or by other means at roughly the same time of the mass murder being perpetrated.[118] Closer to home, he admitted later to having known of the increasingly wanton and debilitating cruelty meted out toward the male laborers and the petty restrictions that harassed the female ones – even though, as survivors confirm, he and his managerial colleagues never entered the barracks and appeared in the compound but rarely and then under escort – and claimed to have

---

nicht erzählen kann," pp. 86–89 and 98–99, and interview with Manya Friedman and William (Wolf) and Helen Luksenberrg, August 14, 1998.

[114] Ibid., pp. 86–91. Rood recalls one suicide (p. 88) and Pross two (his accounts of 1963 and 1996), but they agree on the means: jumping out of a high window in the packaging building of the factory. Lasik et al., Auschwitz 1940–1945, vol. I, p. 125, report two deaths.

[115] DUA, PCA 2/2, Betriebsbericht Nr. 13 für Mai 1944, June 5, 1944, signed by Pross and Dreske.

[116] Ibid., Betriebsberichte Nr. 13–14, 19–20, June 5, July 5, and December 5, 1944, and January 5, 1945.

[117] DUA, PCA 2/2, Betriebsbericht Nr. 18 für Oktober 1944, November 4, 1944, and Pross's Betr. Entwurf zum Jahresbericht Gleiwitz 1944, techn. Teil, December 14, 1945, and the attached graph showing Produktion u. Gestehungskosten in Gleiwitz 1944.

[118] See the statement of Pross's daughter Brigitte Axster reporting her father's admission of the visits in her afterword to Rood, "Wenn ich nicht erzählen kann," pp. 213–14. On his knowledge in 1944, see DUA, BU Robert Pross, his Betr. DGW – Werk Gleiwitz – Einsatz von Häftlingen, January 23, 1996, p. 5.

interceded to change things.[119] Given the workers' importance to him, his contention is plausible that he took the opportunities of visits to Auschwitz to argue for the replacement of successive camp commanders whose brutality cut into the workers' productivity. The story is not, however, corroborated by his admittedly sketchy diary for 1944, and, if it happened, the first change of leadership in September backfired. SS-Oberscharführer Bernhard Becker's successor, a beast of the same rank named Konrad Friedrichsen, tormented the laborers with after-hours calisthenics and savage beatings for trivial infractions, which he forced inmates to witness during extended evening roll calls.[120] By the time he was relieved of command in January 1945, he had taken a terrible toll, even though most of his murders were delayed – that is, they occurred via the now weekly pick-ups from the infirmary and as a result of the pain he ordained more often than in plain view on the DGW site.

Although the surviving statistics provide no sure basis for calculating the mortality rate among workers at Gleiwitz, it clearly differed pronouncedly between women and men. Virtually none of the females, who worked indoors in eight-hour shifts manipulating important machinery and packing the carbon black, died between 1943 and the evacuation of the plant in January 1945. This is not to say that they were treated well; survivors recall being constantly terrified, cold, hungry, and plagued by skin sores resulting from vitamin deficiency, hence by the constant threat of infection owing to the omnipresent soot and the absence of medicines.[121] Attrition among the men, most of whom performed interchangeable tasks outdoors on the building site, was another matter, however. A rough and conservative estimate, and it is no more than that, would be that at least 300 of them died at Gleiwitz or shortly after being carted away from it between 1942 to 1945, not counting those who were "exchanged" in early 1943 and "given up" later in the year (about 230 individuals).[122] Something more than relatively advantageous working assignments seems necessary to account for such divergent fates. It appears that the plant management at Gleiwitz recognized the difference between expendable workers, for whom it would take few risks in dealing

---

[119] Interview with Manya Friedman and William (Wolf) and Helen Luksenberrg, August 14, 1998; DUA, PRO 01/0012, Pross's *Erinnerungen.* . . . , July 4, 1963, especially 4–5.

[120] *Ibid.*, especially p. 6; and his *Notiz betr.* . . . Besuch von Mr. Coen Rood, May 3, 1999; Rood, "*Wenn ich nicht erzählen kann,*" pp. 103–06, 113, and 115 (where he gives the Camp Commanders' names as Friedrichs and Backer and also notes that rations improved unaccountably in the fall of 1944); and Lasik et al., *Auschwitz 1940–1945*, vol. I, p. 125.

[121] Interview with Manya Friedman and Helen Luksenberrg, August 14, 1998.

[122] If at least as many construction workers died on average per month at the Gleiwitz site after April 1943 as before, the minimum toll was between 240 and 300, but considering the worsening conditions in the Lager as the war went on, and the more brutal discipline after the SS took the barracks over in May 1944, it was in all probability higher. Rood also notes that the SS shot the last remaining eight men in the camp as it was being evacuated; Rood, "*Wenn ich nicht erzählen kann,*" p. 120.

with the DAF or SS, and nonexpendable ones. Willing usually to turn a blind eye to malnutrition, illness, and murder on the construction site, the plant's leaders tried to prevent the wasting away and culling out of the more valuable female workers. This attitude may have been fortified by what women survivors experienced as almost chivalrous behavior toward them by senior managers on certain occasions, as, for example, during one tour of the facility by visiting dignitaries, when an executive even held a door open for the Jewish forewoman of a work shift, who was accompanying the group to explain the operations being observed.[123]

Both the criminality of the Nazi forced labor system and the complicity of firms such as Degussa and DGW that made use of involuntary, under- or unpaid laborers are reprehensible facts regardless of whether anyone made money on the arrangements. An unfortunate side effect of the quest for restitution for forced laborers in recent years, however, is the implication that the evil of the system lay in its profitability, as if the conduct described in this chapter would not be subject to condemnation and restitution but for the wealth it generated. In part, this is a distortion imposed by the universe in which the quest has been pursued: the American judicial system, where the language of civil suits emphasizes the "disgorgement" of unjust proceeds from unlawful conspiracies as the principal means of making them good. Ahistorical as the resulting situation is, no discussion of Degussa's implication in forced labor can expect to be taken seriously any longer if it fails to confront the question of how much Degussa "profited" from the use of forced labor.

The question is both easy and difficult to answer on the broadest level. Clearly, in 1942/43, Degussa's gross profits as a percentage of sales were higher than during the last prewar business year (1938/39) and greater still in 1943/44 (see Appendices B–D), despite rising taxes and stricter price controls. However significant the role of rationalization and greater efficiency in this was, lower average labor costs per person also contributed.[124] But how much the firm theoretically "saved" by employing foreigners as opposed to Germans is impossible to determine, in view of the absence of reliable statistics for how many foreign workers Degussa had overall at any given time and the considerable variation in German wage rates by region, gender, and number of dependents. Nor are the available data specific enough to permit firm calculations about comparative productivity, which varied greatly among foreign laborers, with Eastern workers and female camp inmates often performing rather well when measured against their German counterparts, but Western Europeans, Italians, and male inmates used in construction generally

---

[123] Interview with Manya Friedman, August 14, 1998.
[124] It is also true, however, that gross profits per employee (Arbeitnehmer) peaked in 1941/42, which led to increasing concern about overstaffing toward the end of the war (see Chapter 9).

much less so. All in all, the most one can say with assurance regarding Degussa's involvement in the forced labor system is that it contributed to the firm's substantial profitability during World War II and, by thus aiding the accumulation of new equipment and machinery, during the postwar period, as well.[125] But to what degree in each respect is unknowable.

With regard to Degussa's inmate laborers, however, the analytical possibilities are larger, since the numbers of people and relative wage rates involved are clearer. Still, the sums that result from such calculations are startlingly small when set against the corporation's overall earnings during the war, let alone against the human devastation involved. Of course, in the long run, Degussa expected to profit from the brutality in which it partook, in that the plants at Fürstenberg, Oranienburg, Guben, and Gleiwitz were being built or operated to yield appreciable returns, even if only eventually. But the enterprise did not "save" large sums on the exploitation of the inmate laborers. For the reasons given above, there was probably no cost advantage to the use of Jewish construction laborers at the Zentralwerk and Gleiwitz during 1942. At the latter plant for 1943–44, although calculating what the company's retained labor costs might have been is extremely difficult, a very rough way of proceeding is to say that if the sum of the average monthly numbers of Jews working on the site in 1943 comes to 5,755 and their cost, as noted above, to 709,037 RM, then the wage bill for the total of 7,880 Jewish workers obtained by summing the figures given in the individual monthly plant reports during 1944 would have been 970,845 RM, for an overall cost of almost 1.7 million Reichsmarks. Assuming that the wage bill for native German laborers would have averaged out to a figure about three times this high, if they had worked the same number of hours, we may conclude that the Gleiwitz factory "gained" on the order of 3.4 million marks from the use of slave labor, which is to say some U.S. $13.6 million as of the end of the twentieth century. If one makes a similar calculation for the average of some 1,500 exclusively female inmates who labored at Oranienburg for the Auergesellschaft for ten months in 1944–45 at a price of 4 RM per day, their total cost comes to almost 1.8 million Reichsmarks, but the "gain" to probably no more than an equivalent amount, given the prevailing wage rates for women, which translates to U.S. $7.2 million in recent values. Although these are unhistorical calculations, since Gleiwitz would either never have been built or completed much faster and the Auergesellschaft's production would not have been expanded under normal conditions in the labor market, the arithmetic does convey some sense of the extent of what Degussa would have implicitly pocketed by virtue of the inmate labor system, if Germany had won the Second World War. That would be about 5.2 million Reichsmarks at the time, or U.S. $20.8 million in contemporary currency,

[125] Cf. Mark Spoerer, *Zwangsarbeit unter dem Hakenkreuz* (Stuttgart: Deutsche Verlags-Anstalt, 2001), pp. 188–90, 240–41.

along with whatever percentage of the completed value of the installations at Fürstenberg and Gleiwitz could be attributed to the Jewish portion of the labor force that helped build them.

But the Zentralwerk never was completed, Gleiwitz was finished only three months before being conquered by the Red Army, and one cannot label these relative "savings" on labor "profits." Fürstenberg, on which Degussa had spent 23.6 million marks by January 1945, never produced anything more than an indeterminate quantity of formaldehyde in 1944.[126] Gleiwitz's construction costs aggregated to 10.5 million marks and its total expenditures to more than 21 million as of the end of 1944, by which time its total sales to date had come to 2.3 million Reichsmarks in 1943 and, at most, twice as much in 1944. The plant did not begin to produce at a profit over its unit costs until 1944 and "made" money in the simplest sense for some four months, showing an operating profit for the year of 1.2 million marks. All things considered, Gleiwitz was still 3 million marks in the red when it was overrun by the Soviets, who may also have collected the 800,000 RM that the firm had on deposit in local banks.[127] Not only did the plant lose money; it also consumed a large portion of the profits of the DGW's Dortmund factory. Neither did Degussa or DGW retain the physical results of the inmates' labors, since the plant was stripped by the Soviets, then nationalized and run by the Poles until the early 1990s, when a new joint venture agreement returned the only remnant of the initial project, the shells of the buildings, to Degussa's control.[128] Much the same can be said of the Zentralwerk at Fürstenberg, aside from the eventual recovery of the buildings, and of the Auer facilities at Oranienburg and Guben. By any measure, no "profits" on inmate labor remained to disgorge in 1945, though assuredly justified claims to compensation for unremunerated work and extraordinary physical and mental anguish remained to be paid.[129]

Making money was not the reason the Reich's increasingly counterproductive, cruel, cumbersome, and chaotic program of labor exploitation came

---

[126] DUA, TA 2/86, Genehmigte Investitionen, Anlage Fürstenberg/O., January 21, 1945.

[127] DUA, PCA 2/1, Endabrechnung der Bauarbeiten, Stichtag 31. Dezember 1944, July 26, 1945; PRO 1/12, Schlussabrechnung DGW Gleiwitz, October 8, 1945; PCA 2/2, Gegenüberstellung von Gestehungskosten und Erlösen [for 1943]; PCA 2/2, Bisherige Betriebsergebnisse des Werkes Gleiwitz, August 14, 1944; and, for the profit and deficit figures, BET 9/5, Bericht über die Prüfung der Bilanz nebst Gewinn- und Verlustrechnung per 31. Dezember 1944, November 5, 1945. On the outstanding 800,000 RM, see PCA 2/2, Achterath's two memos headed Betr. DGW – Gleiwitz, January 31, and March 1, 1945.

[128] On the stripping of the plant (and the arrest of Fräulein Mittas, Pross's secretary), PCA 2/2, Schenk's Betrifft Schicksal der Gleiwitzer Russfabrik, August 24, 1945. On the joint venture between Degussa and the Polish government, Brigitte Axster's Nachwort in Rood, "*Wenn ich nicht erzählen kann,*" p. 214.

[129] For a similar conclusion, based on a distinct but related line of argument, see Cornelia Rauh-Kühne, "Hitlers Hehler? Unternehmerprofite und Zwangsarbeiterlöhne," *Historische Zeitschrift* 275 (2002), pp. 1–55.

into being, and it is neither morally nor historically sound to measure its evil by its lucrativeness. Precisely because the "slave" labor system emerged out of a vortex of macropolitical not microeconomic forces, international law consistently has defined the German state – and thus its citizens collectively – as the primary party responsible for answering to the financial claims of people exploited under Nazism.[130] It is thus entirely fitting that the German state now carries most of the burden under the German Remembrance Initiative (*Stiftungsinitiative*) of paying restitution claims from former forced laborers.[131] But German corporate leaders, including Degussa's, showed little hesitation about making use of the system Nazism ordained. By cooperating, they encouraged and perpetuated it; in many cases, they aggravated it as they attempted to twist the regime's actions into economically rational and politically beneficial forms.[132] That is why there is also no injustice in the bill that has fallen on German industry fifty years later, regardless of how little a firm such as Degussa may have "profited," in the end, by the sweat and blood its goals exacted.

[130] On the macrocausation of the forced labor system, see especially Ulrich Herbert, *Hitler's Foreign Workers* (Cambridge: Cambridge University Press, 1997), p. 154.

[131] See Susanne-Sophia Spiliotis, *Verantwortung und Rechtsfrieden: Die Stiftungsinitiative der deutschen Wirtschaft* (Frankfurt am Main: Fischer Taschenbuch Verlag, 2003).

[132] See especially Lutz Budrass and Manfred Grieger, "Die Moral der Effizienz. Die Beschäftigung von KZ-Häftlingen am Beispiel des Volkswagenwerks und der Henschel Flugzeug-Werke," *Jahrbuch für Wirtschaftsgeschichte*, Heft 2 (1993), pp. 89–136; and Neil Gregor, *Daimler-Benz in the Third Reich* (New Haven: Yale University Press, 1998).

8

Degesch and Zyklon B

Arguably, the history of Degussa's role in the manufacture of Zyklon B belongs under the heading of war production. From 1939 to 1945, the predominant uses of this vaporizing pesticide were to fumigate military quarters, supplies, uniforms, vehicles, rolling stock, and vessels; to do the like in connection with the forced labor and ethnic German repatriation programs; and to secure food supplies through the disinfestation of storehouses and milling installations. But these now largely forgotten functions do not explain the enduring infamy of the substance. Even today many people instantly recognize the brand name – certainly far more of them than can identify the companies that owned it – because of a purpose to which perhaps 1 percent of the chemical sold during the war years was put. Between 1941 and 1945, the SS applied Zyklon B on a massive scale at Auschwitz – and to lesser extents at Majdanek, Mauthausen, Stutthof, Neuengamme, Natzweiler, and possibly Dachau and Sachsenhausen – to asphyxiate some 1 million people, nearly all of them Jews. Measured by historical impact rather than relative usage at the time, Zyklon B was no mere military or agricultural product, but an instrument of mass murder. Degussa's part in the manufacture and deployment of the commodity therefore demands separate and close analysis.

Both the use of hydrogen cyanide gas as an insecticide and Degussa's interest in the product antedate the First World War, but the conflict greatly accelerated the two developments.[1] Liquid hydrocyanic acid (also known as

[1] The most thorough and reliable account of the history of Zyklon, and Degussa's involvement with it, is Jürgen Kalthoff and Martin Werner, *Die Händler des Zyklon B* (Hamburg: VSA-Verlag, 1998), but a number of other works are also quite useful: Margit Szöllösi-Janze, "Von der Mehlmotte zum Holocaust. Fritz Haber und die chemische Schädlingsbekämpfung während und nach dem Ersten Weltkrieg," in Jürgen Kocka, Hans-Jürgen Puhle, and Klaus Tenfelde (eds.), *Von der Arbeiterbewegung zum modernen Sozialstaat* (Munich: K. G. Saur, 1994), pp. 658–682; Angelika Ebbinghaus, "Der Prozess gegen Tesch & Stabenow. Von der Schädlingsbekämpfung zum Holocaust," *1999*, 13 (1998), pp. 16–71; Hervé Joly, "L'implication de l'industrie chimique allemande dans la Shoah: Le cas du Zyklon B," *Revue d'histoire moderne et contemporaine* 47 (2000), pp. 368–400; and Paul Weindling, *Epidemics and Genocide in Eastern Europe, 1890–1945* (Oxford: Oxford University Press, 2000). Also relevant to the early history of the product are Dietrich Stoltzenberg, *Fritz Haber: Chemiker, Nobelpreisträger, Deutscher, Jude* (Weinheim: VCH, 1994), and Margit Szöllösi-Janze, *Fritz Haber, 1868–1934: Eine Biographie* (Munich: C. H. Beck, 1998). I have drawn on all of these

prussic acid and, in German, *Blausäure* – blue acid – because it was first derived from Prussian blue dye) was recognized as a lethal poison within a few
decades of its discovery toward the end of the eighteenth century. Upon contact with air at temperatures of twenty-six degrees centigrade (seventy-nine
degrees Fahrenheit) and above, the compound evaporates into an imper-
ceptible gas that quickly impedes the transfer of oxygen among the cells
of susceptible organisms. Inhalation of only seventy milligrams (less than
one three-thousandth of an ounce) causes a 150-pound human to lose consciousness, convulse, and die within as little as two minutes unless antidotes
are applied. Although the resistance of small mammals and some insects is
marginally greater than that of people, the chemical's potential as a fumigant
was recognized in the 1880s by California orange growers, who began employing it under coverings placed over individual trees, and its application
spread gradually during the next two decades to mills and ships in the United
States, orchards in Spain and Sicily, and railroad cars in South Africa.[2] These
advances drew the notice of Degussa, which already was the sales agent for
all participants in the international cyanide cartel, and of the company's
sodium cyanide–producing American affiliate, Roessler & Hasslacher. Between 1912 and 1916, in fact, Walter Heerdt, a young German fresh from
his doctoral studies, acquired experience with disinfesting felled trees under
tent sheets while working for Roessler & Hasslacher before returning home
to join the parent firm.

As Heerdt did so, Degussa began devoting considerable attention to the
substance in response to a number of German publications and research initiatives, some propelled by the need to conserve the Reich's strained food
supplies in wartime, others by a desire to deal with the itchy and fever-bearing
lice that proliferated under the conditions of trench warfare and especially
abounded in the newly occupied regions of Eastern Europe. Field tests soon
demonstrated that hydrogen cyanide gas eradicated most pests from silos
and mills without harm to contents or structures and from clothing and
footwear without damage to dyes, metals, and leathers. Thus, even though
the light weight of the toxin made it disperse rapidly unless contained and
therefore relatively useless as a weapon, hydrocyanic acid won the support
of the Kaiser Wilhelm Institute for Physical Chemistry in Berlin, headed by
Fritz Haber, the scientist principally responsible for German gas warfare.
Working in cooperation with Degussa, which placed its experience, apparatus, and chemicals at his disposal, he created a department in the Institute to
combat lice and other vermin, then in early 1917, a Technical Committee for
Pest Control (TASCH) attached to the War Ministry. Supervised by the not

publications and refrained from citing them again except regarding quotations and statistics
or controversial points.
[2] DUA, S/1044, Gerhard Peters, *Blausäure zur Schädlingsbekämpfung* (Stuttgart: Ferdinand
Enke, 1933), pp. 16, 22–23, and 41–42.

yet thirty-year-old Heerdt, whom Haber designated as its managing director at the end of the war, TASCH's specialists conducted numerous gassings at granaries, military installations, and border crossing points, among other locations. Most of these employed the simple but cumbrous pot method that Degussa elaborated for applying *Blausäure* in sealed spaces. When workers wearing protective suits and oxygen masks placed paper-wrapped pieces of sodium cyanide in tubs containing sulfuric acid diluted with water, the resulting reaction released both hydrocyanic acid and enough heat to vaporize it, thus annihilating any vermin present.

Haber was so impressed with the success of the system that he argued for making it generally available through a public corporation. The result was the Deutsche Gesellschaft für Schädlingsbekämpfung (Degesch), founded in March 1919 in Berlin as a state-controlled partnership of corporate investors, taken over in 1920 and moved to Frankfurt by a consortium of chemical firms, and acquired in 1922 by Degussa alone, but managed all the while by Walter Heerdt. However, a web of chemical, political, and practical impediments stood in the way of widespread commercial application of gaseous hydrocyanic acid. In liquid state, the chemical tends to decompose (polymerize) rapidly and to explode if not handled gently; as a gas, its deadliness is matched by its stealth, making leakage and lingering traces ever-attendant dangers. Resourceful scientists therefore quickly hit on the idea of adding an eye irritant to a nonvolatile cyanide derivative that could be transported without risk, then applied as a spray. As the derivative changed in the presence of moisture and warmth into hydrocyanic acid and vaporized, the warning agent supposedly would keep people at bay. The invention was patented for Degesch in 1920 under the name Zyklon, an acronym of the main ingredients (compounds of cyanide and chlorine) that also translates as "cyclone." Uneconomical to produce, however, it also proved problematic on two other grounds: the telltale irritant dissipated more rapidly than the toxin, which led to casualties; and the components had been used in poison gases for the German army and thus soon were banned by the victorious Allies. Degesch's practitioners therefore reverted to the direct use of *Blausäure*, but safety remained a concern, along with the inconvenience of transporting and deploying tubs and the pollution caused by the residues they contained at the end of a gassing.

These difficulties took several years to resolve. The decisive step came in 1922, when Heerdt conceived of soaking absorbent materials, initially pellets of fossilized algae, in the acid and sealing them in tightly packed cans. Prepared in sizes appropriate to many different assignments, the tins could be shipped or carried with little risk, and their contents easily swept up and discarded or reused after dispersal to release the gas. Then, in 1923–24, Heerdt and other chemists, including Bruno Tesch, another veteran of Haber's wartime operations, developed a modified recipe for the warning agent, a stabilizing additive, and the acid. The concoction circumvented the

Allied prohibition of potential chemical weapons and had the fringe benefit of stimulating respiration by insects. Nonetheless, utilizing the newly patented product – still labeled Zyklon, but known among specialists as Zyklon B to differentiate it from the earlier, banned formula that was dubbed retrospectively Zyklon A – remained delicate. Given its lethality, successful fumigation without danger to people in the vicinity required an experienced staff operating under carefully controlled conditions. German law therefore permitted only government-certified practitioners to work with the substance.

Almost from its outset, Zyklon B's commercial history involved three, as matters turned out, distinct dimensions, and these make for a confusing tale featuring multiple corporate actors. For, aside from during the brief start-up period of 1922–24, when Degussa chemists produced and packaged Zyklon under risky and improvised conditions and Degesch dispensed it, the enterprises that owned the patents and trademarks to the product (Degesch for the vaporizing process and the brand name; Degussa for the chemical formulas) were not the firms that made it or that sold and usually applied it. Instead, manufacturing, on the one hand, and retailing, on the other, were farmed out to separate companies, while Degesch oversaw and served as the hub of this system. All the entities eventually involved were tied to Degussa – either directly or via its dominance of Degesch, either through shareholdings or license and other contracts – but all retained a measure of operating independence because Degussa saw little net gain from annexing them.

The pattern regarding production was emblematic. Although during the first third of the twentieth century Degussa continuously ranked second among continental European producers of the sodium cyanide that was a key component of chemically fabricated *Blausäure*, manufacturing 27 percent of their output in 1901–14 and 20 percent in 1920–33, the corporation wished to avoid synthesizing the temperamental acid in densely populated Frankfurt.[3] Fortunately, a different and cheaper manufacturing method existed, in which Degussa had a double financial stake. This alternative, the "*Schlempe* process," took its name from the German word for the nitrogenous remnants of sugar beet plants after the removal of their sucrose. In the 1890s, Julius Bueb had devised a means of obtaining cyanide compounds, along with briquettes and carbon black, from this raw material through dry distillation at extremely high temperatures, then formed a company, Schlempe GmbH, to license the procedure to interested parties. Degussa took a majority participation in the firm (52 percent), in association with the inventor (15 percent) and the Dessau Works for Sugar Refining (30 percent), which began applying the process.[4] So economical were its reliance on the vegetable

[3] Degussa, however, periodically reconsidered this decision. See, for example, DUA, IW 32.15/1, Stiege's successive Berichte concerning Zyklon during 1929.
[4] DUA, DL 13.3/1, Bericht Nr. 2, K. Bonath, "Natriumcyanid," November 1967, pp. 4–5, 7–18. On the apportionment of stock in Schlempe GmbH, see AW 33.2/1, Chem. Fabr. Schlempe

waste of an ongoing industry and relative independence of chemical inputs that licensees dominated European sodium cyanide production during the decades on either side of the First World War, turning out 54 percent and 61 percent of the respective totals.[5] In connection with Zyklon B, two other circumstances surrounding the *Schlempe* process were even more telling. It yielded hydrocyanic acid directly; and, as the sales agent for the cyanide cartel, Degussa was obligated, considering the absence of profitable alternative uses for the perishable *Schlempe*, "always [to] sell the production of all *Schlempe* cyanide factories first."[6]

Thus, Degussa's interests in shifting *Blausäure* output from Frankfurt, pricing Zyklon attractively, collecting dividends from Schlempe GmbH, and stabilizing cartel sales (on which it earned a 4 percent commission) intersected with those of the Dessau Sugar Refining Works in disposing of its cyanide output on predictable terms. Yet Degussa lacked any urge to take over this desirable subcontractor for making Zyklon, since no other aspect of sugar beet processing held allure for Frankfurt. The result was an enduring and complicated production relationship by which Dessau became the sole manufacturer of Zyklon from 1925 to 1936 and remained the principal one until 1944, despite the granting of another license, initially in order to supply the Czech, Austrian, and Balkan markets, to the Kaliwerke Kolin in the meantime.[7] From 1924 to 1928, a young chemist named Gerhard Peters, who had been a work student in Degussa's *Blausäure* operation during the preceding two years while completing his doctorate in chemistry at the University of Frankfurt and who subsequently headed Degesch's research laboratory and, then, the company itself from 1940 to 1945, was employed at Dessau to establish the production process. It called for Dessau to make the acid; to combine it with a stabilizer (from IG Farben's Uerdingen plant), a warning agent (from Schering AG), and the absorptive material, all of which Degesch provided; to pack the Zyklon using containers and labeling and

to its Gesellschafter, June 17, 1926. That the company became more or less a shell over time is suggested by Fritz Roessler's Aktennotiz, August 13, 1928, in the same file, which remarks that toward one of the licensees, the Kaliwerke AG in Kolin, "the Schlempe company does not appear as such any more, instead relations are conducted solely with Degussa."

[5] For these figures, and those previously noted for Degussa, DUA, DL 13.3/1, Bericht Nr. 2, K. Bonath, "Natriumcyanid," November 1967, p. 42. Degussa's own production eventually overtook that of the *Schlempe* producers in 1938 and was, in turn, overtaken by that of IG Farben in 1939; *ibid.*, chart headed NaCN Produktion bezw. abgesetzte Mengen NaCN 100%ig von 1920–1944, between pp. 40–41.

[6] For a schematic representation of the chemistry involved, see DUA, AW 33.5/1, the chart labeled Uebersicht der Arbeitsweise der Kaliwerke Kolin, undated; for the quotation, IW 31.6/1, Degussa to the Kaliwerke AG Prague, May 30, 1907.

[7] For the background to the onset of production at Kolin, see DUA, AW 33.6/1, Stiege's Aktennotiz, April 1, 1935, and Schlosser's Niederschrift, May 24, 1935, as well as AW 33.5/1, Jahresbericht für die Sitzung des Executiv-Ausschusses, August 11, 1944, which dates the first output to 1936.

other machinery that also belonged to Degesch; and, finally, to deliver the ready-to-ship goods to a Degesch branch office on the factory site. At that point, Dessau's connection with the product ceased. It became the property of Degesch, which paid Dessau for its acid and services at a periodically renegotiated rate per 100 kilograms of cyanide content (95 RM in 1927, twice as much ten years later) and reimbursed that firm monthly for the wages and salaries of the local Degesch staff.[8] Somewhat looser procedures later pertained at Kolin, which retained independent sales rights in some markets.

Degussa's and Degesch's readiness to delegate sales and service operations also attested to the dangers of working with hydrogen cyanide gas and to the savings that decentralization could bring. Because of the risks involved, only officially licensed firms could deploy *Blausäure* in Germany or train others to do so, and such enterprises had to maintain staffs of specialists and substantial insurance against possible legal liabilities. Hermann Schlosser, then the Degussa director responsible for chemicals sales, therefore recognized that off-loading these burdens onto selected affiliates would curtail Degesch's expenses and exposure. In 1925, he instigated a reorganization of Degesch by which he succeeded Walter Heerdt as business manager, then handed over exclusive sales and application rights for Zyklon B in Germany and specified export markets to two other companies. One of these recipients, Heerdt-Lingler GmbH of Frankfurt (Heli), was a new partnership between Degesch's departing head and Johannes Lingler, another former Degesch executive. Heli's reserved territory initially encompassed Germany more or less west and south of the Elbe River, along with Austria, Southeast Europe, Poland, Holland, and Egypt, to which Switzerland, Belgium, Luxembourg, and Turkey later were added.[9]

The second Zyklon vendor, Tesch & Stabenow GmbH of Hamburg (Testa), already existed, however. It had begun operations in January 1924, shortly after Bruno Tesch, the former manager of Degesch's branch offices in Berlin and Hamburg, left that firm out of pique at his exclusion from a share in the patent rights to Zyklon B (only Heerdt had gotten an "inventor's contract" entitling him to a portion of the proceeds). Apparently through the good offices of his patron, Fritz Haber, Tesch linked up with Paul Stabenow, the Hamburg sales representative of the Association for Chemical and Metallurgical Production of Aussig in Czechoslovakia. It provided the capital to launch the new enterprise, which specialized in using the pot method to disinfest ships with *Blausäure*. Though Tesch felt little affection for Degesch, it needed his excellent connections with the local authorities in the lucrative harbor city's market, and he wanted access to Zyklon before it drove him

---

[8] For the price figures, DUA, IW 33.2/1, Vertrag zwischen Dessauer Zucker-Raffinerie GmbH und Degesch, January 26, 1927, and Degesch to Dessauer, January 25, 1937.

[9] DUA, IW 57.14/2, Vertrag zwischen Degesch und Heerdt-Lingler GmbH, October 15, 1925.

out of business. A marriage of convenience therefore took place. Degesch bought half of Aussig's shareholding, and Testa obtained a monopoly over dispensing Zyklon in Germany north and east of the Elbe, and in Denmark, Danzig, and the Baltic states, to which Finland, Czechoslovakia, and the naval market in Norway were appended in the following year. In return, Tesch agreed to peddle and use only hydrocyanic acid or Zyklon for fumigation, to pay 40 percent of all promotional costs for the product, and to send Degesch copies of all invoices.[10]

The different origins of the two affiliates largely predicted the subsequent pattern of their respective ties to Degesch. Relations between Frankfurt and Testa proved consistently awkward and acrimonious, even though Degesch spent 100,000 RM to buy out Aussig completely in 1927 as Stabenow was dying, then generously agreed not only to loan Tesch enough money against future profits to buy 45 percent of Testa's capital, but also to let him exercise the voting rights to Degesch's 55 percent as a trustee. Such gestures apparently made little dent in Tesch's resentment toward his nominal masters in Frankfurt and only strengthened his determination to act as independently of them as possible. Contacts with Heli, on the other hand, were continuously close and cooperative, as illustrated by the smooth negotiations by which Degesch acquired 51 percent of the smaller firm's stock in 1931 and reduced the original partners to 24.5 percent each in exchange for augmenting Heli's income by assigning it half of Degesch's meanwhile increased but nonvoting participation in Testa.

Nonetheless, the same basic operational procedures governed Zyklon deliveries by both sales subsidiaries from 1925 to 1942. Customers in the regions reserved to Testa or Heli dealt only with it, as a result of either direct contact or referral by Degesch. Once the needs of a particular project had been estimated, Testa or Heli sent a corresponding order to Degesch, which made a record and forwarded it to Dessau (or Kolin after 1936) for fulfillment. That installation then dispatched the goods, usually directly to the customer for application by Heli's or Testa's technicians, and a copy of the shipping invoice went to Degesch. It thus acted primarily as a holding company and clearinghouse, collecting its revenues from the purchases and dividends of the sales subsidiaries, license fees from foreign producers, and direct exports to countries served by neither Heli nor Testa.

In 1930, the corporate linkages surrounding Zyklon B grew still more complex by virtue of changes in the ownership of Degesch. To contain competition from new variants of calcium cyanide and aethylene oxide that IG Farben and Th. Goldschmidt AG had patented, Degussa ceded shares in

---

[10] DUA, IW 57.14/3, Zusammenfassung des Vertragtextes Degesch-Testa vom 8. Oktober 1925, Aktenvermerk zur Besprechung am 12. Oktober 1926 in Frankfurt, and the summary of contractual relations between Degesch and Testa, headed Tesch & Stabenow Internationale Gesellschaft für Schädlingsbekämpfung mbH, Hamburg and hand-dated February 5, 1961.

Degesch to these firms and turned it into the distributor of all their gaseous pesticides. Farben's holding henceforth came to 42.5 percent, the same figure to which Degussa's dropped, and Goldschmidt received 15 percent. In return, the two new partners agreed to sell their current and future vaporizing insecticides (initially Zyklon, Cartox, Calcid, and T-Gas, and later Tritox, Ventox, and Areginal as well) only to Degesch at cost, and it then made them available through Heli and Testa at coordinated prices so that the products would not undersell one another. To make Degussa's relationship with Degesch exactly analogous to Farben's and Goldschmidt's, Degussa became the formal and momentary buyer of Dessau's (later also Kolin's) Zyklon output as it emerged from that factory, then the reseller to Degesch.[11] At the end of each business year, that firm's pooled profits on the goods acquired from the investors were divided according to their capital shares, which resulted in disproportionate annual earnings for sometimes one partner, sometimes another, depending on how well its gases had sold during the period.

Despite the byzantine quality of these ownership and sales arrangements (schematically presented in Appendix Q), Degesch remained an appendage to Degussa. It supplied two out of the three business managers appointed following the ownership changes, including both Schlosser and the executive who shouldered the day-to-day responsibilities, Heinrich Stiege (ironically, another of the several senior Degussa officials who had a Jewish grandparent). They functioned largely independently of Degesch's Administrative Committee of eleven members (five from Degussa, including Walter Heerdt, five from IG Farben, and Theodor Goldschmidt), which acted as a consultative rather than supervisory body and met irregularly before ceasing to convene altogether after 1941.[12] In fact, Goldschmidt grew so irritated with the group's pointlessness that he briefly resigned, but there was little he could do in the face of his partners' gentlemen's agreement to work out disputed matters among themselves.[13] That they hardly ever disagreed probably reflected the negative game IG Farben was playing. In all likelihood, it traded its gaseous pesticides for stock in Degesch in order to be in a position to block the firm from experimenting in the more promising direction of sprayed liquid insecticides. That was certainly the only subject that ever excited more than passive interest in Degesch on the part of Farben's

---

[11] DUA, IW 57.2/1, Vertrag zwischen der Deutschen Gold- und Silberscheideanstalt und der Deutschen Gesellschaft für Schädlingsbekämpfung, April 21, 1934.

[12] DUA, IW 57.2/1, Peters and Kaufmann to members of the Administrative Committee, July 18, 1941, says that the investors have waived a meeting for that year, and none apparently took place thereafter.

[13] DUA, IW 57.2/1, Schlosser's Aktennotiz, September 8, 1930 (on the Farben-Degussa agreement); and the exchange of correspondance between Goldschmidt and Busemann, March 30 to April 3, 1936, Busemann to Verwaltungsrat and Geschäftsführer of Degesch, April 15, 1936, and Stiege's Aktennotz, October 30, 1936, as well as DL 3.Busemann/5, Busemann's Besuch des Herrn Theo Goldschmidt, April 14, 1936 (on Goldschmidt's irritation).

executives.[14] Meanwhile, Degesch's offices remained in or, after 1943, adjoining Degussa's headquarters building; Degesch's personnel continued not only to come from Degussa, but also in many cases to stay its employees; Degesch's books kept being audited by Degussa alone; and Degesch's monthly business reports and summaries went to Schlosser and to Ernst Bernau, but not to the other investors.[15] In short, despite the broadened partnership of 1930, Degesch was an integral part of the Degussa concern and not of IG Farben's, as erroneously implied at the trial of its executives for war crimes in 1947–48 and generally accepted ever since.

As such, Degesch and Zyklon were not dominant in their industry or prominent within Degussa during the 1930s. Hydrocyanic gas faced considerable competition in Germany from less risky arsenic-, sulfur-, and steam-based preparations that also were easier and cheaper to apply in many settings, if not necessarily as effective. Until 1938, foreign markets provided the majority of Zyklon's earnings, even as these were eroded from 1931 on by the slump in international trade and the overvaluation of the Reichsmark. The quantity sold in 1939 thus was still 15 percent below the level at which it had crested in 1930 (210 tons), despite rising domestic consumption in the meantime (see Appendix R, Table I). Moreover, at an average of 863,000 RM annually in 1937–39, the resulting revenues came to only 39 percent of Degesch's.[16] Even as its other products took up the slack, the little company with a workforce of about thirty-five people remained a minor contributor to Degussa's balance sheets, generating just 85,000 RM in dividends in each of the two most rewarding prewar years (1937 and 1938). Although twice the face value of Degussa's shareholding, the respective payments constituted only about 3 percent of Degussa's income from subsidiaries in either period.[17] Degesch thus retained importance to the parent firm primarily by virtue of Schlosser's personal interest in the company, which reflected Degussa's desire to preserve its dominance of the cyanide field; in commercial terms, both the subsidiary and Zyklon B were no more than dependable, low-cost performers.

World War II did not advance either the product's market share among German vermin-combating agents or Degesch's intramural significance.

[14] See especially DUA, DL 3.H.Schlosser/1, Peters to Schlosser, May 26, 1944; IW 57.2/1, Notiz für Herrn Schlosser, signed by Peters, August 7, 1944.

[15] See, for example, DUA, SCH 01/0004, Bernau and Scherf to Gerhard Peters, November 28, 1946, which remarks "that you have been, not a Degesch, but a Degussa employee." On the acquisition of a new building at Neue Mainzerstrasse 52 in Frankfurt, next door to Degussa's headquarters, see DUA, Bericht über die Prüfung des Jahresabschlusses vom 31. Dezember 1943.

[16] Joly, *Revue d'histoire moderne et contemporaine* 47 (2000), p. 386; and DUA, BET 9/43, Beantwortung der Fragen in der Anweisung der amer. Militärregierung für Deutschland betr. Dekartellisierung, Anlage zu 6a, a table of Degesch's sales by volume and value per product, 1936–47.

[17] *Ibid.*, and Appendix B to this book for Degussa's overall receipts from subsidiaries.

Constrained by shortages of *Schlempe*, sodium cyanide, and absorbent materials, total production of Zyklon increased by a factor of only 2.6 between 1938 and 1943 (from 160 to 411 tons), while that of sulfur-based fumigants rose ten- to twentyfold.[18] Degesch's annual dividend payments to Degussa actually dropped in 1939 and 1940 to 42,500 RM before rebounding to 85,000 RM in 1941 and 1942, then retreating to 63,750 RM in 1943.[19] The total of almost 319,000 RM amounted to 2.7 percent of Degussa's earnings from stockholdings from 1939 to 1943, that is, to roughly the same proportion as in the last peacetime years. Although Degesch's receipts from sales surged to the unprecedented sums of 2.89 million Reichsmarks in 1942 and 3.46 million Reichsmarks a year later, their average annual level in 1940–44 was less imposing. At 2.39 million Reichsmarks, it represented a modest increase of only 7 percent over the figure of 2.22 million for 1937–39. In fact, the overall quantity of goods sold by Degesch peaked in 1939, and net profits, even during the boom years of 1942–43, never replicated the tallies of 1937–38, which helps explain why the subsidiary received no more than passing mention in the minutes of Degussa's managing board meetings from 1940 to 1945.[20]

What mounted strikingly after the war began was not the relative prevalence of Zyklon or the lucrativeness of Degesch, but the enterprise's degree of dependence on the substance, which became overwhelming. As supplies and sales of IG Farben's Calcid and Cartox faltered, and the conflict greatly multiplied the ideal situations for the application of Zyklon – notably in delousing clothing and uniforms in the ten-cubic-meter, mass-producible "circulation chambers" that the firm devised in the mid-1930s and in disinfesting barracks, ships, boxcars, mills, storehouses, and hospitals – the product's proportion of Degesch's total sales revenue climbed. It reached 65 percent in 1943 (and Zyklon provided 70 percent of Degesch's gross profits that year, although the 411 tons sold made up only 47 percent of turnover by volume) and averaged to 60 percent in 1940–44 (7.6 million Reichsmarks out of 12.7 million Reichsmarks altogether). Zyklon grossed an annual average of 1,468,200 RM from 1940 to 1944, a gain of 70 percent over the level of

[18] DUA, BET 9/43, Beantwortung der Fragen . . . der amer. Militärregierung, Anlage zu 6a; and IW 57.8/1, Herbert Rauscher's Bericht über Zyklon B, June 18, 1947, pp. 6–7.
[19] DUA, BET 10/7, Bernau's handwritten and undated tabulations. See also the entries in RFI 4.2/85 and 89, Jahresabschlüsse 1938–39 und 1939–40, which show that these dividends came to 2.3 percent and 1.2 percent of Degussa's total such income in the respective years.
[20] The only significant discussion of Degesch in these records occurred in connection with changes in the firm's management in the spring of 1940; see DL 2/1, Niederschrift über die Vorstandssitzung am 6. Mai 1940, pp. 89–90, and Anlage 9. When Degussa overhauled its organization in 1943, Degesch was not included in the new framework and left responsible to its own Administrative Committee; see DUA 2/1, Niederschrift über die Vorstandssitzung am 1. November 1943, Anlage 1. Interestingly, the only detailed treatment of Zyklon in Degussa's managing board meetings from 1939 to 1945 occurred after the war in Europe ended, when the board discussed transferring production from Dessau to Ludwigshafen; *ibid.*, am 10. Mai 1945, p. 2.

1937–39, or ten times as much as the growth in the firm's average overall sales receipts.[21] So great had demand become by the last quarter of 1942 that Dessau went over to three production shifts per day and Kolin sought to do the same, buttressing its case for a greater part in Zyklon output with the exaggerated claim that "current usage is exclusively by the Wehrmacht."[22]

That not all of Zyklon's gains came in the form of direct military orders is suggested by the sales figures for Heerdt & Lingler in Frankfurt. Because Testa's marketing region embraced the nation's capital and thus most procurement offices, the bulk of military demand fell to that company, whereas Heli's business centered on nominally civilian customers. These ranged from industrial and agricultural installations, including in the occupied countries of the firm's allotted territory, to corporations and municipalities concerned with pest control among foreign laborers brought to the Reich. Yet, Heli's sales of Zyklon thrived. They nearly quadrupled following the annexation of Austria (from 42,114 RM in 1937 to 156,104 RM in 1938), fell back in 1939, surged again in 1940–41 as a result of the conquests of Poland and the Low Countries, then more than doubled between 1941 and 1942 (from 173,636 RM to 410,216 RM) and almost duplicated that feat in 1943 (reaching 708,970 RM) in response to the influx of non-German workers.[23]

Still, the military market, funneled largely through Testa, was not only substantial, but also increasingly pivotal to that firm. The armed services generated an indeterminate but appreciable share of the fumigation contracts that brought in the vast majority of Testa's earnings (e.g., 84 percent from 1941 to 1944; see Appendix R, Table II), as well as a respectable portion of the less rewarding direct sales of Zyklon that accounted for the rest (on which Testa generally enjoyed a sales margin of 20 percent on defense-related orders, or about 1,050 RM per ton through September 1943 and 900 RM per ton thereafter).[24] As a result of both sorts of commissions, the Hamburg company's turnover by volume rose from 27.4 tons in 1937 to 81.2 in 1939 (an increase of 196 percent), compared with figures of only 41.7 to 51.7 tons (plus 24 percent) at its counterpart in Frankfurt. More specifically, the

---

[21] DUA, BET 9/43, Beantwortung der Fragen in der Anweisung der amer. Militärregierung für Deutschland betr. Dekartellisierung, Anlage zu 6a; and, on the share of gross profits in 1943 from Zyklon B, Anlagen zum Geschäftsbericht für 1943.

[22] DUA, IW 33.2/1, Dessauer Zucker-Raffinerie to Degesch, November 12, 1942, and PCA 2/142, Stoecker to Baerwind, September 23, 1942, where the quoted words appear.

[23] DUA, BET 9/43, Gewinn- und Verlustrechnungen, Heerdt-Lingler GmbH, 1936–44.

[24] On the pricing of Zyklon, see DUA, IW 32.2/1, Preisbildungsstelle Kassel to Degesch, February 8, 1941 (establishing a factory price of 5.28 RM per kilogram and a retail price of 6.33 RM per kilogram), and Kalthoff and Werner, *Händler des Zyklon B*, p. 124, which notes that the price control authorities established on October 1, 1943, three retail prices – 4.55 RM per kilogram for defense-related orders, 4.75 RM per kilogram for other public agencies, and 5.28 RM per kilogram for civilian consumers – and noted that it considered the usual 20 percent margin for the sales firms too high, though no further price reductions took place during the war. That suggests that the factory price as of the fall of 1943 was 3.65 RM per kilogram.

Wehrmacht bought forty tons of Zyklon in 1938 for delousing barracks in Austria and the Sudetenland, and fifty-three more tons in 1939 to use in the Protectorate and Poland. Though consumption sagged in 1940 to thirty-two tons and in 1941 to about twelve tons, in part because of increasing use of less-expensive fumigation processes that employed hot air, these totals were more than enough to offset the reduction of Testa's core business in Hamburg's harbor.[25] In 1942 and 1943, military purchases from Testa turned up once more, coming to 20.3 and 35 tons, that is, to 25.7 percent and 29.3 percent of its total external sales (see Appendix R, Table III).

Moreover, another customer spurred Zyklon's and Testa's growth after the war began: the SS. Part of its interest in the product related to the swift expansion of the organization's military formations (the Waffen-SS) after 1939, but the chief impetus stemmed from the swelling of the concentration camp system (from 21,000 inmates in mid-1939 to more than 700,000 in January 1945) and the malignant creep of its mission. That technicians from Tesch & Stabenow were present at Auschwitz as early as the week of July 5 to 11, 1940, when they fumigated the lodgings of the SS guard force for the newly established camp, was thus a dreadful portent.[26] Initially, however, in addition to such contract work, the most attractive offerings of Degesch and Testa to the SS were the circulation chambers that disinfested clothing with warm air and Zyklon and the instruction and demonstrations that the latter firm offered on the use of Zyklon B. By 1940, at least one such installation existed at Sachsenhausen, and Bruno Tesch, extending his usual practice toward the army and the Labor Service, conducted at least two of the annual courses on the product at the SS Disinfectors' School adjacent to that camp in 1941 and 1942.[27] The SS bought another 23 of the 182 such chambers sold in 1941–42 (most went to municipalities and industrial firms), and Auschwitz ordered an additional 19, though these were never delivered.[28] No extant document establishes exactly how many of the 552 such chambers erected on German territory during the war the SS acquired; out of the first 340 commissioned, however, 105 went to either the Wehrmacht or the Waffen-SS.[29]

Although delighted to promote these installations, since they yielded not only instructional fees but also a commission of 12 percent from Degesch on each, Tesch cannot have been happy about one of the unintended consequences of his efforts. In April 1941, his success in persuading the SS of the value of Zyklon led that organization to obtain a decree from the

[25] Joly, *Revue d'histoire moderne et contemporaine* 47 (2000), p. 385; Ebbinghaus, *1999* 13 (1998), pp. 49–50; and Kalthoff and Werner, *Händler des Zyklon B*, p. 105.

[26] *Ibid.*, p. 173.

[27] Ebbinghaus, *1999* 13 (1998), pp. 48–49; Kalthoff and Werner, *Händler des Zyklon B*, p. 152.

[28] Joly, *Revue d'histoire moderne et contemporaine* 47 (2000), pp. 385 and 395 (note 112).

[29] DUA, BET 9/43, E. Wüstinger, "Die spontane Entwicklung der Kammerbegasung," Referat gehalten vor der Gesellschafter-Versammlung der Deutschen Gesellschaft für Schädlingsbekämpfung, September 4, 1942, p. 3.

Agriculture and Interior ministers that added SS disinfection units to the authorized appliers of *Blausäure* and exempted them from official oversight and restrictions regarding its use. Henceforth, Tesch's services to Himmler's Black Corps no longer consisted of conducting fumigations, but primarily of selling it Zyklon, along with occasionally visiting posts or concentration camps to teach personnel, including prisoners, how to operate the circulation chambers. Unfortunately for his company, the latter role was much less profitable than the former (see Appendix R, Table II). In 1942, for example, the forty-two tons of Zyklon applied by Testa's own technicians brought in 11.6 RM more per kilogram than Testa paid Degesch for the substance, whereas the seventy-nine tons Testa sold to other users produced a net income of only 1.17 RM per kilogram. As a result, although purchases by the SS after the decree of April 1941 were substantial – at least 24.9 tons of Zyklon in 1942 and 29.8 tons in 1943, respectively 31.5 percent and 24.9 percent of Testa's external sales in those years (see Appendix R, Table III) – earnings were not. Testa's average gross margin per kilogram retailed of 1.17 RM in 1942 and 1.07 RM in 1943 meant that its gain on sales to the SS during this two-year period, over and above the cost of goods but before deductions for overhead, aggregated to no more than 61,001 RM. This sum represents only 5.5 percent of the 1,103,237 RM in net proceeds from all of the firm's activities in 1942–43 (see Appendix R, Tables II and III). Furthermore, probably incomplete records establish that a minimum of 65.7 tons of Zyklon went to the SS from Testa between 1942 and 1944 (see Appendix R, Tables III and IV). If one posits an average margin of 1.10 RM per kilogram on these sales, the net income of 72,261 RM works out to only 3.9 percent of the firm's total of 1,849,731 RM in this time frame.

   In other words, as so often in the history of the Holocaust, cooperating with its perpetrators was not the royal road to riches for Bruno Tesch. Already in September 1941, when the SS began using its new autonomy regarding hydrocyanic acid to experiment with employing it to kill people at Auschwitz, Tesch's commercial relationship with the organization promised him rather small future profits. Yet, preserving these ties seemed vital to the survival of his company for other reasons in 1941–42, and understanding them is essential to comprehending the decisions he made then, which contributed to the deaths of hundreds of thousands of human beings and ultimately proved fatal to him as well.

   Although Tesch and his subordinates at Testa played no known part in the design, construction, and operation of the gas chambers at Auschwitz and Majdanek that began systematically massacring Jews in early 1942 with the Zyklon B the firm provided, he and at least some of his assistants apparently learned of the SS's intentions during the first half of that year.[30] According

---

[30] For the argument that the ventilation system of the gas chamber in Crematorium II at Birkenau was inspired by that of a Degesch circulation chamber, see Michael Allen, "The Devil

to Anna Uenzelmann's postwar testimony, Tesch returned that June from a trip to Berlin, dictated a report on it to her, and remarked at the end, apparently with some consternation, that "our Zyklon B would be used for killing people." Two other Testa employees later claimed to have seen the document, a clerk named Erna Biagini and Emil Sehm, a bookkeeper at the firm from May 1942 to July 1943, who blew the whistle on Tesch to the British occupiers of Hamburg in 1945. Sehm recalled the contents as saying that an army officer had asked Tesch about the possibility of deploying Zyklon to kill Jews, whereupon he had advised that it could be used exactly as on insects and agreed to show SS personnel how.[31] The alleged text was never found, and Tesch denied it ever existed. If it did, it was burned, perhaps during an air raid that struck Testa's offices or, more probably, by the senior staff just before the Allies arrived in Hamburg. In any case, the defense at Tesch's postwar trial never provided grounds to doubt the three witnesses other than his own denials, and all of the events narrated – the question, Tesch's response and commitment, and even his consternation – are plausible.

Whether he was shaken or not by what the SS proposed, Tesch's record of serving the military and the SS made him the logical expert to ask about such matters in 1942, and his threatened commercial position at the time surely disposed him to act as Sehm claimed. This vulnerability, not such circumstantial evidence as Tesch's Nazi Party membership since May 1, 1933, his coldness and petty tyranny toward his employees, and his unkind treatment of a baptized half-Jewish secretary – much as these facts say about his personality and character – explains his conduct at the moment of truth and thereafter. For he continued to sell Zyklon to the SS, to send his personnel to service its circulation chambers, and to display indifference to reports from returning subordinates about the dreadful treatment of concentration camp inmates (though none claimed later to have known or told him of the mass gassings). And he made sure that his closest aides squelched any suspicions that arose in-house. When a secretary who prepared the bills for various concentration camps openly wondered whether the large quantities of Zyklon being ordered really could be needed for fumigation, chief bookkeeper Alfred Zaun, whom she considered "a 100 percent Nazi," hushed her with the warning that "if you repeat such remarks, I must report you to the authorities."[32] In 1945, no less a personage than Heinrich Himmler rewarded

in the Details: The Gas Chambers of Birkenau, October 1941," *Holocaust and Genocide Studies* 16 (2002), pp. 189–216. Neither Allen nor any other scholar of the subject, however, contends that Testa (or Degesch) played an active part in this process of adaptation.

[31] Kalthoff and Werner, *Händler des Zyklon B*, pp. 148–50. The original quotation of Uenzelmann in the trial record appeared as "was" [wurde] rather than "would be" [würde] used, but her later testimony in the proceedings against Gerhard Peters established that the latter formulation was her intention.

[32] *Ibid.*, p. 205. The first quotation is the authors' paraphrase, the second her version of Zaun's remarks.

Tesch's services with a directive to the building department of the Hamburg police to help him with the reconstruction of his bombed-out offices, and the message concluded with this emphatic testimonial:

The firm Tesch & Stabenow in Hamburg has worked for many years and on a large scale for both the SS and the police in various parts of the Reich. Dr. Tesch always has shown himself ready in absolutely exemplary fashion to comply with the orders of the office of the Reichsführer[-SS].[33]

As the gassings began, and Tesch began truly earning this disreputable ac-colade, he was embroiled in a fight for his economic life with Degesch, from which he emerged weakened and more dependent than ever on his politi-cal connections. Always strained, relations between the prickly businessman and his majority shareholder already had led to two judicial settlements in 1938–39 before deteriorating irrevocably after the German occupation of Bohemia and Moravia in March of the latter year. This event had two transformative effects. It changed the clash between two contractual com-mitments by Degesch – its grant of a production license to Kolin in 1935 and its allotment of Czechoslovakia to Testa's sales territory in 1926 – from a squabble over priority in a small foreign country to a contest over revenues from a portion of the German domestic market with a substantial Wehr-macht garrison; and it increased Degussa's solicitude for Kolin, which was no longer just a source of license income but a participant in the Greater Ger-man economy and, increasingly, the Degussa concern. When Tesch moved to undercut Kolin's role in the Zyklon business by refusing to sell or use that company's output, Degesch countered, no doubt with Hermann Schlosser's consent, by reclaiming the 55 percent of shares in Testa that Frankfurt had allowed Tesch to hold and vote as trustee since 1927.[34] Undaunted, and fur-ther irritated by agreements Degesch had made regarding the use of T-Gas and Tritox by public agencies, Tesch submitted a resolution to the stockhold-ers' meeting in March 1940 that forebade him to accept changes to previous practice "through which the rights of Testa, especially its independence in relations with its customers and in the treatment of its territory, are changed" and authorized him "to take legal steps or other suitable countermeasures immediately" in the event that "the repeated invasions and interventions by Degesch in Testa's field of activity do not stop."[35] Degesch's representatives got the motion tabled until the general meeting a year later, by which time they were prepared. After electing Gerhard Peters of Degesch to chair the

---

[33] Quoted in *ibid.*, p. 154.

[34] The process of repossession began early in the year as part of the settlement of one of the previous disputes, but was then executed in the autumn; see DUA, IW 57.14/3, notarized Annahmeerklärung, February 24, 1939, and Stiege and Peters to Tesch, November 24, 1939.

[35] DUA, IW 57.14/3, Tesch to Degesch, April 8, 1941, Point 1 of which is a repeat of the previous year's submission.

session, they passed two votes that tied Tesch to their preferred courses of action and then rejected his proposal, thus provoking a walkout by his lawyer and presenting Peters with what he considered "a thoroughly flawless lever for his dismissal."[36]

Tesch replied with a volley of lawsuits against the legality of not only the meeting's decisions, but also of Kolin's sales of Zyklon to the Wehrmacht in the Protectorate, and against Degesch, from whom he sought restitution of the 150,000 RM assessed to him after he lost the Kolin case.[37] All failed, but he held two aces, one of which he played in June 1941, when another shareholders' gathering took up the question of his removal as of the end of the year. Because the Hamburg authorities had licensed him personally, not Testa as a company, to carry out fumigations with *Blausäure*, he announced, his departure would render Testa incapable of doing business. That this information came as "an unexpected surprise" to Gerhard Peters is a measure of how poorly he had planned Degesch's attack – and of the weakness of Degesch's institutional memory, since none of its current officials professed to know of this situation, although it was one reason Degesch had allied with Tesch almost twenty years earlier rather than tried to compete with him. After some confusion, the removal of Tesch as of December 31 was approved formally, but all present probably knew that the vote could not take effect without shutting Testa down, except in the unlikely event that another chemist could be found whom Hamburg's government would recognize. Thus, Bruno Tesch hung onto his job and firm into May 1942, when he produced his second ace. At another shareholders' meeting, after trying unsuccessfully to scare Degesch with the possibility that he would respond to his removal by taking up a position with the Wehrmacht that would cut the ground out from under Testa's future business, Tesch presented a brusque (and syntactically garbled) letter from Karl Kaufmann, the Gauleiter and Reichsstatthalter in Hamburg, that checkmated Peters and Degesch:

Your firm is listed as a Defense Works by the Industry and Trade Chamber of Hamburg.... As the obligated person in a position of trust, I set great store by working together with you personally in the future. I consider any change in the organization of your business therefore intolerable.[38]

Both sides now recognized that the only possible settlement was a divorce, from which each could try to take away what mattered to it most. For Tesch, this was control over his company; for Degesch, it was an end

---

[36] DUA, IW 57.14/3, Protokoll der Gesellschafter-Versammlung der Tesch & Stabenow Internationale Gesellschaft für Schädlingsbekämpfung, April 19, 1941; and Peters' Aktennotiz Betr. Gesellschafterversammlung der Testa, April 22, 1941, p. 5 (for the quotation).
[37] DUA, IW 57.14/3, Schiedsspruch des Reichsgerichtes, 17 Juli 1941 (rejecting his claims regarding Kolin).
[38] DUA, IW 57.14/3, Heydorn to Tesch, May 27, 1942 (p. 21 of the notarized protocol of the shareholders' meeting of Tesch & Stabenow, May 30, 1942).

to Tesch's defiance concerning Kolin and the parent firm's arrangements regarding products other than Zyklon. Late in June 1942, probably just after Tesch's fateful trip to Berlin, a contract was hammered out. Degesch sold its 2,750 RM of shares in Tesch & Stabenow for their face value plus 40,000 RM from the firm's profits in 1942; recognized its monopoly on the application and sales of *Blausäure*-based Degesch products in Germany east of the Elbe, Denmark, Norway, Finland, the former Baltic states, and the General Government; and limited its customers for all other Degesch goods to the Wehrmacht, the National Labor Service, and the Waffen-SS. Testa gave up its resistance to ordering Zyklon from Kolin, ceded to Heli the sale of all other Degesch preparations to private consumers and nonmilitary agencies, and pledged to purchase a minimum of twenty-four tons of Zyklon per year and to buy no gaseous cyanide preparations or equipment from any other provider.[39] Henceforth, Tesch's reporting to Degesch regarding Zyklon consisted only of monthly summaries of sales, rather than copies of invoices (though orders still had to be submitted via Degesch until April 1944, and Dessau always kept records of shipments and destinations, which could not be dispatched without Degesch's approval). In other words, he finally had secured the largely free hand he had pursued since becoming tied to Degesch in 1925, as well as full title to his own earnings from 1943 on. But the last battle had been a close call; he had prevailed only by dint of his political connections; and the business remaining to him depended now more than ever on Zyklon in particular and good relations with the military and the SS in general. This context was unlikely to produce any other outcome of his trip to Berlin in June 1942 than the one Emil Sehm described and Heinrich Himmler praised.

Whatever Tesch knew of the goings-on in Auschwitz and Majdanek, he sold them at least 29.4 metric tons of Zyklon B from 1942 to 1944 – almost 90 percent of what the former site obtained in this period and all of what the latter did – along with another 14.8 tons to further concentration camps (more likely 15.2 tons, since the 403 kilograms that Dessau shipped to Stuffhof in January 1945 probably resulted from an order via Testa) and 21.5 tons to other agencies of the SS (see Appendix R, Tables III and IV). Yet, he was not the only supplier of the product to each of these recipient groups. Heli serviced the concentration camps in its sales region, sending almost 2.2 tons of Zyklon to Mauthausen in 1942–43, as well as quantities for which specific figures have not surfaced to Dachau and Buchenwald. Kolin dispatched 400 kilograms to Theresienstadt in 1944 on its own sales authority and relinquished ten times as much in 1943 to one Anton Slupetsky, the operator of a fumigating firm in Linz that served Mauthausen, when he simply appeared at the factory in the Protectorate and, backed by the local

---

[39] DUA, IW 57.14/3, Vertrag signed by Peters and Tesch, June 27, 1942; and notarized Ausfertigung of the sales contract, June 27, 1942.

23   Gerhard Peters

Gestapo leader, laid claim to the entire amount on hand. And Auschwitz supplemented the accumulated surplus it possessed in 1944 with some 1,155 kilograms of Zyklon that a Polish nitrogen factory apparently produced that year, presumably under a license from Degesch (although Degussa's files seem to contain no record of such an arrangement).⁴⁰ Most sensationally, however, quantities of Zyklon began to flow to the SS Main Hygiene Park at Oranienburg outside of Berlin in June 1943 and to Auschwitz directly three months later at the behest of Degesch's chief executive, who acted, so to speak, under the noses of Degussa's leaders in Frankfurt.

Gerhard Peters became one of Degesch's business managers in early 1939, then its principal operating officer early in 1940, after Hermann Schlosser moved up to chair of Degussa's managing board and Heinrich Stiege went into the German navy. In August 1941, the political crisis that led to Walter Heerdt's removal from Heli (see Chapter 2) resulted in Peters assuming leadership of that firm as well, initially on a putatively temporary basis, but ultimately for the duration of the war. Less than a year later, in May 1942, he was named head of the Working Committee for Disinfestation and Epidemic Control in the Armaments Ministry, with responsibility for allocating personnel, raw materials, and output of relevant products, powers that were broadened in 1944 by his appointment as head of the Production Committee for Insecticides and Pesticides in the Economic Group for Chemistry. Aside from personal ambition, two passions appear to have animated

---

⁴⁰ On all of these deliveries, see Appendix R, Table IV, and the references provided there.

Peters's performance in all these posts. First, having built his entire career around *Blausäure*-based products, he was an enthusiast for Zyklon and eager to extend its market, especially in the face of competition from processes relying on steam. Second, having devoted his energies to Degesch since the early 1920s and reached its top, he was determined to make it "into the leading enterprise in its field, that is, an active and influential factor in the technical and organizational development of German pest control."[41] This goal, more than anything else, fueled his conflict with Bruno Tesch.

A third motivation also clearly played a role in Peters's wartime conduct. Having joined the SA in November 1933 and the NSDAP in May 1937, he was by all indications dedicated to the German war effort and to National Socialism, though not politically conspicuous outside his enterprise. A favorable Party evaluation of September 1942 curtly concluded that "he takes part generously in the usual donations. His manner and actions are National Socialist."[42] But postwar descriptions were more forceful. The Works Council formed at Degussa after the fighting ended castigated him as follows:

> Dr. Peters has worked as leader of our pest control department by all available means for National Socialism. Wherever he saw opposition to his person, he cleared it away with drastic threats of the political movement. Among other things, he informed our colleague Amend [who was not a Party member] that he would have to change his attitude or he [Peters] would have to remove him. Our colleague E. Sänger [whom the Party had declared unacceptable as Heerdt's successor at Heli in 1941] . . . made an unfavorable comment and Dr. Peters declared that one should report such a person to the authorities. . . . He held plant assemblies in relatively rapid succession, at which he warned people against defeatism. If anyone was propagandistically active for the Party, it was Dr. Peters, who even outdid our [Nazi] plant foreman. We also note that he once called our colleague Dr. Schulenburg to order, when the Niemöller case was discussed over lunch. . . . [I]n his capacity as a Party member, he said he would have to consider whether or not to report the matter.[43]

Even allowing for a spirit of vengefulness among some Germans in 1946 or for the personal unpopularity produced by Peters's well-documented deficiencies in handling subordinates, these are credible accounts. As Walter Heerdt conceded a few months earlier, despite his refusal to ascribe any role in his downfall in 1941 to his successor or to hold him responsible for his political views, "there can be no doubt that Dr. Peters did what he could for everything related to the Party."[44] The resulting hostility was so great after 1945 that Degesch's chief executives had to reassure the Works Council of

---

[41] DUA, BET 9/43, G. Peters, "Neue Zielsetzungen der Degesch," September 4, 1942, p. 1.

[42] HHW, Sig. 483/10982, Gaupersonalamtsleiter to Gauwirtschaftsberater, 4. September 1942, which also provides the dates of his Party affiliations.

[43] DUA, BR 01/0012, Zirkelbach to the public prosecutor, Minister für Wiederaufbau und politische Befreiung, November 15, 1946.

[44] DUA, BR 01/0012, Heerdt to Betriebsausschuss der Degussa, September 2, 1946.

Degussa that, regardless of the course of Peters's denazification proceedings, "under no circumstances is there an intention to take Dr. Peters into Degesch again."[45]

Peters's related desires to serve himself, his product, his firm, and his political convictions all contributed to shaping his behavior in June 1943, when he, like Bruno Tesch almost exactly a year earlier, became a co-conspirator in the program of murder with Zyklon B.[46] The person who apparently initiated Peters into this criminal partnership was a tormented, thirty-eight-year-old SS-Obersturmführer named Kurt Gerstein.[47] After joining the SS in 1941, in part to escape the political surveillance that resulted from his earlier opposition to the Nazi regime, Gerstein rose rapidly within the antiepidemic staff of the organization's chief sanitation officer, SS-Oberführer Joachim Mrugowsky, who ordered and distributed most of the Zyklon B that went to concentration camps after early 1942. The young man thus became increasingly entangled in the genocide, which proceeded under the cover of combating typhus. In fact, he witnessed one massacre with carbon monoxide at Belzec in 1942. Shocked at the length of time required by the primitive and unreliable equipment involved, he then embarked on a nerve-racking effort to get information on the killing out to the wider world while seeming to carry out his superiors' instructions without actually doing so.

At Mrugowsky's behest, Peters apparently called upon Gerstein at his office in Berlin and, after swearing to keep the "national secret" they were about to discuss, learned from the SS man that he had been delegated to acquire materials clandestinely for the execution of certain categories of people on Himmler's orders. He therefore wanted to obtain Zyklon B without the usual warning agent, as was possible for industries whose products could be adversely affected by it (e.g., some foodstuffs, tobacco), in order to make these killings more "humane." Peters knew better than to believe that the omission of the additive would have any effect on the victims, especially because the amount being included had fallen as a result of wartime shortages. But he does not seem to have paused either to advise Gerstein on ways of administering Zyklon so as to make death swifter or to speculate on other purposes behind Gerstein's request. Following the war, the chief SS pharmacist at Auschwitz, through whose hands the Zyklon used

[45] DUA, BR 01/0012, Degesch to Betriebsrat der Degussa, September 23, 1946.

[46] Except where otherwise indicated, my account of Peters's actions and behavior relies primarily on that presented in DUA, BU Gerhard Peters, judgment of the Schwurgericht des Landgerichts Frankfurt am Main, May 27, 1955, which is generally careful and sound, despite its regrettable (and obviously reluctant) verdict.

[47] The classic authorities on Gerstein are Saul Friedländer, *Kurt Gerstein: The Ambiguity of Good* (New York: Alfred A. Knopf, 1969); and Pierre Joffroy, *A Spy for God: The Ordeal of Kurt Gerstein* (New York: Harcourt Brace Jovanovich, 1970). I have also found Valerie Hébert, "Kurt Gerstein's Actions and Intentions in Light of Three Post-War Legal Proceedings" (M.A. Thesis, McGill University, 1999), very helpful.

in the gas chambers passed, suggested that the real motive was to use them in rapid sequence, which was impeded by lingering traces of the warning agent.[48] In any case, after some hesitation, Peters agreed to the deliveries, disregarding in the process Degesch's contractual commitments to Testa, but told Gerstein that maintaining secrecy was impossible. The best alternative was a standing monthly order to create an appearance of normality. Gerstein insisted on 500-gram containers, and a deal was struck for shipping 200 kilograms per month, that is, 400 cans, to Gerstein's Office for Disinfestation and Decontamination at Oranienburg and billing him personally. In fact, however, in the twelve months from June 1943 to May 1944, Dessau dispatched some 3,790 kilograms pursuant to this arrangement, including not only the regular consignments to Oranienburg, but also slightly more than half as much sent directly to Auschwitz, apparently as a result of either this conversation or follow-up consultations that Peters always denied ever took place.

Peters's postwar accounts give different descriptions of the targeted groups Gerstein listed, but all used the word *inferiors*, all avoided the term *Jews*, and all incriminated him. As Gerstein's request for secrecy implied, and Peters admitted to knowing at the time, none of the actions the SS man contemplated – not gassing as a form of capital punishment, not euthanasia, and not the execution of the physically or mentally handicapped or other "inferiors" – was legally sanctioned in Nazi Germany. That Hitler had issued a personal authorization of "mercy death" for "incurables," dated September 1, 1939, hardly legitimated Peters's course, since that document never had been published and lacked, in any case, the force of law.[49] All Peters had by way of justification was Gerstein's word that such murders had been occurring for quite some time on Himmler's direct authority, backed by Hitler. In the view of the postwar court that ultimately and reluctantly acquitted Peters, "he simply went along" and never considered any other course.[50] Perhaps he acted out of Party and national loyalty; probably he concluded that if he did not cooperate, someone else would; and certainly he wanted to head off possible trouble with the SS, though more for the sake of preserving his official activities and personal standing than because of worries about the consequences for Degesch's business, which, if Heli's experience after 1941 was any guide, would not have suffered. Whether Gerstein mentioned Jews in June 1943 or not – and there are strong arguments for guessing either way – had no bearing, in all likelihood, on Gerhard Peters's behavior. He agreed to abet killings by fiat; indeed, he suggested a way to help conceal them. One category of "inferiors," more or less, would have made little difference.

---

[48] Kalthoff and Werner, *Händler des Zyklon-B*, p. 163.
[49] Henry Friedlander, *The Origins of Nazi Genocide* (Chapel Hill: University of North Carolina Press, 1995), p. 67.
[50] For the quotation, DUA, BU Gerhard Peters, judgment of the Schwurgericht des Landgerichts Frankfurt am Main, May 27, 1955, p. 32.

Here, too, money was not the issue. The price per kilogram for Gerstein's Zyklon was 5 RM, presumably the prevailing rate for defense-related purchases at the time the orders commenced. Thus, the income on 3,790 kilograms came to only 18,950 RM and the probable proceeds, after payments to Dessau, to about 11,500 RM.[51] Furthermore, most of the bill went unpaid, and Peters chose not to pursue the matter. Only two invoices were honored, those of November 9, 1943 for 195 kilograms each, one by the Auschwitz camp administration and one by the Berlin office of the Medical Service of the Waffen-SS.[52] Kurt Gerstein's name appears rather conspicuously on the itemization of accounts outstanding that circulated within Degesch and to Degussa in the final months of Nazi rule.[53] Only as the regime was collapsing, and again after it did so, did Degesch dare try to collect its money, but now from the War Damages Office in Frankfurt.[54]

Whatever Gerstein told Peters about the scope of the SS murder program, he had ample reason to guess at it and chose to acquiesce, as well as to stifle the misgivings of others. Anton Slupetsky, the fumigator from Linz who supplied Mauthausen, apparently was so disturbed by witnessing a gassing of sick prisoners there in 1942 that he later discussed the subject with Peters, who reassured him on the ground that Zyklon caused less suffering than the carbon monoxide used at other camps.[55] His secretary claimed after the war to have overheard a conversation in which Hans-Ullrich Kaufmann of Degesch, whose duties made him aware of the quantities that both it and Testa were having shipped to Auschwitz, asked Peters whether one ought not to get written confirmation that such large amounts really were being used for disinfestation, but Peters allayed his concerns.[56] Kaufmann himself remembered discussing the first delivery to Auschwitz with Peters, presumably because of the intrusion on Testa's sales region, and later drawing the size of Gerstein's unpaid bill to Peters's attention, only to be told on both occasions that all was in order.[57] But Kaufmann confessed after the war to no further knowledge, lest he implicate himself. Nonetheless, another employee also later recalled that people talked openly at Degesch's offices concerning deliveries "to Auschwitz for the gassing."[58] Probably no one did

<hr>

[51] For the quantities shipped, the dates, and the fees (but not the destinations), see DUA, BE 01/0012, copy of the order book page for Konto-Nr. G 36, Obersturmführer Kurt Gerstein, Oranienburg, June 30, 1943, to May 31, 1944. It is clear from the page of Dessau's order book for March 1944 reproduced in Kalthoff and Werner, *Händler des Zyklon-B*, p. 162, that the cans dispatched were, indeed, of 500 grams.
[52] *Ibid.*, p. 25. [53] DUA, BET 10/7, Gewinn- und Verlustrechnung für 1944.
[54] See Kalthoff and Werner, *Händler des Zyklon-B*, p. 216; and DUA, DL 11.5/60, Degesch to Bachmann, July 12 and August 12, 1946.
[55] Weindling, *Epidemics and Genocide*, pp. 262, 314.
[56] Kalthoff and Werner, *Händler des Zyklon-B*, p. 182.
[57] DUA, BU Gerhard Peters, judgment of the Schwurgericht des Landgerichts Frankfurt am Main, May 27, 1955, p. 28.
[58] DUA, BR 01/0012, Zirkelbach's Notiz für Spruchkammerverfahren Dr. Peters, June 17, 1947, although the reliability of the recollection is somewhat undercut by the circumstance

so within Peters's earshot, for his determination to maintain the secrecy Gerstein demanded seems as well substantiated as his studied lack of curiosity about what he was making possible. But there were limits to his and his firm's cooperativeness. On two occasions, employees of Heli, which Peters also headed, declined to draw up or endorse plans for supposed fumigation chambers at Mauthausen and Natzweiler because their specifications, which are suspicious in retrospect, violated the firm's safety guidelines.[59]

In general, as far as Peters was concerned, it was his and Testa's job to supply the SS as far as output and the allocations of his Working Committee allowed, and what the Black Corps did with the substance was none of his business. He clung to this stance while Zyklon, which had been rationed since early 1943, became increasingly scarce. Even so, as air raids and a shortage of raw material shut down Dessau's beet processing works (and thus also the unscathed Zyklon installation there) for most of the period May 28 to October 31, 1944, many of Degesch's circulation chambers, including at concentration camps, had to be converted to Areginal, a new, nontoxic contribution to the firm's product line from IG Farben.[60] Thus, Peters's assurance to Gerstein that the Zyklon he had not yet used in mid-1944 could outlast the three-month shelf life indicated on the product labels is unlikely to have represented any more sinister impulse than a desire to deflect further demands for more product than he could furnish.

In any case, throughout 1944, Peters was preoccupied with managing what he considered Zyklon's bleak postwar prospects. On the one hand, he fought a running battle with IG Farben to get Degesch's operating sphere redefined as "interior disinfestation" rather than merely gaseous pesticides and found himself so stymied by the giant firm's negativism, which he thought "will lead Degesch in the near future onto a dead track," that he asked Hermann Schlosser to furlough him from Degesch so as to devote himself to his unpaid government posts.[61] On the other hand, he labored to exact a price from Kolin's demands for a larger share of what both it and Peters already perceived as a declining postwar appetite for the product, demands that he saw as damaging to the returns Degesch depended on from Dessau.[62] The outcome of the second dispute is not clear from the surviving records; that from the first was surely unsatisfactory, although Schlosser assuaged Peters's desire to withdraw from Degesch. In the course of 1944, he had to look on as

---

that it concerned T-Gas, not Zyklon B. If the German word actually used was *Begasung* rather than *Vergasung*, as quoted, the conversation would have been harmless.

[59] Kalthoff and Werner, *Händler des Zyklon-B*, pp. 188 and 196.

[60] On the damage at Dessau, see DL 3.H.Schlosser/1, Peters' Notiz für Herrn Schlosser, June 19, 1944.

[61] DUA, DL 3.H.Schlosser/1, Peters to Schlosser, May 26, 1944 (two letters), and Peters's Notiz für Herrn Schlosser, May 27, 1944; and IW 57.2/1, Peters's Notiz für Herrn Schlosser, August 7, 1944, from which the second set of quoted words come.

[62] DUA, DL 3.H.Schlosser/1, Stoecker to Schlosser, August 28, 1944.

Degussa secured its future in insecticides via another half-owned subsidiary, the Chemische Fabrik von J. E. Devrient AG of Hamburg, which entered into contracts with the patent holder for a new product called Gesarol (DDT), Geigy S. A. of Switzerland, and its German licensee, Schering AG.[63]

Did Degussa's leaders know that Zyklon B was being used after September 1941 not only to kill lice, but also to kill human beings whom the Nazi regime regarded as such? No extant written record or firsthand testimony so indicates, which is why the arrests in February 1948 of Hermann Schlosser, Ernst Bernau, and Adalbert Fischer, all members of Degussa's managing board and Degesch's Administrative Committee, resulted in criminal charges against them being dropped within weeks. Degussa's managers swore consistently after the war that Peters told them nothing, and he said the same. But one would expect as much in view of the facts that Heinz Scherf combined the roles of a member of Degussa's managing board and Peters's defense lawyer after the war, and Degussa offered to pay up to 150,000 Deutschmarks as bail money in order to keep Peters out of jail during the appeals of his initial convictions as an accessory to first manslaughter, then murder.[64] In truth, he and Schlosser were not particularly close, as Stiege, who was away at the front, and the Degussa chairman were, thus one cannot infer that Peters would have sought the corporate chairman's counsel. If he did not, however, on so grave a matter as the product's application to human beings, the evidence against him becomes still more damning, since such silence suggests either an awareness of illegality or an absence of shock about what was happening.

One thing is sure: if Peters or other Degesch employees did not tell Degussa's chief executives, they could not have deciphered the use to which Zyklon was being put from the sales figures forwarded to some of them. Total known shipments to Auschwitz came to approximately 24.2 metric tons in the years 1942–44 and those to Majdanek to 7.7 (see Appendix R, Table IV); the total revenue from both quantities was probably about 159,500 RM (about U.S. $63,800 at the time and $638,000 at the end of the twentieth century). In contrast, total Zyklon B sales in these years amounted to 963 tons and just over 5 million marks (U.S. $2 million and $20 million, respectively).[65] This means that just over 3 percent of Zyklon sales, by either volume or value, went to the principal sites at which it was used to kill. If one calculates on the basis of the total quantity sold within Germany and its

[63] DUA, IW 63.5/1, Devrient AG, Bericht des Vorstandes über das Geschäftsjahr 1943, May 16, 1944; Notiz über die Besprechung . . . in Berlin, May 25, 1944; Notiz über Besprechungen in Berlin, July 18, 1944; and Róka's Herstellung von Gesarol-Wirkstoff bei der Degussa, June 26, 1945. See also Weindling, *Epidemics and Genocide*, pp. 380–81.
[64] Clariant Werksarchiv Gersthofen, Ordner 125, Heinz Scherf to Theo Goldschmidt, July 4, 1950. I am grateful to Dr. Stephan Lindner for bringing this document to my attention.
[65] DUA, BET 9/43, Beantwortung der Fragen in der Anweisung der amer. Militärregierung für Deutschland betr. Dekartellisierung, Anlage zu 6a.

possessions (some 729 tons; see Appendix R, Table I), the share rises to but 4.4 percent. Even the total quantity dispatched to all concentration camps was only slightly more obvious; at fifty-six metric tons, it composed less than 6 percent of the Zyklon sold from 1942 to 1944 and less than 8 percent of that vended domestically.

What could or should Degesch or Degussa have done if Peters had behaved differently and/or told Schlosser? On the personal level, each man could have contrived a reason to resign, thus forwarding responsibility to a successor. But just stating that possibility indicates how little it would have achieved, aside from individual innocence. If the executives acted alone, they would have been replaced; if the successors also quit, the authorities would have been provoked sooner or later. In theory, Degesch could have claimed that the Zyklon supplies had been exhausted. After all, shortages enabled Peters to stand his ground against the furious demands of SS-Sturmbannführer Pflaum, the head of the Fumigation Department at Auschwitz (whose Zyklon supplies apparently were kept separate from those used for gassing), for more of the product during 1944.[66] In practice, however, stanching the flow to Auschwitz altogether probably would have been impossible thanks to Bruno Tesch, whose interests in preserving good relations with the SS and in embarrassing Degesch were profound. Had he protested and set off an investigation, the ruse would have been found out. Meanwhile, of course, it would have depended on complete loyalty within Degesch and Heli, where fervent Nazis, including Walter Rasch, who handled relations with Mauthausen and Theresienstadt and even visited Auschwitz in 1944, might not have been reliable.

Calculating how much money Degesch and Degussa took in from the murders with Zyklon B is complicated by uncertainty about the proportion of the quantities shipped to Auschwitz and Majdanek that actually was used in the gas chambers. Both Gerstein and SS-Unterscharführer Pery Broad, a veteran of the staff of the Political Department at Auschwitz, calculated on a ratio of one kilogram for each 1,000 people to be killed, which would mean that only one metric ton of Zyklon would have sufficed to annihilate the roughly 1 million persons gassed at the two camps. Dr. Charles Bendel, a Romanian Jewish physician who survived Auschwitz and was an eyewitness to the gassing process, testified after the war that one kilogram was used for each 500 prospective victims, which would raise the quantity needed to but two tons.[67] Commandant Rudolf Höss's postwar estimate of five to seven kilograms per 1,500 deaths under normal conditions, two to three

66 See Kalthoff and Werner, *Händler des Zyklon-B*, pp. 108 and 182–83. Pflaum was angry enough at Peters to launch an apparent inquiry into his background; see Osoby Archive, Moscow, 500-3-764, 1.248, unknown Standartenführer to Pflaum, August 18, 1944. I am indebted to Dr. Ralf Banken for forwarding this document to me.
67 Robert Jan van Pelt, *The Case for Auschwitz* (Bloomington: Indiana University Press, 2002), pp. 427–28.

more kilograms in cold or wet weather, results in a figure of 3.3 to 6.6 tons of Zyklon.[68] And, Joachim Mrugowsky claimed after the war that only 5.6 tons out of 23.8 that arrived at Auschwitz actually were used for fumigation, which indicates the possibility that 18.2 tons were available for killing.[69] Spoilage is likely to have cut heavily into that figure, however, until the SS learned in 1944 that the expiration dates on the Zyklon tins were not hard and fast. All in all, it seems reasonable to assume that the SS over- rather than underdosed, and thus that Höss's totals are not far off. If so, six tons of Zyklon (less than 1 percent of German domestic sales, 1942–44) would have produced sales income to Degesch or Testa of over 30,000 RM (U.S. $12,000 at the time; $120,000 in 1999) and earnings for both of roughly half these amounts, before deductions for overhead and taxes. That figure corresponds to only 1 percent of the total receipts minus the cost of goods sold by Testa alone in the period 1942–44 (see Appendix R, Table II). If one, rather arbitrarily, traces 1 percent of the dividends Degussa collected from Degesch in 1942–44 (148,750 RM), which included those it netted from Testa, to the killings with Zyklon at Auschwitz and Majdanek, the parent firm's proceeds come to 1,487.50 RM (U.S. $595 at the time or U.S. $5,950 in 1999).

Shocking as it is to say, the idea that Degussa made a fortune by providing the means to murder the European Jews is fatuous. Unless accompanied by an assessment of punitive damages, "disgorgement" of profits from this aspect of the *Shoah* would yield little, even if one left out of account the losses inflicted on Degesch in consequence of the war: over 281,000 RM in foreign assets, not counting patents, and some 716,524 RM worth of damages to property and equipment, much of which was not made good by the war damage claim process.[70]

In May 1946, Bruno Tesch and his chief aide, Karl Weinbacher, paid with their lives at the order of a British military court for supplying the SS with Zyklon in full knowledge of its intentions with the product, but Gerhard Peters fared better at the hands of the German judiciary. After no fewer than ten different legal proceedings between 1948 and 1955, although repeatedly convicted as an accessory to manslaughter or murder and forced to spend a total of two years and eight months in jail, he benefited from a change in German law and returned to freedom for the remaining nineteen years of his life. The decision of the court that awarded him a "third-class acquittal" arguably turned, however, on a factual error.[71] The judges concluded that they could not prove that the Zyklon he supplied to Gerstein actually had

---

[68] Wacław Długoborski and Franciszek Piper (eds.), *Auschwitz 1940–1945*, vol. III: *Mass Murder* (Oświęcim: Auschwitz-Birkenau State Museum, 2000), pp. 203–04.

[69] Weindling, *Epidemics and Genocide*, p. 306.

[70] DUA, D 2/18, unsigned, undated memo drawn up for the occupation authorities, headed Deutsche Gesellschaft für Schädlingsbekämpfung m.b.H., Frankfurt/M. (Degesch).

[71] The phrase is that of Kalthoff and Werner, *Händler des Zyklon-B*, p. 168.

been used to kill, since that man demonstrably had tried to destroy much of it, and no witnesses had confirmed that Zyklon without a warning agent and/or in 500-gram tins had been used in the gassings at Auschwitz. Thus, Peters had committed "unsuccessful abetting," which was no longer punishable as a result of amendments to the penal code passed in 1953. Apparently itself uncomfortable with the verdict it felt constrained to render, the court explicitly noted that "the trial has not established the innocence of the accused" and refused to restitute Peters for his costs.[72] Despite this gesture, the court appears to have erred in overlooking or discounting the testimony given in 1949 by Fritz Peter Strauch, a former inmate employed in the SS pharmacy at Auschwitz, who swore that all the Zyklon used for gassing passed through that office and that only Zyklon without the warning agent was employed throughout his time there from April/May 1943 to October 1944.[73] To be sure, he recalled cans of one or five kilograms, not 500 grams, but no surviving record indicates any deliveries of warning-free Zyklon to Auschwitz other than via Peters and Gerstein.

If one measures by deeds and intentions, rather than by the quantities of Zyklon provided, Gerhard Peters's guilt equaled Bruno Tesch's, and the question of whether he deserved the same fate depends more on one's opinion of capital punishment than on the adequacy of the evidence. Both men, one according to multiple witnesses and the other by his own admission, provided the SS knowingly with materials that were to be used for murder. Neither man's life was threatened or demonstrably endangered by the prospect of evading the requests for his assistance. Both acted less out of monetary greed than practical self-interest of a wider sort and perhaps out of a misplaced sense of national solidarity. To be sure, both also probably felt trapped in a tragedy not of their making. But neither showed any sign of exercising imagination to escape his dilemma or even claimed later to have racked his brains in the matter.

Given this, Degussa's role in bringing about Peters's ultimate release is perhaps the most suspect aspect of the corporation's conduct in relation to Zyklon B. If Peters, indeed, acted independently, why did Degussa feel obliged to defend him? He had been granted sick leave in August 1945 as a result of coming to blows with a recently fired workman, who publicly claimed to have been released because he had "seen too much" at Degesch, then allowed to resign from the firm at the end of the year, along with other tainted figures (Rasch of Heli, Kaufmann and Gassner of Degesch).[74] The

---

[72] DUA, BU Gerhard Peters, judgment of the Schwurgericht des Landgerichts Frankfurt am Main, May 27, 1955, especially pp. 33–36 and 44–48. The term of art appears on p. 45, the quoted phrase on p. 46.

[73] Kalthoff and Werner, *Händler des Zyklon-B*, pp. 182–83.

[74] See DUA, BR 01/0022, Schlosser to Peters, August 23, 1945; Schlosser's Aktennotiz Betr. Degesch/Heli of the same date; and the attached Streng vertraulicher Bericht Betreffend: Auseinandersetzung mit Tätlichkeiten by Peters, August 20, 1945.

earlier political miscues of his successor, Walter Heerdt, made that man the ideal leader of Degesch until his death in 1957. By the time of Peters's initial conviction in 1949, the anti–big business phase of the American occupation had ended, and it had hung Zyklon B and Degesch safely around the neck of IG Farben, which was being dissolved. If anything, springing to Peters's defense risked drawing attention to the corporate relationship with Degussa that fortunately seemed forgotten. Nonetheless, the firm provided him with bail money, counsel, and pleas to industrialists for support in 1950. And between October 1951 and June 1954, while free between trials, Peters worked at Degussa's Wesseling subsidiary as a "research assistant" and head of its hydrogen cyanide facility, and that firm pleaded with the court in 1954 not to take Peters into custody in view of his importance to the factory's production.[75]

There is no hard evidence that Degussa's rallying to Peters's defense amounted to paying him hush money. The most durable deals of such a sort are generally implicit in any case. More probably, Degussa's response reflected a self-serving but not altogether false attitude that pervaded the German corporate world after 1945, more or less along the lines of "we all made compromises for the good of the firm or the stockholders or the employees or the family or. . . ." Peters's situation appears to have come to stand, to Degussa's leaders, for their own, perhaps subconsciously guilt-laden sense of innocence, which they felt compelled to assert through him. Only such speculation seems capable of making sense of the presentation of his client by Heinz Scherf, the Degussa managing board member who served as Peters's defense lawyer, as a person in a "desperate situation . . . in which he was thrust through no fault of his own by the chaotic confusion of the Third Reich."[76] This depiction of Peters as victim fit in with a general postwar public relations offensive on the part of German industry that sought to divert attention from the degree to which business had served the Nazi regime by focusing on its coercive nature.[77] The portrait also sought to play on a widespread and self-pitying feeling in many quarters of the fledgling Federal Republic that concentration on the suffering of others under Nazism had obscured the supposedly equal horrors inflicted on the Germans by it.[78]

The tangled story of Degussa and Zyklon B did not end with the fate of Gerhard Peters. Degussa kept operating Degesch after 1945 in association with Bayer AG (a successor firm to IG Farben), and Goldschmidt (although the shareholdings changed in 1955 to 37.5 percent, 37.5 percent, and

[75] Kalthoff and Werner, *Händler des Zyklon-B*, pp. 182–83.
[76] Clariant Werksarchiv Gersthofen, Ordner 125, Scherf to Theo Goldschmidt, July 4, 1950, p. 9.
[77] S. Jonathan Wiesen, *West German Industry and the Challenge of the Nazi Past* (Chapel Hill: University of North Carolina Press, 2001).
[78] Robert G. Moeller, *War Stories: The Search for a Usable Past in the Federal Republic of Germany* (Berkeley: University of California Press, 2001).

25 percent respectively). And the subsidiary resumed production of Zyklon, continuing to sell it under that name in Germany until 1974 (when it was restyled Cyanosil) and for international use until Degussa took over Degesch completely in 1986 and ceded it to Detia-Freyberg GmbH of Laudenbach. In the meantime, Degussa also retained its shares in Heli and acquired 30 percent of the stock in Testa, which was reincorporated after the war under that acronym as Degesch's exclusive representative in the former territory of Tesch & Stabenow. The two sales firms were merged in 1979 into a new Deutsche Gesellschaft für Schädlingsbekämpfung (DGS), in which Degesch obtained 100 percent of the shares in 1986, just before Degussa divested it. Otherwise useful products are, after all, seldom punished for the evil purposes to which people put them.

9

War's End and Aftermath

For Degussa, the beginning of the end of the Nazi era occurred on March 22 to 24, 1944, when successive waves of Allied bombers devastated Frankfurt and loosed "catastrophe...upon the main administration building as well as Works I and II." Within 36 hours, some 18 million Reichsmarks worth of the firm's structures, equipment, and supplies collapsed into ash and rubble. Only the new laboratory building on the Wolf family's former property emerged relatively intact. Also completely or partially destroyed were the homes of Hermann Schlosser, Ernst Bernau, Adalbert Fischer, and Koloman Róka.[1]

Though hardly the first aerial attack on either a Degussa installation or the city of Frankfurt, the onslaught of late March 1944 vastly exceeded anything the firm had experienced or anticipated. Knapsack's military importance and proximity to Britain attracted strikes as early as the summer of 1940, prompting Degussa to sink 130,000 RM into blast- and shrapnel-proofing that muted the effects of renewed assaults in October 1942 and March 1943.[2] The Berlin offices and laboratories of the Auergesellschaft at Fr. Krause Ufer 24 were wrecked the following September, and their staffs then transferred to outlying sites, as were some of Degussa's own operations in the nation's capital.[3] And the metropolis on the Main River suffered through no fewer than thirty-six raids in 1940–42, then was hit repeatedly in 1943–44, including by hundreds of aircraft at a time on October 4, November 26, December 20, January 29, February 4 and 8, and March 2 and 18.[4] Yet early in that month, the managing board's report on the

---

[1] DUA, DL 2/1, Niederschrift über die Vorstandssitzung am 3. April 1944, n.p., for the quotation and the extent of the damage; and am 3. Juli 1944, n.p., for the cost estimates. For an overview of the attack and its effects on the city, see Armin Schmid, *Frankfurt im Feuersturm* (Frankfurt: Frankfurt Societäts-Druckerei, 1965), pp. 124–28, 162–63, and 165.

[2] DUA, DL 2/1, Niederschriften über die Vorstandssitzungen am 5. August 1940, p. 108; am 2. September 1940, p. 124; am 7. Juli 1941, pp. 191–92; and am 5. Oktober 1942, p. 278; and DL 3.Baerwind/26, Besuch im Werk Knapsack, March 10, 1943.

[3] On Degussa's offices, see *ibid.*, am 5. Februar 1944, p. 357; on the Auergesellschaft, DUA, IW 24.9/12, Monatsbericht Nr. 11 für August 1943, October 21, 1943; and IW 24.9/1, Bericht des Vorstandes für das Geschäftsjahr 1942/43, April 5, 1944, pp. 1–2.

[4] Schmid, *Frankfurt im Feuersturm*, pp. 28–30, 81–83, 94–95, 100, and 123–24.

business year 1942/43 noted with obvious relief that "happily, we have been spared... serious war damage."[5] Such good fortune probably contributed to the apparent inability of Degussa's leadership to grasp what lay in store for it, even after the Anglo-American Operation Gomorrah rendered 44 percent of Hamburg's housing uninhabitable and killed some 40,000 of that city's residents within just ten days in July and August 1943; even after Schlosser, Bernau, Róka, Fischer, and Ernst Baerwind viewed "the completely destroyed center of Düsseldorf" a few days later and drove home on a deserted highway in a "very serious mood about the near future"; and even after the Nazi regime evacuated a large share of Frankfurt's prewar population (114,500 people, almost exactly 20 percent of the total in September 1939) during the following October.[6]

Before the Allied air fleets ravaged Degussa's headquarters, its principal preparations consisted of establishing an around-the-clock system of air wardens (in September 1942, even managing board members agreed to spend one or two nights per month in this role), prioritizing buildings to save in the event of fire, assuring the water supply for such efforts, readying an emergency system of communication with other installations, improving the basement shelter at the Gutleutstrasse works, and belatedly deciding, less than three weeks before the March conflagration, to add numerous smaller bunkers at that plant and construct a large one for the people at Works I and the administrative center in the Weissfrauenstrasse.[7] Plans to disperse operations had been applied solely to clerical departments that depended on costly machinery and/or did not need to be in immediate contact with the firm's leadership, for example, bookkeeping, data processing, and several purchasing and sales sections. As a result, only about 320 of the corporation's roughly 700 central employees and virtually none of its manufacturing personnel nearby had been shifted to suburban or remote locations by the

[5] DUA, DL 2/1, Bericht des Vorstandes über das Geschäftsjahr 1942/43, March 6, 1944, p. 2. A few days earlier, Bernau tallied the net losses from air attacks during the preceding business year at just under 1.7 million Reichsmarks, nearly all of them having occurred at Knapsack, Kalscheuren, Düsseldorf, and Berlin; RFI 4.2/104, Bilanzbericht an den Aufsichtsrat über das Geschäftsjahr 1942/43, March 3, 1944.

[6] See Olaf Groehler, *Bombenkrieg gegen Deutschland* (Berlin: Akademie Verlag, 1990), pp. 119 (on the devastation to Hamburg), 269 (on the total number of evacuees from Frankfurt), and 447 (on that city's prewar population). On the directors' visit to Düsseldorf and their knowledge of what had happened in Hamburg a few days earlier, DUA, D 3/2, Baerwind Tagebuch, Abschrift, p. 39, entry nr. 208 for August 5, 1940.

[7] See DUA, DL 2/1, Niederschriften über die Vorstandssitzungen am 7. September 1942, pp. 266–67; am 1. Februar 1943, p. 299; am 1. März 1943, p. 306; am 7. September 1943, p. 335; and am 6 März 1944, p. 360. Also authorized on the last-named date were two large bunkers, each costing 150,000 RM (as did the improvements at the Gutleutstrasse plant) at Rheinfelden and Kalscheuren. Illuminating insight into Degussa's air defense measures is provided by DUA, PCA 2/147, Bericht über die Tätigkeit des Werkschutzleiters der Hauptverwaltung des Werkes I in der Zeit vom 15.3.–6.9.1943, n.d., no signature.

time Frankfurt went up in flames.[8] Whatever the final death toll to Degussa's workforce in March 1944 (no tally appears to have survived), the wonder is that more people did not die. Had the preponderance of the bombs not fallen at night, casualties assuredly would have been greater.

Nonetheless, as with regard to German industry in general, the Allied air offensive proved less successful in smashing Degussa's factories than in strangling them. Declared irreparable, the Degussit installation in Frankfurt had to be reconstructed at Stierstadt, where it reopened in October 1944, but Degussa's other manufacturing facilities on the banks of the Main were all operating again by the end of April.[9] They seldom returned to previous levels of production, however, thanks to the domino effects of the relentless bombing: recurrent interruptions in the flow of gas, coal, electricity, parts, and intermediates; constant diversion of time, energy, laborers, and money to air raid defense measures and increasingly Sisyphean reconstruction tasks; and steady erosion of confidence in the point of pursuing goals other than personal or corporate survival. All these consequences gathered force once "Fortress Europe" was breached in the West in June 1944, Soviet troops began to capture plants in the East (Hainowka fell first in July, then Perecin in October), the task of erecting barriers against these encroaching forces pulled increasing numbers of workers off assembly lines, and tactical air attacks in support of advancing Allied troops both added to the weight of strategic bombing and eliminated time to take shelter.[10] Meanwhile, the immolation of Frankfurt scattered Degussa's administrative units and managing board members to improvised offices in towns and villages surrounding the city, greatly reducing their ability to communicate with each

[8] See DUA, DL 2/1, Niederschrift über die Vorstandssitzung am 5. Juli 1943, p. 326 (on the initial plans for the dispersal of offices and staff from Frankfurt); and am 6. März 1944, pp. 361–62 (on the progress thereafter). Of course, a few manufacturing operations had been transferred from Frankfurt in preceding years, for example, parts of beryllium production to Rheinfelden in early 1941, and protection from air raids had factored into such decisions; see DL 2/1, Niederschriften über die Vorstandssitzungen am 6. Januar 1941, p. 152; and am 3. März 1941, p. 164.

[9] On the Durferrit plant and the revival of production in Frankfurt, see DUA, DL 2/1, Niederschrift über die Vorstandssitzung am 3. April 1944, n.p. [2]; Notizen aus der Vorstandsbesprechungen vom 11. April, vom 19. April, und vom 26. April 1944, unpaginated; Niederschrift über die Vorstandssitzung am 1. Mai 1944, n.p. [1]; Notizen aus dem Vorstandscolloquium am 20. Juni 1944, p. 1; and DL 3/20, Postzettel Nr. 104, October 18, 1944.

[10] On the loss of laborers to work on fortifications, see, for example, IW 33.8/9, [Knapsack] Betriebsbericht für August 1944, September 8, 1944, pp. 15–16; and für September 1944, October 6, 1944, p. 14. On the air raids, DUA, DL 3/20, Postzettel Nr. 100, October 13, 1944, which reports that the Kalscheuren factory had begun suspending production daily at dusk because alarms no longer allowed evacuation of the works by the time planes appeared overhead. Regarding the attacks that month that partially or totally disabled Degussa's Rhineland installations (Kalscheuren, the Marquart subsidiary, and Knapsack), DL 2/1, Niederschrift über die Vorstandssitzung am 6. November 1944, pp. 1–2; and DL 3/20, Postzettel Nr. 105, October 19, 1944.

24   Bomb damage, 1944 (offices in Frankfurt)

25   Bomb damage, 1944 (offices in Berlin)

other or plants and branches in other parts of the country, and making over-all coordination increasingly impossible.[11] Not until October 1944 did the firm again possess anything resembling a central headquarters, housed in the isolated Wächtersbach Castle, a full 50 kilometers northeast of Frankfurt, and its telephone connection with other installations remained imperfect.[12] From midyear on, therefore, the volumes of Degussa's output and deliveries fell inexorably, while the costs of achieving them mounted.[13] Now, the same preoccupation with self-interest that had driven the firm's cooperation and complicity with National Socialism impelled at least some of Degussa's leaders to start decoupling its future from the regime's.

The chaos of competing priorities – sustaining production, strengthening air defenses, creating reserve or replacement plants in the German interior, finding and renting safe quarters for clerical offices, and planning for the future – that overwhelmed Degussa's managers after March 1944 already had them reeling prior to that date. In the autumn of 1943, faced with Bernau's increasingly dire financial projections, a majority on the managing board began declining to advance Degussa's own capital to carry out further investment projects with primarily "defensive" rather than "commercial" value. Among these were not only the backup sodium plant at Rheinfelden and the lamp-black installation Johannes Eckell wanted (see Chapter 6), but also a pilot plant for low-pressure synthesis of methanol, which Albert Speer's Armaments Ministry desired in order to break a short-term bottleneck in output of that product. Though willing, "considering the extraordinary importance that must be attached to maintaining our cyanide fabrication," to spend 250,000 RM on a reserve sodium cyanide installation at Grünau that would be useless in peacetime, Degussa's executives drew the line at appropriating another 450,000 RM to serve only the Ministry's short-range methanol needs and demanded government financing as the precondition for their cooperation.[14] As with regard to the sodium facility, such intransigence did not last long. Within a month, after the corporation's representatives in Berlin

[11] For numerous reports on the rather frantic scattering of directors and offices to Idstein, Kronberg, Kleinkarlbach, Langelsheim, Mombach, Oppenau, Wolfgang, and, more remotely, Konstanz, see DUA, DL 2/1, Niederschriften über die Vorstandssitzungen bzw. Notizen aus den Vorstandsbesprechungen, March 6 to July 27, 1944.
[12] On the inability to establish telephone contact between Wächtersbach and the many offices transferred to Konstanz, see DL 2/1, Niederschrift über die Sitzung des Ausschusses für Verkaufsorganisation am 9. Januar 1945, p. 1.
[13] For the first serious reports of production declines at undamaged plants, such as Mombach, Fürstenberg, and Wolfgang, because of inability to obtain intermediates, see DUA, DL 2/1, Niederschriften über die Sitzungen des Ausschusses für Verkaufsorganisation am 8. August 1944, p. 3; and am 5. September 1944, pp. 2–3.
[14] DUA, DL 2/1, Niederschrift über die Vorstandssitzung am 6. Dezember 1943, pp. 347–48. Cf. the alacrity with which the board agreed to devote 400,000 RM to backup plants for watch stones at Weissenstein and for Degussit at Stierstadt only a few months earlier; *ibid.*, am 5. Juli 1943, p. 325.

weighed in heavily in favor of the project, the board grudgingly sanctioned the expenditure and designated Wolfgang as the site.[15]

But after the cataclysm of March 1944, Degussa's resistance stiffened. By June, the enterprise was trying "to head off completely" a Berlin-inspired demand for a chloride of lime factory at Rheinfelden "that is commercially uninteresting in the future."[16] To be sure, the firm's leaders continued to exert themselves for militarily urgent installations that also promised to give off high returns (e.g., Dissousgas) and/or to sustain or further the prospects of key factories (especially Fürstenberg).[17] Degussa's reluctance to commit funds to less immediately rewarding initiatives, including the practice of exporting large volumes of goods on credit in order to help the Reich's balance of payments, became increasingly apparent over the summer, however, as the Western Allies broke out of Normandy and began racing across France.[18] At the end of September, the ever more irritated and desperate authorities in Berlin reacted. August Kolb, Degussa's managing board member who also supervised national chemicals and explosives production from a post in the Armaments Ministry, sent his corporate colleagues a long letter cataloging their shortcomings from the point of view of his ministerial associates. His message culminated in the general complaint that "Degussa lacks enthusiasm for action."[19]

Schlosser's five-page, single-spaced *cri du coeur* in response set forth the divided loyalties that guided Degussa in the final year of the war so passionately and bluntly that the document deserves quotation at length. After telling Kolb that "like so many other Berlin officials...you have only a very incomplete idea of the conditions that have developed here in the West and that are growing worse daily," Schlosser described the difficulties under

---

[15] *Ibid.*, am 4. Januar 1944, pp. 351–52. On subsequent vacillations regarding this project, see *ibid.*, am 5. Juni 1944, n.p. [6]; and am 3. Juli 1944, n.p. [2–3].

[16] *Ibid.*, am 5. Juni 1944, n.p. [3–4]. For the comparative context of Degussa's actions in this respect and others during the final year of the fighting, see Klaus-Dietmar Henke, *Die amerikanische Besetzung Deutschlands* (Munich: Oldenbourg, 1995), pp. 449–70.

[17] *Ibid.*, am 4. Januar 1944, p. 352; am 6. März 1944, p. 361; and am 3. Juli 1944, n.p. [3]. Especially revealing in this connection is Degussa's eager pursuit of a methanol plant at Fürstenberg as a replacement for an abandoned ammonia-making installation; see Niederschrift über die Vorstandssitzung am 4. September 1944, p. 394; Notizen aus der Vorstandsbesprechung am 22. September 1944; Niederschrift über die Vorstandssitzung am 2. Oktober 1944, n.p. [5]; Notizen aus der Vorstandsbesprechung am 27. Oktober 1944, p. 2. As the managing board noted, "it remains essential to us to drive Fürstenberg forward as far as possible during the war"; Notizen aus der Vorstandsbesprechung am 21. November 1944, p. 1.

[18] On the managing board's decision to cease deliveries to foreign customers without payment in advance or an assurance that the necessary funds were on deposit in a German bank, see DUA, DL 2/1, Fischer to Group Leaders and Members of the Sales Committee, August 1, 1944.

[19] For the quotation, see DUA, DL 2/1, Niederschrift über die Vorstandssitzung am 2. Oktober 1944, n.p. [1].

which Degussa was laboring at a time when "the personnel are so worn out by the continuing attacks and alarms that one can no longer demand intensified performance," and itemized more than 32 million Reichsmarks in losses currently confronting his firm even as its "earning power ... is in the process of rapidly disappearing." He then laid down a strikingly clear demarcation of what Degussa henceforth would or would not do for the Fatherland:

We unanimously concluded at yesterday's managing board meeting, in any case, that the point at which our expenditures exceed our income is approaching with giant steps and that we then must live off the capital just in order to pay wages and salaries.... Our personal engagement, all our expert knowledge, and our entire organization are unconditionally at the service of all tasks essential to the war effort, and, as a veteran of the front in the last war and given my stance throughout this one, I will not let anyone reproach me for lacking enthusiasm for action, especially not in this phase of the war, when we surely must give our all. That cannot mean however, that we use the property of others, namely the money of Degussa's stockholders, to finance things that clearly are tasks of the state alone.... The financing of a factory that is needed solely for the momentary purposes of the war and that will be in peacetime completely superfluous and ... unprofitable is clearly a matter for the state office that demands it.... I am convinced that I can write to you so openly because you understand exactly my entire stance and attitude, which is unchanged concerning the necessity of fighting this war to the last and to the end, and know that I let no one outdo me in consciousness of duty. This sense also applies, however, to my duties as chief executive of Degussa, and in this connection I cannot take, to the best of my knowledge and belief, a different position from the one described above on the fundamental issue of rejecting further financial sacrifices that would ruin Degussa.[20]

True to Schlosser's word, on the preceding day, the managing board made two fundamental decisions concerning its future services to the National Socialist regime: with regard to factories, "to make sure of all possible state financial guarantees before we make new commitments"; and concerning war-related trade deals, to advance no further funds "unless accompanied by a completed guarantee from the state, payable within a short period."[21]

As Schlosser's letter and these decisions suggest, by early October 1944, Degussa's board had begun to act on a realization that the members dared not articulate, namely that the war was lost. Probably the chairman, Baerwind, and Bernau saw the truth earliest, perhaps from the moment the D-day beachheads were secured, and Fischer, Federlin, and Róka may have avoided the conclusion longest. But several developments in late summer shook even the hard-liners. Federlin had to announce in early August that "the coming call-ups as part of the ruthless prosecution of total war will lead to extraordinary personnel reductions, for which replacements are scarcely to be expected."[22] This was followed in September by the withdrawal of all

[20] *Ibid.*, Anlage 1, Schlosser to Kolb, October 3, 1944.   [21] *Ibid.*, n.p. [1, 3].
[22] *Ibid.*, am 7. August 1944, n.p. [2].

foreign laborers from Degussa's exposed plants west of the Rhine, then by government demands that Degussa detail workers to the Westwall border fortifications and release 30 percent of the firm's administrative employees for military duty or war production, and finally by renewed bombing that knocked the Gutleutstrasse plant out for a further two months and forced additional production transfers to Grünau.[23] The worsening situation almost certainly completed the process by which the other active managing board members (Achterath, Robert Hirtes, Geo Hubert, and Ewald von Retze) came to recognize that their principal challenge henceforth was to bring as many of Degussa's assets as possible through the impending collapse without provoking charges of defeatism.

That Schlosser and Bernau already were thinking far ahead is clear from a number of their actions during 1944. Shortly after Degussa's buildings in Frankfurt crumbled, Schlosser warned his colleagues against investing funds in rapid reconstruction, arguing instead in favor of making preparations to erect a temporary barracks complex outside the city and meanwhile entering into negotiations with the nearby town of Isenburg to secure a site for a "future central precious metals works."[24] Such a course would preserve the firm's financial strength "for a perhaps one day to be expected, rapidly occurring peace," after which the firm could weigh the options of returning to its original headquarters site or selecting a less constricted one.[25] An even clearer indication of the chairman's line of thought came over the summer,

[23] *Ibid.*, am 4. September 1944, p. 392 (on the labor drafts); and Notizen aus der Vorstandsbesprechung am 15. September 1944, as well as DL 3/20, Postzettel Nr. 77, September 16, 1944 (on the withdrawals of foreign laborers), and Nr. 79, September 19, 1944 (on the damage to Werk II). The "30 percent action" apparently led to releases of approximately 160 people, see DL 3/20, Postzettel Nr. 105, October 19, 1944, p. 2; and DL 2/1, Notizen aus der Vorstandsbesprechung am 23. Januar 1945, p. 3. On the ninety-nine individuals whom the firm made available for the Westwall work, see BR 01/0012, Liste unserer für die Heranziehung zum langfristigen Notdienst (Westwallaktion) namhaft gemachten Gefolgschaftsmitglieder, September 6, 1944. The move of zirconmetall to Grünau was delayed repeatedly, however, by Johannes Eckell and may never have been carried out; see PCA 1/559, Schmidt's Aktennotiz Betr.: Besprechung...über die Wiedereingangbringung unseres Zirkonmetallbetriebes, November 1, 1944; Fachbereich Seltene Erden to Degussa, December 1, 1944; and Baerwind's Aktenvermerk betreffend Wiederaufbau Zirkonmetall/Gutleutstrasse und Zirkonverlagerung Grünau, December 9, 1944.
[24] DUA, DL 2/1, Niederschrift über die Vorstandssitzung am 1. Mai 1944, n.p. [3].
[25] DUA, DL 3.Schlosser/1, Schlosser's Notiz für Herrn Architekt Ziegler betr. Sammel- und Übergangslager Degussa, May 3, 1944. On the further development of these plans, see DL 2/1, Notizen aus der Vorstandsbesprechung am 9. Mai 1944, p. 2; and Niederschrift über die Vorstandssitzung am 5. Juni 1944, n.p. [1]. At the last managing board meeting before the arrival of American troops in Frankfurt, the group entrusted Ziegler, however, with the task of rebuilding both the administrative building and the metals works, presumably on the original site; *ibid.*, Notizen aus der Vorstandsbesprechung am 20. März 1945, p. 3. The board's decision a few months earlier to expend 275,000 RM on office furniture and equipment in the Protectorate and store the material in Germany probably occurred in preparation for this reconstruction project; see *ibid.*, Niederschrift über die Vorstandssitzung am 4. Dezember 1944, p. 4.

when he launched a review of Degussa's "planned staffing after the war, taking into consideration the [intention] to retain the personnel now at the front," and sanctioned a decision to use the ordered 30 percent reduction in administrative staff as a means of streamlining the firm's organization and achieving a "stronger alignment of our workforce with postwar conditions."[26] In this respect, he soon had the backing of a report by Bernau tracing part of the continuing growth of Degussa's operating costs to declines in the quality of the firm's staff as a result of military call-ups, "which had the consequence that deficient performance had to be offset partially by more personnel."[27] Implicitly the decision to reverse this trend amounted to conceding that such adjustments had become futile. Moreover, Degussa's finance man made several significant, adroit, and politically risky moves just before the end of the 1943/44 business year in September, all of which bespoke his determination to reduce the corporation's financial exposure. He not only applied all of Degussa's 3 million Reichsmarks in accumulated tax rebate certificates to the firm's annual revenue bill, wrote off large portions of the remaining value of Degussa's subsidiaries, authorized a buildup in the firm's precious metal reserves, and began calling in all possible accounts payable from abroad, but also sold all of Degussa's 28 million Reichsmarks in "government bonds and . . . investments in purely war industries" for cash, which he then deposited.[28]

Throughout 1944, Degussa also began disentangling itself from assorted war-related contracts and otherwise reorienting its production around what it projected to be the demands of the postwar economic environment, with a particular eye to prospective competition from the United States. As early as February, the firm granted paid leaves of absence to Dr. Hans Walter, the head of its patent section, along with two of his assistants, to continue their work independently on methylnitrate for rocket propulsion and munitions and renounced Degussa's rights to any previously or subsequently patented military applications of the product. In December, the corporation followed up with a further division of rights to the military and civil forms of Formit, an explosive derivative of methylnitrate.[29] Meanwhile, Degussa wriggled out of

---

[26] *Ibid.*, Niederschrift über die Sitzung des Ausschusses für Verkaufsorganisation am 4. Juli 1944, p. 2 (for the first quotation); and Niederschrift über die Vorstandssitzung am 4. September 1944, p. 392 (for the second).

[27] DUA, BET 10/1, Bernau's Betr.: Unkosten, September 26, 1944, p. 3.

[28] DUA, Bernau's Bilanzbericht an den Aufsichtsrat über das Geschäftsjahr 1943/44, May 24, 1945, pp. 7–8, 11. On the call-in of foreign obligations to Degussa, see DL 2/1, Niederschrift über die Vorstandssitzung am 4. September 1944, p. 393; am 6. November 1944, pp. 3–4; and am 4. Dezember 1944, p. 3.

[29] DUA, BU Hermann Schlosser, patent division agreement between Walter and Degussa, February 3,1944, with Anlagen; Eidesstattlichen Erklärungen Dr. Hans Walter and Dr. Heinz Scherf, February 10, 1947; DL 2/1, Notizen aus der Vorstandsbesprechung am 19. Dezember 1944, p. 2; and SCH 1/32, Fuchs to Schlosser, January 4, 1945, with enclosure, and Degussa to Fuchs February 2, 1945.

commitments to work on two carbon black–related projects of significance to the Wehrmacht, an attempt to develop so-called *Explosionsruss* from methane and the "Chimney Sweep Program" to devise a coating of carbon black or rubber that would make U-boats undetectable by Allied devices using electromagnetic waves.[30] Indeed, regarding the latter case, Schlosser proudly pointed out to the director of Degussa's research operations that "this is quite unambiguous proof of my contention that one very well can free oneself from burdensome research assignments even under difficult conditions, if one definitely wants to do so and above all gives practically clear and persuasive reasons."[31] Equally indicative of the firm's gathering efforts to slough off unwanted activities and prepare itself for new challenges were several developments regarding Degussa's production palette. Shortly after Helmut Achterath reported to the managing board on the importance of Degussa's earnings from the acetic acid syndicate to the "coming peacetime situation," Schlosser revealed his firm intention to abandon Degussa's near-monopoly position in the charcoaling of wood in favor of the synthetic production of formaldehyde and solvents at Fürstenberg. He therefore all but told the responsible subordinate to stop trying to maintain or expand the corporation's position in this "losing business."[32] Most tellingly, the chairman appointed a new development staff under Dr. Max Goecke to begin tackling the firm's most formidable postwar problems, "the extension of the raw materials base and the creation of products that promise a considerable commercial profit," and he circulated to the managing board a list of the current prices of the principal American products likely to compete with Degussa's after the war, "which . . . underlines the dangerousness of this competition in the future."[33]

Because the preeminent goal, according to the managing board's minutes of late January 1945, now was "to lead the Degussa concern through its present war tasks to the future peacetime ones," the firm's foremost challenge became saving its factories from Hitler's increasingly feverish orders to destroy everything in the invading Allies' paths.[34] While Speer maneuvered

---

[30] On *Explosionsruss*, see DUA, DL 2/1, Niederschriften über die Vorstandssitzungen am 1. Februar 1943, p. 299, and am 5. Juni 1944, n.p. [6–7]. On the *Schornsteinfegerprogramm*, PCA 2/144, Untermann's Ber.: Sitzung im OKM Berlin, May 29, 1943; DL 11.5/43, Schlosser to Kühnhold, October 30, 1944; Schlosser to Untermann, December 11 and 20, 1944; Schlosser to Kühnhold, December 21, 1944, and January 16, 1945; and Untermann's Notiz für Herrn Dr. Mayer-Wegelin, July 9, 1957.

[31] DUA, DL11.5/43, Schlosser to Fuchs, December 2, 1944.

[32] DUA, DL 2/1, Niederschrift über die Vorstandssitzung am 7. August 1944, n.p. [1]; DL 3/20, Schlosser to Roos, September 9, 1944.

[33] DUA, DL 2/1, Niederschrift über die Sitzung des Ausschusses für Verkaufsorganisation am 9. Januar 1945, pp. 3–4. On the appointment of the development staff, *ibid.*, am 6. November 1944, pp. 4–5.

[34] DUA, DL 2/1, Notizen aus der Vorstandsbesprechung am 23. Januar 1945, p. 1.

in Berlin to undermine these instructions, the firm's managers did the like, reiterating at every opportunity the line they laid down in mid-September 1944:

We favor trying to preserve plants threatened by the enemy under all circumstances, since the opponent is not dependent on them, but they are extremely valuable for the German economy and Degussa. If necessary, at most paralysis by removal of important parts should occur, but on no account blowing up [of the works].[35]

Three days later, Speer's ministry interceded against the detonation of Knapsack as Allied forces approached, and Degussa's board resolved that "the general policy remains firm: intensified production as long as possible, preservation of the plants, and holding the workforce together."[36] When chaos descended following the turn of the year and Schlosser felt compelled to issue a general directive to all branch and plant leaders for their conduct in the event of becoming cut off from the firm's headquarters, he combined brief and general admonitions to fulfill "our national obligations up to the last possibility" and "your duty to the Fatherland and the Führer up to the last moment" with full and specific instructions regarding the future of their installations:

In addition, there are your obligations to your plant and its workforce and to the entire Degussa Works Community. In fulfilling them, naturally advance agreement with the decisive agencies and Party offices and, if necessary, with the Wehrmacht, is always to be established. Assuming this, the most important thing is to keep the plant and production lines as capable of action as in any way possible, so that, when the other prerequisites for the resumption of production, such as coal, electricity, raw materials, transportation, and so on are again present, work can be resumed in order to provide the workforce with bread and employment.... If a situation arises in which you are again wholly or partially capable of production but have no communication with the responsible sales office or the headquarters, it is entirely within the range of your initiative to look for regional sales possibilities and to develop the resulting business on your own. The most important matter is that you become fully operational again as fast as possible, which means not only producing but also selling, in order to secure the financing of production and especially wage payments.[37]

---

35 *Ibid.*, am 15. September 1944, p. 1. On Speer's efforts, see Joachim Fest, *Speer: The Final Verdict* (New York: Harcourt, 2001), pp. 233–62, but also the more critical account of Henke, *Die amerikanische Besetzung Deutschlands*, pp. 421–35.
36 On Speer's intercession, DL 3/21, Postzettel Nr. 78, September 18, 1944, p. 1; for the quotation, DUA, DL 2/1, Niederschrift über die Vorstandssitzung am 2. Oktober 1944, n.p. [2].
37 DUA, GEH 6/7, Schlosser to all plants and branches of the Degussa concern [an alle Werke und Zweigniederlassungen des Degussa-Konzerns], February 2, 1945, pp. 1–2. See also Schlosser's and Federlin's instruction to Dr. Deppe in Berlin "to refrain from nothing in order to remain operational"; DL 3/20, Postzettel No. 17, January 25, 1945.

That apparently none of Degussa's German installations fell victim to Hitler's scorched earth policy, although much equipment was lost through massive withdrawals of machinery from individual plants, is a testament to the success of Schlosser's and his colleagues' determination not to join in the *Nibelungentod* that the Nazi Führer ordained for the German people.[38] Such thinking also had an ugly side, however, as demonstrated by Robert Hirtes's letter to his colleagues just before Frankfurt fell in late March 1945. Noting that "we have to reckon in the near future with the pulling out of all foreigners," he rejoiced in this "elegant" solution to the problem of protecting the factories from pillaging and advised strongly against attempts to keep on "one or another who has gotten on well."[39]

Yet the losses, both human and material, mounted steadily. Degussa appears never to have tallied its casualties from the fighting, the bombings, the conquests of its works, and the increasingly hasty and hazardous retreats, especially those from the eastern parts of Germany. But fragmentary references in the surviving documents to incidents or individual fates suggest that the number of deaths during the last year of the war probably ran well into the hundreds.[40] With regard to buildings and equipment, the data are somewhat more precise. On February 20, 1945, Bernau put the war's damages to Degussa at 74.5 million Reichsmarks, of which the firm had recovered but 6.5 million Reichsmarks from the government.[41] The latter figure increased by only 1.2 million Reichsmarks in subsequent months, whereas the fighting and subsequent expropriations inflicted another 45 million Reichsmarks in losses on the corporation, according to its own postwar tabulation.[42] The

[38] The losses of equipment shipped out from Knapsack and Fürstenberg appear to have been particularly large; see DL 2/1, Niederschrift über die Vorstandssitzung am 5. März 1945, p. 1 (reporting that only eight of thirty-two wagon loads of goods from the former plant had arrived in Rheinfelden), and Notizen aus der Vorstandsbesprechung am 20. März 1945, p. 2 (on attempts to get machinery away from the Zentralwerk by ship up the Elbe River). The plant in Hungary at Perecin, in which Degussa held a minority of the stock, may have been detonated, however, by retreating German troops; see DL 3/20, Postzettel Nr. 139, December 8, 1944.
[39] DUA, MEN 29, Hirtes's Notiz für die Herren Dr. Truthe u. Dipl. Ing. Giessen, March 15, 1945.
[40] One indication of the personnel losses is the note that only 125 of the 700 called-up members of the Frankfurt workforce alone had reregistered with the firm by July 9, 1945; DL 2/1, Niederschrift über die Vorstandsbesprechung, July 10, 1945, p. 3.
[41] DUA, DL 2/1, Notizen aus der Vorstandsbesprechung am 20. Februar 1945, p. 2; and BET 10/1, Bernau's Betr.: Kriegsschäden, February 15, 1945. For earlier estimates of the destruction and information concerning the reimbursements, see DL 3/20, Postzettel Nr. 78, September 18, 1944; and DL 2/1, Niederschrift über die Vorstandssitzung am 6. Februar 1945, p. 4.
[42] See, on the government payments, DUA, RFI 4.2/146, Zentral-Abteilung, Übersicht über die durch den Krieg verursachten Verluste an Vermögenswerten der Degussa, November 17, 1947, p. 3; and concerning Degussa's final tabulation, DL 11.5/61, Zusammenstellung

total net damage figure of at least 111 million Reichsmarks does not include, however, the value of what was destroyed at the Auergesellschaft, which that firm reckoned later in 1945 at 61 million Reichsmarks.[43] To be sure, Auer's proximity to Berlin and political connections facilitated prompter and greater reimbursement than its owner experienced – the 30 million Reichsmarks that flowed quickly from the Reich War Damages Office enabled the firm to pay off its huge bank loans just before the Russians arrived in Oranienburg and to compile deposits of 11.4 million Reichsmarks.[44] But the near obliteration of Auer's facilities still made a substantial inroad on Degussa's assets, all the more so when most of the cash ended up in Soviet hands.[45]

When the war in Europe ended in May, the concern's managers presided over an eerily disparate corporate remnant, composed in roughly equal measure of wholly or nearly unscathed plants (e.g., Konstanz, Wyhlen, and Rheinfelden near the Swiss border, Bodenfelde, Brilon-Wald, Brücken, Lorch, Mombach, Oeventrop, and Oppenau), burned-out shells (Pforzheim, Hanau, Frankfurt, Auer, and Reinickendorf, to name only some), and semi-intact installations in the Soviet zone of occupation or across the Oder-Neisse Line whose future relationship to the firm was uncertain at best (e.g., Fürstenberg, Grünau, Wildau, and Mölkau), or likely to be nonexistent (e.g., Gleiwitz, Vosswalde – for an overview of the situation, see Appendix M). By then, or within a few additional months, many of these had been stripped of their inventories, the precious metals the concern had hoarded as the war waned, and sometimes even their machinery, either by the occupying forces or the desperate forced laborers marooned in or around the sites.[46]

der Kriegs- und Kriegsfolgeschäden und Vermögenswerte gemäss Gesetz Nr. 53 der Militärregierung bezw. Nr. 5 des Allierten Kontrollrates per 20. Juni 1948 nach Vermögensarten, as well as Anlage V5.

[43] Rainer Karlsch and Zbynek Zeman, *"Urangeheimnisse." Das Erzgebirge im Brennpunkt der Weltpolitik 1900–1960* (Berlin: Ch. Links, 2003), Chapter 1.

[44] On August Kolb's role in effecting this payment, just before Speer released him from ministerial duties and dispatched him to southern Germany on April 12, see DL 3.Fischer/2, Besprechungen mit Dr. Kolb, June 25, 1945.

[45] DUA, BET 10/1 (also IW 24.5/3), Bernau's Betr.: Auergesellschaft, July 24, 1945, pp. 1–5; and IW 24.5/1, Ausführungen anlässlich der [Auergesellschaft] Aufsichtsratsitzung, January 18, 1946, p. 3.

[46] On the shipping of precious metals from Degussa's Vienna branch to Hanau, Reinickendorf, and Frankfurt see GEH 6/14, Hirtes's Notiz Betr.: Edelmetall-Vorräte in Wien, September 11, 1944, and Nees's Notiz betr. Edelmetallbestände bei Degussa-Wien, February 19, 1945; and DL 3/20, Postzettel Nr. 104, October 18, 1944, p. 2; on that from Eastern plants to Berlin, GEH 3.Hirtes/12, Hirtes's Notiz Betr.: Verkaufsstelle Breslau, January 30, 1945, and Deppe to Hirtes, February 8, 1945, which also reports on the transfer of the quantities in Berlin to Wolfen and Wächtersbach. On the stripping of Gleiwitz, see PCA 2/2, Schenk's Betrifft Schicksal der Gleiwitzer Russfabrik, August 24, 1945; of Fürstenberg, Schulze-Nicolai's Aktennotiz Betrifft: Werk Fürstenberg/Oder, April 4, 1946; of Wolfgang, IW 44/6/1, Finck to Fischer, April 14 and 18, 1945; of Welden and Pforzheim, DL 2/1,

Also badly but figuratively damaged in consequence of Nazi rule were many of the firm's leaders, at least in the eyes of portions of Degussa's workforce, the victors, or both. Few of these executives appear to have understood immediately how awkward their presence had become as a result of their earlier political connections. To be sure, Carl Lüer and Wilhelm Aviery, the two most prominent National Socialists on the supervisory board, soon were arrested, and that body retroactively dated their departure from its ranks to March 27, 1945.[47] And Hermann Federlin resigned from the managing board in mid-June.[48] But none of the firm's other principal figures felt obliged to draw personal consequences from their previous conduct or what had befallen their nation and firm. Schlosser, above all, quickly made clear his intention to remain at the helm, as usual tracing the decision to the urgings and interests of others. Only a week after the arrival of American troops, on the same day that he wrote Hirtes, who had remained in Frankfurt, from Wächtersbach to suggest how Degussa could jury-rig its ruined buildings and "open its gates at its old head office in that original area that is marked by its name," Schlosser dispatched a more personal, handwritten letter.[49] It informed his old friend (they were on a first-name basis, though not *per Du*) as follows:

In the view of the colleagues here, I should retain the leadership if at all possible. I am also of the opinion – quite objectively, as you know me – that this certainly would be good on account of my international connections. Personal ambitions have to be set aside in this regard.[50]

This time, Schlosser was thinking too far ahead. By the end of the 1940s, the realities of administering and rebuilding Germany and stemming communism in Europe muted American hostility toward former National Socialists – and the hardships of West Germany's postwar economic situation had the same effect among Degussa's workforce – so Schlosser once again got the chance to make use of his "international connections." But the mood in 1945 was much different. Already in May, a newly constituted Works Council of Degussa's white- and blue-collar personnel obtained management's agreement to the removal of "demonstrable activists and denouncers" and a

Niederschriften über die Vorstandsbesprechungen, June 12 and 26, 1945; and of Rheinfelden, DL 3. H.Schlosser/15, Beschlagnahmung von Fertigprodukten und Rohstoffen von der französischen Militärbehörde, August 10, 1945.

[47] DUA, APR 2, Protokolle der 457. und 458. Aufsichtsratssitzungen August 31, 1945 and January 11, 1946, Abschrift, pp. 56–57.

[48] *Ibid.*, 458. Aufsichtsratssitzung, January 11, 1946, p. 58. Federlin may have taken the hint from Heinz Scherf, Degussa's principal lawyer, who told him shortly after the war ended that "he had been regarded in the firm as solidly for the Party"; DUA, SCH 01/0003, Federlin to Scherf, February 9, 1947, p. 1.

[49] DL 3.Hirtes/2, Schlosser to Hirtes, April 5, 1945.

[50] *Ibid.*, Schlosser to Hirtes, April 5, 1945.

general preference for dropping Party members first whenever layoffs appeared necessary.[51] Although the American authorities who scrutinized the firm's remaining records in detail throughout the summer ultimately chose not to act against the firm collectively, that is, to dismember it like IG Farben, the U.S. Military Government did issue Law Nr. 8 in August, calling for the demotion or complete dismissal of Party members from leadership positions in all business enterprises, including Degussa and its plants and branches.[52] Thereafter, the resignations, retirements, and severances from the corporation's senior ranks came thick and fast. By the end of October, six members of the supervisory board, including all of Henkel's representatives and Felix Warlimont of the Norddeutsche Affinerie, were gone, along with seven members of the managing board: Schlosser, Achterath, and Hirtes by direct order of the Military Government on September 24; Hubert on grounds of ill health a week later; and Fischer, Róka, and von Retze pursuant to Law Nr. 8. After the French occupation administration arrested Kolb, prompting the board to put him on leave and let his term run out in March 1946, only two people remained on that body, the non–Party members Bernau and Baerwind, to whom Heinz Scherf, Degussa's legal specialist, quickly was added.[53]

Lower down the corporate hierarchy, denazification also initially took a toll. At the behest of the Works Council, a number of employees who had held local Party offices were summarily dismissed immediately after the Third

---

[51] Mechthild Wolf *Im Zeichen von Sonne und Mond* (Degussa: Frankfurt am Main, 1993), pp. 213–15.

[52] On the American investigation of Degussa, see DUA, SCH 01/0036, Goecke's Notiz, May 26, 1945; Bernau's Betr.: Besuch einer amerikanischen Kontrollkommission, August 15, 1945; his Betr.: Zweiter Besuch, August 21, 1945; his Betr.: Dritter Besuch, September 7, 1945; his Betr.: Vierter Besuch, September 28, 1945; Dickert's Notiz betr. Aktenprüfung hier [Brilon-Wald, where the corporate records had been sent for safekeeping] durch USA-Kontroll-Commission, September 1, 1945; Albrecht's Notiz betr. Besuch einer fünfköpfigen amerikanisch-englischen Kommission . . . bei Herrn Schlosser, September 7, 1945; Erskine's Verzeichnis der von der Urkundenverwaltung der Degussa-Brilon-Wald mitgenommenen Safeurkundenmappen, October 12, 1945; and Dickert's Notiz über den . . . erneuten Besuch einer vierköpfigen USA-Kontrollkommission, October 13, 1945. On the abandonment of the short-lived American plan to split Degussa into three parts and for a listing of the few divestitures the firm ultimately was forced to carry out, see Wolf *Im Zeichen von Sonne und Mond*, pp. 221–22.

[53] DUA, APR 2, Protokoll der 458. Aufsichtsratssitzung, January 11, 1946, Abschrift, pp. 57–58, 60–61. Bernau's term on the board also was extended through the end of September 1948. Kolb had been entrusted with Degussa's interests in the French zone of occupation only a few months earlier; see DL 2/1, Niederschrift über die Vorstandsbesprechung am 2. September 1945, p. 1, and DL 3.Fischer/2, Fischer to Kolb, 2.x.45. The removals at the Auergesellschaft were equally sweeping: by January 1946, Schlosser, Fischer, and Róka were gone from the supervisory board, along with four members of the managing one (Weise, Vorbau, Zürcher, and Pütter). When the chairman, Karl Quasebart, resigned on March 13, 1946, leadership of the firm fell to the man Schlosser had resolved to remove at the end of that year, Heinrich Paetsch. See IW 24.9/1, Geschäftsbericht des Vorstandes [der Auergesellschaft], September 10, 1947.

316   *From Cooperation to Complicity*

Reich surrendered, including Adolf Hilpert, the firm's Party foreman.[54] But as of early September, Scherf reported that another 150 wage and salary earners still were "politically endangered," and the ensuing white-collar dismissals alone appear to have come to approximately sixty as the firm released all personnel who had joined the NSDAP prior to May 1, 1937, or aroused particular irritation through their fervor.[55] Among the ousted were the plant managers at Brilon-Wald, Hanau, Rheinfelden, and Wolfgang; the heads of the Degesch, Homburg, and Marquart subsidiaries and of Degussa's offices in Vienna and Milan; and the corporation's chief in-house architect, along with at least five senior directors (Goecke, August Schenk, Heinz Schimmelbusch, Emil Wüstinger, and Hans Hinz).[56] Not all suspect salaried employees were let go altogether, however; some were downgraded to wage earners, usually in blue-collar positions.[57]

Over the next few years, however, many of the removed individuals returned to Degussa, often to their former or equivalent posts, thanks to the "fellow-traveler factory" that the denazification process became as the Western occupiers delegated it to German special courts (*Spruchkammer*).[58] Once Scherf learned to provide the right sort of exonerating statements – and even to steer cases involving Degussa personnel to particular jurisdictions and judges – the number of old Degussa employees declared fit for renewed

[54] For example, Ludwig Boedicker, a former procurist in the Durferrit division, who had been an Ortsgruppenleiter; Heinz Grode of the Degussit division, who had held the same office in Eschborn (on both, see their case files in DUA, SCH 01/0003); and Emil Scheller, a chemist with the same Party post in Lorsbach (see DUA, BR 01/12). On Hilpert, SCH 01/0004, Schlosser and Hirtes to Hilpert, May 10, 1945. On the severance payments these men were to receive (albeit to blocked accounts), see SCH 01/0002, Scherf's Vorentwurf zu einem Schreiben an die zu entlassenden Ortsgruppenleiter unserer Firma, May 28, 1945.

[55] DUA, DL 2/1, Niederschrift über die Vorstandsbesprechung am 11. September 1945, p. 1 (for the quotation); Wolf, *Im Zeichen von Sonne und Mond*, p. 216 (for the number dismissed); and SCH 01/0004, Scherf to Betriebsräte Werke I-II, January 4, 1946 (for the policy). See also SCH 01/0002, Degussa-Siebert to Militärregierung Hanau, April 11, 1946, on the dismissals at that plant.

[56] See DUA, DL 2/1, Niederschriften über die Vorstandsbesprechungen am 14. August 1945, pp. 1–2; am 28. August 1945, pp. 2, 4; am 18. September 1945, p. 2; and am 24. September 1945; and DL 3.Schlosser/13, a draft of Schlosser's testimonial letter for the removed head of the Chemiewerk Homburg AG, Karl Beister. See also SCH 01/0002, Zusammenstellung der ordentlichen Zeichungsberechtigten der Degussa der seit der Besetzung Deutschlands . . . aus ihren Aemtern ausgeschieden sind, January 21, 1946, which lists fifty individuals, of whom only two had died or were missing.

[57] See DUA, BR 01/0013, Angestellte, die aufgrund ihrer politischen Belastung ins Lohnverhältnis übernommen wurden, December 4, 1946, which lists thirty-seven individuals, along with their former and current positions and information on their Party membership.

[58] The best study of the process remains Lutz Niethammer, *Die 'Mitläuferfabrik': Die Entnazifizierung am Beispiel Bayerns* (Berlin: Dietz, 1982). The satiric description comes from the five categories into which denazification judgments could fall: principal criminal (*Hauptschuldige*), compromised (*Belastete*, defined as Party activists, militarists, and profiteers), less compromised *(Minderbelastete)*, fellow traveler (*Mitläufer*), and innocent (*Entlastete*).

employment rose steadily.[59] Certainly, the reconstitution of the corporation's managing board offers the most dramatic illustration: though the Works Council managed to slow the pace of reelections and to demand the appointment of one politically uncompromised new member, Erich Altwein, Hirtes rejoined the board in April 1947, Achterath and von Retze in June 1948, and Schlosser himself in June 1949, following the end of his two-year probationary sentence as a "minor collaborator" (*Minderbelastete*) by a denazification court.[60] Eight months later, he became chairman again, just as his firm was beginning to turn a profit and pay dividends, for the first time since the end of the business year 1943/44.[61] All these men already had been exercising managerial functions unofficially or from behind the scenes for long periods prior to their reinstatement, indeed in Schlosser's case, virtually since the end of the war. Meanwhile, Bernau ascended to the supervisory board in 1948, at the same time his former colleague, Adalbert Fischer, was also elected.[62] In the end, among the members of Degussa's managing board

[59] See, in general, the material on particular denazification cases collected in DUA, SCH 01/0003–5. Two sorts of manipulation of the proceedings stand out in Degussa's records. The first involved transferring employees from areas where witnesses could incriminate them to new posts elsewhere; see the case of Dr. Deppe, the figure at Degussa's offices in Berlin who probably knew most about the origins of the precious metals that arrived there. His posting to Düsseldorf immediately after the war provoked an angry controversy in the Works Council; BR 01/0008, Stizung des Betriebsausschusses am 4. März 1946. The second way of rigging outcomes is indicated by SCH 01/0003, Scherf to Bernstorff, January 7, 1947, saying that his case is scheduled to be heard by the court headed by one Dr. Rath, "to whom at my behest, insofar as possible, all Degussa cases are given."

[60] See DUA, APR 2, Protokolle der 461. Aufsichtsratssitzung am 29. Mai 1947, Abschrift, pp. 70 and 72; der 463. Aufsichtsratssitzung am 8. Juni 1948, p. 76; der 465. Aufsichtsratssitzung am 30. März 1949, p. 79, and Ergänzungsbechluss, p. 80. In view of the tendency in Degussa's own versions of its past to emphasize that Schlosser's return was highly popular with the workforce, it is worth quoting the cool tone of the message from the Works Council on March 28, 1949, that was cited in the Aufsichtsrat's decision to reinstate him: "we express the hope that the expectations associated with this appointment may be fulfilled for the best of the enterprise and its workforce." On the role of the Works Council in Altwein's selection and the phasing in of the other reinstatements, see BR 01/0008, Scherf's Entwurf, November 19, 1946.

[61] On the losses in the latter half of the 1940s, which accumulated to 2 million Reichsmarks prior to the currency reform in June 1948, DUA, APR 2, Protokoll der 459. Aufsichtsratssitzung am 19. Dezember 1946, p. 63; der 461. Aufsichtsratssitzung am 29. Mai 1947, p. 71; der 463. Aufsichtsratssitzung am 8. Juni 1948, p. 75; and der 466. Aufsichtsratssitzung am 26. August 1949, p. 82; on the profits, which recommenced in 1948/49 after the introduction of the Deutschmark, and the dividends, which resumed at the end of 1950/51, Heinz Mayer-Wegelin, *Aller Anfang ist Schwer* (Degussa: Frankfurt am Main, 1973), p. 169. The pattern for the Auergesellschaft was identical, but the total accumulated loss in the postwar years only just less than 103,000 RM; see IW 24.9/1, Geschäftsbericht des Vorstandes, September 10, 1947, pp. 1, 5–6; and IW 24.9/2, Bericht der Treuhand-Vereinigung AG, Berlin über die Prüfung... der Auergesellschaft AG, Berlin, June 30, 1949, p. 6.

[62] DUA, APR 2, Protokoll der 463. Aufsichtsratssitzung am 8. Juni 1948, pp. 76–77. The two men finished out their Degussa careers in these posts in 1951 and 1952, respectively.

during the period 1941–45, only Menzel, Federlin (who died in 1949), Kolb, Róka, and Hubert (who was ill) never worked for the firm again. Even Carl Goetz, the former head of the Dresdner Bank who had been driven from the chairmanship of Degussa's supervisory board in 1947 while the Americans investigated him for war crimes, was unanimously reelected to that position at the first opportunity in 1949.[63] He retained his seat until 1965, the same year that Schlosser, who joined him on that body in 1959, finally also retired.

Meanwhile, Degussa showed considerable generosity in alleviating the plight of former employees whose degree of identification with National Socialism ruled out a return to the firm's ranks, despite the laxer atmosphere that prevailed from 1948 on. Hans Hinz, who had been a Party member since May 1933 and instrumental in the processing of plundered precious metals in Berlin, received a premature pension rounded up to 500 Deutschmarks per month immediately following the currency reform of 1948.[64] Friedrich Pressel, the former plant director at Rheinfelden, who had joined the NSDAP in 1931, greeted Hitler's accession enthusiastically, been shunned after 1945 by the Works Council at his plant, then denounced to the French occupation authorities and interned by them for thirty-one months, some of that period at hard labor, found his legal costs covered by the firm and the duration of his employment so interpreted by Degussa as to entitle him to a pension.[65] For a time, the corporation even held open the prospect of a clerical post for him at Kredenbach before suggesting that "it would certainly be good if he would ask around about a job outside Degussa" and promising to continue to pay his legal expenses and pension if he succeeded.[66] Even the corporation's two most notorious National Socialists, Adolf Hilpert and Hans Menzel, benefited from a charitable attitude on the part of the firm. Heinz Scherf wrote a testimonial for Hilpert's denazification case in 1947, and Degussa voluntarily raised the pension to which he was entitled after October 1948 to 200 Deutschmarks per month, then doubled it in January 1950.[67] With regard to Menzel, whose invalid status and recent divorce had made him a pathetic figure by the late 1940s, Degussa's decision to raise his legally prescribed monthly pension of 27 Deutschmarks to 250 Deutschmarks "in memory of your ancestors and in consideration of your children," was almost

[63] *Ibid.*, Protokolle der 461. Aufsichtsratssitzung am 29. Mai 1947, p. 72, and der 466. Aufsichtsratssitzung am 26. August 1949, p. 83.

[64] DUA, SCH 01/0004, Scherf to Hinz, July 5, 1948.

[65] DUA, SCH 01/0004, Baerwind's Aktenvermerk betreffend Dr. Pressel, February 25, 1948, and Spruchkammerverfahren von Dr. Pressel, August 26, 1948; Scherf's Notiz für Herrn Altwein, September 10, 1948.

[66] DUA, SCH 01/0004, Baerwind to Pressel, November 25, 1948; Nunier's Bescheinigung Betreff: Dr. Pressel, January 20, 1949; Scherf to Pressel, February 2, 1949; and Scherf's Notiz für Vorstand. Betr.: Besuch des Herrn Pressel, August 8, 1949 (from which the quotation is drawn).

[67] DUA, SCH 01/0004, Scherf's unheaded testimonial of July 14, 1947; Personal-Abteilung to Hilpert, April 22, 1949; and Scherf and Altwein to Hilpert, January 5, 1950.

certainly a gesture to his mother, a member of the Roessler family.[68] Still, it is remarkable in view of the man's decision to reopen an old quarrel by sending a last-minute letter to the members of Degussa's supervisory board in April 1949 in hopes of heading off Schlosser's reinstatement.[69] A future historian of Degussa's postwar history no doubt will unearth further, perhaps even more sensational examples of this sort.[70]

From the perspective of the present, the most vexing aspect of such grants is that they occurred while the firm was fending off demands from its workforce and restitution claimants with reference to the need for the utmost thrift as the corporation and the nation dug out from under their devastation. In 1950 alone, the pension payments to the four men mentioned in the preceding paragraph would have exceeded in value the single documented voluntary contribution on Degussa's part immediately after the war to the victims of the regime the firm had served. That expenditure is recorded rather tersely in the minutes of the managing board meeting of June 19, 1945, under the heading "donation for concentration camp inmates, etc." as follows: "The Metallgesellschaft has decided on a donation of 15,000 RM. Degussa will donate 10,000. Personally, each [member] can give what he wants."[71] To be sure, the entry reflects conditions at the very nadir of Degussa's fortunes, but the grudging stance toward the suffering that had flowed from German policies in which the corporation took part typified the firm's conduct in ensuing years, as the discussions of restitution proceedings regarding Aryanized properties and precious metals in Chapters 3 and 5 of this book have documented.

What explains Degussa's acceptance of responsibility for the firm's most compromised former employees but rejection of liability for their deeds or for Degussa's acts of complicity, even after the shortages of 1945–49 gave way to the German "economic miracle" of the 1950s and 1960s? The readiness to subsidize former National Socialists is the more easily chronicled aspect of this behavior. For one thing, denazification was as necessary as it was impossible, and its defects bred cynicism and apologetics. Many of the firm's leaders knew how fine and fortuitous the line between being punished and appearing innocent sometimes was. After all, among Degussa's leaders, Walter Roessler, who had mobilized the Gestapo in the takeover of the Aurora refinery (see Chapter 5) and applied for membership in the Nazi Party in March 1938 but been lucky enough to be rejected because of his earlier Rotary membership, emerged in 1945 as "thoroughly clean politically" and

---

[68] DUA, BU Hans Menzel, Schlosser to Charlotte Menzel, September 13, 1950, and Altwein and Scherf to Menzel, October 2, 1950, where the quoted words appear.

[69] DUA, BU Hans Menzel, Degussa Vorstand to Mitglieder unseres Aufsichtsrates, May 5, 1949.

[70] Cf. the forthcoming study by Stephan Lindner, *Höchst angepasst: Ein IG-Farben Werk im Dritten Reich.*

[71] DL 2/1, Niederschrift über die Vorstandsbesprechung am 19. Juni 1945, p. 2.

therefore the Allies' choice to act as trustee for all precious metals stocks in postwar Austria.[72] Ernst Bernau, who plotted to steal the Margulies family's holdings in ÖCW (see Chapter 3), remained on the managing board after 1945 merely because he had not joined the NSDAP, while Pressel and Achterath, to cite but two examples, respectively underwent imprisonment and demotion, primarily because they had failed to resign from the Party after turning away from it.

Willingness to circumvent the strictures of occupiers that allowed such anomalies drew additional strength from a convenient element in German law, the requirement of base intent (e.g., personal gain or sadism) for a finding of deep culpability. Over and over, Degussa's leaders drew a distinction between "idealistic" reasons, however misplaced, for having become and acted as a National Socialist and "corrupt" grounds, a distinction that then was applied to exonerate almost all corporate executives. In essence, their argument amounted to asserting that they did not know the gun was loaded or, more specifically, to claiming that they thought National Socialism was about pageantry, pride, and prosperity, not conquest, oppression, plunder, and what nowadays is called ethnic cleansing, and that this was an honest mistake, for which no one could blame them. Typical of this indulgent stance was Ernst Baerwind's defense of Pressel as a man

who affiliated himself with the National Socialist worldview for idealistic reasons at a time when scarcely anyone, including those today sitting in judgment, could know what one day would become of National Socialism, who remained caught in the net... when the National Socialist idea took earthly form, and who now in consequence of the collapse of the political system and of Germany must suffer incomparably more as in all fairness should be the case considering his entire character.[73]

Such an attitude did not mean that everything was forgotten or forgiven. One does not find among those who rose to the managing board of Degussa after the war, for example, individuals associated with the use of slave labor. Indeed, when Robert Pross retired from the firm at the end of 1970, he ascribed his disappointment at never having achieved that rank to the fact that "I...was marked with the odium of having been professionally successful during the Thousand Years, [which]...seems never to have left me."[74]

But what of the other side of Degussa's postwar conduct, its stonewalling of questions about and compensation payments for its complicity in the

[72] On Roessler's application and rejection, see Ralf Banken, *Die Entwicklung des Edelmetallsektors im "Dritten Reich" 1933–1945* (forthcoming), Chapter 2; for the quotation and his postwar appointment, DL 2/1, Niederschrift über die Vorstandsbesprechung am 21. August 1945, p. 1.
[73] DUA, SCH 01/0004, Baerwind to Drischel, May 21, 1947.
[74] DUA, BU Robert Pross, Anrede, December 16, 1970. That Pross's experience in this regard was not unique within German industry is suggested by Volker Berghahn, *The Americanization of West German Industry* (New York: Cambridge University Press, 1986), pp. 54–55.

Reich's most heinous crimes? Part of the explanation lies in the sheer enormity of the destruction visited on Germany and the firm by the war and the expropriations that followed, which dulled Degussa's executives to the pain their nation had caused and which seemed, in any case, more than sufficient expiation for it. Perhaps these leaders also recognized, although they are not recorded as having done so, a point this book has documented that would have seemed far too subtle for public debate: that Nazi economic policies – including Aryanization, autarky, and armaments – had brought the firm great profits, but participation in the regime's worst crimes (especially the plunder of Jews' precious metals, the use of slave labor at plants the firm lost, and the sale of Zyklon B for murder) had not.[75] Certainly, banishing questions about the past became a contemporary political strategy, as German industrialists, Degussa's managers included, sought to defend themselves against challenges to the capitalist system in the quarter century following the war by cultivating a simplistic and prettified image of corporate behavior during it.[76]

Above all, however, the likelihood is that Degussa's leaders rejected a reexamination of their firm's conduct and resulting obligations on the basis of more straightforward reasoning: these men felt they had done their best and largely succeeded and saw nothing to be gained, even morally, from second-guessing themselves or permitting anyone else to do so. In a sense, they had been faithful followers of Ernst Busemann, never swimming against the stream, but always navigating so as to serve corporate interests as best the situation allowed. They thus had made Degussa's success compatible with either outcome of the Second World War. Had Germany won, the firm could have pointed with pride to all it had done for the war effort and recentered its business around the new Konzernwerk, which would have been located virtually in the middle of an expanded Greater German Reich and represented a corporate analog to Germania, the new capital that Hitler intended to make of Berlin. But, when the nation was defeated, the firm could – and did – accentuate the line it had drawn between direct and indirect military production. Moreover, from the point of view of the managers who survived to lead Degussa after 1945, their conduct had been not only politically shrewd, but materially and morally optimizing, as well. Although Hitler's war had cost Degussa heavily and much work had been wasted, especially on lost plants, the corporation emerged from the Third Reich richer and stronger than it had been in 1933. Whereas many personnel had been killed, the livelihoods of the survivors had been salvaged and new opportunities

---

[75] For an argument similar to mine concerning the use of slave labor, see Cornelia Rauh-Kühne, "Hitlers Hehler? Unternehmerprofite und Zwangsarbeiterlöhne," *Historische Zeitschrift* 275 (2002), pp. 1–55, especially 51–52.

[76] See S. Jonathan Wiesen, *West German Industry and the Challenge of the Nazi Past* (Chapel Hill: University of North Carolina Press, 2001).

for expansion created. Degussa's leaders almost surely told themselves that they had served the interests of its share- and stakeholders, whatever the infringements on the rights and comforts of others, and that prioritizing in this fashion stood first among an executive's duties. That is, at bottom, what Schlosser told Kolb in October 1944 – and that had been the implicit premise of Hans Schneider's behavior in the "Jew Metal Action," Ewald von Retze's disinterest in the conditions of forced laborers, Robert Pross's conduct at Gleiwitz, and perhaps even Gerhard Peters's response to Kurt Gerstein. The special discomfort aroused by Degussa's history in the Third Reich is that, by the standards of practical rationality, Degussa's leaders from 1933 to 1945 could and probably did feel vindicated in their choices, whereas at the most elemental level, these were morally indefensible.

I cannot close this book without a personal story. In the early 1980s, a thirty-something German friend told me that expecting his fellow citizens to acknowledge their society's implication in the crimes of National Socialism was futile until the generation involved had passed from the scene. "We have to wait for them all to die out," I recall him claiming. He exaggerated, of course, for his nation already had made great, if halting and uneven progress in facing up to and learning from its past.[77] But his frustration also was justified. More than any other single factor, the defensive refusal of the wartime generation and its children to reconsider its conduct during the Third Reich accounts for the long delay between the end of that regime and the appearance of books such as this one. Even now that both generations are nearly gone, reticence or denial on the part of some Germans persists, which is the principal reason studies such as this remain to be written about a majority of the nation's major firms (or university faculties, for that matter). Yet, recollecting my friend's comment puts me in mind of Churchill's famous aphorism that democracy is the worst system of government ever devised – except for every other one. When placed in comparative context, German society's collective confrontation with what it did from 1933 to 1945 invites nearly the same evaluation. This book, though written by an American, is an outgrowth of that confrontation, and, I hope, both a contribution and testament to it.

---

[77] See the two most powerful, and somewhat contrasting, recent studies, Jeffrey Herf, *Divided Memory: The Nazi Past in the Two Germanys* (Cambridge: Harvard University Press, 1997), and Norbert Frei, *Adenauer's Germany and the Nazi Past* (New York: Columbia University Press, 2002).

Appendix A

Board Members of Degussa, 1933–1945

Supervisory Board (Aufsichtsrat)
Max Freiherr von Goldschmidt-Rothschild	1897–1934
Alfred Merton (Metallgesellschaft)	1917–35
Carl Bosch (IG Farben)	1919–40
Julius Bueb (Stickstoff-Syndikat)	1919–44
Georg Schwarz (Metallgesellschaft)	1922–33
Max von der Porten (Vereinigte Aluminiumwerke)	1924–34
Fritz Roessler	1924–37
Moritz Freiherr von Bethmann (Bethmann Bank)	1926–45
Felix Warlimont (Norddeutsche Affinerie)	1930–45
Hugo Henkel (Henkel)	1930–45
Paul Hammerschlag	1931–33
Ludwig Deutsch (Dresdner Bank)	1931–37
Adolf Hilpert and Georg Schröder (NSBO)	1933–34
Georg DuBois	1933–43
Rudolf Euler (Metallgesellschaft)	1934–49
Richard Merton (Metallgesellschaft)	1936–38
Rudolf Stahl (Salzdetfurth/Mansfeld)	1936–45
Carl Goetz (Dresdner Bank)	1937–47
Carl Lüer (NSDAP)	1938–45
Franz Traudes (Metallgesellschaft)	1939–41
Max Schmid (Frankfurter Allgemeine Zeitung)	1939–61
Werner Lüps (Henkel)	1941–42
Wilhelm Avieny (Metallgesellschaft/NSDAP)	1941–45
Hermann Richter (Henkel)	1943–45
Jost Henkel (Henkel)	1943–45

Managing Board (Vorstand)
Hans Schneider	1908–41
Carl Riefstahl	1917–37
Ernst Busemann, chair (1930–39)	1919–39
Hektor Roessler	1921–41
Ernst Baerwind	1926–54

(*continued*)

Hermann Schlosser, chair (1939–59)	1926–59 (suspended, 1945–49)
Adalbert Fischer	1930–45
Koloman Róka	1930–45
Ernst Bernau	1930–48
Hans Menzel	1941–43
Hermann Federlin	1941–45
Geo Hubert	1941–45
August Kolb	1941–46
Helmut Achterath	1941–57 (suspended, 1945–48)
Ewald von Retze	1941–59 (suspended, 1945–48)
Robert Hirtes	1941–64 (suspended, 1945–47)

Appendix B

Vital Statistics of Degussa, 1933–1945

	1932/33	1933/34	1934/35	1935/36
Stock capital (million Reichsmarks)	35.6	35.6	35.6	35.6
Published balance sheet value (million Reichsmarks)	75.5	82.6	77.6	82.5
Workforce (with subsidiaries)	c. 1,850	3,895		
Balance sheet values reported on corporate tax returns (ooo RM)				
Total value	89,340	96,778	93,407	100,436
Fixed capital	15,983	14,980	13,677	14,549
Stock participations (subsidiaries)	12,449	19,772	21,279	23,956
Liquid funds	12,135	11,038	10,230	15,121
Government bonds			491	1,002
Tax rebate certificates	1,078			
Reserves	19,437	19,437	19,437	19,437
Bank obligations	36	247	75	665
Excess of assets over liabilities	15,466	16,113	18,080	20,299
Net profit		4,228	5,444	4,577
Profit and loss calculations (ooo RM)				
Gross turnover				124,218
Net turnover				?
Minus manufacturing costs				?
Gross profit	16,990	17,899	16,328	17,153
Minus operating costs				9,891
Operating profit				7,262
Plus other income				3,196
Total proceeds				10,458
Minus taxes/other deductions				6,814
Net earnings	3,914	3,888	3,659	3,644

(*continued*)

	1932/33	1933/34	1934/35	1935/36
Significant income/expense items (000 RM)				
Manufacturing costs				
Depreciation	5,176	6,068	2,819	4,719
Research and development				1,056
Operating costs				
Wages and salaries	10,639	12,246	13,459	5,569
Taxes and social payments				2,411
Other income				
License fees				43
From subsidiaries	325	416	1,106	1,744
Sales of stocks/bonds				446
Taxes/other deductions				
Export promotion payments				1,086
Write-offs of holdings/bills				2,694
Corporation tax				1,704
Winterhilfswerk	50	60	65	115
Adolf Hitler donation	62	23	39	38

	1936/37	1937/38	1938/39	1939/40
Stock capital (million Reichsmarks)	35.6	35.6	35.6	35.6
Published balance sheet value (million Reichsmarks)	88.2	89.1	92.5	95.8
Workforce		4,890		
Balance sheet values reported on corporate tax returns (000 RM)				
Total value	109,076	114,868	124,897	137,455
Fixed capital	15,086	19,443	20,461	22,497
Stock participations (subsidiaries)	25,161	31,035	31,597	34,526
Liquid funds	18,421	14,188	18,229	18,139
Government bonds	3,223	1,843	495	382
Tax rebate certificates			3,925	3,013
Reserves	20,978	21,450	21,450	21,450
Bank obligations	761	3,653	8,469	6,000
Excess of assets over liabilities	23,896	27,149	34,070	47,640
Net profit	8,370	c. 6,200	c. 10,100	12,206+
Profit and loss calculations (000 RM)				
Gross turnover	133,135	?	158,765	160,264
Net turnover	?	129,350	131,257	129,356
Minus manufacturing costs	?	?	110,451	105,473
Gross profit	17,612	17,386	20,806	23,883
Minus operating costs	10,843	12,058	12,902	12,326
Operating profit	6,769	5,328	7,904	11,557
Plus other income	4,684	5,276	6,079	6,377

Total proceeds	11,453	10,604	13,983	17,934
Minus taxes/other deductions	6,639	7,498	10,842	14,764
Net earnings	4,814	3,106	3,141	3,170

Significant income/expense items (000 RM)

Manufacturing costs				
Depreciation	7,022	5,321	5,357	5,065
Research and development	1,074	1,430	1,383	1,366
Operating costs				
Wages and salaries	5,952	6,581	7,188	6,413
Taxes and social payments	2,651	3,365	3,244	3,324
Other income				
License fees	157	983	180	249
From subsidiaries	2,861	2,886	3,821	3,577
Sales of stocks/bonds	524	553	592	582
Taxes/other deductions				
Export promotion payments	1,830	1,408	1,755	1,665
Write-offs of holdings/bills	1,494	1,151	3,982	4,434
Corporation tax	1,697	2,460	3,187	4,701
Winterhilfswerk	110	122	137	147
Adolf Hitler donation	41	45	43	67

	1940/41	1941/42	1942/43	1943/44	1944/45
Stock capital (million Reichsmarks)	68.0	76.5	76.5	76.5	76.5
Published balance sheet value (million Reichsmarks)	127.0	143.9	181.1	194.2	200.1
Workforce (with subsidiaries)		6,098	(20,939)	10,100	
		(17,588)		(27,900)	

Balance sheet values reported on corporate tax returns (000 RM)

	1940/41	1941/42	1942/43	1943/44	1944/45
Total value	155,775	181,929	218,170	226,625	233,913
Fixed capital	23,713	29,341	33,448	35,004	27,447
Stock participations (subsidiaries)	46,001	49,682	53,587	31,391	28,359
Liquid funds	26,717	26,989	48,704	19,748	12,349
Government bonds	9,729	11,433	28,696	1,429	1,534
Tax rebate certificates	3,013	2,934	2,934	14,603	0
Reserves	627	12,000	12,000	12,000	12,000
Bank obligations	5,113	6,264	7,432	10,786	12,066
Excess of assets over liabilities	26,263	47,359	48,416	45,196	46,279
Net profit	14,728	8,536+	5,543+	12,398+	9,793

(*continued*)

	1940/41	1941/42	1942/43	1943/44	1944/45
Profit and loss calculations (000 RM)					
Gross turnover	193,598	204,133	230,603	222,914	65,685
Net turnover	162,014	181,902	207,171	200,846	65,685
Minus manufacturing costs	134,010	154,681	171,587	163,921	56,326
Gross profit	28,004	27,221	35,584	36,925	9,359
Minus operating costs	13,846	14,806	15,880	15,319	8,781
Operating profit	14,158	12,415	19,704	21,606	578
Plus other income	8,224	7,693	6,657	8,150	2,153
Total proceeds	22,382	20,108	26,361	29,756	2,731
Minus taxes/other deductions	19,322	16,622	22,919	29,756	4,828
Net earnings	3,060	3,486	3,442	0	−2,097
Significant income/expense items (000 RM)					
Manufacturing costs					
Depreciation	4,068	5,055	4,899	4,536	1,453
Research and development	1,935	1,858	2,147	1,376	369
Operating costs					
Wages and salaries	7,156	8,559	9,153	8,774	4,354
Taxes and social payments	3,161	2,543	2,078	1,987	1,058
Other income					
License fees	994	906	838	947	215
From subsidiaries	2,376	2,828	2,836	2,987	494
Sales of stocks/bonds	773	841	1,238	1,275	45
Taxes/other deductions					
Export promotion payments	2,120	238	8	1	0
Write-offs of holdings/bills	630	1,851	2,187	22,844	3,534
Corporation tax	8,372	9,956	12,259	1,347	0
Winterhilfswerk	166	194	190	184	0
Adolf Hitler donation	40	96	73	84	0

Sources: Stock capital and balance sheet value: Heinz Mayer-Wegelin, *Aller Anfang ist Schwer* (Frankfurt am Main: Degussa AG, 1973), p. 168.
Workforce: DUA, DL 11.5/21, An alle Zweigniederlassungen und Verkaufsstellen, March 31, 1933 [1932/33 (as of the middle of the business year)]; TLE 1/23, Bernau's memo on Finanzen, February 26, 1938 [1933/34 (as of the end of the business year), 1937/38 (as of December 31, 1937)]; RFI 4.2/99, Dresdner Bank to Reich Economics Ministry, February 24, 1942 (as of that date); DL 2.1, Niederschrift über die Vorstandssitzung am 7. September 1943, p. 334 (as of March 31, 1943, but excluding 4,400 drafted personnel); AW 2.8/1, Federlin to the Reichspostdirektion Wien, May 24, 1944; DL 5/41, Aufstellungen des MOB-Ausschusses, March 3, 1945.
Tax return balance figures: DUA, RFI 4.8/5-6, Körperschaftssteuerberichte 1933–45.
Profit and loss calculations and significant income and expense items – for 1932–35: Geschäftsberichte for 1932/33, 1933/34, 1934/35, and DUA, RFI 4.2/67, 70, and 74 Abschlüsse zu 30. September 1934, 1935, and 1936; for 1935–45: DUA, DL 2/16, Tabelle 4 mit Anlagen, as amended regarding gross profits by D 2/18, Development and Structure of Degussa, undated [1945/46], p. 14.

Appendix C

Degussa's Sales by Product Line, 1935–1943

CHART 1 (000 RM)	1935–36	1936–37	1938–39[b]	1939–40[b]	1940–41[b]	1941–42[b]	1942–43[b]
Investment and Special Income	2,358	2,093	1,317	1,365	1,285	2,158	2,871
Precious Metals Sector							
Precious metals[a]	53,151	49,191	49,747	31,276	43,356	50,332	55,721
Ceramic colors	3,900	5,033	5,078	3,870	4,208	4,458	3,889
Total	57,051	54,224	54,825	35,146	47,564	54,790	59,610
Inorganics Sector							
Rheinfelden/Knapsack	16,319	18,049	17,914	14,260	15,019	15,582	15,925
Chemicals	12,634	14,877	15,432	9,843	9,629	12,704	13,661
Special metals	0	0	0	0	0	748	1,133
Total	28,953	32,926	33,346	24,103	24,648	29,034	30,719
Organics Sector							
Carbide	0	0	0	2,882	3,446	4,371	4,121
Carbon black	0	0	5,171	6,781	8,741	10,828	12,959
HIAG	35,524	43,250	62,512	63,907	73,173	63,807	74,526
Total	35,524	43,251	67,683	73,570	85,360	79,006	91,606
Metals Treating Sector							
Hardeners (Durferrit)	0	0	0	8,870	8,993	11,823	14,430
Thermal ceramics (Degussit)	0	0	0	0	0	1,333	1,834
Oven building (IOB)	332	643	1,595	1,465	4,776	5,605	7,646
Total	332	643	1,595	10,335	13,769	18,761	23,910
Artificial Leathers Sector							
Wolfgang, etc.	0	0	0	15,745	20,974	20,386	21,888
TOTAL	124,218	133,137	158,766	160,264	193,600	204,135	230,604

CHART 2 (percentages)	1935–36	1936–37	1938–39[b]	1939–40[b]	1940–41[b]	1941–42[b]	1942–43[b]
Investment and Special Income	1.9	1.6	0.8	0.9	0.7	1.1	1.2
Precious Metals Sector							
Precious metals[a]	42.8	36.9	31.3	19.5	22.4	24.7	24.2
Ceramic colors	3.1	3.8	3.2	2.4	2.2	2.2	1.7
Total	45.9	40.7	34.5	21.9	24.6	26.8	25.8
Inorganics Sector							
Rheinfelden/Knapsack	13.1	13.6	11.3	8.9	7.8	7.6	6.9
Chemicals	10.2	11.2	9.7	6.1	5.0	6.2	5.9
Special metals	0.0	0.0	0.0	0.0	0.0	0.4	0.5
Total	23.3	24.7	21.0	15.0	12.7	14.2	13.3
Organics Sector							
Carbide	0.0	0.0	0.0	1.8	1.8	2.1	1.8
Carbon black	0.0	0.0	3.3	4.2	4.5	5.3	5.6
HIAG	28.6	32.5	39.4	39.9	37.8	31.3	32.3
Total	28.6	32.5	42.6	45.9	44.1	38.7	39.7
Metals Treating Sector							
Hardeners (Durferrit)	0.0	0.0	0.0	5.5	4.6	5.8	6.3
Thermal ceramics (Degussit)	0.0	0.0	0.0	0.0	0.0	0.7	0.8
Oven building (IOB)	0.3	0.5	1.0	0.9	2.5	2.7	3.3
Total	0.3	0.5	1.0	6.4	7.1	9.2	10.4
Artificial Leathers Sector							
Wolfgang, etc.	0.0	0.0	0.0	9.8	10.8	10.0	9.5
TOTAL	100.0	100.0	100.0	100.0	100.0	100.0	100.0

[a] Includes Weber & Hempel.

[b] Includes Organgesellschaften.

Note: Rounding produces slight variations from the accurate gross profit figures in Appendix B.

Sources: DNA, RFI 4.2/74, 77, 85, 89, 93, 98, and 104 (figures reaggregated for comparability over time, where possible, but the data do not include the sales income from some subsidiaries, e.g., Wyhlen and Durferrit, prior to their absorption into Degussa).

Appendix D

Degussa's Gross Profits by Product Line, 1932–1944

CHART I (million Reichsmarks)

	1932–33	1933–34	1934–35	1935–36	1936–37	1937–38	1938–39	1939–40	1940–41	1941–42	1942–43	1943–44
Investment and Special Income	2.0	1.8	2.1	1.8	2.9	2.7	2.1	3.0	5.5	4.6	7.3	7.2
Precious Metals Sector												
Precious metals	3.5	3.3	3.9	5.1	4.9	4.9	4.8	3.8	5.9	8.3	8.6	8.8
Weber & Hempel	0.2	0.2	0.2	0.2	0.2	0.0	0.3	0.4	0.3	0.3	0.4	0.1
Ceramic colors	0.7	0.9	0.9	0.9	1.1	1.0	1.2	1.1	1.2	1.2	1.2	1.3
Total	4.4	4.4	5.0	6.2	6.2	5.9	6.3	5.3	7.4	9.8	10.2	10.2
Inorganics Sector												
Rheinfelden/Knapsack	9.9	11.0	8.3	7.9	8.7	8.5	8.5	6.5	5.0	4.9	4.3	4.1
Chemicals	0.6	0.7	0.7	1.0	1.3	1.1	2.3	2.9	2.3	2.7	2.5	4.0
Special metals	0.0	0.0	0.0	0.0	0.2	0.0	0.1	0.2	0.1	0.2	0.3	0.1
Total	10.5	11.7	9.0	8.9	10.2	9.6	10.9	9.6	7.4	7.8	7.1	8.2
Organics Sector												
Carbide	0.0	0.0	0.0	0.1	0.4	0.5	0.6	0.6	0.6	0.7	1.0	0.8
Carbon black	0.0	0.0	0.1	0.1	0.2	0.4	1.5	1.9	2.3	2.2	2.9	1.7
HIAG	6.1	6.4	6.6	8.3	9.2	8.6	10.5	13.5	13.6	10.5	12.1	12.5
Total	6.1	6.4	6.7	8.5	9.8	9.5	12.6	16.0	16.5	13.4	16.0	15.0
Metals Treating Sector												
Hardeners (Durferrit)	0.0	0.0	0.1	0.3	0.4	0.5	0.9	2.4	2.5	3.1	3.7	4.2
Thermal ceramics (Degussit)	0.0	0.0	0.0	0.0	0.0	0.0	0.0	0.0	0.3	0.4	0.8	0.6
Oven building (IOB)	0.0	0.0	0.1	0.1	0.2	0.1	0.2	0.3	0.6	1.0	1.5	2.3
Total	0.0	0.0	0.2	0.4	0.6	0.6	1.1	2.7	3.4	4.5	6.0	7.1
Artificial Leathers Sector												
Wolfgang, etc.	0.1	0.1	0.2	0.2	0.5	1.0	0.7	0.4	1.9	1.6	2.7	2.8
TOTAL	23.1	24.5	23.2	26.0	30.2	29.3	33.7	37.0	42.1	41.7	49.3	50.5

CHART 2 (percentages)	1932–33	1933–34	1934–35	1935–36	1936–37	1937–38	1938–39	1939–40	1940–41	1941–42	1942–43	1943–44
Investment and Special Income	8.6	7.4	9.1	6.9	9.6	9.2	6.2	8.1	13.1	11.0	14.8	14.3
Precious Metals Sector												
Precious metals	15.1	13.5	16.8	19.6	16.2	16.7	14.2	10.3	14.0	19.9	17.4	17.4
Weber & Hempel	0.9	0.8	0.9	0.8	0.7	0.0	0.9	1.1	0.7	0.7	0.8	0.2
Ceramic colors	3.0	3.7	3.9	3.5	3.6	3.4	3.6	3.0	2.9	2.9	2.4	2.6
Total	19.0	18.0	21.6	23.9	20.5	20.1	18.7	14.3	17.6	23.5	20.7	20.2
Inorganics Sector												
Rheinfelden/Knapsack	42.8	45.0	35.8	30.4	28.8	29.0	25.2	17.6	11.9	11.8	8.7	8.1
Chemicals	2.6	2.9	3.0	3.9	4.3	3.7	6.8	7.8	5.5	6.5	5.1	7.9
Special metals	0.0	0.0	0.1	0.0	0.7	0.1	0.3	0.5	0.2	0.5	0.6	0.2
Total	45.4	47.8	38.9	34.3	33.8	32.9	32.3	25.9	17.6	18.7	14.4	16.2
Organics Sector												
Carbide	0.0	0.0	0.0	0.4	1.3	1.7	1.8	1.6	1.4	1.7	2.0	1.6
Carbon black	0.1	0.1	0.3	0.4	0.7	1.4	4.5	5.1	5.5	5.3	5.9	3.4
HIAG	26.4	26.2	28.5	32.0	30.5	29.3	31.2	36.5	32.3	25.2	24.5	24.8
Total	26.4	26.3	28.8	32.7	32.5	32.4	37.4	43.2	39.2	32.1	32.5	29.7
Metals Treating Sector												
Hardeners (Durferrit)	0.1	0.1	0.3	1.0	1.3	1.7	2.7	6.5	5.9	7.4	7.5	8.3
Thermal ceramics (Degussit)	0.0	0.0	0.0	0.0	0.0	0.0	0.0	0.0	0.7	1.0	1.6	1.2
Oven building (IOB)	0.0	0.0	0.4	0.4	0.7	0.3	0.6	0.8	1.4	2.4	3.0	4.6
Total	0.1	0.1	0.8	1.3	2.0	2.0	3.3	7.3	8.1	10.8	12.2	14.1
Artificial Leathers Sector												
Wolfgang, etc.	0.4	0.4	0.9	0.8	1.7	3.4	2.1	1.1	4.5	3.8	5.5	5.5
TOTAL	100.0	100.0	100.0	100.0	100.0	100.0	100.0	100.0	100.0	100.0	100.0	100.0

Note: All figures are rounded to the first decimal place.

Sources: DUA, RFI 4.2/64, 67, 70, 74, 77, 80, 85, 89, 93, 98, 104, 108 (figures reaggregated for comparability over time).

Appendix E

Degussa's Export Sales by Product Line, 1935–1943

1. Percentage of sales exported

	1935/36	1936/37	1938/39[c]	1939/40[c]	1940/41	1941/42[c]	1942/43[c]
Precious metals[a]	19.5	22.4	20.0	15.3	6.9	7.7	9.6
Ceramic colors	33.3	31.9	23.3	14.1	19.6	14.8	11.5
Rheinfelden[b]	7.1	4.9	1.9	6.2	1.1	1.3	2.9
Chemicals	58.6	52.6	49.0	31.4	27.6	26.0	24.8
Special metals					2.0	2.0	1.1
Carbon black	14.0	11.6	2.5	10.4	35.0	41.4	47.4
HIAG			8.0	5.9	4.6	4.8	4.8
Hardeners (Durferrit)				9.4	9.5	13.3	11.9
Thermal ceramics (Degussit)						9.8	8.5
Oven building	38.6	22.5	8.7	9.3	6.7	5.4	4.4
Wolfgang group						7.8	4.3
Whole firm	20.4	19.9	15.3	9.8	8.5	9.2	9.7

2. Line's percentage of Degussa's exports

	1935/36	1936/37	1938/39[c]	1939/40[c]	1940/41	1941/42[c]	1942/43[c]
Precious metals[a]	40.8	41.5	40.9	30.6	22.0	18.9	23.4
Ceramic colors	5.1	6.1	4.9	3.5	4.7	3.5	2.0
Rheinfelden[b]	4.6	3.3	1.4	5.3	1.2	1.1	2.1
Chemicals	29.2	29.6	31.1	19.7	20.5	17.5	15.1
Special metals						.1	.1
Carbon black			5	4.5	22.6	23.8	27.4
HIAG	19.6	19.0	20.6	30.2	19.5	16.1	15.6
Hardeners (Durferrit)				5.3	7.0	8.3	7.7
Thermal Ceramics (Degussit)						.7	.7
Oven building	.5	.5	.6	.9	2.4	1.6	1.5
Wolfgang group						8.4	4.5
TOTAL	99.8	100.0	100.0	100.0	99.9	100.0	100.1

[a] Includes Weber & Hempal.
[b] Includes Knapsack.
[c] Includes Organgesellschaften.

Sources: DUA, RFI 4.2/74, 77, 89, 93, 98, and 104 (figures reaggregated for comparability over time).

Appendix F

Aryanizations and Compensation Payments by Degussa, 1933–1960

Property	Aryanizations (Reichsmarks)		Compensations (Deutschmarks)	
	Nominal value	Price paid	By Degussa	Total
Firms				
Homburg	237,240	803,824[a]	290,000	440,000
Auer	7,000,000	9,224,000	385,000	385,000
Wyhlen		1,555,000	No claim made	
Hirsch		163,422[a]	18,495	245,000
Marquart	800,000	1,550,000	Restitution made in trade	
Grünau	262,500	364,600	256,000 + license fees	
Hydrocarbon	99,000	198,000	Seized by the German Democratic Republic (GDR)	
ÖCW	572,000	339,000	457,600[b] + profit & resale	
Kulzer (50%)	150,000	143,300	367,500	835,000
MG (2)	1,140,000	1,180,750	(Profitable sale)	
Aurora	100,000	0	Seized by Czechoslovakia	
Fröhlich (53%)	318,900	335,039	Seized by Czechoslovakia	
Prag-Dewitz (Auer)		380,000	Seized by Czechoslovakia	
Real estate				
Neptunhaus	791,600	716,250	30,000	30,000
NM Str. Ecke	36,600+	165,000+	10,000	10,000
Vogelweidstr.	37,000	25,000	25,000	25,000
Adlerbau	114,300	125,000	75,000	75,000
Siegburgerstr.		36,000[a]	Claim withdrawn	
Weisensee			Seized by the GDR	
Hamburg			?	?
Karlsplatz		129,000	Seized by Austria	
Stern house (Kulzer)		220,000	10,000	
Prag (Auer/ shoe polish)		45,000	Seized by Czechoslovakia	

(continued)

Property	Aryanizations (Reichsmarks)		Compensations (Deutschmarks)	
	Nominal value	Price paid	By Degussa	Total
Patent				
Kramer		6,500	?	?
Totals		17,704,695	2,153,595	

Summary: Of twenty-five Aryanization cases, no restitution claims were made in four, restitution was paid in twelve, confiscations took place in seven, and two cases remain unclarified.

[a] Degussa's share of total payments of 1,860,703 RM (Homburg), 453,950 RM (Hirsch), and 100,000 RM (Siegburgerstr.).

[b] Converted from Reichsmarks to Deutschmarks on a ratio of 5:4.

Appendix G

Growth of the Auergesellschaft, 1933–1945

	1933/34	1934/35	1935/36	1936/37	1937/38	1938/39[a]
Stock capital (000 RM)	7,000	7,000	7,000	7,000	7,000	7,000
Balance sheet value (000 RM)	8,688	12,174	13,226	18,229		27,101
Sales (000 RM)		20,000	24,500	31,000	50,000	87,600
Depreciation (000 RM)	(1000)	977	604	884	(1,597)	(5,000)
Net profits (000 RM)	425	528	606	625	542	846
Borrowed funds (000 RM)				3,500	7,000	6,000
Gas defense % of sales		78	80		85	90
Military % of sales						
Workforce	2,713		(+25%)			c. 3,250

Note: Figures in parentheses are inferred from the remainder of the firm's documented total depreciation, 1933–43, after deducting the annual entries.

[a] Fifteen months owing to the change of the close of the business year from June 30 to September 30.

	1939/40	1940/41	1941/42	1942/43	1943/44	1944/45
Stock capital (000 RM)	7,000	7,000	11,000	11,000	11,000	11,000
Balance sheet value (000 RM)	39,336	44,531	45,483	51,909	60,227	
Sales (000 RM)	95,000	100,000	117,000	109,600	129,582	
Depreciation (000 RM)	5,143	3,030	5,860	4,593	4,920	
Net profits (000 RM)	518	502	524	488	558	−10,406
Borrowed funds (000 RM)	11,186	5,600	4,569	21,492	20,132	18,500
Gas defense % of sales	92	87	86	85	82	
Military % of sales	75+	90	77	79+		
Workforce	8,600	9,065	9,218	10,601	13,700	11,500

Sources: IW 24.9/1 and 24.5/5, Bernau's Betr.: Bilanz Degea, January 16, 1934; Berichte des Aufsichtsrates bezw. des Vorstandes für die Geschäftsjahre 1933/34–1942/43; Berichte des Vorstandes zur Bilanz, November 15, 1938, January 4, 1940; Bilanzentwurf zum 30. September 1944 and Umsätze nach ausgehenden Rechnungen, January 11, 1945; IW 24.8/2, Busemann's Notiz betr. Bilanz Auergesellschaft, July 2, 1936; DL 3.Busemann/5, Notiz Betr. Geldbedarf der Auergesellschaft, April 23, 1937, Finanzlage der Auergesellschaft, April 4, 1938, Betr. Auergesellschaft, April 1, 1939; IW 24.5/5, Bernau's Betr.: Auergesellschaft, June 10, 1940, and October 2, 1943; BET 10/1, Bernau's Betr.: Auergesellschaft, July 24, 1945; and IW 24.5/3, Bernau's Betr.: Auergesellschaft, April 16, 1947.

Appendix H

Main Products of the Wood Carbonization Industry and Their Uses as of 1936

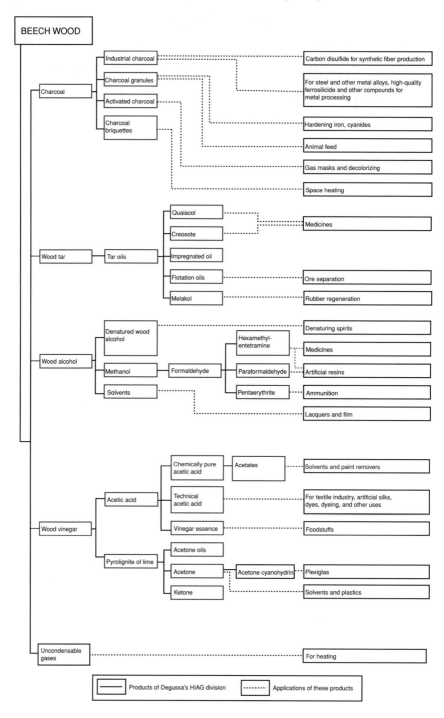

Appendix I

Development of Degussa's Output (Selected Plants and Products), 1933–1943

Plant and products	Metric tons produced		
	1933	1938	1943
Rheinfelden			
Hydrogen peroxide (100% pure)	114	486	965
Sodium peroxide	2,046	2,294	3,151
Sodium perborate/percarbonate	13,706	15,557	4,146
Knapsack			
Sodium	3,204	5,841	7,650
Chlorine	4,929	8,917	11,420
Wyhlen – carbide	0	10,624	11,598
Kalscheuren			
Gas-based carbon black	0	3,550	4,719
Lampblack	0	3,048	4,803
HIAG plants in postwar West Germany[a]			
Charcoal	32,120	72,980	72,510
Activated charcoal	80	250	610
Wood tar	7,630	19,600	19,960
Tar oils	640	1,370	9,120
Quaiacol	0	20	60
Creosote	280	60	20
Flotation oils	0	50	810
Denatured wood alcohol	740	790	560
Solvents	600	890	600
Methanol	1,370	2,190	1,770
Formaldehyde	1,620	3,180	7,120
Paraformaldehyde	0	0	10
Acetates	3,100	6,940	9,770
Acetone	1,120	1,510	1,400
Acetone cyanohydrin	0	430	1,600

[a] Bodenfelde, Brilon-Wald, Bruchhausen, Brücken, Konstanz, Kredenbach, Lorch, Mombach, Oeventrop, Schleiden, and Züschen. The figures include the totals for both charcoal and wood tar and the end products derived from them, but only the end products of wood vinegar and wood alcohol, which were entirely distilled into these by the plants.

Sources: DUA, ZVS 1/10, memo from Technische Abteilung II to Z.S.V. [Zentral-Statistische Verwaltung?], Betr.: Fragebogen der Militärregierung, October 25, 1946 (for the carbonization and distillation plants); and memo by Harant and Bonath, October 24, 1946 (on the other installations). The figures for the former refer to the business years ending in 1933, 1938, and 1943; those for the latter apparently to the calendar years.

Appendix J

Degussa's Precious Metals Refining and Inventories, 1932–1945 (in kilograms)

Production from Raw Inputs (i.e., other than already-purified silver)

Business year	Fine silver	Fine gold	Fine platinum
1935/36	492,956	16,955	168
1936/37	445,155	11,651	170
1937/38	391,577	10,372	117
1938/39	288,180	11,176	135
1939/40	328,715	5,412	96
1940/41	331,945	6,740	91

Sources: DUA, GEH 5/5, Degussa to Reichskommissar für die Preisbildung, December 1, 1939, November 19, 1940, and August 27, 1941.

	Refining						On hand[a]	
Year	Gold in	Gold out	Net flow	Silver in	Silver out	Net flow	Gold	Silver
1932	28,351	28,374	−23		c. 425,000		2,390	120,767
1933	28,740	28,408	+332		c. 680,000		2,317	121,701
1934	16,595	16,556	+39				2,150	121,743
1935	15,477	15,652	−175				2,059	97,207
1936	15,440	15,663	−223		c. 519,000		2,150	108,892
1937	10,776	10,966	−190	547,687	571,838	−24,151	2,055	106,365
1938	11,130	11,409	−279	409,588	252,869	+156,719	2,041	96,991
1939	9,496	9,400	+96	379,100	337,072	+42,028	2,177	123,504
1940	5,716	5,955	−239	307,267	335,208	−27,941	2,060	110,901
1941	6,687	6,416	+271	434,147	446,706	−12,559	2,087	135,069
1942	7,325	7,527	−202	271,796	322,879	−51,083	2,304	264,978
1943	8,456	8,912	−456	365,552	372,079	−6,527	2,389	282,364
1944	3,680	3,853	−173	358,673	331,545	+27,128	1,635	18,873
1945	627	380	+247	23,001	47,310	−24,309	−755	−101,894
Total	168,496	169,471	−975	3,096,811	3,017,506	+79,305		

[a] As of September 30 of each year.

Sources: DUA, Scheidebücher: Edelmetall Ein- und Ausgänge, and RFI 4.8/5, Steuerbilanzen, Anlagen 2b or f; Ralf Banken, Die Entwicklung des Edelmetallsektors im "Dritten Reich" 1933–1945 (forthcoming), Chapter 2.

Appendix K

Degussa's Gold and Silver Separation Processes, 1941

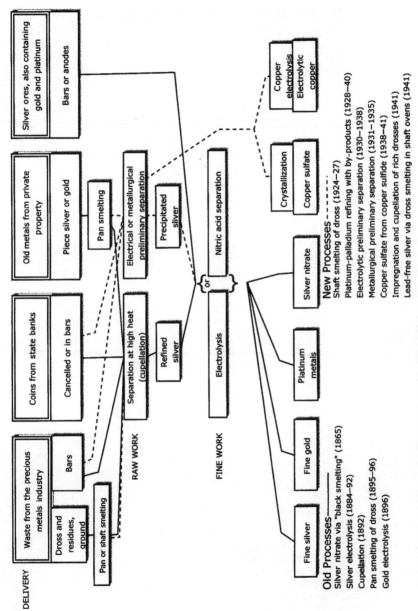

DELIVERY

Silver ores, also containing gold and platinum — Bars or anodes

Old metals from private property — Piece silver or gold — Pan smelting

Coins from state banks — Cancelled or in bars

Waste from the precious metals industry — Bars

Dross and residues, ground — Pan or shaft smelting

RAW WORK

Electrical or metallurgical preliminary separation — Precipitated silver

Separation at high heat (cupellation) — Refined silver

FINE WORK

Nitric acid separation

Electrolysis

or

Fine silver — Fine gold — Platinum metals — Silver nitrate

Crystallization — Copper sulfate

Copper electrolysis — Electrolytic copper

Old Processes

Silver nitrate via "black smelting" (1865)
Silver electrolysis (1884–92)
Cupellation (1892)
Pan smelting of dross (1895–96)
Gold electrolysis (1896)

New Processes

Shaft smelting of dross (1924–27)
Platinum–palladium refining with by-products (1928–40)
Electrolytic preliminary separation (1930–1938)
Metallurgical preliminary separation (1931–1935)
Copper sulfate from copper sulfide (1938–41)
Impregnation and cupellation of rich drosses (1941)
Lead-free silver via dross smelting in shaft ovens (1941)

Source: DUA, GEH 3.Hirtes/1, Hirtes to General Major H. Klein, June 16, 1943, enclosure (modified).

Appendix L

Organizational Chart of Degussa, 1943

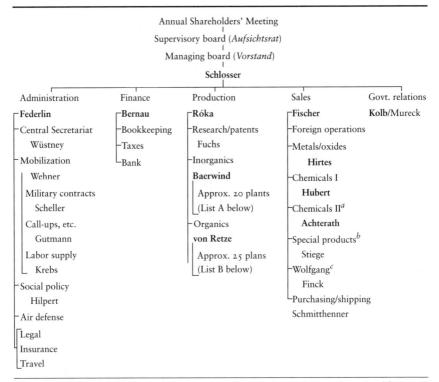

Annual Shareholders' Meeting

Supervisory board (*Aufsichtsrat*)

Managing board (*Vorstand*)

Schlosser

Administration	Finance	Production	Sales	Govt. relations
Federlin	**Bernau**	**Róka**	**Fischer**	Kolb/Mureck
Central Secretariat	Bookkeeping	Research/patents	Foreign operations	
Wüstney	Taxes	Fuchs	Metals/oxides	
Mobilization	Bank	Inorganics	**Hirtes**	
Wehner		**Baerwind**	Chemicals I	
Military contracts		Approx. 20 plants	**Hubert**	
Scheller		(List A below)	Chemicals II[a]	
Call-ups, etc.		Organics	**Achterath**	
Gutmann		**von Retze**	Special products[b]	
Labor supply		Approx. 25 plans	Stiege	
Krebs		(List B below)	Wolfgang[c]	
Social policy			Finck	
Hilpert			Purchasing/shipping	
Air defense			Schmitthenner	
Legal				
Insurance				
Travel				

List A: Beuel (Marquart), Blankenburg (Hydrocarbon), Dortmund (DGW), Dossenheim, Frankfurt I & II, Gleiwitz (DGW), Grünau, Hanau, Kalscheuren, Knapsack, Kolin, Raudnitz, Reinickendorf, Rheinfelden, Weissenstein (ÖCW), Wesseling, Wien, Worms, and Wyhlen.

List B: Bodenfelde, Brilon-Wald, Bruchhausen, Brücken, Frankfurt/Oder, Fürstenberg, Fürstenwalde, Greifenhagen, Hainowka, Konstanz, Kredenbach, Lorch, Mölkau, Mombach, Oeventrop, Paraxol (A, B, W, and Z), Ratibor, Schleiden, Treuen, Vosswalde, Wildau, Wolfgang, and Züschen.

Bold names = members of the managing board.

[a] Carbide, carbon black, charcoals, acetic acid.

[b] Thermal and metals-treating products.

[c] Artificial leathers, water-resistant cloths, etc.

Sources: DUA, DL 2/1, Niederschrift über die Vorstandssitzung am 5. Juli 1943, Anlage 1; PCA 2/144, Federlin's Notiz. Personalamt, January 28, 1943; and TLE 1/23, Federlin's Notiz Betr.: Organisation, October 21, 1943.

Appendix M

Locations of Degussa's Principal Plants, 1939–1943

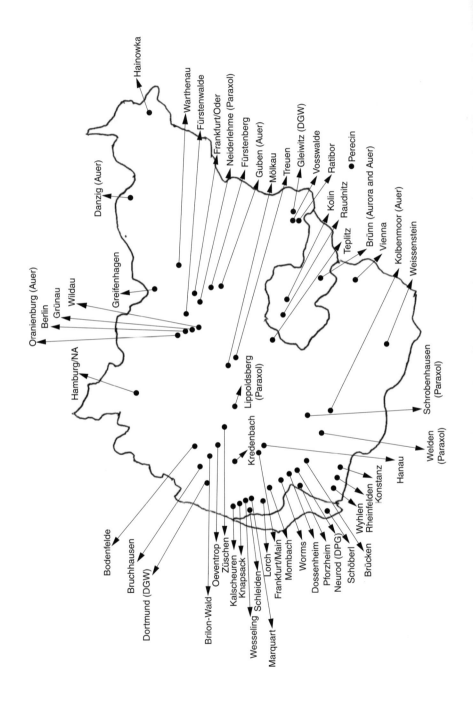

Hainowka

Warthenau

Fürstenwalde

Frankfurt/Oder

Neiderlehme (Paraxol)

Fürstenberg

Guben (Auer)

Mölkau

Treuen

Gleiwitz (DGW)

Vosswalde

Ratibor

Perecin

Kolin

Raudnitz

Brünn (Aurora and Auer)

Teplitz

Vienna

Kolbenmoor (Auer)

Weissenstein

Danzig (Auer)

Oranienburg (Auer)

Grünau

Berlin

Wildau

Greifenhagen

Hamburg/NA

Schrobenhausen
(Paraxol)

Lippoldsberg
(Paraxol)

Welden
(Paraxol)

Kredenbach

Hanau

Konstanz

Rheinfelden

Wyhlen

Bodenfelde

Bruchhausen

Dortmund (DGW)

Brilon-Wald

Oeventrop

Züschen

Kalscheuren

Knapsack

Wesseling

Schleiden

Lorch

Frankfurt/Main

Mombach

Worms

Dossenheim

Pforzheim

Neurod (DPG)

Schöberl

Brücken

Marquart

Appendix N

Female, Foreign, and Forced Labor at Degussa (Sample Plants and Dates), 1940–1945

Frankfurt/ Gutleutstrasse	7/41	12/42	9/43	3/44	9/44	1/45
National service on date	118	139	138	155	167	175
On site						
Clerical/admin.	178 (?)	74 (18)	78 (20)	79 (21)	76 (22)	81 (24)
Workers	422 (71)	419 (99)	582 (172)	532 (172)	551 (191)	538 (180)
Total	600 (?)	493 (117)	670 (192)	611 (193)	627 (213)	619 (204)
Germans	580 (?)	384 (87)	495 (136)	460 (122)	437 (148)	441 (150)
POWs	20	49	0	0	0	0
Eastern workers	0	60 (30)	78 (55)	99 (70)	78 (55)	73 (49)
Other foreigners	0	0	86 (1)	60 (1)	112 (10)	105 (5)
Percent German	97	78 (18)	74 (20)	75 (20)	70 (24)	71 (24)
Percent Female	?	24	29	32	34	33
Called-up as % of German males present	?	47	38	37	58	60

Note: Figures in parentheses represent women.
Source: DUA, IW 2.8/8, Betriebsberichte for the respective months (apprentices included in all categories).

Knapsack	1/41	12/41	8/42	1/43	8/43	2/44	9/44
National service on date	26	35	47	54	72	84	94
On site							
Workers/apprentices	201	220	218	222	331 (24)	359 (26)	373 (38)
Germans	186	190	176	125	189 (23)	179 (25)	179 (35)
POWs	15	19	25[a]	50	86	98	93
Foreigners	0	11	17	47	56 (1)	82 (1)[b]	101 (3)
Percent German	93	86	81	56	57 (7)	50 (7)	48 (9)
Percent Female	?	?	?	?	8	7	10
Called-up as % of German males present	14	18	27	43	43	55	61

Note: Figures in parentheses represent women.
[a] Russian POWs replaced Polish.
[b] *Ostarbeiter* arrived 11/43.
Source: DUA, IW 33.8/7, Betriebsberichte for the respective months (figures adjusted to include foreign assembly workers consistently).

Kalscheuren	6/40	9/41	2/44	8/44	1/45
National service on date	38		84	85	88
On site					
Clerical/admin.	25		44	54	55
Workers	183		314 (20)	321 (27)	232 (16)
Total	208	233	358 (20)	375 (27)	287 (16)
Germans	208	216	137 (20)	130 (27)	110 (16)
POWs	0	27	14	14	0
Ostarbeiter	0		144	153	114
Other foreigners	0		19	24	8
Percent German	100		38 (6)	35 (7)	38 (6)
Percent Female	?		6	7	6
Called-up as % of German males present			71	83	85

Note: Figures in parentheses represent women.
Source: DUA, IW 34.2/1–3, Betriebsberichte bzw. Erläuterungen zu den Kalkulationen for the respective months.

Brilon-Wald	5/40	1/43	4/43	9/44	3/45
National service on date					
On site					
Clerical/admin.		18 (9)			
Workers		283 (80)			
Total	229	301 (89)	371 (89)	321	
Germans	229	?	186 (24)	169	
POWs		57	52	42	50
Ostarbeiter		?	73 (65)	70 (61)	91 (60)
Other foreigners		?	60	40	
Percent German	100	?	50 (6)	53	
Percent Female			30	24	
Called-up as % of German males present					

Note: Figures in parentheses represent woman.
Sources: DUA, D 2/3, Hiagwerk Brilon-Wald to Degussa Vorstand, November 12, 1947; IW 40.10/1, handwritten roster of French POWs, 1941–45; Gefolgschaftsstand am 10.3.43; Werk Brilon-Wald to Wirtschaftsamt der Stadt Brilon, October 1, 1944; Brilon-Wald to Gemeinschaftslager Dortmund-Hamm, February 17, 1945; and DL 5/41, Aufstellungen des Mob-Ausschuss-Büro, January 5 and March 3, 1945.

Rheinfelden	8/39	10/39	8/40	8/42	2–3/43	8/43	11/43	7/44
National service on date		178	214	240	247	253		
On site								
Clerical/admin.	60			84				
Workers	622			501				
Total	682 (15)	438 (14)	480 (73)	468 (86)	585 (84)	646 (107)	669 (132)	701 (154)
Germans	659 (15)	415 (14)	458 (73)	449 (86)	437 (84)	474 (107)	459 (86)	435 (84)
POWs							0	
Ostarbeiter					153	172	74 (35)	266
Other foreigners	23	23	22	19			136 (11)	(70)
Percent German	97	95 (3)	95 (15)	96 (18)	75 (14)	74 (17)	69 (13)	62 (12)
Percent Female	2	3	15	18	14	17	20	22
Called-up as % of German males present	0	44	56	66	70	69	?	?

Note: Figures in parentheses represent women.

Sources: DUA, PCA 2/144, Rheinfelden/Bd., Gesamte Arbeiterbestand, March 6, 1943; Anlagen zum Bericht über den Besuch des Herrn. Gen. D. Inf. V. Unruh, November 10, 1943; IW 29.10/1, Gefolgschaftsbewegung, September 1943; PCA 1/536, Anlage zum Schrb. an Bez. Obm. d. Wigru. Chem. Ind. H. Oberbürgerm. Renninger, July 22, 1944.

Appendix O

Degussa's Work Force circa
September 30, 1944

Installation	Total staff	Installation	Total staff
Branches (*Zweigniederlassungen*)		Wien-Liesing	89
Berlin	101	Wildau	216
Hamburg	29	Wolfgang	450
Hanau (Siebert)	890	Worms	62
Soden-Salmünster	193	Wyhlen	104
Hanau (IOB)	222	Züschen	167
Pforzheim	298	Owned 51%–100%	
Vienna	138	Auergesellschaft	10,614
Degussa plants		Aurora/Brünn	??
Bodenfelde	375	Fröhlich/Raudnitz	??
Brilon-Wald	321	Grünau	??
Bruchhausen	182	Hydrocarbon	63
Brücken	164	Marquart	418
Dossenheim	97	Mölkau	330
Fürstenberg/Oder	354	Paraxol	934
Fürstenwalde	??	Perecin	??
Frankfurt I/II/admin.	2,045	Treuen	111
Greifenhagen	334	Wesseling	237
Kalscheuren	355	= 12,707+	
Knapsack	404	Owned 50%	
Konstanz	27	Aufbereitung	13
Kredenbach	136	DGW/Dortmund	694
Lorch	205	DGW/Gleiwitz	1,037
Mombach	190	Devrient	122
Oeventrop	219	DPG	19
Ratibor	78	Kulzer	110
Reinickendorf/Bürmoos	684	Schöberl	??
Rheinfelden	721	= 1,995+	
Schleiden	88	Owned 25%–49%	
Teplitz	??	Aktivkohle (33%)	170
Vosswalde	127	Degesch (42.5%)	43

Essigsäure (41%)	45	Nordd. Affin. (37.5%)	1,900
Fränkische	171	Weissenstein (47%)	132
Warthenau	154	Oswaldowski (31%)	32
Homburg (43%)	??	Speyer & Grund (36%)	20
Kolin (13%)	approx. 300	Zwiesel (25%)	136
			= 3,103+

[Already lost: Hainowka 353 (as of September 30, 1943)]

Subtotals	10,065+	17,805
		= 27,870+

Sources: DUA, D 2/15–18, Answers to Questions from the Decartellization Branch, 1946–48; DL 5/41, Aufstellungen des Büro des MOB-Ausschusses, January 5 and March 3, 1945; PERS 02/0016, Degussa Berlin to Degussa Frankfurt, November 4, 1944 (ZN Berlin); IW 24.6/1, Quasebart to Schlosser, November 11, 1944 (Auer); PCA 2, Betriebsbericht Nr. 17, October 5, 1944 (Gleiwitz); AW 5.8/10–12, Betriebsbericht für Dezember 1944 (Weissenstein). As far as possible, these figures exclude employees called up for national service or transferred from other sites.

Appendix P

Principal Holdings of the Degussa Concern, 1945

100%	51%–99%	50%
MARQUART AG 1 mRM, Beuel/Bonn	WESSELING AG 1.6 mRM, 51% Wesseling/Köln	DGW (carbon black) 13 mRM, w/rubber industry Dortmund
Auergesellschaft 11 mRM, Berlin (GDR)	SCHLEMPE GmbH .1 mRM, 52% Frankfurt a.M.	DEVRIENT AG (pesticides) 1.2 mRM, w/Nordd.
Hydrocarbon .1 mRM, Berlin (GDR)	*Grünau AG*	Affinerie Hamburg
Atlas-Ago AG 1.5 mRM, Mölkau (GDR)	4 mRM, 86% Grünau (GDR)	**KULZER & CO.** .4 mRM, w/Heraeus Frankfurt a.M.
Carbon GmbH .3 mRM, Ratibor (Poland)	*Fröhlich, Jermár* .5 mRM, Prague/ Raudnitz (Czech.)	D. PULVERMETALL. .1 mRM, w/MG Frankfurt a.M.
Ch.W. Dr. Becker .3 mRM, Fürstenwalde (GDR)		*Ges. für Aufbereitung* .1 mRM, w/IG Farben
Wachs- und Ledertuch Fabriken .2 mRM, Treuen (GDR)	*Less than 50%:*	
Ch. Fa.Vosswalde .15 mRM, Vosswalde (Poland)	DEGESCH (pesticides) .1 mRM, 42.5%, w/IG and Goldschmidt, Frankfurt	**HOMBURG AG** 1 mRM, 43%, w/IG Farben Frankfurt a.M.
Paraxol GmbH .1 mRM, four sites	*ÖCW, Weissenstein* ??, 47% w/IG Farben Vienna (Austria)	NORDD. AFFINERIE 22.5 mRM, 37.5% w/MG and two others, Hamburg
Aurora ? mRM, Brünn	*Kaliwerke Kolin* ??, 13% w/Spiritus Syn. Kolin (Czech.)	**FRÄNK. WEINESSIG** 1.8 m, 41% w/IG Farben and two others, Schweinfurt
	Deutsche Aktivkohle, 33%, w/MG and IG Farben, Premnitz (GDR)	

bold = Aryanized; *italics* = dissolved or largely expropriated; CAPS = retained by Degussa; Figures = total capitalization; ( ) indicate the country to which installations lost in 1945; mRM = million Reichsmarks; GDR = German Democratic Republic.
Source: Adapted from DUA, D 2/18, organizational chart, January 1, 1947, signed by Büttgen.

356

Appendix Q

Corporate Relations in the Manufacture and Sale of Zyklon B

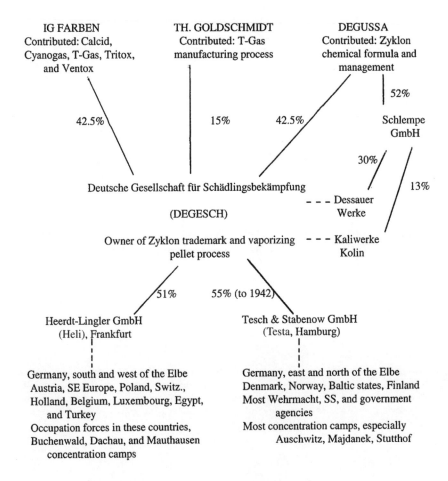

IG FARBEN
Contributed: Calcid,
Cyanogas, T-Gas, Tritox,
and Ventox

TH. GOLDSCHMIDT
Contributed: T-Gas
manufacturing process

DEGUSSA
Contributed: Zyklon
chemical formula and
management

52%

42.5%   15%   42.5%   Schlempe
GmbH

30%   13%

Deutsche Gesellschaft für Schädlingsbekämpfung

– – – Dessauer
Werke

(DEGESCH)

Owner of Zyklon trademark and vaporizing   – – – Kaliwerke
pellet process   Kolin

51%   55% (to 1942)

Heerdt-Lingler GmbH
(Heli), Frankfurt

Tesch & Stabenow GmbH
(Testa, Hamburg)

Germany, south and west of the Elbe
Austria, SE Europe, Poland, Switz.,
Holland, Belgium, Luxembourg, Egypt,
and Turkey
Occupation forces in these countries,
Buchenwald, Dachau, and Mauthausen
concentration camps

Germany, east and north of the Elbe
Denmark, Norway, Baltic states, Finland
Most Wehrmacht, SS, and government
agencies
Most concentration camps, especially
Auschwitz, Majdanek, Stutthof

Solid lines = shares of capital and profits   Broken lines = flows of orders and goods

Source: Adapted from DUA, SCH 1/44, Chart headed Stand 1942/43, March 1, 1948, signed by Büttgen.

Appendix R

Significant Statistics Concerning Zyklon B

I. Zyklon Sales and Profits of Degesch and Degussa, 1928–44

Year	Metric tons Domestic	Metric tons Total	Zyklon sales (ooo RM)	Zyklon % of Degesch sales	Degesch net profits (ooo RM)	Degussa dividend (ooo RM)
1928	38	*158*				
1929	52	*195*				
1930	60	210				
1931	35	*135*				
1932	26	*124*		72		
1933	27	*117*				
1934	50	*125*		59	41,850	
1935	50	*130*			85,709	
1936	60	148	808		95,135	
1937	54	133	721	37	251,743	85,000
1938	83	160	875	38	202,545	85,000
1939	95	180	994	42	104,462	42,500
1940	215	242	1,325	65	102,679	42,500
1941	163	194	1,014	56		85,000
1942	249	321	1,664	58	200,327	85,000
1943	290	411	2,224	65	150,338	63,750
1944	*190*	231	1,094	64	− 23,791	0

Note: Italicized figures are approximate.
Sources: Hervé Joly, "L'implication de l'industrie chimique allemande dans la Shoah: Le cas du Zyklon B," *Revue d'histoire moderne et contemporaine* 47 (2000), pp. 380, 386, 392; BET 9/43, Anlage zu 6a; BET 10/7, handwritten tabulation of dividends; IW 57.2/1, Protokolle der Verwaltungsausschuss-Sitzungen, 1935–41; Prüfung des Jahresabschlusses, December 31, 1943; BET 10/7, Bernau and Luft to Degesch, November 1, 1945.

II. Sales and Profits in Reichsmarks of Tesch & Stabenow GmbH, 1941–44

	1941	1942	1943	1944	Total
Receipts[a] from fumigations	282,345	485,897	396,673	390,490	1,555,405
Receipts[a] from Zyklon sales	45,736	92,681	127,986	27,923	294,326
Total	328,081	578,578	524,659	418,413	1,849,731
Net profits (*Reingewinn*)	60,523	174,231	73,651[b]	35,534	343,939

[a] Income minus the cost of goods.
[b] Originally 142,598 RM before a retrospective reduction for taxes in August 1944.
Source: NI-11,369, reproduced in Angelika Ebbinghaus, "Der Prozess gegen Tesch & Stabenow. Von der Schädlingsbekämpfung zum Holocaust," *1999* (1998), p. 69 (all figures have been rounded off).

III. Zyklon Sales in Kilograms by Tesch & Stabenow GmbH, 1942–43

	1942	1943
Exports	16,297	32,484
Misc. govt. clients	17,550	22,205
Misc. army and navy	9,082	15,012
Hauptsanitätspark, Berlin	11,232 = 37,864	19,982 = 57,199
Auschwitz		12,183
(Other) concentration camps	9,132	6,120
SS	15,776 = 24,908	11,472 = 29,775
Total	79,070	119,458

Source: NI-11,880–81, reproduced in Angelika Ebbinghaus, "Der Prozess gegen Tesch & Stabenow. Von der Schädlingsbekämpfung zum Holocaust," *1999* (1998), pp. 67–68 (all figures rounded off).

IV. Documented Deliveries of Zyklon to Concentration Camps, in Kilograms, 1942–45

	1942	1943	1944	1945	1942–45
By Tesch & Stabenow					
Sachsenhausen/Oranienburg	1,438	2,914			4,352
Neuengamme	180	427			607
Gross-Rosen		430			430
Majdanek[a]	360	1,628			7,711
Ravensbrück		352			352
Auschwitz	7,479	12,174	1,999		21,652
Others	35	380	6,928		7,343
Zentralsanitätslager der SS			1,720		1,720

(*continued*)

	1942	1943	1944	1945	1942–45
By Degesch (Gerstein orders)					
To SS-Zentralsanitätslager		830	1,580		2,410
To Auschwitz		590	790		1,380
By Heli					
To Mauthausen	804	1,362			2,166
To Dachau					
To Buchenwald					
By Slupetsky, Linz					
To Mauthausen		4,000?			4,000
From Dessau					
To Stutthof				403	403
From Kolin					
To Theresienstadt			400		
From Azot, Jaworzno					
To Auschwitz			1,155		1,155
Subtotal from Testa	9,492	18,305	10,647		44,167
Subtotal from Degesch		1,420	2,370		3,790
Subtotal from others	804	5,362	400	403	6,969
Subtotal to Auschwitz	7,479	12,691	4,017		24,187
Subtotal to other camps[a]	2,817	12,396	10,555	403	31,894
Minimum total to all camps from all sources					56,081

[a] Entries do not add up horizontally because the documented totals for Majdanek exceed the sums of the documented yearly deliveries to it.

Sources: (a) on Testa's sales, NI-11,937, reproduced in Angelika Ebbinghaus, "Der Prozess gegen Tesch & Stabenow. Von der Schädlingsbekämpfung zum Holocaust," *1999* (1998), p. 70, and Wacław Długoborski and Franciszek Piper (eds.), *Auschwitz 1940–1945*, vol. III: *Mass Murder* (Oświęcim: Auschwitz-Birkenau State Museum, 2000), p. 201 (for 1942–43), and DUA, BU Gerhard Peters, judgment of the Schwurgericht des Landgerichts Frankfurt am Main, May 27, 1955, p. 10 (for 1944); (b) on Testa's sales to Majdanek in 1942 and overall, Jürgen Kalthoff and Martin Werner, *Die Händler des Zyklon B* (Hamburg: VSA-Verlag, 1998), pp. 155 and 185; (c) on Degesch's sales and the amount that went to Auschwitz, DUA, BU Peters, trial judgment of 1955, p. 33 (this figure is well documented and higher than that presented in Długoborski and Piper (eds.), *Auschwitz 1940–1945*, vol. III, p. 203); (d) on sales by Dessau, Heli, Slupetsky, and Kolin, Kalthoff and Werner, *Händler*, pp. 170, 186–87, and 199; and (e) on deliveries to Auschwitz from Azot, Długoborski and Piper (eds.), *Auschwitz 1940–1945*, vol. III, p. 203. Because of what I believe to be some double counting, my total for Zyklon received by Auschwitz is less than the 25 tons described as the likely minimum in the last-named source, but slightly more than the 23.8 tons that SS-Oberführer Joachim Mrugowsky, the person best placed to know as the chief of hygiene for the Waffen-SS, gave as the total in 1946; see Paul Weindling, *Epidemics and Genocide in Eastern Europe, 1890–1945* (Oxford: Oxford University Press, 2000), p. 306. Raul Hilberg, *The Destruction of the European Jews*, third ed. (New Haven: Yale University Press, 2003), vol. III, p. 957, refers to two orders of five and six metric tons, respectively, in April 1944, the first without a warning odor, the second to be sent to Auschwitz, but I have found no confirmation that these actually were fulfilled. Readers should be aware that laborious reconstruction of the data on these shipments is necessary because all three of the principal firms involved — Degesch, Dessau, and Testa — intentionally destroyed most surviving records in 1945.

Index